THE
WEST POINT
HISTORY
OF THE
CIVIL WAR

THE UNITED STATES MILITARY ACADEMY

EDITORS: CLIFFORD J. ROGERS, TY SEIDULE, AND SAMUEL J. WATSON

SIMON & SCHUSTER

NEW YORK LONDON TORONTO SYDNEY NEW DELHI

Simon & Schuster
1230 Avenue of the Americas
New York, NY 10020

First Simon & Schuster hardcover edition October 2014

SIMON & SCHUSTER and colophon are registered trademarks of Simon & Schuster, Inc.

The West Point Crest is a registered trademark of the Department of the Army

For information about special discounts for bulk purchases, please contact Simon & Schuster Special Sales
at 1-866-506-1949 or business@simonandschuster.com.

The Simon & Schuster Speakers Bureau can bring authors to your live event. For more information or to book an event
contact the Simon & Schuster Speakers Bureau at 1-866-248-3049 or visit our website at www.simonspeakers.com.

Interior design by Ruth Lee-Mui
Jacket design by Eric Fuentecilla
Jacket photograph courtesy of the Library of Congress

Manufactured in the United States of America

10   9   8   7   6   5   4   3   2   1

Library of Congress Cataloging-in-Publication Data is available.

ISBN 978-1-4767-8262-1
ISBN 978-1-4767-8265-2 (ebook)

CONTENTS

Dedicated to those West Point graduates who "freed a race and welded a nation."

ACKNOWLEDGMENTS

The *West Point History of the Civil War* comprises six chapters of the *West Point History of Warfare* that have been revised and expanded for the general reader, and for the requirements of publication on paper. *The West Point History of Warfare* is a seventy-one-chapter enhanced e-book survey of military history from ancient times through the present day, designed to be used by cadets in the core History of the Military Art course at West Point. Because of the close relationship between the two projects, all those who have contributed to making *The West Point History of Warfare* the best possible product have also helped make *The West Point History of the Civil War* the exceptional book it is. We therefore offer our gratitude to all of them here.

The West Point History of Warfare and *The West Point History of the Civil War* are the products of an extraordinary public-private partnership between the Department of History at West Point and Rowan Technology Solutions, created by the Viola Foundation. We took the best aspects of government service and paired them with the best aspects of philanthropy. Then we mixed in a healthy dose of business savvy. The result is the book you see before you.

This project required a visionary who believed that cadets at West Point deserved the best education possible and that providing the best education required employing the latest technology. Mr. Vincent Viola not only provided the money to put together this formidable project but also realized that a bunch of historians—both in uniform and out—would need help to run the business of managing an immense, cutting-edge, high-technology endeavor. He started a company called Rowan Technology Solutions to create this book. Vinnie named the company for the famed Lieutenant Rowan from the Elbert Hubbard pamphlet *A Message to García*. In 1898 President William McKinley gave Andrew Rowan, an 1881 West Point graduate, a message to deliver to the Cuban leader Calixto García. With no idea of García's location, Rowan left Washington to accomplish his mission. And accomplish it he did. Since then, army officers have known that "taking a message to García" is shorthand for taking initiative.

The team at Rowan lives up to his redoubtable legacy of initiative. Vinnie gave the project to his West Point classmate Anthony Manganiello to execute. Tony, as the Rowan CEO, gave the team a laser-like focus: create the best possible product for cadets and make sure, above all, that it improves cadets' understanding of military history. Tony's best work was picking the leader of day-to-day operations for Rowan, Timothy Strabbing, the lone Naval Academy graduate and the lone marine on the project. Tim, the executive director of the Viola Foundation, has driven this project to heights we did not believe possible when we started. He has assembled a crack team. The cartographers—Therese Diede, Michael Bricknell, and Jeremy Goldsmith—have created some of the greatest military history maps ever. To insure that they met those high standards, we brought in a maestro of mapmaking, Bruce Daniel. In the project's early days, Bob Pratt created a prodigious number of maps. The designers for this project—Terry O'Toole, Axelle Zemouli, and Nicholas Lituczy—helped the historians see new ways of presenting information effectively and beautifully. Their design infuses everything we do. Chase Stone drew the soldiers that help bring the book to life. Looking at his art, one can almost hear each soldier speak. With so many endnotes and so much text, we needed strong copy editors to wrangle the words into shape. Matthew Manganiello and Grace Rebesco have done that job superbly. During our first summer, we had two interns who did far more substantive work than typical interns do. Thanks to Dan Vassallo and Peter Seidule.

One person on the team deserves special mention. Our senior adviser, Gen. John Abizaid (a Rowan partner) saw issues long before we did, protecting us from problems we didn't know about until after he had already fixed them.

The West Point History of the Civil War is, of course, a history book, and we had the finest historians working on it. We picked the best Civil War historian possible for each chapter, and thankfully each agreed to work with us. Professors Mark Neely, Joseph Glatthaar, Stephen Woodworth, Earl Hess, and James Hogue provided us with crisp text reflecting the very latest scholarship. We hired the "A" team, and it shows. We also needed historians to design the maps, choose the images, and interpret for cartographers and designers. The two associate editors, Dr. Joseph Stoltz and Dr. Keith Altavilla, did astonishing work beyond our wildest expectations in finding images, storyboarding maps, and turning text into an interactive experience. Dr. Rebecca Forrestal also served as a superb assistant editor and helped us think through GIS maps. Professor John Hall read every word and provided valuable comments and suggestions. Col. (Ret.) Paul Melody, senior adviser to the project, also read every page. His counsel regarding the "soldier experience" texts was especially valuable. Professors John Stapleton and Steve Waddell and Col. Gail Yoshitani, volume editors for other sections of *The West Point History of Warfare*, made very important contributions to the overall design, structure, and pedagogical underpinnings of the work.

One reason this book is, in our not-so-humble opinion, a great book is because we tested *The West Point History of Warfare* with 1,200 cadets and 30 instructors over the course of a year. With cadet and instructor focus groups, we found out what worked and what needed improvement. Lt. Col. Jason Musteen led the Military History Division at West Point. He had the complex task of getting the text into cadet hands, which was no easy thing. Maj. Rick Anderson served as the course director for HI301: History of the Military Art. He created study questions, set up a course structure on iTunes U, and generally insured that such a major transition in technology and pedagogy went off without a hitch. Maj. Chuck Bies served ably as assistant course director and Maj. Greg Jenemann led our robust assessment process to make sure we found errors and corrected them. Maj. Dave Musick took point on a variety of technology-related issues. Our iron majors made this a far better book. Every faculty member who taught using the text has provided comments and insights and helped make this project a success. So too did the many other members of our faculty who participated in the vigorous discussions as we reexamined the nature and structure of our History of the Military Art course before we launched into creating *The West Point History of Warfare*. We thank every one of you, but especially Professor Dan Franke, who was the first to teach the History of the Military Art course with a draft version of the new text during the summer of 2013, and Professor Eugenia Kiesling, who offered especially thorough and valuable comments on many chapters. We also want to thank the 1,200 cadets who used the text and helped us improve it. They had no choice—we are an obedience-based organization, after all—but they really did give us great feedback. In the Department of History, we had a formidable admin team that supported the entire project. Lt. Col. Ray Hrinko, Ms. Deb Monks, Mr. Rich Stephenson, Ms. Melissa Mills, Ms. Yvette O'Neal, and Ms. Loretta Woody helped make this project go smoothly. We had two Military History Division chiefs who provided great assistance getting the project started. Thanks to Cols. Kevin Farrell and Gian Gentile.

In less than a year, we had a new textbook on the iPad in the hands of cadets. West Point is the trifecta of bureaucracy: army, federal, and academic. Although the complex rules and structures of bureaucracies are intended to make organizations work reliably and effectively, all historians know that they can sometimes act to stifle innovation. We were lucky, however, to work with dedicated and competent administrators and staffers who understood what we were trying to do and helped us do it. Two individuals who made especially important contributions were West Point's chief information officers, Col. Chuck Grindle and Col. Ron Dodge. They surmounted every obstacle, helped by Lt. Gen. Rhett Hernandez, the then chief of Army Cyber Command. Another brilliant West Point graduate, Guy Filippelli, was our go-to man for tech issues. While the technological challenges were tough, the legal challenges proved equally daunting. West Point is lucky to have two superb lawyers working to insure innovation can occur legally. Our thanks to Lori Doughty and Laura Heller for their fine work. Justin Waldie at Virtu Financial provided superb pro bono counsel for the project as well.

To create the interactive widgets and animated maps for the e-book versions of our texts, we needed the best technologists in the business. Luckily, we found The 42. Led by CEO Christopher Kingsley and COO Jackie Miller, The 42 has taken our vision to places we couldn't imagine. When we first started this project, we cold-called dozens of companies until we found Adrian Perica at Apple. Adrian is a West Point graduate and provided us access and insights that were crucial to our success. Apple opened its doors to us. He introduced us to Greg Christie, who provided superb feedback on our book. He also makes a mean Manhattan. Our liaison at Apple, Deirdre Espinoza, helped guide us through the entire process of creating an enhanced e-book.

When we started this project to write a million words and create new maps by the hundreds, we needed to draw on a wide range of expertise. We would like to gratefully thank our advisory team, Susan Poulton, Elizabeth Samet, Roger Spiller, and Joe Glatthaar, who helped us with contacts, steered us away from dangerous waters, gave us great encouragement, and, occasionally, told us to paddle faster. For maps, Col. Steve Fleming, Col. Mike Hendricks, and Frank Martini provided sage counsel.

West Point's leaders have provided us with great support. Brig. Gen. (Ret.) Lance Betros, then head of the Department of History, started this project by bringing it to Vinnie Viola and served as an adviser even after leaving West Point. Col. Mat Moten, Gen. Betros's successor as department head, oversaw the launch of the active development of the book and provided his fullest support to it. Brig. Gen. Tim Trainor, our dean, approved our plan for *The West Point History of Warfare* and then made sure that we had the support we needed to execute a very complex rollout of technology. Lt. Gen. Robert Caslen, our superintendent, is one of the project's biggest fans. His help has been invaluable in getting our book to a military audience outside West Point.

Two other people have been crucial to *The West Point History of the Civil War*. We can't thank Thomas LeBien enough. Our editor at Simon & Schuster saw the potential for this book early. His excellent editing made it a far better book, and his patience dealing with multiple authors, editors, cartographers, and designers was Job-like. Kudos to his assistant editor, Brit Hvide, as well. The book is indebted to the publishing professionals at S&S, especially Mike Kwan, Ruth Lee-Mui, Jonathan Evans, Phil Bashe, Bryan Miltenberg, and Jonah Tully. Our agent at the William Morris Endeavor agency, Eric Lupfer, was, literally, born for this job. He made his earthly debut in Keller Army Community Hospital at West Point when his father, Tim, was teaching history here. He has shepherded the neophytes through the valley of mass-market publishing with no casualties.

Finally, Cliff and Ty would like to thank the *West Point History of Warfare* widows: our wives, Shelley Reid and Shari Seidule. We spent nearly every evening and nearly every weekend for the past two years on this project. Their forbearance and support made this possible.

The West Point History

of the

Civil War

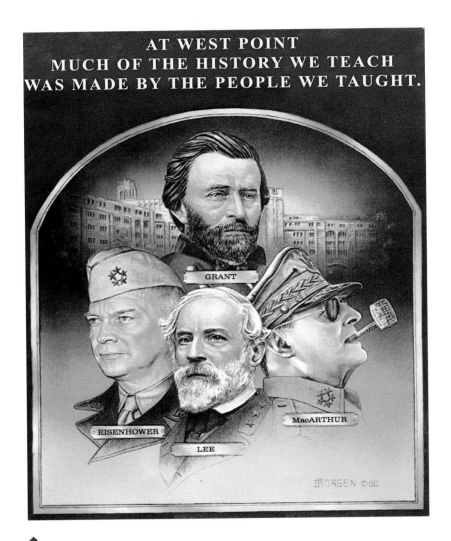

▲

"Much of the History We Teach Was Made by the People We Taught"

West Point's most effective recruiting poster makes a direct link between the "Long Gray Line" of famous graduates and the cadets of today. All cadets take a two-semester military history course called "The History of the Military Art."

"Much of the history we teach was made by the people we taught."

West Point's most effective recruiting poster draws its power from the Civil War of 1861 to 1865. Ulysses S. Grant and Robert E. Lee seem to stare down with Olympian resolve, backed by the granite solidity of West Point itself. Walking through the campus, the visitor may feel as though the Civil War occurred last year. The number of buildings, statues, memorials, and paintings heralding the Civil War could be termed obsessive. Cadets live in barracks named for Grant, Lee, William T. Sherman, and Winfield Scott, all Civil War veterans. The student union is also named for Grant. The memorial building, Cullum Hall (after another Civil War veteran), has a ballroom filled with enormous portraits of the Union generals. Collectively, they glare down at the visitor with a singular message: if not for West Point, if not for these dedicated professional soldiers, there would be no United States of America. The Civil War generation of West Point officers, after making an immense contribution to insuring that the Union would survive and that government of the people, by the people, and for the people would not perish from the earth, went on to make certain that the most important war in the nation's history would have the proper recognition at the nation's military academy. Ever since, the Civil War has been a constant presence here at West Point. And it always will be.

THE CIVIL WAR AT WEST POINT

The Civil War was the most traumatic event in the United States Military Academy's history. During the 1850s, the Academy had changed from an institution that promoted nationalism to a bitterly divided school. In the early 1850s, James Ewell Brown "J. E. B." Stuart praised the nationalizing effect of West Point, claiming that there was "no North or South" among the cadets. That soon changed, however. Peter Michie, who would later spend three decades teaching at West Point, arrived at the Military Academy as a cadet in 1859. He described how the corps of cadets split "into two parties, hostile in sentiment and even divided in barracks."[2] By November 1859, when abolitionist John Brown raided the arsenal at Harpers Ferry hoping to begin a massive slave uprising, the corps of cadets was no longer a unified body. Cadet Pierce Young from Georgia told several cadets, "By God, I wish I had a sword as long as from here to Newburgh, and the Yankees were all in a row. I'd like to cut off the head of every damn one of them."[3]

Southern cadets became even more vocal before the 1860 presidential election, cowing cadets who supported Abraham Lincoln's Republican ticket. Cadet George Custer reported that after the election in 1860, southern cadets burned the president-elect in effigy as they looked to assail "Republican Abolitionists in the Corps." One 1862 graduate who later fought at Gettysburg wrote that it took more courage to vote for Lincoln at West Point than it did to face Pickett's Charge.[4]

West Point in 1860 was more violent and ill disciplined than at any other time in its history. Although few cadets were openly Republican, their number included Emory

INTRODUCTION:

THE

WEST POINT

HISTORY

OF THE

CIVIL WAR

COL. TY SEIDULE,
*Professor and Head,
Department of History,
United States Military
Academy*[1]

One of the few openly abolitionist cadets, Upton fought with Wade Hampton Gibbes on the eve of the Civil War. He later became one of the best tactical commanders of the Civil War and among the most influential officers of the postwar era.

Upton, who would later become influential at the Academy and in the army. Upton was involved in one of the most famous brawls of that era, with Wade Hampton Gibbes from South Carolina. Gibbes resigned a few months later and fired one of the first shots of the Civil War at Fort Sumter. Gibbes accused Upton of "intimate association with negroes" while he was a student at Oberlin College, the first college in the country to admit African Americans. Upton was an avowed abolitionist, but nonetheless he found that assertion so offensive that he challenged the much larger Gibbes to a duel. Despite a deep cut on his face caused by a bayonet, the feisty Upton held his own during the brawl as southern cadets hurled abuse.[5]

Henry C. Farley of South Carolina was the first cadet to leave West Point following Lincoln's election, on November 19, 1860.[6] By the summer of 1861, sixty-five of the eighty-six southern cadets had departed, often for high rank in the Confederate army.[7] Louisiana-born and avowed secessionist Pierre Gustave Toutant Beauregard arrived at the Academy to assume duties as superintendent on January 23, 1861. He never decamped from the West Point Hotel; the new secretary of war, Joseph Holt, ordered the

previous superintendent, Richard Delafield, to relieve Beauregard of his post after only five days. Holt rightly questioned Beauregard's loyalty and did not want him to assume the superintendency and then resign his commission, taking cadets with him.[8] Among the faculty, no senior professor resigned. Dennis Hart Mahan, the longest-serving member, stayed at West Point despite his Virginia roots.[9] Although only 23 of the 155 officers assigned to the West Point faculty from 1833 to 1861 joined the Confederacy, the resignation of high-profile officers such as former superintendent Robert E. Lee left the Academy open to criticism.[10]

While the internal trauma was terrible, the external attacks were even more dangerous to West Point. President Lincoln and Secretary of War Simon Cameron criticized West Point because so many of its graduates left the U.S. Army to fight for the Confederates. Radical Republican senators railed against the Academy and twice brought a vote to the floor of Congress to stop all funding to West Point and close the Military Academy. Senators argued that West Point was an incubator for secession and treason, and that it produced an aristocratic caste of officers to the detriment of volunteer citizen-soldiers. Senator Zachariah Chandler of Michigan declared that he "was prepared to abolish West Point Academy. I believe that but for this institution the rebellion would never have broken out." Senator Benjamin Wade of Ohio believed that a string of southern secretaries of war and Military Academy superintendents

CADET REVIEW PARADE
Prior to the mid-1850s, West Point had a nationalizing effect on the country. After 1855, cadets took control of the assignment process for the companies. Southerners went into two, and northerners went into the other two. Even on parade, the two sides began to separate.

I, Cadet *U. S. Grant* of the State of *Ohio*, aged *Seventeen* years and *two* months, do hereby engage, with the consent of my guardian, to serve in the Army of the United States, for eight years, unless sooner discharged by the proper authority. And I, Cadet *U. S. Grant* do hereby pledge my word of honor as a gentleman, that I will faithfully observe the Rules and Articles of War, the Regulations for the Military Academy; and that I will in like manner, observe and obey the orders of the President of the United States, and the orders of the officers appointed over me, according to the rules and discipline of War.

Subscribed to at West Point, N.Y., this *14 th.* day of *September* eighteen hundred and *thirty nine*, in presence of

U. S. Grant

CADET OATH TAKEN BY CADET ULYSSES S. GRANT

Grant signed this oath at the age of seventeen when he entered West Point in 1839. He pledged to follow the rules and articles of war and obey the orders of the president of the United States.

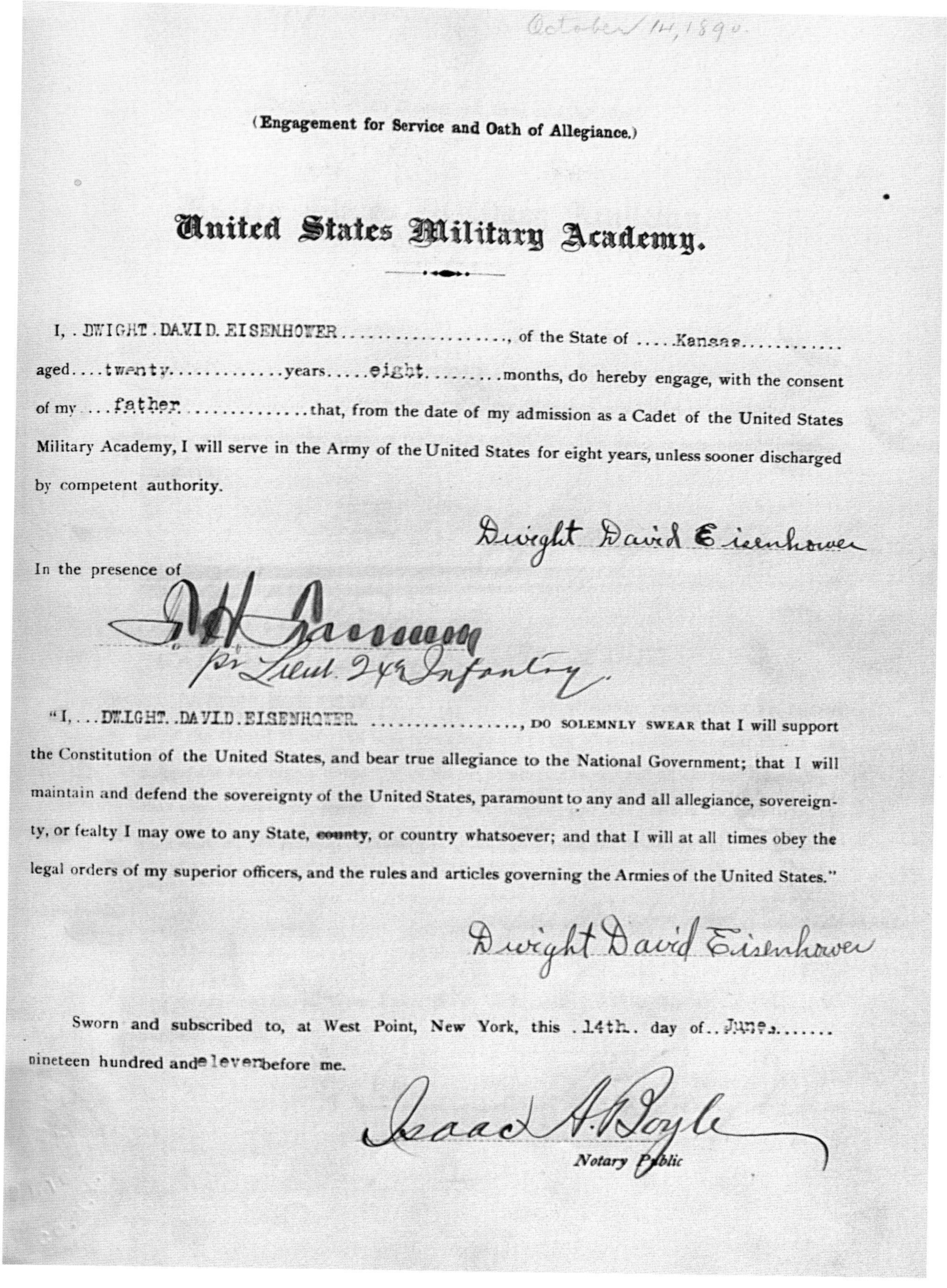

October 14, 1890.

(Engagement for Service and Oath of Allegiance.)

United States Military Academy.

I, DWIGHT DAVID EISENHOWER, of the State of Kansas aged twenty years eight months, do hereby engage, with the consent of my father that, from the date of my admission as a Cadet of the United States Military Academy, I will serve in the Army of the United States for eight years, unless sooner discharged by competent authority.

Dwight David Eisenhower

In the presence of

W.H. Garmann
1st Lieut. 24th Infantry.

"I, DWIGHT DAVID EISENHOWER, DO SOLEMNLY SWEAR that I will support the Constitution of the United States, and bear true allegiance to the National Government; that I will maintain and defend the sovereignty of the United States, paramount to any and all allegiance, sovereignty, or fealty I may owe to any State, ~~county~~, or country whatsoever; and that I will at all times obey the legal orders of my superior officers, and the rules and articles governing the Armies of the United States."

Dwight David Eisenhower

Sworn and subscribed to, at West Point, New York, this 14th day of June nineteen hundred and eleven before me.

Isaac A. Boyle
Notary Public

▲ DWIGHT D. EISENHOWER'S CADET OATH, 1911
Congress's dismay at the number of USMA officers and cadets who renounced their oaths and fought against the federal government caused it to mandate, by an 1861 statute, the Cadet Oath. For more than 150 years, West Point cadets, and only West Point cadets, have sworn this oath.

WEST POINT CONFEDERATES

Until July 1863, Congress and the public associated West Point strongly with prominent Confederate leaders, including Jefferson Davis (center), Robert E. Lee (right of Davis), P. G. T. Beauregard (right of Lee), and Joseph E. Johnston (second from right). After the dual victories at Gettysburg and Vicksburg by two Academy graduates, George Meade and Ulysses S. Grant, the general opinion of the Academy in the North improved markedly.

had so deeply molded the culture of the Academy that "you can hardly find a graduate of West Point who is not heartily now the supporter of southern institutions . . . the whole batch were imbued with the southern secession doctrine." Not only did he denounce the "perjured traitors" who had resigned their commissions and gone to serve the Confederacy, he worried that hundreds of other graduates who had remained in Union blue were "treacherous and rotten at the heart, and . . . doing us infinitely more mischief than any number of them who have turned and resigned their commissions." While most loyal officers thought such attacks were unfair, many did believe that the cadets and officers educated and nurtured at West Point who left for the Confederacy were traitors who brought shame to the Academy.

The vote to shutter the Academy failed, as many rose to West Point's defense, but the defections of many graduates to the Confederacy were widely seen as suggesting a problem with the institution and did lead to some remedial legislation.[11] On August 3, 1861, Congress passed legislation requiring an oath solely for West Point cadets. The bill's author, Representative Abraham Olin, a Republican from New York, asserted, "This oath will not permit that . . . [a cadet] shall set aside his allegiance to the general Government whenever a band of traitors and rebels shall choose to set up a defiant authority."[12] To make the point, the bill declared that any cadet or graduate of the Military Academy who took up arms against the United States after swearing the oath would be court-martialed.[13] If convicted, the graduate would be sentenced to death.[14] Cadets at West Point, and only at West Point, continue to use this oath. The U.S. Air Force and Naval Academy oaths are not prescribed by law.

West Point proved a lightning rod in the early years of the war, when Academy graduates Robert E. Lee and Thomas J. "Stonewall" Jackson continued to prove their worth to the Confederate side, while Union generals and West Pointers George Mc-Clellan and John Pope seemed hopeless and hapless. In 1863 the fortunes of the Union changed with the ascendency of Grant, Sherman, Philip Sheridan, and George Thomas—all West Point graduates. By the end of the war, West Point's reputation was set. It had produced the great generals who "freed a race and welded a nation," as one professor proclaimed. The treason of the Confederates, an issue that loomed so large at the beginning of the war and through the nineteenth century, faded from memory after the Spanish-American War in 1898, replaced by pride at the martial prowess of West Point graduates in both the Union and Confederate armies.

TEACHING THE CIVIL WAR AT WEST POINT

Before the Civil War ended, professors were teaching its campaigns to cadets. Professor Mahan's second edition of his elementary treatise on the military art, *Outposts*, written in 1864, incorporated examples from several Civil War campaigns. Another professor, Gustav Fieberger, wrote a pamphlet on Gettysburg at the turn of the twentieth century and later a book. At the same time, cadets began visiting Gettysburg for a staff ride that combined classroom study of the campaign with a visit to the battlefield. Cadet George Patton's copy of the Gettysburg book contained not only the history of the campaign but also the very strict instructions cadets had to follow on the trip, especially where they could smoke (almost anywhere) and when they could drink alcohol (never).[15]

By 1915, the military history course had failed to keep up with the educational currents of the time. Dwight D. Eisenhower wrote in his memoirs that he hated history because the course at West Point forced him to memorize the location of every general officer and his unit for each hour of the Battle of Gettysburg. "If this was military history," Eisenhower wrote later, "I wanted no part of it." Instead, Ike wanted to know the "meaning of the battle" and why commanders made the choices they did.[16]

The teaching of the Civil War became much improved in the late 1950s when Brig. Gen. Vincent Esposito teamed with cartographer Edward Krasnoborski to create *The West Point Atlas of American Wars*. The book was the best example to date of how maps and text could be integrated to create something greater than the sum of their parts. Yet despite the superb maps and insightful narrative, cadets could read the entire book and not know that slavery had anything to do with the Civil War. The emphasis was on the operational and tactical levels of war: how armies move and how they fight. Little attention was paid to the strategic and political levels. Later textbooks created for West Point cadets studying the history of the military art offered more well-rounded

▼
Cullum Memorial Hall
The ballroom of Cullum Hall has portraits of the great Civil War Union generals. Pride of place goes to Ulysses S. Grant, with William T. Sherman on the opposite wall. No Confederate officers are permitted in the ballroom because George Cullum's will prohibits "unworthy subjects." Two Confederates, Joseph Wheeler and Fitzhugh Lee, are excepted, because they fought wearing U.S. Army blue in the Spanish-American War.

Visit of First Class to Gettysburg Battlefield.

INSTRUCTIONS.

1. No unauthorized article will be allowed on the train. If necessary an inspection will be made.
2. Each cadet will bring with him his text-book and a copy of this circular. They will be carried by him in visiting the field.
3. Cadets are prohibited from leaving the train en route and from smoking in any but the day car.
4. Upon reaching Gettysburg, each cadet shall go at once to the hotel assigned to him. Breakfast has been ordered at 7 a. m.
5. At 8 a. m., each day, the class will be formed by sections at the Gettysburg Hotel and will be assigned to the carriages. No change shall be made by any cadet after this assignment.
6. Smoking is prohibited while visiting the field.
7. When directed, cadets shall leave the carriages promptly, and while on foot will not loiter on the way. At Reynolds' statue, at Little Round Top, at Armistead's monument, and at the Michigan monument on the cavalry field the cadets shall assemble promptly.
8. Dinner will be served at 1 p. m. and the carriages will leave at 2:30 p. m.
9. While in Gettysburg, cadets are prohibited from entering any place where intoxicating liquor is sold. Smoking will be allowed when not visiting the field. All cadets shall retire before 10 p. m., when an inspection will be made.
10. Cadets who desire to purchase photographs of the class taken at Gettysburg, must submit permits before leaving West Point.
11. When not on duty, cadets are authorized to visit the rooms of the Gettysburg Park Commission where a large relief map of the field, and plates giving the hourly positions of the troops, may be inspected.
12. The train will leave Gettysburg   at 7:30 p. m. The class will be formed at the station at 7:15 p. m.
13. On arrival at West Point, cadets shall leave the train promptly and shall be formed by the senior cadet officer and marched to barracks.
14. Cadet officers in charge of the cars and the hotels shall see that these instructions are complied with by cadets under their charge.

GEORGE S. PATTON'S COPY OF INSTRUCTIONS TO FIRST-CLASS CADETS

At the beginning of the twentieth century, each senior class ("firsties," in West Point speak) traveled to Gettysburg to study the campaign. West Point kept a close eye on cadets' morals as well as their training and education, including this 1909 insistence on no alcohol. What West Point wanted it did not always receive, however, as the members of Patton's class of "Aught Nine" called themselves "Naughty Nine" because of their raucous parties.

treatments. Now with the latest mapmaking technology and generous support, we can make an even better contribution to cadet education.

THE WEST POINT HISTORY OF THE CIVIL WAR

The West Point Department of History is proud of the innovative book we (and our partners, Rowan Technology Solutions) developed to educate and inspire our cadets to understand their chosen profession. With all-new text by leading military historians, new maps, rich illustrations, and innovative graphics, cadets can learn more about the Civil War and more about their roles as army officers. But in a democracy like the United States, it is important for all citizens, not just professional soldiers, to know something about warfare in general—and about this seminal American conflict in particular, which did so much to shape our national history. We have therefore developed *The West Point History of the Civil War*, taking chapters from the *West Point History of Warfare* and expanding and adapting them for the general reader. Professor Samuel J. Watson, one of the original volume editors, took the lead in that process, in consultation with the chapter authors.

Americans are not a militaristic people—we don't cotton to fancy uniforms or the

pomp of Soviet-style military parades—but as a nation, we do go to war quite often. An informed citizen, even if he or she deplores war, should know about a subject that informs who we are in the most elemental way. We are, after all, a country born in war during the American Revolution and united as a nation by the Civil War. War is the most complex, dangerous, and unpredictable activity undertaken by humans, and humans are the most complex, dangerous, and unpredictable animals on the planet. Understanding war makes for a more informed citizenry, and informed citizens may influence their elected leaders the next time the nation rallies to the flag with calls for battle.

A project of the scope of *The West Point History of Warfare*—almost a million words and almost a thousand new maps—was beyond the means of the faculty at West Point. *The West Point History of Warfare*, and so *The West Point History of the Civil War*, were made possible by the generosity of Vincent Viola and the Viola Foundation. Not only did Mr. Viola provide the money for this project, he started a company, Rowan Technology Solutions, to create a military history textbook for West Point by enlisting an extraordinarily talented team of historians, designers, cartographers, programmers, and project managers. They took the text and made it beautiful, immersive, and instructive.

The other partner in the creation of *The West Point History of Warfare* was the

◀ THE PANORAMA OF MILITARY HISTORY, MESS HALL MURAL
The mammoth mural in the southwest wing of the Cadet Mess Hall, seventy feet long and thirty-five feet tall, shows the importance of military history at West Point by depicting twenty important battles. The Civil War is represented in Meade's victory at Gettysburg, bottom right. Completed in 1936 using egg tempera over plaster, the panorama remains one of the largest unbroken murals in the world.

Department of History at the United States Military Academy at West Point. Faculty created the chapter list, selected the authors, designed the new version of the History of the Military Art course that the textbook was designed to support, and retained editorial control throughout. Then we tested the book with thirty instructors and 1,200 cadets taking the History of the Military Art course at West Point to insure that the book worked. It did. Cadets gave the text glowing reviews.

We created *The West Point History of Warfare* to educate and inspire cadets at West Point. We hope that *The West Point History of the Civil War* has the same effect on you.

◤ **Our Banner in the Sky**

Frederic Edwin Church painted *Our Banner in the Sky* following the attack on Fort Sumter to rally support for defense of the flag and the country. The history of the Civil War retains an important position in the memory of West Point, and of the nation it serves.

◀ **West Point Cadets**

The United States Military Academy's mission is to educate, train, and inspire the Corps of Cadets so that each graduate is a commissioned leader of character committed to the values of Duty, Honor, and Country, and prepared for a career of professional excellence and service to the nation as an officer in the United States Army.

BRITISH NORTH AMERICA
(CANADA)

OREGON
TERRITORY
1846

UNORGANIZED
TERRITORY
1803

MEXICAN CESSION
(UNORGANIZED
TERRITORY)
1848

GADSDEN PURCHASE 1853

TEXAS
(ANNEXED 1845)

Pacific
Ocean

MEXICO

WISCONSIN

MICHIGAN

IOWA

ILLINOIS INDIANA OHIO

MISSOURI

KENTUCKY

ARKANSAS

TENNESSEE

MISSISSIPPI

LOUISIANA

ALABAMA GEORGIA

FLORIDA

VERMONT MAINE

NEW YORK

NEW
HAMPSHIRE

MASSACHUSETTS

RHODE ISLAND

CONNECTICUT

NEW JERSEY

PENNSYLVANIA

DELAWARE

MARYLAND

DISTRICT OF
COLUMBIA

VIRGINIA

NORTH
CAROLINA

SOUTH
CAROLINA

Atlantic
Ocean

Gulf of Mexico

The United States in 1848

United States

United States Territories

0   250   500 Miles

BRITISH NORTH AMERICA
(CANADA)

OREGON
TERRITORY

MINNESOTA
TERRITORY

WISCONSIN

MICHIGAN

UTAH
TERRITORY

CALIFORNIA

UNORGANIZED
TERRITORY

IOWA

ILLINOIS INDIANA OHIO

MISSOURI

NEW MEXICO
TERRITORY

GADSDEN PURCHASE 1853

MISSOURI COMPROMISE LINE (1820)

36° 30'

UNORGANIZED
TERRITORY

ARKANSAS

TEXAS

KENTUCKY

TENNESSEE

MISSISSIPPI

LOUISIANA

ALABAMA GEORGIA

FLORIDA

VERMONT MAINE

NEW
HAMPSHIRE

NEW YORK

MASSACHUSETTS

RHODE ISLAND

CONNECTICUT

NEW JERSEY

PENNSYLVANIA

DELAWARE

MARYLAND

DISTRICT OF
COLUMBIA

VIRGINIA

NORTH
CAROLINA

SOUTH
CAROLINA

Atlantic
Ocean

Pacific
Ocean

MEXICO

Gulf of Mexico

The Compromise of 1850

Free State or Territory

Slave State or Territory

Free or Slave Status to be
Determined by Popular Vote.

0   250   500 Miles

INTRODUCTION

All wars are extensions of politics, but the political background of the Civil War is especially important to understanding its conduct and outcome. Was secession a planter coup or a broadly popular movement? On the other side, we have to explain the explosive growth of the Republican Party in only half a decade before 1860. Given the extent of racism among the white electorate even in the North, how did a political party critical of slavery capture the presidency? These are essentially political rather than military questions, but the American Civil War was the first war in which *both* belligerents intensively mobilized their citizens to engage in a struggle that the population as a whole, through democratic mechanisms, had chosen to fight. Then there are the more specifically military problems of the opening phase of the war: what advantages and disadvantages did each side possess, and how did they influence strategy? Why did the first major campaigns of the war, culminating at the battles of First Bull Run and Shiloh, not bring the decisive results each side expected?[1]

THE ROOTS OF SECESSION

As the two-year war with Mexico drew to a close in 1848, Abraham Lincoln of Illinois was serving his only term in Congress. Along with most other Whigs, he opposed the war as unconstitutional and unnecessary. But the Treaty of Guadalupe Hidalgo of 1848 cemented the country's acquisition of vast Mexican territories in the West. That territorial expansion, for which Lincoln (though a westerner) had little appetite, would come close to undoing the United States. The Wilmot Proviso of 1846, the traditional place to begin discussion of the causes of the Civil War, was a congressional measure that would have prohibited slavery in the new territories. Although defeated in the Senate, it introduced an issue that never went away—until there was war.

In the 1840s, American politics were dominated by two fiercely competitive parties, called Whigs and Democrats, each of which had support both in the North and in the South.[2] Beginning in 1846, political debates over the expansion of slavery into former Mexican territory strained the cohesion of both parties and put the country on the road to civil war.[3] Yet racism was spreading in the North: resentment or hatred of slavery did not entail belief in the equality of blacks and whites, even among some abolitionists. Historians have trouble reconciling those two developments. How could the

1

ORIGINS OF THE CIVIL WAR AND THE CONTEST FOR THE BORDERLANDS

MARK E. NEELY JR.

◤ THE UNITED STATES IN 1848

◀ THE COMPROMISE OF 1850

Efforts to resolve the issue of California's statehood, coming quickly after the Mexican-American War, led to the unsatisfying Compromise of 1850. This compromise saw California become a free state, included a tougher Fugitive Slave Law to return runaway slaves, and introduced the concept of popular sovereignty into federal law.

same voters who lived in states that excluded African Americans from settlement, such as Indiana and Illinois, come to support a political party pledged to stopping the spread of slavery to the territories?

Secession—the proximate cause of the war—is also difficult to explain. From 1787 to 1860, slavery thrived under the protection of the United States Constitution. The slave population of the United States grew from 697,681 (in a total population of 3,929,214) in the 1790 census, to 3,953,760 (of 23,191,876 people, including 488,070 free African Americans) in 1860.[4] The price of what was called a "prime field hand" in the New Orleans slave market reached the great sum of about $1,800, reflecting the productive potential of slave labor.[5] There was a provision in the Constitution for returning runaway slaves to the South, and laws to do so had been passed in 1793 and 1850. The U.S. Army had fought two wars in Florida as much to destroy refuges for runaway slaves as to expel Spaniards and Indians. Slavery, as a matter of practice and economics, was deeply embedded in antebellum America.[6]

During the 1830s and 1840s, amid a political system that usually worked to minimize clashes over slavery, slaveholders had little reason to believe that their property would be better protected through secession, which would entail setting up a new nation-state, than by remaining in the United States. The radical secessionist "fire-eaters," long a minority, needed to convince cautious slaveholders to take the risk of losing that protection and perhaps provoking war with the United States. They also needed to convince those southerners who held no slaves themselves—about three-quarters of the white population—to risk war over secession.[7] This was accomplished by political parties with platforms that often stressed issues other than the perceived threat to slave property: for example, including economic issues such as banking, transportation infrastructure, and commercial regulations disadvantageous to the South, and especially the threat of northern "tyranny" to all white southerners' rights. A similar broadening of appeal was necessary if the North was to be organized against the growth of slavery.[8] Antislavery politicians had to find ways around direct discussion of the fate of the African Americans in the United States. They tended not to focus on the suffering of the slaves, which would not have been much understood at all had it not been for the efforts of one brilliant woman: abolitionist Harriet Beecher Stowe.[9]

Her book, *Uncle Tom's Cabin*, published in 1852, put a spotlight on the most important characteristics of slavery in the United States in the 1850s, just as sectional conflict and secessionist agitation intensified.[10] Vigorous growth, not (despite what some historians have claimed) stagnation or decay, characterized this old institution. Between 1800 and 1860, planters moved or sold about a million slaves from the old settlements in the Upper South to the "cotton kingdom" of the Deep South and the

▲

UNCLE TOM'S CABIN

A harsh depiction of slave life, *Uncle Tom's Cabin* was a bestselling novel and popular stage show. Performances of the show were produced worldwide, and revivals persisted into the twentieth century.

◄ A SLAVE FAMILY IN A GEORGIA COTTON FIELD, CA. 1860

The explosive growth of cotton as a cash crop in the United States led to the expansion of slavery in the Deep South, deeply influencing national discussions on westward expansion.

Southwest, where the slaves endured bitter new hardships.[11] Northern women like Stowe were particularly sensitive to the destruction of families this great migration entailed—husbands separated from wives and parents from children—and of the slaves' struggle to gain religious consolation from the Bible when laws in southern states criminalized teaching them to read. Stowe's novel described movingly the flight of a mother across treacherous ice on the Ohio River to keep her child from being sold away from her, and the old slave Uncle Tom's Christian patience under ultimately fatal whippings on a remote Louisiana plantation.

Although slavery was much discussed in the politics of the 1850s, it was not generally discussed in the emotional terms that Stowe used in her novel. The political system of the day was entirely the province of men. Only males could vote or hold office, and when men argued about slavery, they tended not to stress theology or the rights of blacks and their families but white rights, liberties, jobs, and property.

The direct inspiration for *Uncle Tom's Cabin* was the Fugitive Slave Act of 1850, itself a consequence of the presidential election of 1848, in which Whig and Mexican War hero Zachary Taylor, a southerner and a slaveholder, defeated northern Democrat

KANSAS-NEBRASKA ACT

Stephen Douglas's proposed division of the Nebraska Territory in 1854 used popular sovereignty as a way to resolve the slave controversy. Instead, it only created further rancor, as the proposal overturned the old Missouri Compromise regarding slavery's expansion.

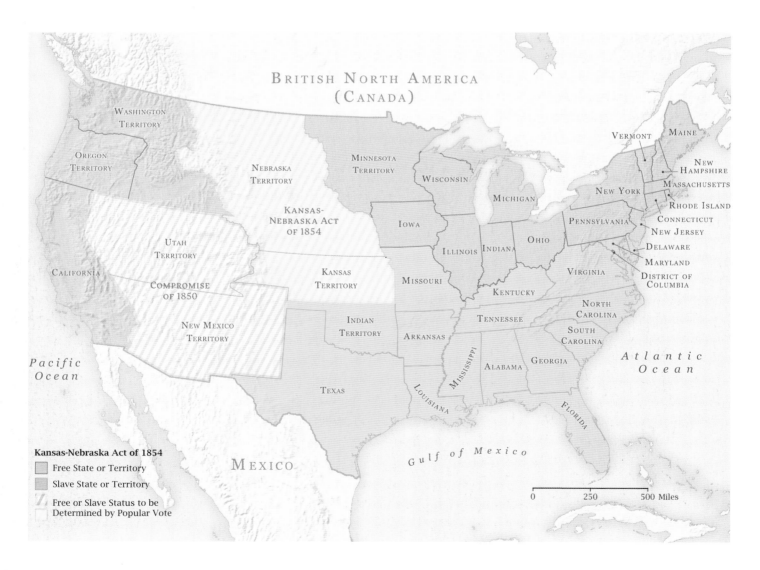

Kansas-Nebraska Act of 1854

- Free State or Territory
- Slave State or Territory
- Free or Slave Status to be Determined by Popular Vote

0   250   500 Miles

Lewis Cass (as well as Martin Van Buren, the candidate of the Free Soil Party, a coalition of antislavery Democrats and Whigs that prefigured the Republican Party of Abraham Lincoln). An ensuing crisis over the extension and security of slavery was resolved by the Compromise of 1850, which provided for the admission of California as a free state but allowed slavery in the newly acquired New Mexico and Utah Territories. It also abolished the slave trade in the District of Columbia but strengthened the Fugitive Slave Law, requiring northerners to aid in the capture of slaves who had escaped to the North.[12]

The compromise did not last very long. One party to the compromise, the Whigs, was greatly weakened by losing the presidential election of 1852. Their candidate, Gen. Winfield Scott, proved inept and unpopular, and lost to northern Democrat Franklin Pierce, a volunteer general during the Mexican War. In 1854 Democratic senator Stephen A. Douglas of Illinois, eager to promote western development and his own presidential prospects, introduced the most disastrous single piece of legislation passed in United States history: the Kansas-Nebraska Act, which opened those territories to slavery, subject to votes by the settlers. In 1820 Congress had passed the Missouri Compromise, forbidding slavery in the area of the Louisiana Purchase north of the 36° 30' line of latitude (with the exception of Missouri itself). The area that Douglas wanted to organize lay north of the line.

Opponents were shocked at the removal of an old and hallowed prohibition against slavery in lands where the question had long been settled. Douglas defended the measure ferociously as an exercise in "popular sovereignty." He thought that the voters most directly concerned should settle the slavery question locally. The most powerful

Stephen A. Douglas, a lifelong Democrat, served as U.S. Senator from Illinois from 1847 until his death. He proved to be the practical enabler behind the Compromise of 1850. In the Senate, he became chairman of the Committee on Territories and identified himself with the development of the American West. In 1854 he introduced what became the Kansas-Nebraska Act to organize territories that stood in the way of connecting East and West securely. The act required him to make expressly null and void the restriction on slavery expansion in the Missouri Compromise. He thought that the principle of "popular sovereignty" would work the sort of magic that the Compromise of 1850 had done. Instead, it brought warfare in Kansas and helped cause the formation of the Republican Party.

Antislavery men despised him for the act, and yet in 1857 Douglas entered into a feud with President James Buchanan over Kansas that would eventually split the Democratic Party. In 1858 he ran against Abraham Lincoln for Illinois's Senate seat, engaging in a famous series of political debates. Douglas emphasized race, asking, "Do you desire to strike out of our State Constitution that clause which keeps slaves and free negroes out of the State, and allow the free negroes to flow in, and cover your prairies with black settlements? Do you desire to turn this beautiful State into a free negro colony?" Douglas retained his seat.

Douglas hoped to gain the Democratic presidential nomination in 1860, but a rule requiring a two-thirds majority at the convention thwarted him, and the party split. Later he was nominated by the northern wing of the party. In the subsequent four-party presidential election, he came in second in the popular vote but won few electoral votes. Shortly after the Civil War began, Douglas died, but not before pledging support for the war to Lincoln's Republican administration.

STEPHEN ARNOLD DOUGLAS

APRIL 23, 1813–JUNE 3, 1861

opposing argument, persuasive among many northern Democrats as well as Whigs, was the idea of "free soil": that the immense resources of the West should be reserved for free men, without their having to face unfair competition from slaveholding "aristocrats." For some free-soilers, keeping slavery out of unsettled territories was a moral imperative. It was widely assumed that if slavery could not move ceaselessly to new lands, it would gradually die out, having grown unprofitable on exhausted soils. For other free-soilers, particularly those whose political roots lay in Jacksonian Democracy (which emphasized equality among whites), the most important point was to ensure that non-slave-owning farmers would not have to compete at a disadvantage with those holding slaves. For them, free soil had little to do with racial equality. Preventing slaves from entering new territories kept out most African Americans, and legislatures could forbid immigration by free blacks. This "white man's solution" to the problem of western expansion appealed to those who disliked slavery but still harbored strong prejudices against blacks.[13]

All of these positions on the expansion of slavery could be said to be constitutional. Northern Whigs noted that article IV, section 3 of the Constitution declared that "Congress shall have power to dispose of and make all needful rules and regulations respecting the territory or other property belonging to the United States." This, they thought, meant that Congress could forbid slavery in the territories, as it had done in the Northwest Ordinance of 1787 and the Missouri Compromise of 1820. Others disagreed, noting that the clause did not mention "government" of the territories expressly. The southern position on slavery's expansion into the lands of the West, devised a generation earlier by South Carolina's John C. Calhoun, was called the "common property" doctrine. The territories, Calhoun argued, had been acquired by the

EXPANSION OF SLAVERY, 1790–1860 ▶
The spread of slavery across the South to the western states contributed to a constitutional crisis.

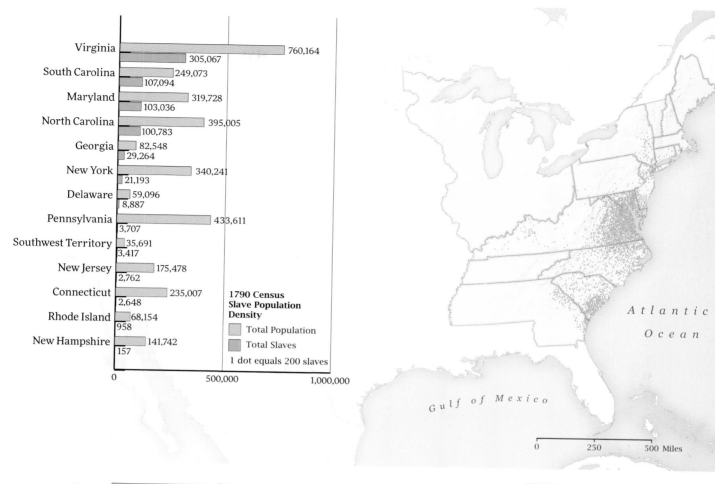

1790 Census
Slave Population
Density

Total Population
Total Slaves

1 dot equals 200 slaves

State	Total Population	Total Slaves
Virginia	760,164	305,067
South Carolina	249,073	107,094
Maryland	319,728	103,036
North Carolina	395,005	100,783
Georgia	82,548	29,264
New York	340,241	21,193
Delaware	59,096	8,887
Pennsylvania	433,611	3,707
Southwest Territory	35,691	3,417
New Jersey	175,478	2,762
Connecticut	235,007	2,648
Rhode Island	68,154	958
New Hampshire	141,742	157

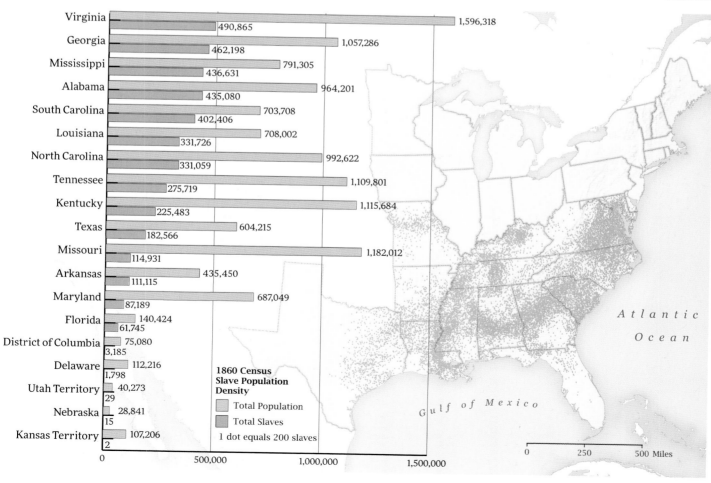

1860 Census
Slave Population
Density

Total Population
Total Slaves

1 dot equals 200 slaves

State	Total Population	Total Slaves
Virginia	1,596,318	490,865
Georgia	1,057,286	462,198
Mississippi	791,305	436,631
Alabama	964,201	435,080
South Carolina	703,708	402,406
Louisiana	708,002	331,726
North Carolina	992,622	331,059
Tennessee	1,109,801	275,719
Kentucky	1,115,684	225,483
Texas	604,215	182,566
Missouri	1,182,012	114,931
Arkansas	435,450	111,115
Maryland	687,049	87,189
Florida	140,424	61,745
District of Columbia	75,080	3,185
Delaware	112,216	1,798
Utah Territory	40,273	29
Nebraska	28,841	15
Kansas Territory	107,206	2

ARREST IN BOSTON.

THE ESCAPE ON SHIPBOARD.

DEPARTURE FROM BOSTON.

THE SALE.

THE ADDRESS.

AUCTION

THE PRISON.

Anthony Burns.

DRAWN BY BARRY FROM A DAGUERREOTYPE BY WHIPPLE & BLACK.

JOHN ANDREW

blood and treasure of southerners as much as northerners. Who then was to say that southerners could not move to them with their lawful property, just as northerners could? Anything else made southerners second-class citizens.

The most powerful argument against the Kansas-Nebraska Act was articulated by Ohio senator Salmon P. Chase. The North, he maintained, was defending the republic from a "Slave Power Conspiracy."[14] The number of southerners in the 1860 census who could be classified as "planters"—holding twenty slaves or more—was only 46,274.[15] Were these few to rule or ruin all 31,513,114 Americans? This wealthy aristocracy, a growing number of northerners said, cared nothing for American values and rights and wanted to throttle any movement or institution that thwarted slavery. A free press that might criticize slavery? That had not existed in the slave states for years.[16] The right to petition Congress against slavery? The Slave Power Conspiracy had prevented that for almost a decade until it lost the struggle over the "gag rule" in Congress in 1844.[17] These telling antislavery arguments did not focus on the suffering of African Americans in slavery but on the threat to the liberties that white men had always enjoyed.[18] Besides, the argument went, the country's founders never intended for slavery to last. The word *slavery* does not appear in the Constitution. The drafters of the document, Republicans argued, always referred to it by clumsy circumlocutions such as "people held to service or labor" because they had hoped—even expected—that it would end, whether by economic exhaustion or gradual individual emancipation.

The Kansas-Nebraska Act helped destroy what was left of the Whig Party in the North. In 1854 the Republican Party began to form in opposition, but it initially made slow progress. In the mid-1850s, many American voters were focused on problems other than slavery and sectional conflict. Indeed, in 1854–55 another new mass political party, the anti-immigrant, anti-Catholic American Party (commonly called the Know-Nothing Party) gained more support than the Republicans. Their success reflected widespread concern over the enormous influx of foreigners into the United States between 1845 and 1854—many of them Catholic Irish and Germans, of whom American Protestants (the vast majority of the population) were often deeply suspicious.[19] For many Americans, the fear of a Papal Plot was more vivid than the fear of a Slave Power Conspiracy.[20]

But the Republican Party, blessed with able politicians like Lincoln, coped effectively with the Know-Nothing competition, eventually absorbing most of those voters without conceding any platform principles to their bitter prejudices. The Republicans also crafted an economic platform that appealed to many northerners, supporting

◄ **ANTHONY BURNS**

Anthony Burns escaped slavery in Virginia in 1853 but was captured in Boston and, after a trial, re-enslaved under the Fugitive Slave Law. Bostonians stormed the courthouse to free him, forcing the federal government to send troops on the day of his trial. The case ignited antislavery feeling across the North. As Amos Adams Lawrence described the case, "We went to bed one night old-fashioned, conservative, compromise Union Whigs & waked up stark mad Abolitionists."

Anti-immigrant feeling was another critical component of American politics during the 1850s. Many former Whigs, uneasy about the Republicans' abolitionist leanings, considered the nativist Know-Nothings as potential challengers to the Democrats.

government aid to railroads, greater protection against imports for manufacturers, and a "homestead act" to encourage western settlement by small farmers. Democrats, who blocked or vetoed these measures, steadily lost support in the North. The collapse of the Whigs left the North open to control by a party without support in the South.[21]

ESCALATION TO VIOLENCE

Violence aggravated sectional controversy. Slave catchers, aided by U.S. marshals and sometimes federal troops, clashed with free blacks and white abolitionists when they tried to return fugitive slaves to the South. In Kansas, a bloody civil war broke out as settlers from both sides surged into the territory, making a mockery of the idea of "popular sovereignty." The U.S. Army was deployed to keep the peace but could not prevent an assault on the free-soil stronghold of Lawrence in May 1856.[22] Republicans exploited the bloodshed for great political gains that year when they ran their first presidential candidate, former army engineer and explorer John C. Frémont, against Democrat James Buchanan and Know-Nothing Millard Fillmore. Violence also broke out in Congress. South Carolina representative Preston Brooks became incensed by what he perceived to be a personal insult to a relative made by Senator Charles Sumner of Massachusetts in a speech about "Bleeding Kansas." Brooks beat Sumner bloody with a cane on the very floor of the Senate. These events lent credibility to Republicans' warnings against the arrogance and intolerance of the Slave Power.

Law failed to calm the situation. The Supreme Court sought to settle matters by issuing the *Dred Scott* decision in 1857. A Missouri slave, Scott (owned by an army surgeon), had first sued for his freedom in 1846, claiming he was a free man because

he had once lived in a free state and a free territory. In 1857 the chief justice, Roger B. Taney, led a Supreme Court dominated by southern slaveholders to a 7–2 decision declaring that an African American could not be a citizen of the United States (and therefore lacked standing to sue in federal court) and that Congress lacked the power to prohibit slavery from the territories. The decision enraged Republicans and threatened the northern Democratic doctrine of popular sovereignty, because Taney stated that neither Congress nor a territorial legislature could prohibit slavery. Not only did the Constitution make no mention of race, it explicitly authorized Congress to make legislation for the territories, and Congress had been exercising the power to regulate slavery since the Northwest Ordinance in 1787. Many found the decision baseless.[23]

President James Buchanan, like Franklin Pierce, was a "doughface": one of the northern Democrats sympathetic to southern fears who were coming under increasing criticism from Douglas's wing of the Democratic Party. Buchanan fed the flames by pressing for the ratification of a proslavery constitution for Kansas in 1858. That Lecompton Constitution was rejected by both Kansas voters and the House of Representatives, where the Republicans had gained control in the 1858 elections. More violence ensued. In 1859 the radical abolitionist John Brown, who had murdered proslavery settlers in Kansas, attacked the federal arsenal at Harpers Ferry, Virginia, with twenty-two men. Brown had imagined that slaves throughout the South would rush to join his band in rebellion. Instead, a small military force under Col. Robert E. Lee recaptured the arsenal, and Brown was hanged. But rumors of slave insurrection became common in the South, fostering an atmosphere of crisis and the formation of volunteer military groups during the election year 1860.[24]

The Republicans had grown rapidly, combining former Whigs and Know-Nothings with some Free Soil Democrats. Like any party successful over the long term, the Republicans were a coalition. Whigs brought their desire to use the federal government to promote economic development through the Homestead Act, the tariff, land grants to railroads, and a more stable banking and monetary system. Antislavery advocates and free-soilers immediately preferred the Republicans over the Know-Nothing antagonism toward Catholicism and immigration, and as the Republicans coalesced, many Know-Nothings began to realize that the road to office was more likely to come within the wider coalition that the Republicans were assembling. At the local level, depending on the ethnic and religious composition of a community, the Republicans might pander to nativist sentiments, but party leaders kept strident nativism out of the national platform. Indeed, the Republicans began to gain adherents among Protestant German immigrants, one of the three largest of the new immigrant groups, many of whose leaders had participated in attempted democratic revolutions in Germany in 1848. These men were sympathetic to the Republicans' antislavery message.[25]

John C. Frémont had done well for the first presidential candidate of a new party, winning a third of the popular vote in a three-party race against the American Party and the Democrats. In the electoral college calculus, the Republicans needed only Pennsylvania and one of several other states to win the presidency in 1860—and it was unlikely that many Know-Nothings would turn to the Democrats. The tariff, targeted at the electorally critical state of Pennsylvania, also helped the Republicans win congressional seats there in 1858. As the 1860 election approached, the Republicans had made such gains that southern leaders feared the Democrats would lose the White House, which they had held for twenty-four of the last thirty-two years. With the presidency would eventually go the Supreme Court (whose justices rarely remained on the bench into their seventies and eighties), and perhaps the *Dred Scott* decision.[26]

The slaveholders handed Lincoln the election. Stephen A. Douglas had been outraged by Buchanan's abrogation of popular sovereignty, and southern Democrats were no longer willing to accept a northern candidate. The northern majority rejected a platform plank that would have permitted slavery in all the territories (making the *Dred Scott* decision, rather than popular sovereignty, Democratic policy), so

THE LAST MOMENTS OF JOHN BROWN ▶
Brown's Harpers Ferry raid touched off a wide range of responses, from respectful mourning, such as this idealized postwar painting of Brown being led to the gallows, to horror and condemnation across the South.

ABRAHAM LINCOLN
FEBRUARY 12, 1809–APRIL 15, 1865

By the time Abraham Lincoln became commander in chief in 1861, he had served as a volunteer officer and enlisted man in the Black Hawk War of 1832 against the Sac and Fox Indians, and had helped elect military hero Zachary Taylor president. He had also criticized the Mexican-American War as unconstitutional and unnecessary, made fun of military heroes as presidential candidates, and even made fun of his own early military experience (all in a speech in Congress in 1848).

From his Black Hawk War experience, Lincoln had seen the results of gruesome atrocities, and he was not particularly shy of blood. As a onetime frontier wrestling champion in New Salem, Illinois, he saw warfare as simple: he told Grant in 1864, "Hold on with a bull-dog grip, and chew & choke, as much as possible."[28] On the other hand, even in the Black Hawk War, Lincoln had also observed the civilized laws of war and once protected an Indian who had come into his camp with a good-conduct pass from being murdered by the vengeful militiamen around him.

Though he is often described as inexperienced (as compared with his Confederate counterpart, Jefferson Davis), Lincoln had learned important lessons about war. While suffering under the administration of Democrat James K. Polk and his war in Mexico, Congressman Lincoln learned to ignore partisanship in choosing military commanders; as commander in chief Lincoln clung to George B. McClellan as commander of the Army of the Potomac longer than most Republicans thought wise. Lincoln possessed the inner resources to withstand the public-opinion impact of long casualty lists and an indomitable determination to do whatever was necessary to restore the Union—but he made it a point to observe the laws of war in an internecine conflict.

southerners walked out of the nominating conventions in Charleston and Baltimore, and the northern and southern Democrats nominated different candidates. That fall, the Republicans, led by Lincoln, won 1,866,452 votes; the northern Democrats, led by Douglas, 1,376,957; the southern Democrats, led by John C. Breckinridge, 849,781 (18 percent of the vote, largely in the Lower South); and the Constitutional Union ticket, led by John Bell, 588,879 (12 percent, largely in the Upper South, where he won Tennessee, Kentucky, and Virginia). Lincoln's support, concentrated in populous northern states, earned him 180 of 303 electoral votes and the White House. Douglas, the odds-on favorite just a year before, won only Missouri. Though Lincoln won a mere 39 percent of the popular vote, more than 80 percent of the voters cast their ballots against the candidate (Breckinridge) widely thought to represent secession.[27]

Although Lincoln proclaimed repeatedly that he would not interfere with slavery in the states where it existed, southerners refused to accept the election of a president heading a party pledged to end the expansion of slavery. A clear majority of whites in the Deep South responded immediately to the call for secession. Despite the sense of crisis, secessionist leaders rarely had to resort to strong-arm tactics or political dirty tricks to persuade the slaveless majority to go along with secession. Indeed, what is most notable about this revolutionary movement was how orderly and parliamentary in method it turned out to be. Secession amounted to deratification of the Constitution, as the secessionists, state by state, called for elections of conventions that met and, adhering to familiar legislative rules, voted to annul their previous ratifications of the Constitution and form a new confederation.[29]

South Carolina seceded on December 20, 1860, followed, in order, by Alabama,

Jefferson Davis was born in Kentucky in 1808. After attending Transylvania University, Davis graduated from the U.S. Military Academy in 1828, ranking twenty-third out of thirty-two graduates, and served seven years as an infantry lieutenant. Resigning his commission and moving to Mississippi, Davis became wealthy operating plantations worked by slave labor, and was elected to the House of Representatives in 1845.

In 1847 Davis formed a one-year volunteer infantry regiment, and his fellow soldiers elected him colonel. At Buena Vista, in northern Mexico, Davis's battlefield leadership gained national renown, and during the 1850s, he served as senator and secretary of war, initiating a five-year curriculum at West Point that ended due to the demands of the Civil War. In 1860 Davis supported secession as a last resort to protect slavery. In February 1861, after considering several presidential prospects, the Provisional Confederate Congress selected Davis as president of the Confederate States of America.

He implemented controversial policies including conscription, impressing (requisitioning) food and livestock for the Confederate army, suspending habeas corpus, approving congressional funds to build Confederate factories, and requiring slave labor to work on Confederate projects. As commander in chief, he mixed defensive and offensive strategies. After the war, Davis wrote a two-volume memoir to justify secession and his policies as president. He died in Mississippi in 1889. Extremely intelligent, Davis was also very prickly, and had poor relations with many of his generals and with several governors of important Confederate states. Given his position, it is not surprising that many historians assign him significant responsibility for Confederate defeat, though it is not clear that any other southern politician might have done better.

JEFFERSON FINIS DAVIS
JUNE 3, 1808–DECEMBER 6, 1889

Mississippi, Florida, Georgia, Louisiana, and Texas. By the beginning of February, seven slave states had seceded, but eight had not: Virginia, with its grain and industry; Tennessee, with its pork and grain; North Carolina, with yet more grain; Arkansas; and the border states of Missouri, Kentucky, and Maryland. (Delaware had very few slaves and was unlikely to secede.) No one knew what would happen next. The outcome of the war might well be determined by how many of these states (which collectively had far more white citizens, and potential combatants, than the Lower South) remained in the Union.[30] For the next eighteen months, U.S. policy makers were preoccupied with keeping the border states in the Union.

At this point, the Constitution, which would serve the United States well during the war and shape victory for the North, let the new president down. The document said nothing about secession and did not explicitly state that the Union was perpetual.[31] Lincoln condemned secession as "the essence of anarchy,"[32] without having the real clincher in any constitutional argument: text from the document itself.

The legal argument over secession was not so much an argument over the Constitution as an argument over *theories* of the Constitution. Southern secessionists held to the "compact theory" or "state rights" theory. They argued that the individual states were sovereign and had joined together in a compact in 1787 to create a confederation in which the central government was expressly delegated certain powers.[33] All other powers were retained by the states—including the power to nullify laws or withdraw from the confederation if the government overstepped the boundaries of the prescribed powers. That was a historical argument, not one based on the text of

The Constitution of the Confederate States of America

The C.S.A. Constitution shared much of its language with the U.S. constitution except for one major difference: slavery. The Confederate Constitution made explicit that slavery was allowed.

the Constitution (which never said anything explicit about "sovereignty"). In his inaugural address, Lincoln, echoing Andrew Jackson before him, countered with a parallel historical argument:

The Union is much older than the Constitution. It was formed in fact, by the Articles of Association in 1774. It was matured and continued by the Declaration of Independence in 1776. It was further matured and expressly declared and pledged to be perpetual, by the Articles of Confederation in 1778. And finally, in 1787, one of the declared objects for ordaining and establishing the Constitution, was "*to form a more perfect union*." But if destruction of the Union, by one, or by a part only, of the States, be lawfully possible, the Union is *less* perfect than before, which contradicts the Constitution, and therefore is absurd.[34]

Lincoln thus carefully reserved an important place for the Declaration of Independence in the history of the Union, which by his reasoning was "matured" by a document that declared that "all men are created equal."

Hoping to attract the Upper South into their slave republic, the Confederates played it safe by adopting most of the old U.S. Constitution but adding explicit guarantees of slavery and lengthening the presidential term to six years (but forbidding reelection). Jefferson Davis of Mississippi became their president. Unlike Lincoln or anyone in Lincoln's cabinet, Davis—a West Point graduate—had substantial military experience both in combat (as a regimental commander in the Mexican War) and as secretary of war under President Pierce.

As southerners abandoned Congress, Republicans rejected several attempts at compromise that might still have permitted the expansion of slavery—at least south of the old Missouri Compromise line (which Lincoln expected would lead to expansionist wars in Latin America and the Caribbean)—and prohibited in perpetuity any amendments interfering with slavery in the states.[35] Yet Confederates did not necessarily expect secession to end in war: the growth of sectional chauvinism encouraged the belief that Yankee shopkeepers would refuse to sacrifice their businesses or their lives to force unwilling southerners to remain in the Union. Instead, would northerners not say good riddance to slaveholders and slaves alike?

The country drifted. Lincoln's inauguration would not take place until March. Buchanan was still president but had no moral authority, and he could not resolve a crisis over the federal government's possession of Fort Sumter, in the harbor at Charleston, South Carolina. State militias seized many federal military installations in the South; federal troops withdrew from or surrendered others, leaving only Fort Pickens, guarding Pensacola Bay, Florida, and Sumter in U.S. hands come spring. When the Confederacy fired on Sumter on April 12, 1861, it unleashed a whirlwind of

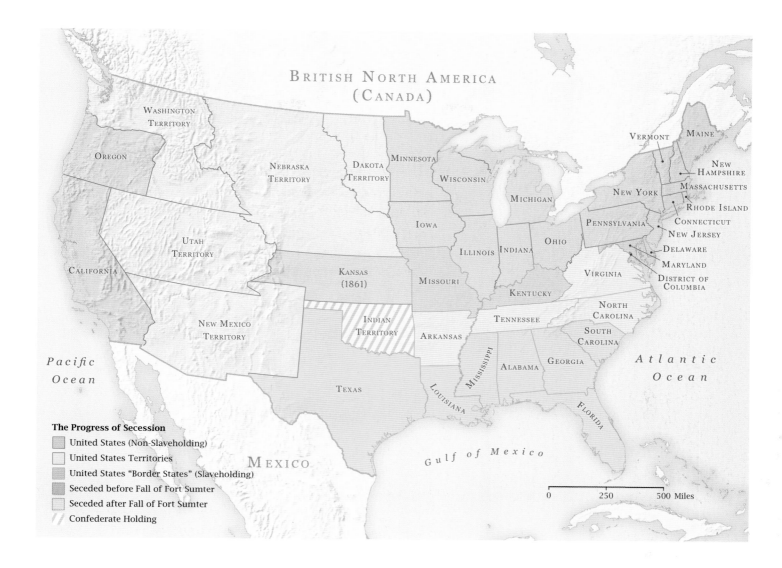

The Progress of Secession

- United States (Non-Slaveholding)
- United States Territories
- United States "Border States" (Slaveholding)
- Seceded before Fall of Fort Sumter
- Seceded after Fall of Fort Sumter
- Confederate Holding

0   250   500 Miles

outraged nationalist sentiment in the North, irrespective of political party. Two days later, Stephen A. Douglas met with Lincoln and issued a public statement backing the war; he viewed secession as an attempt to overthrow the United States government. Douglas then went on a speaking tour to the West, vowing that "every man must be for the United States or against it; there can be no neutral in this war—only patriots and traitors." But the United States would have to cross the Upper South to defeat the rebellion. When Lincoln called for 75,000 volunteers the day after Sumter fell, Virginia, Tennessee, North Carolina, and Arkansas seceded rather than participate in the "sub-jugation" of their fellow southerners.[36]

By 1860, Americans north and south both felt their counterparts were treating them as second-class citizens. The sectional crisis would be decided by politics rather than by law or the Constitution. The secessionists had rejected electoral politics in the United States, but elections would continue to determine whether the northern states would sustain their effort to reunite the nation—and ultimately to destroy slavery.

WAVES OF SECESSION

Seven states of the Deep South seceded between December 1860 and February 1861, following Lincoln's election. The four states of the Upper South did not secede until after Lincoln's call for a volunteer army following Fort Sumter. The four slaveholding Border States remained in the Union.

S.S.BALTIC.OFF SANDY HOOK APR.EIGHTEENTH.TEN THIRTY A.M. .VIA

NEW YORK. . HON.S.CAMERON. SECY.WAR. WASHN. HAVING DEFENDED

FORT SUMTER FOR THIRTY FOUR HOURS UNTIL THE QUARTERS WERE EN

TIRELY BURNED THE MAIN GATES DESTROYED BY FIRE.THE GORGE WALLS

SERIOUSLY INJURED.THE MAGAZINE SURROUNDED BY FLAMES AND ITS

DOOR CLOSED FROM THE EFFECTS OF HEAT .FOUR BARRELLS AND THREE

CARTRIDGES OF POWDER ONLY BEING AVAILABLE AND NO PROVISIONS

REMAINING BUT PORK. I ACCEPTED TERMS OF EVACUATION OFFERED BY

GENERAL BEAUREGARD BEING ON SAME OFFERED BY HIM ON THE ELEV

ENTH INST.PRIOR TO THE COMMENCEMENT OF HOSTILITIES AND MARCHED

OUT OF THE FORT SUNDAY AFTERNOON THE FOURTEENTH INST.WITH

COLORS FLYING AND DRUMS BEATING.BRINGING AWAY COMPANY AND

PRIVATE PROPERTY AND SALUTING MY FLAG WITH FIFTY GUNS. ROBERT

ANDERSON.MAJOR FIRST ARTILLERY.COMMANDING.

In an age of passionate nationalism, raising armies was easy—at first. Many Democrats joined, as well as Republicans. Although the universal militia system had declined ever since the Revolution, volunteer militia companies had become popular, north and south, as sectional antagonism grew. The process of mobilizing troops was shaped by federalism and was much like that employed since 1775. Once Congress authorized a call for soldiers, the state governments oversaw raising them. Politicians and local notables recruited troops personally, often staging mass rallies in public squares and spending their own money. The state governments paid and supplied the recruits until a regiment reached sufficient strength to be mustered into federal service. The governors appointed the regimental officers.[37] Only the generals were appointed by the president, with the advice of Congress. Politics played a role in their selection, but the Regular Army ultimately retained most senior operational and strategic commands: in fifty-five of the sixty largest battles of the war, the generals commanding on both sides were West Point graduates.[38]

In the United States, bounty payments were eventually required for recruiting, as they had been in previous wars, but the bounties were commonly raised by states and localities in order to help meet the state troop quotas agreed on by their representatives in Congress. The bounties, raised by taxation, loans, and voluntary contributions, demonstrated the patriotism and sense of duty of communities across the nation. The process in the Confederate states was similar, though the Confederacy lacked the capital for cash bounties, and southern soldiers elected their officers more often than in the North.

Despite their exclusion from voting, officeholding, and most other civil rights, women proved no less patriotic than men, encouraging enlistment and providing much of the clothing and camp equipment for the first regiments. Some women saw connections between their struggle for rights and the African American struggle for freedom: despite her many reservations about the fairness of the political system, staunch women's rights advocate Elizabeth Cady Stanton, also an abolitionist, vowed, "War, pestilence, famine, anything but an ignoble peace!"[39] Women's eager contributions to the Union are best symbolized by the United States Sanitary Commission. In 1861 President Lincoln ordered the creation of this public-private partnership dedicated to raising medical supplies and enhancing medical services for the armed forces. The officers of the organization were men, often doctors, but women performed most of its work. Eventually they organized great "sanitary fairs" in northern cities, raising

◀ MAJOR ANDERSON'S TELEGRAM SURRENDERING FORT SUMTER
The Confederates fired on Fort Sumter first, starting the war. The northern public lionized Robert Anderson for his role. A proslavery Unionist, he returned the thirty-three-star flag from Fort Sumter to New York. Anderson's appearance in Union Square with the flag was the largest single gathering in North America to that date.

THE UNION VOLUNTEER.

O'er Sumters walls OUR FLAG again we'll wave; | OUR UNION and OUR LAWS maintain we must;
And give to traitors all a bloody grave. | And treason's banner trample in the dust.

NEW YORK PUBLISHED BY CURRIER & IVES. 152 NASSAU ST

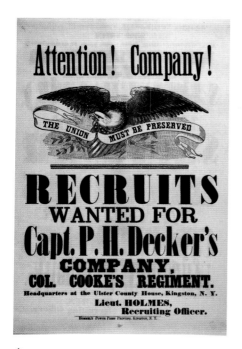

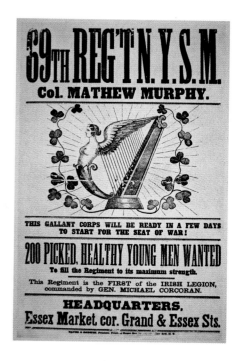

RECRUITING POSTERS

Civil War armies were recruited at the lowest levels, with potentially several towns furnishing a company of men. This local connection created strong bonds within the unit, but significant casualties could be devastating to the community.

Southerners, especially those in Upper South states such as Tennessee, rallied to support the Confederacy not necessarily out of devotion to a new nation but for the protection of their homes from what this poster calls "The Yankee War."

Some volunteer calls played to ethnic sentiment, such as this poster for the 69th New York, a part of the famous Irish Brigade, which served from First Bull Run in 1861 through Appomattox in 1865.

GRANT ENLISTS IN THE WAR EFFORT

This letter from Ulysses Grant to his father-in-law, Frederick Dent (a Missouri states' rights Democrat and slaveholder), of April 19, 1861, shows a typical mix of military, political, and economic considerations at war's outbreak. Grant wrote it the day after presiding over an enlistment rally, where he had warned potential recruits that volunteering meant accepting poor food, hard marching, and obedience even to seemingly unjust orders—and then announced that he intended to reenlist himself.

The times are indeed startling but now is the time, particularly in the border Slave states, for men to prove their love of country. I know it is hard for men to apparently work with the Republican party but now all party distinctions should be lost sight of and evry true patriot be for maintaining the integrity of the glorious old Stars & Stripes, the Constitution and the Union. The North is responding to the Presidents call in such a manner that the rebels may truly quaik. I tell you there is no mistaking the feelings of the people. The

Government can call into the field not only 75,000 troops but ten or twenty times 75,000 if it should be necessary and find the means of maintaining them too. It is all a mistake about the northern pocket being so sensative. In times like the present no people are more ready to give their own time or of their abundant means. No impartial man can conceal from himself that in all these troubles the South have been the aggressors and the Administration has stood purely on the defensive . . . In all this I can but see the doom of Slavery. The North do not want, nor will they want, to interfere with the institution. But they will refuse for all time to give it protection unless the South shall return soon to their allegiance, and then too this disturbance will give such an impetus to the production of their staple, cotton, in other parts of the world that they can never recover the controll of the market again for that comodity. This will reduce the value of negroes so much that they will never be worth fighting over again.[40]

◀ PATRIOTIC PRINT

Volunteer sentiment ran high in the days following Fort Sumter. Men in the North and the South rushed to defend the causes of Union or independence, slavery or abolition. This early rush of patriotic fervor, though, was not sustainable, and recruitment efforts would turn to monetary inducements.

"Drum of the Gray Reserves, First Regiment Pennsylvania Infantry"
Music played an important role during the Civil War, from stoking patriotic sentiment in recruitment to communicating orders on the battlefield. Regiments attempted to supply their own bands to accompany the march.

immense sums to aid soldiers and sailors by auctioning donated goods. Along the way, women devised a new way of stoking patriotism among civilians: the fairs made patriotic sacrifice fun.[41]

Free African Americans in the North were also eagerly patriotic, but in 1861 and 1862, their desire to serve the nation remained frustrated by prejudice that kept them out of the army (but not the navy, which was always desperate for recruits and had employed black sailors since the Revolution). There was no counterpart to the Sanitary Commission in the Confederacy, though white women there were equally dedicated to the national cause. Union soldiers were often surprised by their defiant spirit.[42]

If the two sides were fairly balanced in patriotic enthusiasm, the North enjoyed great material advantages. In an essay entitled "God and the Strongest Battalions," historian Richard N. Current summarized them this way:

When war began in 1861, the statistics from the latest federal census decidedly favored the twenty-three states remaining in the Union as against the eleven that had withdrawn from it. In population the North had an advantage of almost five to two, and this advantage appears even greater if the slaves (more than one-third of the southern people) are counted as somewhat less than the same number of freemen. In wealth and capacity to produce, the North held a still greater edge: in value of real and personal property, more than three to one (even with the inclusion of $2 billion for the slave property of the South); in capital of incorporated banks, more than four to one; in value of products annually manufactured, more than ten to one. The seceded states . . . contained only about a third of the total railroad mileage and practically none of the registered shipping.[43]

As for population numbers, military historian Richard McMurry has contrasted them in this unforgettable way:

Over 80 percent of the military-age population in 1860 lived in the states and territories that were to remain loyal to the Federal government. New York State's military population alone was three-fourths that of the entire Confederacy. New York, Massachusetts, and Vermont alone could have fielded an army that outnumbered the military-age population of the eleven Rebel states by 51,687 men. When those eastern Yankees needed to rest from the fatigues of war, they could have been replaced by a force from Illinois, Indiana, and Ohio that exceeded total Confederate strength by 35,662 men. Pennsylvania's half a million military-age men would have provided adequate replacements for any casualties, and the military-age men in the other sixteen northern states could have gone about their normal business.[44]

The United States also enjoyed far more liquid capital, a far more developed financial and transportation infrastructure, and far greater experience with large-scale, translocal organizations and institutions. Militarily, the large majority of antebellum regular

officers, especially artillerymen, staff officers, and quartermasters, remained loyal to the United States.[45] Thus, the Union had more capable people to run a more developed system employing more resources to support what became a much longer war than the combatants first expected.

One might conclude from such comparisons that the outmatched Confederacy did not stand a chance. It is true that the Confederates squandered one important asset on the very first day of the war: they lost the moral advantage as the victim of aggression by firing the first shot at Fort Sumter.[46] But as the four-year duration of the war and the great casualties suffered by the North attest, it would be an error to think that southern politicians had led their fellow citizens into a war they had no chance of winning. Comparisons of population and industry do not accurately predict the winners of wars. In fact, Confederates could argue that manufacturing capacity was largely irrelevant to winning a war in the middle of the nineteenth century. The qualities they thought most important were cultivated in agrarian societies and were not really "modern": the ability to shoot a rifle, to march long distances on skimpy rations, and to ride a horse well.[47]

The Confederates, moreover, enjoyed several compensating advantages. They thought history was on their side, likening their cause to that of George Washington and the colonists in their struggle for independence in 1776. (Both sides tended to think that God was on their side.) The conventional military wisdom of the era emphasized the advantage of "interior lines," which the Confederacy possessed. That is, if we consider the perimeter of the Confederacy as an arc to be defended, the Confederates could rush troops from inside the arc to this threatened place or that along a radius, or

"SANITARY FAIRS"

Sanitary fairs became a regular feature of the war effort among civilians in the North. The fair in Philadelphia raised over $1 million in three weeks.

DISTRIBUTION OF ▶ WHITE MALES, AGES 15 TO 39, 1860; VALUE OF CASH CROP PRODUCTION, 1860

The nation's population, especially the white population, was concentrated in the North. The South, however, generated the majority of the country's non-food cash crops (mostly cotton), especially in the Deep South and the Mississippi River Valley.

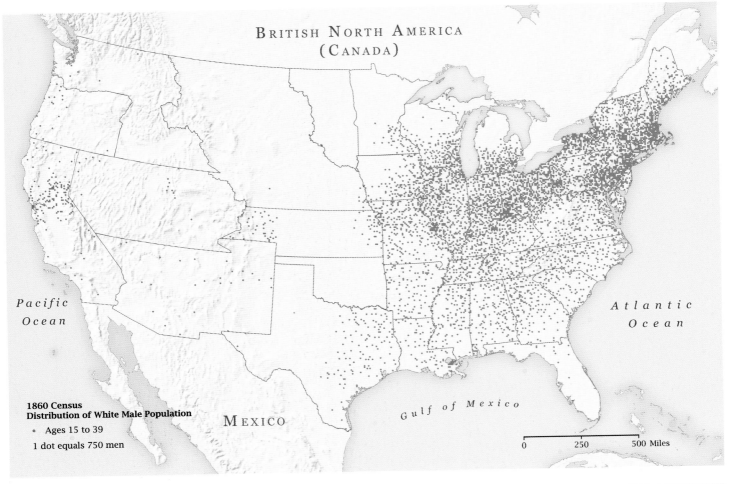

1860 Census
Distribution of White Male Population

- Ages 15 to 39

1 dot equals 750 men

1860 Census
Cash Crop Value Dot Density

- Crop, Orchard, and Market Garden Products
- Ginned Cotton
- Tobacco
- Cane Sugar

1 dot equals $350,000

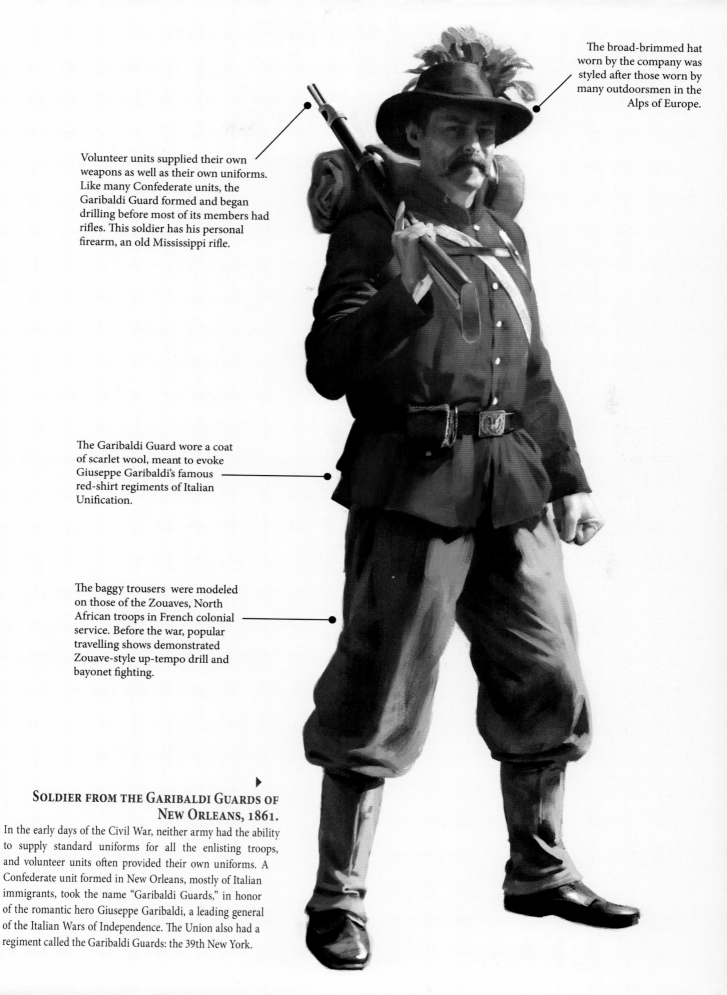

The broad-brimmed hat worn by the company was styled after those worn by many outdoorsmen in the Alps of Europe.

Volunteer units supplied their own weapons as well as their own uniforms. Like many Confederate units, the Garibaldi Guard formed and began drilling before most of its members had rifles. This soldier has his personal firearm, an old Mississippi rifle.

The Garibaldi Guard wore a coat of scarlet wool, meant to evoke Giuseppe Garibaldi's famous red-shirt regiments of Italian Unification.

The baggy trousers were modeled on those of the Zouaves, North African troops in French colonial service. Before the war, popular travelling shows demonstrated Zouave-style up-tempo drill and bayonet fighting.

▶

SOLDIER FROM THE GARIBALDI GUARDS OF NEW ORLEANS, 1861.

In the early days of the Civil War, neither army had the ability to supply standard uniforms for all the enlisting troops, and volunteer units often provided their own uniforms. A Confederate unit formed in New Orleans, mostly of Italian immigrants, took the name "Garibaldi Guards," in honor of the romantic hero Giuseppe Garibaldi, a leading general of the Italian Wars of Independence. The Union also had a regiment called the Garibaldi Guards: the 39th New York.

shift them across a shorter chord. Meanwhile, the Union forces had to traverse greater distances around the outside of the circumference to concentrate forces for an attack, though this problem would be diminished by U.S. advantages in railroads and naval power.

The Confederacy also enjoyed the advantage of the defensive. This advantage was magnified by the nature of the terrain, especially in the East. Gouverneur Warren, the chief engineer in the Union's Army of the Potomac, described the Virginia theater this way:

> [T]he entire region from the Potomac to the James River, and from the Blue Ridge to the Chesapeake . . . is a dense forest of oak or pine, with occasional clearings, rarely extensive enough to prevent the riflemen concealed in one border from shooting across to the other side; a forest which, with but few exceptions, required the axmen to precede the artillery from the slashings in front of the fortifications of Washington to those of Richmond . . . [Appreciating this] will aid those seeking to understand why the numerous bloody battles fought between the armies of the Union and of the Secessionists should have been so indecisive. A proper understanding of the country, too, will help to relieve the Americans from the charge so frequently made at home and abroad of want of generalship in handling of troops in battle—battles that had to be fought out hand to hand in forests, where artillery and cavalry could play no part; where the troops could not be seen by those controlling their movements.[48]

Such terrain—and the lack of good maps—might have posed even more difficulties for the Union army had it not been for the help of African Americans in the South, who often risked their lives to guide and inform northern soldiers.

The benefit of the intelligence gained from slaves did not eliminate the difficulties posed by space and terrain. Historian Richard McMurry has made us keenly aware of that factor. These dilemmas were especially serious in the East. It was about 160 miles from the Chesapeake to the Blue Ridge Mountains, but the manageable front for assault by large forces was much narrower, extending roughly from Fredericksburg to that dense wilderness Warren described: less than 10 miles across. The other potential axis of advance, the Shenandoah Valley, shielded Confederate troops when they moved north toward Harrisburg and Washington but funneled Union troops away from the Confederate capital in Richmond, Virginia, toward Lynchburg, Virginia.

By contrast, the Confederates in the West were responsible for a potential front of 600 miles, reaching from the Appalachian Mountains to Arkansas. The rivers in

◀ ZOUAVE PARADE
Zouave troops (volunteers whose uniforms and drill were modeled after those of French North African soldiers) parade to the battlefield in front of the unfinished Capitol building.

The "Reliable Contraband"
Because maps of the South were not widely published and were riddled with errors, Union armies relied on scouting and the advice of locals, particularly slaves eager to assist the war effort and possibly gain their freedom.

Virginia ran more or less east to west, creating obstacles across the obvious Union line of advance. In the West, they penetrated south into the Confederacy and invited attack, especially down the Mississippi, Tennessee, and Cumberland Rivers. They were valuable highways for a country with a strong navy, a great advantage that the North exploited immediately by imposing a naval blockade along the Confederate coast. Soon the Union would exploit that advantage on inland waters too.[49]

WARFARE IN 1860: CAPABILITIES AND EXPECTATIONS

Military options and choices were conditioned by technology, institutional experience, and international example. Naturally, nations wanted to put the new railroads, rifles, ironclad ships, and telegraph to effective use. These had had little impact in the war with Mexico, but the Crimean War, pitting Britain and France against Russia between 1853 and 1856, and Austria's defeat at the hands of France and Piedmont (northern Italy) in the war of 1859 amply demonstrated the value of steam power for long-distance troop deployment and supply, and of the telegraph for strategic communication.[50]

At the tactical level, another recent invention had the potential to effect equally great changes in warfare. The Minié ball, invented at the beginning of the 1850s, was a conoidal bullet with a hollow base that expanded to grip the grooves of a rifled musket when fired. Unlike the rifles of the American Revolution and the Napoleonic Wars, a Civil War rifle musket could be loaded in the same manner as a smoothbore, and in the hands of a skilled marksman was accurate out to 400 yards—at least four times as far. Yet these weapons were still loaded one cartridge at a time into the muzzle, at about the same speed as smoothbore muskets throughout the preceding century, producing the same clouds of black powder smoke to obscure aim. Perhaps most important, due to the parabolic trajectory of the Minié ball when fired at targets more than 125 yards away, soldiers who did not use their sights properly were likely to send their bullets over the heads of their enemies. The potential of the weapon could not be reached without training, and Civil War soldiers had very little. British rifle fire broke up dense Russian formations in the Crimea, but in 1859, poorly trained Austrian troops were unable to use their rifles effectively against hard-charging French infantry. Hastily raised Civil War armies were not trained to the standard of long-service British infantrymen, and on the wooded terrain of the typical American battlefield, commanders often initiated firefights at ranges not much greater than those of the Napoleonic era. The average Civil War firefight for which data are available began at under 130 yards. Moreover, attackers adopted somewhat looser formations and more rapid advances to compensate for that accuracy, a response that reached the public in the vogue for "Zouave" tactics and uniforms (modeled on those of the Algerian light infantry in French service) just before the Civil War. As a result, the new rifle musket did not favor the defense as much as initially seemed likely, and attackers' casualties were no higher (though still remarkably high by today's standards) than in the battles of Napoleon and Prussia's Frederick the Great fifty to a hundred years before.[51]

Ordnance development was a strength of the antebellum U.S. Army, like engineering and logistics. New rifled cannon, and very large-caliber, shell-firing cannon like the Dahlgren gun, gave artillery new range, accuracy, and power during the 1850s, but artillery was still normally aimed by direct line of sight. Most of the United States east of the Mississippi was still wooded, and heavy artillery could reach its offensive potential only during sieges. Yet there were enough good riflemen that cannon could no longer be advanced into canister range (350 yards or less), from which U.S. cannon had devastated Mexican formations only fifteen years before. Thus artillery proved most effective on the defensive, when it was in position to fire canister at troops advancing at close range outside of entrenchments or other field fortifications. American cavalry usually fought dismounted, and had virtually no experience of the mounted charges that had scattered infantry and decided some battles in the days of Napoleon.[52] As a result, the employment of combined arms attacks (coordinating infantry, artillery, and cavalry) had limited effect on Civil War battlefields, diminishing the potential for decisive victories in the Napoleonic style that Americans on both sides hoped to emulate.

The greatest problem of adjustment was not to technology but to scale. The army was the most far-flung organization within the United States, and expeditions in the West gave army quartermasters experience on a continental scale more than a decade before the Civil War. Prewar officers were also experienced drillmasters, which often led to their being given command of volunteer units. Yet most of the army's combat experience, even in Mexico, was in small-scale engagements rather than the "grand tactics" of the Napoleonic warfare they idealized. Nor did abstract knowledge compensate for this deficiency. While cadets at West Point drew maps and diagrams explaining how they would arrange large units in battle, Americans had virtually no experience actually doing so. Only Winfield Scott and Maj. Gen. John E. Wool remained from those who had orchestrated conventional battles against Mexico, and there was no one else with division-level command experience, much less experience in coordinating the maneuver of corps to set up and exploit battlefield success. Command and control—coordinating combat power—would prove the most difficult task that Civil War commanders faced.[53]

American military education remained in relative infancy. Officers were experts at frontier skirmishes and constructing coastal fortifications, not at planning and fighting large-scale battles and campaigns. West Point was a school for lieutenants, devoted to engineering, with a lot of practice in infantry and artillery drills and some instruction in building field fortifications. Even Dennis Hart Mahan, who taught engineering and the "science of war," paid little attention to strategy, except in seminars for faculty like the "Napoleon Club." The work of Swiss theorist Antoine-Henri Jomini influenced Mahan but was taught directly to cadets for only a few years just before the war.[54]

Predispositions drawn from popular culture were ultimately more important than the specifics that Mahan taught. Tactically, soldiers and commanders alike often preferred to stand and fight in the open, fearing a diminution of offensive spirit if they entrenched—at least during the first two years of the war. Perhaps the greatest influence on American warfare was the memory of Napoleon, the beau ideal of decisive offensive action. Battles would decide the war, and one had to attack to win battles. Yankees and Rebels alike yearned to prove their courage and manliness, to family, neighbors, comrades, and themselves, to prove themselves true Americans to their counterparts on the other side. Patient strategies of economic warfare and resource exhaustion, like Scott's Anaconda Plan to strangle the Confederacy from the Atlantic and the Mississippi or the naval blockade the Union imposed beginning in 1861, found little purchase among either soldiers or civilians, particularly those in Congress and the press.[55]

The Confederacy had several ways to win the war. They might lure the four border states (Maryland, Kentucky, Missouri, and Delaware, all slaveholding states) into their confederation, which would add potentially decisive resources and spatial depth. They might imitate their Revolutionary forefathers and persuade a European power to win their independence for them, as France had done in the American Revolution. The Confederacy's greatest asset for this strategy was "King Cotton." In 1861 the British economy was dependent on southern cotton for the heart of its industry: textile mills. If the Union blockade curtailed cotton supplies and caused an economic depression, surely, southerners thought, Britain would have to intervene.

The Confederates had other, more vague hopes based on perceived cultural differences between North and South. Would the capitalists of the greedy North tolerate a downturn in the economy for the sake of subduing the Confederacy? Would the antagonistic political parties in the North ever agree to cooperate and fight the war? The Confederacy, on the other hand, had no political parties and was proud of it.[56] Some

▼
"KING COTTON"
King Cotton sits on his throne, fanned by African American slaves, while Great Britain and France prostrate themselves before the king. Although this cartoon was drawn by Thomas Nast in 1866, it reflects one of the Confederacy's biggest hopes: that France and Great Britain would support the CSA because of their great need for raw cotton.

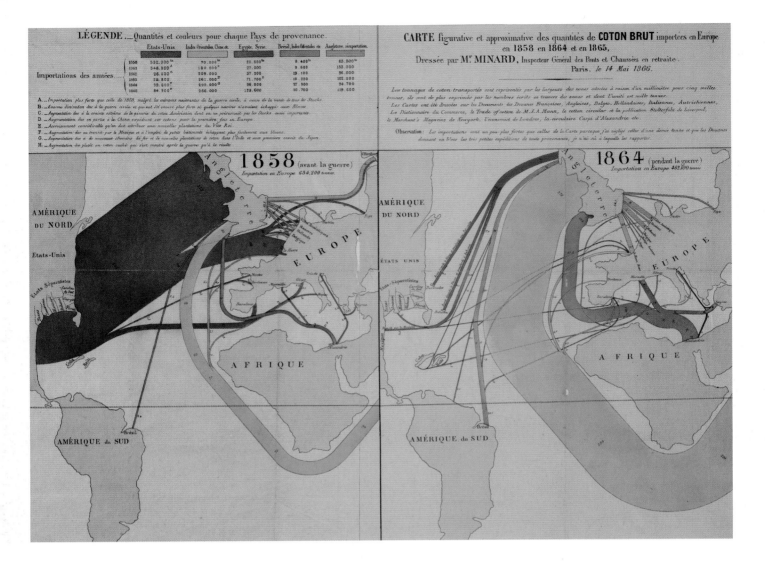

THE COTTON TRADE

Before the Civil War, the South provided much of the cotton processed in the industrial mills of Europe (left). The Confederates failed to anticipate that the British would be able to replace American cotton with supplies from Egypt and India (right).

thought that the clerks and recent immigrants of the North did not have the heart and stamina to win. With all these advantages, perhaps the Confederacy could simply repel northern attacks and wait for the Union to lose the will to fight.

THE BORDER STATES

The allegiances of the northernmost ("border") slave states were thus of key strategic importance. Delaware, Maryland, Kentucky, and Missouri remained in the Union after Fort Sumter. It was clear to all, especially Lincoln, that without the border states, the Union might have been unable to subdue the Confederacy. As the great Civil War historian James M. McPherson put it, just the three states of Maryland, Missouri, and Kentucky "would have added 45 percent to the white population and military manpower of the Confederacy, 80 percent to its manufacturing capacity, and nearly 40 percent to its supply of horses and mules."[57] They could have constituted the margin of victory. Concern for the politics of the border states colored nearly every policy and strategy decision for the first eighteen months of the war. Therefore the history of the

border states is crucial to understanding how the North succeeded.[58] Put simply, amid the turmoil of 1861, Missouri, Kentucky, and Maryland were retained as much by force as by sentiment.

The Union kept the deeply divided state of Missouri by using force (which some historians have labeled a coup d'etat) against force.[59] Missourians had elected a convention to consider secession before the war broke out. The convention rejected secession and adjourned, but the governor remained secessionist. When war commenced, attention focused on St. Louis, the only area in the slaveholding South where significant numbers had voted for Lincoln in 1860. (However, Missouri as a whole voted for Stephen A. Douglas in 1860 rather than the secessionist Breckinridge.) When the pro-Confederate state militia formed up in a camp near St. Louis, citizens sympathetic to the Union feared for the safety of the city's federal arsenal. Republican politician Francis P. Blair Jr. and Regular Army captain Nathaniel Lyon boldly mobilized a local militia, composed mostly of German Americans, surrounded the secessionists' camp, and forced their surrender. When they marched the prisoners through the streets of the city, a riot broke out, and thirty people were killed in the ensuing melee.

Soon afterward, the Unionist forces marched on the Missouri capital, Jefferson

BATTLE OF WILSON'S CREEK
Like First Bull Run, Wilson's Creek was a confused fight in which attacking Union forces gained an initial advantage but ultimately suffered defeat. The Federal commander, the aggressive Nathaniel Lyon, was the first Union general to be killed in the war (depicted above). Although most Missourians supported the Union, the victorious army included around five thousand members of the Missouri State Guard, a generally pro-secession militia.

City, in the state's plantation belt, and drove out the pro-secession governor. They then recalled the old secession convention and had that body choose a governor. (Not until 1864 would the governor be popularly elected.) From time to time over the course of the war, the convention reconvened to act on key measures, including emancipation. Lyon, promoted to brigadier general overnight, went on to surprise the Confederate camp at Wilson's Creek with a dawn attack on August 10 but was heavily outnumbered. When Lyon was slain, the Federal troops were forced to retreat, but Union reinforcements soon drove organized Confederate forces from the state. Nevertheless, Missouri suffered the worst guerrilla violence of any state in the Civil War.[60]

Maryland's Civil War history also began with violence. Like most of the Upper South, Maryland was deeply divided along regional and economic lines. Its government was of uncertain loyalty. The state's largest city, Baltimore, was the Union's biggest problem. (Maryland west of the city, populated mostly by small farmers, was overwhelmingly Unionist.) After Fort Sumter, troops from Massachusetts rushed to secure the nation's capital, but they had to change trains in Baltimore, and on April 19, 1861, a secessionist mob attacked a Massachusetts regiment. Sixteen people were killed. Baltimore's authorities subsequently burned the railroad bridges into town, ostensibly to prevent further incidents, leaving Washington isolated and without military protection. To secure the railroad routes to the capital, President Abraham Lincoln issued his first suspension of the writ of habeas corpus: along railroad routes to the city, military commanders could now arrest civilians and detain them indefinitely without filing criminal charges.

After the Baltimore riot, Union soldiers arrested and imprisoned a Maryland secessionist named John Merryman.[61] Chief Justice Taney, the author of the *Dred Scott* opinion, sought to challenge the constitutionality of Lincoln's suspension and issued a writ of habeas corpus on Merryman's behalf. Taney then traveled to Baltimore to receive the prisoner in court, but the officer in charge of the fort where Merryman was held refused to comply, because the writ of habeas corpus had been suspended by the president. Taney wrote subsequently an opinion saying that the president had no power to suspend the writ, because the provision for suspension appeared in article I of the U.S. Constitution, which described the powers of Congress—not the executive branch. But this was the opinion of a single justice, not the Supreme Court, and it did nothing to halt the suspension of the writ of habeas corpus, which later spread throughout the Union and the Confederacy. For the remainder of the war and long after, the president's suspension would become the focus of profound debate over the restriction of civilian liberties.[62]

At the end of the summer, the railroad bridges were rebuilt, Baltimore was occupied by Union troops and put under martial law, and Washington, D.C., was secured by strong garrisons. Nevertheless, even as late as September, the administration had thirty-one members of the Maryland legislature arrested to prevent them from meeting and perhaps passing a secession ordinance. The wartime Maryland government was not quite the result of a coup d'etat, but Lincoln had made it clear that he was prepared to retain the state by force.

A colossal Confederate strategic mistake helped keep Kentucky voluntarily loyal to

MASSACHUSETTS MILITIA PASSING THROUGH BALTIMORE

Baltimore was a center of pro-Confederate sentiment, which exploded into mob violence against the 6th Massachusetts Militia in April 1861. Violence in the state led to Lincoln's suspension of habeas corpus, the first in a series of controversial legal actions during the war.

THE 7TH REGIMENT LANDS AT WHARF OF THE NAVAL ACADEMY AT ANNAPOLIS, MARYLAND

Under a Confederate threat, Union forces occupied many parts of Maryland, including Annapolis. The Naval Academy decamped for the war to Newport, Rhode Island.

JOHN C. FRÉMONT
A committed abolitionist, John Frémont's 1861 order declaring the slaves of Missouri rebels to be free created a series of political headaches for Lincoln. The president's revocation of the order caused trouble with his party's radical faction.

the Union. After the state effectively declared neutrality, both Union and Confederate forces lined up on its borders, watching for signs of the balance of popular sentiment in the state. Anxious to retain command of the Mississippi River, the Confederates blinked first, occupying the river port of Columbus on September 3, 1861. Their invasion shifted Kentucky sentiment decisively in the Union's favor, forcing the secessionist governor to flee the state. As in Missouri, guerrilla warfare would wrack Kentucky for the remainder of the war. The Lincoln administration asserted emergency war powers, and civil liberties suffered, but about twice as many Kentuckians and Marylanders served in the military forces of the United States as in those of the Confederacy. Communications with Washington were secure, and the path to Tennessee lay open.

THE EMANCIPATION QUESTION

It was in the border states that emancipation first emerged as a political issue. The strategic importance of retaining these slaveholding states in the Union led to a noticeable conservatism in the policies of the early Lincoln administration. In a carefully worded message to a special session of Congress convened on July 4, 1861, President Lincoln laid out the case for resorting to war in order to sustain the Union. Of that message, the African American abolitionist Frederick Douglass commented, "No mention is, at all, made of slavery. Any one reading that document, with no previous knowledge of the United States, would never dream from anything there written that we have a slaveholding war waged upon the Government."[63]

Douglass was not alone in this observation. A large faction within the Republican Party, who called themselves the Radicals, followed the logic that slavery had sundered the nation and threatened democracy, and concluded that slavery had to be destroyed. John C. Frémont, the 1856 Republican presidential candidate and now the commanding general in Missouri, was among them. On August 30 he issued an order declaring martial law, threatening guerrillas with execution, and declaring the slaves of Missouri rebels free.

President Lincoln wasted little time in telling Frémont to execute no one without presidential consent: Lincoln's view of such summary judgments was that they only invited retaliation, and the situation would spiral down "indefinitely." Frémont refused to alter the emancipation order, so Lincoln revoked it himself.

Some Republicans objected loudly to Lincoln's action, and on September 22, 1861, the president wrote a long, confidential letter to an old political ally explaining why he had done it:

Genl. Frémont's proclamation, as to confiscation of property, and the liberation of slaves, is *purely political*, and not within the range of *military* law, or necessity. If a commanding General finds a necessity to seize the farm of a private owner, for a pasture, an encampment, or a fortification, he has the right to do so, and to so hold it, as long as the necessity lasts; and this is within military law, because [it is] within military necessity. But to say the farm shall no longer belong to the owner, or his heirs forever; and

this as well when the farm is not needed for military purposes as when it is, is purely political, without the savor of military law about it. And the same is true of slaves. If the General needs them, he can seize them, and use them; but when the need is past, it is not for him to fix their permanent future condition. That must be settled according to laws made by law-makers, and not by military proclamations. The proclamation in the point in question, is simply "dictatorship" . . . You speak of it as being the only *means of saving* the government. On the contrary it is itself the surrender of the government. Can it be pretended that it is any longer the government of the U.S.—any government of Constitution and laws—wherein a General, or a President, may make permanent rules of property by proclamation?[64]

In exactly one year's time, President Lincoln would do what he here called dictatorship.

The price of retaining the border states in the Union was high; higher than historians usually point out. It eroded civil liberties everywhere in the North and kept the war one between two slaveholding republics, preventing the Union from seizing the moral high ground. But the alternative was possible military defeat. Life was difficult, sometimes harsh, for many citizens of Missouri and Kentucky during the war, but by late 1862, the effective border with the Confederacy was established, and these states thereafter became a sideshow, of no special consequence to the war's outcome.[65]

PIERRE GUSTAVE TOUTANT BEAUREGARD

MAY 28, 1818–FEBRUARY 20, 1893

Born on a sugar plantation in Louisiana, P. G. T. Beauregard graduated from West Point and fought in the Mexican-American War. He entered Confederate service in 1861 and oversaw the bombardment of Fort Sumter. His able biographer, the great Civil War military historian T. Harry Williams, characterized Beauregard as given to grandiose plans that called for greater numbers, discipline, and organization than his generally modest-sized amateur armies possessed.

His plans at Bull Run made little sense, and he improvised during the battle. (Beauregard shared honors for the victory with his superior, Joseph E. Johnston.) Publishing his report of the Battle of Bull Run prematurely poisoned his relationship with Jefferson Davis.

Davis sent him to the West, where his penchant for ringing public declarations served him well. While in the Mississippi Valley in March 1862, Beauregard issued a call for the planters to contribute to the nation their plantation bells, used to call slaves to work, to be cast into cannon. The metal was not really needed, but the appeal to sacrifice captured the imagination of the Confederacy for a time.

Beauregard was second in command to Albert Sidney Johnston in Tennessee, and in an attempt to defeat U. S. Grant at Shiloh on the Tennessee River before he was joined by another Union army under Don Carlos Buell, Beauregard and Johnston attacked Grant and even overran his camp. Johnston was killed on the afternoon of April 6, 1862, and Beauregard assumed command. At night, Buell's forces arrived; outnumbered, Beauregard was forced to retreat after another bloody day of fighting.

Victory thus eluded Beauregard. He fell seriously ill afterward, and President Davis eventually sent him to coastal defense duty at Charleston.

For a short time, it seemed that the Confederacy might do better in acquiring foreign allies than it had in gaining the border states. The greatest diplomatic crisis of the war occurred in November and December 1861. Among the many Confederate vessels that, early on, managed to evade the Union navy was a blockade runner carrying James M. Mason and John Slidell, two diplomats trying to get to Europe to represent the Confederacy there. The Confederate runner was successful in carrying Mason and Slidell to Cuba, where they transshipped to the British *Trent*. The U.S.S. *San Jacinto* stopped the *Trent* and seized the diplomats. Mirroring American anger fifty years before, Great Britain was enraged by U.S. interference with a neutral ship sailing from a neutral port (Havana). War threatened, but after a daylong cabinet meeting on Christmas Day 1861, the Lincoln administration artfully backed down and released the diplomats.[66]

Afterward, British diplomacy was determined not by need for cotton, not by the aristocracy's sympathy with the slaveholding Confederacy, and not by the enthusiasm of Great Britain's antislavery reformers (supported by the factory workers), but by the traditional wait-and-see method of Old World diplomacy, unaffected by ideals: the British government would wait to see whether the Confederacy was likely to achieve its independence before risking intervention and war with the United States. The battlefield would be the arbiter of diplomacy.[67]

STRATEGY AND OPERATIONS IN THE FIRST YEAR OF THE CIVIL WAR: THE EAST

During the first weeks of the war, Winfield Scott, general in chief of the U.S. Army, had identified the Mississippi River as an offensive opportunity. He came up with a plan,

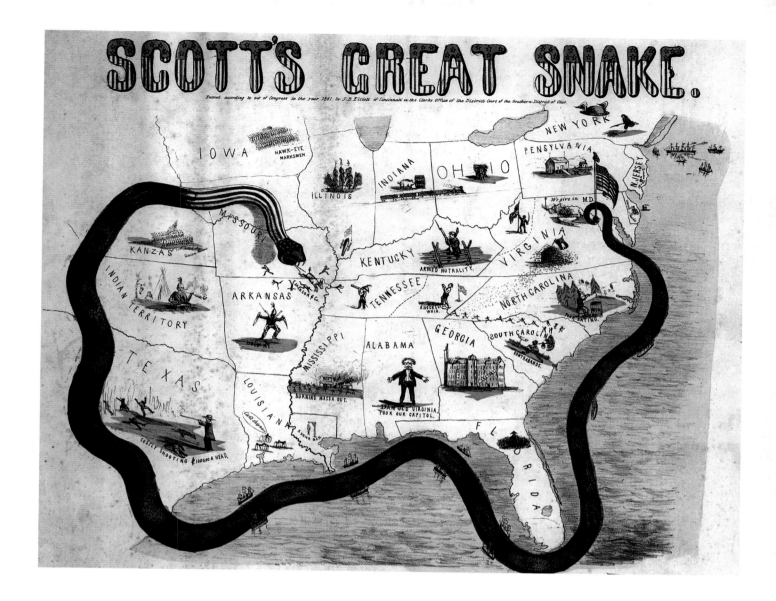

popularly called the Anaconda, which envisioned first encircling the Confederacy with a naval blockade and then advancing down the Mississippi, cutting the Confederacy in two, followed by passive economic strangulation. Like Lincoln and many other northern leaders, Scott believed that secession had been a coup, that few southerners were truly committed to the Confederacy, and that most would return to their former allegiance if faced with deprivation or defeat. Scott hoped to avoid direct, heavy fighting or widespread territorial occupations, which might embitter southerners even if Union armies won clear-cut victories. Scott's attention to the West was forward looking, but media attention and public opinion were fixated on the war in the East. Harking back to Napoleon and to the war with Mexico, both sides expected that battles—indeed, "a single grand victory"—would quickly decide the war. In the North, the cry of the day was "On to Richmond." This vision of war as a simple, face-to-face contest drove the first major U.S. offensive of the conflict against Confederate positions along Bull Run, a creek just east of the road junction at Manassas in northern Virginia, twenty-five miles from Washington. Victory would force the Confederates away from the capital and open the road to Richmond. Brig. Gen. Irvin McDowell, in charge of the army in

WINFIELD SCOTT'S ANACONDA PLAN

Though criticized in some quarters for its deliberate pace, Winfield Scott's plan to squeeze the Confederacy through land and sea pressure had many supporters, and some of its early steps would prove crucial to winning the war.

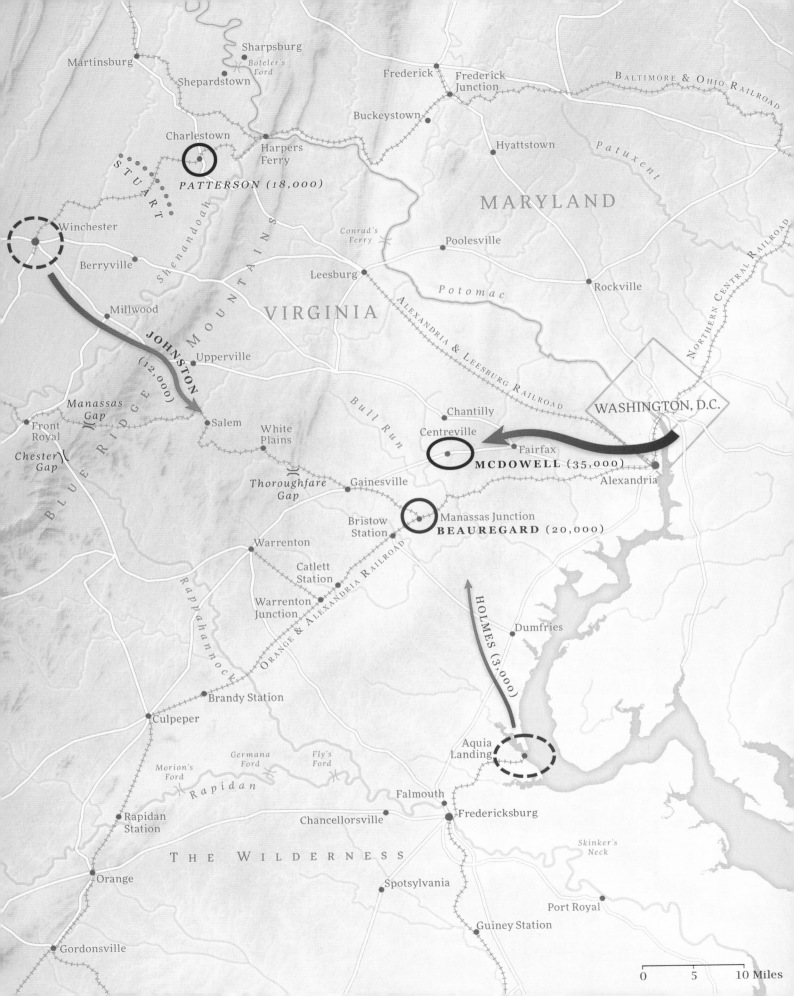

Martinsburg

Sharpsburg

Boteler's Ford

Shepardstown

Charlestown

Harpers Ferry

PATTERSON (18,000)

STUART

Winchester

Berryville

S T U A R T

Frederick

Frederick Junction

Buckeystown

BALTIMORE & OHIO RAILROAD

Hyattstown

Patuxent

MARYLAND

Conrad's Ferry

Poolesville

Rockville

NORTHERN CENTRAL RAILROAD

Millwood

JOHNSTON
(12,000)

Shenandoah

Upperville

Manassas Gap

Salem

Chester Gap

Front Royal

BLUE RIDGE MOUNTAINS

MOUNTAINS

VIRGINIA

Leesburg

Potomac

ALEXANDRIA & LEESBURG RAILROAD

Bull Run

Chantilly

Centreville

Fairfax

McDOWELL (35,000)

WASHINGTON, D.C.

Alexandria

White Plains

Thoroughfare Gap

Gainesville

Bristow Station

Manassas Junction
BEAUREGARD (20,000)

Warrenton

Rappahannock

Catlett Station

Warrenton Junction

ORANGE & ALEXANDRIA RAILROAD

Dumfries

HOLMES (3,000)

Brandy Station

Culpeper

Germana Ford

Fly's Ford

Morton's Ford

Rapidan

Rapidan Station

Aquia Landing

Falmouth

Chancellorsville

Fredericksburg

Skinker's Neck

THE WILDERNESS

Orange

Spotsylvania

Port Royal

Gordonsville

Guiney Station

0   5   10 Miles

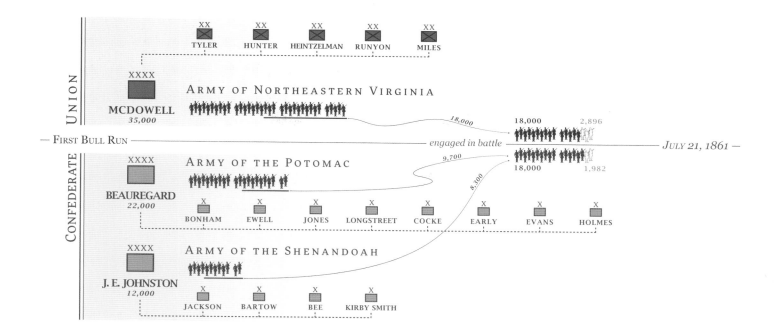

UNION

XXXX
MCDOWELL
35,000

ARMY OF NORTHEASTERN VIRGINIA

18,000

18,000   2,896

— FIRST BULL RUN ———————————————————— *engaged in battle* ———————— *JULY 21, 1861* —

CONFEDERATE

XXXX
BEAUREGARD
22,000

ARMY OF THE POTOMAC

9,700

18,000   1,982

X BONHAM   X EWELL   X JONES   X LONGSTREET   X COCKE   X EARLY   X EVANS   X HOLMES

8,300

XXXX
J. E. JOHNSTON
12,000

ARMY OF THE SHENANDOAH

X JACKSON   X BARTOW   X BEE   X KIRBY SMITH

Washington, warned Lincoln that his troops were not ready for offensive operations, but the president insisted: "You are green, it is true, but they are green also; you are all green alike."[68]

Launching 35,000 soldiers against 25,000 Confederates, McDowell divided his advance into three parts, intending to fix the Confederate center and right while his main effort of 12,000 troops turned their left (passed beyond their left flank and threatened their rear) at Sudley Springs. Marching well before dawn, the Union center column (8,000 strong) ran into and held up the left column, which was unable to cross Bull Run until 9:30 in the morning. Nevertheless, the Confederates were surprised and had to rush troops to delay the Federals left at Matthews Hill. Some 900 Rebels became 2,800, before a flank attack by Col. William Tecumseh Sherman drove them back to Henry House Hill at 11:30.

Then the U.S. attack broke down. Cautiously, McDowell began an artillery bombardment of the hill, but thirteen Confederate guns faced eleven Federal ones. Though fifteen U.S. regiments were deployed around the hill, no more than two attacked at the same time. Meanwhile, 8,500 Confederate reinforcements arrived by rail from the Shenandoah Valley to the west, where a separate Union army had failed to pin them down. Thus supported, with the numbers actually engaged roughly even, Rebel brigadier Thomas J. Jackson stood "like a stone wall" for several hours on the reverse slope of Henry House Hill. At 3:00, the 33rd Virginia attacked the Union artillery; wearing

◀ **FIRST BULL RUN CAMPAIGN**

The two armies lurched toward a confrontation in northern Virginia. The battle that followed was so close to Washington that Union civilians camped above the battlefield, hoping to witness a grand victory in what many of them believed would be the war's decisive (and only) battle.

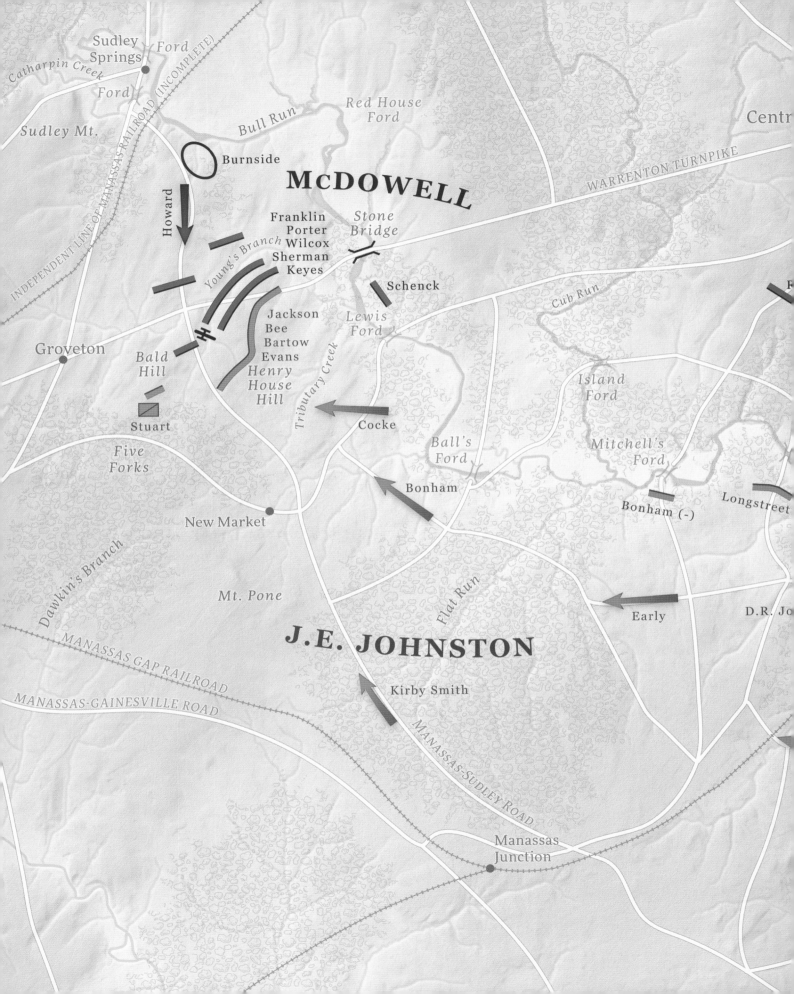

blue uniforms, they were mistaken for Federals, and the cannon were captured. The Federal offensive collapsed, and emboldened Confederates drove forward. Confusion turned to chaos, and retreat to rout, as Union soldiers and wagons jammed a bridge and the spectators fled from nearby vantage points.[69]

The First Battle of Bull Run brought several crucial dynamics to light. The battle was fought in front of the media, which amplified the defeat and contributed to the overreaction of northern politicians. A well-laid battle plan failed when commanders proved unable to coordinate formations, and thus combat power. The U.S. commanders charged with fixing the Confederate right and the Confederates in the Shenandoah, failed to do so. The Confederates then combined operational agility—using a railroad to bring troops to within several miles of the battle—with the defender's advantage of being set in place, with less maneuvering and coordinating to do. But they were too exhausted and disorganized to press the advantage of victory by pursuing the defeated U.S. forces to Washington, much less to seize the capital.

It is difficult to recover a sense of just how disastrous this battle looked at the time, because the size of later armies and their larger casualties made those at Bull Run—about 1,250 total dead—seem almost insignificant. But at that point, it was the largest number of Americans ever slain in a single day. Before the war, the Republicans had devised a telling critique of southern society, blaming its weakness, economic backwardness, and lack of population growth on the blight of slavery.[70] The U.S. Army's panicked flight made it clear that, despite the North's material advantages, the Confederacy had what it took to fight a war.

Congress panicked too. With the border states in mind, the House of Representatives sent a clear signal by passing what came to be called the Crittenden Resolutions, which stated, in part:

◀ **FIRST BATTLE OF BULL RUN**
Most of the fighting took place near Henry House Hill, as the two armies hurled themselves piecemeal into a confused back-and-forth struggle. Late in the afternoon, it was the Union troops who finally broke, fleeing back to Washington.

That the present deplorable civil war has been forced upon the country by the disunionists of the southern States, now in arms against the constitutional Government, and in arms around the capital; that in this national emergency, Congress, banishing all feelings of mere passion or resentment, will recollect only its duty to the whole country; that this war is not waged on their part in any spirit of oppression, or for any purpose of conquest or subjugation, nor for the purpose of overthrowing or interfering with the rights or established institutions of those States, but to defend and maintain the supremacy of the Constitution, and to preserve the Union with all the dignity, equality, and rights of the several States unimpaired; and that as soon as these objects are accomplished the war ought to cease.[71]

In other words, the North had no designs on slavery and wished only to save the Union.

The resolutions proved a terrible political mistake. The Republican-dominated Congress soon passed legislation confiscating slave property in the Confederacy, but the Democrats treated the Crittenden Resolutions as a solemn declaration of war aims and used them to oppose expanding the war to pursue abolition, arguing that such a step would profoundly alter the understanding under which men of all parties had rushed to the colors. A panicked Congress had handed the Democrats an electioneering issue they would use until the end of the war.

FORT DONELSON
Ulysses S. Grant earned the nickname "Unconditional Surrender Grant" after defeating and capturing a Confederate army at Fort Donelson. Very few Civil War battles ended with the capture of the enemy's army, but Grant managed to do it three times.

THE WESTERN THEATER

U.S. operations were far more successful in the West. Demonstrating unusual aggressiveness and backed by Illinois political patrons, Ulysses S. Grant rose quickly from shopkeeper to regimental and ultimately army-level command. Responding to political pressure, the Confederates sought to defend the breadth of Tennessee with a cordon of posts, which required dispersing their limited forces. After the Rebel invasion of Kentucky, Grant and Admiral Andrew H. Foote brought crucial victories through joint operations, using steamboats to supply riverine advances, capturing Fort Henry on the Tennessee River on February 6, 1862, and driving a wedge between the main Confederate forces concentrated at Columbus and Bowling Green.[72]

Flooded by the river, Fort Henry surrendered to Federal gunboats before Grant's troops could attack. Fort Donelson, on the Cumberland River, proved more difficult. Delayed by the flooding, Grant marched 25,000 soldiers across the twelve miles between the positions on February 13, but Donelson was well fortified, and its guns repulsed a Union naval bombardment the following day. Nevertheless, the 12,000 troops that P. G. T. Beauregard sent from Columbus could not be fed, and the Rebel commanders, Gideon Pillow and John Floyd, launched a breakout attempt on the fifteenth. Grant was absent consulting with Foote and had not designated a second in command.

CAMPAIGN FOR FORTS HENRY ▶ AND DONELSON

Moving quickly, and in coordination with the navy, Grant was able to capture both Fort Henry and Fort Donelson early in the war, which opened up the Tennessee and Cumberland Rivers to further advances in the West.

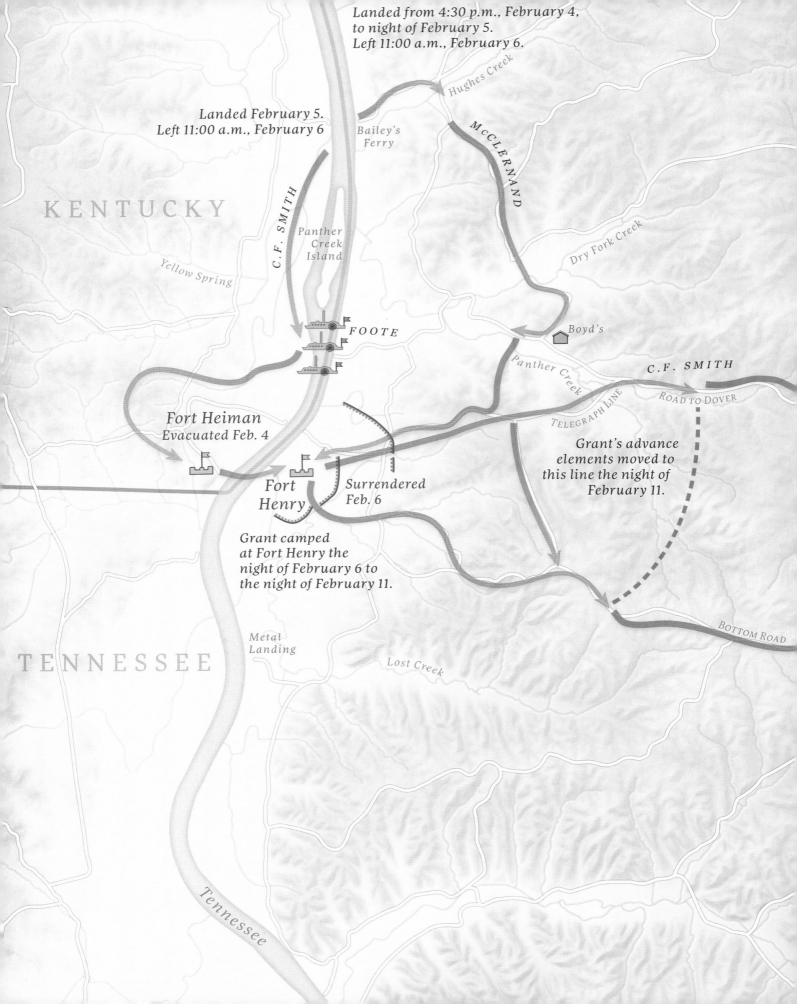

Landed from 4:30 p.m., February 4,
to night of February 5.
Left 11:00 a.m., February 6.

Landed February 5.
Left 11:00 a.m., February 6

Hughes Creek

McCLERNAND

Bailey's
Ferry

KENTUCKY

C.F. SMITH

Panther
Creek
Island

Dry Fork Creek

Yellow Spring

FOOTE

Boyd's

Panther Creek

C.F. SMITH

TELEGRAPH LINE

ROAD TO DOVER

Fort Heiman
Evacuated Feb. 4

Grant's advance
elements moved to
this line the night of
February 11.

Fort
Henry

Surrendered
Feb. 6

Grant camped
at Fort Henry the
night of February 6 to
the night of February 11.

Metal
Landing

Lost Creek

BOTTOM ROAD

TENNESSEE

Tennessee

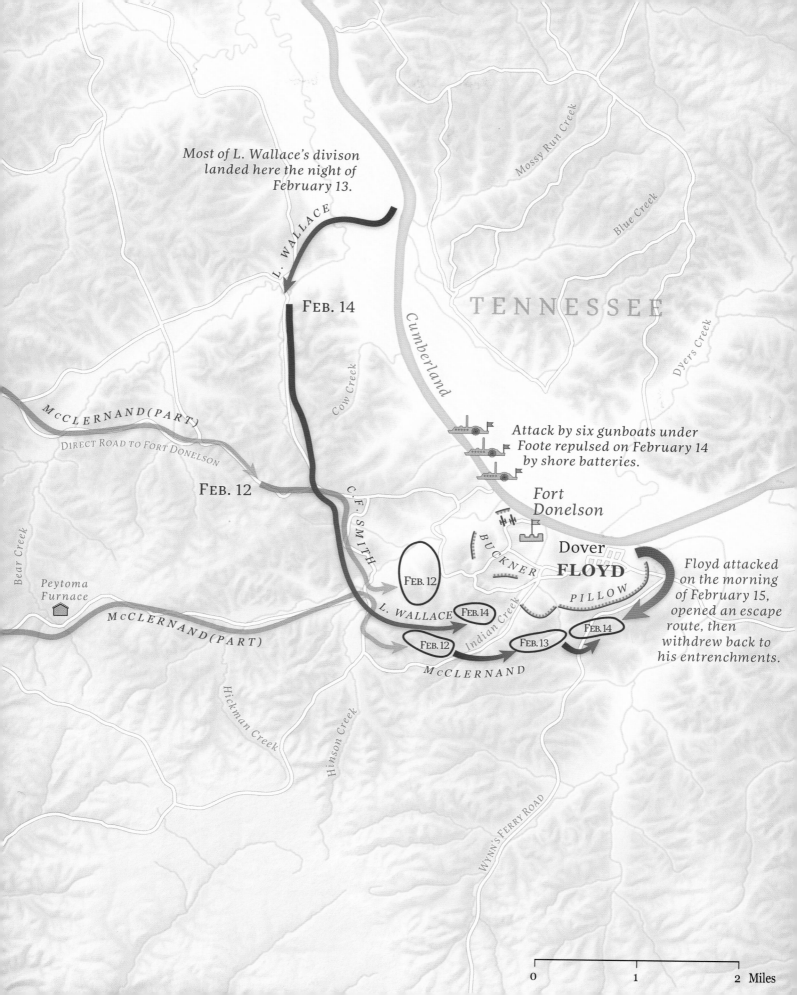

Most of L. Wallace's divison landed here the night of February 13.

L. WALLACE

FEB. 14

TENNESSEE

Mossy Run Creek

Blue Creek

Dyers Creek

Cumberland

Cow Creek

McCLERNAND (PART)

DIRECT ROAD TO FORT DONELSON

FEB. 12

Attack by six gunboats under Foote repulsed on February 14 by shore batteries.

C. F. SMITH

Fort Donelson

Bear Creek

Peytoma Furnace

McCLERNAND (PART)

FEB. 12

L. WALLACE

FEB. 14

BUCKNER

Dover
FLOYD

PILLOW

Floyd attacked on the morning of February 15, opened an escape route, then withdrew back to his entrenchments.

FEB. 12

Indian Creek

FEB. 13

FEB. 14

McCLERNAND

Hickman Creek

Hinson Creek

WYNN'S FERRY ROAD

0   1   2 Miles

ANDREW HULL FOOTE
SEPTEMBER 12, 1806–JUNE 26, 1863

Andrew Foote's father, Senator Samuel A. Foote, secured an appointment to West Point for Andrew, but the younger Foote left after six months to become a midshipman in the navy. Among his many postings, from 1849 to 1851 he helped to suppress the slave trade off the African coast. The experience made him a committed abolitionist, in addition to being a prominent advocate for temperance. He observed British naval actions during the Second Opium War, and after Chinese batteries fired upon his ships, he stormed the beaches to briefly occupy Chinese territory.

Foote commanded the New York Naval Yard when the Civil War began, and was transferred to command of the Mississippi River Squadron. Officially under the authority of the army, Foote effectively coordinated with Ulysses Grant in capturing Forts Henry and Donelson in February 1862. The navy's new ironclad gunboats proved especially effective in bombarding Fort Henry, and forced the Confederate surrender before much of the army could arrive. The better-constructed Fort Donelson provided a sterner defense, and his fleet took significant damage. His own flagship, the U.S.S. *St. Louis*, was left rudderless, and Foote was wounded. He later combined with John Pope to capture Island No. 10 by April of that year.

Foote received the thanks of Congress twice during this period, once following Henry and Donelson, and again after Island No. 10. Late in 1862 he became one of the navy's first rear admirals. In New York, on his way to take command of the North Atlantic Blockading Squadron, Foote was suddenly struck by Bright's disease, a kidney ailment, and died.

John A. McClernand's division was unentrenched, and the Confederates had nearly broken through the Union line when Floyd and Pillow lost their nerve and withdrew to their trenches. Galloping to the scene, Grant seized the initiative and launched Charles F. Smith's division against the Rebels, seizing their earthworks (field fortifications typically constructed by digging a trench and throwing the dirt forward to make an embankment) and threatening the fort. That night, Pillow and Floyd (who as U.S. secretary of war had sent arms to southern arsenals in 1860 and now feared being tried for treason) escaped, along with Nathan Bedford Forrest's cavalry. The next-ranking Confederate officer, Simon Bolivar Buckner, asked for terms the following morning. Buckner, who had loaned Grant money to return east when Grant resigned from the army in California in 1854, probably hoped for the "honors of war," by which his soldiers would be paroled and could serve the Confederacy away from the battlefield. Instead, Grant replied, "No terms except unconditional and immediate surrender can be accepted. I propose to move immediately upon your works." Nearly 13,000 Rebels became prisoners, the largest surrender in American military history to that point.[73]

These advances opened Tennessee, the breadbasket of the Confederacy and a major source of recruits, to Union occupation. Outflanked, the Confederates withdrew from Kentucky, and, indeed, from Nashville, a major railroad junction. Despite a counteroffensive that autumn, the Confederacy would never recover the state. Even better for the Union, its navy and army were working together to take control of the Mississippi River, on which the Confederates had a half-dozen major forts. Digging canals and employing naval gunboats and mortar boats in a bombardment lasting three weeks, Andrew Foote and Brig. Gen. John Pope surrounded and seized Island No. 10 south of New Madrid on April 8, taking about 4,500 prisoners (out of 5,350 defenders) at a cost of fewer than a hundred casualties from their force of 25,000—an achievement that helped win Pope command of an army in Virginia the following summer.

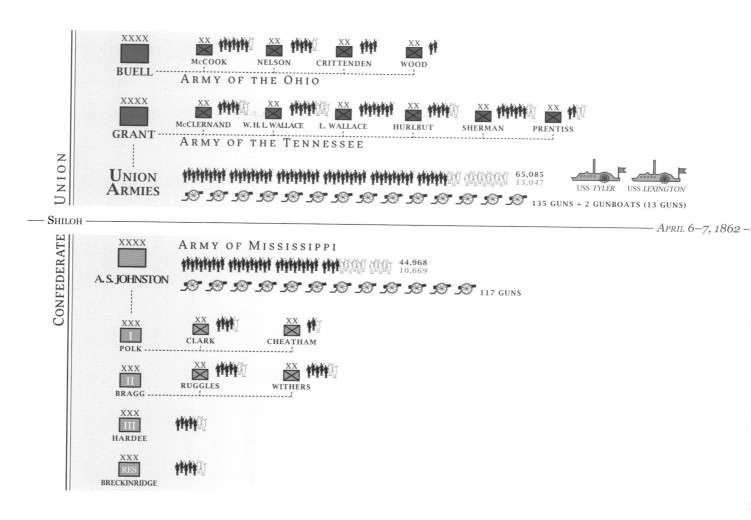

At the other end of the river, after a month spent moving heavy ships across the sandbar at its main entrance, a naval flotilla led by David G. Farragut entered the Mississippi on March 27, with mortar boats bombarding the principal Rebel forts beginning on April 18. Six days later the squadron advanced to move past the forts; the Confederates attacked, but with only gunboats and an ironclad ram (first employed the previous October, when it had scattered the Federal flotilla), they were defeated, losing eight vessels against a Union loss of only one ship out of seventeen. Four days later, the Union captured the greatest maritime prize of all: the largest city in the South, New Orleans.[74]

Washington was thrilled by the good news, but the administration remained preoccupied with the East. Secretary of War Edwin M. Stanton used a proclamation celebrating Grant's western victory to chastise George B. McClellan, commander of the Army of the Potomac, who planned to move by water to attack Richmond indirectly from the southeast, rather than overland from the north:

> Much has recently been said of military combinations and organizing victory. I hear
> such phrases with apprehension . . . We owe our recent victories to the Spirit of the

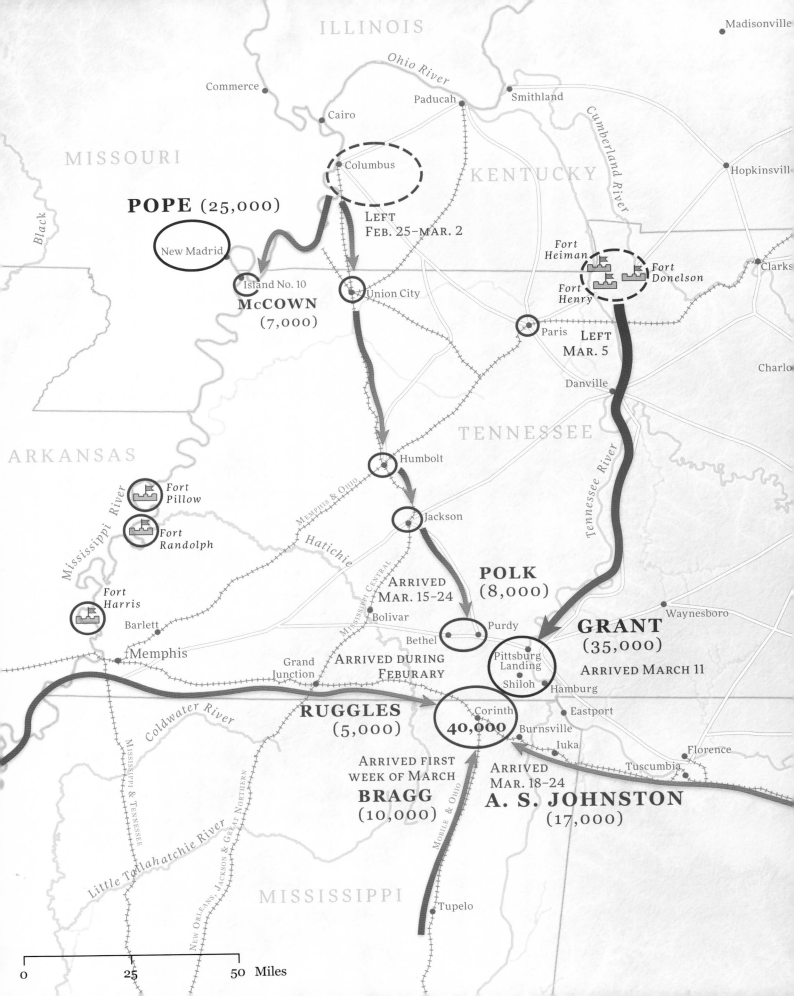

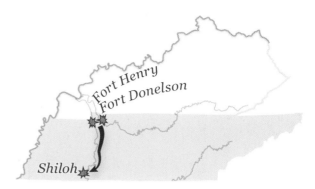

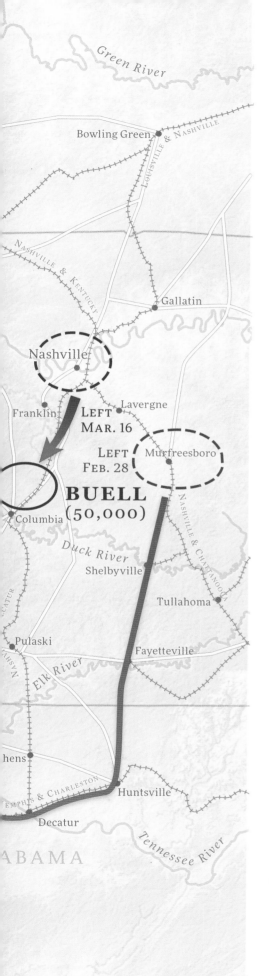

Lord . . . Patriotic spirit with resolute courage in officers and men is a military combination that never failed.

> We may rejoice at the recent victories, for they teach us that battles are to be won now and by us in the same and only manner that they were ever won by any people or in any age since the days of Joshua, by boldly pursuing and striking the foe.[75]

Time-consuming organization and the development of strategy were not top priorities for the Lincoln administration, the media, or the public. Fighting was. Anything less seemed weak, if not treasonous.[76]

Grant's attempt to press farther south, toward the railroad junction at Corinth, Mississippi, met surprising Confederate resistance at the Battle of Shiloh, along the Tennessee River, fought April 6–7, 1862. Grant only narrowly avoided defeat. Learning from the failure of their cordon defense, the Confederates now concentrated their forces and seized the initiative, launching about 40,000 troops against an unsuspecting army of near-equal size under Grant. But this operational maneuver collapsed at the tactical level; Shiloh demonstrated yet again the difficulty of synchronizing combat power in Civil War battles. The Confederates, commanded by Albert Sidney Johnston, arrayed their assault in four long lines, each composed of a corps. This arrangement denied the corps commanders reserves or the ability to shift troops once engaged, and confusion was amplified by dense woods and occasional ravines clouded by powder smoke. These conditions prevented U.S. troops from using their rifle muskets as effectively as possible, but they also slowed Confederate movement, broke up

◀ **ADVANCE TO SHILOH**
As Grant moved south along the Tennessee River, Confederate troops in the West raced to gather at Corinth, aiming to halt his advance somewhere near the Alabama border.

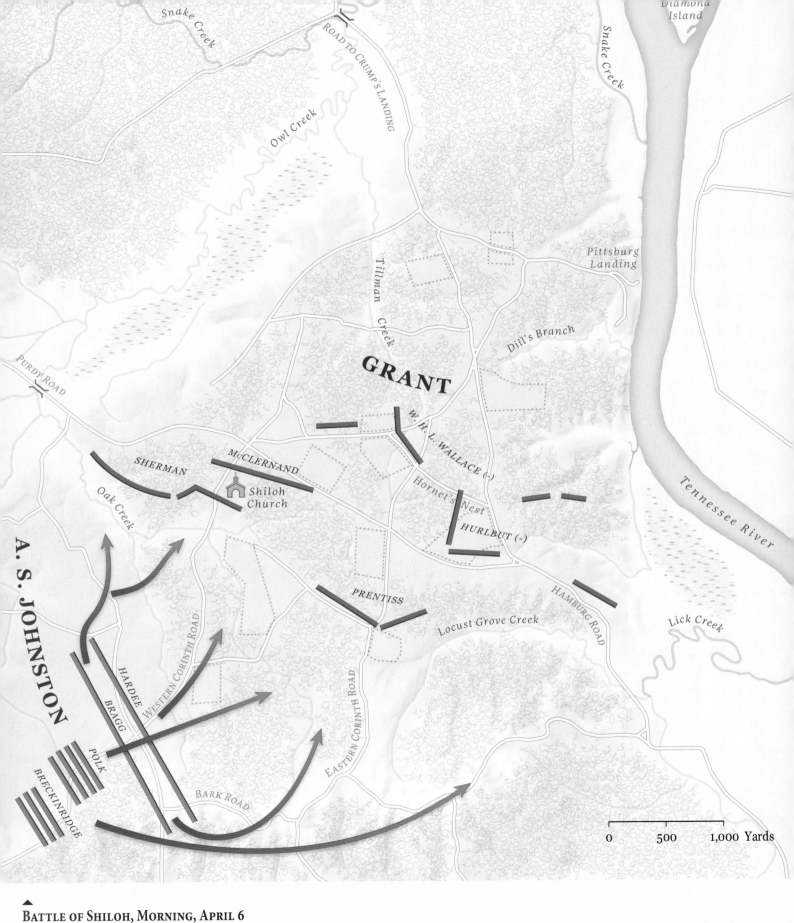

Snake Creek

Diamond Island

Road to Crump's Landing

Owl Creek

Snake Creek

Tilman Creek

Pittsburg Landing

Dill's Branch

GRANT

Purdy Road

W. H. L. Wallace (-)

Tennessee River

SHERMAN

McCLERNAND

Oak Creek

Shiloh Church

Hornet's Nest

HURLBUT (-)

A. S. JOHNSTON

PRENTISS

Locust Grove Creek

Hamburg Road

Lick Creek

HARDEE

WESTERN CORINTH ROAD

BRAGG

EASTERN CORINTH ROAD

POLK

BRECKINRIDGE

BARK ROAD

| 0 | 500 | 1,000 Yards |

▲ BATTLE OF SHILOH, MORNING, APRIL 6

Albert Sidney Johnston's Confederates surprised an unprepared Union army at Pittsburg Landing. Johnston stacked his corps, which provided a significant initial punch but prevented effective use of reserves.

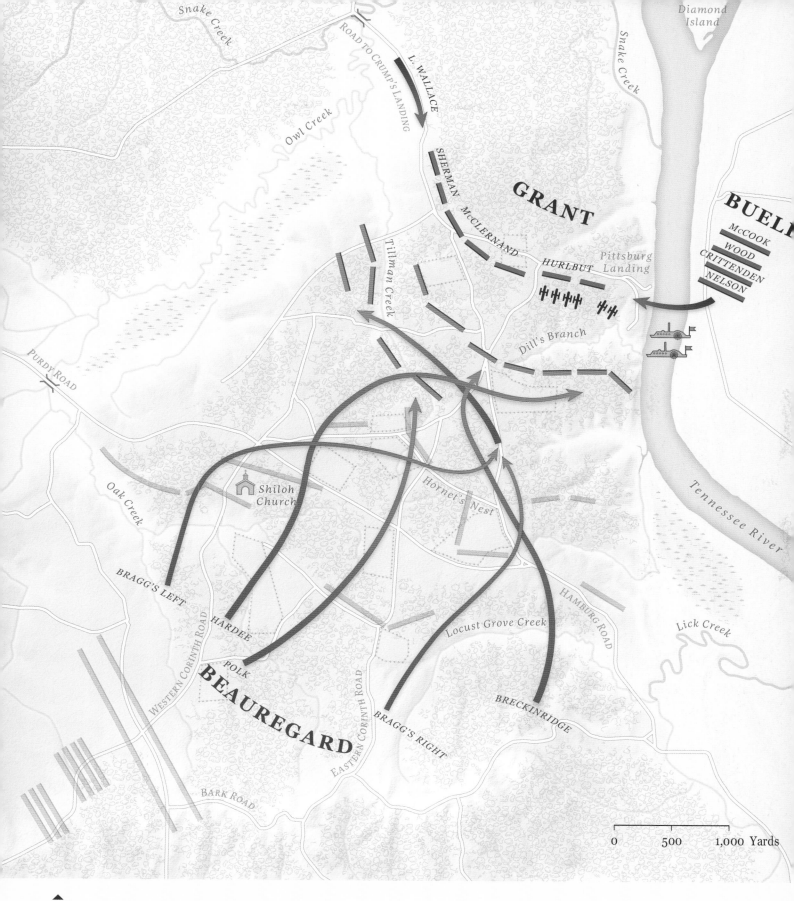

Snake Creek

Diamond Island

Snake Creek

ROAD TO CRUMP'S LANDING

L. WALLACE

Owl Creek

SHERMAN

GRANT

BUELL

McCLERNAND

McCOOK

WOOD

HURLBUT

Pittsburg Landing

CRITTENDEN

NELSON

Tillman Creek

Dill's Branch

PURDY ROAD

Tennessee River

Oak Creek

Shiloh Church

Hornet's Nest

BRAGG'S LEFT

HARDEE

Locust Grove Creek

Hamburg Road

Lick Creek

WESTERN CORINTH ROAD

POLK

BEAUREGARD

BRAGG'S RIGHT

EASTERN CORINTH ROAD

BRECKINRIDGE

BARK ROAD

0   500   1,000 Yards

BATTLE OF SHILOH, EVENING, APRIL 6

The Confederates' advance quickly became intermixed and lost organization, though they pushed back the Union army. Johnston was wounded in the leg and died from blood loss. Intense fighting took place in an area known as the Hornet's Nest, where Confederates managed to capture a Union division.

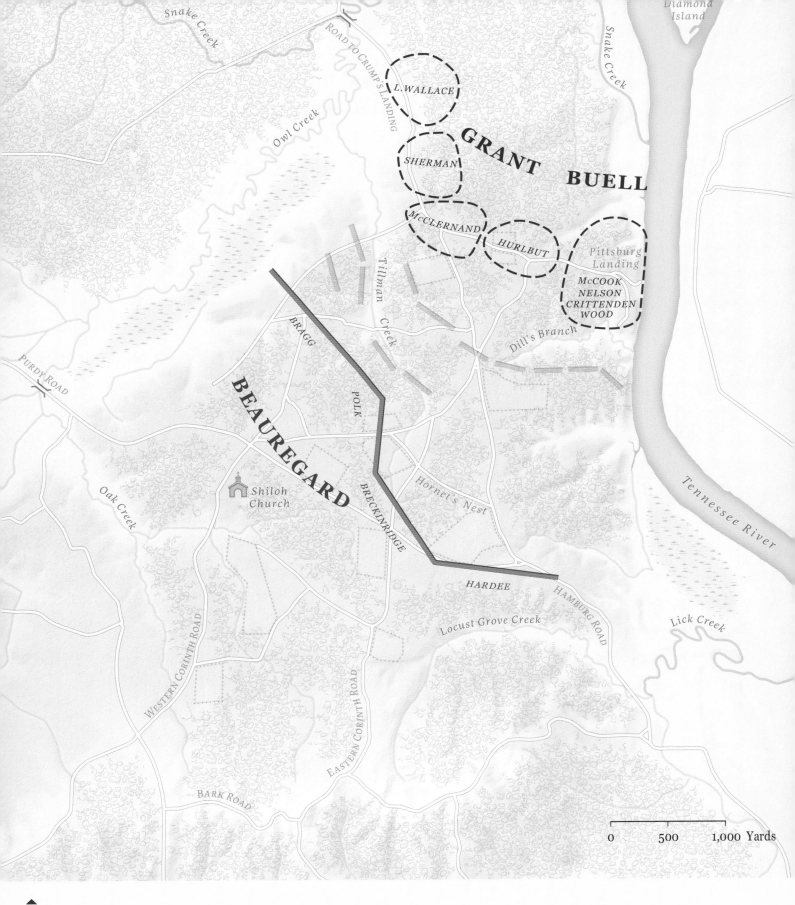

BATTLE OF SHILOH, MORNING, APRIL 7

Confederate delays brought on by confusion and nightfall allowed Grant to reform his lines near the river. In addition, he received reinforcement in the form of Lew Wallace's division from the north, and Don Carlos Buell's Army of the Ohio. Grant now outnumbered his foes.

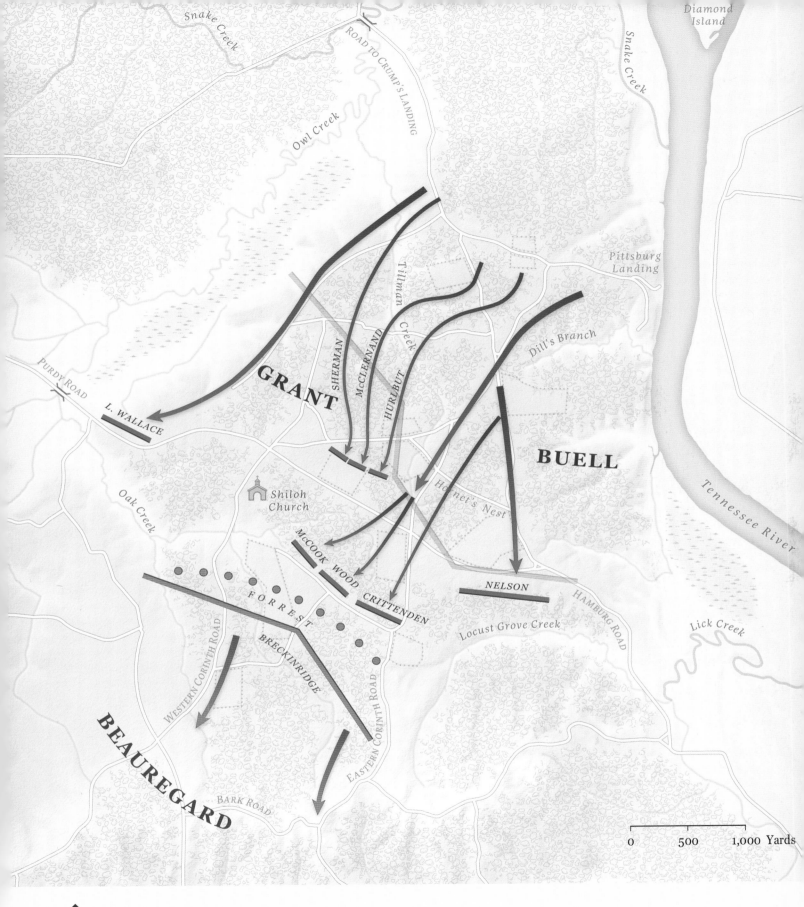

BATTLE OF SHILOH, AFTERNOON, APRIL 7

Though he had called the battle a victory the previous evening, Beauregard saw his men pushed back throughout the day, and he eventually retreated. Grant was unable to continue the pursuit, his men exhausted by two days of hard fighting.

Confederate formations, and made it difficult for Confederate artillery to support the advance.[77]

The Confederates achieved complete tactical surprise and local numerical superiority when they attacked early on the morning of the sixth, but Union troops fell back slowly, while the Rebels became increasingly disordered amid the woods. Johnston, mortally wounded that afternoon, had never been able to exercise army-level command and control across the battlefield. Confederate units became jumbled together, losing momentum when they encountered Federals in sunken roads and ravines such as "the Hornet's Nest." Only numbers and determination remained Confederate advantages, and even those were lost when (after some delays) Don Carlos Buell's Army of the Ohio arrived during the evening with 28,000 fresh U.S. troops. Yet the Rebels finally massed sixty-two cannon to blast open the Hornet's Nest and had nearly reached the Federal supply depot at Pittsburg Landing before dark. Rain began to fall, and William Tecumseh Sherman, a division commander who had thought a Confederate attack unlikely and now pondered retreat, asked Grant what he thought of the situation: "We've had the devil's own day, haven't we?"

Grant replied quietly, with the determination that would raise him eventually to command the armies of the United States, that the army would "lick 'em tomorrow, though."[78]

Reinforced by Buell, Grant's soldiers, outnumbering the Confederates nearly two to one, ground forward the next day (April 7), and the Rebels withdrew. The Union had suffered over 13,000 casualties (about 20 percent of its force); the Confederates, over 10,500 (25 percent). Winfield Scott had conquered Mexico with an army of only 14,000 men. The Civil War had become a great war indeed. Yet nothing was decisive, in the Napoleonic sense expected by generals, politicians, and the public: the woods and casualties now hampered Federal cohesion and coordination, precluding an effective pursuit.

Despite the heavy losses, and criticism that Grant had been surprised, Lincoln was pleased that he had come to grips with the enemy. Grant now knew that the war was changing: "Up to the battle of Shiloh I . . . believed that the rebellion . . . would collapse suddenly and soon, if a decisive victory could be gained over any of its armies. . . . [After Shiloh] I gave up all idea of saving the Union except by complete conquest."[79]

▚ **THE BATTLE OF SHILOH**
On the first day, Confederate forces had pushed the Union forces almost to Pittsburg Landing. The intensity of battle would prove to be an important lesson for men on both sides. This print shows the lethal effect of artillery used against linear formations at close distances.

◀ **THE BATTLE OF SHILOH**
The intense fighting and high casualties at Shiloh (by far the bloodiest battle of the war to that point) shocked the nation and nearly led to Grant's removal.

Grant's observation captured the shifting sentiments of many northerners, particularly the Republicans in Congress.

CONCLUSION

The Union and the Confederacy each brought formidable assets to the war. These were rooted in potent economies but perhaps above all in mobilizing popular sentiment on both sides. The Confederacy had the advantage of spatial depth; the Union, of institutional depth and infrastructure. Northern naval power, a product of industry, would permit the Union to exploit its numerical advantage in multiple attacks on exterior lines (usually condemned in nineteenth-century military thought for diffusing effort) against Confederate interior lines—*if* the Union command could coordinate them. Despite the telegraph, that coordination would prove difficult, between theaters (strategically), within theaters operationally, and tactically, as at Bull Run and Shiloh.

"A people's contest," as Lincoln called it, meant political pressure but also a level of popular support not seen since the days of the *levée en masse* (a national mobilization of civilians and volunteer soldiers during the French Revolution). Secession and war began because the slaveholders had underestimated the will of the citizens of the northern states. In mid-1862 Abraham Lincoln was fortunate still to be head of the government of the United States. In a parliamentary system, instead of a constitutional one, he might have lost a vote of confidence after the defeat at the Battle of Bull Run. But under article II of the Constitution, Lincoln would be president and commander in chief for at least four years, and in the spring of 1862, the Union was taking the offensive. Only impeachment (highly unlikely with a Republican-controlled Congress) or assassination (never yet the fate of an American president) could change the determined leadership of the North. Lincoln could weather the criticism of a disappointed public and the watchful Democratic Party. Lincoln could search for able generals and victory. He was bound to do so, or die trying.[80]

INTRODUCTION

After the Battle of First Bull Run, both the Union and the Confederacy began to build and train large armies. For the Confederacy and Brig. Gen. Joseph E. Johnston, it was a daunting challenge as they confronted the problems of a small, predominantly agricultural economy with a transportation network that was mostly suited to moving nonperishable goods. The Union, with its large population, impressive industrial base, efficient transportation network, and extraordinary production of food crops and livestock, possessed the resources necessary to develop a large, well-equipped military force. To head this massive Army of the Potomac, President Abraham Lincoln selected George B. McClellan, West Point graduate, Mexican War veteran, and railroad president. Yet it was a former U.S. Army officer, now a Confederate general, Robert E. Lee, who reshaped the course of the war. A nation's ability to prosecute a war effectively depends on manpower, materiel, morale, and leadership. Lee's extraordinary leadership during the Peninsular, Second Bull Run, and Antietam campaigns compensated for inferior numbers and resources, buoyed morale, and altered the momentum of the war, one of the greatest achievements in American military history.

REORGANIZATION AFTER FIRST BULL RUN: THE CONFEDERATES

In the afterglow of the resounding Rebel triumph in the Battle of First Bull Run, a Mississippi private who knew no better crowed, "We have won the greatest victory that has ever been recorded in history." Johnston thought otherwise. His troops had earned a victory, but they had also squandered a great opportunity to pursue the Federals more aggressively. As he wrote President Jefferson Davis confidentially, "The victory disorganized our volunteers as utterly as defeat would do in an army of regulars."[1]

Johnston realized that the Confederates must make significant changes to the army. He believed the great advantage his soldiers possessed was their motivation. Southerners fought for independence and their rights against invaders; in the eyes of Confederates, Yankees were hirelings who fought solely for money. Johnston's men had fired high in the battle, but with experience they would calm down and take more deliberate aim. Next time, Johnston's soldiers would be better drilled and disciplined. If they continued to occupy this advanced location around Bull Run, they would also need improved defensive positions and more troops, especially cavalry. Had the Rebels possessed just a few more mounted brigades, the haul of Union prisoners and equipment would have been exponentially greater.[2]

Although victory at First Bull Run triggered a resurgence of enlistments, some of them for the duration of the war, the great obstacle that confronted the Confederacy over the next nine months was manpower. Most of those who enlisted in 1861 did so for a one-year term. After limited success offering incentives to keep them in uniform, in April 1862 the Confederate Congress passed the first conscription act in American

2

THE WAR IN THE EAST, JULY 1861– SEPTEMBER 1862

JOSEPH T. GLATTHAAR

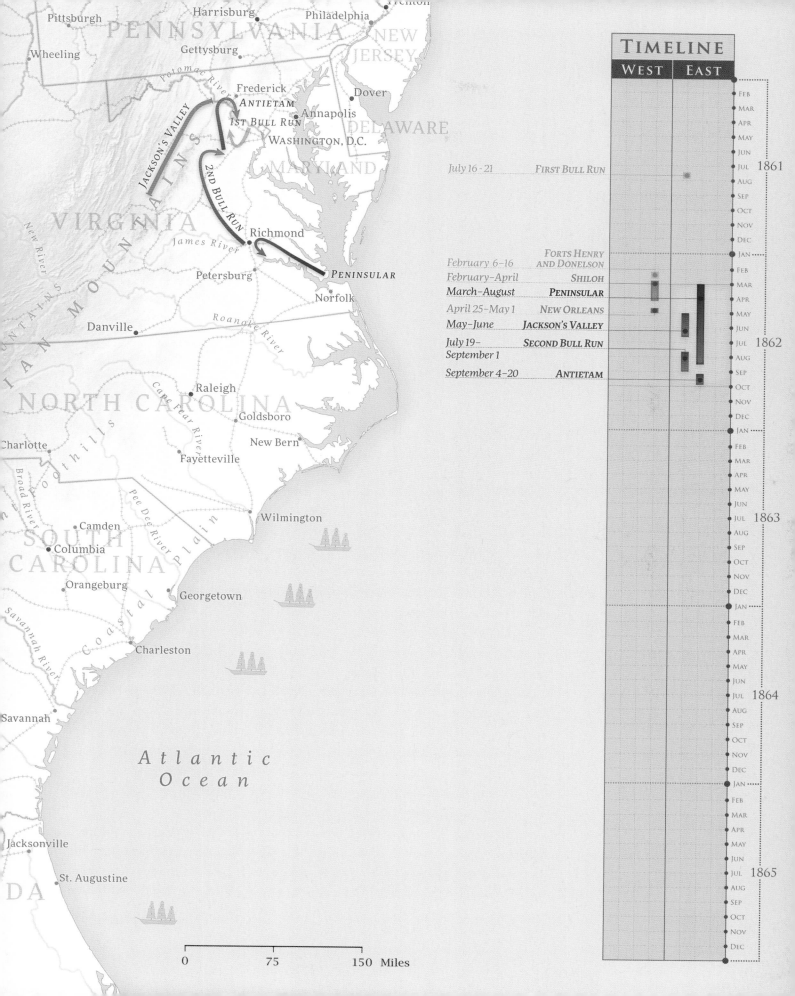

PENNSYLVANIA

Pittsburgh
Harrisburg
Philadelphia
Wheeling
Gettysburg
NEW JERSEY
Dover

Potomac River

Frederick
ANTIETAM
Antietam
1ST BULL RUN
Annapolis
DELAWARE
WASHINGTON, D.C.
MARYLAND

JACKSON'S VALLEY

VIRGINIA

New River

2ND BULL RUN

Richmond
James River

PENINSULAR

Petersburg
Norfolk

Danville
Roanoke River

APPALACHIAN MOUNTAINS

NORTH CAROLINA

Raleigh
Goldsboro

Charlotte
New Bern

Fayetteville

Cape Fear River

Pee Dee River

Broad River

Camden
SOUTH CAROLINA
Columbia

Wilmington

Orangeburg

Georgetown

Savannah River

Charleston

Coastal Plain

Savannah

Atlantic
Ocean

Jacksonville

St. Augustine

FLORIDA

0   75   150 Miles

TIMELINE

WEST	EAST	

July 16 - 21	*FIRST BULL RUN*	1861 FEB MAR APR MAY JUN JUL AUG SEP OCT NOV DEC
February 6–16	*FORTS HENRY AND DONELSON*	JAN
February–April	*SHILOH*	FEB
March–August	**PENINSULAR**	MAR
April 25–May 1	NEW ORLEANS	APR MAY
May–June	**JACKSON'S VALLEY**	JUN
July 19– September 1	**SECOND BULL RUN**	JUL 1862 AUG
September 4–20	**ANTIETAM**	SEP OCT NOV DEC

1863

1864

1865

Joseph Eggleston Johnston

February 3, 1807–March 21, 1891

Born near Farmville, Virginia, Johnston was a classmate of Robert E. Lee in the U.S. Military Academy class of 1829. He fought in Mexico and served as quartermaster general of the U.S. Army. With P. G. T. Beauregard, Johnston masterminded the Confederate victory at First Bull Run and later commanded the Army of Northern Virginia. He was the fourth-highest-ranking officer in the Confederate army.

While superb on the defensive, Johnston lacked aggressive spirit. He retreated in the face of McClellan's advance during the Peninsular campaign and launched an ill-coordinated attack at Seven Pines–Fair Oaks on May 31, 1862, which failed to achieve significant advantages. Johnston was severely wounded by artillery fire on May 31, and Robert E. Lee eventually succeeded him. When Johnston recovered, Jefferson Davis placed him in charge of two large departments in the West, but he was unable to save Vicksburg, Port Hudson, or Middle Tennessee.

Still under a dark cloud, Johnston replaced Gen. Braxton Bragg as commander of the Army of Tennessee in December 1863. He rejuvenated the army and conducted a defensive campaign against Sherman during the Atlanta campaign, giving up large areas of territory but maintaining the effectiveness of his army. Nevertheless, Davis grew alarmed and replaced him with Hood.

Johnston was restored to command of the Army of Tennessee in February 1865. His last battle, at Bentonville, North Carolina, only temporarily halted Sherman's march through the Carolinas. He surrendered his troops on April 26 after news of Lee's surrender was confirmed. Johnston remained one of the more controversial generals of the Civil War until his death.

history. Those who had served a year were required to remain in the service for two additional years. They received furloughs at the army's convenience and could elect new officers and even change branches of service. Other able-bodied white males between eighteen and thirty-five years of age were subject to conscription, unless the number of volunteers met each state's manpower quota. Several months later, legislation allowed substitutions and created exemptions for government workers, clergymen, physicians, selected skilled workers, and farmers, and, controversially, for one white male adult wherever twenty or more slaves resided within a five-mile radius.[3] Nevertheless, the draft managed to keep the Rebel army together for the upcoming campaign and provided essential manpower throughout the war.[4]

Maintaining good health among the soldiers was another challenge. Johnston, the former quartermaster general of the U.S. Army, began constructing a massive army camp—a kind of mobile city—larger than any southern city in 1860 other than New Orleans. Initially, the Confederates had remained camped on the battlefield after their victory. But pollution from dead animals and men, poor sanitary practices, and dense populations resulted in woeful rates of disease, sometimes reaching 75 percent in regiments. Eventually the army dispersed over a nine-square-mile area. By December, some 75,000 officers and men were camped within it. Many succumbed to childhood illnesses that rural soldiers had avoided in their youth, but the biggest killer was typhoid fever, spread usually through a contaminated water supply.[5]

Civil–military relations posed a third problem, as relations deteriorated between Jefferson Davis and his key subordinates, Brig. Gens. Beauregard and Johnston. The friction stemmed from a mix of prickly personalities, powerful senses of southern honor, and different perceptions of duties and prerogatives. In August Beauregard

complained to two former volunteer aides who were also Confederate congressmen of supply problems, asserting that shortages prevented the Confederates from capturing Washington. The ensuing firestorm in Congress painted Davis as incompetent, even though Beauregard's claims were gross exaggerations. Embers of the dispute had just begun to stop glowing when Davis read Beauregard's report on the Bull Run campaign in the newspapers. There Beauregard repeated an absurd proposal he had submitted for the capture of Washington, which Davis had declined to pursue. Once again, the public howled, and Congress erupted in fury. Davis defended himself, but the damage was done. In January 1862, he transferred Beauregard to the west.[6]

Johnston, too, ran afoul of Davis early in the war. The Confederate general feared becoming trapped at Harpers Ferry by Union forces. He wanted to retreat but worried that the order to withdraw would damage his reputation, so he dodged responsibility and sought to have Davis himself issue the order instead. Johnston also rejected, in writing, orders from Robert E. Lee, who held the position of military adviser to the president, because he believed that he outranked Lee. Davis considered the acts "insubordinate" and wrote so on Johnston's replies.[7] In September, after Congress created the rank of general, Johnston exploded with an intemperate and inappropriate letter to Davis when he learned that he ranked fourth behind Adjutant Gen. Samuel Cooper, Albert Sidney Johnston, and Lee—all of whom he had outranked in the antebellum army. Though Davis had determined Johnston's rank in accordance with Confederate laws, he declined to justify himself to the general. That winter, Johnston flagrantly refused to obey directives to rearrange regiments into brigades by state to promote recruitment, and he obstructed the secretary of war's directive to grant extensive winter furloughs to promote reenlistment, claiming that he had the right to determine which orders to obey and when to obey them. Then, in early March 1862, miscommunication between Johnston and Davis resulted in a Confederate retreat from the Manassas-Centreville area to an unprepared position south of the Rappahannock River. Staggering quantities of food, clothing, and equipment were destroyed or abandoned, largely due to sloppy planning and unnecessary haste.[8]

Reorganization After First Bull Run: The Union Side

Union Col. William Tecumseh Sherman anticipated disaster when he witnessed the ill-disciplined, destructive behavior of many soldiers on the march toward Bull Run. "No curse could be greater than invasion by a Volunteer Army," he wrote his wife. "No goths or vandals ever had less respect for the lives & property of friends and foe, and henceforth we ought never to hope for any friends in Virginia . . . Our men are not good Soldiers—They brag, but dont perform."[9]

To instill organization and discipline, the War Department called on Maj. Gen. George B. McClellan. Second in his West Point class, assigned to Maj. Gen. Winfield Scott's staff in Mexico, and an observer of European warfare in the Crimean War, McClellan had given up a promising military career for a railroad engineering position. In time, he rose to president of the Ohio & Mobile Railroad, before joining the war as a major general of volunteers. In early July 1861, he stumbled through a victory at Rich Mountain, part of a campaign that would ultimately secure West Virginia for the Union.[10] In the aftermath of the rout at First Bull Run, his triumph looked considerable, and he received orders to take command of the Army of the Potomac.[11]

McClellan took charge quickly. In the aftermath of defeat, the government recruited vast numbers of regiments and batteries; McClellan oversaw their incorporation into the army. He made sure that his men received quality clothing and equipment and sufficient food. He scrutinized their drill and imposed discipline. A man of enormous energy and organizational ability, McClellan seemed to be everywhere. He made a mob of volunteers feel and begin to act like soldiers, and they loved him for it.

McClellan also instituted changes in two areas that proved critical. First, on the recommendation of Maj. William F. Barry, his chief of artillery, McClellan ordered the concentration of four batteries in each division, to concentrate firepower for division commanders. Batteries generally consisted of six but never fewer than four guns. Later, when McClellan consolidated divisions into corps (the first time in American history

▼ CONFEDERATE CAMP
Confederate camps initially suffered from significant hygiene problems from the dead animals and soldiers, poor sanitary practices, and close quarters. Over time soldiers learned to make their encampments healthier and more comfortable, as shown in the photograph.

◄ HEROES OF MANASSAS
This image celebrates the victorious Confederate leadership—Beauregard, Jackson, Davis, Stuart (or possibly Col. Turner Ashby), and J. E. Johnston—following First Bull Run (which Confederates called the First Manassas). It certainly does not hint at the men's disagreements over strategy and other personal differences that plagued Confederate high command throughout the war.

this was done), at least one-half of all artillery would constitute the corps artillery reserves, giving corps commanders the same control over firepower. Barry preferred smoothbore twelve-pound Napoleons to rifled cannon. With relatively small cleared areas surrounded by woods throughout Virginia, Barry believed that the army would seldom need ranges beyond a mile, making rifled guns, with a three-mile range but firing smaller projectiles, less useful.[13]

The second organizational change occurred when McClellan increased his proportions of wagons and animals to troops far beyond those of Napoleon Bonaparte's army fifty years earlier. American citizen-soldiers demanded a comparatively high standard of living for their service,[14] and the reliability of percussion caps (the new ignition mechanism that had replaced the shower of sparks and pan of priming powder of the older flintlock muskets) enabled troops to fire more rapidly, utilizing more ammunition. Thus the army had to haul more food and supplies, hence more wagons and animals. The scattered farms and limited acreage under cultivation in Virginia offered minimal forage for the army. A horse consumed twenty-six pounds of hay and fodder per day, and a soldier's daily ration weighed three pounds. If the army marched rapidly, it could draw a fair proportion of the forage from the countryside, but in operations over terrain that armies had already picked clean, or when advances were slow, or when the acreage traversed was sparsely cultivated, the army had to haul more forage. Collectively, this necessitated a huge increase in the numbers of wagons, mules, and horses. Heavy fighting also required more ambulances and draft animals. Napoleon usually employed an average of twelve wagons per thousand men; McClellan and his quartermasters planned for forty-five wagons per thousand men and took nearly twenty-five thousand horses and mules for all three branches of service.[15]

McClellan's Men ▶

Prints such as this one, produced and sold to generate popular support for the war, illustrate the favor McClellan enjoyed early on. He looked like a general, and soldiers would cheer as he went by, demonstrating their gratitude for his training and support.

TWELVE-POUNDER NAPOLEON ▶

McClellan reorganized his artillery to allow for more concentrated firepower. Each division received a battalion of four batteries, each consisting of four or six cannon. The most common artillery pieces used by both sides during the Civil War were the twelve-pounder Napoleons (named for Napoleon III of France). They were durable, reliable, and relatively easy to make.

These transportation demands slowed marches over the narrow, muddy dirt roads and led to massive traffic jams. Yet many commanders, including McClellan's successors in command of the Army of the Potomac, feared abandoning their wagons and relying on foraging, in case forage proved insufficient as more men picked over the same farms. Nor could armies bring all the supplies they needed with them. Wagon trains followed them from secure bases to supplement their needs. The result was a vicious cycle: officers and men demanded and consumed a large amount of supplies, which required more wagons, but the horses and mules that pulled those wagons also consumed a huge amount of food, requiring more wagons and additional animals. These logistical demands slowed down the army, limiting its ability to outmaneuver enemy armies or to catch them and force them to fight at a disadvantage. Civil War armies probably averaged no more than ten miles per day on the march, and the larger the army, the slower it moved. The slower it moved, the more supplies it needed to sustain an advance over a given distance, and the less it could rely on foraging.

Union commanders tried repeatedly to reduce their supply columns, hoping that twenty wagons per thousand men might prove adequate. When commanders were able to find solutions the increase in army mobility could be decisive, as with U.S. Grant near Vicksburg and Sherman after he captured Atlanta. But these solutions depended on agricultural density and were hard to sustain, particularly in the face of a powerful enemy within a limited space, as in northern and central Virginia. More often, lack of supplies eroded armies, particularly those of the less well-resourced Confederacy. For most Union army commanders, who were trained as engineers and who doubted that they had advantages sufficient to outmaneuver their opponents, the choice was clear. They hoped that slow and steady would win the race; that their advantages in numbers and firepower would outweigh Rebel agility.

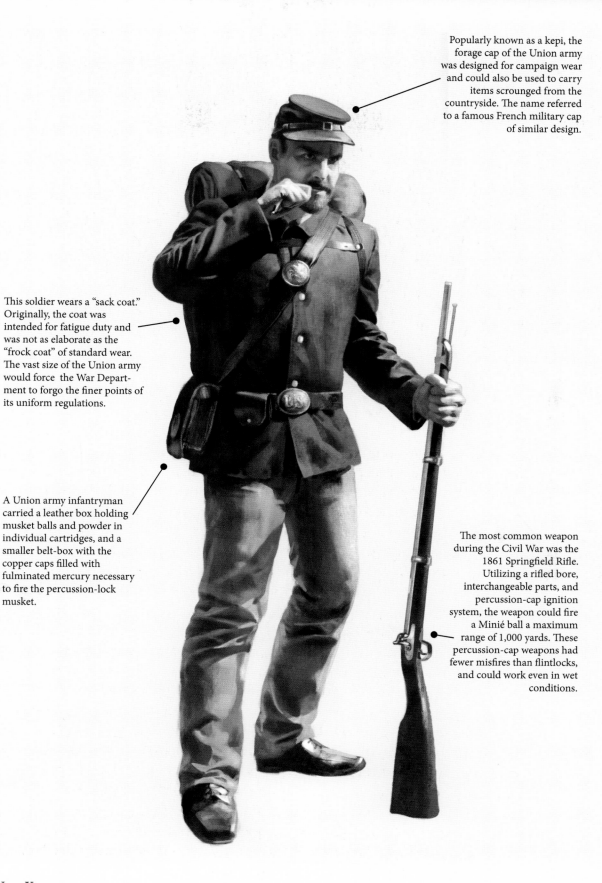

Popularly known as a kepi, the forage cap of the Union army was designed for campaign wear and could also be used to carry items scrounged from the countryside. The name referred to a famous French military cap of similar design.

This soldier wears a "sack coat." Originally, the coat was intended for fatigue duty and was not as elaborate as the "frock coat" of standard wear. The vast size of the Union army would force the War Department to forgo the finer points of its uniform regulations.

A Union army infantryman carried a leather box holding musket balls and powder in individual cartridges, and a smaller belt-box with the copper caps filled with fulminated mercury necessary to fire the percussion-lock musket.

The most common weapon during the Civil War was the 1861 Springfield Rifle. Utilizing a rifled bore, interchangeable parts, and percussion-cap ignition system, the weapon could fire a Minié ball a maximum range of 1,000 yards. These percussion-cap weapons had fewer misfires than flintlocks, and could work even in wet conditions.

39TH NEW YORK

In the years after First Bull Run, few volunteer units retained the gaudy uniforms they had joined with. The need to replace the garish coats and pants of 1861, combined with the growing industrial capacity of Union uniform manufacturers, created a more standardized appearance among the North's soldiers.

GEORGE BRINTON McCLELLAN

DECEMBER 3, 1826–OCTOBER 29, 1885

McClellan graduated second in his class from USMA in 1846 and served in the Mexican War on Winfield Scott's staff. He observed the Crimean War. A railroad president, he was a strong supporter of Stephen A. Douglas in 1860. After a minor victory at Rich Mountain, he was appointed commander of the Army of the Potomac. He soon began to inflate enemy numbers and criticize Scott, and succeeded him as commanding general in November 1861.

McClellan built a massive army around Washington and trained it well, but he refused to campaign. He also acted contemptuously toward most politicians, including the president. Lincoln removed him as commanding general of the Union Army but left him in place as commander of the Army of the Potomac for the spring 1862 amphibious offensive known as the Peninsular campaign. McClellan eventually landed at Yorktown, Virginia, and fought his way to the outskirts of Richmond, only to be driven back in the battles of Seven Days. After insubordinate behavior and demanding absurd numbers of troops, he was ordered to support John Pope's force south of Washington, D.C., and contributed to his defeat at Second Bull Run. Lincoln nevertheless reinstated McClellan as commanding general because he needed someone to restore order in the army. After discovering Lee's invasion plans, McClellan launched an uncoordinated attack at Antietam. When he failed to follow up that lackluster victory aggressively, Lincoln removed him. McClellan had great difficulty getting along with superiors and lacked the kind of strong character necessary for combat command.

RHODE ISLAND CAMP

With volunteer units commissioned and raised by the states, new regiments would train within their own borders for several months before receiving an assignment and heading to their new locations.

For all his motivational successes and organizational improvements, McClellan nonetheless fell out of the good graces of his superiors. Never a loyal subordinate,[16] he let his ego run wild, and he soon clashed with Winfield Scott (commanding general of the U.S. Army since 1841), President Lincoln, and anyone else who disagreed with him. Upon his arrival in Washington, McClellan wrote to his wife about how everyone deferred to him: "I almost think that were I to win some small success now I could become Dictator or anything else that might please me—but nothing of that kind would please me—*therefore* I *won't* be Dictator. Admirable self denial!" He informed Lincoln that he wanted 273,000 troops in Virginia. Without evidence, he insisted that the Confederates numbered 100,000, and he feared the loss of Washington. In mid-July he fawned over Scott as a great military mind. Three weeks later, after Scott insisted that the capital was safe, McClellan wondered whether Scott "is a *dotard* or a *traitor!*" Meanwhile, his assessment of enemy numbers continued to escalate. On August 16,

▼
LINCOLN AND MCCLELLAN
Lincoln regularly met with McClellan and his generals to discuss strategy. The general found these meetings tedious, and they helped to build his antipathy toward the president.

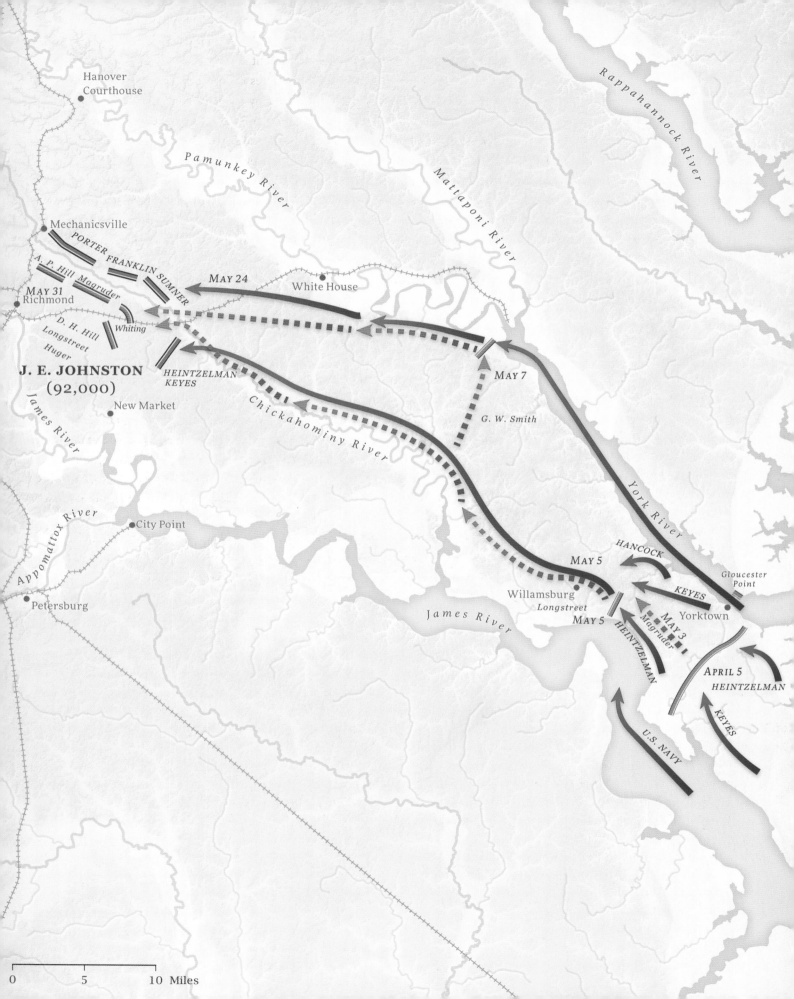

Hanover
Courthouse

Pamunkey River

Mattaponi River

Rappahannock River

Mechanicsville

PORTER FRANKLIN SUMNER

A. P. Hill Magruder

MAY 24

White House

MAY 31
Richmond

D. H. Hill
Longstreet
Huger

Whiting

MAY 7

J. E. JOHNSTON
(92,000)

HEINTZELMAN
KEYES

New Market

Chickahominy River

G. W. Smith

James River

York River

Appomattox River

City Point

HANCOCK

*Gloucester
Point*

MAY 5

KEYES

Petersburg

James River

Willamsburg
Longstreet

MAY 5

Magruder

Yorktown

MAY 3

HEINTZELMAN

APRIL 5
HEINTZELMAN

KEYES

U.S. NAVY

0   5   10 Miles

Chesapeake
Bay

McCLELLAN
(105,000)

MARCH 17
Hampton

Fort
Monroe

Norfolk

when McClellan had an aggregate present force of well over 100,000, he claimed that Confederates had "3 to 4 times my force"; three days later, they had 150,000; in mid-September, "The enemy probably have 170,000!" By late October, Scott had had enough, retiring after fifty-three years' service. Lincoln offered Scott's position to McClellan, who also continued to command the Army of the Potomac. "I can do it all," he replied.[17]

Others, too, came under McClellan's attack. The secretary of state was a "meddling, officious, incompetent puppy"; the attorney general, "an old fool"; and the secretary of the navy, "weaker than the most garrulous woman you were ever annoyed by." The president was "an idiot," "a well-meaning baboon," and "*the original gorilla.*" Lincoln endured the general's disdain for the good of the cause, but McClellan's stock plummeted in his eyes.[18]

TO THE PENINSULA

When McClellan finally got the Army of the Potomac moving in the spring, it took one misstep after another. He planned to transport his army by water from Washington to Urbanna, on the shores of Chesapeake Bay, and then position his command between Johnston's army and Richmond. The move would bypass Rebel defenses along the Manassas-Centreville line, enable him to supply his army easily by water, and compel Johnston to attack the Union forces. Before McClellan moved, however, Johnston fell back behind the Rappahannock, which was closer to Richmond, derailing the Urbanna plan. When Federal troops occupied the positions abandoned by Johnston, the size of the fieldworks indicated that Confederate strength was nowhere near what McClellan had asserted, but this had no impact on his estimates.

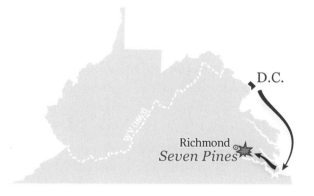

D.C.

Richmond
Seven Pines

◀ **PENINSULAR CAMPAIGN, JUNE 1862**
McClellan advanced up the Peninsula slowly, first capturing Yorktown and then moving on Richmond. The outnumbered Confederates under Joe Johnston retreated, looking for an opportunity to strike back.

IRONCLADS

The Confederate ironclad was the captured Union vessel *Merrimack*, renamed *Virginia* and covered with iron plating, while the Union ship, *Monitor*, had a unique design. The two ships battled to a draw at Hampton Roads on March 9, after the *Virginia* had wreaked havoc on wooden ships in the region.

McClellan next chose Yorktown as his amphibious destination, which would bring his army even closer to Richmond and still permit it to draw supplies by water. But before he could begin transporting his troops, the Confederacy launched the C.S.S. *Virginia*, with four inches of iron plating protecting its sides. The U.S. Navy had urged a joint expedition to regain the Norfolk Navy Yard, where the Confederacy was refitting the *Virginia*, but McClellan had rejected the proposal. The decision came back to haunt him. The *Virginia* wreaked havoc on the blockaders, and only when the ironclad U.S.S. *Monitor* was completed and fought the *Virginia* to a standstill at Hampton Roads could McClellan move. Lincoln, his confidence shaken, removed McClellan as commanding general just before the campaign began but left him as commander of the Army of the Potomac. The president, assisted by Secretary of War Edwin M. Stanton, would act as commanding general of all U.S. armies.[19]

As McClellan landed some 55,000 troops, the Confederate commander on the peninsula, Maj. Gen. John B. Magruder, perpetrated a brilliant bluff with only 14,000 troops. Nicknamed Prince John for his theatrics, Magruder used "Quaker guns"—logs painted black to look like artillery—employed train whistles and cheering soldiers to indicate the arrival of reinforcements, and paraded the same troops through different

trenches that stretched across the Peninsula to suggest powerful defenses. A wary McClellan declined to attack the fortified position and advanced by regular siege approaches, giving Johnston enough time to shift his army east of Richmond.

After Johnston inspected the defensive works near Yorktown, he recommended a retreat to the vicinity of Richmond. He did not like the defenses and feared that the Federals would outflank the batteries across the York River at Gloucester Point, landing behind his command and trapping it on the Peninsula. Robert E. Lee, still serving as principal military adviser to Jefferson Davis, argued otherwise. The Gloucester batteries would block movement up the York while the *Virginia* prevented advances up the James. If the Confederates retreated, they would lose Norfolk Navy Yard and the *Virginia*. Moreover, on the narrow Peninsula, McClellan could not deploy his overwhelming strength. Davis sided with Lee, but it was not long before Johnston fell back anyway, fighting off a small but nasty Union attack at Williamsburg. Federal troops then pursued cautiously to within five miles of Richmond.[20]

QUAKER GUN

Quaker guns—that is, logs painted to resemble artillery—were part of a series of theatrics that helped to slow the Union advance on the Peninsula and to feed McClellan's belief that the Confederates had significantly more men.

MORTARS

The Union army used mortars like these to fire rounds over the walls and into besieged towns such as Yorktown.

Thomas Jackson graduated from USMA in 1846 and had a distinguished combat record in the Mexican War. In 1851 he resigned from the army to take a faculty position at the Virginia Military Institute. A devout Presbyterian, he was appointed a Confederate brigadier general, he disciplined and trained his brigade rigorously, and at First Bull Run it stood its ground beautifully, earning him his nickname Stonewall Jackson and his troops the moniker the Stonewall Brigade. He was promoted to major general.

Eccentric and arbitrary, Jackson ran afoul of the secretary of war and the president, and submitted his resignation, which was not accepted. Jackson then collaborated with Lee and conducted a brilliant campaign known as Jackson's Valley campaign. At the Seven Days, Jackson was too exhausted to fight well, but he redeemed himself at Cedar Mountain, Second Bull Run, and in the Maryland campaign.

Promoted to lieutenant general, he led a corps at Fredericksburg and again at Chancellorsville, where he directed a flank march that rolled up the Union right. He was badly wounded by friendly fire and died subsequently of pneumonia. Enormously popular with the troops, Jackson's secretiveness and inflexibility most likely would have impaired his ability to command a major army.

THOMAS JONATHAN JACKSON

JANUARY 21, 1824–MAY 10, 1863

THE VALLEY CAMPAIGN

Meanwhile, events in the Shenandoah Valley created new problems for the Union. In late March 1862, Stonewall Jackson and 4,500 men struck a Union force at Kernstown. Although Jackson based his attack on faulty intelligence and suffered a repulse, the fight worked to Confederate advantage. McClellan had shortchanged the defenses of Washington to augment his troop strength near Richmond, double counting, adding incorrectly, and including troops that were in the Shenandoah Valley to achieve the agreed-upon defensive strength. Jackson's attack alerted Lincoln that the defenses around Washington were weaker than he thought. When the president responded by withholding a corps from McClellan's army to protect the capital, Lee saw an opportunity.

Emerging as a master of the operational art, Lee realized that he could influence Lincoln and northern public opinion and reduce McClellan's troop strength with a bold drive into the Lower (northern) Shenandoah Valley. On April 25 Lee explained the entire military situation to Jackson and then spelled out his agenda: with Union commands scattered throughout Virginia, "I have hoped in the present divided condition of the enemy's forces that a successful blow may be dealt them by a rapid combination of our troops before they can be strengthened themselves either in their position or by re-enforcements." He wanted Jackson to combine with Brig. Gen. Richard S. Ewell's command of 8,500[21] and advance on the enemy in the Valley. An attack on the Federal concentration around Warrenton, northwest of Fredericksburg, offered a second option. Either plan would relieve the pressure on the defenders near Fredericksburg and keep reinforcements from McClellan. "The blow, wherever struck, must be successful, be sudden and heavy," Lee explained. "The troops used must be efficient and light." The general then concluded with revealing words, "I cannot pretend at this distance to direct operations depending on circumstances unknown to me and requiring the exercise of discretion and judgment as to time and execution, but submit these suggestions

FOOT CAVALRY

To delay their pursuers even further, Jackson's men destroyed bridges and blocked roads, giving them a greater opportunity to prepare for a fight on ground of Jackson's choosing.

for your consideration." Lee established a superb command relationship. He offered options and advice; Jackson decided and executed.[22]

Jackson quickly joined a small Confederate command near Staunton and repulsed a Federal attack at McDowell, Virginia. Lee urged Jackson to combine with Ewell and advance on 35,000 Union troops in the Valley under Maj. Gen. Nathaniel P. Banks. "Whatever movement you make against Banks," Lee advised, "do it speedily, and if successful drive him back toward the Potomac, and create the impression, as far as practicable, that you design threatening that line." Jackson slipped through a gap in the Massanutten Mountains undetected, joined with Ewell, and marched rapidly northward with his 17,000 men to surprise and crush a Union detachment at Front Royal on May 23. Banks, suddenly aware of the threat, retreated northward. With Rebels nipping at their heels, Banks's men discarded vast quantities of equipment and supplies, earning Banks the derogatory nickname Jackson's Quartermaster. The Confederates delivered another powerful blow at Winchester, but confusion in victory and Ewell's failure to execute a direct order enabled Banks's columns to escape. By midafternoon on May 26, the Federals had crossed the Potomac to safety.[23]

Even in defeat, Lincoln perceived opportunity. With Jackson at Harpers Ferry, if Maj. Gen. John C. Frémont's command pushed east through a gap in Shenandoah Mountain and occupied Strasburg, Maj. Gen. Irvin McDowell's corps could advance west and join forces, trapping the Confederates. Yet in one of the great marches of the war, Jackson's men hustled 100 kilometers in three days, before the Federals could cover half that distance. Jackson's army then defeated the Federal columns piecemeal

JACKSON'S VALLEY CAMPAIGN ▶

After a failed initial attack on Nathaniel Banks at Winchester, Jackson retreated south through the Shenandoah Valley.

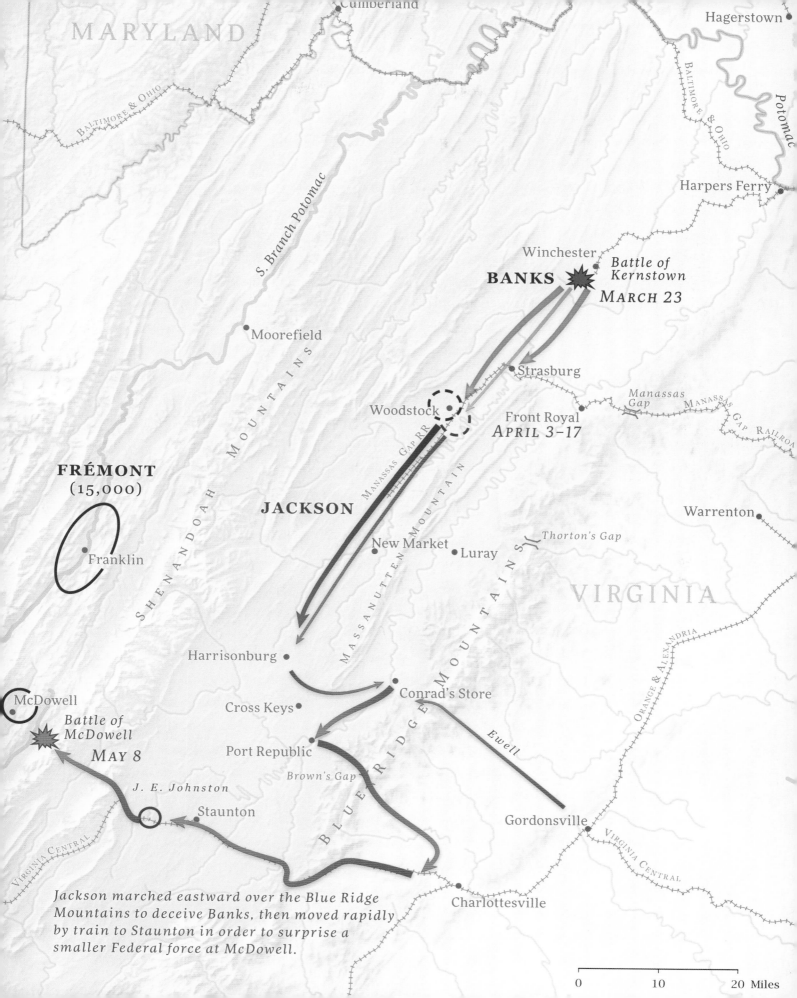

MARYLAND

Cumberland

Hagerstown

BALTIMORE & OHIO

Potomac

BALTIMORE & OHIO

Harpers Ferry

S. Branch Potomac

Moorefield

Winchester

BANKS

Battle of Kernstown

MARCH 23

Strasburg

Manassas Gap

MANASSAS

FRÉMONT
(15,000)

Woodstock

Front Royal

APRIL 3–17

GAP RAILROA

Manassas Gap RR

JACKSON

Franklin

New Market

Luray

Thorton's Gap

Warrenton

VIRGINIA

Harrisonburg

McDowell

Cross Keys

Conrad's Store

Battle of McDowell

MAY 8

Port Republic

Ewell

J. E. Johnston

Brown's Gap

Staunton

Gordonsville

VIRGINIA CENTRAL

BLUE RIDGE MOUNTAINS

ORANGE & ALEXANDRIA

SHENANDOAH MOUNTAINS

MASSANUTTEN MOUNTAIN

VIRGINIA CENTRAL

Charlottesville

Jackson marched eastward over the Blue Ridge Mountains to deceive Banks, then moved rapidly by train to Staunton in order to surprise a smaller Federal force at McDowell.

0   10   20 Miles

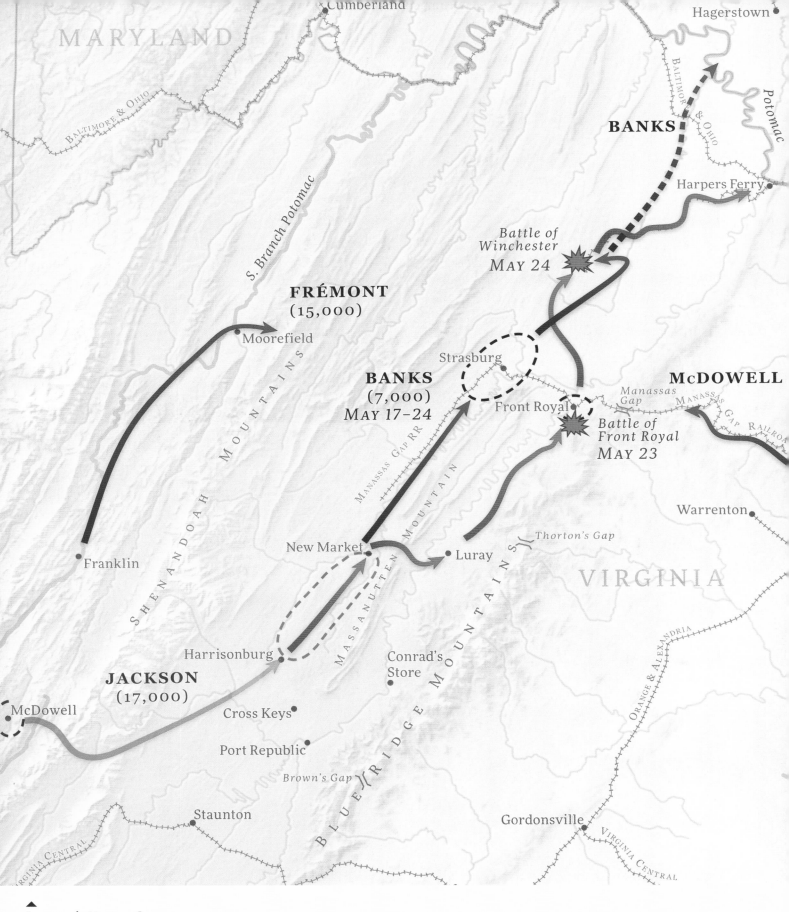

JACKSON'S VALLEY CAMPAIGN

Joining with Richard Ewell's force at Luray, Virginia, Jackson's men pushed down the valley, driving Banks into Maryland. Meanwhile, Lincoln ordered Frémont and McDowell to converge at Strasburg, Virginia, and trap the Confederates.

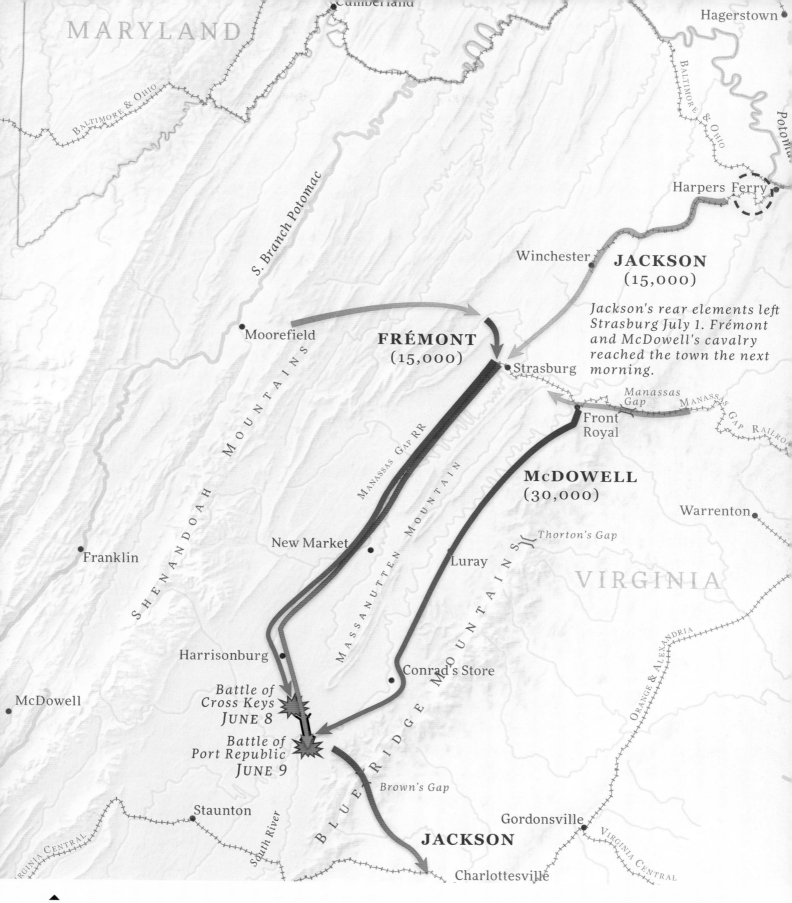

MARYLAND

VIRGINIA

Baltimore & Ohio

S. Branch Potomac

Hagerstown

Cumberland

Potomac

Harpers Ferry

Winchester

JACKSON
(15,000)

Jackson's rear elements left Strasburg July 1. Frémont and McDowell's cavalry reached the town the next morning.

Moorefield

FRÉMONT
(15,000)

Strasburg

Manassas Gap

Manassas Gap Railroad

Front Royal

McDOWELL
(30,000)

Warrenton

Thorton's Gap

Franklin

SHENANDOAH MOUNTAINS

Manassas Gap RR

New Market

Massanutten Mountain

Luray

Conrad's Store

BLUE RIDGE MOUNTAINS

Orange & Alexandria

McDowell

Harrisonburg

Battle of
Cross Keys
JUNE 8

Battle of
Port Republic
JUNE 9

Brown's Gap

Staunton

South River

Virginia Central

JACKSON

Gordonsville

Virginia Central

Charlottesville

▲
JACKSON'S VALLEY CAMPAIGN
Jackson's famous "foot cavalry" raced past the attempted trap. Frémont and McDowell pursued slowly, and Jackson defeated their piecemeal attacks successively at Cross Keys and Port Republic.

on consecutive days at Cross Keys and Port Republic. In six weeks, Jackson's men had fought five battles and numerous skirmishes against three separate Union commands. The Confederacy rejoiced in his success, which delayed troops from reinforcing McClellan, at least temporarily.[24]

THE BATTLES OF SEVEN PINES AND THE SEVEN DAYS

As McClellan and his massive army inched closer to Richmond, Johnston had to act to prevent a siege that might choke the Confederate capital. On May 31 he launched a complicated attack on the Union forces near Seven Pines, east of Richmond. The attack was poorly planned and executed at nearly every level. Johnston wrote no plan of battle,[25] and Maj. Gen. James Longstreet advanced along the wrong route, obstructing other movements and delaying the attack. Brig. Gen. Daniel Harvey Hill[26] waited for reinforcements for five hours before finally attacking without them, hammering back the Federal line. At 6:00, Johnston rode out to investigate and called a halt to the attack. Moments later, a musket ball crashed into his shoulder, and shell shards struck him in the chest and thigh. Meanwhile, Union troops re-formed and checked the Rebel advance. Only ten of twenty-two Confederate brigades had seen action. The next day, Johnston's second in command, Maj. Gen. Gustavus W. Smith, launched uncoordinated assaults once again with little success. In two days of fighting, the Union lost

McCLELLAN SQUEEZE ▶
This cartoon demonstrates the apparent distress faced by the Confederacy as McClellan sat on the outskirts of Richmond. Jefferson Davis is the devil-horned figure in the center of the coils. Any dissatisfaction that northern politicians and civilians may have had with McClellan would have dissipated if he had captured the Confederate capital.

5,000 men; the outnumbered Confederates suffered over 6,000 casualties, including their commander.[27]

It was clear to Jefferson Davis that Smith was not up to the job of army commander, and he replaced the wounded Johnston with Davis's own military adviser, Lee. The general had had a great prewar reputation: second in his West Point class, Corps of Engineers, Mexican War hero and the best officer on Scott's staff in Mexico, superintendent of West Point, and regimental commander in Texas. By early 1861, perhaps sooner, Lee had decided to leave the U.S. Army if Virginia seceded. At the beginning of the war, Scott offered Lee the principal field command in the East, but Lee declined and resigned his commission, certain that Virginia would leave the Union.[28]

Yet doubts about Lee were common throughout the Confederacy. One West Point graduate called Lee's appointment as commander of Virginia forces "unfortunate." He thought that Lee struggled to make decisions. South Carolina governor Francis W. Pickens believed, "The truth is Lee is not with us at heart, or he is a common man, with good looks, and too cautious for practical Revolution."[29]

Army command was both a learned science and an art that few could master. In the prewar army, Lee had never led more than a regiment, and it would take time to make the leap to army command. Like other soldiers in the war, he would have to learn on the job, and those harsh lessons usually cost lives. As Lee quickly discovered, the Rebel public and soldiery had extremely high expectations and were not very forgiving. In Lee's first major field-command assignment in 1861, he attempted to coordinate three separate columns in the rugged terrain of western Virginia. Lee formed a complicated plan, far too difficult for his subordinates to execute, and eventually retreated without delivering a powerful blow. The press and public howled over Lee's incompetence. One officer, a student at West Point when Lee was superintendent, reported to his father that people called Lee a dirt dauber: a small insect that leaves a soiled trail in its wake.[30]

◀ THOMAS MEAGHER AT THE BATTLE OF FAIR OAKS (SEVEN PINES)
Thomas Meagher commanded the Irish Brigade, composed mostly of men of Irish descent. Representatives of various ethnic and immigrant groups, such as Meagher or the German Franz Sigel, received high rank within the army to demonstrate their importance to the Union cause and encourage enlistment from within those communities.

ROBERT EDWARD LEE

JANUARY 19, 1807–OCTOBER 12, 1870

Robert E. Lee was the son of a famous Revolutionary War officer and graduated second in his class from West Point in 1829. In the Mexican War, he served brilliantly. Winfield Scott called him the best officer in the army. After the war, he was superintendent of West Point, as well as lieutenant colonel and then colonel of the 2nd U.S. Cavalry. In 1861, he declined command of the principal U.S. field army and instead took command of Virginia's state forces, assisting President Jefferson Davis.

Lee failed as a field commander at Cheat Mountain and was roasted by the media. Davis sent him to the southeast but recalled him as military adviser in March. He helped design Jackson's Valley campaign. After Joe Johnston's wounding, Lee took command and achieved stunning successes, driving the Union army back from Richmond in the Seven Days Battles and then clearing Federal forces out from nearly all of Virginia.

An aggressive commander who seized the initiative, utilized the element of surprise, and commited all his forces in battle to defeat the larger and better-resourced Union army, Lee proved too aggressive at Antietam and Gettysburg. Despite heavy losses, his army still inflicted 124,000 casualties on the Union forces from May 1864 to April 1865. In the end, his army was trapped and surrendered at Appomattox Court House on April 9, 1865.

Such attacks damaged Lee's reputation to the point that Davis decided to send him away from Richmond to oversee the defense of Charleston and the rest of South Carolina, in addition to Georgia and Florida. Davis, however, recalled Lee as his chief military adviser before the 1862 spring campaign season opened. Communications between Davis and Johnston had broken down, and Davis felt that he needed someone both Johnston and he respected. Yet memories in Virginia were long. One staff officer thought the appointment of Lee "looks like a fatal mistake." He then beseeched, "May God in mercy protect us." Even McClellan rejoiced when he heard mistakenly in April 1862 that Lee would replace Johnston as field commander. "I prefer Lee to Johnston," he explained to Lincoln in a letter. "[T]he former is *too* cautious & weak under grave responsibility—personally brave & energetic to a fault, he yet is wanting in moral firmness when pressed by heavy responsibility & is likely to be timid & irresolute in action."[31]

McClellan completely misread Lee. As a military commander, Lee could assume responsibility, plan thoroughly, and act decisively. Over the course of three and a half decades of military service, employing the experience of active duty in Mexico and the Confederacy, wide reading about the Napoleonic Wars, and mature reflection, Lee had sharpened his skills as a campaign planner. He could see how each command related to another, and how he could employ them in combination to achieve success. Lee also had an uncanny talent for anticipating enemy movements. He understood the possibilities that confronted his opponents, studied their decisions, and thereby gained insight into how they would respond to specific situations that he created.[32]

With the army's back to Richmond, Lee quickly took charge of what he called the Army of Northern Virginia. He cracked down on waste, knowing that the Confederacy had limited resources and a narrow margin of error, and he established routines so that soldiers received food and supplies reliably. Lee demanded that officers devote themselves to the well-being of their men, to insure that everyone was rested and healthy for the inevitable battle. Despite resistance, Lee compelled soldiers to dig trenches and

MILITARY BALLOON
Union forces began using observation balloons during the Peninsular campaign, but to limited effect. McClellan still used inaccurate assessments of Confederate strength, which justified his slow retreat from Richmond during the Seven Days Battles.

prepare rifle pits, abatis (defensive obstacles formed by felling trees and interlacing the branches), and other obstructions. He also gathered intelligence on the enemy and drew in reinforcements for combat from secondary theaters.[33]

Lee's plan was bold. McClellan's army straddled the Chickahominy River, making it difficult for those Federals north of it to retreat or to receive reinforcements. Lee would leave just 25,000 entrenched men to hold at bay the mass of the Union army south of the Chickahominy, while he hurled some 65,000 men against the exposed right flank of McClellan's force, a single corps commanded by Fitz John Porter. To buttress the attack, Lee summoned Jackson's columns from just outside the Valley to fall on the exposed Union flank. Jackson rode fifty-two miles in fourteen hours to meet with Lee and then rode all night to rendezvous with his command. He then pushed his troops and himself too hard to make the unreasonable deadline he had set. Jackson's exhausted soldiers arrived late, and neither they nor their commander, who had slept only ten hours in the previous four days, performed with their usual aggressiveness.

Lee pulled three divisions from the trenches and positioned them to attack. Once Maj. Gen. A. P. Hill[34] heard Jackson's gunfire, he was to hurl his men directly into the Union line. Lee believed pressure from Hill in the front and Jackson in the rear would dislodge the Federals. Longstreet's division would attack the enemy as it retreated, and Daniel Harvey (D. H.) Hill's division and J. E. B. Stuart's cavalry would reinforce Jackson. Lee wanted no letup until they cut McClellan's supply line, which ran to the small hamlet of White House on the Pamunkey River. The plan involved tremendous risks, but Lee knew McClellan and doubted that his cautious counterpart would attack the lightly defended trenches while his flank was under assault by the Army of Northern Virginia.

On June 26 Jackson failed to attack on schedule, making Lee's situation more risky by the moment, until A. P. Hill finally crossed Chickahominy River and attacked frontally, without Jackson's support. By nightfall, Jackson finally got in position on McClellan's right flank, where his presence compelled Porter to order his exposed corps to withdraw. McClellan, however, was spooked, and he began to shift his supply base and his army to the James River and the protection of Union gunboats.

Once again, Federals occupied high ground behind a waterway, this time Boatswain's Swamp, and they strengthened it with rifle pits and abatis. On June 27 Jackson's command was again tardy, arriving in the late afternoon. Meanwhile, Confederates under A. P. Hill and Longstreet launched a series of unsuccessful frontal assaults. Near sunset, with the Confederates pressing all along the line, men from the Texas Brigade[35] waded through a supposedly impassable swamp, stormed a steep hill, and crashed through the Union line at its crest. At the opposite end of the battlefield, Jackson's men also penetrated the defenses, and the Federal line collapsed. In this Battle of Gaines's Mill, Lee's army won a clear victory, but it suffered some 9,000 casualties, while inflicting losses of only 6,000 men on the larger Federal force.

On the Union side that day, McClellan made noises about striking the Confederates who shielded Richmond, but the ferocity of Lee's attack and Magruder's theatrics in the trenches again confirmed his beliefs that the Rebel army greatly outnumbered his own, scaring him into a defensive posture. McClellan remained well to the rear at

STUART'S RIDE ◥
Ordered to scout McClellan's flank, Stuart was able to take his cavalry on a full ride around the entire Army of the Potomac. This revealed the weakness of McClellan's position and made the dashing Stuart a hero to the Confederacy.

WHITE HOUSE ON THE PAMUNKEY ▶
This appropriately named building was McClellan's headquarters at White House Landing during the Seven Days. McClellan abandoned the base as Lee pushed on his army.

his headquarters and failed to rush reinforcements to Porter, whose corps bore the brunt of the Confederate attack. Porter finally received an additional division that afternoon, raising his strength to some 35,000, but no others arrived before the Confederates shattered his lines. At least 60,000 Union troops remained inactive while Porter battled to extricate his command.[36]

The strain of the campaign shattered McClellan. He slept little and exhausted himself. As he confessed in a letter to his wife, "You can't tell how nervous I became." Two weeks after the campaign ended, he elaborated. "I *did* have a terrible time that week—for I stood alone, without anyone to help me—I felt that on me rested everything & I felt how weak a thing a poor mortal erring man is!" The pressure and sense of isolation caused him to collapse emotionally. He abdicated his responsibilities as army commander and lapsed into the more familiar role of a staff officer. Instead of coordinating the fighting of his corps, he oversaw the shifting of his supply base from the York River to the James River.[37]

Lee also felt frustration, but his came from losing opportunities to strike devastating blows against the enemy. His plans required a degree of timing and coordination that would have challenged a veteran army. Although the area had been settled for nearly 250 years, Lee and his subordinates had poor maps, leading to confusion. The Army of Northern Virginia was organized in divisions rather than in corps, so too many separate commands reported directly to Lee, and his inexperienced staff officers failed to communicate his intent to subordinates. Nor did the division commanders always fight with the aggressiveness that Lee expected of them. At Savage's Station on June 29, Lee tried to sandwich the Federals between Jackson's wing and the divisions of Magruder and Maj. Gen. Benjamin Huger, with Longstreet and A. P. Hill in support. Conflicting orders and vague information detained Jackson, and, without Jackson's support, Magruder advanced cautiously and committed only a portion of his troops to battle. The results proved inconclusive.[38]

The next day, June 30, Lee's army again failed to coordinate effectively. Huger acted hesitantly while Jackson was too exhausted to formulate command decisions. This placed the burden onto Longstreet's and A. P. Hill's soldiers. They advanced toward Glendale and encountered stiff resistance. The battle seesawed as Confederates assaulted and seized portions of the Union line, only to lose them to counterattacks.

GAINES'S MILL ◥

Artist Alfred Waud's sketch of Union forces withdrawing after the Battle of Gaines's Mill, with commissary stores on fire in the background.

GUNBOAT CANDIDATE ▶

When he ran for president in 1864, McClellan saw his actions during the Seven Days mocked, particularly the fact that he was already on board a gunboat headed back to the ocean during Malvern Hill, the campaign's final battle, and a Union victory.

Some fought hand to hand. As nightfall descended, the Rebels seized a critical battery and forced the Federals to withdraw. In the Battle of Frayser's Farm, the two sides racked up a combined 6,400 casualties.

Time after time, Lee had attempted to crush a portion of McClellan's army, and in each instance, the Federals had managed to escape. The next morning, the Confederates discovered Union forces occupying a wheat-covered slope called Malvern Hill. Lee knew that as the Federals retreated close to the James River, Federal gunboats would enhance Union firepower considerably, making it nearly impossible to defeat them. This would be his last opportunity to deliver a devastating blow. But the Federals occupied an outstanding defensive position, with steep slopes on three sides, and had concentrated perhaps thirty-five cannon on the crest. McClellan's decision to consolidate his artillery into battalions at the division level and retain a corps reserve now paid dividends.

Lee intended to create artillery crossfire to silence enemy batteries and soften the position, and then to have infantry assault up the slope. Once again, his command could not concentrate at the right time and place. Artillery never reached position in sufficient numbers to silence anything. Overwhelming Union firepower, benefitting from the commanding terrain, quickly silenced the few Rebel guns that fired. Nonetheless, Magruder ordered a North Carolina brigade forward, followed by others, and began a series of ill-coordinated assaults. In the face of overwhelming fire, none reached the crest; the attacking soldiers were mowed down along the slope or dropped to the ground, unwilling to advance farther, and made their way back when they thought it was safe. Mercifully, the attack started late in the day, and darkness brought it to a halt. The sight of 5,600 Confederate casualties strewn across the field outraged the cantankerous D. H. Hill so much that twenty-five years later he recollected, "It was not war—it was murder."[39]

The scope and intensity of the fighting during the Seven Days exceeded anyone's imagination. "We used to think that the battle of Manassas was a great affair," a South Carolinian wrote to his wife, "but it was mere child's play compared with those in which we have been engaged lately."[40] A Pennsylvanian wrote home of his miraculous escape amid absolute horror: "Three guns, one after another, were shot to pieces in my hands, and one of these was struck twice before I threw it away. My canteen was shot through, and I was struck in three places by balls, one over the left eye, one in the left shoulder, and one in the left leg, and the deepest wound was not over half an inch, and I came off the field unhurt."[41] A Georgia private wrote his wife, "I have heard talk of war & read of war but never could realize its horrors until I experienced it. I have been in four fights in one week & marched all the time, have seen thousands of dead men & horses, and even the Woods cut to peaces by the heavy Artilery."[42] The two sides suffered a combined 36,000 casualties, a total surpassed only by the Battle of Gettysburg.

Despite the victory at Malvern Hill, McClellan remained unnerved. The next day, Union forces evacuated Malvern Hill, falling back to a position on the James River, with protection from their gunboats and ready access to supplies. Lee and his army had driven the Federals back over twenty miles and secured Richmond. Confederate

newspapers were loath to give Lee credit, instead heaping praise on Jackson, Long-street, A. P. Hill, and even Johnston. But published letters in newspapers from soldiers in the Army of Northern Virginia provided a different reason for success: Lee.

McClellan, meanwhile, was convinced that he had done all anyone could have done. Throughout the campaign, his messages to authorities in Washington degener-ated from cockiness to near hysteria. After the first day, despite commanding eleven divisions, he blustered, "If I had another good Division I could laugh at Jackson." Two days later, as Confederate attacks compelled his army to retreat, McClellan defended his leadership: "Had I (20,000) twenty thousand fresh & good troops we would be sure of a splendid victory tomorrow." He was not responsible for the retreat, he wrote the next day to the secretary of war, and if the government wanted victory, "you must send me very large reinforcements & send them at once." With melodrama, he insisted that he felt "too earnestly tonight" because he had seen too many dead and wounded,

though he had never left his headquarters. His concluding remark, which was so outrageous that the telegraph operator in Washington deleted it, shifted the entire burden of defeat onto Lincoln and Stanton: "If I save this Army now I tell you plainly that I owe no thanks to you or any other persons in Washington—you have done your best to sacrifice this Army." By July 1, despite commanding more troops than his enemy, he insisted, "I need *50,000* more men, and with them I will retrieve our fortunes. More would be well, but that number sent at once, will, I think enable me to assume the offensive." Three days later, he wanted 100,000. His demands had reached absurd proportions.[43]

Blame always rested elsewhere. He dispatched his father-in-law and chief of staff, William L. Marcy, to Washington to answer questions and to pass along his letter seeking 100,000 reinforcements. After Marcy's dire briefing, a worried Lincoln decided to examine the condition of the army personally. He caught a steamer for McClellan's army and stayed only a day, during which he conversed with McClellan and his corps commanders and examined the troops. The condition of the army surpassed Lincoln's expectations; the soldiers remained confident. But when he asked the corps commanders what they should do next—whether to continue the campaign from there or to return to Northern Virginia and operate along the Washington–Richmond axis—no consensus existed. Lincoln declined to tip his hand, but McClellan suspected that the president was planning to bring the army back to Washington.[44]

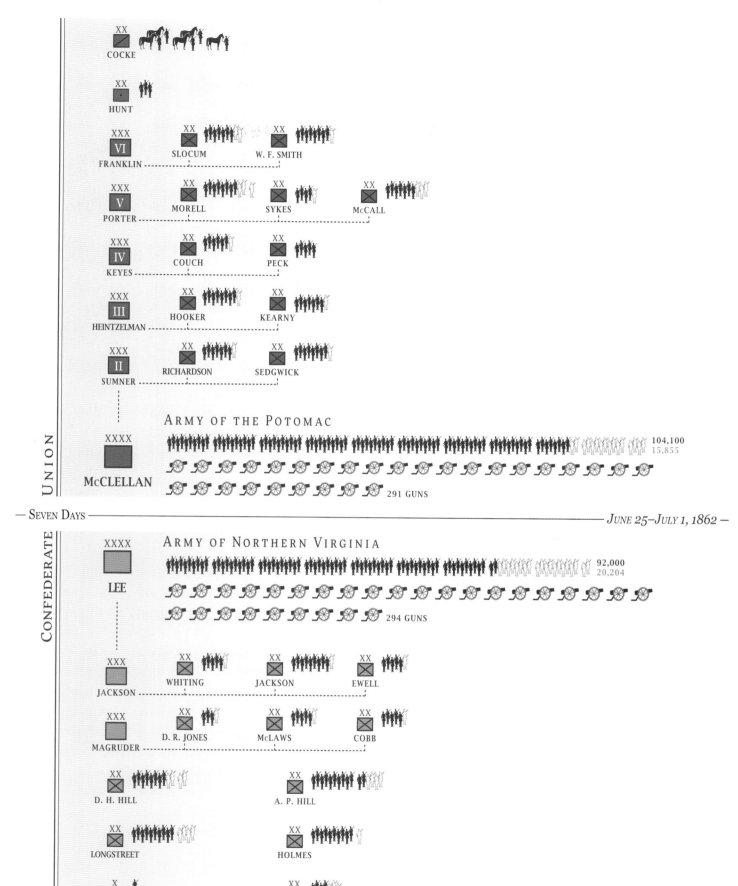

COCKE

HUNT

XXX
VI
FRANKLIN — SLOCUM — W. F. SMITH

XXX
V
PORTER — MORELL — SYKES — McCALL

XXX
IV
KEYES — COUCH — PECK

XXX
III
HEINTZELMAN — HOOKER — KEARNY

XXX
II
SUMNER — RICHARDSON — SEDGWICK

ARMY OF THE POTOMAC

XXXX
McCLELLAN

104,100
15,855

291 GUNS

UNION

— SEVEN DAYS —   — JUNE 25–JULY 1, 1862 —

CONFEDERATE

XXXX   ARMY OF NORTHERN VIRGINIA

LEE

92,000
20,204

294 GUNS

XXX
JACKSON — WHITING — JACKSON — EWELL

XXX
MAGRUDER — D. R. JONES — McLAWS — COBB

D. H. HILL   A. P. HILL

LONGSTREET   HOLMES

PENDLETON   HUGER

STUART

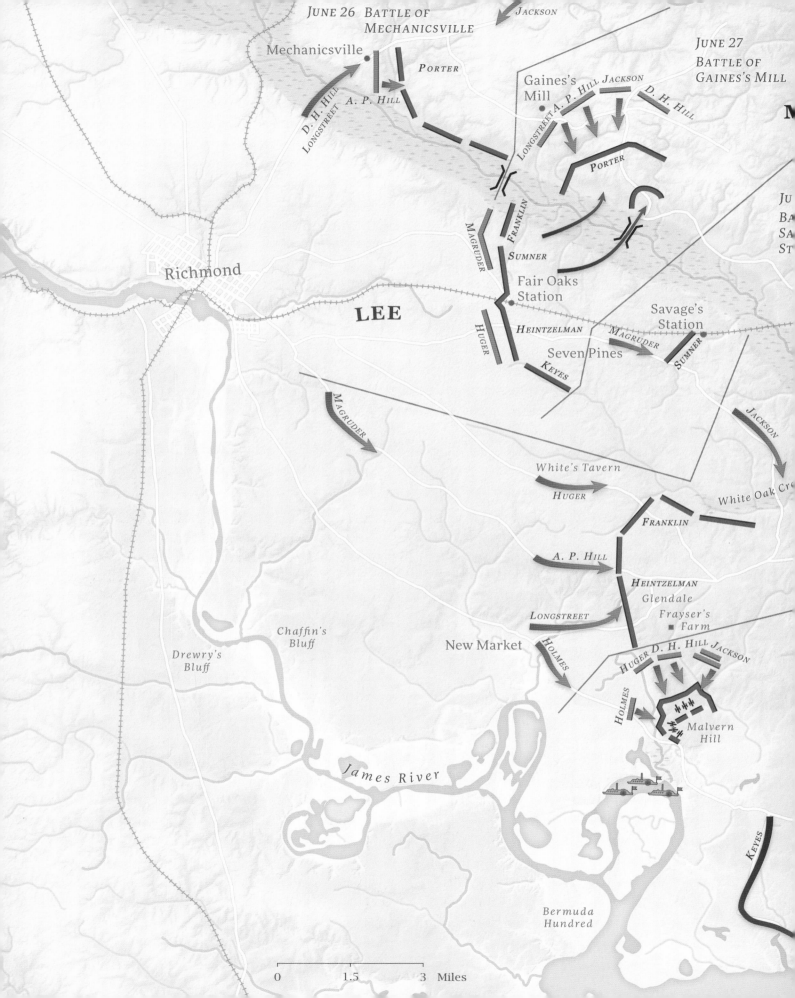

JUNE 26 BATTLE OF MECHANICSVILLE

JACKSON

Mechanicsville

PORTER

D. H. HILL

A. P. HILL

LONGSTREET

JUNE 27 BATTLE OF GAINES'S MILL

Gaines's Mill

LONGSTREET *A. P. HILL* *JACKSON* *D. H. HILL*

PORTER

FRANKLIN

MAGRUDER

SUMNER

Fair Oaks Station

Richmond

LEE

HUGER

Savage's Station

MAGRUDER *SUMNER*

HEINTZELMAN

Seven Pines

KEYES

MAGRUDER

JACKSON

White's Tavern

HUGER

White Oak Cre

FRANKLIN

A. P. HILL

HEINTZELMAN

Glendale Frayser's Farm

LONGSTREET

Chaffin's Bluff

New Market

HOLMES

HUGER *D. H. HILL* *JACKSON*

Drewry's Bluff

HOLMES

Malvern Hill

James River

Bermuda Hundred

KEYES

0   1.5   3   Miles

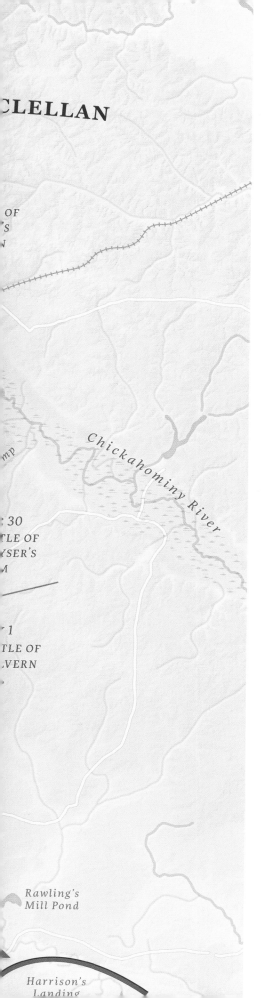

A few days before the Confederate attack, McClellan had requested an opportunity to offer his views on the conduct of the war, and Lincoln consented. As the president boarded his vessel to return to Washington, McClellan handed him a letter that, he later boasted to his wife, would "save the country" if Lincoln acted on it. The president coolly scanned the document, tucked it securely in his coat pocket, and thanked McClellan. The policy paper called for a war that narrowly targeted the Confederate army and its government. No effort should be undertaken to "subjugate" secessionists or confiscate civilian property, including slaves. "A declaration of radical views, especially upon slavery, will rapidly disintegrate our present armies," McClellan predicted.[45]

Critics of McClellan have accused him of transcending proper civil-military boundaries by offering advice on war policy, but he surely had that right and obligation.[46] Even though Lincoln had removed him as commanding general, McClellan still reported directly to the secretary of war and the president. He offered confidential advice that he believed would advance the Union military cause. Still, there were two problems with McClellan's letter. First, in the wake of defeat, his timing could not have been more dreadful. Second, McClellan, a conservative Democrat, championed a continuation of the original, limited-war policies at a time when the president and Congress were deciding to escalate the war.

Back in April 1861, three slaves who had labored on a Confederate military project slipped away from camp, stole a boat, and rowed to Union lines at Fort Monroe, Virginia. The next day, a Confederate officer under flag of truce approached Union lines, seeking return of the fugitive slaves. The Union

◀ **SEVEN DAYS BATTLES**
In a series of battles, Lee pushed McClellan's army away from Richmond, until the Union commander finally withdrew from Harrison's Landing, Virginia. Although Confederate casualties were higher than Union losses, McClellan fell back after each confrontation.

commander, Brig. Gen. Benjamin Butler, refused. A clever lawyer and politician, Butler pointed out the obvious: if you secede from the Union, federal laws no longer protect you. More importantly, Butler insisted on his right to confiscate the slaves as "contraband of war" for their work on behalf of the Confederate army, just as he could confiscate Rebel muskets or gunpowder. Butler then hired the fugitives to build a bakery for Federal troops. In one swoop, he had emancipated three slaves and put them to work for the Union army. Later that summer, Congress endorsed Butler's decision in the First Confiscation Act.[47]

Once the Union opened that door, it began transforming the war. Slaves who had worked on Confederate military projects came to Union lines with families in tow. Few Union officers would retain the male and return the family into slavery, so the emancipation door creaked further open. In late 1861 Congress began considering legislation to use blacks in military service. In early 1862 it abolished slavery in the District of Columbia and the territories, and in the spring it debated two important pieces of legislation: the Militia Act,[48] which would authorize the use of blacks "for any military or navy service for which they may be found competent," and the Second Confiscation Act,[49] which authorized the seizure of all Confederate property, including slaves. Both

LINCOLN AT ANTIETAM
Lincoln and McClellan clashed over war policy through the rest of the general's tenure. This picture from after the Battle of Antietam (September 17, 1862) shows Lincoln visiting with officers from the Army of the Potomac, though it would not be long until the president fired McClellan from that command.

bills passed, and Lincoln signed them into law on July 17, 1862, ten days after he'd left with McClellan's letter. Within a week of their passage, Lincoln notified his cabinet of his intention of issuing an emancipation proclamation. McClellan was on the wrong side of the issue. He advocated a restrictive war, while Lincoln, the majority in Congress, many Union soldiers, and some generals were moving toward an expanded war that targeted Confederate people and property, not just its army, as the enemy. They had come to the realization that most southern whites were committed Rebels, not Unionists, as they had thought early in the war.[50]

THE SECOND BULL RUN CAMPAIGN

On July 11 Lincoln appointed Henry W. Halleck, the former commander of the Department of the Mississippi (the regional command comprising all the Union territories from the Appalachian Mountains to Kansas) and victor in the campaign for Corinth, as the new general in chief. His first job was to resolve McClellan's status on the Peninsula. Lincoln explained the situation and sent Halleck to McClellan with an

▼
CONTRABANDS
In 1861 the U.S. Army began referring to escaped slaves as "contrabands"—that is, describing them as confiscated property that would otherwise be used by an enemy to assist in its war efforts. Through this declaration, the government was no longer under any legal obligation to return them to slavery.

offer of no more than 20,000 reinforcements; otherwise they would shift McClellan's army back to Washington. McClellan insisted that he needed more men, but Halleck would not budge. Before Halleck left, McClellan vowed to try resuming the offensive with the 20,000 reinforcements that the general in chief had offered, but within a week, he called for more men, and on August 3 Halleck ordered McClellan to move the army back to Washington expeditiously. McClellan and his subordinates had insisted that Lee commanded 200,000 men and was receiving reinforcements. If that were true, Halleck reasoned, then both the 40,000 men shielding Washington and the 115,000 under McClellan were in jeopardy and needed to unite.[51]

In the aftermath of Jackson's Valley campaign, Lincoln had appointed Maj. Gen. John Pope to command all the forces in Virginia outside McClellan's army. A pompous West Point graduate who had earned a victory at Island No. 10 out west, Pope embraced a harsher type of war. He quickly insulted his soldiers, crowing, "I have come to you from the West, where we have always seen the backs of our enemies," and outraged his enemies with orders to confiscate foodstuffs from civilians, to punish locals for any destruction done by guerrillas, to execute guerrillas summarily, and to arrest all disloyal persons in the army's rear, whether peaceable or not.[52]

As Pope maneuvered his columns to threaten Gordonsville, Virginia, and Lee's vital supply line, the Virginia Central Railroad, Lee detached Jackson and indicated that he wanted Pope "suppressed." On August 9 Jackson struck with three divisions and narrowly won the Battle of Cedar Mountain against one of Pope's corps.[53]

Shortly after Jackson's victory, Lee detected the withdrawal of Union troops from the Peninsula and responded boldly. Once again he saw an opportunity to alter the

◀ ESCAPED SLAVE OUTSIDE A CAMP TENT
"Contrabands" would also provide various services to Union soldiers, such as cooking, cleaning, sewing, or other general assistance.

JOHN POPE
A brash general who had won at New Madrid and Island No. 10 in the West, Pope alienated his new eastern command with unfavorable comparisons to his former army. Promising to establish his "headquarters in the saddle," Pope had much less success against Lee in Virginia.

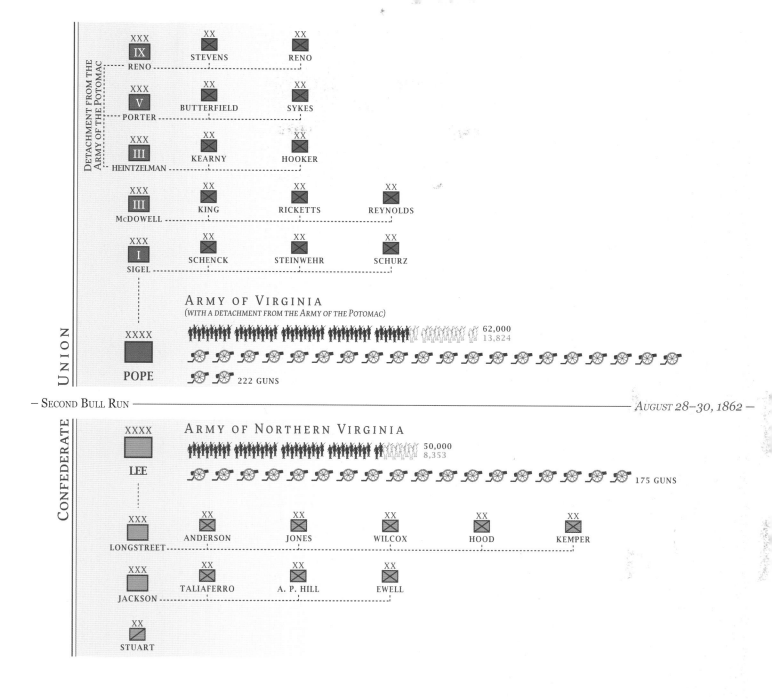

Detachment from the Army of the Potomac

XXX IX RENO	XX STEVENS	XX RENO
XXX V PORTER	XX BUTTERFIELD	XX SYKES
XXX III HEINTZELMAN	XX KEARNY	XX HOOKER

| XXX III McDOWELL | XX KING | XX RICKETTS | XX REYNOLDS |
| XXX I SIGEL | XX SCHENCK | XX STEINWEHR | XX SCHURZ |

XXXX POPE

ARMY OF VIRGINIA
(WITH A DETACHMENT FROM THE ARMY OF THE POTOMAC)

62,000
13,824

222 GUNS

UNION

— SECOND BULL RUN —
— *AUGUST 28–30, 1862* —

CONFEDERATE

XXXX LEE

ARMY OF NORTHERN VIRGINIA

50,000
8,353

175 GUNS

| XXX LONGSTREET | XX ANDERSON | XX JONES | XX WILCOX | XX HOOD | XX KEMPER |
| XXX JACKSON | XX TALIAFERRO | XX A. P. HILL | XX EWELL |

XX STUART

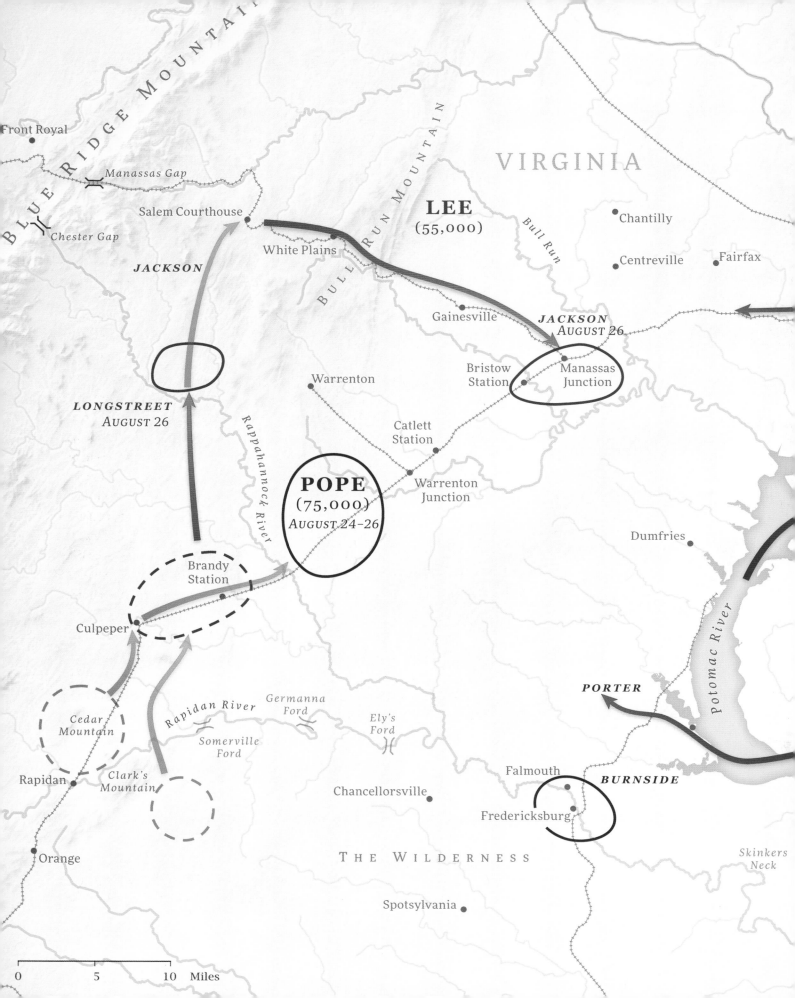

Front Royal

BLUE RIDGE MOUNTAINS

Manassas Gap

Chester Gap

VIRGINIA

Salem Courthouse

White Plains

BULL RUN MOUNTAIN

LEE
(55,000)

Chantilly

Bull Run

Centreville

Fairfax

JACKSON

Gainesville

JACKSON
AUGUST 26

JACKSON
AUGUST 26

Warrenton

Bristow
Station

Manassas
Junction

LONGSTREET
AUGUST 26

Catlett
Station

Rappahannock River

POPE
(75,000)
AUGUST 24–26

Warrenton
Junction

Dumfries

Brandy
Station

Culpeper

PORTER

Potomac River

Cedar
Mountain

Rapidan River

Germanna
Ford

Ely's
Ford

Somerville
Ford

Clark's
Mountain

Falmouth

BURNSIDE

Rapidan

Chancellorsville

Fredericksburg

Orange

THE WILDERNESS

Skinkers
Neck

Spotsylvania

0   5   10   Miles

shape and scope of the war in the East by seizing the initiative. For some time, Lee and Davis had hoped to raid into Maryland and Pennsylvania to give northerners a taste of war. Lee sent Longstreet with most of the troops around Richmond to join Jackson, and then followed with the remainder of the army when it was clear that Richmond was safe. Although Lee missed a chance to trap Pope near the Rappahannock River, Stuart's horsemen seized Pope's headquarters wagon and a bounty of information on Union strength and plans. Lee then sent Jackson on a fifty-mile march around Pope's western flank, capturing the huge Union supply depot at Manassas Junction. Longstreet and Lee followed.[54]

Pope tried to concentrate his army to meet the Confederates, but he was hindered by unaggressive subordinates and uncertainty over Lee's whereabouts. On August 28 and 29, Pope and Jackson fought, often desperately, near Manassas, with Pope launching repeated piecemeal attacks against Rebel positions along a railroad cut to Pope's north. In a classic showdown, the Confederate Stonewall Brigade and the Federal Iron Brigade slugged it out in open ground, inflicting dreadful casualties on each other with no real success for either side. As one Federal soldier described it, "It seemed as if the heavens was a furnace."[55] Two Union corps from McClellan's army could have aided Pope immensely, but McClellan, assigned the task of funneling troops to Pope as they arrived by boat in northern Virginia, quibbled with Halleck and blatantly withheld the troops, suggesting to Lincoln that perhaps the best option was to "leave Pope to get out of his scrape" and instead use the troops to protect Washington.[56] On the twenty-ninth, Longstreet approached the battlefield and prevented Porter's corps from striking Jackson's exposed western flank.[57] Then, late in the day, Longstreet attacked the Union left with a reinforced division, knocking the Federals off the high ground east of Groveton, valuable terrain that positioned the Confederates to launch a larger assault the following day.[58]

Early the next afternoon, Pope again struck at Jackson's command, employing Porter's fresh troops. To aid Jackson, Longstreet increased Col. Stephen Dill Lee's artillery to eighteen guns. From some high ground to the south and west of Jackson's position, Col. Lee's artillerists pounded Union attackers against the right portion of Jackson's line. Devastating cannon fire cut

◀ **Second Bull Run Campaign**

In order to eliminate the threat to Richmond from the north, Lee sent Jackson on a long march around Pope's Union force. Jackson captured Pope's supply depot at Manassas Junction, while the Union general moved north to meet him.

SECOND BULL RUN CAMPAIGN ▶

As Pope gathered his army near Manassas, Jackson swung
around and prepared to engage him at Bull Run.

down many who tried to cross the artillery front; Federals who made it across
the open ground found themselves trapped between Jackson's troops and Col.
Lee's unrelenting artillery fire. Twice Pope attempted to reinforce the attack
against Jackson, and both times Col. Lee's artillerists halted the advance.[59]

At 4:00, as Porter's momentum began to wane, Longstreet unleashed his
own attack, with 25,000 relatively fresh soldiers. Wave after wave of shouting
Rebel infantrymen stormed down on the exposed Union flank. The Federals
resisted but could not halt the onslaught. Pope managed to cobble together a
strong defense with Regular Army regiments along Henry House Hill on the
field of the Battle of First Bull Run, delaying the attackers enough for the onset
of darkness. Later that night, he retreated toward Washington. Jackson tried to
pursue, but his weary men could not catch Pope's army. At the Battle of Second
Bull Run, Lee inflicted about 15,000 casualties on Pope's forces. The cost
was some 9,000 Confederate soldiers.

Lincoln believed that McClellan had wanted Pope to lose. Stanton demanded a court martial, and nearly the entire cabinet called for McClellan's
removal. Yet Lincoln refused. Although McClellan's conduct toward Pope was
"unpardonable," the president considered him "too useful just now to sacrifice." Pope's shattered command required rapid rejuvenating, which was Mc-
Clellan's forte. "If he can't fight himself," Lincoln told his private secretary, "he
excels in making others ready to fight." Lincoln ordered McClellan to assume
command of the Washington defenses and take charge of Pope's army as it fell
back into the city.[60]

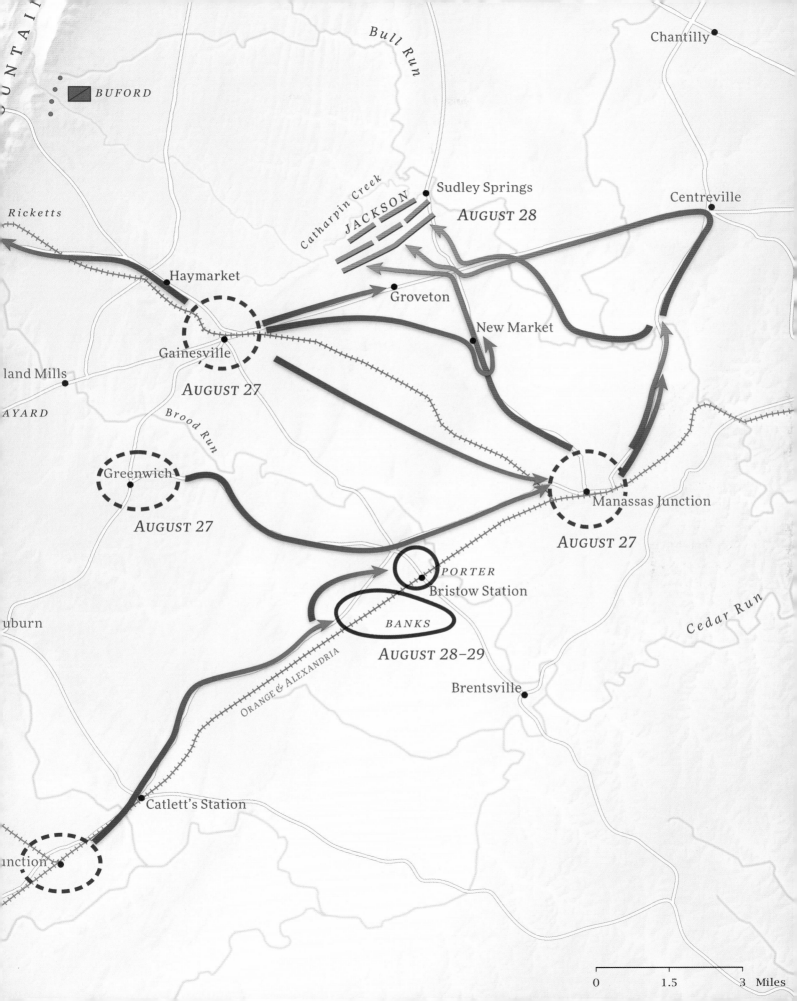

BUFORD

Ricketts

Bull Run

Chantilly

Catharpin Creek

JACKSON

Sudley Springs

AUGUST 28

Centreville

Haymarket

Groveton

New Market

Gainesville

AUGUST 27

land Mills

AYARD

Brood Run

Greenwich

AUGUST 27

Manassas Junction

AUGUST 27

uburn

PORTER

Bristow Station

BANKS

AUGUST 28–29

Brentsville

Cedar Run

ORANGE & ALEXANDRIA

Catlett's Station

nction

0   1.5   3 Miles

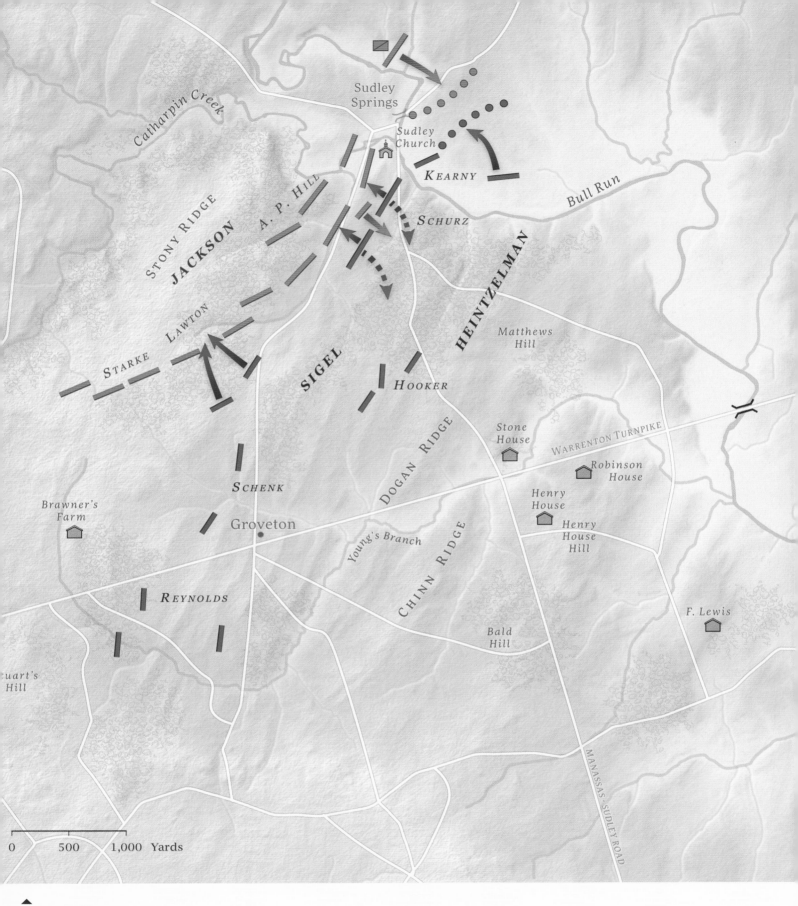

Catharpin Creek

Sudley
Springs

Sudley Church

KEARNY

Bull Run

STONY RIDGE

A. P. HILL

JACKSON

SCHURZ

Lawton

HEINTZELMAN

Matthews
Hill

Starke

SIGEL

HOOKER

Stone
House

WARRENTON TURNPIKE

Robinson
House

Schenk

DOGAN RIDGE

Henry
House

Brawner's
Farm

Groveton

Young's Branch

CHINN RIDGE

Henry
House
Hill

F. Lewis

Reynolds

Bald
Hill

tuart's
Hill

MANASSAS - SUDLEY ROAD

0   500   1,000 Yards

SECOND BATTLE OF BULL RUN

Jackson and Pope fought on August 29, both waiting for reinforcements. Jackson waited for James Longstreet to protect his flank, while Pope sought reinforcements from McClellan, who had two additional corps within supporting distance.

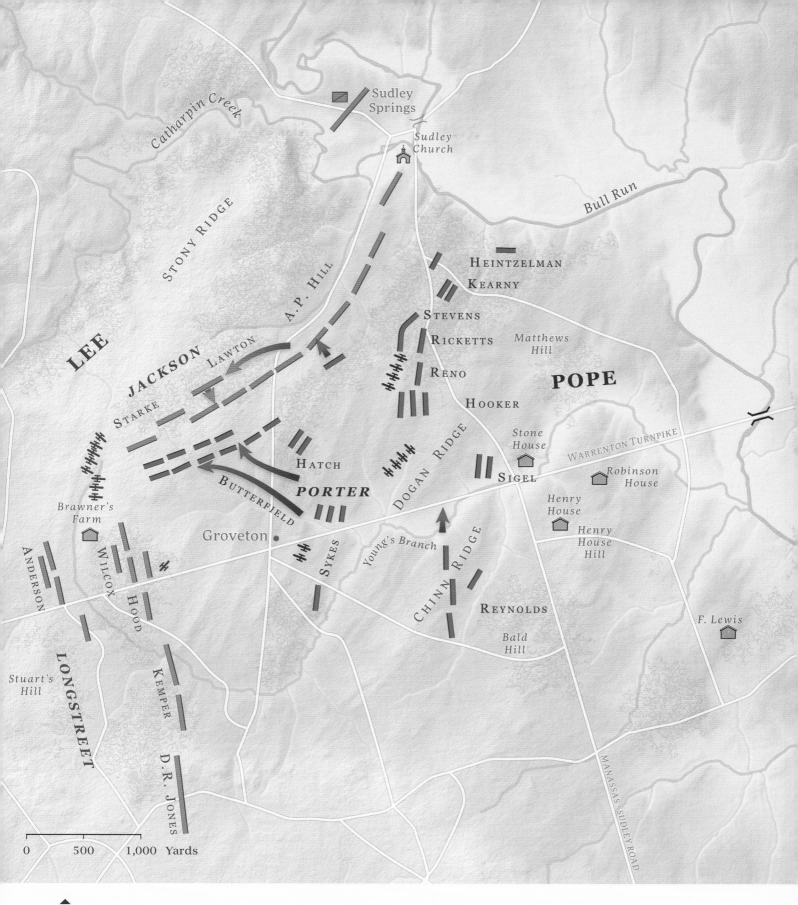

Catharpin Creek

Sudley Springs

Sudley Church

Bull Run

STONY RIDGE

HEINTZELMAN

KEARNY

A. P. HILL

LEE

STEVENS

RICKETTS

Matthews Hill

JACKSON

LAWTON

RENO

POPE

STARKE

HOOKER

Stone House

WARRENTON TURNPIKE

HATCH

DOGAN RIDGE

SIGEL

Robinson House

BUTTERFIELD

PORTER

Henry House

Brawner's Farm

Groveton

Young's Branch

CHINN RIDGE

Henry House Hill

F. Lewis

ANDERSON

WILCOX

SYKES

REYNOLDS

HOOD

Bald Hill

Stuart's Hill

KEMPER

LONGSTREET

D. R. JONES

MANASSAS–SUDLEY ROAD

0   500   1,000 Yards

SECOND BATTLE OF BULL RUN

As Pope moved to envelop Jackson's flank, Longstreet arrived to blunt the attack, and suddenly it was Pope whose flank was exposed.

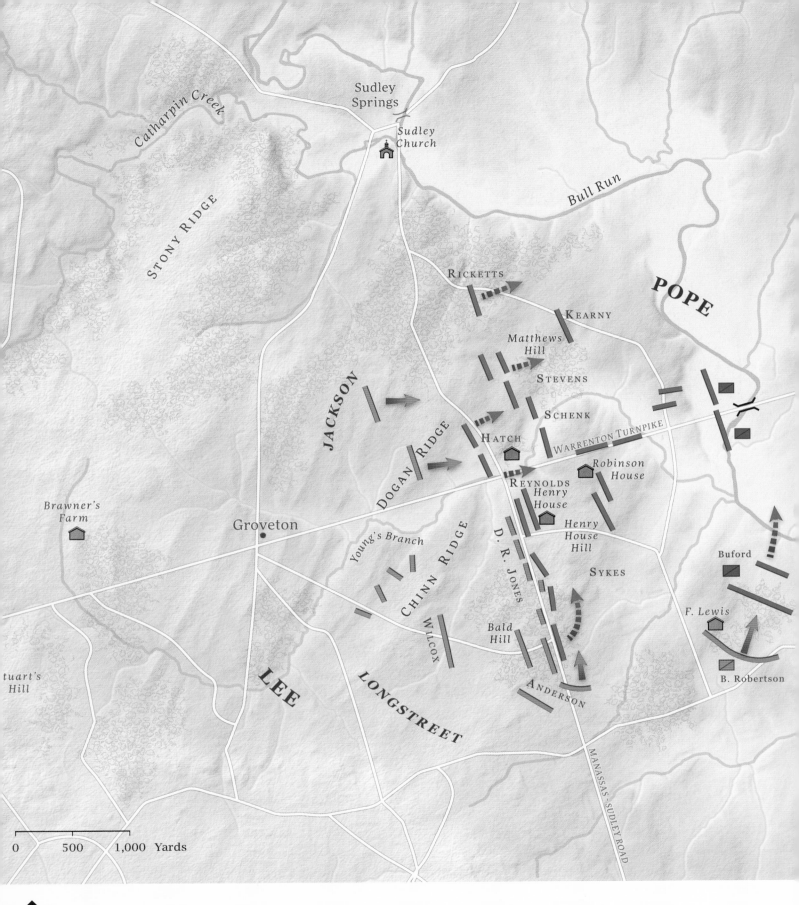

Sudley
Springs

Catharpin Creek

Sudley Church

Bull Run

STONY RIDGE

POPE

RICKETTS

KEARNY

Matthews
Hill

STEVENS

JACKSON

SCHENK

WARRENTON TURNPIKE

DOGAN RIDGE

HATCH

Robinson
House

Brawner's
Farm

REYNOLDS
Henry House

Groveton

Young's Branch

CHINN RIDGE

Henry
House
Hill

D. R. JONES

Buford

SYKES

F. Lewis

WILCOX

Bald
Hill

tuart's
Hill

LEE

ANDERSON

B. Robertson

LONGSTREET

MANASSAS - SUDLEY ROAD

0   500   1,000   Yards

▲
SECOND BATTLE OF BULL RUN
With both Longstreet's and Jackson's corps in place, the Confederates swept Pope's army from the field. Darkness and a strong defense near Henry House Hill halted the
Confederate pursuit, and Pope retreated to Washington.

THE ANTIETAM CAMPAIGN

In three months, Lee and his army had completely reversed the course of the war in the East. By seizing the initiative and dictating the flow of operations, they had alleviated the threat to Richmond and driven Union troops from most of Virginia. With momentum on his side, Lee now pushed across the Potomac River into Maryland. The Union had congressional elections coming up, and the presence of Confederate soldiers on Federal territory might damage Union morale on the home front and tilt the electoral outcome to antiwar Democrats. After two months of uninterrupted Confederate victories, diplomatic recognition from Britain and France—perhaps even military intervention—seemed more possible than ever before. If the Army of Northern Virginia could live off Maryland and Pennsylvania farmers, Lee could ease the burden on Confederate farmers. Finally, some Confederates believed that Maryland, a slaveholding state, might be fertile recruiting ground for the Confederacy.[61]

Lee advanced northward to the east of the Shenandoah Valley, intending to shield his lines of communication behind the Blue Ridge Mountains, and expecting the Federals to withdraw the garrison of Harpers Ferry before it could be trapped. Halleck, however, vetoed any evacuation, and Lee targeted the exposed garrison. On September 9 Lee ordered three columns led by Jackson to converge on Harpers Ferry, seize the high

SECOND BATTLE OF BULL RUN
Union soldiers who returned to the battlefield of Second Bull Run in 1863 found the remains of their fallen comrades still lying near the railroad embankment defended by Stonewall Jackson's corps.

ground overlooking the garrison, and lay siege. Meanwhile, Longstreet's troops and D. H. Hill's division marched northward toward Boonsboro, Maryland; Stuart's cavalry covered them. By splitting his army, Lee certainly incurred some risks, but he believed it would take weeks for the Federals to revive their army after the rout at Second Bull Run, and he had to disperse his forces to feed them properly from the countryside.

It took McClellan just two short weeks to reenergize the Federal army and begin a cautious pursuit. That changed on September 13, when the lucky break of the war fell into his lap. A corporal rummaging through an abandoned Confederate campsite in Frederick, Maryland, discovered a paper tied around several cigars. He unraveled the sheet and discovered a copy of Lee's invasion plans. It had fallen out of a staff officer's pocket. Within hours, McClellan knew that Lee had divided his forces—with Jackson attacking the Union garrison at Harpers Ferry and Longstreet's command pushing farther north—and he devised a scheme to defeat Lee's army in detail. By a swift march, McClellan could have seized a central position, cutting off and ensnaring a sizeable chunk of Lee's army. Instead, he tarried and failed to exploit the revelation fully.[62]

On the morning of September 14, two Union corps challenged D. H. Hill's troops for control of Turner's Gap at South Mountain. Lee, who knew of the lost order within twenty-four hours, promptly warned division commander Lafayette McLaws to beware of a Federal advance on his flank in the valley between South Mountain and Harpers Ferry. Lee also dispatched Longstreet to assist D. H. Hill, but too late. The Union IX Corps overwhelmed Hill's command and pried open the mountain gaps. By nightfall, Union forces stood only eight miles from Harpers Ferry.[63]

Lee elected to concentrate at Sharpsburg on the northern bank of the Potomac River. From there, he could buy Jackson time by threatening the flank of any Union relief expedition. Jackson did not need it. Securing high ground all around Harpers Ferry, Rebel gunners opened a bombardment at dawn on September 15. Within a couple of hours, the Union garrison of 11,000 surrendered, along with 73 cannon, 13,000 small arms, and extensive military stores: the largest surrender of U.S. forces

"Maryland, My Maryland" ▶

The Army of Northern Virginia hoped to find support among the secessionist population of Maryland. The song "Maryland, My Maryland" was part of that effort to encourage the state to join the Confederacy. Lee also invaded Maryland for supplies, for as this image suggests, his army was short of food and fodder. The cartoon contrasts the Confederate horsemen as Marylanders envisioned them before the invasion (left) with how they actually appeared (right)

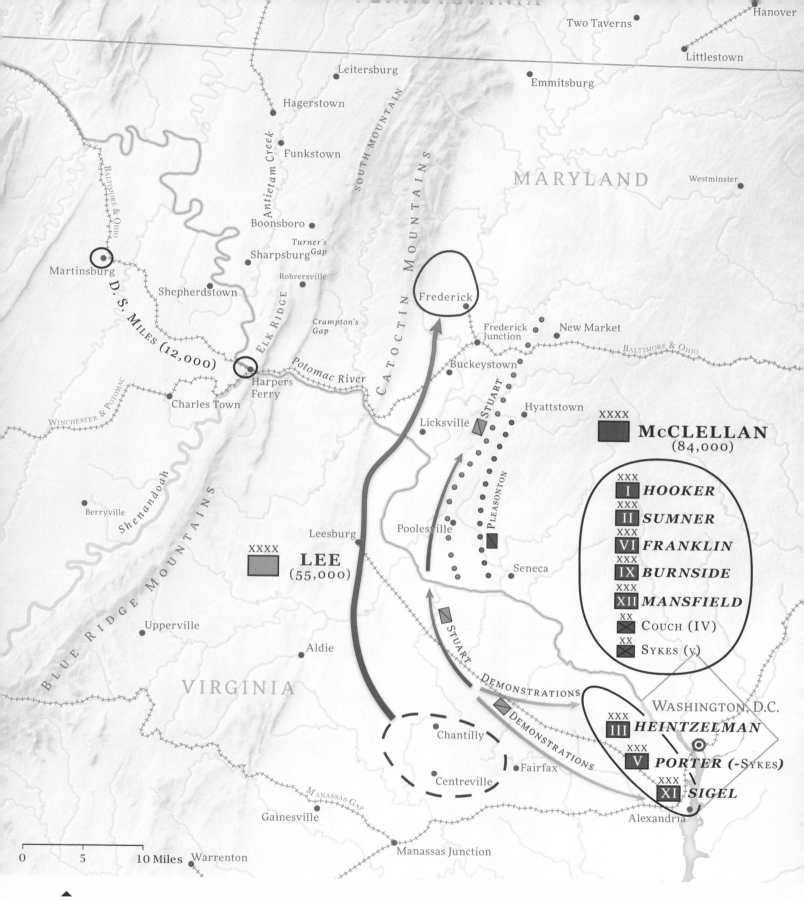

PENNSYLVANIA

Hanover

Two Taverns

Littlestown

Leitersburg

Emmitsburg

Hagerstown

MARYLAND

Westminster

Funkstown

Antietam Creek

SOUTH MOUNTAIN

Boonsboro

Sharpsburg *Turner's Gap*

Martinsburg

Rohrersville

D. S. MILES (12,000)

Shepherdstown

ELK RIDGE

Crampton's Gap

Frederick

Frederick Junction

New Market

BALTIMORE & OHIO

CATOCTIN MOUNTAINS

Potomac River

Buckeystown

Harpers Ferry

Hyattstown

Charles Town

WINCHESTER & POTOMAC

Licksville

STUART

XXXX

McCLELLAN
(84,000)

Berryville

Shenandoah

Poolesville

PLEASONTON

XXX
I   *HOOKER*
XXX
II   *SUMNER*
XXX
VI   *FRANKLIN*
XXX
IX   *BURNSIDE*
XXX
XII   *MANSFIELD*
XX
COUCH (IV)
XX
SYKES (V)

Leesburg

XXXX

LEE
(55,000)

Seneca

BLUE RIDGE MOUNTAINS

Upperville

Aldie

VIRGINIA

STUART

DEMONSTRATIONS

WASHINGTON, D.C.

Chantilly

DEMONSTRATIONS

XXX
III   *HEINTZELMAN*

Fairfax

XXX
V   *PORTER* (–SYKES)

Centreville

XXX
XI   *SIGEL*

MANASSAS GAP

Gainesville

Alexandria

0   5   10 Miles   Warrenton

Manassas Junction

▲ ANTIETAM CAMPAIGN

Lee launched an invasion of Maryland in early September, intending to gain supplies and recruits in Maryland and hoping to inflict a decisive blow on the Army of the Potomac.

Two Union corps overwhelmed Confederate brigades in three gaps controlling South Mountain. Lee then ordered his forces to concentrate near Sharpsburg.

until World War II. Jackson designated A. P. Hill's division to oversee the surrender and remove the captured "property"—including 2,000 blacks, whom the Army of Northern Virginia enslaved or re-enslaved—while he led the remainder of his forces on an all-night march to Sharpsburg.[64]

McClellan concentrated his army amid some rolling hills at Antietam Creek. Late on September 15 and throughout September 16, he elected to probe Confederate lines rather than strike a blow, giving Jackson time to reinforce Lee. On September 17 he launched his only attack of the war. McClellan wrote no plans, but he wanted Maj. Gen. Joseph Hooker on the Union right flank and Maj. Gen. Ambrose P. Burnside on the far left to close like a vice. Unfortunately, no one told Burnside, and he failed to reconnoiter properly before the attack.[65]

Hooker opened the battle on Lee's far left at dawn. Three batteries of horse artillery that Stuart had positioned on the commanding ground of Nicodemus Heights had perfect flanking fire, weakening Hooker's assault and enabling Confederates to inject sufficient troops to blunt the charge. Confederate John Bell Hood's division struck with a fury. According to an officer in the 6th Wisconsin, "As we appeared at the edge of the corn, a long line of men in butternut and gray rose up from the ground. Simultaneously, the hostile battle lines opened a tremendous fire upon each other. Men, I cannot say fell; they were knocked out of the ranks by the dozens. But we jumped over the fence, and pushed on, loading, firing, and shouting as we advanced." They advanced well into the cornfield, fell back, and with the aid of reinforcements stormed through the cornfield again, until they encountered men from Hood's Texas Brigade and Evander C. Law's Alabama Brigade. The Confederates delivered a blow that the Wisconsin officer described as "like a scythe running through our line."[66] But the counterattack quickly proved costly. Hood's Texas Brigade, which had stormed Gaines's Mill in the Seven Days Battles, suffered disastrously, including the loss of 82 percent of the

HARPERS FERRY
Lee captured Harpers Ferry with 11,000 Union soldiers and its extensive military stores. Over the course of the war, Harpers Ferry changed hands eight times.

men in the 1st Texas Infantry, the highest percentage of casualties suffered by any Confederate regiment in a single battle in the war.

As Hooker's I Corps was used up, the XII Corps entered the fray, too late for coordinated action. At 9:00 a.m. Maj. Gen. Joseph Mansfield's division of Maj. Gen. Edwin Vose Sumner's II Corps attacked on Hooker's left. It barged through devastated Confederate ranks and into the West Woods, where it met vicious resistance and was forced to withdraw. At the same time, the rest of Sumner's command struck Rebels in a sunken road near the center of the battlefield. At about 1:00 p.m., the Federals finally broke into the road and fired along its length, cutting down defenders until they abandoned the position. "The Minnie balls, shot & shell rained upon us from every direction except the rear," a North Carolina sergeant later jotted in his diary.

Among the heroes was the commander of the 6th Alabama Infantry, Col. (and future corps commander) John B. Gordon. Gordon was struck in the calf, the thigh, the left arm, and the shoulder by Minié balls. One of his men wrote, "Our gallant Col. [John] B. Gordon, though wounded and bleeding profusely in four places, continued cheering his men, though oft entreated to leave the field."[68] As troops on his right began to waver, Gordon moved over to buoy their spirits, when a ball struck his face and passed through his neck, leaving a disfiguring wound. Gordon collapsed unconscious. When he awoke, the colonel crawled one hundred yards to

▲
Antietam Woods

Intense fighting in the West Woods at Antietam, near Dunker Church, began the bloodiest single day in American history.

the rear, where he finally received medical attention. By then the Rebel line in the sunken road, known forever after as the "Bloody Lane," had collapsed. Lee's center was open.

The great opportunity was suddenly there. McClellan contemplated committing reserves—an entire corps and part of another—which could have split the Confederate army in two and possibly trapped most of Lee's men north of the Potomac River. Yet McClellan hesitated. He was still convinced that Lee's army was much larger than his own and that the hilly terrain concealed a large part of it. McClellan turned to Sumner, who counseled against tapping the reserves, bolstering McClellan's predilections for caution, and the army commander decided against it.

Meanwhile, on the far Union left, Burnside tried to storm a stone bridge across Antietam Creek at 10:00 a.m. and was stopped cold by 400 Confederates on some high ground above occupying hastily constructed defenses and supported by some artillery. Rather than waiting for troops to ford the creek to the south and turn the Confederates from their position, Burnside unimaginatively hurled column after column onto the bridge, only to see them slaughtered. Five hundred Union soldiers fell in the attack. On the Confederate side, nearly one-third of the defenders became casualties, indicative

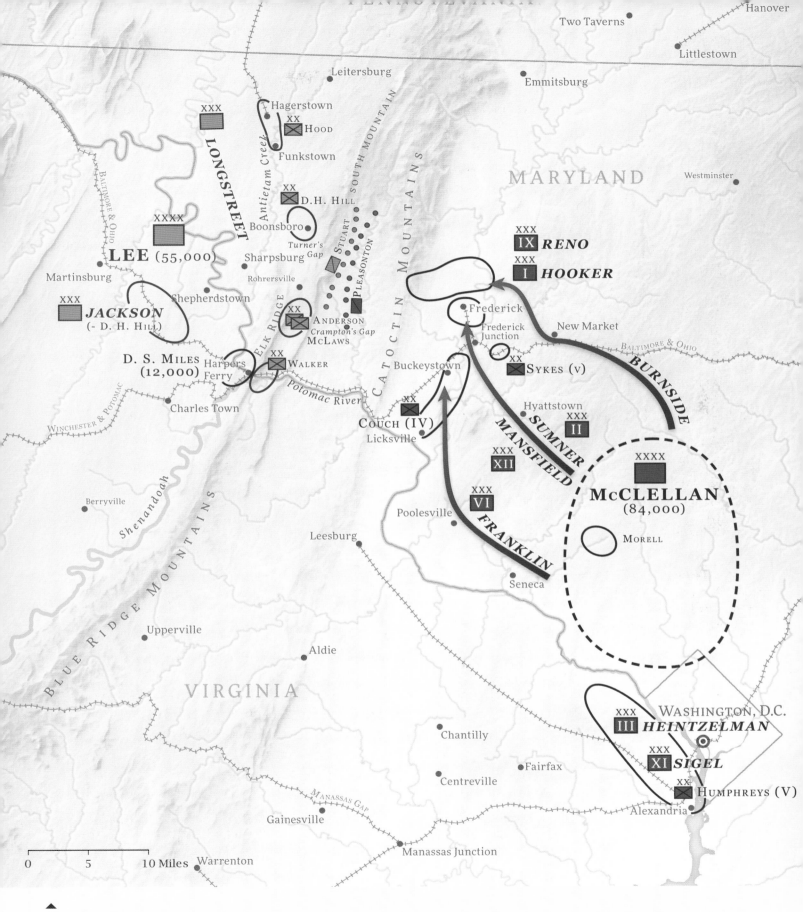

PENNSYLVANIA

Hanover

Two Taverns

Littlestown

Leitersburg

Emmitsburg

MARYLAND

Westminster

XXX LONGSTREET

Hagerstown

XX HOOD

Funkstown

Antietam Creek

SOUTH MOUNTAIN

XXXX
LEE (55,000)

XX D.H. HILL

Boonsboro

Turner's Gap

Sharpsburg

Stuart

Rohrersville

Pleasonton

CATOCTIN MOUNTAINS

Frederick

XXX IX RENO

XXX I HOOKER

Martinsburg

Shepherdstown

XXX
JACKSON
(- D. H. HILL)

ELK RIDGE

XX ANDERSON
Crampton's Gap
McLAWS

Frederick
Junction

New Market

BALTIMORE & O HIO

XX SYKES (V)

BURNSIDE

D. S. MILES
(12,000)

Harpers
Ferry

XX WALKER

Potomac River

Buckeystown

XX
COUCH (IV)

Hyattstown

XXX
II

SUMNER

BALTIMORE & OHIO

WINCHESTER & POTOMAC

Charles Town

Licksville

MANSFIELD

XXXX
McCLELLAN
(84,000)

XXX
XII

Shenandoah

Berryville

XXX
VI

FRANKLIN

Poolesville

Morell

BLUE RIDGE MOUNTAINS

Leesburg

Seneca

Upperville

VIRGINIA

Aldie

Chantilly

WASHINGTON, D.C.

XXX III HEINTZELMAN

Fairfax

XXX XI SIGEL

Centreville

XX HUMPHREYS (V)

Gainesville

MANASSAS GAP

Alexandria

0   5   10 Miles   Warrenton

Manassas Junction

▲ ANTIETAM CAMPAIGN

On September 13, an Indiana soldier discovered a copy of Special Order No. 191, which revealed Lee's plans and dispositions. Even after gaining the information, McClellan delayed. Lee recognized the danger and began to gather his army together near Sharpsburg.

▲

BURNSIDE'S BRIDGE

The fighting at Burnside's Bridge, a critical crossing of Antietam Creek, was some of the fiercest of the battle. After two hours, the defending Confederates ran out of ammunition, and Ambrose Burnside's corps forced its way across the bridge.

COMBAT AT ANTIETAM

With approximately 23,000 casualties for both sides, Antietam was the bloodiest day in American history. The battle was marked by fierce fighting all along the field. This was the experience of a Union private who fought near the cornfield in the battle's northern section:

My ramrod is wrenched from my grasp as I am about to return it to its socket after loading. I look for it behind me, and the Lieutenant passes me another, pointing to my own, which lies bent and unfit for use across the face of a dead man. A bullet enters my knapsack just under my left arm while I am taking aim. Another passes through my haversack, which hangs upon my left hip. Still another cuts both strings of my canteen, and that useful article joins the debris now thickly covering the ground. Having lost all natural feeling I laugh at these mishaps as though they were huge jokes, and remark to my nearest neighbor that I shall soon be relieved of all my trappings. A man but a few paces from me is struck squarely in the face by a solid shot. Fragments of the poor fellow's head came crashing into my face and fill me with disgust. I grumble about it as though it was something that might have been avoided.[67]

of the viciousness of the fighting there. With too few troops left, Confederate officers picked up rifles and began firing to blunt the Union advance. About 1:00 p.m., as the defenders ran out of ammunition, Burnside's men were able to force their way across the bridge. It then took time for Burnside to move three divisions across the narrow bridge. By 3:00 p.m., Burnside was in position to press his attack, and Lee, who had drawn from his right to aid his beleaguered left and center, had little strength to resist. Confederates fought valiantly, but by 4:00 p.m., Burnside was on the verge of capturing the road to Harpers Ferry and Lee's line of retreat. Suddenly A. P. Hill's division raced up from the rear, having covered seventeen miles from Harpers Ferry in seven hours. Hill's men slammed into Burnside's inexperienced soldiers, rolled up his flank, and saved Lee from disaster. McClellan considered reinforcing Burnside but decided against it. The fight was over.

Before the battle, Lee had hoped to smash the Federals and continue with the raid, but that was now impossible. He had suffered 13,000 casualties out of approximately 40,000 soldiers, compared with McClellan's losses of almost 11,000 from an army of 78,000 troops. Both armies had fought courageously. The next day, the two sides stared at each other, and that night, Lee withdrew south of the Potomac River.

THE DEAD OF ANTIETAM

Following the battle, famed photographer Mathew Brady sent Alexander Gardner to the battlefield to document the aftermath. A public exhibition of the photographs, "The Dead of Antietam," opened in October 1862 in New York and drew huge crowds. It was the first time that the realities of war had been presented to the public in such a graphic fashion.

FIRST READING OF THE EMANCIPATION PROCLAMATION

Francis Bicknell Carpenter's painting depicts Lincoln revealing the Emancipation Proclamation to his cabinet in July 1862. Carpenter carefully arranged the cabinet officials based on their position on Lincoln's announcement. The two men at Lincoln's right side (the left of the painting), Edwin Stanton and Salmon Chase, were the strongest supporters of emancipation.

McClellan pronounced Antietam a great victory. "Those in whose judgment I rely tell me that I fought the battle splendidly & that it was a masterpiece of art," he crowed to his wife. McClellan debated seriously whether he should demand that Lincoln dump Stanton and reappoint himself general in chief over Halleck. In truth, he had attacked piecemeal and squandered his overwhelming manpower advantage and perhaps the best Union opportunity to crush Lee's army until 1865.[69]

The president reacted to McClellan's "masterpiece of art" less enthusiastically, but the victory served his political purpose. Back in July, Seward had convinced him not to announce his emancipation decree until after the next Union victory; otherwise it might look like a desperate act of a losing side. On September 22, 1862, Lincoln issued the Preliminary Emancipation Proclamation. All slaves in areas of rebellion on January 1, 1863, would become free, but that freedom depended on Union battlefield success. The war for reunion was now also one to destroy slavery. It would target the property of secessionists as well as enemy soldiers, transforming the nature of the war.

Conclusion

In the sixteen months since the Battle of First Bull Run, the Union had forged a massive army and had driven to the doorsteps of Richmond. The wounding of Johnston and his replacement by Lee transformed the war in the East. Against superior manpower, resources, and firepower, Lee utilized his exceptional leadership skills, relying on initiative, speed, and audacity to reverse the course of the war and earn the adoration of his soldiers and the Confederate people; military effectiveness derives from morale and leadership at least as much as from manpower and materiel. Lee's bold attacks in the Seven Days campaign drove the Union army back fifty miles and temporarily shattered McClellan. Lee then "suppressed" Pope at Second Bull Run and pushed into Maryland, capturing the garrison at Harpers Ferry and liberating nearly all of Virginia from the U.S. Army. While McClellan's forces inflicted heavy losses at Antietam, his caution, reinforced by Lee's string of successes, convinced him to withhold reserves at the critical moment of the battle.

These setbacks had taught Union soldiers and many politicians and generals that to conquer the rebellion they needed to embrace a harsher approach to warfare. By late 1862, the Union was doing just that. Yet merely repulsing Lee's raid into Maryland did little toward suppressing the rebellion. The Union needed offensive operations, and Lincoln wondered whether McClellan could conduct one effectively.

Introduction

The Confederates had achieved great success under Robert E. Lee's leadership as he executed Confederate president Jefferson Davis's military strategy, delivering powerful blows against invading armies as close to the border as possible to discourage other attempts at conquest and to protect the lives and property of Confederate citizens. But the burdens of war were taking their toll on the Confederacy. The strain of sustaining large armies and enduring substantial losses of men on and off the battlefield took a terrible toll on Rebel society, with its greatly inferior resources and more limited manpower—and therefore a limited margin of error. By contrast, the Union possessed the resources but lacked effective military leadership in the eastern theater to utilize those advantages in manpower, supply, and equipment. Lincoln was growing increasingly impatient with his generals' failure to campaign aggressively. His greatest concern was preserving a strong commitment among soldiers, sailors, and the public to the cause of reunion, now complicated by the Preliminary Emancipation Proclamation, and the surest way to boost morale was success on the battlefield.

International Context and Confederate Strategy

The failure of Lee's raid into Maryland, coupled with the Emancipation Proclamation, badly damaged Davis's foreign policy plans. Confederates had always hoped to secure foreign intervention, convinced that cotton was crucial to the world economy. Without it, they believed, European textile mills would lay off tens of thousands of workers, creating economic, social, and political chaos. Thus, the Confederacy planned to use cotton not only to purchase weapons and machinery but also to leverage a breakup of the Union blockade and induce foreign military intervention.

The key to this plan was Great Britain, the largest cotton importer. Without Britain, France lacked the naval and economic power to intervene in the Civil War. In December 1861, those two nations, along with Spain, invaded Mexico, seeking repayment of debts while the Union was too preoccupied with its war to enforce the Monroe Doctrine, President James Monroe's 1823 warning that the United States would not permit European powers to interfere in the affairs of independent nations in the Americas. Britain and Spain soon withdrew, but France remained and set up a puppet regime in Mexico. Yet violating a unilateral U.S. proclamation was a far cry from intervention on the Confederacy's behalf, which would almost certainly enmesh the meddling European powers in war with the United States.

Initially, Great Britain indicated its intent to avoid active intervention in the Civil War, though British shipyards did build ships for the Confederacy, and Rebel blockade runners brought in Enfield rifles from British factories. By late summer 1862, however, several prominent British leaders, including Foreign Secretary Lord John Russell and Chancellor of the Exchequer William Gladstone, wanted stronger action: British

3

Lee's War in the East

Joseph T. Glatthaar

OHIO

Columbus

ILLINOIS

Peoria

Quincy

Springfield

Indianapolis
INDIANA

Dayton

Hannibal

Cincinnati

Missouri River

St. Louis

Illinois River

Wabash River

Evansville

VI

Jefferson City

Louisville
Frankfort
Lexington
Perryville

Osage River

Ohio River

KENTUCKY

STONES RIVER

MISSOURI

Cairo
Paducah

HENRY - DONELSON

Kentucky River

Cumberland River

STONES RIVER

BRAGG'S INVASION OF KENTUCKY

OZARK PLATEAU

White River

Black River

Fort Donelson

Mississippi River

Fort Henry

SHILOH

Nashville

Murfreesboro

PERRYVILLE

ARKANSAS

Jackson

TENNESSEE

BLUE RIDGE

Pittsburg Landing

TULLAHOMA-CHATTANOOGA

CUMBERLAND PLATEAU

Memphis

Chattanooga

Greenville

Little Rock

Arkansas River

Corinth
Holly Springs

Tennessee River

Huntsville

APPALACH

Pine Bluff

VICKSBURG

Tombigbee River

Columbus

Atlanta

Oconee River

Piedm

August

Camden

MISSISSIPPI

ALABAMA

GEORGIA

Milledgeville

Alabama River

Chattahoochee River

Macon

Pearl River

Old Kingston

Columbus

Altamaha R

Vicksburg
Jackson

Selma

Montgomery

Natchez

Red River

Sabine River

St. Landry

Port Hudson

Mobile

Tallahassee

Baton Rouge

PORT HUDSON

Pensacola

FLO

LOUISIANA

New Orleans

NEW ORLEANS

Apalachicola

Gulf of Mexico

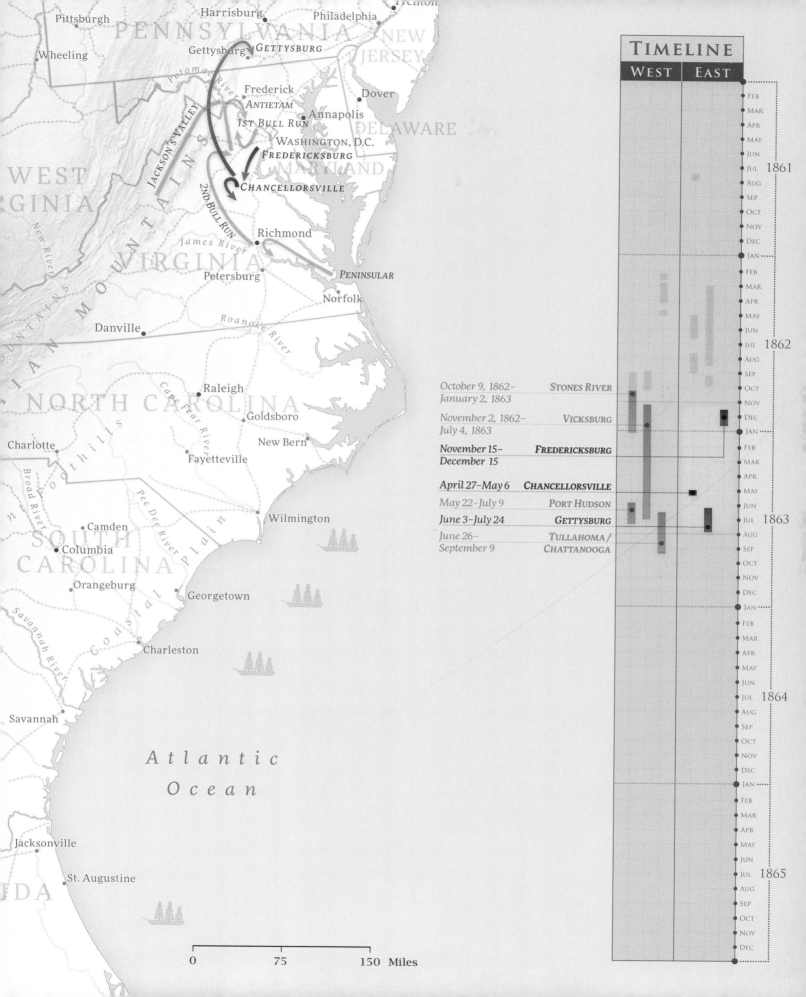

PENNSYLVANIA

Pittsburgh
Wheeling
Harrisburg
Philadelphia
Trenton

Gettysburg *GETTYSBURG*

Potomac River

NEW JERSEY

Frederick
Dover

ANTIETAM

1ST BULL RUN

Annapolis

DELAWARE

WASHINGTON, D.C.

JACKSON'S VALLEY

FREDERICKSBURG

MARYLAND

WEST VIRGINIA

2ND BULL RUN

CHANCELLORSVILLE

New River

Richmond

James River

VIRGINIA

Petersburg

PENINSULAR

Norfolk

Roanoke River

Danville

BLUE RIDGE MOUNTAINS

Raleigh

NORTH CAROLINA

Cape Fear River

Goldsboro

Charlotte

New Bern

Fayetteville

Pee Dee River

Broad River

SOUTH CAROLINA

Camden

Columbia

Orangeburg

Georgetown

Savannah River

Charleston

Coastal Plain

Wilmington

Atlantic
Ocean

Savannah

Jacksonville

St. Augustine

FLORIDA

0   75   150 Miles

TIMELINE

WEST	EAST

FEB
MAR
APR
MAY
JUN
JUL **1861**
AUG
SEP
OCT
NOV
DEC
JAN
FEB
MAR
APR
MAY
JUN
JUL **1862**
AUG
SEP
OCT
NOV
DEC
JAN
FEB
MAR
APR
MAY
JUN
JUL **1863**
AUG
SEP
OCT
NOV
DEC
JAN
FEB
MAR
APR
MAY
JUN
JUL **1864**
AUG
SEP
OCT
NOV
DEC
JAN
FEB
MAR
APR
MAY
JUN
JUL **1865**
AUG
SEP
OCT
NOV
DEC

October 9, 1862–
January 2, 1863   *STONES RIVER*

November 2, 1862–
July 4, 1863   VICKSBURG

November 15–
December 15   **FREDERICKSBURG**

April 27–May 6   **CHANCELLORSVILLE**

May 22–July 9   PORT HUDSON

June 3–July 24   *GETTYSBURG*

June 26–
September 9   TULLAHOMA /
CHATTANOOGA

Uncle Sam catches John Bull (Britain) trying to sneak cotton out of the South while supplying arms to the Confederacy. Napoleon III (the French rooster), looks on while two Confederates (P. G. T. Beauregard and Jefferson Davis) hang in the background. Uncle Sam also wields a club labeled "Principle of Non Interference."

recognition of the Confederate States of America as an independent nation. They hoped that Britain would establish strong ties with the cotton-growing Confederacy and open the door for British loans, investment, and trade. Dismayed by the bloodshed within an advanced nation, other British leaders demanded intervention or mediation on humanitarian grounds. But Prime Minister Viscount Palmerston hesitated to act until Confederate victory seemed likely. That situation did not occur. Gen. Braxton Bragg raided into Kentucky, fought to a draw at Perryville, and then fell back into Tennessee. Lee's march into Maryland, which seemed so promising, resulted in a defeat at Antietam that September. These Confederate setbacks, followed by the Preliminary Emancipation Proclamation, undercut any prospect of British action.[1]

Many British leaders perceived the Proclamation as a desperate act to curry international favor, but four factors prevented Britain from intervening on behalf of the Confederacy. First, the British working people rallied enthusiastically behind the Union and the Emancipation Proclamation. They saw it as a means of elevating debased people and united behind it. Second, Britain found new sources of cotton in Egypt and India, and a drought made Great Britain and much of Europe dependent on U.S. grain exports, and hence Union goodwill.[2]

Third, while some British leaders favored diplomatic recognition, what the Confederacy needed was military intervention, and that was extremely unlikely. British Secretary of War George Cornewall Lewis came out against even diplomatic intervention, arguing that the British government had no practical solution to the conflict and that intervention would probably lead Great Britain, which had abolished slavery in 1833, into war against the United States on the side of a slaveholding nation. There were strategic considerations, too. A decade earlier, Great Britain had struggled to project a

ABE LINCOLN'S LAST CARD

Though Lincoln hoped to avoid having the Emancipation Proclamation seem like a desperate action, this cartoon from the British magazine *Punch* suggests he did not entirely succeed. Lincoln, portrayed with his hair in devilish horns, plays his final card. (A black face can be seen on the ace of spades card.)

THE POSSIBILITIES OF KING COTTON

The Confederate government made King Cotton the center of its diplomacy, hoping to force Britain to recognize the new nation when it could not receive the crop for textile production. In this critical Northern cartoon, the normally anti-slavery John Bull is willing to look the other way on slavery in order to gain access to cotton.

small military force into the Crimea. Two previous wars against the United States had demonstrated that without control of the Great Lakes, Britain could not support an invasion from Canada, the obvious staging ground. The advent of ironclads insured at best a stalemate along the Canadian border, which would be tantamount to a Union victory on that front. Even if Britain broke the blockade temporarily, it still lacked the strength to inject sufficient manpower or the essential materials into Confederate territory to alter the war's outcome, especially against a rapidly growing Union navy.

Fourth, Lincoln and his administration handled diplomatic issues shrewdly. In November 1861 a U.S. naval officer had removed a mail packet and two Confederate "diplomats" from the RMS *Trent,* heading to Great Britain. The British were furious, but Lincoln deftly defused the situation. Citing the fact that the British were interpreting the rights of neutrals just as the United States had prior to the War of 1812 against Britain, he released the Confederate diplomats. This event taught Lincoln and Secretary of State William Seward a valuable lesson: that Britain was deeply concerned about precedents for conduct on the high seas. England did not want to protest over a matter of lesser importance and then have those protests come back to haunt it when something vital was at stake. That element of restraint ensured that the two countries would strive to maintain relatively good relations throughout the Civil War.[3]

THE MISCEGENATION BALL ▶
Though this cartoon was from 1864, Democratic success in 1862 was driven by similar fears over the degree to which Lincoln and the Republicans would promote social equality. Lincoln and other so-called Black Republicans were regularly accused of promoting emancipation in order to intermingle with (and perhaps even marry) black women.

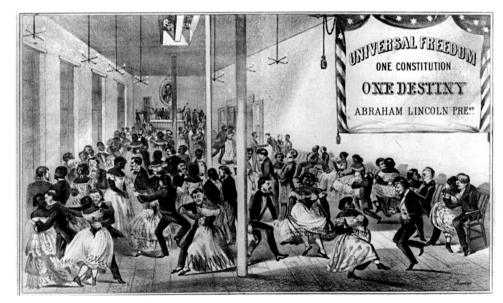

Back at home, General George B. McClellan was furious over the Preliminary Emancipation Proclamation, which ran counter to his conservative vision of Union war aims. He prepared a vigorous protest, but friends talked him out of sending it. Instead, he issued a general order that reminded his troops of the relationship between soldiers and the government: "The remedy for political errors, if any are committed, is to be found only in the action of the people at the polls."[4] McClellan overestimated the impact of emancipation on Union soldiers. There was some political backlash against emancipation, yet despite that and all the Confederates' successes over the summer, the people of the Union maintained their commitment to the war. In the midterm elections of 1862, the Republicans lost 20 of their 108 seats in the House of Representatives, but, combined with the Unionists, a group of strongly prowar Democrats, they still controlled 60 percent of the House. And in the Senate, the Republicans and Unionists actually gained seats, giving them 80 percent of the chamber.[5]

In the days and weeks after his victory at Antietam, McClellan rested and refitted his army. Lincoln implored and then scolded him to advance. After Antietam, Lee had retreated to the northern part of the Shenandoah Valley, where his army could eat well and draw supplies by rail. Lincoln, who had mastered Euclidean geometry in his

McClellan Takes Leave of the Army

After Lincoln finally relieved McClellan, the general wrote to his wife, "I feel I have done all that can be asked in twice saving the country . . . I feel some little pride in having, with a beaten & demoralized army, defeated Lee so utterly . . . Well, one of these days history will, I trust, do me justice."

younger days, noted that McClellan's army was closer to Richmond than the Confederates. With the Confederate army in the Shenandoah Valley, its "route is the arc of the circle, while yours is the chord." If McClellan drove into Virginia east of the Blue Ridge, he would threaten Lee's communications with Richmond. If Lee advanced north, the Federals could follow behind him, threatening his communications and compelling Lee to fight on McClellan's terms. If Lee shifted to protect his communications, McClellan could race him to Richmond, gain the "inside track," and engage the Army of Northern Virginia on ground of McClellan's choosing. Roads, railroads, and waterways from Washington could supply Union forces like "spokes of a wheel extending from the hub towards the rim." Lincoln concluded, "It is all easy, if our troops march as well as the enemy; and it is unmanly to say they can not do it." Yet McClellan declined to move. In late October he complained about ill and worn-out horses. Lincoln lost his patience. "I have just read your dispatch about sore-tongued and fatigued horses," he telegraphed. "Will you pardon me for asking what the horses of your army have done since the battle of Antietam that fatigues anything?"[6] Finally, on October 27 McClellan began crossing the Potomac. It took a week to do so, alerting Lee and enabling him to shift Lt. Gen. James Longstreet's men to block the advance. On November 5 Lincoln, his patience exhausted by delays, ordered a reluctant Maj. Gen. Ambrose Burnside to replace McClellan. The "Little Napoleon" would never command again.[7]

Burnside insisted that he was not qualified for the job of army commander. He was not being modest. A loyal officer whose notable whiskers gave us the inverted name of sideburns, he could plan large-scale operations but lacked the ability to command them effectively. Nevertheless, he finally agreed to succeed McClellan because the high command of the Army of the Potomac suffered deep rifts, and Burnside feared that Maj. Gen. Joseph Hooker, an egotistical corps commander highly critical of his superiors, coveted the slot. With Hooker's strong standing among Radical Republicans, he likely would receive the appointment and only worsen divisions in the army.[8]

AMBROSE EVERETT BURNSIDE

MAY 23, 1824–SEPTEMBER 13, 1881

Burnside graduated from USMA in 1847 and resigned in 1853 to manufacture weapons, including the breech-loading rifle he called the Burnside carbine, in Rhode Island. He entered the war in command of the 1st Rhode Island Infantry but commanded a brigade at First Bull Run. He then led an expedition and captured Roanoke Island in North Carolina and was promoted to major general of volunteers. He refused command of the Army of the Potomac but led a mishandled attack on Lee's right at Antietam.

Commanding the Army of the Potomac after McClellan's relief, he developed a good operational plan, but the delayed arrival of pontoons for bridging foiled his effort to slip across the Rappahannock unopposed. After the disastrous battle of Fredericksburg, he tried again to take the offensive in the infamous "Mud March." He was then relieved of command after the mismanagement and assigned to command the Army of the Ohio, where he repulsed Longstreet's attack at Knoxville in November 1863. He returned east as commander of the IX Corps and handled it poorly in the Wilderness. Eventually Burnside was relieved after the mismanagement of the Petersburg Mine assault in July 1864. After the war, he served as governor of Rhode Island and U.S. Senator.

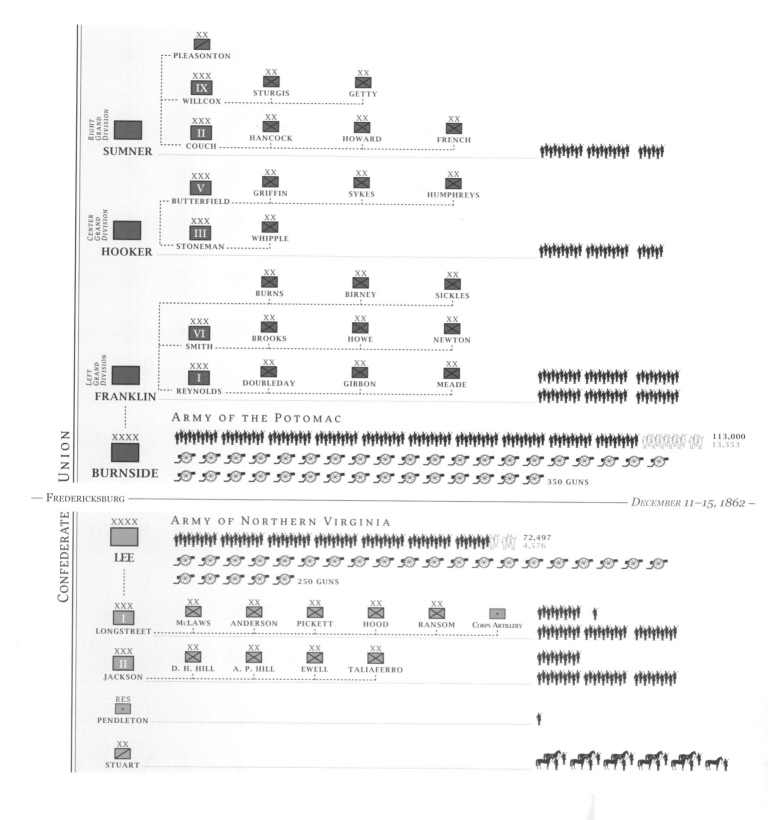

UNION

RIGHT GRAND DIVISION — SUMNER

- **PLEASONTON** (XX)
- **IX — WILLCOX** (XXX)
  - **STURGIS** (XX)
  - **GETTY** (XX)
- **II — COUCH** (XXX)
  - **HANCOCK** (XX)
  - **HOWARD** (XX)
  - **FRENCH** (XX)

CENTER GRAND DIVISION — HOOKER

- **V — BUTTERFIELD** (XXX)
  - **GRIFFIN** (XX)
  - **SYKES** (XX)
  - **HUMPHREYS** (XX)
- **III — STONEMAN** (XXX)
  - **WHIPPLE** (XX)

LEFT GRAND DIVISION — FRANKLIN

- **BURNS** (XX)
- **BIRNEY** (XX)
- **SICKLES** (XX)
- **VI — SMITH** (XXX)
  - **BROOKS** (XX)
  - **HOWE** (XX)
  - **NEWTON** (XX)
- **I — REYNOLDS** (XXX)
  - **DOUBLEDAY** (XX)
  - **GIBBON** (XX)
  - **MEADE** (XX)

ARMY OF THE POTOMAC

BURNSIDE (XXXX)

113,000
13,353

350 GUNS

— FREDERICKSBURG —
— DECEMBER 11–15, 1862 —

CONFEDERATE

ARMY OF NORTHERN VIRGINIA

LEE (XXXX)

72,497
4,576

250 GUNS

I — LONGSTREET (XXX)
- **McLAWS** (XX)
- **ANDERSON** (XX)
- **PICKETT** (XX)
- **HOOD** (XX)
- **RANSOM** (XX)
- **Corps Artillery**

II — JACKSON (XXX)
- **D. H. HILL** (XX)
- **A. P. HILL** (XX)
- **EWELL** (XX)
- **TALIAFERRO** (XX)

RES — PENDLETON

STUART (XX)

D.C.
Fredericksburg
Richmond

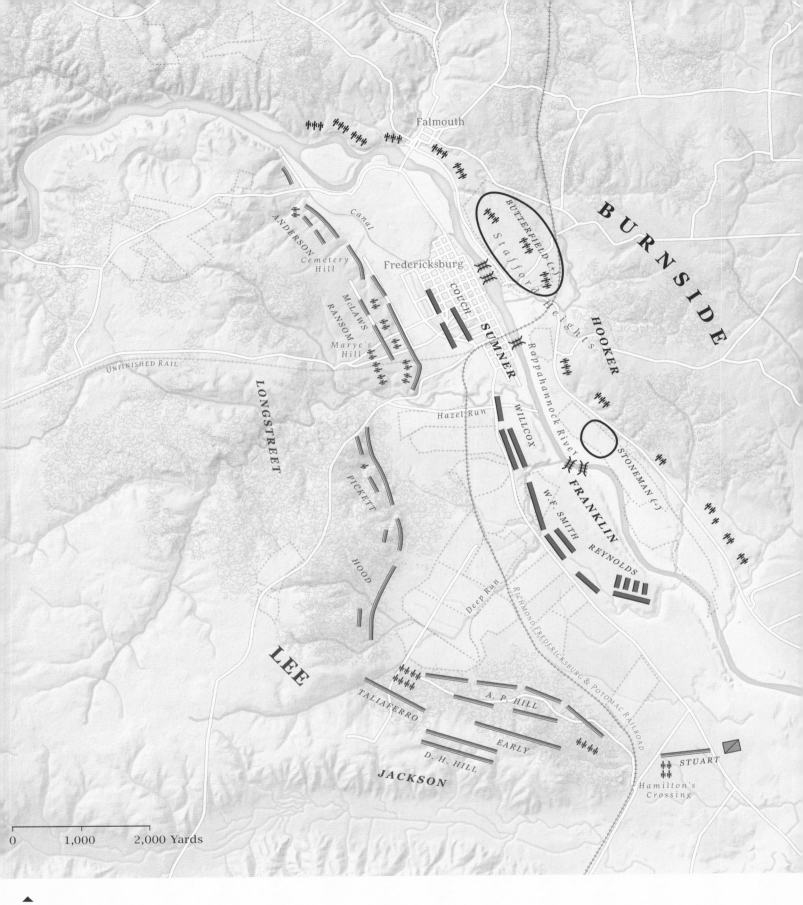

▲ FREDERICKSBURG

Burnside's overall plan was for Franklin's massive grand division (two corps plus reinforcements) to turn the Confederates' right flank while frontal attacks by Sumner's men pinned Lee's strongly positioned left. Hooker's Grand Division provided a large reserve.

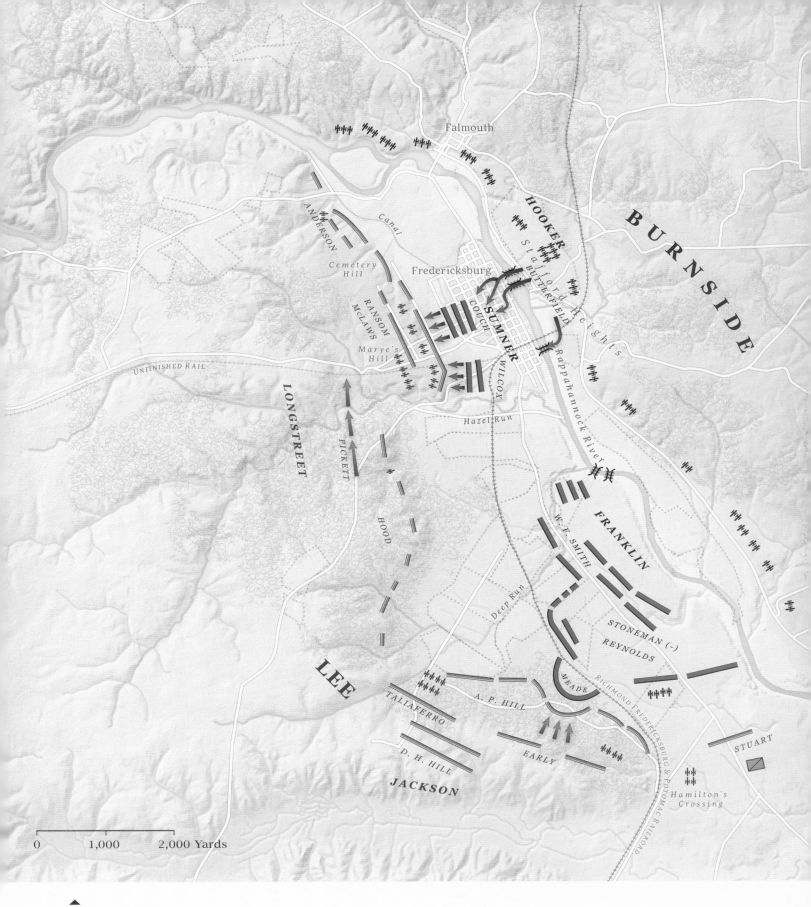

Falmouth

BURNSIDE

HOOKER

Stafford Heights

BUTTERFIELD

Fredericksburg

SUMNER

COUCH

WILCOX

ANDERSON

Canal

Cemetery
Hill

RANSOM

McLAWS

Marye's
Hill

Unfinished Rail

LONGSTREET

PICKETT

Hazel Run

Rappahannock River

HOOD

W. F. SMITH

FRANKLIN

STONEMAN (-)

REYNOLDS

Deep Run

LEE

TALIAFERRO

A. P. HILL

MEADE

RICHMOND FREDERICKSBURG & POTOMAC RAILROAD

STUART

D. H. HILL

EARLY

JACKSON

Hamilton's
Crossing

0   1,000   2,000 Yards

▲ FREDERICKSBURG

One by one, divisions from Sumner's grand division advanced up Marye's Heights, and one by one they were slaughtered by Confederate artillery and musketry. Farther south, Union troops broke a segment of Jackson's forward line, but his reserves were able to retake the lost ground.

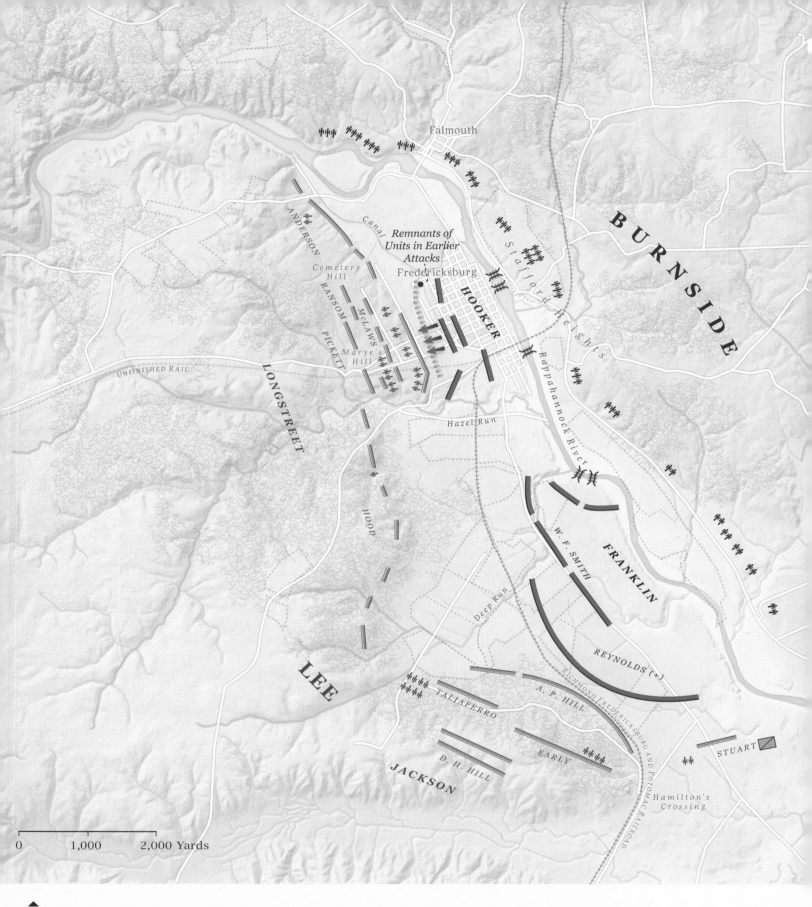

Falmouth

BURNSIDE

Remnants of
Units in Earlier
Attacks
Fredericksburg

Canal

Stafford Heights

HOOKER

ANDERSON

Cemetery
Hill

RANSOM

McLAWS

Marye's
Hill

PICKETT

Rappahannock River

LONGSTREET

Unfinished Rail

Hazel Run

HOOD

W. F. SMITH

FRANKLIN

Deep Run

REYNOLDS (+)

RICHMOND, FREDERICKSBURG AND POTOMAC RAILROAD

LEE

TALIAFERRO

A. P. HILL

JACKSON

D. H. HILL

EARLY

STUART

Hamilton's
Crossing

0   1,000   2,000 Yards

▲
FREDERICKSBURG

Butterfield's V Corps followed up Marye's Heights, with similar results. Most divisions attacked one brigade at a time. Only nightfall ended the futile assaults.

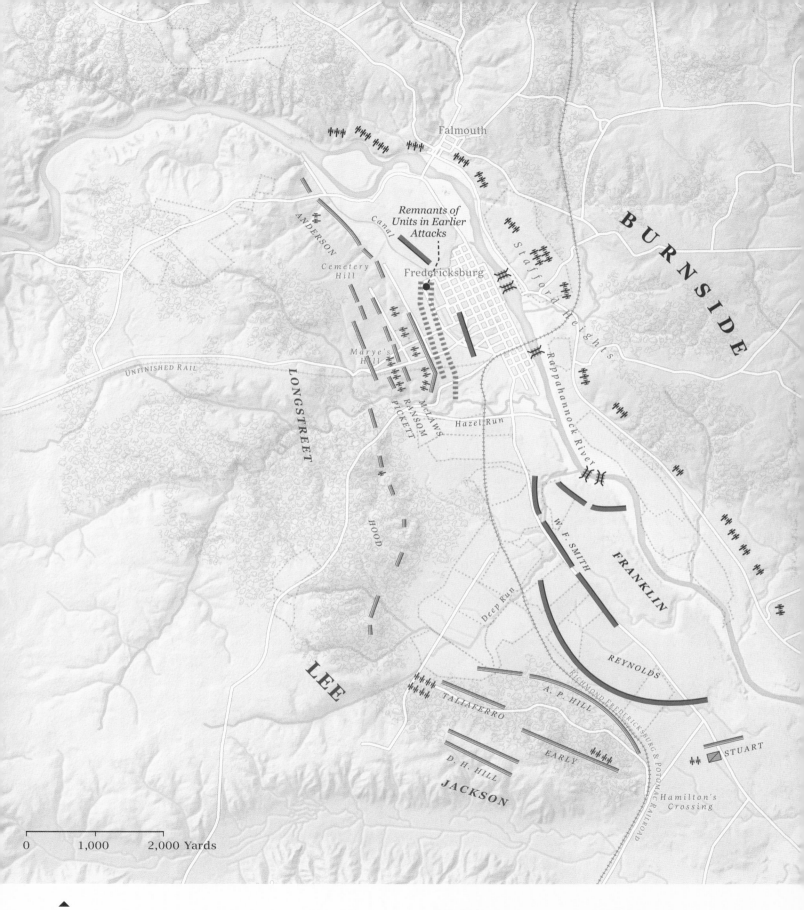

Falmouth

BURNSIDE

ANDERSON

Canal

Remnants of Units in Earlier Attacks

Cemetery Hill

Fredericksburg

Stafford Heights

Marye's Hill

Unfinished Rail

LONGSTREET

Ransom

McLaws

Pickett

Rappahannock River

Hazel Run

HOOD

Deep Run

W. F. Smith

FRANKLIN

REYNOLDS

LEE

RICHMOND, FREDERICKSBURG & POTOMAC RAILROAD

TALIAFERRO

A. P. HILL

STUART

EARLY

D. H. HILL

JACKSON

Hamilton's Crossing

0   1,000   2,000 Yards

▲ Fredericksburg

Both sides held their positions for two days, with the wounded and dead between the lines. On December 15, in a rainstorm, Burnside withdrew back across the river.

CROSSING THE RAPPAHANNOCK

The late arrival of pontoon bridges delayed the Union army's crossing of the Rappahannock River and allowed the Confederates to reinforce Fredericksburg. Union artillery shelled the town, and eventually soldiers pushed their way across using the pontoons as boats.

His self-critical reservations notwithstanding, Burnside devised a clever operational plan to feint toward Gordonsville and slip across the Rappahannock River at Fredericksburg. At first the plan worked. Burnside beat Lee to the river, but the pontoon bridges that General in Chief Henry Halleck had promised were not there. In a classic example of what the military theorist Carl von Clausewitz called "friction," poor planning, miscommunication, and foul weather delayed their arrival by ten days. Burnside could have forded with part of his army, but he feared that rising water from rainfall to the west might trap it south of the river. The delay enabled Longstreet and Lt. Gen. Thomas J. Jackson to concentrate their corps around Fredericksburg. The surprise lost, Burnside nonetheless elected to bull his way over the river and through Lee's army. He divided his army into three "grand divisions": one under Maj. Gen. Edwin V. Sumner, to cross near the city and fix the main Confederate line; another under Maj. Gen. William B. Franklin, to cross farther to the southeast, hoping to drive into Lee's rear; and the third commanded by Hooker as the army reserve. Under heavy fire from the city of Fredericksburg, Federal troops tried unsuccessfully to bridge the river. Burnside had to shell the town and send soldiers across in boats to uproot the snipers—a rare case of urban fighting and river crossing under fire in the war. Crews of infantry and engineers were then able to complete the pontoon bridges and rush men across the Rappahannock and into the city. On the Union left, Franklin had far less difficulty crossing the river, but he was under orders not to attack until Sumner was ready. This delay allowed Jackson to concentrate his

troops, who were scattered along the river from Hamilton's Crossing to Port Royal, a distance of about fifteen miles.[9]

The main fight began the next morning, December 13, when Franklin's troops initiated the attack. Jackson deployed his soldiers along a ridgeline overlooking a wide, open space, yet neglected to fortify his position with abatis or entrenchments. His men repulsed the Union assault along most of the line, except for a swampy area where his defenses were thin. There Maj. Gen. George Gordon Meade's division penetrated Jackson's line, but Jackson tapped his extensive reserves, and, after a vicious fight, they sealed the breach.[10]

On the Rebel left, Longstreet's corps occupied high ground and strong defenses. Part of his line benefitted from a stone wall and a sunken road; in other areas, he had his men throw up entrenchments at Marye's Heights. On the extreme left of the line, Brig. Gen. Cadmus M. Wilcox, whose troops had suffered so badly in the Bloody Lane, prepared zigzag trenches so that any attacker who penetrated them could not fire up and down them, as the Federals had done at Antietam. To augment the defenses, well-positioned artillery dominated the viable routes of attack. The Union assault was a slaughter. Brigade after brigade, division after division attacked head-on and failed. To protect themselves, Federals "actually dragged their dead in a line," a Rebel artillerist described, "piled them up like logs, dug a trench behind & thrown the dirt upon them, & thus made a *fortification* out of *their own dead.*"[11] Other divisions attacked nearby and suffered similar results. Longstreet's defensive position was superb. Only a deep

BURIAL SCENE AFTER THE BATTLE OF FREDERICKSBURG
The Battle of Fredericksburg was a perfect disaster for Burnside and the Army of the Potomac, with failure and heavy casualties resulting from a poorly executed plan. The worst losses came at Marye's Heights outside the town, where division after division failed to break the Confederate defenses on the slope of the hill.

Mud March

Following the embarrassing result at Fredericksburg, Burnside tried to launch a new offensive, striking for the fords above the town. Heavy winter rains turned the roads into a muddy mess, and the Army of the Potomac could not make any significant advance. Following the failed "Mud March," Lincoln replaced Burnside with Joe Hooker.

penetration on the Union left by Franklin could have unhinged Longstreet's command, and Jackson had snuffed out any hope of victory there.

For two days, the opposing sides held their ground, with wounded and killed scattered over no-man's-land. On December 15, amid a nighttime rainstorm, Burnside withdrew his forces across the river. Confederate losses totaled more than 5,000; Union casualties surpassed 12,600, many of them abandoned on the field. A Virginian informed his father, "one might have walked a ¼ of a mile stepping from dead Ye.[Yankee] to dead Ye. without once touching the ground."[12]

Though defeated, Burnside did not give up. He planned another feint and crossing, this one six miles below (south of) Fredericksburg. Lincoln caught wind of the plan from two complaining generals and requested a meeting. Burnside offered to resign, the president backed down, and on January 20 Burnside tried again, this time northwest of Fredericksburg. Heavy rains converted the roads into quagmires, and the delay cost Burnside the element of surprise. Not willing to risk a reprise of the Fredericksburg debacle, he called off the Mud March on January 22. Several days later, Lincoln replaced Burnside with Joseph Hooker.

DISCIPLINE AND SUPPLY IN THE ARMY OF NORTHERN VIRGINIA

Despite the victory, Lee knew he had to change the culture and improve the discipline of the Army of Northern Virginia. Since the Seven Days Battles of June and July 1862, straggling had deprived the army of considerable combat punch, and during the

Maryland campaign that September, it reached epidemic proportions, almost ending in disaster. One Rebel cavalry brigade in Virginia alone gathered up 5,000 to 6,000 men who had fallen out of the march, and as many as 15,000 were absent from the Battle of Antietam—many because they lacked footwear.[13]

Plundering, too, had been a serious problem as far back as First Bull Run. Early on, soldiers plundered for money and mementos. As the war dragged on and shortages became more rampant, Lee's troops plundered out of necessity, seeking food, clothing, and valuables to purchase essential items. After Fredericksburg, Lee's men resembled locusts, swooping in to pick clean northern casualties left behind.[14] A North Carolina officer admitted, "Our men went to work robbing the dead without ceremony,"[15] while a staff officer explained to his grandmother, "They were stripped to the skin by our Soldiers who have long since lost all delicacy on the subject."[16] In some instances, Confederates dug up buried Union dead to get their clothes. Scavengers sought garments, U.S. money (increasingly valued as Confederate currency depreciated), watches, and jewelry. One disgusted Virginian lamented to his wife that "a Mississippian cut a dead Yankees finger to get his ring."[17] Nor were these plunderers simply enlisted personnel. "Officers, Cols. Majors, etc, forgot their positions and quarrelled about the distribution of the booty," according to a Georgian.[18] Robbing from the dead, prisoners of war, and southern and northern civilians had become commonplace, as had straggling. Both practices represented a severe breakdown in discipline that would come back to haunt the Confederate armies, especially in a war with such a very narrow margin for error.[19]

Immediately after Antietam, Lee reinvigorated his efforts to change the army culture, urging his corps commanders to "infuse a different spirit among our officers, and to inspire them in making every necessary effort to bring about a better state of discipline."[20] Yet Rebel soldiers came from a society that cherished personal independence and honor and resented authority and discipline. Confederate military culture flowed from the bottom up, reflecting the priority of individual rights in southern white society, and despite all Lee's efforts, he could not alter it. The culture of indiscipline had established itself long before he assumed command, and despite his best efforts throughout the war, in the face of rampant shortages and woeful losses, especially among officers, discipline never quite took hold.[21]

Although social and cultural factors help explain the widespread plundering, the basic driving force was necessity. The Confederacy entered the war with limited resources and struggled to supply and feed its troops. It compensated with battlefield spoils. By the end of 1862, the army in Virginia had picked up more than 100,000 small arms and 174 pieces of artillery on battlefields, enough to offset the manufacturing and importation shortfall and place quality weapons in the hands of troops. Soldiers gathered necessary food and clothing from Union dead and captured, along with pocket money that bought additional clothing and sustenance. With winter setting in, Confederates needed pants, shirts, shoes, overcoats, and blankets just to cope with the cold, and many were eager for a fight just so they could plunder from the battlefield.[22]

The army also suffered from a severe shortage of animals and wagons. The Union Army of the Potomac had one wagon for every forty men and one horse or mule—many of those for cavalry—for every two to three men. By comparison, a field officer

The 1853 Enfield rifle was a popular weapon in the Confederate army. Similar in design and function to the Springfield, these British-made weapons were imported by Confederate blockade runners, due to the lack of significant industry in the southern states.

Many states, both Union and Confederate, provided their volunteer regiments with distinctive insignia representing their home government. This soldier of the 1st Texas wears the "Lone Star" on his broad-brimmed hat.

Confederate soldiers often lacked proper load-bearing equipment like packs. This soldier has bundled his belongings into a long blanket roll he carries on his shoulder.

As denoted by the stripes on his sleeve, this soldier has been promoted to corporal. Led as it was mostly by West Point graduates, the Confederate army had mostly the same rank-structure, organization, and traditions as the U.S. Army.

1ST TEXAS ▶

Nicknamed "the Ragged Old First," the 1st Texas served from the Seven Days to Appomattox. The unit gained particular note as part of the Army of Northern Virginia's renowned Texas Brigade, famous for its time under John Bell Hood.

▲
LEE IN UNIFORM

Though Lee's image and success had the power to inspire Confederate soldiers (and even the nation) to fight, it was not enough to effectively instill military discipline on individually minded southern soldiers.

in Lee's army complained that his brigade had only thirty-seven wagons, six of which were worn out; a Union brigade of comparable size would have had fifty serviceable wagons. One Confederate brigade had two-mule teams instead of four pulling each wagon, except for those wagons that had no animals at all. Similar hardships afflicted the cavalry. More than a third of the Hampton Legion, for example, lacked mounts.[23]

Food for troops was also at a premium that winter and well into the spring of 1863. No longer could they supplement their diet from local purchases, because those few civilians who remained in the area had nothing to offer. On Christmas Day 1862, a Virginian informed his parents that for a good mackerel, "I think I'd risk letting a whole company have one fire at me from one hundred yards off." Men lived on half rations or less; coffee was a luxury. Nor were rations good quality. Pvt. Lewis Leon jotted in his diary one February day, "got one day's rations, hard enough to fell a bull."[24]

War had so disrupted wheat production in Virginia that farmers harvested only a quarter of what they did in peacetime. Manpower shortages, campaign disruptions, wartime refugees, and occupied territory limited the number of acres under cultivation. In an average year before the war, 800,000 to 1,000,000 bushels of wheat were shipped to Richmond. In 1862, even though the city's population doubled and it became the supply depot for the army, only 250,000 to 300,000 bushels arrived. One full-grown cow provided a full meat ration to two hundred soldiers. By mid-January 1863, the army supply of cattle had dwindled down to enough to last through the end of the month only, and those had become very thin due to insufficient grazing.[25]

The limits of the logistic network exacerbated these problems. Railroads were not built for speed, and, unlike in the North, connecting lines often had different gauges, so that locomotives and cars could not transfer from one track to the other. The road system offered few macadamized or planked turnpikes, and dirt thoroughfares became quagmires after rainfall, making travel in the winter and spring particularly burdensome. By the winter of 1862–63, the Virginia rail system had deteriorated badly and was increasingly unreliable. Lee's army encamped that winter along the Rappahannock River. The Richmond, Fredericksburg & Potomac Railroad ran directly there, but it was not designed to carry much freight, so teamsters had to haul most supplies thirty-five miles over muddy roads. The Virginia Central Railroad, arguably the most important railroad in the state and a viable alternative, intersected with the Richmond, Fredericksburg & Potomac at Hanover Junction, Virginia. From there, it ran to Charlottesville and through the Shenandoah Valley, the richest region for food production in the state. Two years of overuse and lack of repairs, however, left its efficiency "most seriously impaired," as the railroad president (a Union spy who reported regularly to Federal authorities on railroad issues) informed Jefferson Davis. In mid-March 1863, the line suffered four derailments in a five-day

▼

HARDTACK

Tough, long lasting, and generally tasteless, hardtack, a sort of cracker made from water, flour, and salt, was the base of a Civil War soldier's rations.

▲
WHEAT HARVEST

This drawing shows slaves stacking wheat in Culpeper, Virginia, in 1863. The overall harvest dropped dramatically in the South during the Civil War.

span. A severe shortage of workers exacerbated the overuse problem. The railroad employed only about half the number of laborers as it had before the war, and many of the slaves who made ties to secure the rails and prevent derailments had run away. Railroad officials had to reduce the weight in each car by 25 percent and slow down their speed.[26]

Into the spring, tight supplies translated into meager rations. It took thirty cars, which in turn required two or three trains, to carry one million rations, enough for Lee's soldiers for two weeks. Animals in Jackson's corps alone required four cars of forage per day. With all the demands for the Richmond area and the difficulty of procuring and loading that quantity on a regular basis, soldiers and animals usually lived on reduced daily rations: often a quarter pound of bacon, some bread, and a little rice and molasses. Union intelligence learned of the shortages through interrogations of deserters. On the eve of the spring campaign in 1863, Federal soldiers taunted that the Rebels "have a new Gen[eral] in command of [their] army & say his name is General Starvation."[27]

Hoping to ease the burden, Lee sent Virginia cavalrymen home with their horses that winter so they could feed them. He also detached two divisions (15,000 soldiers, a quarter of the army) under Longstreet and sent them to southeastern Virginia to block Federal troops from Burnside's old corps massed at Norfolk from advancing on Petersburg and Richmond. This prevented Union troops from severing the vital railroad between Petersburg and Weldon and enabled Longstreet's men to gather food for themselves from an area untouched by the ravages of war, while also collecting

**DAMAGED CONFEDERATE ▶
TRAIN**

Railroads throughout the South were in poor condition, and suffered as a result of a disparity in gauges and capabilities. The lack of significant industrial production in the Confederacy made it difficult to replace damaged materials, or to retire decrepit machines like this locomotive.

critical supplies for the main army. Lee was thus able to reduce the burden of supplying his troops along the Rappahannock by 20 percent. It also meant, however, that Long-street's divisions would miss the Battle of Chancellorsville in April and May.[28]

For all the army's problems, perhaps its greatest was Lee's health. Just before the first march into Maryland, the Confederate general broke both wrists when his horse fell. He could not write, he could not ride, he could not even dress himself. In February 1863, doctors thought Lee had caught pneumonia, which they later rediagnosed as neuralgic rheumatism, but it was most likely a heart attack. Over the next two months, his condition was weak, and he could not muster the strength to work normal hours. In mid-April a staff member reported that Lee was doing better but still resided in a house a few miles from the army headquarters. Meanwhile, he had mountains of

CONFEDERATE HORSE ▶

Thanks in part to the strong equestrian tradition in the South, Confederate troopers in the first half of the war proved generally superior to their Union counterparts. Since Rebel horsemen provided their own mounts (receiving in return higher pay and allowances), they often procured the best horses they could afford, giving them an advantage over Federals on government-issue mounts. But when expensive horses were lost, Confederate soldiers often could not afford replacements of equal quality.

paperwork and extensive planning to do. Since it was almost campaign season, authorities kept Lee's true condition from nearly everyone.[29]

Meanwhile, following the recommendation of key artillery officers, Lee consolidated every four batteries into a battalion, with one battalion assigned to each division. In addition, each corps had two reserve artillery battalions, which it could employ in conjunction with division battalions for heavy, concentrated fire. This reorganization of the army's "long arm," a huge leap forward, would greatly improve the coordination of the army's firepower in the upcoming campaign.[30]

BATTLE OF CHANCELLORSVILLE

Hooker, the new commander of the Army of the Potomac, had undercut his superiors to get the job. A hard-drinking officer whose notorious camp followers took on his name as "hookers," he had foolishly told a reporter that what the country needed to win the war was a dictator. When Lincoln appointed him to command the army, the president scolded Hooker for infusing a spirit of dissension among high-ranking officers yet promised him full support. "What I ask of you is military success," Lincoln chided him, "and I will risk the dictatorship."[31]

As active and enterprising as he was ambitious, Hooker reinvigorated his 130,000-man army with better food, clothing, and health care, new furloughs, and a whiskey ration. He also instituted corps badges. Intended to help identify deserters, these insignia became symbols of honor among the troops.

Yet Hooker brought baggage with him that ultimately undermined him and his efforts. He was a sharp critic of McClellan and Burnside, and his hostility predisposed him against good officers who were close to both men. By criticizing his superiors, he had helped to poison the atmosphere among general officers in the Army of the

JOSEPH HOOKER
November 13, 1814–October 31, 1879

Joe Hooker graduated from USMA in 1837. He fought in the Second Seminole War, served as adjutant at USMA, and served on various generals' staffs in the war with Mexico. He commanded a division during the Peninsular, Seven Pines, and Seven Days operations. Hooker also served in the Second Bull Run campaign. Promoted to major general, United States Volunteers, he led a corps at Antietam and a grand division at Fredericksburg.

A sharp critic of his superiors, Hooker was named commander of the Army of the Potomac, where he improved morale and restored order, but he also foolishly injured the command and control of his artillery. He was defeated at Chancellorsville, and then his resignation as army commander was accepted in a dispute with Lincoln and Halleck. He later commanded the XX Corps at Lookout Mountain in the fall of 1863. During the Atlanta campaign, Hooker continued as head of the XX Corps but was relieved at his request when his former subordinate Maj. Gen. Oliver Otis Howard was assigned command of the Army of the Tennessee. He finished out the war in the Northern Department. His nickname "Fighting Joe" came from a typographical error that read "Fighting Joe Hooker" instead of "Fighting—Joe Hooker."

Potomac. McDowell, McClellan, and Pope were gone for unsatisfactory performance; Fitz John Porter was under arrest for having disobeyed orders at Second Bull Run; Franklin, a sharp critic of Burnside, was removed as grand division commander. Sumner, another grand division commander, could no longer tolerate the stress of the job and the in-fighting and asked to be relieved. Hooker, who had curried favor with the Radical Republicans, now had the chief position, but he had also helped establish a precedent of undercutting the senior leadership of the army.[32]

Hooker instituted two organizational changes that hurt his army. With all three grand division commanders gone (he had been one of them), he scrapped Burnside's organization so that all eight corps commanders now reported directly to him. This re-created a problem of command and control that Lee had confronted during the Seven Days Battles, with too many people reporting to the commanding general directly.

Worse, Hooker effectively demoted his talented and experienced artillery commander Brig. Gen. Henry J. Hunt. Hooker perceived Hunt as a McClellan man, and when Hunt wanted to further consolidate artillery into a corps, and argued vociferously for it, Hooker relegated him to administrative duties—thus removing the one person who could insure that the gunners acted in concert in battle.[33]

Hooker's campaign plan was to send his cavalry, 10,000 strong, and a maneuver force of three corps across fords well upriver from Fredericksburg while the bulk of the army, approximately 65,000 men, held Lee's troops in place or drew his attention below the town. The cavalry would drive on Richmond and disrupt Lee's rear; the three corps would roll up Lee's left flank, uncovering more fords. Hooker wanted them to press east through a tangled second-generation forest known as the Wilderness into open ground. That would trap Lee between two huge Federal commands or compel the Army of Northern Virginia to retreat and suffer attacks in flight.[34]

Initially, everything went according to Hooker's plan. Three flanking corps crossed the Rappahannock and Rapidan Rivers before Lee could react, and, near Fredericksburg, Federals quietly laid pontoons and crossed the Rappahannock. By April 30, the Federals had skillfully shifted the bulk of their army below the Rappahannock-Rapidan line and created a pincer that threatened Lee's rear and supply line.

Ever since his retreat across the Potomac River, Lee had sought another opportunity to advance northward into Maryland and Pennsylvania. With this goal in mind, Lee refused to fall back. To do so would prevent him from launching another offensive into the North. Lee decided to leave Maj. Gen. Jubal Early with just 9,000 troops and fifty-six guns to hold the defenses at Fredericksburg, while the bulk of his army focused on Hooker's flanking force, which he perceived as the greater threat.

Unexpected resistance in the Wilderness convinced Hooker to slow his advance, effectively abandoning his plan. On May 1, as Federals encountered Rebels advancing westward, the Army of the Potomac assumed a defensive posture, and the initiative passed to Lee. That day, Confederates tested the center and eastern part of the main Federal line and discovered a strong Union position, with an almost impenetrable combination of tangled growth, felled trees, and breastworks. That left only the far Federal right, the western end of Hooker's convex line, as a target.

Rebel cavalryman Brig. Gen. Fitz Lee (Lee's nephew) had detected that the Union's

CORPS BADGE

Hooker's system of corps badges, originally designed to help stragglers identify their units, created symbols of honor for the corps and divisions. Badges appeared on uniforms, flags, and even envelopes to foster cohesion and pride. The badge on the envelope here identifies the sender as a member of VI Corps (the cross), 3rd Division (blue cross, with red for 1st Division; white for 2nd).

CHANCELLORSVILLE

Jackson's surprise attack on the Union flank caused the near-collapse of Oliver O. Howard's XI Corps. Troops from Hiram G. Berry's division of III Corps checked the retreat, but the damage to XI Corps's psyche and reputation had been done. Thereafter, the German-American XI Corps was derisively called the "Flying Dutchmen."

right flank was unfortified. On the night of May 1, seated on a cracker box, Lee proposed that Jackson strike it. The next day, with locals as guides, Jackson took 28,000 soldiers on a circuitous twelve-mile route around the Federal right. Since the march absorbed most of the day, Lee, with 13,000 troops and twenty-four cannon, kept five Union corps at bay.[35]

For ten hours, Jackson's lengthy column hiked around the Federal flank. On several occasions, Federal troops observed the movement, but no one alerted Maj. Gen. Oliver Otis Howard, commander of the XI Corps. Jackson discovered the unsuspecting Union troops lounging around camp, protected only by some thin abatis and without cavalry cover. He carefully arranged his men and, around 6:00 p.m., swooped down to attack. Some Rebels slowed to plunder the Federal camp, but most pressed on, rolling up the Union flank. However, as darkness descended, Federal resistance stiffened, and the attack slowed. Jackson rode forward with a small party to observe the Federal positions, hoping to cut off the Army of the Potomac from the fords across the Rappahannock. Skittish Confederates heard the noise and, assuming the party was Federals, fired. Jackson sustained three wounds: in his right hand, his left wrist, and above the left elbow. Although he survived the amputation of his arm, eight days later Stonewall Jackson died of pneumonia.[36]

Jackson had won a resounding victory, crushing Howard's corps, but Lee was still in a precarious position: heavily outnumbered and with his army divided into three

WOUNDED AT CHANCELLORSVILLE

Rice C. Bull of the 123rd New York suffered two wounds in the Battle of Chancellorsville in fighting around the Chancellor House on May 3, 1863. Confederates under Brig. Gen. Stephen Dodson Ramseur overran the Union position, and Bull fell into Confederate hands. Union prisoners were paroled and turned over to Union authorities. They bounced around in ambulances over corduroyed roads. Bull was placed in a hospital and received a wounded furlough. He returned to his command in mid-October 1863 and fought the rest of the war, rising to the rank of sergeant.

May 3: The bullet that entered my right cheek had glanced along the jaw bone and came out of my neck near the jugular vein. My second wound was in my left side above the hip; the bullet came out near the back bone and making a ragged wound.

. . .

The morning of May 5th, [four] Surgeons, under flag of truce, reported at the camp . . . The Surgeons then went among the wounded looking for those that required amputation; they said they could do nothing at that time for the other wounded . . . The Surgeons began their bloody work at once in the immediate view of the wounded, some of whom were not more than ten feet from the table. As each amputation was completed, the wounded man was carried to the old house and laid on the floor; the arm or leg was thrown on the ground near the table, only a few feet from the wounded who were laying near by.

. . .

May 8: By May 8th our wounds had all festered and were hot with fever; our clothing which came in contact with them was so filthy and stiff from the dried blood that it gravely aggravated our condition. Many wounds developed gangrene and blood poisoning; lockjaw caused suffering and death . . . Finally, not the least of our troubles were the millions of flies that filled the air and covered blood-saturated clothing when they could not reach and sting the unbandaged wounds. I want to say again that the Confederate soldiers were always kind and helpful.[39]

segments. That night, Lee emphatically directed Maj. Gen. J. E. B. Stuart, commanding in Jackson's place, to reunite with him. Stuart had already taken steps to seize the hill at Hazel Grove, which separated the two portions of the Confederate army, but he did not have to fight for it. Though Hazel Grove was the critical piece of ground on the battlefield, Hooker ceded it in order to tighten his own line. There, on May 3, Stuart planted twenty-eight cannon under the direction of Col. Edward Porter Alexander, later concentrating fourteen more guns near the Orange Plank Road. The Hazel Grove position solved a recurrent problem: Confederate case shot and shells[37] often exploded prematurely, so infantry commanders refused to allow artillery to fire over their heads. The artillery positions of Hazel Grove and Orange Plank Road gave the Confederates an extraordinary converging fire on the Union infantry and artillery occupying the cleared high ground known as Fairview, even while it permitted Stuart's infantry to advance during the bombardment. The combined arms worked unusually well together, shattering the Federal position at Fairview despite stiff resistance and high Rebel casualties. The victory would have been impossible without Lee's reorganization of his "long arm."[38]

As the two Confederate forces linked up, Lee and Stuart rode through the lines. For the first time, the troops cheered Lee. The sight, wrote a Georgia sergeant, "was inspiring beyond anything you can imagine." One of Lee's aides observed the spontaneous outpouring and later confessed, "I thought that it must have been from such a scene that men in ancient days rose to the dignity of gods." Meanwhile, on the Federal side, a cannon shot struck near Hooker and knocked him unconscious. Hooker quickly recovered his senses, but any aggressive spirit he had was now lost.[40]

Jackson's death following his wounds from Chancellorsville shook Confederate leadership and was a major blow to future operations. Upon hearing of the general's demise, Lee remarked, "I have lost my right arm."

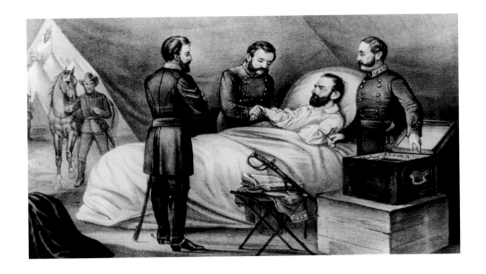

Back at Fredericksburg, Union Maj. Gen. John Sedgwick's 24,000 men finally crossed the river on the night of May 2, under orders to unite with the rest of the army. It took three assaults the next morning before the Federals slammed through Early's undermanned lines at Marye's Heights. When the Federals regrouped and launched another strong attack to exploit the breakthrough, they ran into Brig. Gen. Cadmus M. Wilcox's Alabamians. An 1846 West Point graduate and a Regular Army officer, Wilcox conducted perhaps the most skillful delaying action of the war. Along Orange Plank Road leading into Lee's rear, his men fought obstinately, falling back and rallying three times. The last time, around Salem Church, Wilcox received help from four other brigades and repulsed the Union advance. The next day, however, a Confederate counterattack failed when Maj. Gen. Lafayette McLaws disregarded orders and refused to advance.[41]

That was the last real fighting at Chancellorsville. On the night of May 5, having suffered more than 17,000 casualties, "'Fighting'—*fainting*—fleeing" Joe Hooker, as a Virginia private called him, retreated over the Rappahannock. Once again, a Union army commander had failed to commit all his troops, as some 40,000 north and east of the Rappahannock River did not fight. Lee lost 13,000 soldiers out of 60,000 engaged, Jackson among them. Although Lee's losses were much greater proportionally, Hooker's retreat marked the fifth time that the Federals had launched an offensive campaign in the East and lost.[42]

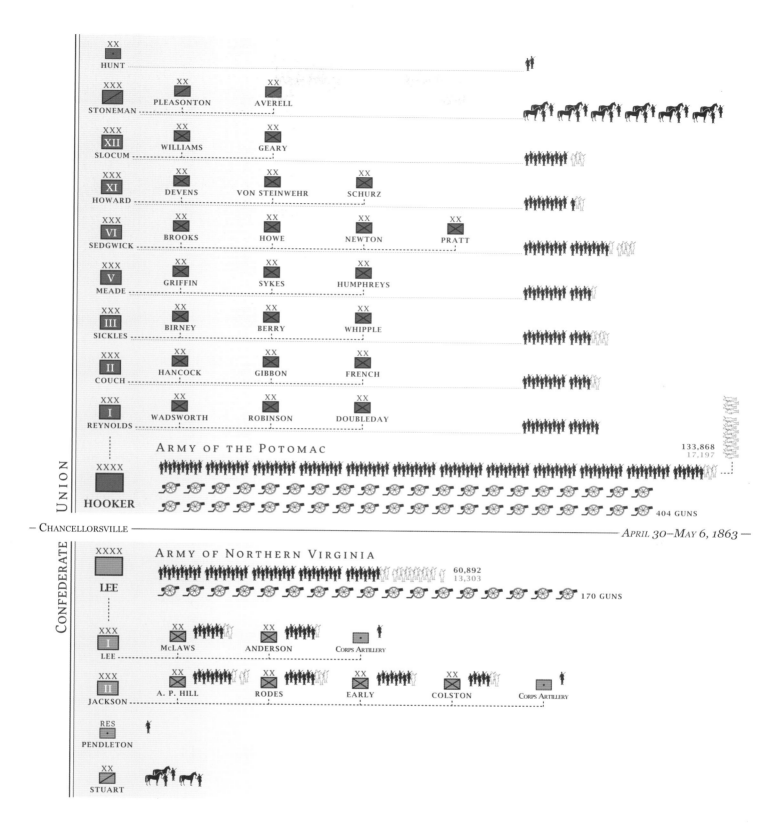

XX
HUNT

XXX
STONEMAN — PLEASONTON — AVERELL

XXX
XII
SLOCUM — WILLIAMS — GEARY

XXX
XI
HOWARD — DEVENS — VON STEINWEHR — SCHURZ

XXX
VI
SEDGWICK — BROOKS — HOWE — NEWTON — PRATT

XXX
V
MEADE — GRIFFIN — SYKES — HUMPHREYS

XXX
III
SICKLES — BIRNEY — BERRY — WHIPPLE

XXX
II
COUCH — HANCOCK — GIBBON — FRENCH

XXX
I
REYNOLDS — WADSWORTH — ROBINSON — DOUBLEDAY

ARMY OF THE POTOMAC

133,868
17,197

XXXX
HOOKER

404 GUNS

Union

— CHANCELLORSVILLE —   — *APRIL 30–MAY 6, 1863* —

Confederate

XXXX
LEE

ARMY OF NORTHERN VIRGINIA

60,892
13,303

170 GUNS

XXX
I
LEE — McLAWS — ANDERSON — CORPS ARTILLERY

XXX
II
JACKSON — A. P. HILL — RODES — EARLY — COLSTON — CORPS ARTILLERY

RES
PENDLETON

XX
STUART

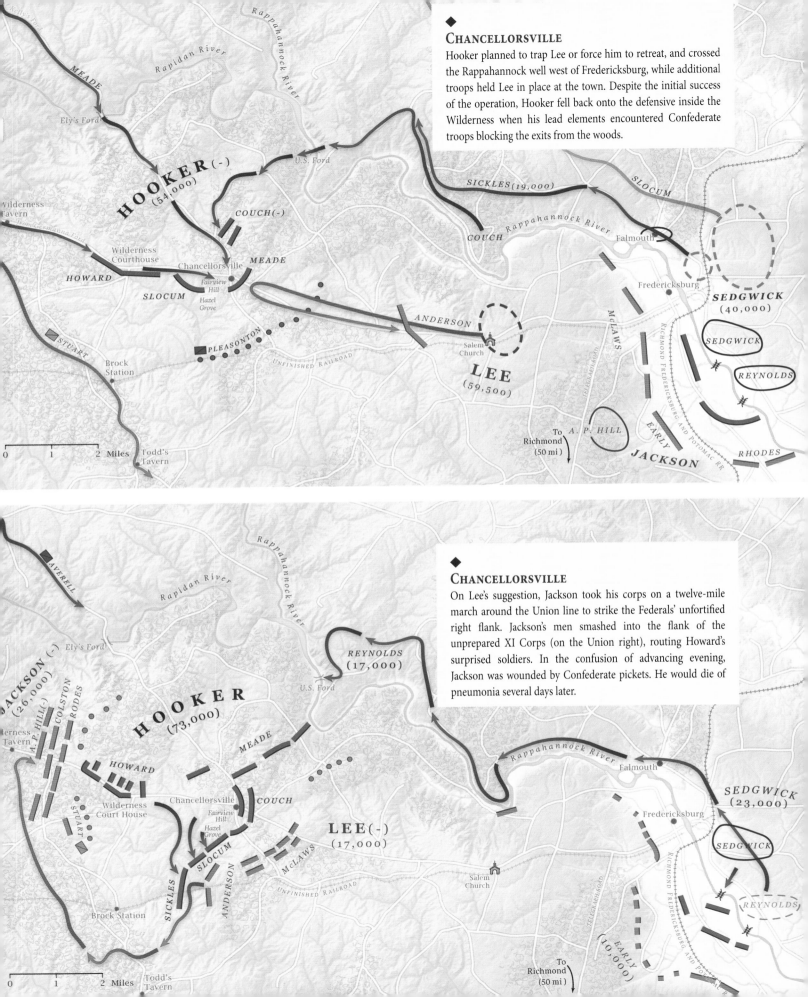

◆ CHANCELLORSVILLE

Hooker planned to trap Lee or force him to retreat, and crossed the Rappahannock well west of Fredericksburg, while additional troops held Lee in place at the town. Despite the initial success of the operation, Hooker fell back onto the defensive inside the Wilderness when his lead elements encountered Confederate troops blocking the exits from the woods.

Map labels (top): Rapidan River · Rappahannock River · MEADE · Ely's Ford · U.S. Ford · SICKLES (19,000) · SLOCUM · HOOKER (-) (54,000) · COUCH (-) · Rappahannock River · Falmouth · SEDGWICK (40,000) · Wilderness Tavern · Wilderness Courthouse · COUCH · Fredericksburg · SEDGWICK · HOWARD · Chancellorsville · MEADE · REYNOLDS · SLOCUM · Fairview Hill · Hazel Grove · ANDERSON · McLAWS · STUART · PLEASONTON · Salem Church · LEE (59,500) · UNFINISHED RAILROAD · Brock Station · To Richmond (50 mi) · A. P. HILL · EARLY · JACKSON · RHODES · Todd's Tavern

Scale (top): 0 1 2 Miles

◆ CHANCELLORSVILLE

On Lee's suggestion, Jackson took his corps on a twelve-mile march around the Union line to strike the Federals' unfortified right flank. Jackson's men smashed into the flank of the unprepared XI Corps (on the Union right), routing Howard's surprised soldiers. In the confusion of advancing evening, Jackson was wounded by Confederate pickets. He would die of pneumonia several days later.

Map labels (bottom): AVERELL · Rapidan River · Rappahannock River · Ely's Ford · REYNOLDS (17,000) · U.S. Ford · JACKSON (-) (26,000) · A.P. HILL (-) · COLSTON · RODES · Wilderness Tavern · HOOKER (73,000) · MEADE · Rappahannock River · Falmouth · SEDGWICK (23,000) · HOWARD · Chancellorsville · COUCH · Fredericksburg · STUART · Wilderness Court House · Fairview Hill · Hazel Grove · SLOCUM · SEDGWICK · SICKLES · ANDERSON · McLAWS · LEE (-) (17,000) · Salem Church · REYNOLDS · UNFINISHED RAILROAD · Brock Station · EARLY (10,000) · To Richmond (50 mi) · Todd's Tavern

Scale (bottom): 0 1 2 Miles

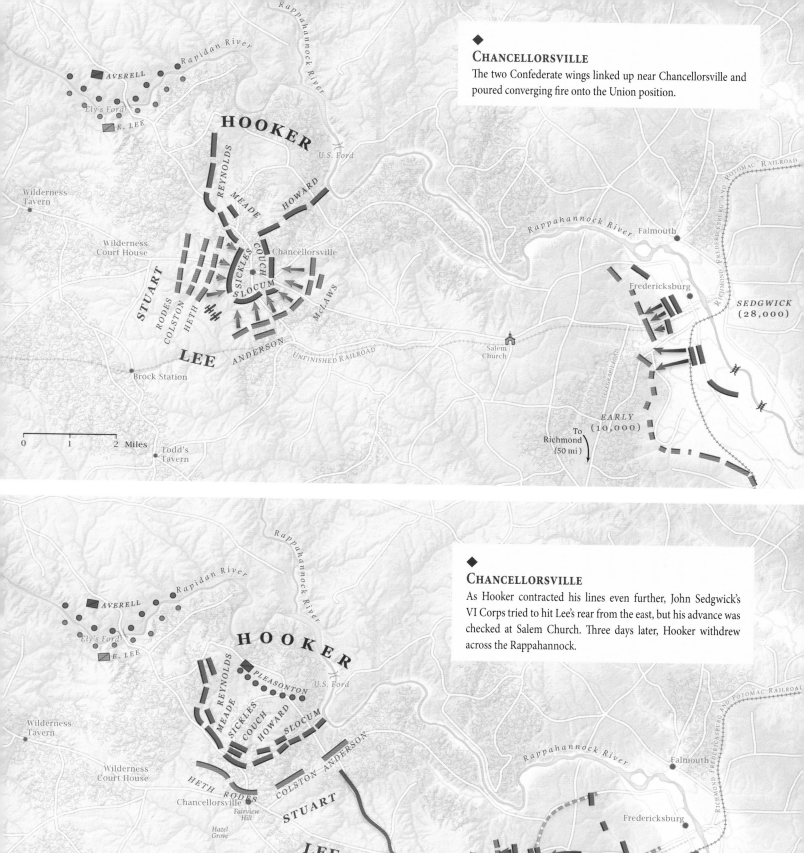

◆

CHANCELLORSVILLE

The two Confederate wings linked up near Chancellorsville and poured converging fire onto the Union position.

◆

CHANCELLORSVILLE

As Hooker contracted his lines even further, John Sedgwick's VI Corps tried to hit Lee's rear from the east, but his advance was checked at Salem Church. Three days later, Hooker withdrew across the Rappahannock.

With Hooker licking his wounds, Lee took immediate steps to seize the strategic initiative. He had multiple objectives for launching a raid into Maryland and Pennsylvania. In the West, Union general Ulysses S. Grant was conducting a brilliant campaign and hammering Confederate armies in Mississippi, threatening to besiege Vicksburg, the critical Confederate position on the Mississippi River.[43] When the secretary of war proposed that Lee ship a division to Mississippi, the army commander resisted. "The uncertainty of its arrival and the uncertainty of its application cause me to doubt the policy of sending it," Lee responded.[44] The distance was over 700 miles on indirect and debilitated rail lines, and the division would be exposed to malaria if it reached the Vicksburg region. Nor did Lee think a single division would make an appreciable difference. He felt his army could accomplish more with those troops than could the commanders in Mississippi.

If the Army of Northern Virginia could instill fear among the people of Pennsylvania, the Lincoln administration might feel compelled to detach large forces from Grant to save critical industrial centers back east and to protect potential voters from an invading enemy. Certainly a raid northward would spare southern farmers and ease commissary burdens, enabling the Confederacy to feed its largest army on northern grain and livestock. Lee also sought an opportunity to defeat the Federal army far away from its base, where he could follow up his victory with repeated attacks and devastate the Army of the Potomac. Even if Vicksburg fell, the effect of that victory on northern public opinion might well be outweighed by the impact of a series of crushing defeats in Pennsylvania.[45]

For some time, Lee had thought that his two corps were too large for his commanders to direct properly. Stonewall Jackson's death made that concern more acute, so the general now decided to reorganize the army into three smaller corps. Longstreet, who returned from the Suffolk area, would continue to command I Corps. Maj. Gen. Richard S. Ewell would take over Jackson's old II Corps. The new III Corps, made up of one division transferred from I Corps, a second from II Corps, and a newly formed third division, would be led by Maj. Gen. A. P. Hill. The army now had 75,000 troops, its greatest strength since the Seven Days Battles outside Richmond nearly a year before.

Lee had begun his advance north when 8,000 Union cavalry and 3,000 infantry under Maj. Gen. Alfred Pleasonton struck the unsuspecting Confederate cavalry, 9,500 strong, at Brandy Station on June 8. In the largest cavalry battle ever fought in North America, Union and Confederate horsemen engaged in charge and countercharge. Stuart and his horsemen eventually repulsed Pleasonton, but in one blow, the Federals had shattered the Confederate cavalry's aura of invincibility. As a member of Stuart's staff pithily summed up the affair, the Battle of Brandy Station "made the Federal cavalry." Pleasonton also learned that Lee's army was on the move.[46]

Moving on toward Pennsylvania, Lee pushed into the Shenandoah Valley, and on June 14 Ewell captured a Union garrison at Winchester, Virginia, along with supplies

Longstreet graduated near the bottom of his class from USMA in 1842 and was wounded in the Mexican War. He led a brigade at First Bull Run and was one of Joseph E. Johnston's favorites. As major general, he commanded a division at Yorktown and Williamsburg. At Seven Pines, he botched the attack plans and blamed others. During the Seven Days, Second Bull Run, and Maryland campaigns, he fought well. Promoted to lieutenant general and corps command, he fought his corps extremely well at Fredericksburg.

His first foray in independent command at Suffolk was disappointing, and Longstreet rejoined the army for the Gettysburg campaign. Sent west, his troops broke through the Union lines at Chickamauga, but he quarreled with Braxton Bragg and led the failed campaign against Knoxville. In the aftermath, he trumped up charges and court martialed several officers who would have been valuable contributors during the spring and summer campaigns of 1864. Longstreet and his troops returned to Lee's army in time for the Wilderness, where he was badly wounded by friendly fire. Longstreet returned to the army in October and surrendered at Appomattox six months later. A postwar Republican, he was (after Lee's death) blamed unfairly for the defeat at Gettysburg.

JAMES LONGSTREET
JANUARY 8, 1821–JANUARY 2, 1904

there and in Martinsburg. By June 15, Ewell had crossed the Potomac into Maryland and then marched into Pennsylvania; Longstreet and then Hill followed. Lee had his corps commanders disperse their troops to forage on the countryside, where Confederates discovered lush fields and fat livestock. Despite Lee's specific directive authorizing only official confiscation, with officers issuing receipts to civilians, soldiers plundered widely. Hungry Rebels fed themselves lavishly, retaliating for massive Union destruction in Virginia. It was time, they felt, for northerners to endure the brutal effects of war, which might convince them to bring the conflict to an end.[47]

Lee's army advanced largely ignorant of Union movements. On June 23 Stuart had received permission to take three of his five brigades and strike into Hooker's rear. He wanted to redeem himself after the embarrassment of Brandy Station. His cavalry had accomplished the feat before against stationary armies (riding around McClellan's army before the Seven Days Battles and into John Pope's rear during the Second Bull Run campaign), but this time the Federals were marching northward in pursuit of Lee's main force. It took the Rebel horsemen much longer to swing around the Army of the Potomac than Stuart had anticipated, and then he had difficulty locating his own army. Stuart's absence had important consequences. Without those three brigades and their leader, and the essential scouting information they could have provided, Lee struggled to ascertain the location of the Union army during his march into Pennsylvania, placing his scattered forces in a precarious situation.[48]

Lincoln, meanwhile, had lost faith in Hooker. The army commander wanted to strike at Richmond, but Lincoln directed otherwise, reminding him that Lee's army was the proper target. Taking umbrage, Hooker offered to resign, expecting a chastened president to accede to his campaign designs. Instead, Lincoln readily accepted. On June 27 Lincoln placed Maj. Gen. George Gordon Meade in command.

A Regular Army topographical engineer before the war, Meade did his duty well and never intrigued for higher command. In this situation, Lincoln placed an enormous burden on the temperamentally cautious general. Meade pursued Lee northward

GETTYSBURG CAMPAIGN ▶
Lee again struck into the North, looking for another opportunity to destroy the Army of the Potomac. Using the Blue Ridge Mountains as a shield, his army advanced into Pennsylvania, capturing York and threatening the state capital, Harrisburg.

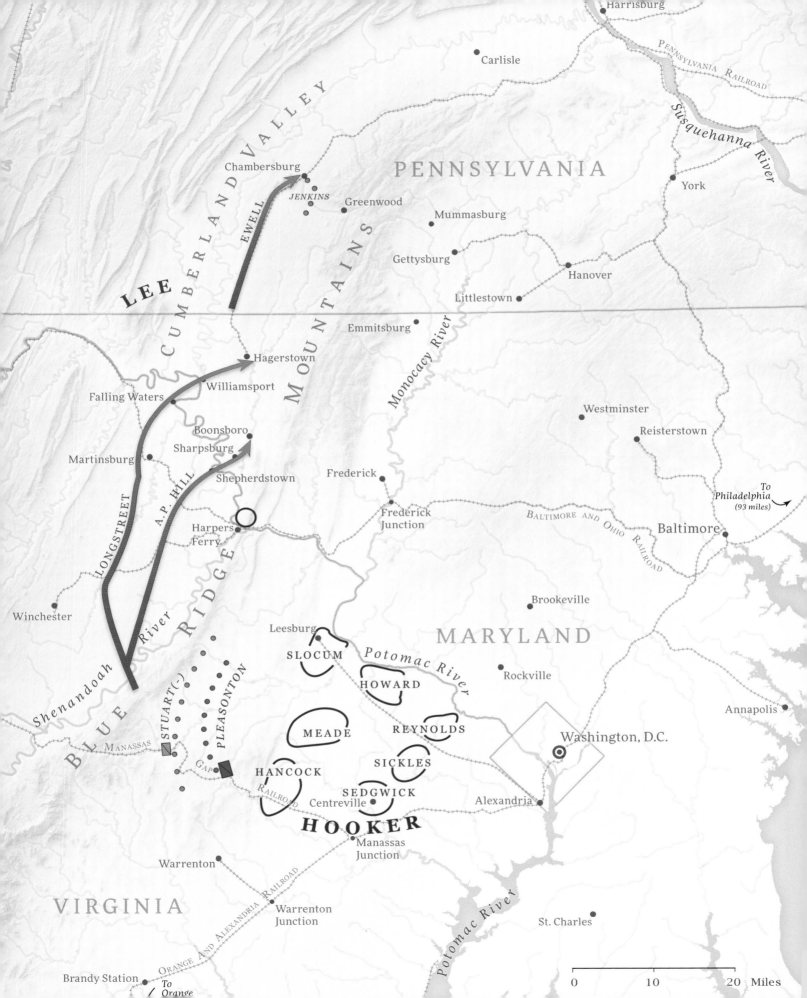

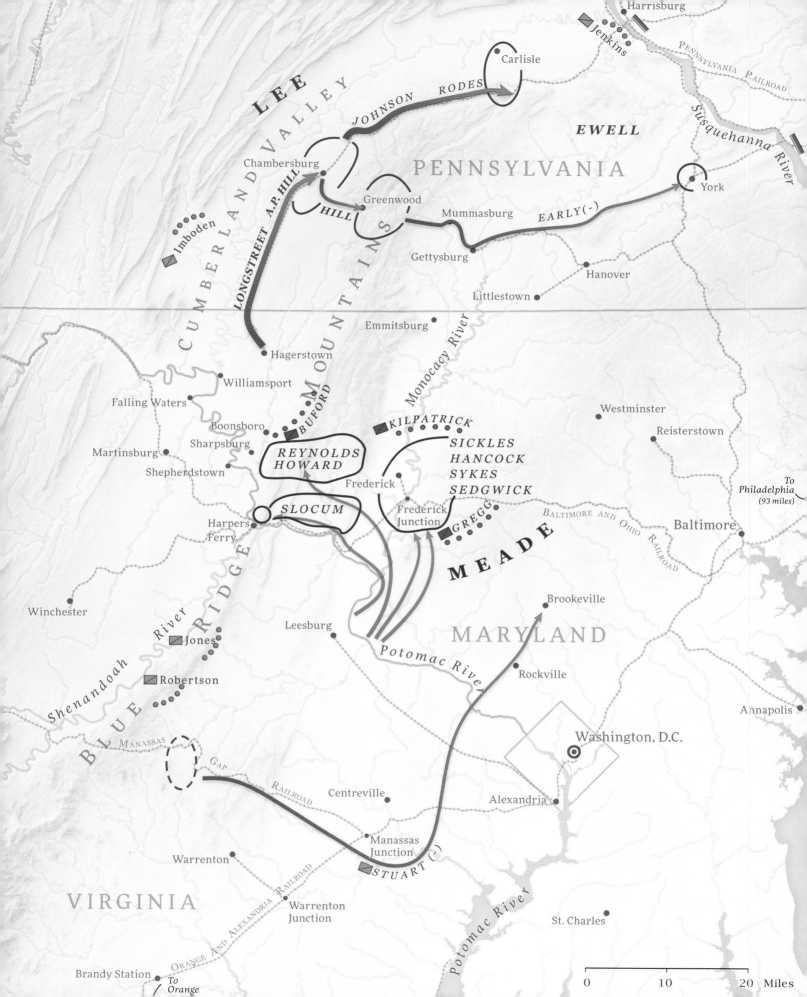

LEE

Carlisle

Harrisburg

Jenkins

PENNSYLVANIA RAILROAD

Susquehanna River

JOHNSON RODES

EWELL

PENNSYLVANIA

CUMBERLAND VALLEY

Chambersburg

LONGSTREET A.P. HILL

HILL

Greenwood

Mummasburg

EARLY (-)

York

Imboden

Gettysburg

Hanover

Littlestown

Hagerstown

Emmitsburg

MOUNTAINS

Monocacy River

Westminster

Williamsport

Falling Waters

BUFORD

KILPATRICK

Reisterstown

Boonsboro

Sharpsburg

Martinsburg

**REYNOLDS
HOWARD**

***SICKLES
HANCOCK
SYKES
SEDGWICK***

Shepherdstown

Frederick

*To
Philadelphia
(93 miles)*

SLOCUM

Harpers
Ferry

GREGG

BALTIMORE AND OHIO RAILROAD

Baltimore

Frederick
Junction

MEADE

Winchester

Shenandoah River

BLUE   RIDGE

Jones

Brookeville

MARYLAND

Leesburg

Robertson

Rockville

Annapolis

Manassas

Washington, D.C.

GAP

RAILROAD

Centreville

Alexandria

Warrenton

Manassas
Junction

STUART (-)

VIRGINIA

Warrenton
Junction

St. Charles

Potomac River

Brandy Station

*To
Orange*

ORANGE AND ALEXANDRIA RAILROAD

0   10   20   Miles

JAMES EWELL BROWN STUART

FEBRUARY 6, 1833–MAY 12, 1864

Stuart was born in southern Virginia, where his father, Archibald, was a veteran of the War of 1812 and a prominent local politician. In 1850 he obtained an appointment to West Point, graduating in 1854. His time at the academy coincided with Robert E. Lee's term as superintendent, and Stuart became a friend of the Lee family. He served with the 1st Cavalry in Kansas, fighting Cheyenne raiders and Kansas guerrillas. In 1859, while in Washington to discuss government contracts, he volunteered to be Lee's aide-de-camp during John Brown's raid at Harpers Ferry.

Stuart resigned from the army after Virginia's secession and organized the 1st Virginia Cavalry regiment, which fought at First Bull Run. In June 1862, after Lee took command of the Army of Northern Virginia, Stuart completed his famous ride around the Army of the Potomac, identifying the Union force's exposed flanks. He launched several more raids on Union supply lines in the years that followed, also fighting in the eastern theater's major battles. He briefly commanded Jackson's corps after the latter's mortal wounding at Chancellorsville.

Stuart's legend began to wane during the Gettysburg campaign, first when his troopers fought the inconclusive Battle of Brandy Station, and then after his attempted ride around the enemy resulted in his arriving late to the battle. During the 1864 Overland campaign, Stuart was mortally wounded during the Battle of Yellow Tavern.

Known by his initials as "Jeb," Stuart was the most famous Confederate cavalry commander. He cultivated the image of a cavalier, wearing a cape and an ostrich feather in his hat. Stuart was also a good officer, and Lee would remark that Stuart had never given him a bad piece of information.

but ensured he kept his army of 90,000 between the Confederates and Washington and Baltimore. At Pipe Creek, some twenty miles southeast of the crossroads town of Gettysburg, Meade laid out a strong defensive position, in case his army had to retire, and then pushed beyond it, fanning out his forces in all directions in search of the enemy. To assist Meade, the Pennsylvania governor called out his militia, and they prepared defensive positions in various locations. By June 30, Maj. Gen. John Buford's cavalry division occupied Gettysburg. The next morning, with Meade's corps anywhere from five to twenty-five miles away, he issued instructions to be ready for either offensive or defensive operations.[49]

The Battle of Gettysburg was an encounter engagement, in which neither side knew the enemy's true strength or dispositions. Lee specifically directed his corps commanders not to bring on a general engagement before his forces were concentrated. Unless the Army of Northern Virginia won a resounding victory with minimal losses, a major battle, with the resulting heavy casualties, would bring an end to the campaign. As soon as he learned that Meade's army was nearby, Lee directed his subordinates to concentrate around Gettysburg. On July 1, men in Hill's corps trudged toward the crossroads town along the Chambersburg Pike looking for shoes and ran into Buford's horsemen, who occupied Herr's Ridge just west of town. Buford's horsemen were able to keep the Confederate infantrymen at bay until later that morning, when Maj. Gen. John F. Reynolds's Union I Corps arrived. Replacing the cavalrymen, Union troops struck with a fury. They plowed into Herbst Woods just south of the pike, capturing a large portion of Brig. Gen. James J. Archer's Tennessee Brigade. They then had to help drive out Confederates in a railroad cut that ran parallel to the pike. Ordered to "go like hell" and dislodge those "kowardly sons of bitches," they did so, but not without heavy losses.[50]

Meade graduated from USMA in 1835 and served largely as a topographical engineer. He was a staff officer under Zachary Taylor during the Mexican War. He commanded a brigade in the Peninsula and Second Bull Run campaigns, and was wounded in the Seven Days Battles. He led a division at Antietam and Fredericksburg, and headed the V Corps at Chancellorsville. At each stage, Meade demonstrated competence and kept out of the political fray. He became commander of the Army of the Potomac in late June and directed it for the remainder of the war. His failure to follow up against Lee at Gettysburg earned him Lincoln's ire, and the president never quite trusted him again.

When Grant was appointed lieutenant general, he kept Meade, an insider who knew the strengths and weaknesses of subordinate officers, and traveled in the field with Meade, placing Meade in an awkward position. An excellent administrator, Meade freed Grant to plan. His problem was his personality under stress. Nicknamed Old Snapping Turtle, he had a "shoot-the-messenger" quality that alienated him from others. His personality became so problematic that Grant sought to move him to command of a new department, but Lincoln, who had little faith in Meade, refused.

GEORGE GORDON MEADE

December 31, 1815–November 6, 1872

Although Reynolds was killed, his corps held on McPherson's Ridge and Oak Ridge, west and northwest of the town. Howard's XI Corps arrived on the scene and extended the Union line to the east to form an L-shaped position north and west of Gettysburg. As a precaution, Howard also left a division south of town on Cemetery Hill. That afternoon, the Federals repulsed an attack by one of Ewell's Confederate divisions from the north, but then Early's division passed beyond the Union right flank from the northeast and buckled the entire line. Over three thousand Union troops were captured that day; the remainder formed a new position south of town, anchored on Cemetery Hill.[51]

Although Lee had arrived in the vicinity of Gettysburg in midafternoon, he could not organize a coordinated attack before nightfall. He had hoped to take advantage of momentum and gave Ewell an order to carry Cemetery Hill "if practicable." But losses were so severe in both Ewell's and Hill's corps that regiments—and, in a few cases, brigades—almost disintegrated. Discipline broke down as Confederates looted shops and homes, and others abandoned the attack to plunder dead and wounded Union troops. Additional Confederate troops were needed to escort the massive number of prisoners to the rear. Ewell examined the ground and declined to launch an attack, a decision that generated considerable controversy years later.[52]

The first day at Gettysburg came to an end with a tactical triumph for the Army of Northern Virginia, yet it was only a precursor of the fighting to come. That evening and throughout the night, Federal forces streamed into the area, anchoring the right at Culp's Hill and extending south from Cemetery Hill along Cemetery Ridge to form a fishhook-shaped position. Meade arrived at 1:00 a.m., and by sunrise, five of the six Union corps had reached the scene.[53]

With most of his army concentrated near Gettysburg, Lee planned to renew the battle the next day. After an early morning reconnaissance of the Union position spotted an exposed left flank, Lee ordered two of Longstreet's divisions to swing around and roll up the Federal line. But the initial route that Longstreet followed would have revealed his march to Meade. To preserve surprise, Confederate troops had to backtrack, thus wasting much of the afternoon on a lengthy trek under a broiling sun and in stifling humidity that drained them of precious energy. By 4:00 p.m., when the attack finally began, Longstreet's troops were already tired.[54]

The key piece of terrain was a rocky hill with trees largely cleared from the top that soldiers came to call Little Round Top, at the southern end of the Union line. Confederate artillery placed there might enfilade the Union line. Foolishly, Union Maj. Gen. Daniel Sickles had advanced his III Corps a half-mile west of Cemetery Ridge to occupy some high ground in his front, bowing the Union position and leaving Little Round Top unoccupied. Yet Meade's chief engineer noticed the problem and rushed soldiers from V Corps, waiting in reserve, to secure the hill just as the Rebel assault began.[55]

On the Confederate right, west of Little Round Top, Texans and Arkansans from Maj. Gen. John Bell Hood's division attacked a rocky outcropping called Devil's Den. Nasty fighting drew in two Georgia brigades, leaving Brig. Gen. Evander Law's Alabamians to assault the wooded southern end of Little Round Top against Maine and New York troops. The Confederates attacked aggressively; the Federals resisted stoutly.

Then an earlier oversight altered the outcome of the battle. During their long march, the Alabamians had crossed a creek but neglected to replenish their canteens. After firing ten or so rounds apiece, the Alabamians' musket barrels clogged with gunpowder residue. Without water, they could not clean the barrels. Yet the Federals were running out of ammunition. When two hundred soldiers from Col. Joshua Chamberlain's 20th Maine Infantry counterattacked down the hill with fixed bayonets, four hundred exhausted Confederates, virtually defenseless without usable muskets or bayonets, surrendered. The Federals held Little Round Top.[56]

To the northwest, Maj. Gen. Lafayette McLaws's Confederate division carried the

First Day at Gettysburg

After several hours of fierce fighting, the Confederates were finally able to drive Union troops back through the town. The delay, though, allowed much of the Army of the Potomac to reach the field.

Peach Orchard with considerable losses and shattered Sickles's III Corps, but stout Union resistance and massive reinforcements from II and V Corps prevented a breakthrough at the Wheatfield, between the Peach Orchard and Little Round Top. Late in the afternoon, Brig. Gen. William Barksdale's Mississippi brigade threatened to break through the Union line on Cemetery Ridge, but a charge by the 1st Minnesota Infantry saved the day, at a cost of 82 percent casualties. Before entering combat, officers in Brig. Gen. John Gibbon's division had read a circular from Meade, reminding the soldiers, "The whole country now looks anxiously to this army to deliver it from the presence of its foe" and exhorting them to do their duty. According to a soldier in

DEVIL'S DEN
A rock formation near the foot of the two rocky hills known as Little Round Top, Devil's Den saw intense fighting as Longstreet's advance moved toward the Union left.

the 1st Minnesota, those were exactly the right words. "One thing our armies lack is enthusiasm, and no efforts are made to create it, when, in many cases, it would accomplish more than real bravery or bull dog courage," he applauded.[57]

On the Confederate left, to the north, Ewell did little throughout the day, enabling Meade to concentrate his reserves against Longstreet. When one of Ewell's divisions took part of the XII Corps's trenches at Culp's Hill during the night, Union troops returning from Longstreet's defeat quickly recaptured them. Lee gained little from fighting in that quarter.

The Rebels had squandered too much daylight and failed to exploit their opportunities. Tired from prolonged marching and sapped by the heat, Lee's columns fought aggressively at first, but they could not muster the strength or coordinate effectively enough to exploit openings like that at the Peach Orchard. Meade, on the other hand, had taken advantage of his interior lines and had deployed his ample reserves masterfully.[58]

That night, Lee faced a difficult choice. He could withdraw in the face of an undefeated enemy, a risky proposition that would preclude further foraging and probably end the campaign, or he could attempt one more desperate assault. With unshakeable faith in his troops, Lee elected to fight one more day. The reinforcements Longstreet had faced suggested that Meade had stripped the Union center to bolster his flanks. Lee planned for Ewell to attack on the north end of the line. Stuart's cavalry, just arrived, would strike the Union rear, unnerve the defenders, and capture prisoners and supplies. Despite qualms on Longstreet's part, his corps, supported by concentrated artillery fire, would assault the Union center and left. Lee modified this plan when harassing fire from Little Round Top struck Longstreet's right; his southernmost troops were withheld, and, instead, soldiers from Hill's Corps joined in the assault.

The day proceeded badly for the Confederates. At Culp's Hill, the day opened with a thirty-minute Union bombardment. When the artillery fire lifted, Ewell's command launched three assaults, but Federals from the XII Corps, reinforced by comrades from I and VI Corps, repulsed the attack. A Union spoiler attack at Spangler's Spring at the extreme right end of the Federal line achieved nothing significant from a tactical standpoint, but it did discourage Ewell from continuing to attack. On the third day, just as on the second, Ewell's corps failed to contribute significantly to the Confederate effort.

After assembling some 170 artillery guns, the Confederates launched the largest concentrated bombardment in the history of mankind up to that time. "All at once it

◄ LITTLE ROUND TOP

Little Round Top, on the south end of the Gettysburg battlefield, formed the anchor of the Union line. The just-in-time dispatch of V Corps to the hill prevented the Confederates from seizing the ground and breaking the Union line.

seemed as though all the artillery in the universe had opened fire and was belching forth its missiles of death and destruction," a Connecticut soldier reported. Meade's artillery chief, Henry Hunt, back in command of a potent artillery reserve, responded with his guns but then slowly tapered off his fire, conserving ammunition and giving the impression that the Confederate bombardment had been successful.

Once the cannon duel ended, some 12,000 men from three Rebel divisions rose and advanced in line. The charge soon exposed their extreme left, and they suffered devastating fire from front and flank. On the Confederate right, two Union regiments from Vermont advanced and poured in enfilading fire that disrupted those attackers. In the center, undulating ground frequently hid the Confederates from Union fire, but Federal artillery, which the Rebels thought their bombardment had silenced, suddenly resumed fire and ripped gaping holes through the Confederate ranks. Finally, Federal infantrymen poured a withering musket fire into the attackers at close range. With the assault weakening, a few Rebels reached the center of the Union line and engaged the defenders in hand-to-hand fighting, but Union reinforcements crushed

WHEATFIELD ▶

Some of the fiercest fighting at Gettysburg took place in the Wheatfield, where Union troops held off a potential breakthrough. The 1st Minnesota took the most casualties, losing 80 percent of its force in the fighting.

CULP'S HILL

Union forces on Culp's Hill secured the northern portion of the field on the morning of Gettysburg's third day. Ewell's defeat helped weaken Lee's overall plan for the day.

them. Thousands of Rebel casualties littered the field and thousands more hugged the ground until nightfall made retreat possible. As one Confederate captain claimed, "It was a second Fredericksburg affair, only the wrong way."[59]

The day after the battle, ordnance officers in Richmond conducted some tests on artillery ammunition that help to explain the failure of the assault. Back in mid-March 1863, a massive explosion and fire had rocked the Richmond Laboratory and Arsenal, shutting it down. Officials had to ship shells and fuses from Charleston to the Army of Northern Virginia. The new tests demonstrated that Charleston fuses burned slower than those made in Richmond, but Lee's veteran gunners did not know it. They estimated distances accurately, packed the appropriate gunpowder, and cut the fuses the correct length, but the shells with the Charleston fuses carried up to 200 yards farther before they exploded.[60] According to a Minnesotan, the Confederates "tried to explode their shells directly over us, but fortunately, most of them just went far enough to clear us."[61] The massive Confederate bombardment had blown up Union wagons in the rear but failed to soften the defensive positions.

On the fourth, Meade braced for a renewed attack that never came. The Army of the Potomac had fought beautifully, but it had also suffered very heavy losses—23,000 men, or 25 percent of the entire army at Gettysburg—and Meade preferred to remain on the defensive. Lee adjusted his lines in the event of a Union attack, but he was in no position to resume the offensive. The Army of Northern Virginia had suffered 28,000 casualties, more than a third of its strength. Lee remained on the battlefield mainly to give his wagons and ambulances a head start in their retreat to Virginia. The next day, July 5, Lee's army withdrew; Meade pursued tentatively. He had a chance to strike Lee again at the Potomac River, when high water prevented Lee from crossing, but after probing the Confederate line, Meade declined to attack.

On July 14 Lincoln drafted a letter to Meade, complaining that he had had Lee "in his grasp" and could have "ended the war" with another attack.[62] Lincoln wrote it to release his sense of frustration over the inability of commanders of the Army of the Potomac to fight effectively and aggressively, but then he placed the note in a drawer to think about whether he was overreacting or his arguments were just. As Lincoln

LONGSTREET AT GETTYSBURG

Longstreet's behavior at Gettysburg has been the subject of significant historical debate. Many historians criticize the general for his slowness and lack of enthusiasm for Lee's plans. Accusing him of sulking during the battle and when ordering Pickett to attack (as depicted below), some even blame Longstreet for the Confederacy's defeat. In this letter, written several years afterward, brigade commander General James Kemper defends his corps commander's behavior prior to the charge:

During the firing of the artillery (which yet reminds me of Milton's description of the war of artillery between the contending hosts of Heaven) I made my men lie flat on the ground, a precaution which poorly protected them from the enemy's hail of shot pelted them and plowed through them, and sometimes the fragments of a dozen mangled men were thrown in and about the trench left by a single missile. While this was going on, Longstreet rode slowly and alone immediately in front of our entire line . . . As he neared me, I walked up to him, intending to remind him of his peril which he seemed really unconscious, and said "General, this is a terrible place." Said he, "What! Is your command suffering?" "Yes," I answered. "A man is cut to pieces here every second while we are talking; sometimes a dozen men are killed at one shot." "Is it possible," said he with a distressed air, "can't you find any safer position for your men?" "No we are exactly behind the line of this crest—the very safest place around here." "I am greatly distressed at this—greatly distressed at this; but let us hold our ground a while longer; we are hurting the enemy badly, and we'll charge him presently;" . . .

Grand old Longstreet! The rabble, the volatile, may hoot at and hound you for political errors which I deplore; but I will never cease to love, honor and admire you as one of the loftiest types of the truest heroism![63]

▲

PICKETT AND LONGSTREET

George E. Pickett's division was one of several involved in the charge on July 3, though it is his name that gets attached to the action. Longstreet, his corps commander, did not believe the attack would work but ordered Pickett and his men forward nonetheless.

viewed it, Meade had lost a golden opportunity to crush Lee's army, which had become the embodiment of the Confederate cause; only when it was destroyed would the Confederacy give up the fight. The president's confidence in Meade was never fully restored. Yet Lincoln doubtless realized that if he sent the letter, Meade would likely resign, and that he had no one with whom to replace Meade. So he never sent it.

Lincoln was not the only one who was upset with the commanding general. The Union troops felt good about the way their senior officers had fought the battle itself. As one Union soldier noted, they "are now practicing war not theorizing it." But after Meade failed to go over to the attack and then delayed his pursuit, Federal soldiers saw a great opportunity slipping through their hands. "Meade was no longer equal to the situation," a New Yorker grumbled.[64] As evidence about the poor condition of Lee's army mounted, soldiers became hostile. "The Prisoners that come in this morning say that we might have took their whole army just as well as not," another soldier complained to his parents. "[I]t is just as I expected Mead was very fraid of A little rain and laid over 24 hours to[o] long and they sliped away from him evry Solgier is growling about it because we might just as well had him as not and now they will march us like light[n]ing to catch him but Shit let it go."[65] When Lee's army escaped south of the Potomac River, a staff officer complained, "Our army is an anomaly—it is an army of Lions commanded by jackasses."[66]

On the Confederate side, Lee submitted his resignation on August 8, asserting that his removal was the appropriate response for military failure. He also confessed that

▲
ARMISTEAD

Lewis Armistead's brigade was the only Confederate unit to break through the defense on Cemetery Ridge, an area now memorialized as "The High Water Mark of the Rebellion." Armistead was mortally wounded during the assault, and the Confederate breach did not last long.

his health impaired his ability to command. Davis replied that finding an adequate replacement was "an impossibility," and rejected the offer.[67]

While Lee's army was badly damaged at Gettysburg, it soon recovered reasonably well. A month later, Lee sent Longstreet with two divisions to Georgia to reinforce Braxton Bragg's Army of Tennessee, where Confederate fortunes had been crumbling. They proved critical in the Rebel victory at Chickamauga but failed to crush Union reinforcements under Burnside at Knoxville. Meanwhile, Lee and Meade battled once more in October at Bristoe Station, Virginia. Confederate general A. P. Hill mismanaged his troops and lost 1,300 men, much to Lee's fury. Six weeks later Meade attempted another offensive, and Lee blocked his path at Mine Run. When the Federals probed and discovered strong defensive positions, Meade canceled the attack. It would be the last major offensive in the East until the spring of 1864—a Union presidential election year.[68]

HOME FRONTS

The battlefield and the home front were inextricably linked. By mid-1863, mounting casualties and hardship began to create significant divisions within Union and Confederate societies. The Confederacy, with its already limited resources and as the target of invasion and occupation, suffered much worse. As more and more Confederate territory fell into Union hands, valuable agricultural areas were lost, and Rebel soldiers suddenly had loved ones under enemy control. President Davis's strategy of protecting territory and citizens while discouraging Federals from prosecuting the war required his army to strike powerful blows as close to the border as possible. As strategy, it made sense, but it incurred heavy combat losses that further undermined morale.

For example, North Carolina, a state that seceded with considerable reluctance, sent the second most troops to the Army of Northern Virginia. At Chancellorsville, 30 percent of all North Carolinians fighting became casualties (3,801 of 13,460)—by far the greatest total and percentage in the army. The seven highest totals of killed and wounded fell to North Carolina regiments. After two huge North Carolina brigades joined the army, nearly half of all the North Carolinians at Gettysburg became casualties (6,582 of 14,182). The four highest regimental totals and six of the seven highest were in North Carolina regiments. In fact, North Carolina lost 1,782 more men than the state with the next highest total—and that difference alone exceeded the losses of eight Confederate states at Gettysburg. Then, at Bristoe Station, nearly all

◄ **DEAD AT GETTYSBURG**

Both commanders prepared their armies to resist an assault on the Fourth of July, but neither was capable of attacking. The next day, Lee withdrew his army back toward Virginia. Meade pursued, but when he caught up with Lee's army, he felt that his own force was not strong enough to attack.

the casualties were North Carolinians (another 10 percent of those in the army). Thus, over a five-and-a-half-month period, some 70 percent of all North Carolinians in the most successful and visible institution in the Confederacy, the Army of Northern Virginia, became casualties. The impact of these losses was devastating to that state's home front. Draft dodging became rampant, locals sheltered army deserters, Unionism or disillusionment increased, and folks at home encouraged desertion. Bands of draft dodgers, deserters, and Unionists violently resisted efforts by authorities to enforce the laws.[69]

Moreover, the Union policy of emancipation encouraged slaves to run away to Federal armies. As slaves learned through their grapevine that this was a war for their freedom, they took whatever steps they could to aid the Union cause: flee to Federal lines, aid northern armies, assist escaped Union prisoners of war, disrupt work, and upset white women and the elderly on the Rebel home front while so many adult white males served in the army.[70]

Wartime policies and hardships afflicted the poor the most and accentuated class divisions. The Confederate Congress had to extend the draft ages from seventeen to forty-five, with men from forty-five to fifty serving in the militia Home Guard. By 1864, substitution had ended, but exemptions shielded large slaveholders, state and local officials, doctors, clergymen, and selected other skilled occupations, creating animosity and social and political strife.[71]

The loss of manpower and the slow breakdown of slavery resulted in a decline in food production and supply, especially in cities, as prices soared. Wealthy Confederates had a financial cushion; poor people had no such luxury. Efforts to impress foodstuffs for

◀ **LINCOLN AT GETTYSBURG**

The only confirmed photograph of Lincoln at Gettysburg. He is just left of the center of the photograph, hatless and looking downward, seated between the row of soldiers facing one way and the line of dignitaries facing the other. The large man in the tall hat on his left-hand side (to the right in the picture) is his friend and bodyguard, Ward Hill Lamon.

GETTYSBURG ADDRESS

Lincoln had been invited to give "a few appropriate remarks" at the dedication of the Soldiers' National Cemetery in Gettysburg on November 19, 1863, an opportunity he used to lay out his understanding of the war's meaning and purpose. Following the address, renowned speaker Edward Everett, whose oration preceded Lincoln, told the president, "I should be glad if I could flatter myself that I came as near to the central idea of the occasion, in two hours, as you did in two minutes." There are several copies of the address; printed below is the Bliss copy,[72] drafted afterward, and the only copy Lincoln signed.

Four score and seven years ago our fathers brought forth on this continent, a new nation, conceived in liberty, and dedicated to the proposition that all men are created equal.

Now we are engaged in a great civil war, testing whether that nation, or any nation so conceived and so dedicated, can long endure. We are met on a great battle field of that war. We have come to dedicate a portion of that field, as a final resting place for those who here gave their lives that that nation might live. It is altogether fitting and proper that we should do this.

But, in a larger sense, we can not dedicate—we can not consecrate—we can not hallow—this ground. The brave men, living and dead, who struggled here, have consecrated it, far above our poor power to add or detract. The world will little note nor long remember what we say here, but it can never forget what they did here. It is for us the living, rather, to be dedicated here to the unfinished work which they who fought here have thus far so nobly advanced. It is rather for us to be here dedicated to the great task remaining before us—that from these honored dead we take increased devotion to that cause for which they gave the last full measure of devotion—that we here highly resolve that these dead shall not have died in vain—that this nation, under God, shall have a new birth of freedom—and that government of the people, by the people, for the people, shall not perish from the earth.

the army only exacerbated the problem. In Richmond in April 1863, women stormed commercial establishments to take food and other essential items. Military forces came out, and Davis confronted the crowd, casting his pocket money among them. A few weeks earlier in Salisbury, North Carolina, a similar riot had erupted. With so many men in the army, local food production had declined, and the creation of a prisoner of war camp there increased demand and therefore prices. Women armed with hatchets and other weapons broke into shops and demanded "donations" of food and salt.[73]

On the Union home front, opposition to the war increased during 1862 and 1863. Many, particularly Democrats, objected to fighting a war to free slaves; others felt that Lincoln's war policies trampled civil liberties; and as defeats and losses increased, others lost hope of Union victory. Opponents of the war, known as Copperheads, led by an Ohio congressman named Clement L. Vallandigham, objected to the administration's abrogation of civil liberties and the changes that Union policy wrought in race relations. They split the Democratic Party into War and Peace Democrats, and Vallandigham was ultimately banished to the Confederacy for his antiwar speeches. He then ran for governor of Ohio in 1863, but lost.[74]

Along with emancipation and black enlistment, the most divisive element of wartime policy was conscription. Volunteering slowed dramatically as casualties mounted. To expand the ranks, the Union adopted a combination of bounties and, by 1863, conscription. The draft operated on the local level, with communities receiving a manpower quota. When enlistments failed to meet that quota, the community held a draft. Federal, state, and local bounties induced many to enlist, and draftees could

hire substitutes or pay a commutation fee. Bounties became so large that a volunteer received enough to purchase a farm. While only 5.5 percent of all Union soldiers were drafted, opposition to wartime policies and especially the draft erupted in riots.

In New York City in mid-July 1863, a riot over the draft turned into a race riot, with white workers killing an estimated one hundred African Americans, whom they blamed for job competition and for the war. In the coal mines of Pennsylvania, ethnic Irish and Germans also violently resisted the draft. The racist cast to draft resistance is particularly ironic given that recruitment of African American soldiers offset state draft quotas and eased the burden on poor and working-class whites.[75]

The Union economy adjusted to the diversion of manpower into the army in part by shifting to greater use of technology. Women and machinery substituted for farm laborers and maintained a high output of foodstuffs. Factories, too, relied on machinery for greater manufacture. With its much greater margin for error, the Union financed the war better (using means including an income tax and bond sales), maintained high employment, and kept inflation at a manageable level.[76]

CONCLUSION

While the Union secured its flanks on the international scene, keeping foreign nations from intervening on behalf of the Confederacy, the Federals failed to generate significant success on eastern battlefields until Gettysburg. They suffered a disastrous defeat at Fredericksburg, and Hooker's promising spring offensive resulted in yet another defeat at Chancellorsville. Even the bloody repulse of Lee's attacks

THE DIS-UNITED STATES OF THE SOUTHERN CONFEDERACY
Having been formed using the rhetoric of states' rights, the Confederate government struggled to forge a coherent national wartime policy. States were most interested in protecting their own borders and interests, which made the creation of a uniform strategy difficult.

DAVIS'S APPEAL
Though considered a strong choice for leadership at the outbreak of war, Jefferson Davis struggled to lead the Confederacy. Davis's call to arms is met sarcastically with a similar request from veterans of Gettysburg, Vicksburg, and Port Hudson.

▲
COPPERHEADS

Peace Democrats, or Copperheads, believed that the South would not return to a nation run by the radical Lincoln and his Republican Party. Rumors of sabotage and sedition circulated throughout the North, and Union officials targeted numerous groups and individuals in highly publicized treason trials.

▲
DRAFT RIOTS

The draft rioters in New York targeted pro-war newspapers, homes of the wealthy, and the city's African American population. Lincoln sent several regiments to the city to put down the riot and maintain order so that the draft could go on.

at Gettysburg, undoubtedly a Union victory, offered no assurance that the Army of the Potomac could conduct effective offensive operations, which were essential to crushing Lee's army and the rebellion. The Union's only consolation—aside from extensive progress in the West (which will be described in the next chapter)—was that although its army had suffered very heavy casualties, it had inflicted irreplaceable losses, including the death of Stonewall Jackson, on the Confederates.

Lee's army continued to fulfill Davis's strategy of punishing the invaders, but the losses it sustained placed a huge strain on the Confederacy. With a much smaller manpower pool and fewer resources, the Rebel margin for error was shrinking rapidly, with significant consequences. Yet 1864 was a Union presidential election year: a chance for northerners to hold a referendum on the war. Stout resistance might compel the Union to concede Confederate independence, but military defeat for the Confederacy would reinforce pro-war elements in the Union and most likely doom the rebellion.

During a period of nineteen months almost exactly in the middle of America's forty-nine-month Civil War, Union and Confederate forces waged a seesaw struggle in the nation's midsection, the region between the Appalachian Mountains on the east and the Mississippi River on the west. Before the start of this crucial period, the Union had made impressive advances in the region, but after the May 1862 Union capture of Corinth, Mississippi, the Federal offensive in the western theater stalled. A year and a half later, however, the Union had seized control of the Mississippi, made extensive territorial gains, won the climactic battle of Chattanooga, and was poised for a war-winning drive into Georgia. Ulysses Grant, more than any other individual, deserves the credit for these victories, which entitle him to recognition as the greatest of the nation's nineteenth-century generals.

The reasons why the Civil War was decided in this western theater are frequently overlooked. The region west of the Mississippi, known during the war as the Trans-Mississippi, was too sparsely populated to be either side's center of gravity. On the other hand, the region east of the Appalachians was quite densely populated by the standards of the time, containing all of the nation's oldest and largest settlements, the bulk of its industry and wealth, and its most-read newspapers, as well as the rival capitals. Operations in the eastern theater therefore attracted (and still attract) attention out of proportion to their military significance and produced disproportionate effects on public opinion, foreign and domestic.

In addition, decisive military results were elusive in the East. Because of the proximity of population centers and the rival capitals, each side fielded its largest army in that theater, but maneuvering room for these armies was limited, and the need to protect Washington and other cities hamstrung Union operations there. Moreover, the eastern theater's geography favored the defender. From Fredericksburg, at the practical eastern limit of operations, to the foot of the Allegheny Mountains on the theater's western edge, was little more than sixty miles. Within that area of operations, most of the rivers ran from west to east, forming obstacles in the path of advancing armies, and none of the streams was navigable for gunboats or supply vessels, except on the theater's eastern coastal rim, along the Chesapeake Bay and the Atlantic. The Confederates could quickly move laterally to meet Federal offensives, as they had at Fredericksburg and Chancellorsville, while threatening the North with invasion through the Shenandoah Valley, as they had in the Antietam and Gettysburg campaigns, and would do again in the early summer of 1864.

The western theater, by contrast, stretched more than three hundred miles, offering ample room for offensive maneuver. Union armies advanced down two distinct axes: near and along the Mississippi, and from Nashville southeast toward Atlanta. Several of the rivers were navigable and, instead of being obstacles, provided avenues of advance from north to south for Union armies, allowing for joint operations with naval gunboats as well as providing almost unbreakable supply lines via the civilian steamboats the army leased. The most important of these rivers were the Mississippi, Tennessee, and Cumberland. At the same time, the western theater contained important

4

GRANT'S WAR
IN THE WEST

STEVEN E.
WOODWORTH

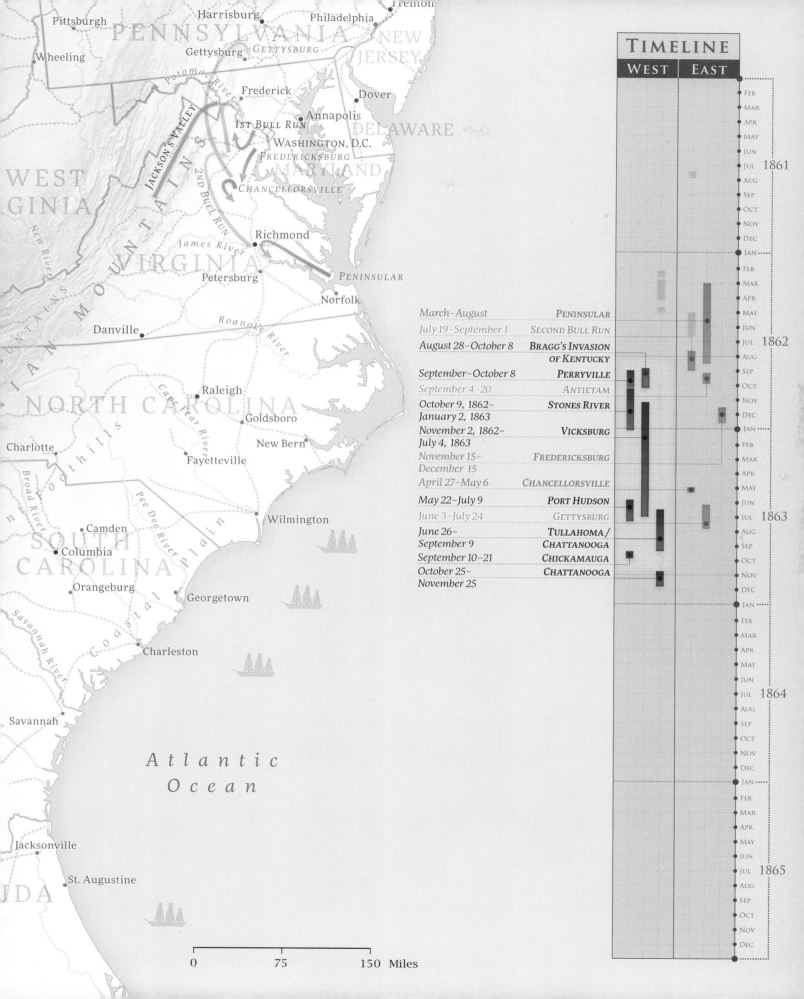

TIMELINE

WEST	EAST

March–August	PENINSULAR
July 19–September 1	SECOND BULL RUN
August 28–October 8	BRAGG'S INVASION OF KENTUCKY
September–October 8	PERRYVILLE
September 4–20	ANTIETAM
October 9, 1862–January 2, 1863	STONES RIVER
November 2, 1862–July 4, 1863	VICKSBURG
November 15–December 15	FREDERICKSBURG
April 27–May 6	CHANCELLORSVILLE
May 22–July 9	PORT HUDSON
June 3–July 24	GETTYSBURG
June 26–September 9	TULLAHOMA / CHATTANOOGA
September 10–21	CHICKAMAUGA
October 25–November 25	CHATTANOOGA

1861
1862
1863
1864
1865

FEB MAR APR MAY JUN JUL AUG SEP OCT NOV DEC JAN
FEB MAR APR MAY JUN JUL AUG SEP OCT NOV DEC JAN
FEB MAR APR MAY JUN JUL AUG SEP OCT NOV DEC JAN
FEB MAR APR MAY JUN JUL AUG SEP OCT NOV DEC JAN
FEB MAR APR MAY JUN JUL AUG SEP OCT NOV DEC

assets, the loss of which would prove fatal to the Confederacy. New Orleans was the South's largest city and its financial capital. Nashville began the war as its second most important industrial city (after Richmond); the surrounding Nashville Basin was a vital food-producing area; and Atlanta became a major industrial center during the war. The Mississippi River was the continent's most important trade and transport corridor, and in Union hands it would sever the beef- and leather-producing hinterland of the Trans-Mississippi. Northern Alabama provided the Confederacy with increasingly important military-industrial assets. Perhaps most important, the western theater of the war included most of the Deep South cotton states, whose zeal to protect the rights of slaveholders had led to the creation of the Confederacy. There was little chance that the slaveholders' republic would long survive the loss of its spiritual and ideological heartland.

RIVERBOATS

The many navigable rivers in the western theater made joint land-naval operations an important part of Union campaigning in that region. Control of the rivers was vital to conquering the region, and gunboats played a critical role in capturing important river sites.

THE CAPTURE OF CORINTH AND THE CONFEDERACY'S LATE-SUMMER OFFENSIVES, MAY TO OCTOBER 1862

THE FIRST CORINTH CAMPAIGN

In February 1862, Grant's victories at Forts Henry and Donelson had shifted the war's momentum decisively in favor of the North. Cautious western theater commander

Henry J. Halleck had then demanded a pause in Union operations, supposedly to gather strength for the next offensive. But this had given Confederate theater commander Albert Sidney Johnston time to concentrate his forces and launch a counterattack against Grant's Army of the Tennessee at Shiloh in early April. Johnston was mortally wounded, Don Carlos Buell's Army of the Ohio reinforced Grant, and the Rebels were driven back, with tremendous casualties on both sides. Thereafter, Union forces continued to hold all they had gained in the preceding months' advances, but they had lost their earlier offensive momentum.

A few days after the Battle of Shiloh, Halleck arrived at Pittsburg Landing and assumed active field command of the Army of the Tennessee, the Army of the Ohio, and John Pope's Army of the Mississippi. Halleck incorporated all three armies into a force of 120,000 men, which he reorganized, without reference to the previous field armies, into a left, right, center, and reserve. A military theoretician without combat experience, Halleck disliked Grant's aggressive style of warfare and had been envious of his more successful subordinate since Forts Henry and Donelson fell. The vocal public criticism of Grant triggered by the shocking casualties at Shiloh gave Halleck an opportunity to sideline him. Halleck assigned Grant the meaningless position of second in command without specific duties, which, as Grant observed, was not much different from being under arrest.[1] Deeply dispirited, Grant contemplated resigning, but his friend William T. Sherman, a division commander in the Army of the Tennessee, encouraged him to hang on, and Grant persevered.[2]

Ulysses S. Grant blossomed in war but was a wallflower in peace. He was as unmilitary in appearance and attitude as a general could get. Though Grant did not command large units in the Mexican-American War, he learned much from it, as Lincoln did. He admired General Zachary Taylor's indifference to appearance and military finery, and that Taylor did not bombard his superiors with messages and correspondence. Though disgusted by the Polk administration's obvious desire to get the (victorious) Whig generals out of the way for Democratic generals, and though Grant considered the Mexican war "unholy" (as was the southern rebellion later) and "a conspiracy to acquire territory out of which slave states might be formed," he did his duty. When it was over, as he recalled later, "I had been in all the engagements in Mexico that it was possible for one person to be in," and had received two brevet promotions for gallantry.

Unable to support his family on a peacetime officer's salary, Grant resigned from the service in 1854. He did not fare well in farming or business, partly because of long stretches of poor health. A patriot and a man who felt his obligation for his West Point education, Grant volunteered at the beginning of the war and became a colonel of an Illinois infantry regiment. His superior in the Department of the Missouri in 1862, General Henry W. Halleck, did not recognize Grant's abilities or his ambition, and Grant had to press hard and line up support from the navy's flag officer, Andrew Foote, to convince Halleck that he could capture Fort Henry, on the Tennessee River. After he captured Fort Henry and then Fort Donelson, it proved difficult to ignore Grant's abilities; he went on to command Union armies at Shiloh, and then in the 1863 Vicksburg and Chattanooga campaigns. In 1864–65, as Lincoln's general in chief of the Union armies, he directed the overall military strategy that won the war and also supervised Meade's Army of the Potomac as it defeated Lee's Army of Northern Virginia.

ULYSSES S. GRANT
APRIL 27, 1822–JULY 23, 1885

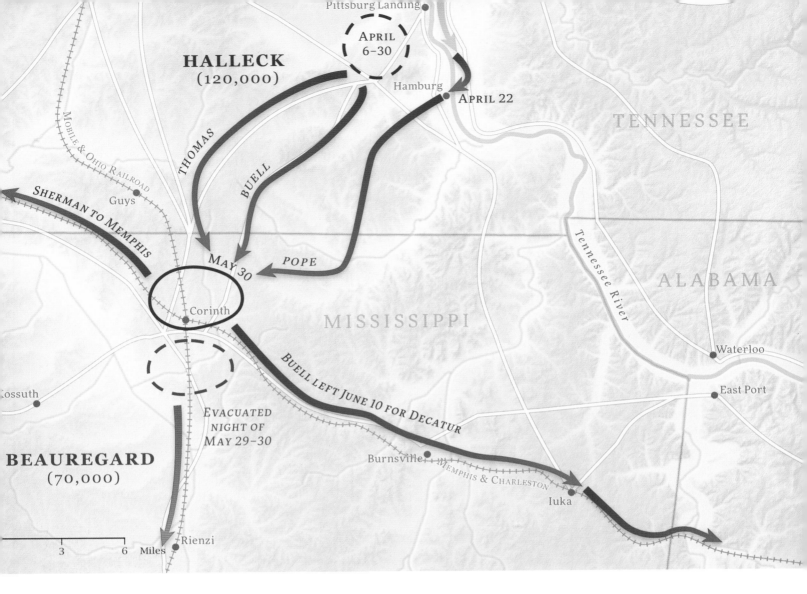

CORINTH

Halleck's three-pronged advance toward Corinth succeeded in capturing the key rail junction, but Beauregard was able to withdraw his force largely intact.

Meanwhile, Halleck moved his enormous force cautiously toward the strategically important rail-junction town of Corinth, Mississippi, at the intersection of the north-south Mobile & Ohio Railroad and the Confederacy's most important east-west railroad, the Memphis & Charleston. Control of Corinth would yield important advantages for movement and supply within northern Mississippi and West Tennessee. Halleck's army began moving from its camps around Pittsburg Landing on April 29 (twenty-three days after Shiloh) and for the next thirty days advanced essentially unopposed, at an average speed of about a thousand yards per day. After each day's advance, Halleck had his troops entrench, and the next morning, he had them in the trenches before dawn to guard against the possibility of another surprise attack. Halleck's opponent, General P. G. T. Beauregard, contemplated no such thing. Badly outnumbered, he made a stealthy evacuation of Corinth on the night of May 29–30, withdrawing his army to Tupelo, Mississippi, fifty miles south. The next morning, Union troops found Corinth devoid of Confederate soldiers and took possession without firing a shot.[3]

Both sides were dissatisfied with the outcome of the first Corinth campaign. On the Confederate side, the discontent came from the highest level. President Davis, who had transferred Beauregard to the West after the Louisianan had demonstrated himself prone to play politics in Virginia, was disgusted that Beauregard had given up Corinth without a fight. Davis wrote privately that Beauregard lacked the nerve to handle great responsibility, and the Confederacy would have to make a desperate effort to regain what had been lost on Beauregard's watch. Davis may have had a point about Beauregard's nerve, though the challenge facing the Louisiana general had been extreme.[4] The Confederate president was also correct that the Rebel loss of territory and resources in the past four months had been catastrophic, though it had come as much on the watch of his old friend Johnston as on that of the prickly and vainglorious Beauregard. Davis did not see matters in that light, however, believing that Johnston would have regained all the Confederate losses had he not fallen at Shiloh. Beauregard, Davis was convinced, had thrown away the fruits of a victory already won. Several weeks after the withdrawal from Corinth, when Beauregard granted himself sick leave to recover from a chronic, probably stress-induced illness at a popular resort in Bladon Springs, Alabama, Davis relieved him and turned the Confederate army in Mississippi over to Gen. Braxton Bragg.[5]

On the Union side, Lincoln wanted a general to coordinate strategy and operations across the continent, or at least to serve as a senior military adviser with a broader vision than those of the army commanders. His seniority and reputation as a military intellectual capped by the capture of Corinth, Halleck was promoted to commanding general of all the Union armies, with his headquarters in Washington, D.C. The wider public, however, as well as many of the soldiers, were disgusted that the campaign had netted the Union only a disease-ridden town beside a railroad junction, allowing Beauregard's army to escape intact.[6]

THE KENTUCKY CAMPAIGN

Halleck's move to Washington did not bring the benefits Lincoln had anticipated. "Old Brains," as Halleck was by then nicknamed, proved as hesitant, indecisive, and lacking in aggressiveness at the national capital as he had in the Mississippi Valley, and Lincoln soon came to characterize him as "little more than a first-rate clerk."[7] Even the most promising consequence of the move—Grant's having replaced Halleck in the Mississippi Valley—did not immediately produce good results. Halleck had left the force under Grant's command scattered in small garrisons holding down West Tennessee and northern Mississippi, and, from Washington, Old Brains kept Grant saddled with orders to occupy territory. Thus deployed, Grant's force was in no position to seize the initiative.

Virtually the only aggressive movement that Halleck had set in motion before leaving for Washington—or since arriving there—was to send Buell's Army of the Ohio eastward along the route of the Memphis & Charleston Railroad through northern Alabama toward Chattanooga. Another rail-junction town, Chattanooga lay astride the

EDMUND KIRBY SMITH
After summoning Bragg's army to his assistance in East Tennessee, instead of combining with it (and placing himself under Bragg's command), Kirby Smith launched an independent invasion of Kentucky, forcing Bragg to follow his lead.

KENTUCKY CONFEDERATES

Kentucky was neutral when the war began, starkly divided over the secession question. Although the state had tipped to the Union when its neutrality was violated by Confederate general Leonidas K. Polk in 1861, the next year Kirby Smith still believed pro-secession Kentuckians would flock to his banners. But the reinforcements he hoped for did not materialize: those most sympathetic to the Confederacy (such as the 3rd Kentucky Infantry, pictured here) had already joined.

direct rail route between Virginia and the Confederate heartland and occupied a gap in the mountains that made it the gateway both to the interior of Georgia and, from the south, to East Tennessee. The latter region contained a large number of loyal Unionists whose brutal suppression by Confederate authorities had filled Lincoln with frustration. The president hoped to begin the South's political reconstruction by forming new state governments, and the Unionists made Tennessee a prime target for this political strategy. Lincoln had been pressing his generals for months to reach East Tennessee, and Buell's movement was at least a start in that direction—and a direct threat to Maj. Gen. Edmund Kirby Smith's scant Confederate East Tennessee command. Buell's force outnumbered Kirby Smith's by a wide margin, but the Union general advanced very slowly. In part that was because Buell, a general after Halleck's own heart, simply operated that way, and in part it was because Halleck had directed Buell to repair and maintain the Memphis & Charleston as his army advanced. Confederate guerrillas could break the railroad faster than Buell's men could fix it, while striking at far more places than the Federals could hope to defend. The task would have hamstrung the advance of a far speedier general than Buell.

Further threatened by the advance of a Union division from the north via the Cumberland Gap, the badly outnumbered Kirby Smith pleaded with Bragg for help, offering to place himself under Bragg's command if that general would bring his army to East Tennessee.[8] Seeing little prospect of effective action against Grant's defenses in

Born in Warrenton, North Carolina, Bragg graduated fifth out of the fifty-man West Point class of 1837 and was assigned to the 3rd Artillery. In the Mexican-American War, he won particular distinction at the battle of Buena Vista. Entering Confederate service, Bragg commanded at Pensacola, Florida, before transferring with his command to join Albert Sidney Johnston's army at Corinth in the spring of 1862. He won praise for his role as a corps commander at Shiloh, and after Beauregard left the army for health reasons, Jefferson Davis gave Bragg the command.

In a bold and innovative use of rail transport, Bragg moved his army to Chattanooga and then marched into Kentucky, turning Don Carlos Buell and forcing his retreat. Unsupported by fellow Confederate commander Edmund Kirby Smith and meeting no general pro-Confederate rising of the Kentucky population, Bragg retreated into Tennessee. After initial success at the Battle of Stones River, he had to retreat to Tullahoma.

Undercut by jealous subordinates, Bragg was unable to stop William S. Rosecrans's midsummer campaign and retreated to Chattanooga. When Rosecrans advanced again in August, Bragg retreated but, receiving reinforcements, turned against Rosecrans's widely separated columns. Disobedience by subordinate generals prevented him defeating Rosecrans in detail, but he drove much of the united Army of the Cumberland from the battlefield of Chickamauga and besieged Rosecrans in Chattanooga. After Grant took command there, Bragg suffered defeat. Davis relieved him of command and assigned him to duty as the president's military adviser in Richmond. In January he briefly and unsuccessfully commanded Confederate troops in North Carolina.

BRAXTON BRAGG
MARCH 22, 1817–SEPTEMBER 27, 1876

northern Mississippi, Bragg agreed to move into East Tennessee. Buell's slow progress toward Chattanooga, like his slow progress toward Pittsburg Landing the preceding spring, gave the Confederates the opportunity to seize the initiative. Sending his supply wagons and artillery across northern Alabama, Bragg shipped his infantry by rail via Mobile, Alabama, to arrive in Chattanooga well ahead of Buell. It was by far the longest use of rail mobility up to that point in military history. Once his artillery arrived, Bragg planned to turn Buell by advancing into Middle Tennessee, threatening the Army of the Ohio's supply line and forcing it to fight at a disadvantage. Then Bragg's and Kirby Smith's combined forces would defeat Buell, opening the way for the Confederacy to reconquer much of the vast swath of territory it had lost as a result of the defeats at Forts Henry and Donelson.[9]

That coordination never came about. Instead of cooperating with Bragg as he had promised, Kirby Smith took his entire force—along with the lead division of Bragg's army (sent ahead to ease his supposedly desperate situation)—and headed straight for the Kentucky bluegrass on August 14. Kirby Smith acted entirely on his own: the Confederate western fall offensive of 1862 was largely the product of his personal lust for fame.[10]

Nevertheless, under Confederate as well as Union military regulations, if two officers were assigned to separate commands, the senior officer could not give orders to the junior unless the two forces physically joined and combined into a single force. Though he urged Kirby Smith not to undertake such a sweeping turning maneuver until they had dealt with Buell, Bragg had no choice but to follow his fellow Confederate, keeping his army between Buell and Kirby Smith's smaller force.[11]

The deep Confederate turning maneuver forced Buell to give up his advance on

KENTUCKY CAMPAIGN ▶
Kirby Smith left Knoxville in August 1862, moving north into Kentucky. Bragg followed in September from Chattanooga, acting as a screen to protect Kirby Smith's smaller force. Bragg finally engaged Buell's Army of the Ohio at Perryville in October.

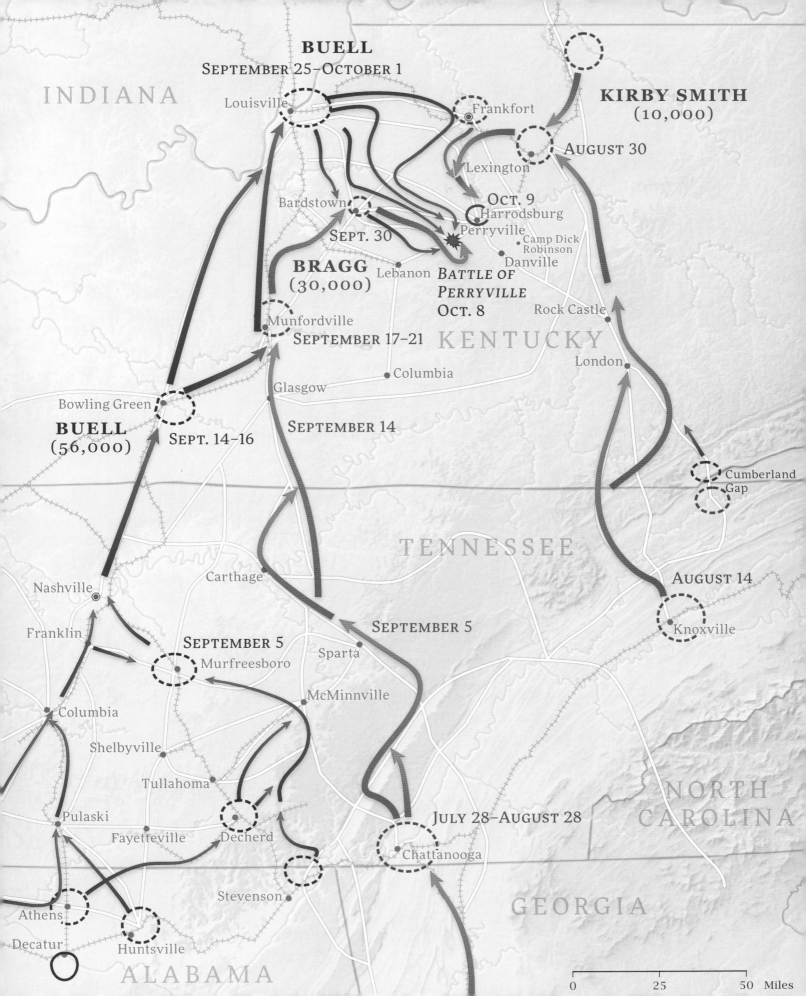

BUELL
SEPTEMBER 25–OCTOBER 1

INDIANA

Louisville

KIRBY SMITH
(10,000)

Frankfort

AUGUST 30

Lexington

OCT. 9

Bardstown

Harrodsburg

SEPT. 30

Perryville

Camp Dick
Robinson

BRAGG
(30,000)

Danville

Lebanon

*BATTLE OF
PERRYVILLE*
OCT. 8

Rock Castle

Munfordville

SEPTEMBER 17–21

KENTUCKY

Columbia

London

Glasgow

SEPTEMBER 14

BUELL
(56,000)

Bowling Green

SEPT. 14–16

Cumberland
Gap

TENNESSEE

Carthage

AUGUST 14

Nashville

SEPTEMBER 5

Franklin

Knoxville

SEPTEMBER 5

Sparta

Murfreesboro

Columbia

McMinnville

Shelbyville

Tullahoma

NORTH
CAROLINA

Pulaski

JULY 28–AUGUST 28

Fayetteville

Decherd

Chattanooga

Stevenson

GEORGIA

Athens

Decatur

Huntsville

ALABAMA

0   25   50 Miles

WILLIAM STARKE ROSECRANS

SEPTEMBER 6, 1819–MARCH 11, 1898

Born in rural Delaware County, Ohio, Rosecrans graduated fifth in the fifty-six-man West Point class of 1842. He served in the Corps of Engineers and as an instructor at West Point until his resignation in 1854. In 1861 Rosecrans became a brigadier general in the U.S. Regular Army and served successfully in the Department of Western Virginia. Transferred to Mississippi, Rosecrans in September 1862 failed to block the retreat of Confederate forces at Iuka, as Grant had ordered. Three weeks later, Rosecrans's troops defended Corinth against Confederate attack. After the battle, Rosecrans failed to pursue as Grant had ordered. Though Grant was displeased, Lincoln promoted the victor of Corinth to command the Army of the Cumberland at Nashville.

In December Rosecrans advanced against Braxton Bragg, who attacked him at Stones River, where Rosecrans held on until Bragg retreated. Thereafter, he angered Lincoln by remaining idle for six months. When he finally advanced, he maneuvered Bragg nearly out of Tennessee in the relatively bloodless Tullahoma campaign. Resuming his advance in mid-August, he crossed the Tennessee River and took Chattanooga before suffering defeat by a heavily reinforced Bragg at Chickamauga. Drawing his forces back into Chattanooga, Rosecrans allowed Bragg to besiege him until Grant relieved him of his command. Rosecrans served out the rest of the war in an insignificant command in Missouri. He resigned in 1867.

Chattanooga and move north, and within a few weeks, the armies had shifted more than 150 miles into central Kentucky. Kirby Smith was serenely occupying the abundant Bluegrass region around Lexington, a hundred miles to the northwest, but sent Bragg neither troops nor supplies. Without reinforcement from Kirby Smith or the mass of Kentucky recruits he had hoped to gain, Bragg lacked enough troops to assault the Army of the Ohio, had insufficient supplies to continue waiting in its path, and had to retreat.[12]

As he began his withdrawal, his army of 18,000 clashed indecisively with that of a much reinforced Buell—55,000 strong—near Perryville on October 8. Mistakenly believing that he faced only part of Buell's army, Bragg launched a series of attacks against the flanks of a single Federal corps. These initially did well because Buell, at his headquarters in his army's rear, remained unaware that an action was in progress, while his subordinates failed to inform him or move to the aid of the lone corps—only 13,000 strong—that the Rebels were assailing. Gradually, the Union army stiffened and held, and Bragg, learning that he faced a much larger army, broke off the action after incurring 3,400 casualties.[13] Thereafter, the Confederate armies, at last combined, continued their retreat toward East Tennessee via the Cumberland Gap. Buell's caution had been confirmed by 4,200 casualties, and after a brief and languid pursuit, he turned away and marched to Nashville.[14]

THE SECOND CORINTH CAMPAIGN

While the Kentucky campaign was progressing toward its anticlimactic conclusion, action had flared in Mississippi, where Bragg had left two small Confederate armies. Maj. Gen. Sterling Price commanded about 16,000 men in northern Mississippi, while Maj. Gen. Earl Van Dorn had a force of similar size in the west-central part of the state. Van Dorn's job was to hold Vicksburg against Union naval forces that had converged there in midsummer.[15]

After the Federal flotilla withdrew to replenish its supplies, Van Dorn turned his

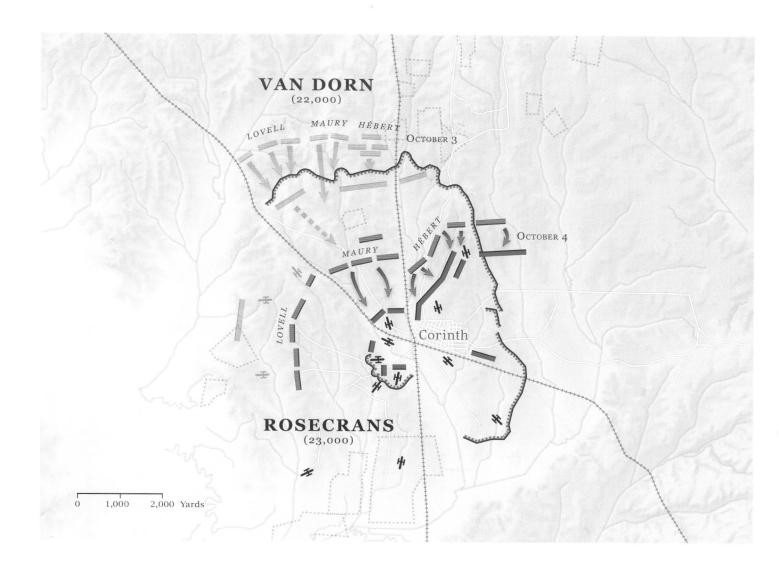

VAN DORN
(22,000)

LOVELL MAURY HÉBERT

OCTOBER 3

OCTOBER 4

MAURY HÉBERT

LOVELL

Corinth

ROSECRANS
(23,000)

0   1,000   2,000 Yards

attention northward, hoping to combine with Price in a campaign that would comple-ment Bragg's foray into Kentucky. Like Kirby Smith with Bragg, Price refused to coop-erate with the higher-ranking Van Dorn, and the two waged a disjointed campaign.[16] On September 19 Price was defeated and narrowly escaped Grant's forces at Iuka, Mississippi.[17] Chastened, he finally combined his force with Van Dorn's for an attack on Corinth.[18]

Fought on October 3–4, the Battle of Corinth proved a bloody repulse for the Con-federates, who lost 4,200 soldiers versus 2,500 Union casualties. Grant had anticipated the attack and reinforced his garrison commander at Corinth, Maj. Gen. William S. Rosecrans. Rosecrans subsequently received much recognition for the victory, though he had performed badly during the battle.[19] Then, despite Grant's repeated orders for a prompt pursuit, Rosecrans delayed until it was too late, when Grant had to stop him from making an ill-advised effort for which the opportunity had passed.[20]

▲
BATTLE OF CORINTH
Confederate forces under Earl Van Dorn attempted to trap the Union garrison at Corinth. Vigorous Confederate assaults pushed Rosecrans's defenders back, but the Union troops ultimately halted and threw back the Rebels with heavy losses. Union control of Corinth was secure from then on.

Corinth

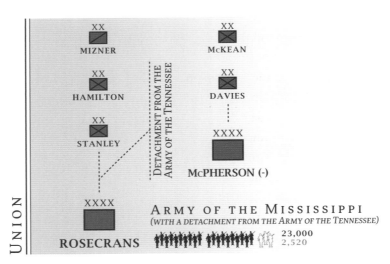

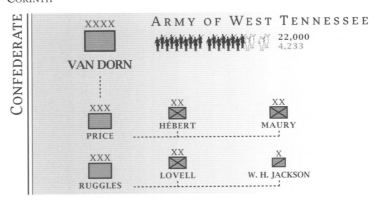

THE STRUGGLE FOR VICKSBURG, JULY 1862–JULY 1863

THE MISSISSIPPI CENTRAL AND CHICKASAW BAYOU CAMPAIGNS

Lincoln was displeased with his generals that fall. From the Atlantic to the Mississippi, Union armies seemed to have made little or no progress during the summer, and the president was, as he put it, tired of trying "to bore with an auger too dull to take hold."[21] The remark referred specifically to Army of the Potomac commander George McClellan, whom Lincoln would send packing in November, but the attitude reflected the president's overall frustration with the progress of the war and, especially, his generals. On October 24 he sacked Buell, who had exhausted Lincoln's patience by allowing Bragg to escape Kentucky. In his place, Lincoln chose Rosecrans, who, when viewed from the distance of Washington, appeared to have been the architect of victory at Corinth.[22]

Lincoln did not remove Grant, who had brought victory at Forts Henry and Donelson as well as at Shiloh and had showed himself more aggressive than any other

Federal general. On the other hand, Union forces in Mississippi, now under Grant's command, had accomplished little since the capture of Corinth the preceding May. This inaction was largely due to the standing orders Halleck had imposed on Grant, but that was not clear in Washington.[23]

Such reflections may have made Lincoln susceptible to the blandishments of an ambitious Illinois politician, now turned general, John A. McClernand, who promised to recruit an army of Democrats—some of whom, McClernand suggested, had previously not felt particularly invested in the war—and lead them down the Mississippi to capture Vicksburg.[24] The town on the bluffs overlooking a hairpin bend of the Mississippi had become the key Confederate link to the Trans-Mississippi, and blocked the commerce of the Union's midwestern states. Lincoln had recognized Vicksburg's strategic importance almost a year before, telling U.S. Navy flag officer David Porter and several other top commanders in November 1861, "See what a lot of land these fellows hold, of which Vicksburg is the key . . . The war can never be brought to a close until that key is in our pocket."[25] Yet Lincoln's commanders had not been winning him the prizes he sought: Richmond, East Tennessee, and Vicksburg. Instead, self-proclaimed professionals such as McClellan and Buell had been doing little while plying Lincoln with complaints and reasons why nothing more could be done. Like many northern politicians, Radical Republicans as well as Democrats, McClernand maintained that

TERRAIN AT VICKSBURG

Though the city itself is not visible, this image shows the high terrain along the Mississippi River (background) that made Vicksburg so difficult to take. As long as the Confederates controlled the city, Union ships could not pass through, and Union commerce could not reach the lucrative ports farther south.

DAVID DIXON PORTER

JUNE 8, 1813–FEBRUARY 13, 1891

David Dixon Porter was a West Pointer's kind of sailor: his career in the Civil War stood as a monument to interservice cooperation. In fact, Ulysses S. Grant, recalling the Vicksburg campaign and Porter's role in it in his memoirs, said, "The most perfect harmony reigned between the two arms of service." Porter's successes were mostly achieved off the oceans, and sometimes while hiding behind trees to shell an enemy.

Yet another veteran of the Mexican-American War, Porter was present for the siege of Veracruz in 1847, the first of many joint military-naval operations with which he would be associated in his successful career. In early 1862 the secretary of the navy, Gideon Welles, chose Porter to command a squadron of mortar schooners that would be towed to their destination to lob their shells into the forts guarding New Orleans. Mortars were heavy siege artillery used in land warfare, and, in the end, the boats with them mounted on their decks would be hidden behind a forest at a bend in the river. The masts of the schooners would be camouflaged with limbs of trees. It was naval warfare hardly in the mode of British admiral Horatio Nelson, the naval hero of the era whose fame resembled Napoleon's in land warfare. But it did contribute to one of the Union's great successes: the capture of New Orleans.

The following year, Porter's energy and courage earned him command of the Mississippi River Squadron that helped Grant capture Vicksburg; later he led the naval contingents participating in the Red River campaign and in the capture of Fort Fisher outside Wilmington, North Carolina. After the war, he reformed the U.S. Naval Academy along the lines of West Point.

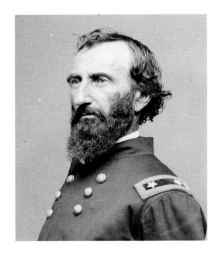

▲

JOHN A. MCCLERNAND

As most Civil War armies were raised as volunteer regiments, political considerations played a significant role in promotions and other appointments. A number of these soldiers, like McClernand, were Democrats, and their presence in the army was important to demonstrate Lincoln's commitment to uniting the nation.

Lincoln's professional officers were ineffective because their West Point educations had disposed them to seek artful solutions (which they labeled "strategy," in a pejorative sense) rather than the hard fighting that commonsense civilians knew would be necessary to win the war. This McClernand promised to rectify.[26]

Without removing Grant from command of the department, Lincoln authorized McClernand to lead an expedition down the Mississippi and told Halleck to draw up orders. Halleck was not a great general, but he had been a pretty good lawyer in California before the war and was a firm believer in military professionalism. He had treated Grant very badly earlier that year, but now he atoned somewhat. Included within the order he drew up were provisions that Grant would still command all the troops operating within the department's boundaries. The expedition would consist of whatever troops Grant did not believe he needed for duty elsewhere, and Grant was still free to make his headquarters anywhere in his department, including with McClernand's column.[27]

Grant had been preparing a campaign of his own against Vicksburg, unaware of the machinations in Washington. By advancing into northern Mississippi along the line of the Mississippi Central Railroad, he hoped to force the new Confederate commander, Lt. Gen. John C. Pemberton, to give battle.[28] Instead, Pemberton, rather than fight superior forces, retreated more than sixty miles into the interior. Concerned at the growing length of his supply line, with Vicksburg still 150 miles to the southwest, Grant paused in December to consider a different approach.[29]

By that time, Grant had begun to get wind of McClernand's planned operation from newspaper reports.[30] He queried Halleck, who reassured him of his continued

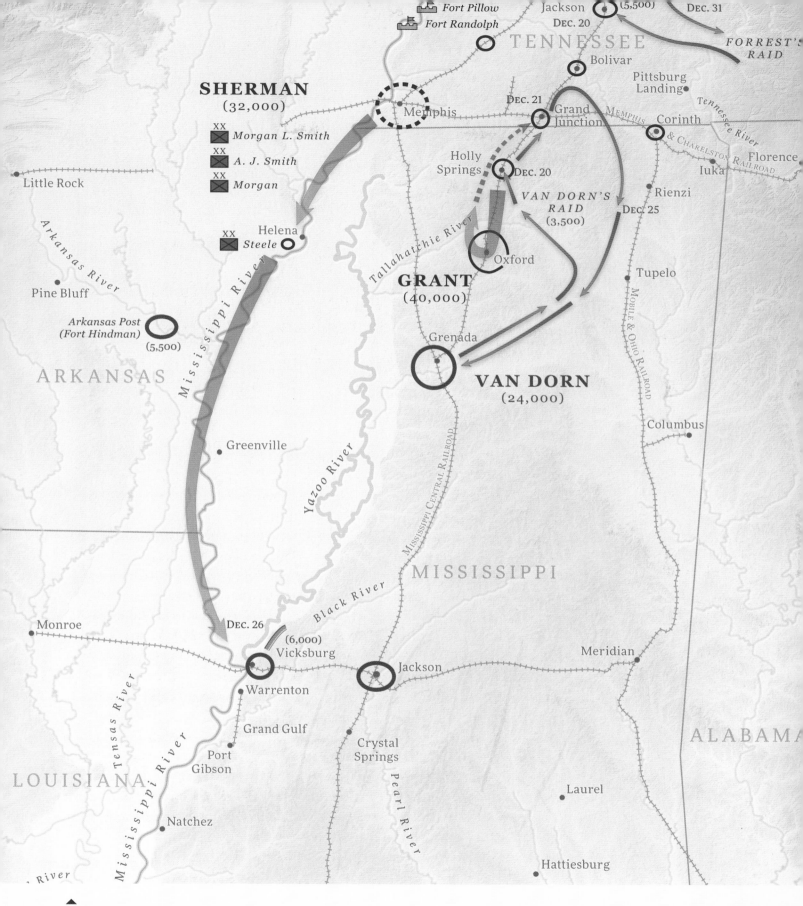

Fort Pillow
Fort Randolph

Jackson (5,500) DEC. 31
DEC. 20

TENNESSEE

Memphis

Bolivar
DEC. 21

Pittsburg
Landing

Grand
Junction

Corinth

FORREST'S
RAID

Tennessee River

MEMPHIS

& CHARLESTON RAILROAD

Florence

Iuka

Rienzi

SHERMAN
(32,000)

XX *Morgan L. Smith*

XX *A. J. Smith*

XX *Morgan*

Little Rock

Arkansas River

Pine Bluff

Helena

XX *Steele*

Holly
Springs
DEC. 20

VAN DORN'S
RAID
(3,500)

DEC. 25

GRANT
(40,000)

Oxford

Mississippi River

Tupelo

Arkansas Post
(Fort Hindman)
(5,500)

ARKANSAS

Grenada

VAN DORN
(24,000)

Columbus

Greenville

Yazoo River

Mississippi Central Railroad

MISSISSIPPI

Mobile & Ohio Railroad

Black River

Monroe

DEC. 26

(6,000)
Vicksburg

Warrenton

Grand Gulf

Tensas River

Port
Gibson

Jackson

Crystal
Springs

Meridian

Mississippi River

LOUISIANA

Natchez

Pearl River

Laurel

ALABAMA

Hattiesburg

GRANT'S FIRST VICKSBURG CAMPAIGN

Grant began his overland advance to Vicksburg in November, reaching Oxford, Mississippi. Earl Van Dorn and Nathan Bedford Forrest launched a series of raids on Grant's supply lines in late December, forcing him to withdraw to Tennessee. Meanwhile, Sherman advanced by water toward Chickasaw Bayou.

GUERRILLAS

Within the western theater of the war, guerrillas were active behind Union lines throughout Tennessee, in Mississippi and Arkansas, and especially in Missouri. Guerrillas used violence to intimidate Unionists and disrupt Union supply lines. The reality was bad, but this propaganda print concentrates images of the worst excesses of the guerrillas.

authority within his department. Grant decided on an alternate plan, one that would satisfy the apparent desire of his superiors for a direct expedition downriver and head off McClernand's play to upstage him. While Grant continued to threaten Pemberton along the railroad, Sherman would take one division back to Memphis, add the troops now collected there, put them on steamboats, go down the river, and take Vicksburg.[31] Grant issued the order on December 8. By hard marching, Sherman had his division back in Memphis by the fifteenth, and by the twenty-first, the expedition was headed downriver, with three divisions in more than forty steamboats.[32]

The trip downriver showed the new character the war had taken during 1862. Union authorities, from Lincoln on down, had started the war with the hope that the great mass of southern whites were Unionists at heart and that a firm but conciliatory policy would bring them back into the fold. Federal commanders had practiced conciliation and restraint during the first year of the war. Disillusionment had begun when Federal troops first came in contact with large numbers of white southerners; the common Union soldiers, especially those of Grant's army who had penetrated farthest into the Confederacy, found local whites implacably hostile and slaves their only reliable friends. As they realized this, the soldiers became less inclined to show restraint. The persons of rebellious southern civilians might still be sacrosanct, and would continue so throughout the war, but their property was another matter.[33]

As the summer had progressed, their superiors had begun to catch on. Sherman,

Guerrilla Warfare and Retaliation

Confederate use of guerrilla warfare was a nuisance to Union forces, but it probably did not have the potential to be a decisive factor in the war. The greatest effect of guerrilla warfare was to make the war more destructive, especially for civilians. Although the level of destructiveness in this war almost never extended to the lives or persons of civilians, it brought some of the earliest incidents of wholesale destruction of civilian property, including the occurrence at Friar's Point, Mississippi. On December 20, Confederate guerrillas there took one of the transports under small-arms fire and were suppressed by naval artillery on the escorting gunboats. A corporal from the 114th Ohio later described what happened next:

> Early the next morning we started, and, running six or eight miles, came in sight of Friar's Point. Here for the first time to many of us was presented a realistic picture of war. It would require an abler pen than mine to properly describe the scene. A number of soldiers had been landed, a portion of the town fired, and, as the flames and smoke rose from the burning buildings, the newly risen sun cast his rays upon a picture that was at once grand and terrible.

While the flames on shore seethed and surged in the destruction of the doomed village, the river in front was filled with steamboats, each loaded to its fullest capacity with blue-coated soldiers, while a fleet of a dozen gunboats, some at anchor and others moving slowly and majestically up and down the river, formed a fitting background to the picture of destruction. Through the open portholes in the dark sides of the gunboats peered out the mouths of the cannon . . . Luckily for the village, no further hostile demonstrations were made by anyone on shore, and, after destroying five or six large buildings on the river front, the flames were stayed, and the fleet of transports, loaded with blue-coated "Yankees" from Ohio, Indiana, Illinois, Kentucky, and other States west of the Alleghenies, with their convoy of gunboats, moved slowly down the great river, leaving the few inhabitants of Friar's Point to reflect that in some cases the paths of discretion might be the proper ones to travel.[35]

who had commanded the Federal garrison of Memphis, finally became fed up with the fact that many families of known members of the Confederate army were living within Union lines at Memphis, often subsisting on rations issued by the U.S. Army, while the unarmed steamboats that brought supplies, including those rations, down the river to Memphis were often the targets of fire from Rebel bushwhackers along the banks.

This development was symptomatic of the growing numbers of Confederate guerrillas in several theaters of the war. Within the western theater, they were active behind Federal lines throughout Tennessee, in Mississippi and Arkansas, and especially in Missouri. Because they could not hold territory, such guerrillas could never fulfill the implicit Confederate war aim of preserving southern society with slavery intact. The passage of Union armies necessarily disrupted slavery, and guerrilla warfare itself intensified the effect, as counterinsurgency forces surged back and forth across the regions where the guerrillas were active in a way that was doubly corrosive to all the structures of southern society. Guerrillas hid among the civilian population and often disguised themselves as civilians, an added factor pushing Federal forces toward harder treatment of civilians.[34]

Sherman's response to the guerrillas who fired on unarmed steamboats in the Mississippi that summer was an example. He announced that henceforth he would respond to each incident by expelling several Rebel families from the city. Though the exiles were given time to pack their belongings and safe conduct beyond Union lines,

FORMATION OF GUERRILLA BANDS

Union soldiers responded to bushwhacker violence with retribution of their own. This was an important part of the transition toward the "hard war" that characterized the Civil War's later stages. This cartoon, from Confederate artist Adalbert Volck, blamed such violence for inciting further guerrilla activity.

the hue and cry against Sherman's supposed cruelty has never ceased. He did not relent. Grant approved.[36]

On December 21, leading elements of Sherman's flotilla came under fire from riflemen apparently sheltering among the buildings of Friar's Point, Mississippi. The navy's gunboats returned fire with heavy artillery. Then an army landing party went ashore and torched several buildings from which the shots were thought to have come. Later that day and early the next, as other transports in the column tied up for wood and water, undisciplined troops, hearing garbled accounts about hostile activity in the settlement, engaged in unauthorized arson and looting. Strenuous efforts by officers and provost guards put a stop to the disorder, divested the looters of their booty, and extinguished the fire, saving at least part of the town, but a similar pattern played out at Milliken's Bend, Louisiana, only a few miles upstream from Vicksburg.[37]

Vicksburg's natural strength lay in the fact that the town was perched atop a steep, two-hundred-foot bluff that looked down onto a hairpin curve of the Mississippi. The bluff represented the northernmost point at which Mississippi's interior plateau stood immediately adjacent to the great river. North of Vicksburg the plateau's rim slanted off to the northeast, leaving between it and the river a swath as much as sixty miles wide of low, swampy, but very fertile country known as the Mississippi Delta.

The bayou's nearly impassable terrain made it difficult for Sherman's force to advance on Vicksburg. Though they vastly outnumbered the Confederate defenders, Union troops were unable to gain any ground.

Since no general wanted to think of landing an assaulting column directly at the foot of the bluff in front of the dozens of heavy guns emplaced on the Vicksburg waterfront, the only way to come at the city was somehow to get onto the plateau behind it and attack its landward defenses. That would mean either getting transports past Vicksburg's powerful batteries to carry the army across the river and reach the plateau below the town or else landing the troops above the town and crossing the Delta. The Delta was narrowest near the mouth of the Yazoo River, a couple of miles north of Vicksburg, so the day after Christmas, Sherman's fleet disgorged its troops several miles up the Yazoo.[38]

Over the next few days, Sherman's army struggled through the tangle of bayous on the Yazoo floodplain between the river and the Chickasaw bluffs. Confederates were entrenched on the crest, and the difficult terrain defeated every effort to advance anywhere except where the Rebel works were strongest. The Confederates easily repulsed

NATHAN BEDFORD FORREST

Nathan Bedford Forrest's cavalry rode behind Grant's lines during the Vicksburg campaign, disrupting supply and communication lines and forcing Grant to withdraw his men in December 1862.

the attack, inflicting nearly 2,000 casualties while suffering very few. This easy Confederate victory came to be known as the Battle of Chickasaw Bayou, after the last and most prominent of the subsidiary watercourses that had obstructed and channeled the Union advance. Unwilling to risk running the Confederate batteries to land south of the town, Sherman on January 2 put his troops back on the transports and returned to the Mississippi.[39]

During the fortnight since he had left Memphis, the situation in the rest of the western theater had changed. A month earlier, Jefferson Davis had appointed Gen. Joseph E. Johnston to command the Confederate forces in the West, hoping to coordinate Bragg's army at Murfreesboro, south of Nashville, as well as Pemberton's, defending Mississippi. Davis wanted Johnston to exploit the Confederacy's interior lines by shifting troops between Bragg and Pemberton as needed. When Davis explained this concept to Johnston in Richmond, the general replied immediately that it would not work, because of inadequate rail lines and the difficulty of securing accurate intelligence.[40] Davis appointed him nevertheless, and on December 4 Johnston established his headquarters in Chattanooga.[41]

When Johnston did not reinforce Pemberton in the face of Grant's advance, Davis decided to go west himself. Leaving Richmond on December 10, he found Bragg's army in fine shape. Despite protests from Bragg and Johnston, as well as their promises that cavalry raids would force Grant's retreat, on December 16 Davis ordered a quarter of Bragg's infantry to join Pemberton.[42]

Bragg and Johnston were right. The cavalry raid that Bragg dispatched, led by Brig. Gen. Nathan Bedford Forrest, wrought havoc in West Tennessee, tearing up railroads and telegraph lines. And the raid that Johnston had launched, under Van Dorn, not only broke the Mississippi Central Railroad in Grant's rear but also, on December 20, destroyed Grant's supply depot at Holly Springs, Mississippi, leaving the Union general little choice but to turn around and march back out of the state, feeding his troops by foraging on Mississippi's farms and plantations along the way. That left Pemberton free to shift forces to meet Sherman near Vicksburg, though the extra troops were not

BATTLE OF STONES RIVER ▶

Bragg struck Rosecrans's line hard from Murfreesboro, but fierce resistance prevented a Confederate breakthrough. After two days of fighting, Bragg retreated, and Rosecrans claimed victory—a critical one coming in conjunction with the issuance of the Emancipation Proclamation.

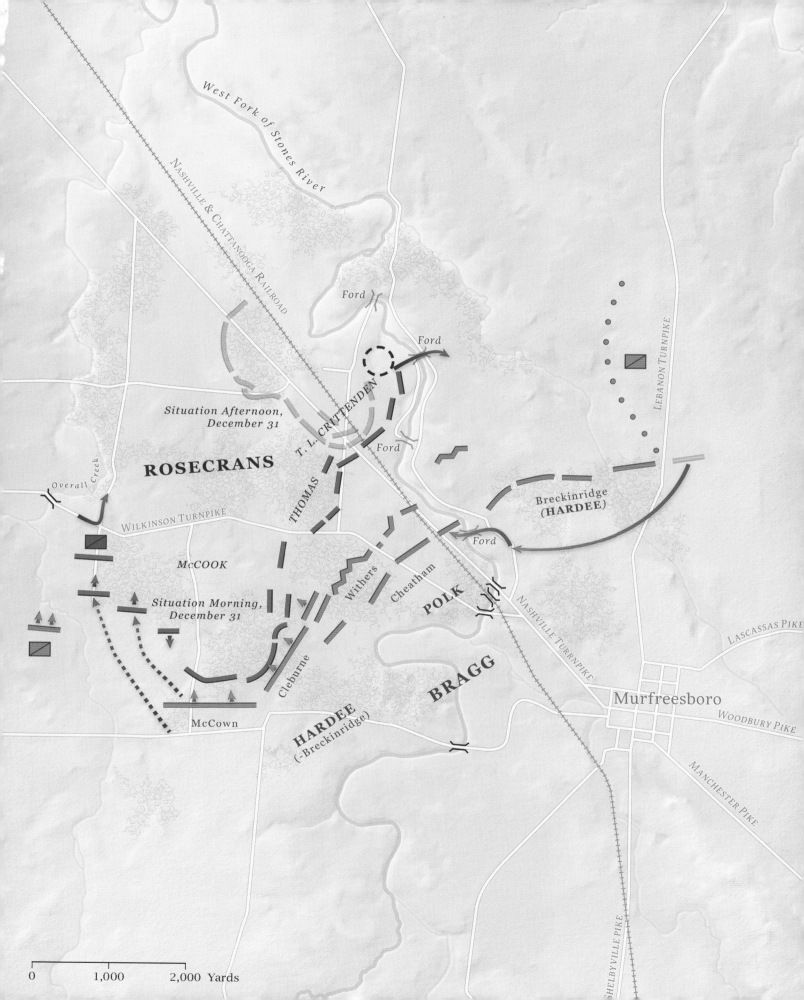

West Fork of Stones River

NASHVILLE & CHATTANOOGA RAILROAD

Ford

Ford

Ford

Situation Afternoon, December 31

T. L. CRITTENDEN

ROSECRANS

THOMAS

Overall Creek

WILKINSON TURNPIKE

Breckinridge
(HARDEE)

Ford

McCOOK

Situation Morning, December 31

Withers

Cheatham

POLK

LEBANON TURNPIKE

LASCASSAS PIKE

Cleburne

BRAGG

NASHVILLE TURNPIKE

McCown

HARDEE
(-Breckinridge)

Murfreesboro

WOODBURY PIKE

MANCHESTER PIKE

SHELBYVILLE PIKE

0   1,000   2,000 Yards

needed, as the difficult terrain provided all the assistance the small garrison required. The troops that Davis sent from Bragg arrived after the assault at Chickasaw Bayou had failed.[43]

News of Davis's transfer of troops from Bragg to Pemberton quickly found its way to Rosecrans.[44] Already under pressure from Washington to advance, he marched from Nashville for Murfreesboro with 44,000 soldiers out of a force of 81,000; the others garrisoned key points against guerrillas.[45]

Rosecrans's troops set off on December 26, but it took them four days to cover thirty miles due to muddy roads and the constant harassment of Rebel cavalry. The Army of the Cumberland, as Rosecrans's command was now known, arrived in front of Murfreesboro on December 29, and deployed the following day facing Bragg's army of 35,000, which was in line a little more than two miles northwest of the town, straddling shallow Stones River. Rosecrans planned to open the fight the next morning, the last of 1862, by attacking Bragg's right, but Bragg beat him to the punch by attacking the Union right instead. Surprised and outflanked, the Federals fell back. Bragg had things much his own way that morning but still struggled with the assortment of problem subordinates that had plagued his army in Kentucky, whom Davis had refused to allow him to remove. A drunken division commander's blunder forced Bragg to commit his reserve early, and another division commander's irrational misapprehensions prevented Bragg from shifting troops to a key sector. The Confederates folded the Army of the Cumberland's right wing almost back on its left but could not finish it off or break its grip on the vital Nashville Pike. That night, Rosecrans and his generals discussed the possibility of retreat but decided to stay put.

Both armies rested on their arms on New Year's Day. On January 2 Rosecrans moved artillery onto an advantageous hill east of Stones River. Bragg sent John C. Breckinridge's division, including the "Orphan Brigade" of Kentuckians, to evict him, but fifty-five cannon decimated the Rebels, bringing their total to nearly 12,000 casualties over the entire course of the battle. With only about 20,000 troops left, and anticipating Federal reinforcements, Bragg then withdrew under pressure from his subordinates, taking up new positions near Tullahoma, forty miles to the southeast.[46] Always cautious, wearied after taking nearly 13,000 casualties in the bloodiest major battle (proportional to the forces engaged) of the war, Rosecrans made no pursuit, but the Union now had a secure grip on Nashville.

GRANT'S SECOND VICKSBURG CAMPAIGN

Meanwhile, back on the Mississippi, McClernand returned from leave to find that Sherman had taken "his" army south without him. He met Sherman's returning forces near the mouth of the Yazoo, and then used them to strike at the Confederate fortress of Arkansas Post on January 11. The successful operation netted 5,000 prisoners and helped secure Grant's water communications for operations against Vicksburg.[47]

Grant arrived a few days later and took command of the expedition, relegating the outraged McClernand to command one of its three corps. Grant was keenly mindful of home-front politics. The disappointments of the preceding summer and fall, followed by Ambrose Burnside's December debacle at Fredericksburg and Sherman's repulse at Chickasaw Bayou, had brought northern morale to its lowest ebb.[48] Alert to the national mood, Grant decided there could be no appearance of retreat, not even to go back to Memphis and resume the campaign with more attention to the security of supply lines, as Sherman and others advised. Instead, he determined to go back downriver to Vicksburg, encamp along the west bank above the town, and stay until he found a way to reach the plateau behind it.

From late January through mid-April, Grant's Army of the Tennessee endured wet, muddy camps, suffering greatly from disease and the discouragement that was afflicting the rest of the country. Grant and Porter tried one scheme after another aimed at getting their flotilla onto the Mississippi below Vicksburg or into the Yazoo above the town, so that they could ferry Grant's troops to the foot of the plateau at a place where it was undefended. They tried digging a canal across a bend of the river opposite Vicksburg—without success. They tried cutting the levees and letting gunboats and transports into the maze of interlocking bayous among the swamps on either side of the river. Sailors stood on deck with poles, fending off the banks to steer the vessels in the narrow, winding waterways barely wide enough for their passage. Two attempts on the east bank strove to reach the upper Yazoo, and one on the west bank aimed at the Mississippi below Vicksburg. All failed.[49]

▼

VICKSBURG CANAL

An illustration of Grant's proposed canal, one of several attempted ways to get the riverboats away from the Vicksburg guns in order to land troops on the other side of the river and assault the town from the land.

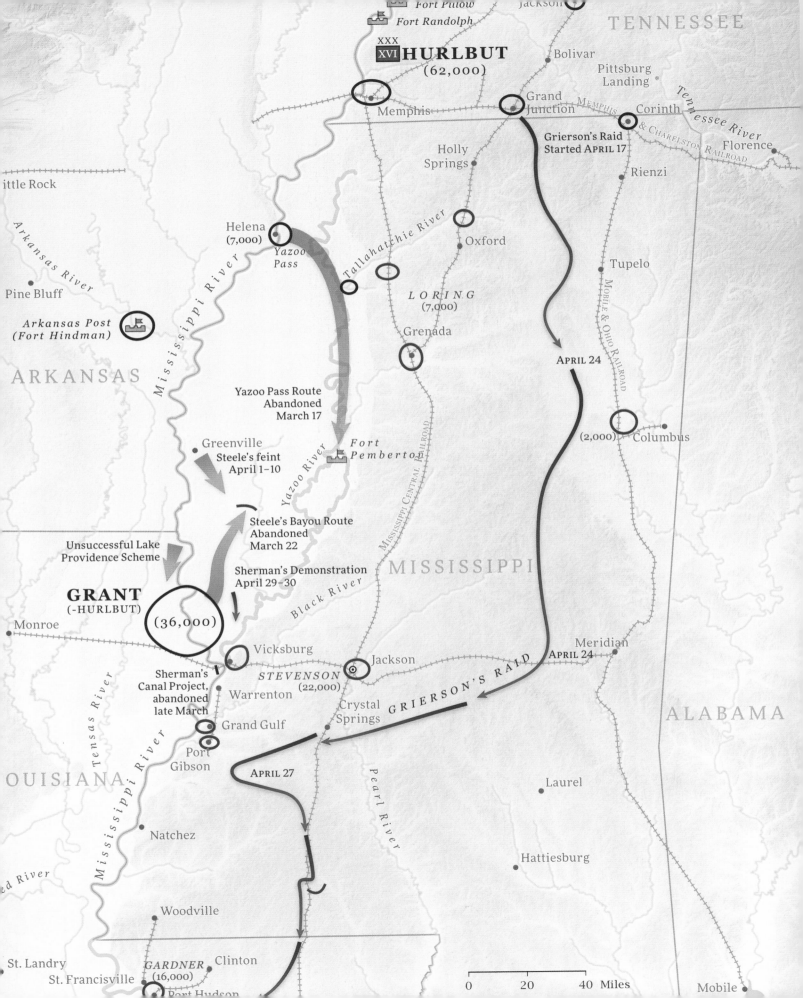

TENNESSEE

Fort Pillow
Fort Randolph

Jackson

XXX
XVI **HURLBUT**
(62,000)

Bolivar

Pittsburg
Landing

Memphis

Grand
Junction

Corinth

Grierson's Raid
Started APRIL 17

Florence

Holly
Springs

Rienzi

Little Rock

Helena
(7,000)

Yazoo
Pass

Tallahatchie River

Oxford

Tupelo

Arkansas River

Pine Bluff

LORING
(7,000)

Grenada

*Arkansas Post
(Fort Hindman)*

APRIL 24

ARKANSAS

Yazoo Pass Route
Abandoned
March 17

Mississippi River

Greenville
Steele's feint
April 1-10

Fort
Pemberton

(2,000)

Columbus

Yazoo River

Steele's Bayou Route
Abandoned
March 22

Sherman's Demonstration
April 29-30

MISSISSIPPI

Unsuccessful Lake
Providence Scheme

Black River

GRANT
(-HURLBUT)

Monroe

(36,000)

Meridian

Vicksburg

Jackson

APRIL 24

Sherman's
Canal Project,
abandoned
late March

STEVENSON
(22,000)

ALABAMA

Warrenton

Crystal
Springs

GRIERSON'S RAID

Tensas River

Grand Gulf

APRIL 27

Port
Gibson

LOUISIANA

Pearl River

Laurel

Natchez

Hattiesburg

Red River

Woodville

St. Landry

GARDNER
(16,000)

Clinton

St. Francisville

Port Hudson

0   20   40 Miles

Mobile

◀ RUNNING THE GUNS AT VICKSBURG

◀ RUNNING THE GUNS AT VICKSBURG
Unable to find another way around, Grant asked Admiral David D. Porter to have his ironclads run past the batteries, hoping to avoid their fire. The gunboats ran successfully on April 16, with the transports following several nights later.

Near the end of March, Grant determined to have the navy run directly past the Vicksburg batteries while his army marched down the west bank to meet the gunboats and transports below the town. Grant asked Porter, who was not under his orders, to run the Vicksburg batteries with his most powerful gunboats. Porter readily agreed, and on the night of April 16, successfully ran the batteries. Six nights later, several of the leased transports, manned by crews of army volunteers instead of their usual civilian complements, also got past Vicksburg. Grant now had the gunboats and transports in place to cross his army below Vicksburg. While a Union cavalry brigade under Col. Benjamin Grierson ranged the length of Mississippi, cutting railroads and telegraph wires and distracting Pemberton, Grant on April 30 began landing on the east bank and got his soldiers onto the plateau before Confederate forces could intervene.[50]

GRANT'S FINAL VICKSBURG CAMPAIGN

Grant advanced into the interior of Mississippi in a campaign of maneuver that became the war's foremost masterpiece of the operational art. For the next two and a half weeks, each time that Pemberton received a report of what Grant was doing, decided how to counter it, and began to move his troops for that purpose, Grant had already completed that movement and was doing something else even more threatening. On May 1 he met a detachment of Pemberton's army under Maj. Gen. John Bowen at Port Gibson. Despite terrain that greatly favored the defender, Grant brought superior force to bear at the point of decision and routed Bowen's troops by the end of the day. But then, rather than proceed directly north toward Vicksburg through the broken terrain

◀ GRANT'S SECOND VICKSBURG CAMPAIGN
Topography and active Confederate resistance made it very difficult for Grant to reach the key fortified city of Vicksburg. His first six approaches all failed, but Grant was nothing if not persistent.

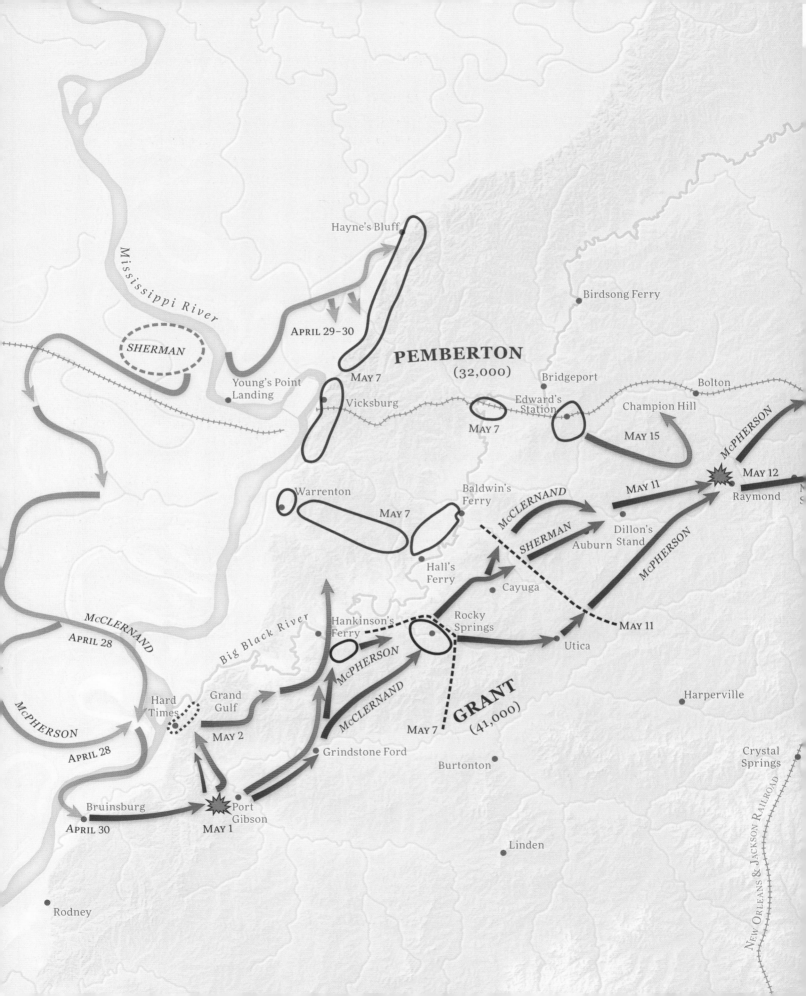

Mississippi River

Hayne's Bluff

Birdsong Ferry

SHERMAN

APRIL 29–30

PEMBERTON
(32,000)

Young's Point
Landing

MAY 7

Bridgeport

Bolton

Vicksburg

Edward's
Station

Champion Hill

MAY 7

MAY 15

McPHERSON

MAY 12

Warrenton

MAY 7

Baldwin's
Ferry

McCLERNAND

MAY 11

Raymond

Hall's
Ferry

SHERMAN

Dillon's
Stand

McPHERSON

Cayuga

Auburn

McCLERNAND

Harperville

Big Black River

Hankinson's
Ferry

Rocky
Springs

MAY 11

McCLERNAND

McPHERSON

Utica

APRIL 28

McPHERSON

Hard
Times

Grand
Gulf

McPHERSON

GRANT
(41,000)

McPHERSON

APRIL 28

MAY 2

McCLERNAND

MAY 7

Crystal
Springs

Grindstone Ford

Burtonton

Bruinsburg

Port
Gibson

APRIL 30

MAY 1

Linden

Rodney

NEW ORLEANS & JACKSON RAILROAD

along the edge of the plateau, Grant angled northeast into the interior of Mississippi.[51]

On May 12 the Confederate garrison of Jackson, an oversized brigade under Brig. Gen. John Gregg, struck the head of Maj. Gen. James B. McPherson's XVII Corps column near the town of Raymond. Gregg mistakenly thought he was attacking a single brigade on the Union flank, and the battle was over as soon as McPherson brought up additional troops from farther back in his column and routed Gregg.[52] The Battle of Raymond, however, convinced Grant that he dared not leave the city of Jackson in his rear as a potential Confederate base while he turned against Vicksburg. On the morning of May 14, after another short but sharp battle, Grant's troops took control of the city.[53]

Retreating from Jackson along with Gregg's troops was Joseph E. Johnston, whom Davis had ordered to Mississippi in frustration at the theater commander's continued unwillingness to exercise the role to which Davis had assigned him: to focus his attention on crucial areas under immediate attack. Yet upon arriving in Jackson, Johnston telegraphed Richmond that he was too late. He ordered Pemberton to withdraw in order to link up with his own force to the east. For reasons never explained satisfactorily, Johnston then marched his troops north, a course that took him away from where he had ordered Pemberton to meet him.[54]

One of the two couriers carrying copies of Johnston's dispatch to Pemberton was a Union agent, who carried the message to Grant instead. Grant aimed to defeat Pemberton's force of about 23,000 before he could join Johnston. Leaving Sherman's corps to finish destroying factories, depots, and railroad facilities in Jackson, Grant marched west with McClernand's and McPherson's corps, 32,000 strong. The armies clashed on May 16 near Champion Hill, about twenty miles east of Vicksburg and the same distance west of Jackson, in the decisive battle of the campaign.

The commanding generals faced each other with roughly equal numbers actually engaged. McClernand was in a sulk that day because Grant had forbidden him to start a battle on his own. He remained aloof a few hundred yards from the battle with three of his four divisions, leaving Grant to face Pemberton with four of the seven divisions present. Pemberton had his own

◀ GRANT'S FINAL VICKSBURG CAMPAIGN
After crossing the Mississippi below Vicksburg, Grant turned inland, marching on the city of Jackson. In response, Johnston evacuated Jackson, while John C. Pemberton began preparing to make a stand at Champion Hill, hoping to trap Grant between his army and Johnston's.

problems with subordinates. The Confederate commander was not the sort to inspire confidence in any case, and some of his fellow Rebels never forgave him for having been born in Pennsylvania. Maj. Gens. William W. Loring and John Bowen at first refused Pemberton's orders and held their divisions unengaged near the southern end of the battlefield while the decisive action swirled back and forth across the key terrain feature, Champion Hill, a couple of miles to the north.[55]

At last Bowen, Pemberton's most able subordinate, relented and brought his division into the fight. Its onset briefly swung the tide in the Confederacy's favor, sweeping the Federals from Champion Hill and down the north slope, but the arrival of McPherson's last division, along with Grant's timely shift of the forces already engaged, combined to halt the Confederate onslaught and hurl it back. Loring still refused to join the fight, and Pemberton had no other reserve with which to stem the surging Federals, who soon swept the field.

During the course of the battle, Pemberton's engineers had constructed a makeshift bridge over Baker's Creek, in the Confederate rear. Now the bridge was all that saved Pemberton from being trapped. His battered army withdrew to the west. Without notifying Pemberton, however, Loring withdrew to the south and then swung east to find Johnston.[56]

The next morning, May 17, Grant pursued Pemberton and found the Confederates holding a hastily fortified bridgehead on the east bank of the Big Black River about ten miles from Vicksburg. Pemberton had taken this position with part of his forces in hopes that Loring's division, of which he had heard nothing since the evening before, might rejoin his army.

Grant's troops advanced aggressively and overran the bridgehead. Most of the Confederates fled across the bridge, torching it behind them. More than a thousand were captured—some, it seemed, not altogether unwillingly.[57] That night, Grant's engineers built their own makeshift bridge over the Big Black, while McPherson's XVII Corps improvised a crossing a couple of miles upstream and Sherman's XV Corps followed in its wake. By that evening, all three corps of the Army of the Tennessee were filing into positions facing the Confederate fortifications on the landward side of Vicksburg. The overstretched Rebels were compelled to give up their outlying batteries overlooking the Yazoo River and Chickasaw Bayou, enabling Grant's army to open a direct supply line to the Mississippi above the town. Contrary to later legend, Grant had not moved

▼ **COKER HOUSE, CHAMPION HILL**

Coker House was used as a field hospital by Union troops during the battle; afterward, some departing soldiers looted the residence.

◄ **CHAMPION HILL**

Champion Hill was the decisive battle of Grant's Vicksburg campaign. Following their defeat, Confederate forces withdrew to the city, and Grant began his siege.

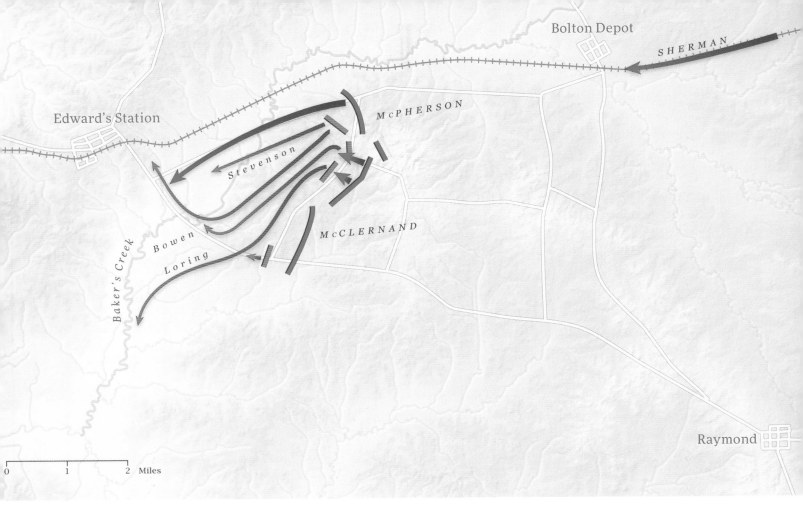

Battle of Champion Hill

In the major battle of the Vicksburg campaign, Pemberton's men pushed back the initial assault from James McPherson's XVII Corps. The belated arrival of the rest of the corps, plus a slow-developing attack by McClernand, pushed back the Confederates. Though Grant was victorious, he failed to trap Pemberton's men.

his army without a supply line during its march through the interior of Mississippi, but he did not allow the supply situation to dictate his movements. Supplies had been somewhat attenuated as wagon trains of coffee and cartridges wound down the west-bank roads, were ferried across the Mississippi River to Grand Gulf, and then wended their way along the roads to try to overtake Grant's fast-advancing army. His troops had, of necessity, helped themselves to much food from local farms. Now, with a short and secure supply line reestablished, the soldiers could again receive their accustomed rations of hardtack, salt pork, and beans.[58]

Grant hoped that the demoralization shown by some of the Confederate troops at the Battle of Big Black River Bridge was widespread within the Rebel ranks, and that the Vicksburg fortifications would not be strongly defended. He also hoped to avoid a prolonged siege in the summer heat of the lower Mississippi Valley, where sickness might lay waste to his army. So he ordered an all-out assault on the Vicksburg fortifications for the next day, May 19. The result was anticlimactic. The terrain around Vicksburg was complicated. Deep, narrow ravines choked with vines and canebrakes wound between flat-topped ridges. Movement by large formations was practical only along the ridgetops, but they were swept by Confederate fire. When officers chose to struggle through the ravines instead, they often found themselves moving in a different direction than intended, and some failed to engage the defenses at all. Those who did

ATTACK AT VICKSBURG
This print from after the war shows a Union advance against the strong Confederate entrenchments at Vicksburg. Desperate Confederate defenders held the ground, necessitating Grant's two-month siege.

"FIRST AT VICKSBURG"
The 1st Battalion, 13th Infantry was a Regular Army unit that took part in the May 22 assault on Vicksburg. Its 43 percent casualty rate during the battle was the highest of any Regular Army unit during the Civil War and led to its special designation "First at Vicksburg."

met bloody repulse. Among the latter, the 1st Battalion, 13th U.S. Infantry (a Regular Army unit raised during the war) lost 43 percent of its men, advancing all the way to the Confederate parapet before being forced to retire.[59]

Undeterred, Grant ordered his officers to spend the next two days preparing for an all-out assault to go in precisely at 10:00 on the morning of May 22. The result was disappointing and much more costly. The Confederates fought stubbornly behind their breastworks and repelled the attack all along the line.[60]

Rebuffed in his attempts to take Vicksburg by storm, Grant settled down to a siege. Over the next six weeks, his troops kept up constant bombardment and sharpshooting and dug their zigzag approach trenches ever closer to the Rebel works. By the end of June, only the width of the earthen parapet separated the opposing lines in many sectors of the front. Union troops had twice tunneled under Confederate fortifications, placing powder charges that destroyed a key Rebel fort. The Rebel lines had held after each explosion, and Confederates built new earthworks behind the craters, but during the early days of July, a half dozen more tunnels extended under the Confederate lines, ready to be loaded with powder.[61]

Meanwhile, Jefferson Davis desperately tried to get Johnston to raise the siege. He reinforced the general's army to almost 30,000 men and repeatedly urged him to act—all to no avail. Johnston hovered north of Jackson, but Grant was ready. Heavily reinforced, he continued to confront Vicksburg with 45,000 men while entrenching another 35,000 under Sherman, facing Johnston. In the end, Johnston did nothing.

On July 3 Pemberton requested terms, and the following day the capitulation took effect. Grant paroled the 30,000-man garrison rather than incur the logistical burden of shipping them north.[62] Celebration swept the North, especially the Midwest, while gloom and bitterness settled over the South. Davis bitterly remarked that the city had fallen because of a general, Johnston, "who wouldn't fight."[63]

Five days after Vicksburg's surrender, the smaller Confederate Mississippi River bastion of Port Hudson, Louisiana, also capitulated. Major Gen. Nathaniel P. Banks's Army of the Gulf had laid siege to Port Hudson on May 22. As at Vicksburg, the Confederates at Port Hudson repulsed several infantry assaults. Among the Union attackers were several regiments of black troops, and the assaults, though unsuccessful, offered one of the first demonstrations that African Americans would fight bravely. On July 9, having heard of

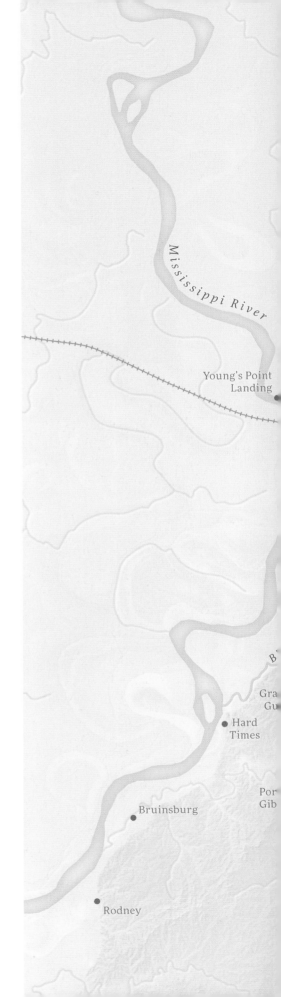

GRANT'S FINAL VICKSBURG CAMPAIGN ▶

After taking Jackson, Grant swung west and drove Pemberton back from Champion Hill into the defenses of Vicksburg itself. When initial assaults failed, the Union troops dug in for a siege of the Confederate stronghold.

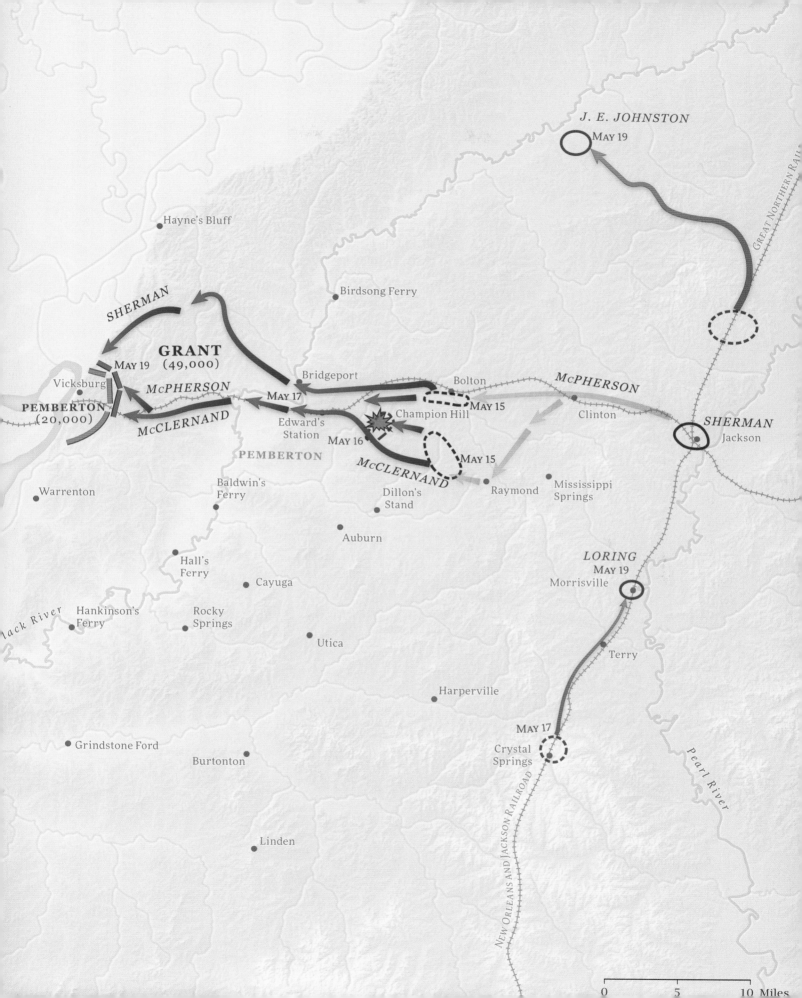

J. E. JOHNSTON
May 19

GREAT NORTHERN RAILROAD

Hayne's Bluff

Birdsong Ferry

SHERMAN

GRANT
(49,000)
Bridgeport
Bolton
McPHERSON
May 19
McPHERSON
May 17
May 15
SHERMAN
Vicksburg
McPHERSON
Champion Hill
Clinton
Jackson
PEMBERTON
(20,000)
Edward's
Station
May 16
McCLERNAND
May 15
McCLERNAND
PEMBERTON

Warrenton

Baldwin's
Ferry
Dillon's
Stand
Raymond
Mississippi
Springs

Auburn

LORING
May 19
Morrisville

Hall's
Ferry

Cayuga

Black River
Hankinson's
Ferry
Rocky
Springs
Terry

Utica

Harperville

Grindstone Ford
Burtonton
May 17
Crystal
Springs
Pearl River

Linden

NEW ORLEANS AND JACKSON RAILROAD

0   5   10 Miles

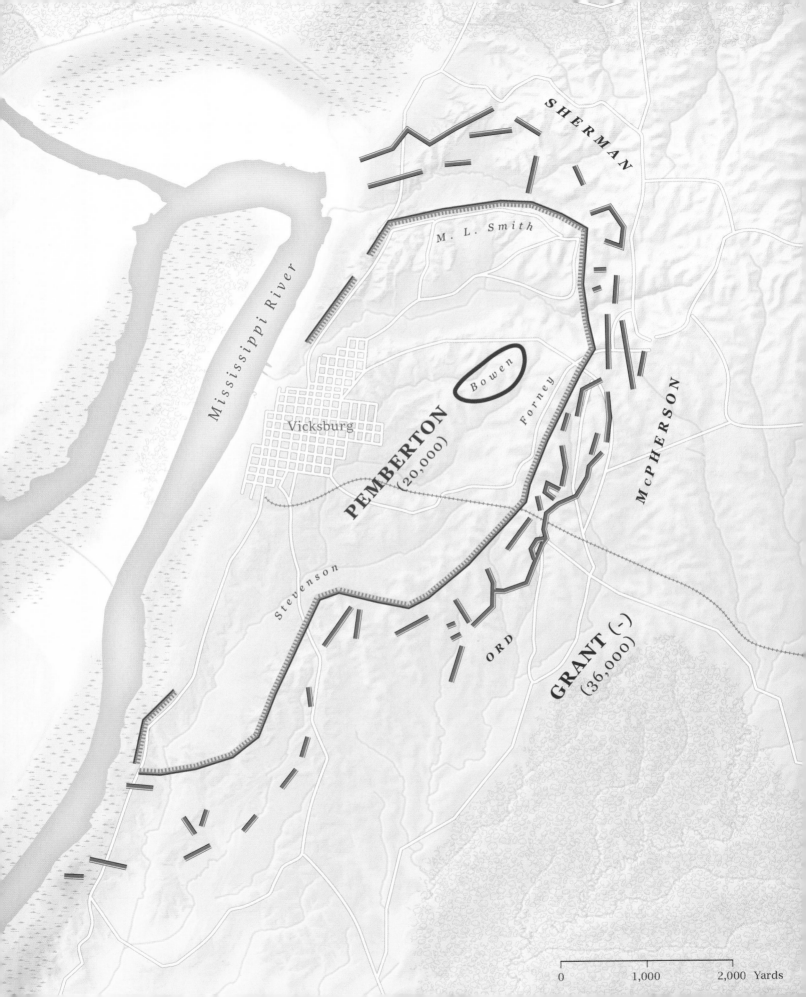

SHERMAN

M. L. Smith

Mississippi River

Bowen

Forney

Vicksburg

PEMBERTON
(20,000)

McPHERSON

Stevenson

ORD

GRANT (-)
(36,000)

0   1,000   2,000   Yards

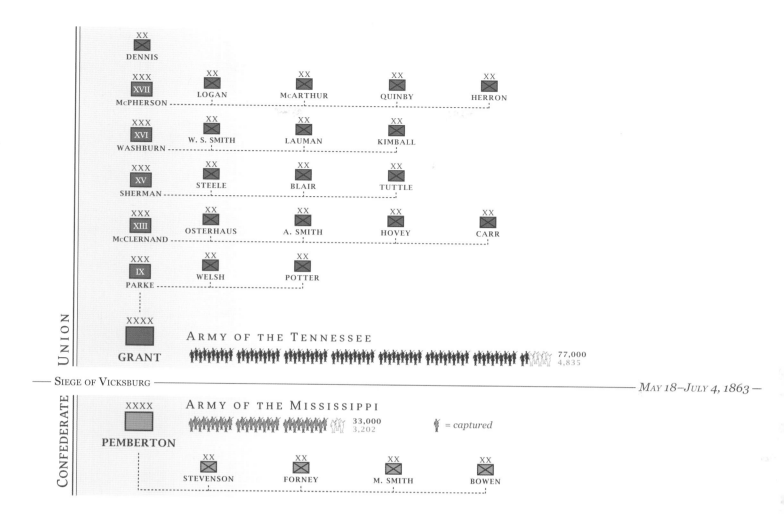

UNION

XX **DENNIS**				
XXX **XVII** McPHERSON	XX **LOGAN**	XX **McARTHUR**	XX **QUINBY**	XX **HERRON**
XXX **XVI** WASHBURN	XX **W. S. SMITH**	XX **LAUMAN**	XX **KIMBALL**	
XXX **XV** SHERMAN	XX **STEELE**	XX **BLAIR**	XX **TUTTLE**	
XXX **XIII** McCLERNAND	XX **OSTERHAUS**	XX **A. SMITH**	XX **HOVEY**	XX **CARR**
XXX **IX** PARKE	XX **WELSH**	XX **POTTER**		

XXXX **GRANT**

ARMY OF THE TENNESSEE

77,000
4,835

—— SIEGE OF VICKSBURG ——————————————————————————— *MAY 18–JULY 4, 1863* —

CONFEDERATE

XXXX **PEMBERTON**

ARMY OF THE MISSISSIPPI

33,000
3,202

= captured

XX **STEVENSON**	XX **FORNEY**	XX **M. SMITH**	XX **BOWEN**

Vicksburg
Jackson

◀ **SIEGE OF VICKSBURG**

Beginning the siege in May, Grant worked to close off the city and starve its defenders. Without relief coming, and with the military and civilian population of Vicksburg starving, Pemberton surrendered the city and his army on the Fourth of July.

THE CRATER OF FORT HILL

During the siege of Vicksburg, Grant tried several tactics to break the Confederate lines, including digging a tunnel underneath the defenses in the hopes of blowing a hole there. The explosions successfully destroyed a Confederate fort, but the defenders were able to reinforce the line.

LOUISIANA COLORED REGIMENT AT PORT HUDSON

Even after the Union began to accept black enlistments, many African American regiments served only as manual labor. A few regiments did make their way to the fighting, such as the troops depicted here at Port Hudson (which the picture incorrectly identified as the 2nd Louisiana).

INSIDE BESIEGED VICKSBURG

The following diary entries are from the diary of an anonymous civilian woman who lived through the siege in Vicksburg, published in 1885. Historians have speculated on the author's identity without coming up with any very compelling answers. She was foreign born, probably British, and her husband, whose initials were H. L., was probably a lawyer and a silent Union sympathizer. Martha was their slave. The *Vicksburg Daily Citizen* was the local newspaper.

May 28th.—Since that day [May 17] the regular siege has continued. We are utterly cut off from the world, surrounded by a circle of fire. Would it be wise like the scorpion to sting ourselves to death? The fiery shower of shells goes on day and night. H_'s occupation, of course, is gone, his office closed. Every man has to carry a pass in his pocket. People do nothing but eat what they can get, sleep when they can, and dodge the shells. There are three intervals when the shelling stops, either for the guns to cool or for the gunner's meals, I suppose—about eight in the morning, and the same in the evening, and at noon. In that time we have both to prepare and eat ours. Clothing cannot be washed or anything else done . . . I think all the dogs and cats must be killed, or starved, we don't see any more pitiful animals prowling around . . . The cellar is so damp and musty the bedding has to be carried out and laid in the sun every day, with the forecast that it may be demolished at any moment. The confinement is dreadful. To sit and listen as if waiting for death in a horrible manner would drive me insane. I don't know what others do, but we read when I am not scribbling in this. H_ borrowed somewhere a lot of Dickens's novels, and we reread them by the dim light in the cellar. When the shelling abates H_ goes to walk about a little or get the "Daily Citizen," which is still issuing a tiny sheet at twenty-five and fifty cents a copy . . . I am so tired of corn-bread, which I never liked, that I eat it with tears in my eyes. We are lucky to get a quart of milk daily from a family near who have a cow they hourly expect to be killed. I send five dollars to market each morning, and it buys a small piece of mule-meat. Rice and milk is my main food; I can't eat the mule-meat. We boil the rice and eat it cold with milk for supper. Martha runs the gauntlet to buy the meat and milk once a day in a perfect terror.[64]

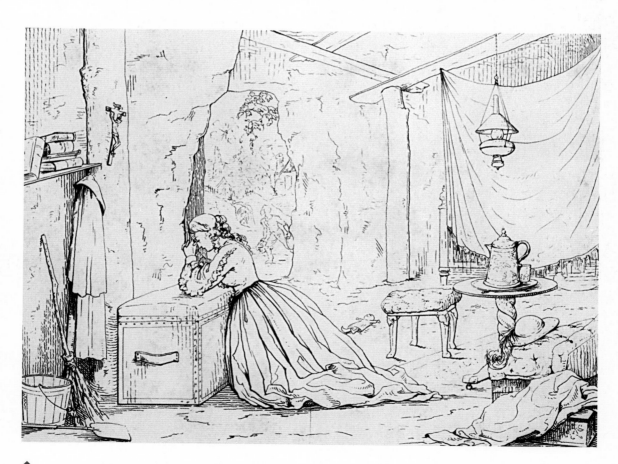

▲
CAVE LIFE IN VICKSBURG
Continual bombardment of the city during the Union siege of Vicksburg led many civilians to seek shelter underground to avoid the fight. Both they and Confederate soldiers in the city suffered from starvation and other problems as the siege dragged on until the eventual surrender on July 4.

Vicksburg's fall, Confederate maj. gen. Franklin Gardner surrendered Port Hudson and its 7,500-man garrison. With that, the Mississippi River was completely lost to the Confederacy, and Union shipping along the river faced no hostile impediments beyond the occasional actions of guerrillas. The benefit to the Union economy, and to Union morale, was immense.

THE CAMPAIGNS FOR CHATTANOOGA, JUNE TO NOVEMBER 1863

THE TULLAHOMA AND CHICKAMAUGA CAMPAIGNS

While Grant was taking Vicksburg, the ever-cautious Rosecrans did nothing despite a steady stream of exhortations from Lincoln, Halleck, and Secretary of War Stanton.[65] While Rosecrans remained idle, Davis detached thousands of Bragg's troops to reinforce Johnston's army intended to relieve Vicksburg. Finally, in late June, with Vicksburg's fate sealed, Rosecrans advanced through Middle Tennessee in what became known as the Tullahoma campaign. Within nine days, he had adroitly maneuvered Bragg all the way back to Chattanooga, just above the Georgia line, with only light skirmishing.[66] Rosecrans halted his army around Winchester, Tennessee, about fifty miles northwest of Chattanooga, concluding an almost bloodless offensive.[67]

If Rosecrans thought the territory he had gained would satisfy his superiors in Washington, he was mistaken. Why had he not followed up his advantage and

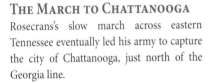

THE MARCH TO CHATTANOOGA
Rosecrans's slow march across eastern Tennessee eventually led his army to capture the city of Chattanooga, just north of the Georgia line.

pursued Bragg until he caught and destroyed his army? Dissatisfaction reached a fever pitch by the time Rosecrans, after a six-week pause to rest and refit, again put the Army of the Cumberland in motion. Bragg now realized that the Cumberland Plateau served better to screen the true axis of an advance than as ramparts for resistance. Further distracted by the need to keep an eye on Ambrose Burnside's simultaneous advance toward Knoxville with the small Army of the Ohio, Bragg found his position turned. His only means of escaping capture was to abandon Chattanooga and retreat into Georgia.[68]

With the same propensity he had displayed after Corinth for trying to pursue after the opportunity for pursuit had passed, Rosecrans now went all out to catch Bragg.[69] Yet Bragg was much closer than Rosecrans suspected, not running but at bay—and reinforced. For months a number of political and military leaders had been trying to persuade Davis that the Confederacy's best strategy was massive reinforcement of its geographic center, via the Army of Tennessee, so as to break the Union's center, held by the Army of the Cumberland. Davis at last agreed and, for the only time in the war, took troops from Lee's Army of Northern Virginia: two divisions under Lt. Gen. James Longstreet. Other reinforcements were on their way to Bragg from all over the Confederacy. They had not all arrived as Rosecrans's widely separated corps began to descend the east side of Lookout Mountain, but their prospect induced Bragg to halt his retreat at LaFayette, Georgia, which happened to be immediately in front of the gap where Rosecrans's center column descended.

Rarely in military history had a general received a better opportunity to defeat his opponent in detail. Bragg gave the orders that would bring overwhelming force down on the front and flank of Rosecrans's central column, the XIV Corps, but his fractious generals refused to obey before the Union commanders recognized their danger and withdrew. In the days that followed, Bragg had an opportunity almost as good to catch and destroy Rosecrans's isolated left-wing column, the XXI Corps. Again his generals balked, and the enemy escaped.[70]

With the Army of the Cumberland reunited at the eastern foot of Lookout Mountain, Bragg attempted to interpose his now-reinforced army, soon to number about 68,000 men, between Rosecrans's 62,000 men and the newly acquired Union base at Chattanooga. As the armies maneuvered, the Federals faced east, moving northward by the left flank, trying to regain a secure connection to Chattanooga, which lay due north of them. The Confederates faced west. Between the two armies was Chickamauga Creek, crossable at a number of bridges and fords. Bragg hoped to cross the Chickamauga north of Rosecrans, turn his left flank, and cut him off from Chattanooga. On September 18 Bragg sent his army across the creek at several points. Union cavalry delayed the advance throughout the day, and Rosecrans sent Maj. Gen. George Thomas's XIV Corps northward on a night march to block Bragg's flanking maneuver. The next morning, when Bragg resumed his advance, he immediately clashed with Thomas, and the engagement quickly became general.

What followed was a two-day battle (September 19–20) in the valley of Chickamauga Creek. Most of the fighting was poorly coordinated, with assaults hampered by the woods, and the battle was shaping up as a stalemate, until near the middle of the

ROSECRANS'S ADVANCE TO ▶
CHATTANOOGA
Over late summer 1863, Rosecrans methodically drove Bragg toward Chattanooga. Though he had maneuvered Bragg to fall back on and then surrender the city, northern leadership chided him for the slowness of his advance.

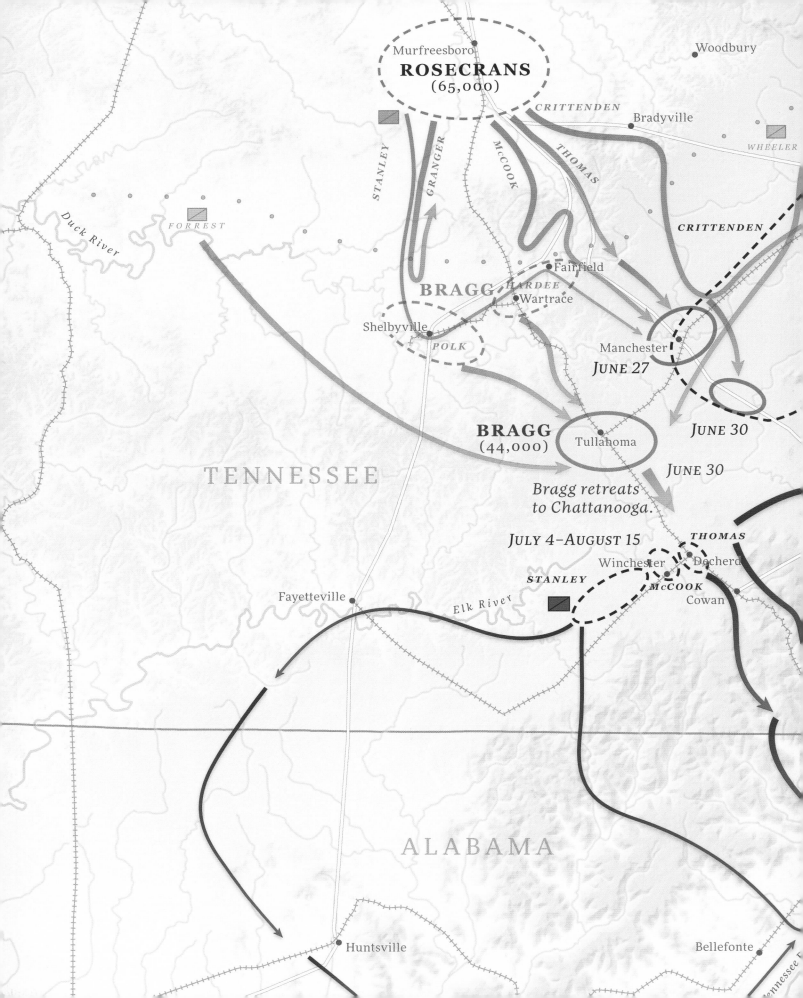

Woodbury

Murfreesboro
ROSECRANS
(65,000)

CRITTENDEN

Bradyville

STANLEY

GRANGER

McCOOK

THOMAS

WHEELER

CRITTENDEN

FORREST

Duck River

Fairfield

BRAGG

HARDEE
Wartrace

Shelbyville

POLK

Manchester

JUNE 27

JUNE 30

BRAGG
(44,000)   Tullahoma

JUNE 30

JUNE 30

Bragg retreats
to Chattanooga.

JULY 4–AUGUST 15

THOMAS

Winchester   Decherd

STANLEY

McCOOK
Cowan

TENNESSEE

Fayetteville

Elk River

ALABAMA

Huntsville

Bellefonte

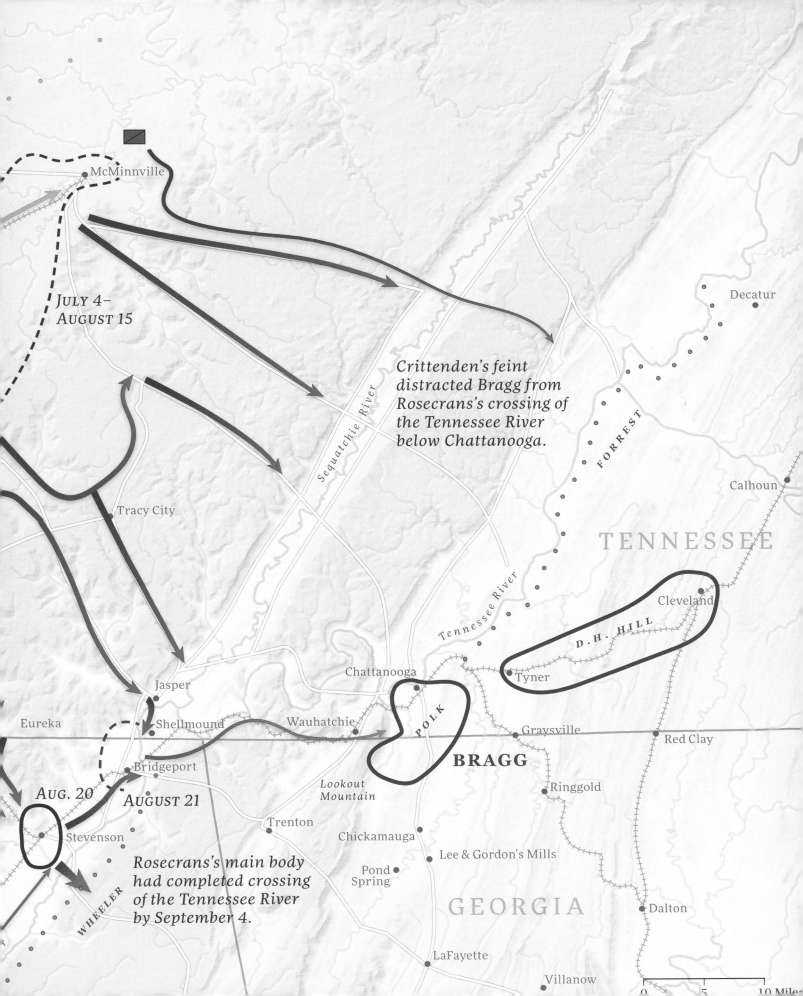

McMinnville

**JULY 4–
AUGUST 15**

Tracy City

Jasper

Eureka

Shellmound

Bridgeport

AUG. 20

AUGUST 21

Stevenson

*Rosecrans's main body
had completed crossing
of the Tennessee River
by September 4.*

Decatur

Sequatchie River

*Crittenden's feint
distracted Bragg from
Rosecrans's crossing of
the Tennessee River
below Chattanooga.*

FORREST

Calhoun

TENNESSEE

Cleveland

D. H. HILL

Tyner

Tennessee River

Chattanooga

Wauhatchie

POLK

Graysville

Red Clay

BRAGG

Lookout
Mountain

Ringgold

Trenton

Chickamauga

Lee & Gordon's Mills

Pond
Spring

GEORGIA

Dalton

WHEELER

LaFayette

Villanow

0   5   10 Miles

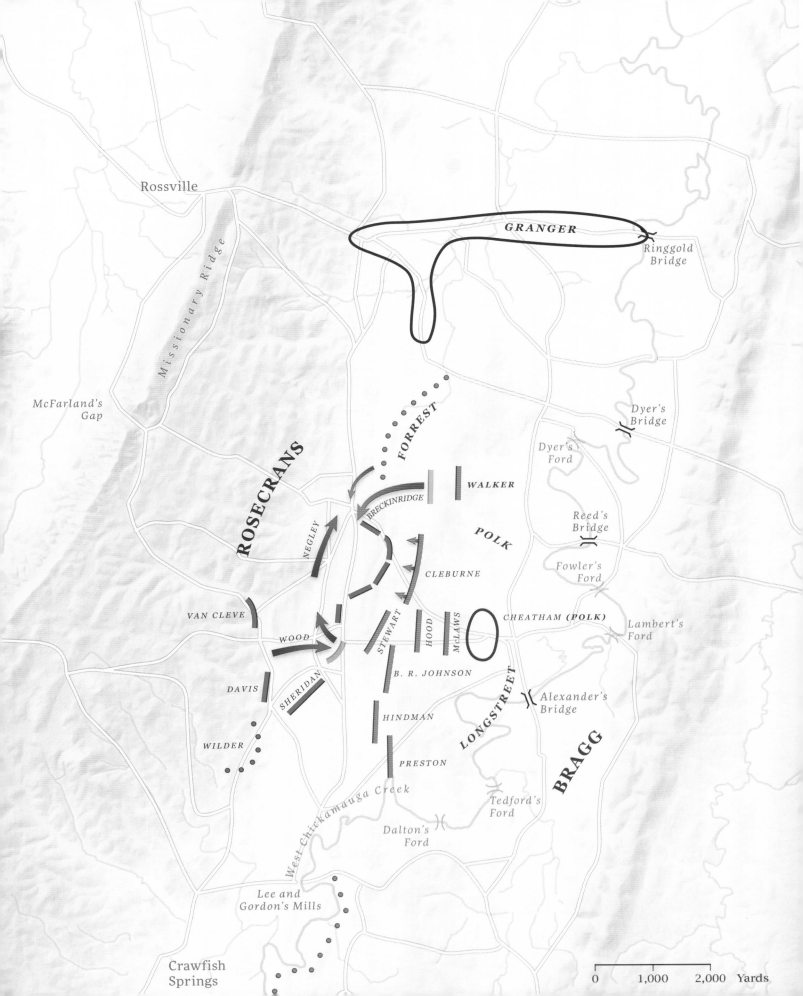

Rossville

Missionary Ridge

McFarland's
Gap

GRANGER

Ringgold
Bridge

Dyer's
Bridge

Dyer's
Ford

FORREST

ROSECRANS

Negley

WALKER

Breckinridge

POLK

Reed's
Bridge

CLEBURNE

Fowler's
Ford

VAN CLEVE

WOOD

STEWART

HOOD

McLAWS

CHEATHAM (POLK)

Lambert's
Ford

DAVIS

SHERIDAN

B. R. JOHNSON

LONGSTREET

Alexander's
Bridge

WILDER

HINDMAN

PRESTON

BRAGG

West Chickamauga Creek

Tedford's
Ford

Dalton's
Ford

Lee and
Gordon's Mills

Crawfish
Springs

0   1,000   2,000   Yards

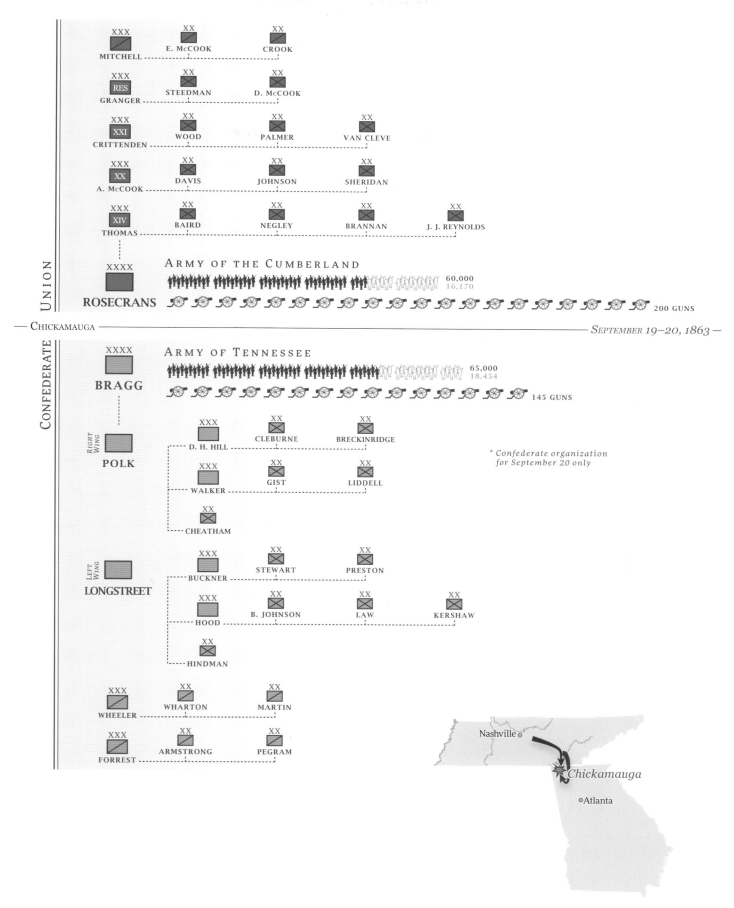

UNION

XXX MITCHELL	XX E. McCOOK	XX CROOK
XXX RES GRANGER	XX STEEDMAN	XX D. McCOOK
XXX XXI CRITTENDEN	XX WOOD	XX PALMER	XX VAN CLEVE
XXX XX A. McCOOK	XX DAVIS	XX JOHNSON	XX SHERIDAN
XXX XIV THOMAS	XX BAIRD	XX NEGLEY	XX BRANNAN	XX J. J. REYNOLDS

XXXX ROSECRANS — ARMY OF THE CUMBERLAND

60,000
16,170

200 GUNS

— CHICKAMAUGA —

SEPTEMBER 19–20, 1863

CONFEDERATE

XXXX BRAGG — ARMY OF TENNESSEE

65,000
18,454

145 GUNS

RIGHT WING XXX POLK

XXX D. H. HILL	XX CLEBURNE	XX BRECKINRIDGE
XXX WALKER	XX GIST	XX LIDDELL
XX CHEATHAM		

* *Confederate organization for September 20 only*

LEFT WING XXXX LONGSTREET

XXX BUCKNER	XX STEWART	XX PRESTON
XXX HOOD	XX B. JOHNSON	XX LAW	XX KERSHAW
XX HINDMAN		

XXX WHEELER	XX WHARTON	XX MARTIN
XXX FORREST	XX ARMSTRONG	XX PEGRAM

Nashville ○

★ *Chickamauga*

○ Atlanta

◀ **BATTLE OF CHICKAMAUGA**

After indecisive fighting on September 19, Bragg struck hard against the Union left early on September 20. Although the initial Confederate attacks were repulsed, Rosecrans had to shift troops from his right wing to sustain his defense.

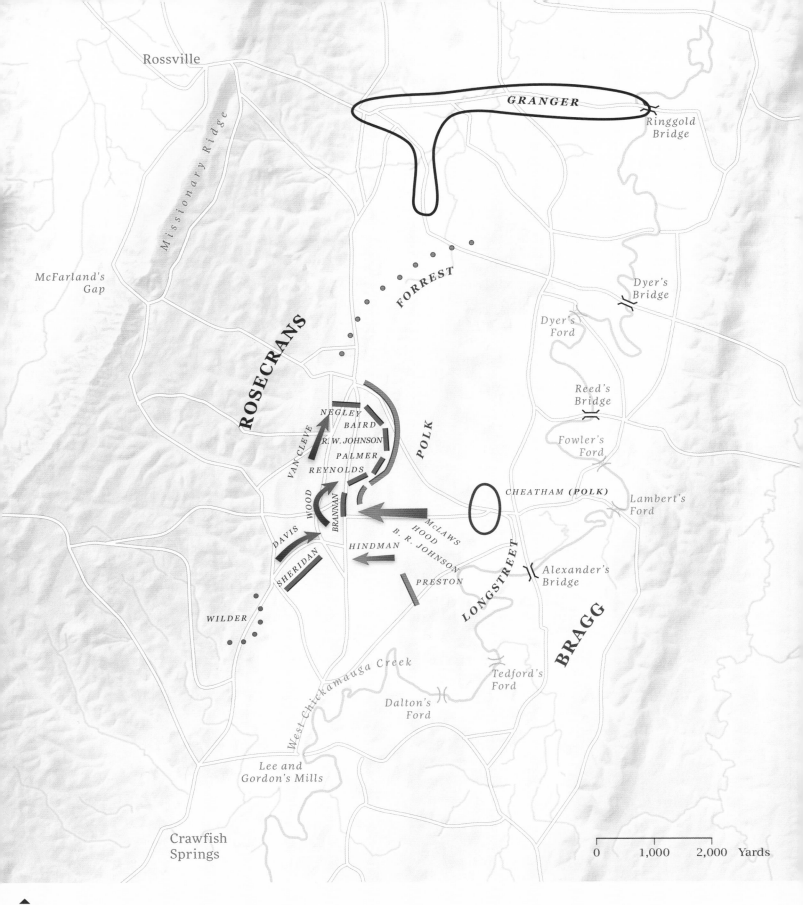

Rossville

Missionary Ridge

McFarland's
Gap

GRANGER

Ringgold
Bridge

FORREST

Dyer's
Bridge

ROSECRANS

Dyer's
Ford

Reed's
Bridge

NEGLEY
BAIRD
R. W. JOHNSON
PALMER
REYNOLDS

POLK

Fowler's
Ford

VAN CLEVE

CHEATHAM (POLK)

Lambert's
Ford

WOOD

BRANNAN

McLAWS
HOOD

DAVIS

HINDMAN

B. R. JOHNSON

Alexander's
Bridge

SHERIDAN

PRESTON

LONGSTREET

BRAGG

WILDER

West Chickamauga Creek

Tedford's
Ford

Dalton's
Ford

Lee and
Gordon's Mills

Crawfish
Springs

0   1,000   2,000   Yards

▲

Battle of Chickamauga

A mistaken order by Rosecrans caused Wood to pull out of line in the middle of the day, just as Longstreet's divisions attacked at that very point.

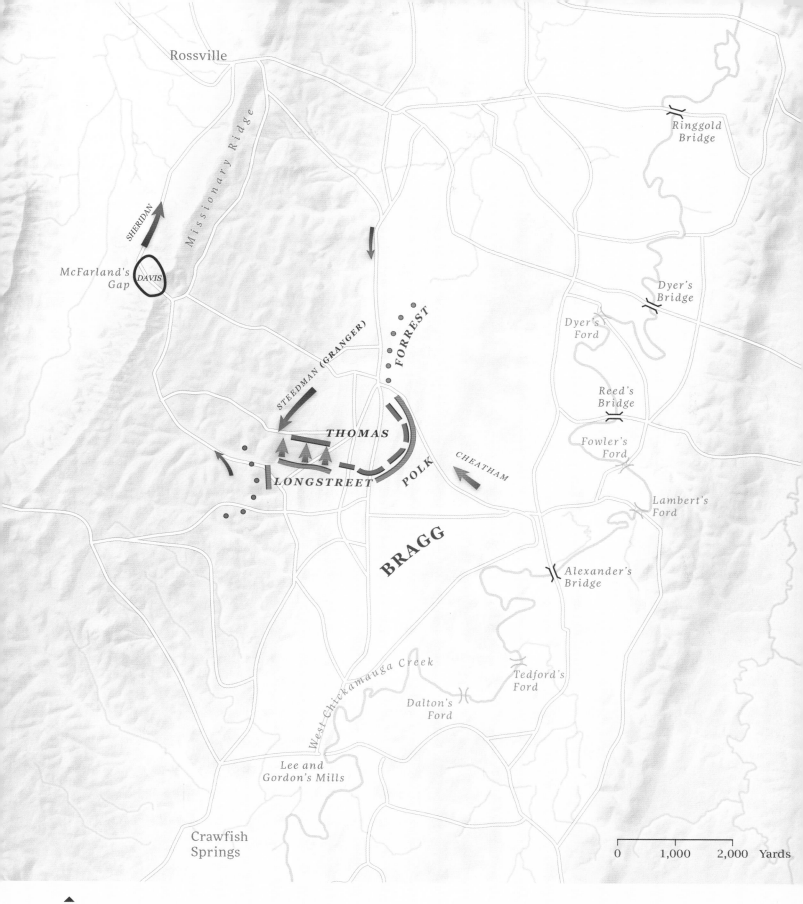

Rossville

Missionary Ridge

Ringgold
Bridge

SHERIDAN

McFarland's
Gap   DAVIS

Dyer's
Bridge

STEEDMAN (GRANGER)

FORREST

Dyer's
Ford

Reed's
Bridge

THOMAS

Fowler's
Ford

LONGSTREET   POLK   CHEATHAM

Lambert's
Ford

BRAGG

Alexander's
Bridge

West Chickamauga Creek

Tedford's
Ford

Dalton's
Ford

Lee and
Gordon's Mills

Crawfish
Springs

0   1,000   2,000   Yards

▲

BATTLE OF CHICKAMAUGA

Though the Union right and center collapsed and withdrew, the left held, again preventing the Confederates from trapping their foe away from Chattanooga. The desperate rearguard action directed by George Thomas protected the line of retreat and earned him the nickname "the Rock of Chickamauga."

CHICKAMAUGA

This sketch by Alfred Waud shows a Confederate line advancing through the trees toward Union troops during the battle of Chickamauga.

second day a nervous and rattled Rosecrans (now in his fourth major battle) ordered a division out of line, inadvertently creating a gap just as the weight of Bragg's attack fell on that sector. The entire southern half of the Army of the Cumberland was routed. Most of the troops rallied a few miles from the battlefield, but Rosecrans himself kept going all the way to Chattanooga. Thomas, commanding the left (northern) wing of the army, held on until nearly nightfall, earning the nickname "the Rock of Chicka-mauga." Only orders from Rosecrans, sent back to the battlefield from Chattanooga, compelled him to withdraw.

Though loud Rebel yells sounded when the two wings of Bragg's army met on the ground that Thomas had previously held, Confederate officers did not know until the following morning that Thomas had withdrawn from the field in good order and was ready to block any effort to pursue his retreating comrades. In any case, successful pursuit was unlikely. As it turned out, the Confederates had won the battle by crushing

CHATTANOOGA AND LOOKOUT MOUNTAIN ▶

Chattanooga was one of the larger cities in Tennessee, and an important railroad junction connecting with the Union army's supply base in Nashville. So long as the Confederates held their strong position on Lookout Mountain outside the city, however, it was very difficult to supply the Union troops inside the town.

Born in Southampton County, Virginia, Thomas graduated twelfth in the forty-two-man West Point class of 1840. Assigned to the 3rd Artillery Regiment, he served with distinction in the Mexican War. Promoted to major in 1855, Thomas was transferred to the newly organized 2nd (later redesignated 5th) U.S. Cavalry.

Remaining loyal at the outbreak of the Civil War, Thomas was assigned to command a division in Kentucky and in January 1862 won the small battle of Mill Springs. Two and a half months later, he led his division in action on the second day of the Battle of Shiloh. That fall, Lincoln offered him command of the Army of the Ohio in place of the plodding Don Carlos Buell, but Thomas refused. Thomas commanded a corps at Stones River, holding a key sector.

Thomas performed well in the Tullahoma and Chickamauga campaigns, in the latter making a stand that secured the retreat of the beaten Union army. Promoted to command the Army of the Cumberland, Thomas throughout most of 1864 exercised that command under William T. Sherman's direct supervision. Detached to deal with John B. Hood in Tennessee that fall, Thomas routed the outnumbered Hood at the Battle of Nashville. After the war, Thomas commanded occupation troops in several southern states and in 1869 was at his own request assigned to command the Military Division of the Pacific and died in San Francisco the following year.

GEORGE HENRY THOMAS

JULY 31, 1816–MARCH 28, 1870

▲

GRANT AT CHATTANOOGA
Ulysses Grant (pointing in the center) watches the assault up Missionary Ridge.

the right and center of the Union line. They had not, however, turned or defeated the all-important Union left, which guarded Rosecrans's line of retreat to Chattanooga. So the result of the Confederate victory was not to cut off the Federals from Chattanooga but to push them back toward it. All told, 18,000 Rebel and 16,000 Federal soldiers had fallen or been captured, in the war's second bloodiest battle.[71]

The Confederacy's only major victory in the western theater throughout the war, Chickamauga might have been entirely barren save for the effect it had on Rosecrans, who seemed to be near emotional collapse during the forty-eight hours or so immediately after the battle. He ordered his army to pull back from positions holding the high ground that commanded the approaches to Chattanooga, enabling the Rebels to seize that high ground and all but cut off his supplies. Confederates holding Lookout Mountain controlled the Tennessee River Gorge downstream from Chattanooga, with the town's only practical road, river, and rail links to Nashville. Confederates on Missionary Ridge controlled the rail link to Knoxville. All that remained in Union hands was a difficult wagon road through the mountains north of town, where supplies trickled into Chattanooga. Rosecrans's soldiers went on short rations.[72]

GRANT'S CHATTANOOGA CAMPAIGN

In Washington, Lincoln was concerned, commenting later that Rosecrans was acting "confused and stunned, like a duck hit on the head."[73] Stanton determined to send two corps of the Army of the Potomac to Chattanooga by rail, a strategic use of

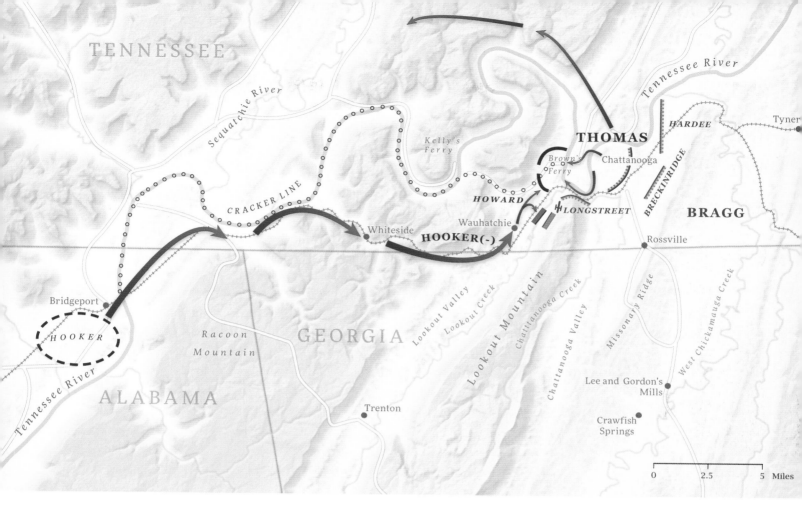

rail transport surpassing that by the Confederates before Chickamauga. Stanton and Lincoln also decided to send a new commander, Grant, who was put in charge of all Union forces west of the Appalachians. The orders specifically gave Grant the option of keeping Rosecrans as commander of the Army of the Cumberland or replacing him with Thomas. Grant chose the latter.[74]

Reaching Chattanooga on October 23, Grant immediately implemented a plan that Rosecrans's staff had worked out for taking key ground west of Lookout Mountain and opening a supply line through the Tennessee River Gorge. The plan succeeded, and the new supply line, dubbed the "Cracker Line" by the soldiers in honor of the hardtack that would traverse it, was soon in full operation.[75]

Grant then made his plans to defeat Bragg. He ordered Sherman, now commanding the Army of the Tennessee, to join him at Chattanooga with four divisions of his Vicksburg veterans. When Sherman arrived, Grant assigned him to cross the Tennessee River northeast of town and attack the right flank of the Confederate position on Missionary Ridge, rolling it up. Thomas's Army of the Cumberland would threaten Missionary Ridge from the front and join the attack when the time was right. A contingent composed of one division each from the Army of the Potomac, the Army of the Tennessee, and the Army of the Cumberland—all under the command of Maj. Gen. Joseph Hooker—would divert Rebel attention by advancing from the west to attack the Confederate positions on the lower slopes of Lookout Mountain.

OPENING THE CRACKER LINE

Rebel control of the railroad and river approaches to Chattanooga left the Union forces there on short rations. Grant's first priority after taking command was to reopen the supply lines. He executed a plan developed by Rosecrans to cross the Tennessee River and seize the area west of Lookout Mountain. Once Hooker accomplished that mission, supplies (including hardtack or "cracker") could flow into the city along the so-called Cracker Line.

MISSIONARY RIDGE

Seen in the distant background, with the town of Chattanooga in the foreground, Missionary Ridge seems to pose a daunting challenge to any direct attack. In fact, however, it proved more difficult for the Confederates to defend the length of the ridge against a frontal attack than to block Sherman's advance along its narrow top.

CONFEDERATE PRISONERS AT CHATTANOOGA

The successful assault up Missionary Ridge netted about 5,000 Confederate prisoners, who were then shipped north to be held in prison camps until traded, or, more likely, until the war ended.

On November 24 Grant launched his offensive, scoring quick initial successes. Hooker's force drove the Rebels from the slopes of Lookout Mountain with surprising ease. While Bragg's attention was thus drawn to his left, Sherman's crossing of the Tennessee went off without a hitch, and by the last light of a short autumn afternoon he took up a position at the north end of Missionary Ridge, squarely athwart Bragg's right.[76]

The next morning Sherman launched his attack to roll up the Confederate line but quickly ran into trouble. Missionary Ridge looked simple from a distance but was actually a complicated series of humps and saddles. Counterintuitively, the ridge was most defensible against a force attempting to advance along its narrow crest, as Sherman's men tried and failed to do throughout most of the day. Inspired defense by Confederate division commander Maj. Gen. Patrick R. Cleburne, who held the flank and dug in his command on a hump of the ridge, also played a major role in Sherman's lack of progress.[77]

From his headquarters atop a small hill in the middle of the plain between

Chattanooga and the ridge, Grant watched Sherman's repulse. Assuming that Bragg must have reinforced Cleburne to achieve that result (though in fact Cleburne neither needed nor could have used more troops within the narrow confines of the ridgetop), Grant decided it was time for Thomas to implement the next part of the overall plan by placing pressure on the central sector of Missionary Ridge. The first step would be for four divisions of the Army of the Cumberland to advance across the plain and capture a line of rifle pits (actually, continuous trenches) the Confederates held near the base of the ridge. Thomas seemed unenthusiastic, but after some delay sent his soldiers forward.[78]

Missionary Ridge was not as strong a position as it appeared. The Confederate defensive arrangements were defective, with troops divided between the line of rifle pits at the base of the ridge and a main line of resistance on the crest, too far back to offer effective support. In addition, some of the Confederate defenders had ambiguous orders whether they were to make a determined stand at the rifle pits or fall back quickly to the crest. Those factors, along with a heavy Union advantage in numbers, made the rifle pits an easy conquest for Thomas's men.

As the Rebel defenders fled up the slope and Thomas's Federals took possession of the trenches at the foot of the ridge, the situation became more complicated than anyone had anticipated. The rifle pits were exposed to heavy Confederate fire from the crest, and it soon became apparent that the bluecoats could not stay there. They would have to go forward or back. On top of that, at least two of Thomas's four division commanders had received no orders regarding where their advance should stop. While they hastily sent to the rear for clarification, brigade commanders all along the line began ordering their troops up the ridge on their own responsibility.

The blue line swayed and became uneven as some men climbed faster than others.

▼
THE OLD BULLDOG ON THE RIGHT TRACK

After Grant's successes in the West, Lincoln promoted him to overall command of Union armies. This cartoon, from the 1864 presidential election, contrasts Grant—the "bull dog" who would tenaciously attack the Confederates (at a doghouse labeled "Richmond")—with the cautious George McClellan, Lincoln's electoral opponent.

Watching the Federals scrambling up the long, steep slope, Grant turned to Thomas to ask who had ordered the advance beyond the rifle pits. Thomas replied that he did not know, and Grant muttered that someone would pay if they were repelled.

But they were not. The steep slopes of Missionary Ridge proved a weaker defensive position than its narrow crest. Their steepness provided abundant defilade, especially because the Confederate line lay on the topographical rather than the military crest of the ridge: in other words, the highest line and not the one providing the best fields of fire against attackers.[79] Spurs projecting down the slope gave additional cover in the folds between them. Confederates fleeing from the rifle pits further obstructed the defenders' fire. Thomas's soldiers were bent on showing that despite Chickamauga, they were as capable as soldiers as Sherman's men. Almost simultaneously they broke the Confederate line at several places, and it began to disintegrate. Bragg vainly attempted to rally his troops, but resistance quickly collapsed. At almost the same time, Hooker, who had spent the day marching from Lookout Mountain, got astride Missionary Ridge, flanking Bragg's line on the south. His arrival was just in time to greatly increase the Union haul of prisoners, some 5,000 in all.

Cleburne's division maintained its cohesion and performed well covering the Confederate retreat, soon aided by the onset of darkness. Bragg's line of retreat led to his right-rear. Since it was his center and left that had broken, the Federals had no real chance of trapping him, and he was able to make good his army's escape, though it lost many cannon. The following day, Union troops under Hooker's command caught up with the rear of Bragg's army, but here Cleburne and his division turned in another superlative performance in rear-guard duty, securing the Army of Tennessee's escape.[80]

CONCLUSION

The Chattanooga campaign ended the middle portion of the Civil War in the West. Never again would the Confederacy launch a serious attempt to recover the territory and resources it had lost in the first massive debacles triggered by the fall of Forts Henry and Donelson nineteen months before.

The outcome was largely due to Grant's unrelenting determination and operational skill at Vicksburg—the first time in the war an entire army was eliminated—and his application of superior resources and logistical capability to rescue Rosecrans's nearly besieged forces after the unexpected setback at Chickamauga. Thanks to these victories, Union forces were now poised to advance into the Deep South state of Georgia, toward the industrial complex that had developed around Atlanta. Along the border of Mississippi, the Mississippi River, the Father of Waters, flowed again, in Lincoln's phrase, "unvexed to the sea."[81] Perhaps most important, the Union's winning team of generals had finally emerged. Sherman, Thomas, and Philip Sheridan were all present at Chattanooga. Their performances in that final battle of 1863 distinguished them as the leaders Lincoln had been seeking since the war began. The president now knew who would be the chief military architect of final Union victory. "Grant is my man," he said, "and I am his for the rest of the war."[82]

Introduction

Ulysses S. Grant took charge of the Union war effort as general in chief with a determination to destroy the Confederacy as quickly as possible. He achieved a remarkable degree of coordination in Federal strategy, pursued a policy of continuous operations, and authorized the implementation of "hard war" policies (as historians have come to call them): deliberate destruction of southern war resources. In all of these efforts, he was most ably supported by William T. Sherman, commander of Union forces in the West. Rebel armies in both the East and the West largely remained on the defensive to slow this mighty effort, hoping that the presidential election in the fall of 1864 might place a man less resolute than Abraham Lincoln in the White House. Despite delays, some battlefield defeats, and incredibly heavy losses, Union forces brought down the Confederacy in less than one year after the start of the spring campaigns in 1864.

Resources and Strategy

When Ulysses S. Grant was promoted to lieutenant general and assumed command of all United States forces on March 9, 1864, he took on a task more complex than any previous American commander had faced.[1] Over the past three years, both belligerents had mobilized nearly all the manpower and material possible to prosecute the war. The major field armies were arguably at the peak of their strength and experience. Yet both sides faced the possibility that their war efforts could unravel in the next few months. In the Union and the Confederacy alike, manpower procurement efforts had largely taken in the available volunteers. During the last year of the war, both sides were plagued by draft evasion, bounty jumpers, and poorly motivated conscripts.[2]

The Federals were in better shape than their opponents. Grant controlled more military power than any previous commander in American history. Remarkably, most of the Union soldiers whose initial term of enlistment was expiring in 1864 opted to reenlist, and nearly 180,000 blacks would join the Federal army by war's end. But the Union war effort was expensive. The nation spent on average $1.24 million every day to sustain it: almost six times the level of prewar Federal expenditures. Many observers wondered how much longer the government could afford the war. Grant understood that speed was of greater consequence than it had been earlier in the conflict.[3]

Moreover, Grant knew that the Union war effort in the East had lagged behind that in the West. The U.S. troops serving in the West were disappointed that their counterparts seemed to make little headway against Robert E. Lee's Army of Northern Virginia, even failing to prevent the transfer of two divisions that had enabled the Rebels to gain the strategic initiative for a short period during and after Chickamauga.[4]

"From an early period in the rebellion," Grant later wrote in his official report as general in chief, "I had been impressed with the idea that active and continuous operations of all the troops that could be brought into the field, regardless of season and

5

Coordinated Strategy and Hard War

Earl J. Hess

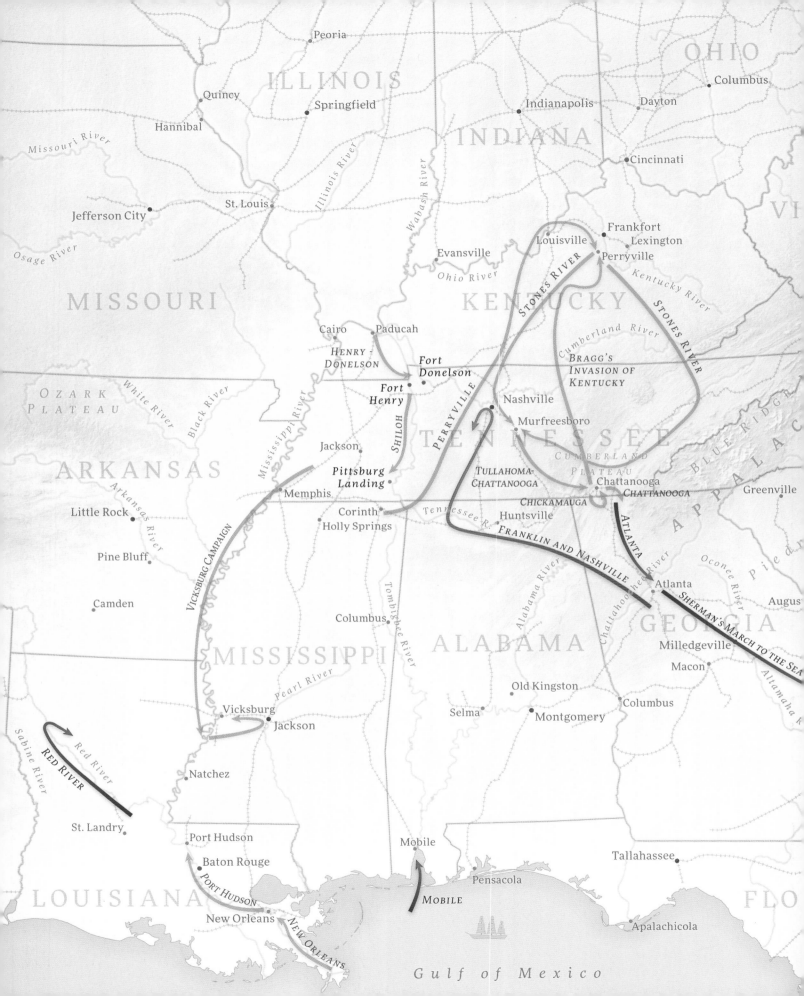

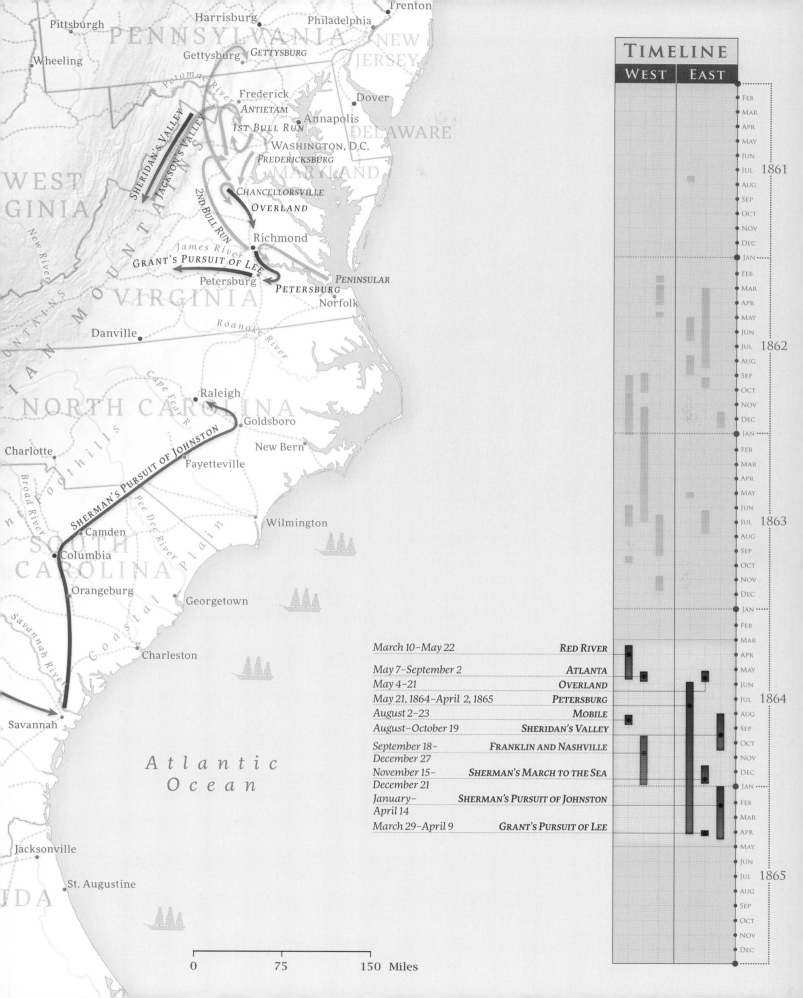

Pittsburgh
Harrisburg
Philadelphia
Trenton
Wheeling
PENNSYLVANIA
NEW JERSEY
Gettysburg *Gettysburg*
Frederick
Dover
ANTIETAM
1ST BULL RUN
Annapolis
DELAWARE
WASHINGTON, D.C.
FREDERICKSBURG
MARYLAND
CHANCELLORSVILLE
OVERLAND
WEST VIRGINIA
SHERIDAN'S VALLEY
JACKSON'S VALLEY
2ND BULL RUN
New River
James River
Richmond
GRANT'S PURSUIT OF LEE
PENINSULAR
Petersburg
PETERSBURG
Danville
VIRGINIA
Norfolk
Roanoke River
Cape Fear R.
Raleigh
NORTH CAROLINA
Goldsboro
SHERMAN'S PURSUIT OF JOHNSTON
New Bern
Charlotte
Foothills
Fayetteville
Broad River
Pee Dee River Plain
Camden
SOUTH CAROLINA
Columbia
Wilmington
Orangeburg
Georgetown
Coastal Plain
Savannah River
Charleston
Atlantic Ocean
Savannah
Jacksonville
St. Augustine
FLORIDA
Potomac River

TIMELINE

WEST	EAST

FEB
MAR
APR
MAY
JUN
JUL 1861
AUG
SEP
OCT
NOV
DEC
JAN
FEB
MAR
APR
MAY
JUN
JUL 1862
AUG
SEP
OCT
NOV
DEC
JAN
FEB
MAR
APR
MAY
JUN
JUL 1863
AUG
SEP
OCT
NOV
DEC
JAN
FEB
MAR
APR
MAY
JUN
JUL 1864
AUG
SEP
OCT
NOV
DEC
JAN
FEB
MAR
APR
MAY
JUN
JUL 1865
AUG
SEP
OCT
NOV
DEC

March 10–May 22	**RED RIVER**
May 7–September 2	**ATLANTA**
May 4–21	**OVERLAND**
May 21, 1864–April 2, 1865	**PETERSBURG**
August 2–23	**MOBILE**
August–October 19	**SHERIDAN'S VALLEY**
September 18–December 27	**FRANKLIN AND NASHVILLE**
November 15–December 21	**SHERMAN'S MARCH TO THE SEA**
January–April 14	**SHERMAN'S PURSUIT OF JOHNSTON**
March 29–April 9	**GRANT'S PURSUIT OF LEE**

0   75   150 Miles

THE PEACEMAKERS

Lincoln met with Sherman, Grant, and Porter on board the *River Queen* during the abortive Hampton Roads peace negotiations in March 1865. By then, the strategy of simultaneous offensives adopted by Grant in 1864 had nearly completed the defeat of the Confederacy.

weather, were necessary to a speedy termination of the war. The armies in the East and West acted independently and without concert, like a balky team," Grant continued, "no two ever pulling together, enabling the enemy to use to great advantage his interior lines of communication for transporting troops from east to west, re-enforcing the army most vigorously pressed."[5] After three years of having made the same point to general after general, Lincoln strongly supported Grant's efforts to coordinate Federal operations across the continent. As the president told Grant, "Those not skinning can hold a leg."[6]

A desire to accelerate the pace of the war and the need to prevent Confederate commanders from helping each other drove Grant's strategic thinking. He could achieve these goals only by exerting personal influence. Grant therefore made his headquarters with George Meade's Army of the Potomac (about 120,000 strong) to give direction and energy where it was most needed, against Lee's army (about 65,000 men). Grant knew he could keep in touch with other field forces by telegraph. More importantly, he could count on Sherman to command the Military Division of the Mississippi and lead an army group of 100,000 troops (consisting of the Armies of the Cumberland, the Tennessee, and the Ohio) against Joseph E. Johnston's Army of Tennessee in Georgia.

Part of the 114th Pennsylvania, some of the over 120,000 men Grant directed and Meade commanded in the Army of the Potomac at the start of the 1864 Overland campaign.

Grant's relationship with other Union commanders was uncertain, and his influence over their movements less effective. As long as Grant and Sherman coordinated their efforts, the Federals could deal with the main Confederate armies effectively.[7]

Rebel prospects of achieving independence had waned a great deal since the start of the war, but ultimate success was by no means out of the question. Jefferson Davis had no general in chief; he himself essentially filled that role. The Army of Northern Virginia and the Army of Tennessee each had about 65,000 men and was arguably at the peak of efficiency, but in the larger strategic context, the Confederacy had suffered a great deal in the past three years. The Union naval blockade of the Rebel coast was increasingly effective, cutting off the Confederacy from needed imports of war materiel and medical supplies and limiting exports that might have earned foreign currency and reduced inflation.[8] The loss of the Mississippi Valley and most of the Upper South had denied the Richmond government an important source of food (especially protein), draft animals, and manpower. Inflation hit southern consumers very hard. By the spring of 1864, it took $46 in Confederate currency to buy what had cost $1 in 1861. By the spring of 1865, consumer prices were ninety-two times higher than they had been before the war.[9]

By early 1864, the Confederacy was at a pivotal point. It had lost a lot of ground in the West but had held its own in the East. Most importantly, Rebel armies still enjoyed high morale. If Davis's best chance to win the war lay in draining the North's will to fight, that strategy also demanded staying power from the Confederates. It was a question as to which side would collapse first if the war continued without decisive results. The Rebels no longer had the manpower or resources to attempt an offensive strategy. They were dependent on a defensive policy that might exhaust them before it did their enemy. Their only true hope lay in the possibility that Lincoln might lose the presidential election in November 1864, and a less resolute chief executive might replace him.[10]

The U.S. government mobilized manpower more effectively than did the C.S. government. The full effect of enlisting black men as soldiers, for example, was felt in the

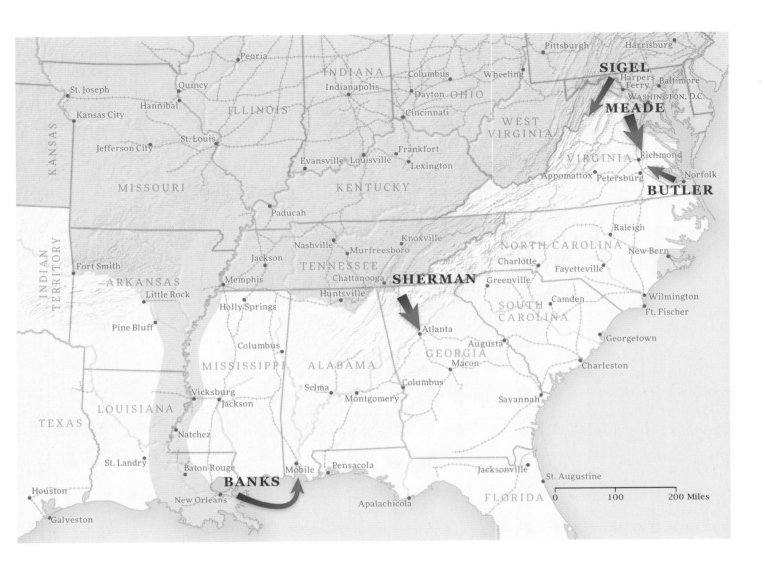

Grant's Plan

The two main pushes would be made by Meade's Army of the Potomac toward Richmond, and Sherman's three armies (the Army of the Tennessee, the Army of the Ohio, and the Army of the Cumberland) toward Atlanta. Both forces were ordered to target the Confederate armies in their way as higher priorities than geographic objectives. Meanwhile, smaller forces under Banks (moving against Mobile), Sigel (in the Shenandoah), and Benjamin Butler (approaching Richmond from the south) would tie down other Confederate forces. In the event, Banks instead moved up the Red River.

last year of the war. In the West, black soldiers were mostly used to garrison towns and other significant points, especially along the Mississippi River, but they rarely saw combat. In the East, a division of U.S. Colored Troops (USCT) served in the Army of the Potomac while more than a division served in the Army of the James. After participating in several Petersburg offensives, these USCT regiments were consolidated into the all-black Twenty-Fifth Corps of the Army of the James. Rebel troops sometimes killed unarmed blacks after they surrendered, as at Fort Pillow in Tennessee and in the Battle of the Crater at Petersburg, but this failed to deter black men in blue from contributing significantly to defeat the Confederacy.[11]

The breakdown of the prisoner exchange system also worked to limit Rebel manpower. In accordance with common military practice of the time, the Union and Confederate armies had agreed in 1862 on a system whereby prisoners of war were promptly released on parole and returned to their own side. If the numbers were equal, the prisoners were considered exchanged and could return to service. But if the Union captured and released a thousand more prisoners than the Confederacy did, then a thousand Confederates would remain "on parole," forbidden to perform any military

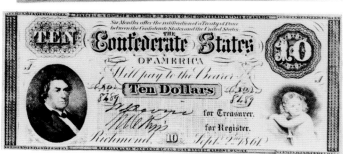

service until an equivalent number of Union soldiers was taken prisoner and paroled. The system worked but was dependent on mutual trust and full disclosure. When the Confederates lost 35,000 prisoners at the surrender of Vicksburg and Port Hudson, they were so desperate to recover their losses that they cut corners and arbitrarily declared the parolees exchanged without the full cooperation of Federal authorities. Many of those parolees then fought at Chattanooga.

In April 1864, with a new offensive about to begin, Grant ordered that all prisoner exchanges cease until the Confederacy recognized the validity of the Vicksburg and Port Hudson paroles. The system also broke down because of Confederate refusal to exchange captured African Americans, insisting that they should be returned to their former masters or used as laborers for Confederate military purposes. The result of Confederate racism and duplicity was overcrowding and suffering in both Union and Rebel prison camps. At Andersonville, Georgia, disease aggravated by supply shortages and a commander later executed by the U.S. government as what we would today call a war criminal, led to the death of 13,000 of 45,000 Federal prisoners. Nevertheless, in an effort to deny the Richmond government much-needed manpower, Grant refused to resume general exchanges that August. By the end of the war, 30,218 out of 194,743 prisoners held by the Confederacy, and 25,976 out of 214,865 Confederates held in Union prisons, had died in enemy hands.[12]

CONFEDERATE PAPER CURRENCY

The increasing effectiveness of the Union blockade in preventing foreign trade and coastal shipping, and the continued printing of money to compensate for the Confederate government's limited revenues from taxes and bond sales, contributed to massive inflation throughout the South. Annual inflation ran at 295 percent in 1862, 268 percent in 1863, and (reduced by currency reform) at merely 107 percent in 1864. The Union also printed enough "greenback" paper money to cause some inflation, but the problem was not nearly as serious in the North.

GRANT MOVES SOUTH: OPERATIONS IN VIRGINIA

Grant set the Army of the Potomac into motion against Lee on May 4, while Sherman initiated his move toward Atlanta at about the same time. Two supporting campaigns also began in the Virginia theater. Benjamin Butler's Army of the James, consisting of troops drawn from coastal enclaves in the Carolinas and Florida, was transported to Norfolk in southeast Virginia, a hundred miles from Richmond. Grant hoped that Butler's army could strike quickly at Richmond or Petersburg, the latter a railroad town twenty-five miles south of the capital that was crucial for Lee's logistical support. Butler disappointed these expectations. A political general with scant field experience, he failed to seize Petersburg when it was sparsely defended and then allowed the outnumbered enemy to drive him back from his position between the two cities on May 16. The Confederates easily neutralized the 30,000 men under Butler's inept command in an area known as Bermuda Hundred.[13]

◀ **CONFEDERATE PRISONERS WITH FREEDMAN**

The prisoner exchange system had broken down during the war, and the Union held on to a large number of Confederate prisoners. Here an African American offers food to hungry prisoners—especially interesting given that the arming of black troops contributed significantly to the end of the prisoner exchanges.

VIRGINIA MILITARY INSTITUTE CADETS IN ACTION AT NEW MARKET

At the Battle of New Market, May 15, 1864, Confederate general John C. Breckinridge supplemented his force with 257 cadets from the Virginia Military Institute. John Sergeant Wise, a VMI cadet and later a Virginia congressman, recorded his experiences during the battle, during which he was knocked unconscious by a shell, in his autobiographical memoir of the war.

"At-ten-*tion-n-n!* Battalion forward! Guide center-r-r!" shouted Shipp, and up the slope we started. From the left of the line, Sergeant-Major Woodbridge ran out and posted himself forty paces in advance of the colors as directing guide, as if we had been upon the drill ground. That boy

would have remained there, had not Shipp ordered him back to his post; for this was no dress parade. Brave Evans, standing six feet two, shook out the colors that for days had hung limp and bedraggled about the staff, and every cadet leaped forward, dressing to the ensign, elate and thrilling with the consciousness that this was war. . . .

Then came a sound more stunning than thunder. It burst directly in my face: lightnings leaped, fire flashed, the earth rocked, the sky whirled round. I stumbled, my gun pitched forward, and I fell upon my knees. Sergeant Cabell looked back at me pityingly and called out, "Close up, men!" as he passed on. I knew no more.[15]

Another column of Federal troops under Franz Sigel advanced up the Shenandoah Valley. That rich breadbasket of Virginia was still a crucial source of food for the Confederacy. Sigel had more experience than Butler but little more ability. At New Market on May 15, a smaller Rebel force—including the 257-man Cadet Corps of the Virginia Military Institute—soundly defeated the Federals and compelled them to retreat down the valley.[14]

Success in Virginia thus rested firmly on Grant's shoulders, and he was keenly aware of the responsibility. Grant preferred sweeping maneuvers to put his forces in the best position for battle (as he had done at Vicksburg), but the constricted geographic theater in the East allowed him less room to maneuver than he had enjoyed in the West. Several of Grant's western victories had been enabled by cooperation with the navy, so when he was asked to develop a campaign plan before his appointment as general in chief, Grant proposed to move 60,000 men inland from the North Carolina coast against Lee's principal supply line, the Weldon and Petersburg Railroad. Lincoln rejected that proposal in favor of keeping the Army of the Potomac between Lee and Washington. Grant accepted political realities (an important reason why Lincoln chose him for the top command) and so he adopted a direct approach over land toward Richmond—the Overland campaign—which required the Federals to engage in prolonged combat, head to head against the Army of Northern Virginia.[16]

Grant expressed his plan for implementing the president's strategic directive in blunt terms. "Lee's Army will be your objective point," he told Meade. "Wherever Lee goes there you will go also."[17] From the banks of the Rapidan, he told Butler, "I shall

THE OVERLAND CAMPAIGN, MAY 3–26 ▶
Grant and Meade led the Army of the Potomac across the Rapidan River and, after fighting in the Wilderness, continued to press south by attempting to turn Lee and the Army of the Northern Virginia.

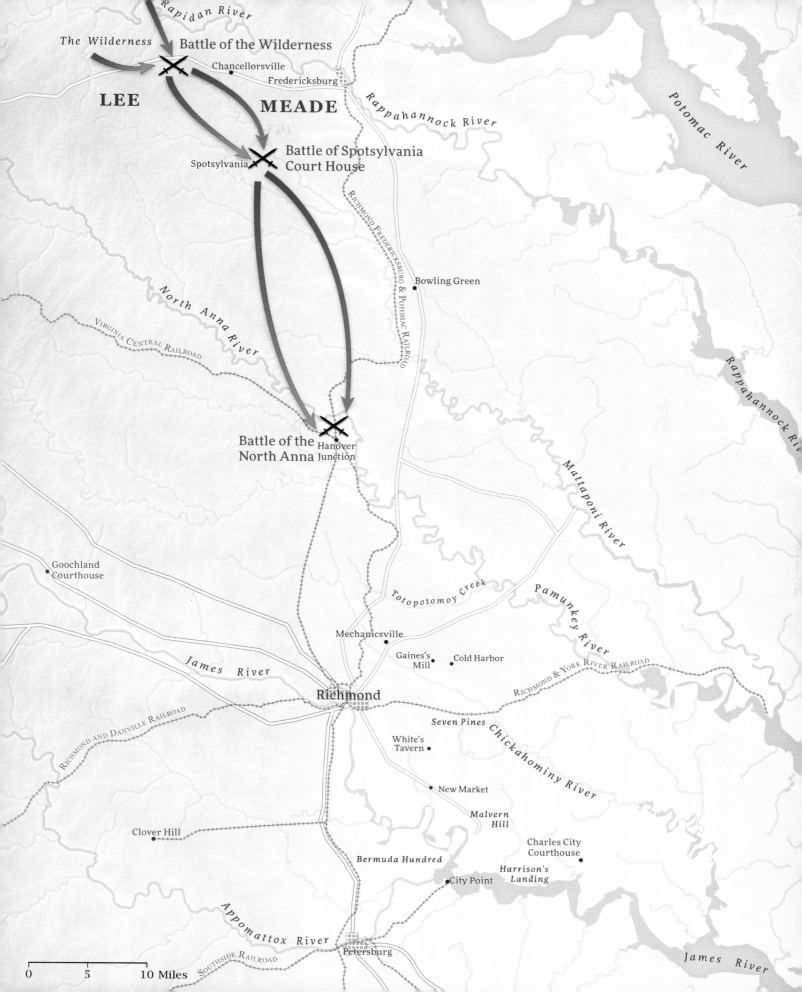

Rapidan River

The Wilderness   Battle of the Wilderness

Chancellorsville
Fredericksburg

LEE   **MEADE**

Rappahannock River

Spotsylvania   Battle of Spotsylvania
Court House

RICHMOND FREDERICKSBURG & POTOMAC RAILROAD

Bowling Green

North Anna River

VIRGINIA CENTRAL RAILROAD

Rappahannock R

Battle of the   Hanover
North Anna   Junction

Mattaponi River

Goochland
Courthouse

Totopotomoy Creek

Pamunkey River

Mechanicsville

Gaines's   Cold Harbor
Mill

RICHMOND & YORK RIVER RAILROAD

James River

Richmond

RICHMOND AND DANVILLE RAILROAD

Seven Pines   Chickahominy River

White's
Tavern

New Market

Malvern
Hill

Clover Hill

Charles City
Courthouse

Bermuda Hundred

Harrison's
Landing

City Point

Appomattox River

Petersburg

James River

SOUTHSIDE RAILROAD

0   5   10 Miles

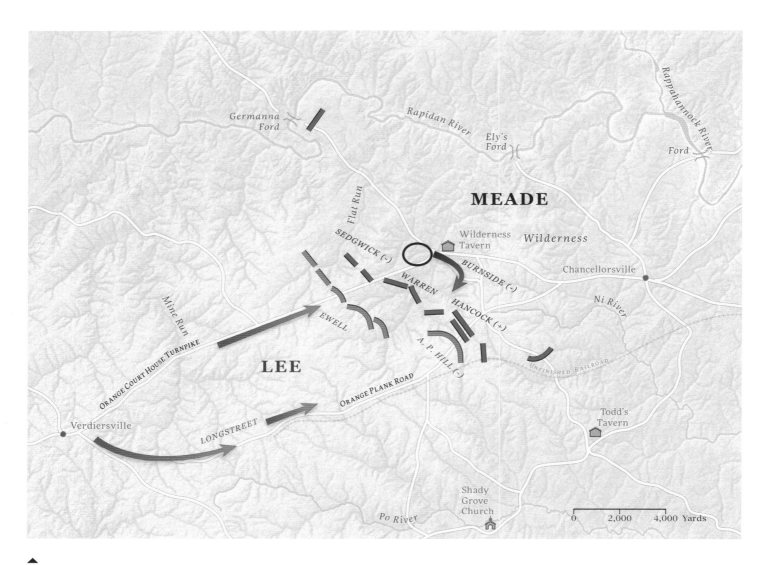

The Battle of The Wilderness

The first battle in the Overland campaign was a bloody fight in the tangled woods where the Battle of Chancellorsville had been fought the year before. More significant than the fight itself was Grant's reaction afterward, moving around Lee's flank to continue south instead of retreating, despite heavy losses.

aim to fight Lee between here and Richmond if he will stand. Should Lee however fall back into Richmond I will follow up and make a junction with your Army on the James River." Presumably a siege would follow, and U.S. resources would triumph.[18]

The first confrontation between the best Union commander and the best Confederate commander occurred on May 5 and 6, 1864, in the tangled vegetation of the Wilderness, where Hooker had been defeated a year earlier. Most of the Army of Northern Virginia was encamped to the west, in order to move between defending the Rapidan and threatening to advance down the Shenandoah Valley toward Maryland. The Army of the Potomac was able to cross the river easily, and Lee had to attack from the west to drive it back. In the ensuing Battle of the Wilderness, both sides traded blows, seeking each other's flanks with attacks and counterattacks that littered the forest floor with casualties. Grant lost nearly 18,000 men, while Lee lost about 11,000. After two days of bloodletting, neither side could claim a victory, but Grant refused to retreat. Instead, he sent the Army of the Potomac south to Spotsylvania Court House on May 8, bypassing Lee's right flank to the east.[19] The initial reaction of Union soldiers was very positive; they were ready for Grant's strategy of continuous operations and liked his combative spirit. "Instantly all of us heaved a sigh of relief," wrote an artilleryman upon learning that Grant was heading south instead of retreating.[20] A Union engineer soldier confessed, "I do not know that during the entire war I had such a real feeling of delight and satisfaction as in the night when we came to the road leading to Spotsylvania Court House and turned to the right."[21] Lee had no choice but to follow, but his intelligence gathering and intuition served him well. He anticipated the Federal move and used his interior lines to shift troops just in time to deny Grant possession of the crossroads at Spotsylvania.[22]

THE BATTLE OF SPOTSYLVANIA

The nature of military operations shifted dramatically at Spotsylvania. At the Wilderness, both sides attacked and counterattacked with only scant fieldworks to impede their movements, but at Spotsylvania, Lee, outnumbered two to one, chose to remain almost entirely on the defensive. The Confederates held their ground and inflicted a heavy toll on the constantly attacking Yankees.[23] But Grant's refusal to admit defeat and retire on May 8 demonstrated that a new attitude had taken hold among the Federals. The Army of Northern Virginia now contented itself with digging trenches and exacting a steep price in blood. On the tactical level, this was a sound decision, protecting Lee's outnumbered soldiers, but the Rebel general knew that conceding the operational initiative to an aggressive commander who had greater resources would doom his army. His only hope lay in the marginal chance that Grant would make a mistake that Lee could take advantage of to compel a retreat, as he had done with Hooker at Chancellorsville.

Indeed, Grant doubted the aggressiveness of some commanders in the Army of the Potomac and tended to be impatient throughout the Overland campaign, ordering

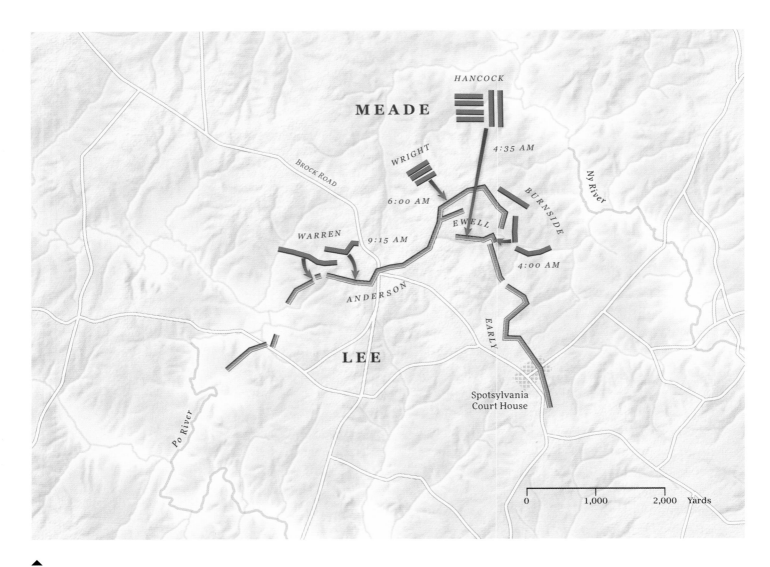

▲

THE BATTLE OF SPOTSYLVANIA COURT HOUSE

Lee had been able to entrench at Spotsylvania, and Grant again hurled his army at the Confederates. Early assaults broke into a bulge in Lee's lines, the so-called Mule Shoe, but could not hold the ground against Rebel counterattacks. The next day (not shown), a larger attack drove in the point of salient, but Lee was able to restore a new line across its base.

TRENCH FIGHTING AT SPOTSYLVANIA

The battles fought during the Overland campaign were a new kind of warfare for the combatants. Union Brig. Gen. Lewis A. Grant described the desperate fighting that took place along the line when he led an assault on the Mule Shoe, Lee's defensive salient, on May 12, 1864:

Nothing but the piled-up logs or breastworks separated the combatants. Our men would reach over the logs and fire into the faces of the enemy, would stab over with their bayonets; many were shot and stabbed through crevices and holes between the logs; men mounted the works, and with muskets rapidly handed them kept up a continuous fire until they were shot down, when others would take their places and continue the deadly work . . . It was there that the somewhat celebrated tree was cut off by bullets; there that the bushes and logs were cut to pieces and whipped into basket-stuff; there that fallen men's flesh was torn from the bones and the bones shattered; there that the rebel ditches and cross sections were filled with dead men several deep.[26]

attacks with scant intelligence about Lee's position or time for his subordinates to plan assaults. The relatively small-scale attacks that took place along the Spotsylvania line from May 8 to May 21 were punctuated by two large assaults against a pronounced bulge in Lee's entrenchments: the Mule Shoe salient. On May 10, Emory Upton—three years out of West Point and already commanding a brigade—organized an assault on the left shoulder of the bulge with 5,000 men of the VI Corps arrayed in four lines. While successive lines were a common formation in the Civil War, Upton worked out what each of those lines was supposed to do in far more detail than most officers. He nearly succeeded in cracking Lee's position but was stymied by two further lines of earthworks and effective Rebel countermoves. When his first line captured a section of the forward trench, the Confederates rushed artillery and reserves to contain the breach. Lacking further reinforcements and under concentrated artillery fire, Upton had to withdraw that night. Yet the results seemed promising to Grant, who ordered a larger attack on the apex of the bulge. Winfield Scott Hancock massed 20,000 troops of his II Corps on the night of May 11, forming them in a combination of columns and lines, before the massive assault rolled forward at the crack of dawn.[24]

The attack on May 12 initially achieved great success, crushing the point of the salient like an eggshell, capturing 3,000 Confederate prisoners and twenty-four guns. Lee's line was in imminent danger of collapse. But then the Union advance disintegrated as 20,000 Federals crowded into a small space, crippling their command and control. The resulting delay in following up the victory allowed Lee to shift several brigades to the salient and launch counterattacks that contained the Union breakthrough. For the rest of this rainy, muddy day, thousands of blue- and gray-clad soldiers were locked in static positions, often separated only by the width of an earthen parapet. They continued to fire at one another for hours as Lee constructed a new line of earthworks across the base of the salient. After more than twelve hours of vicious combat, the Confederates retired to their new position under cover of darkness, leaving the shattered bulge in Union hands. The Federals lost 9,000 men and Lee lost 8,000 in this bloody combat. An oak tree between the opposing forces, twenty-two inches thick, was literally split in two by rifle fire.[25]

EARTHWORKS AT THE WILDERNESS

Richard S. Ewell's II Corps line, just north of Orange Turnpike at the western edge of Saunders's Field. Note the parapet (the bank of earth) with logs used as a revetment (a retaining wall), and smaller logs supporting the upright posts to keep the revetment straight.

Constant sniping and artillery fire and another failed attack on the base of the Mule Shoe salient on May 18 completed the attrition at Spotsylvania. After 18,000 losses, the Army of the Potomac had about 84,000 men left; Lee's losses of 13,000 men left the Army of Northern Virginia with about 41,000 troops. In other words, though Union losses were higher in absolute numbers, the Confederates lost a higher proportion of their strength. Though Lee as well as Grant made up at least part of their losses through reinforcements over the course of the campaign, the Confederacy could not count on doing so for long.

When Grant broke away on May 21, instead of attempting another short end run around Lee's flank, he executed a longer flanking march that took the action to the North Anna River. Lee frustrated Grant, however, staying in front of his movement and constructing a massive line of earthworks just south of the stream that was so well sited by his chief engineer, Martin L. Smith, as to convince Grant that assaults would be futile. No major fighting took place at the North Anna.[27]

FROM COLD HARBOR TO PETERSBURG

When Grant moved south again, on May 26, he met Lee at Cold Harbor—only about ten miles northeast of Richmond. The opposing armies confronted each other for three weeks on level, sandy ground that made for easy entrenchment. The Virginia landscape became scarred by miles of earthworks in multiple lines. Large Union attacks on June 1 came close to breaking Lee's position, but the major Federal assault on June 3 failed to dent the Rebel line. Even Grant later admitted that this attack, which cost 3,500 men, had been a mistake. Union newspapers, which inflated the casualty figure to 7,000 men, made it seem even worse. Stories about Yankee soldiers writing their names on slips of paper and pinning them on their clothes to aid identification of their bodies were postwar fabrications.[28]

After the attack of June 3, the Federals dug in ever closer to their enemy, and elements of siege warfare emerged: constructing approach trenches, digging an underground mine designed to blow up a salient in the Confederate works, and constant sniping and mortar firing. Rather than relying solely on siege approaches, however,

Near the West Angle, the photographer stands on top of the parapet as two of his assistants stand in what was either an artillery emplacement or a bay created by traverses. Heavy logs were used to create the revetment. Much of the fighting on May 12 took place in this environment, with only the parapet or traverse separating antagonists.

**GRANT AT HIS HEADQUARTERS ▶
IN COLD HARBOR**

Grant's tenacious attempts at flanking Lee's army took a toll on both men's forces, but Grant felt compelled to pin down Lee's army to prevent it from sending reinforcements to other theaters of operation. He accepted the heavy losses that resulted from his numerous frontal attacks as a necessity of war.

on June 12 Grant launched yet another wide flanking movement to cross the James River and strike at Petersburg. Union engineers assembled the longest pontoon bridge of the Civil War to span the tidal portion of the James. Lee was unable to penetrate the strong rearguard screening Grant's maneuver. For several days, he lost contact with the Army of the Potomac, holding the Army of Northern Virginia north of the river long enough to give the Federals a head start on one of the great engineering feats of the war.[29]

Grant relied on William F. ("Baldy") Smith's XVIII Corps, detached from Butler's Army of the James, to spearhead his drive toward Petersburg. Although Smith took his time, he managed to capture a section of the formidable but thinly manned earthworks guarding Petersburg on the evening of June 15, in part by using African American troops. Lee's men played no role in the initial defense of Petersburg; the town lay within the department commanded by P. G. T. Beauregard, whose men had to bear the brunt of Grant's attacks for several days.

Unfortunately for Grant, Meade was unable to capitalize on his advantage. Union troops attacked between June 16 and 18 without success, in what came to be called Grant's First Offensive at Petersburg. Though Meade brought 80,000 men to the battle-field by June 18, Beauregard was able to repel every Union assault with only 20,000

DIGGING IN AT COLD HARBOR

Note the methodical way of construction employed by the Federals: constructing the revetment first and then digging a ditch in front to use dirt to pile up a parapet. You can also see the line of abatis (cut branches arranged in a line with limbs interlocked) in front, the use of picks and spades, and the tents set up just behind the line.

BATTLE OF YELLOW TAVERN

In one of the major cavalry actions of the Overland campaign, Phil Sheridan's troops clashed with J. E. B. Stuart on May 11 during a raid targeting Richmond. Stuart was mortally wounded during the battle.

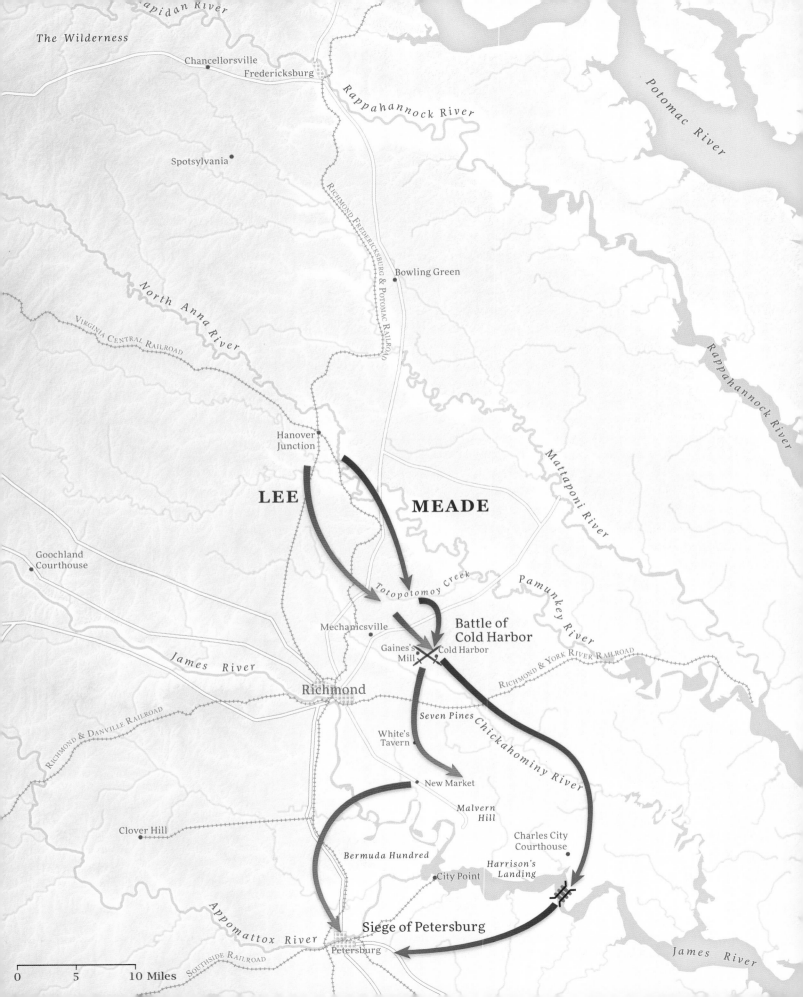

The Wilderness

Chancellorsville
Fredericksburg

Rappahannock River

Spotsylvania

Potomac River

RICHMOND, FREDERICKSBURG & POTOMAC RAILROAD

Bowling Green

North Anna River

VIRGINIA CENTRAL RAILROAD

Rappahannock River

Mattaponi River

Hanover Junction

LEE   **MEADE**

Goochland Courthouse

Totopotomoy Creek

Pamunkey River

Mechanicsville

Battle of Cold Harbor

Gaines's Mill   Cold Harbor

RICHMOND & YORK RIVER RAILROAD

James River

Richmond

Seven Pines   Chickahominy River

White's Tavern

RICHMOND & DANVILLE RAILROAD

New Market

Malvern Hill

Clover Hill

Charles City Courthouse

Bermuda Hundred

Harrison's Landing

City Point

Appomattox River

Siege of Petersburg

Petersburg

SOUTHSIDE RAILROAD

James River

0   5   10 Miles

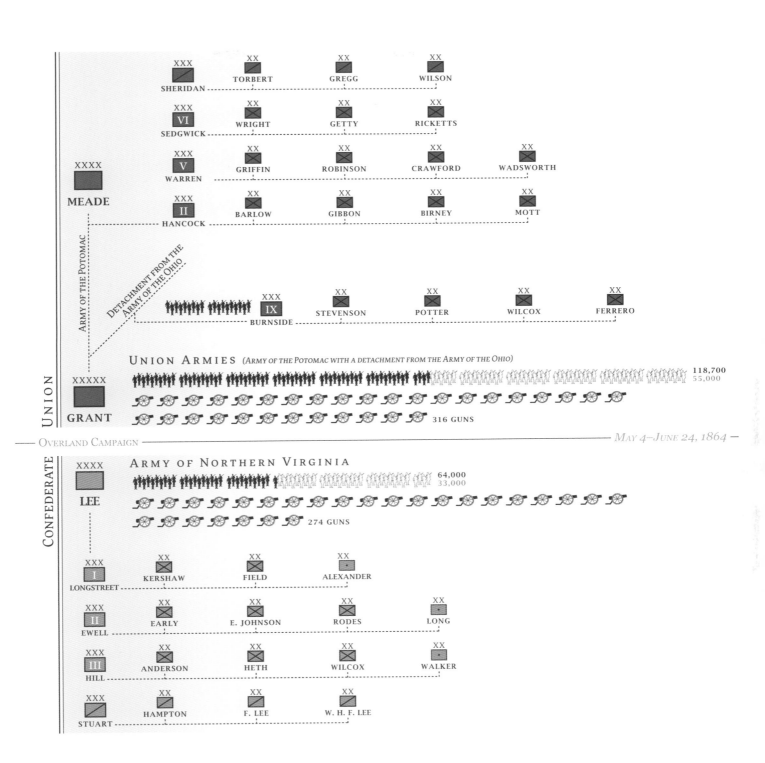

SHERIDAN (XXX)	TORBERT (XX)	GREGG (XX)	WILSON (XX)	
SEDGWICK VI (XXX)	WRIGHT (XX)	GETTY (XX)	RICKETTS (XX)	
WARREN V (XXX)	GRIFFIN (XX)	ROBINSON (XX)	CRAWFORD (XX)	WADSWORTH (XX)
HANCOCK II (XXX)	BARLOW (XX)	GIBBON (XX)	BIRNEY (XX)	MOTT (XX)

DETACHMENT FROM THE ARMY OF THE OHIO.

| BURNSIDE IX (XXX) | STEVENSON (XX) | POTTER (XX) | WILCOX (XX) | FERRERO (XX) |

ARMY OF THE POTOMAC

UNION ARMIES (*ARMY OF THE POTOMAC WITH A DETACHMENT FROM THE ARMY OF THE OHIO*)

118,700
55,000

GRANT (XXXXX)

316 GUNS

MEADE (XXXX)

UNION

— OVERLAND CAMPAIGN —   — *MAY 4–JUNE 24, 1864* —

CONFEDERATE

LEE (XXXX) **ARMY OF NORTHERN VIRGINIA**

64,000
33,000

274 GUNS

LONGSTREET I (XXX)	KERSHAW (XX)	FIELD (XX)	ALEXANDER (XX)	
EWELL II (XXX)	EARLY (XX)	E. JOHNSON (XX)	RODES (XX)	LONG (XX)
HILL III (XXX)	ANDERSON (XX)	HETH (XX)	WILCOX (XX)	WALKER (XX)
STUART (XXX)	HAMPTON (XX)	F. LEE (XX)	W. H. F. LEE (XX)	

◀ **THE OVERLAND CAMPAIGN, MAY 27–JUNE 18**

After avoiding battle at the North Anna River, Grant and Meade continued to push south, swinging around Richmond to strike at Petersburg, the capture of which would sever Lee's principal line of supply and force him to abandon the capital.

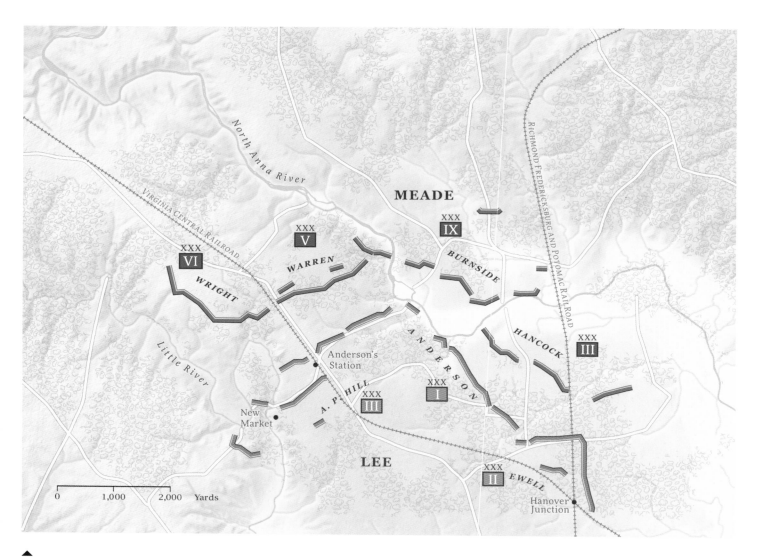

▲
BATTLE AT THE NORTH ANNA RIVER

Grant arrived at the North Anna River to find Lee there once again, with even stronger entrenchments. The terrain was ill suited to another frontal assault, so Grant decided against a major attack, instead swinging south again.

BATTLE OF COLD HARBOR ▶

A major attack on June 1 nearly succeeded, encouraging Grant to try again. But Lee's position was too strong for a frontal attack to succeed, and the Federals lost 3,500 men. Grant was used to ordering attacks that incurred heavy losses, but this was one of two that (as he later wrote) he always regretted.

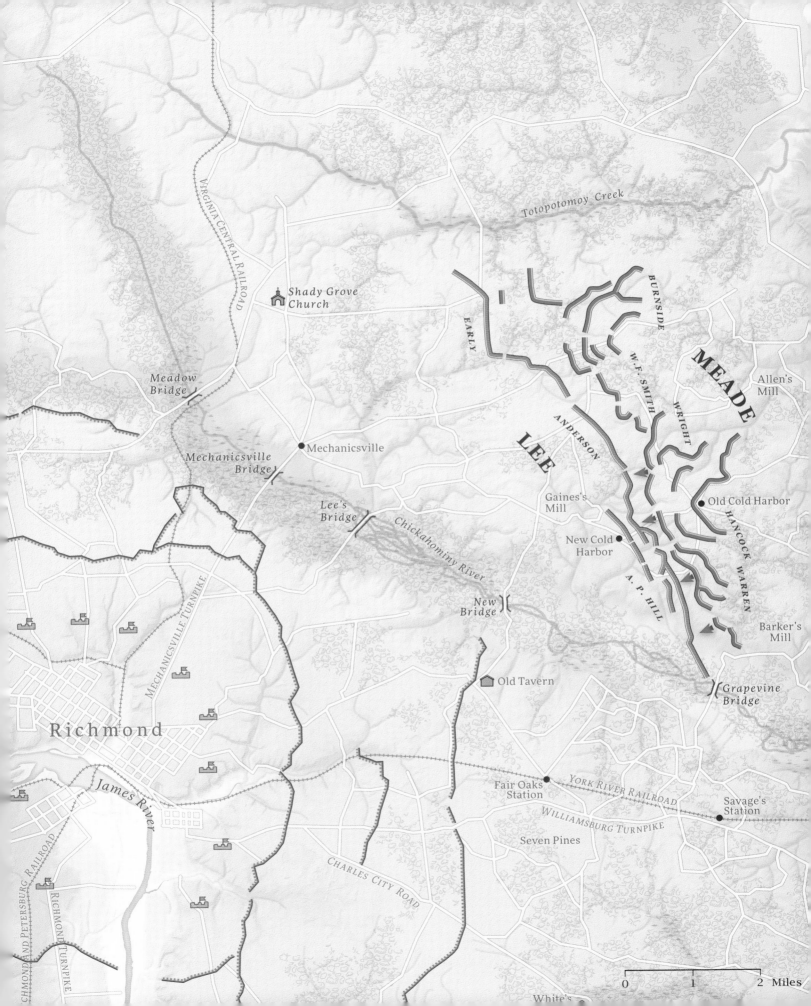

Totopotomoy Creek

VIRGINIA CENTRAL RAILROAD

Shady Grove Church

BURNSIDE

EARLY

MEADE

W. F. SMITH

Allen's Mill

Meadow Bridge

ANDERSON

LEE

WRIGHT

Mechanicsville

Mechanicsville Bridge

Gaines's Mill

Old Cold Harbor

Lee's Bridge

Chickahominy River

New Cold Harbor

HANCOCK

WARREN

New Bridge

A. P. HILL

Barker's Mill

MECHANICSVILLE TURNPIKE

Old Tavern

Grapevine Bridge

Richmond

James River

Fair Oaks Station

YORK RIVER RAILROAD

Savage's Station

WILLIAMSBURG TURNPIKE

RICHMOND AND PETERSBURG RAILROAD

Seven Pines

CHARLES CITY ROAD

RICHMOND TURNPIKE

White's

0   1   2 Miles

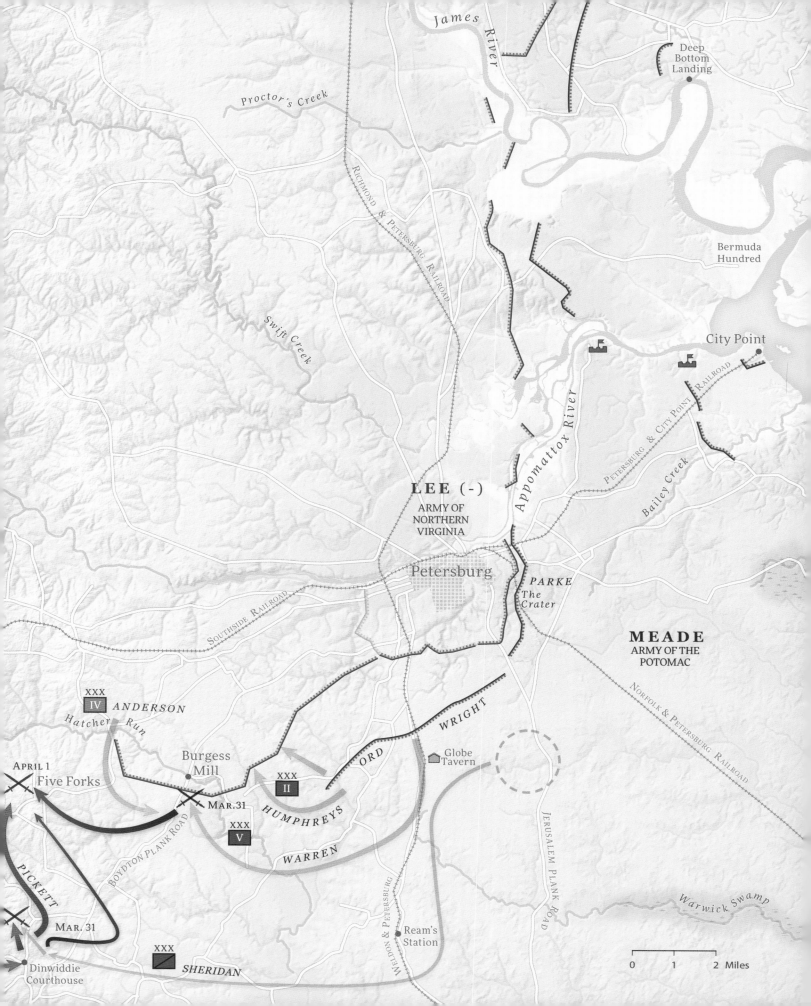

James River

Deep Bottom Landing

Proctor's Creek

RICHMOND & PETERSBURG RAILROAD

Swift Creek

Bermuda Hundred

City Point

Appomattox River

PETERSBURG & CITY POINT RAILROAD

Bailey Creek

LEE (-)
ARMY OF
NORTHERN
VIRGINIA

Petersburg

PARKE
The Crater

SOUTHSIDE RAILROAD

MEADE
ARMY OF THE
POTOMAC

NORFOLK & PETERSBURG RAILROAD

XXX
IV   *ANDERSON*

Hatcher's Run

WRIGHT

ORD

Globe
Tavern

*Burgess
Mill*

APRIL 1
Five Forks

XXX
II

MAR. 31

XXX
V

HUMPHREYS

BOYDTON PLANK ROAD

WARREN

Jerusalem Plank Road

PICKETT

MAR. 31

WELDON & PETERSBURG

Warwick Swamp

Dinwiddie
Courthouse

XXX
SHERIDAN

Ream's
Station

0   1   2 Miles

Rebels. The reasons were many: inadequate information about the terrain and Confederate positions, a near breakdown of coordination between corps and divisions (aggravated by Meade's desperate effort to push his men before the advantage evaporated), and physical and emotional exhaustion after six weeks of intense campaigning. Several brigades in Hancock's II Corps even refused orders to attack.[30]

After June 18, Lee shifted the Army of Northern Virginia to Petersburg, the Federals dug in opposite his line, and both armies settled in for much-needed rest. The Overland campaign had ended; the Petersburg campaign had begun. Grant had lost 64,000 troops in six weeks of ferocious fighting. That was about half the men he started out with on May 4. Lee had lost about 30,000 troops, also half his strength, but many residents of the North and their newspaper editors were appalled at the cost of Grant's campaign, labeling the general a butcher. Rarely do historians find the difference between contemporary opinion and hindsight—or retrospective military analysis—so great. The combination of high casualties and the apparent stalemate of the campaign made Lincoln's Democratic opponents feel the fall election might go in their favor. If it did, the peace plank in the Democratic platform might lead to an end to the war with the Confederacy intact, or to the repudiation of the Emancipation Proclamation in order to readmit the seceded states to the Union with slavery restored.[31]

With hindsight, it is easier to see that when Grant landed outside Petersburg, he had already accomplished a vital shift in the course of the war, one that even a Democratic presidential victory might not have reversed. "I shall take no backward step," he informed chief of staff Henry Halleck on May 10. "We can maintain ourselves at least and in the end beat Lee's Army."[32] Grant was right. His predecessors in the Virginia theater had not fared well against Lee. The Confederate commander had seized and largely held the strategic initiative from the time of the Seven Days campaign, in June 1862, until May 1864, either by blunting Federal efforts to take the initiative or by invading Union territory. Grant reversed that trend, held the initiative for the remainder of the war, and reduced Lee's effective strength by 50 percent in only six weeks of fighting. McClellan, Burnside, Hooker, and Meade had lost 82,600 men in two years of

◀ PETERSBURG CAMPAIGN, JUNE 18
Confederate troops under Beauregard arrived just in time to protect Petersburg and dig in, setting the stage for a nearly ten-month campaign.

failing to master Lee; Grant lost only 64,000 men while gaining and keeping the upper hand over his opponent.[33]

Grant's willingness to accept heavy losses underlay the success of his strategy. Two years later, he spoke about this aspect of his record. "My object in war was to exhaust Lee's army. I was obliged to sacrifice men to do it. I have been called a butcher. Well, I never spared men's lives to gain an object; but then I gained it and I knew it was the only way."[34] His opponents recognized this feature of the Overland campaign. "Half such a whipping [as the Wilderness and Spotsylvania] would have sent McClellan, Hooker, Burnside or Meade crossing to the other side of the Rappahannock," commented a North Carolina officer in Lee's army. "It seems that Grant is determined to sacrifice his army or destroy Lee's."[35]

Lee was the only opponent that Grant failed to completely outmaneuver during the war, but he came very close to doing so when he crossed the James River and struck at Petersburg. Although the city was not captured until April 1865, Grant's relentless maneuvers southward compelled Lee to retreat to Petersburg, which was the best outcome that could be expected once the Confederate general refused to fight in the open. When Lee stopped retreating and the armies faced off at Petersburg, the result was a siege-like situation that the Confederates could not win.

THE ATLANTA CAMPAIGN

Despite his exacting duties during the Atlanta campaign, William Tecumseh Sherman was keenly aware of what was happening in the East. "Grant's Battles in Virginia are fearful but necessary," he told his wife in a letter. "Immense slaughter is necessary to prove that our northern armies can & will fight. That once impressed will be an immense moral power."[36] But Sherman had other ideas about how to conduct his own drive against the Confederate Army of Tennessee.

Western Federals had long before established a morale advantage over their opponents with a string of battlefield victories. Yet Sherman's 100,000 men were dependent on a single-track railroad stretching more than 300 miles to Louisville, Kentucky. Given his tenuous line of communications, Sherman felt he could not afford heavy losses. Moreover, Sherman was usually a careful commander who relied on logistics, maneuver, and strategic context rather than bitter fighting to achieve his objectives.[37]

As a result, Sherman conducted the Atlanta campaign with an effective mix of tactical caution and operational boldness to penetrate 100 miles of Confederate territory in four months, almost constantly within firing range of his enemy. After several years of reacting to Rebel cavalry raids against their lines of communication, the Federals now seized the initiative to prevent Confederate cavalry in Mississippi from threatening Sherman's supply line by launching several raids of their own from Memphis and other points along the Mississippi River deep into the interior of the state. Indeed, Nathan Bedford Forrest was on his way north to raid Sherman's rail link when one of

Born in Lancaster, Ohio, Sherman was raised mostly as a foster child in the family of the influential Whig politician Thomas Ewing. After West Point, Sherman joined the 3rd U.S. Artillery and served in the Second Seminole War. In transit by ship during the Mexican War, he saw no action but was part of the occupation force in California. Promoted to captain in 1850, he resigned from the army in 1853.

When the Civil War came, Lincoln appointed Sherman brigadier general and assigned him to command Union forces in Kentucky. He was soon overcome by stress and relieved of his command. Restored to command a division within Grant's army, Sherman erred in not anticipating the Confederate attack at Shiloh but performed well in the battle, winning Grant's increased respect. Thereafter, he continued to be Grant's most trusted subordinate, commanding a corps in the first and second Vicksburg campaigns. After Grant's promotion to command the Military Division of the Mississippi in October 1863, Sherman succeeded him as commander of the Army of the Tennessee and led a detachment at the Battle of Missionary Ridge.

With Grant's promotion to general in chief, Sherman succeeded him again to command the Military Division of the Mississippi and led its combined forces in the Atlanta campaign and then the Savannah (March to the Sea) and Carolinas campaigns. After the war, Grant's election to president brought Sherman promotion to general of the army, in which capacity he served until retirement.

those Union raids began, forcing him to cancel his plans. The largest Federal incursion, by 25,000 troops led by Sherman himself, culminated in the destruction of military and economic targets in Meridian, Mississippi, in mid-February, aggravating Jefferson Davis's fears for the important war industries in Selma, Alabama, and the vital food-growing regions in the rest of the state. It made him reluctant to divert forces for raids into Tennessee.[38]

Outnumbered by at least two to one, Rebel commander Joseph E. Johnston acted almost purely on the defensive, employing a Fabian strategy of repeated withdrawals to conserve his limited forces and draw the Federals farther away from their base of supplies, hoping that Confederate cavalry could cut the vulnerable railroad line. Yet the expected cavalry strikes never occurred because Sherman directed his subordinates in Mississippi to keep Nathan Bedford Forrest so busy he could not ride northward against the tracks. The Richmond authorities gradually grew frustrated that Johnston was giving up territory without a major battle, and Davis eventually replaced him with the more aggressive John Bell Hood.[39]

Until then, however, Johnston delayed Sherman's advance while maintaining the effectiveness of his army and his men's morale. Sherman employed a turning maneuver to flank his enemy out of Dalton, Georgia, but launched several large-scale attacks on Johnston's next position at Resaca, losing 4,000 troops. Resuming his turning movements, Sherman crossed the Etowah River on May 23 and entered a tangled landscape with few roads. Here Johnston slowed the Federals to a crawl as both armies were locked in extensive fieldworks within yards of each other for weeks, skirmishing and sniping. When the lines reached Kennesaw Mountain, Sherman experimented with a three-pronged attack on June 27 that racked up 3,000 casualties and accomplished nothing. In contrast, Johnston lost only 700 men. Sherman then returned to maneuver, turning Johnston out of the Kennesaw Line (the six-mile arc of field fortifications the

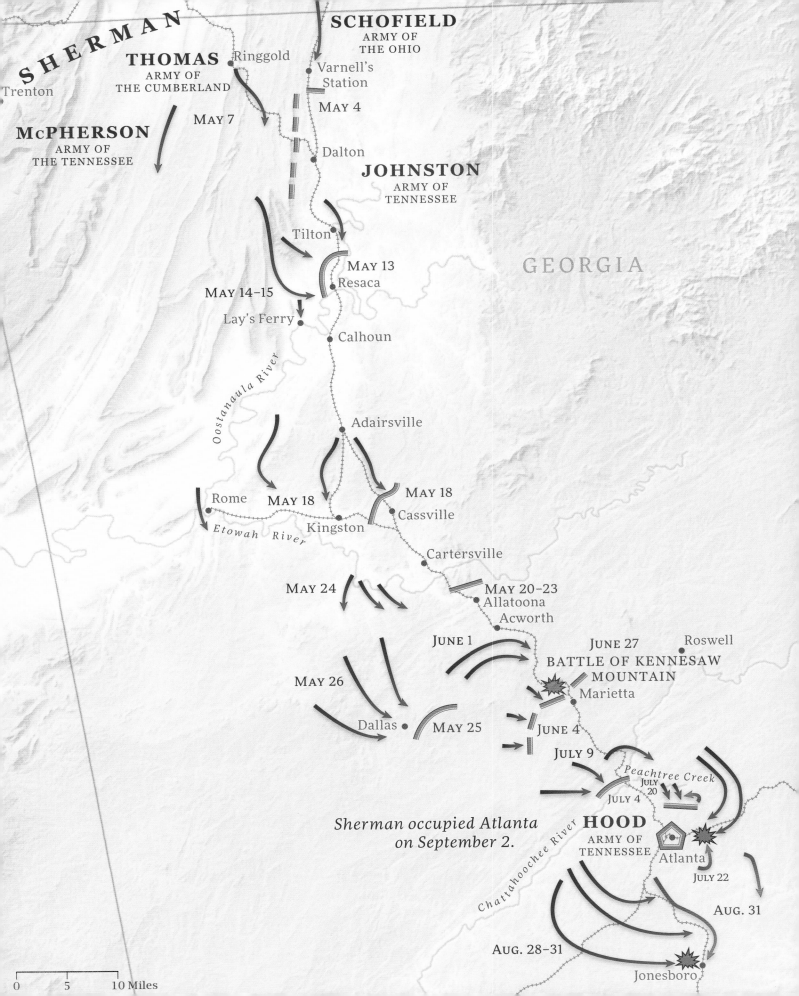

SHERMAN

THOMAS
ARMY OF
THE CUMBERLAND

Trenton

McPHERSON
ARMY OF
THE TENNESSEE

Ringgold

MAY 7

SCHOFIELD
ARMY OF
THE OHIO

Varnell's
Station

MAY 4

Dalton

JOHNSTON
ARMY OF TENNESSEE

GEORGIA

Tilton

MAY 13

Resaca

MAY 14–15

Lay's Ferry

Calhoun

Oostanaula River

Adairsville

Rome

MAY 18

MAY 18

Cassville

Etowah River

Kingston

Cartersville

MAY 24

MAY 20–23
Allatoona
Acworth

JUNE 1

Roswell

JUNE 27
**BATTLE OF KENNESAW
MOUNTAIN**

MAY 26

Marietta

Dallas

MAY 25

JUNE 4

JULY 9

Peachtree Creek

JULY
20

JULY 4

*Sherman occupied Atlanta
on September 2.*

HOOD
ARMY OF
TENNESSEE

Atlanta

JULY 22

AUG. 31

AUG. 28–31

Jonesboro

0   5   10 Miles

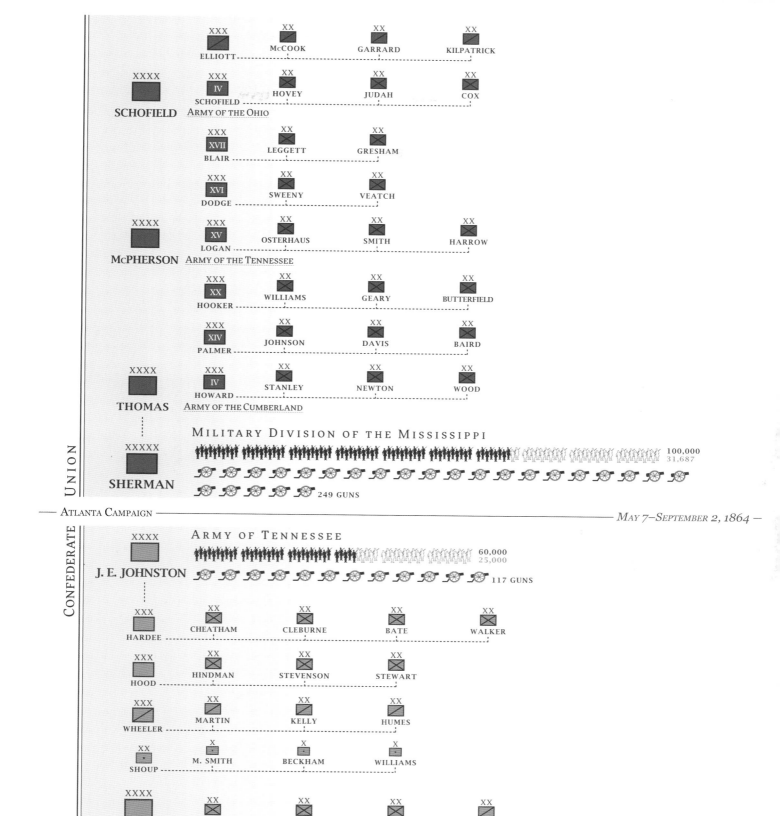

| | XXX ELLIOTT | XX McCOOK | XX GARRARD | XX KILPATRICK |

SCHOFIELD — ARMY OF THE OHIO
XXXX SCHOFIELD — XXX IV SCHOFIELD — XX HOVEY — XX JUDAH — XX COX

XXX XVII BLAIR — XX LEGGETT — XX GRESHAM

XXX XVI DODGE — XX SWEENY — XX VEATCH

McPHERSON — ARMY OF THE TENNESSEE
XXXX McPHERSON — XXX XV LOGAN — XX OSTERHAUS — XX SMITH — XX HARROW

XXX XX HOOKER — XX WILLIAMS — XX GEARY — XX BUTTERFIELD

XXX XIV PALMER — XX JOHNSON — XX DAVIS — XX BAIRD

THOMAS — ARMY OF THE CUMBERLAND
XXXX THOMAS — XXX IV HOWARD — XX STANLEY — XX NEWTON — XX WOOD

MILITARY DIVISION OF THE MISSISSIPPI

SHERMAN XXXXX — 100,000 / 31,687 — 249 GUNS

UNION

— ATLANTA CAMPAIGN —   — MAY 7–SEPTEMBER 2, 1864 —

CONFEDERATE

ARMY OF TENNESSEE

J. E. JOHNSTON XXXX — 60,000 / 25,000 — 117 GUNS

XXX HARDEE — XX CHEATHAM — XX CLEBURNE — XX BATE — XX WALKER

XXX HOOD — XX HINDMAN — XX STEVENSON — XX STEWART

XXX WHEELER — XX MARTIN — XX KELLY — XX HUMES

XX SHOUP — X M. SMITH — X BECKHAM — X WILLIAMS

XXXX POLK — XX LORING — XX FRENCH — XX WALTHALL — XX W. H. JACKSON
POLK — ARMY OF MISSISSIPPI

◀ **ATLANTA CAMPAIGN**

Reluctant to engage in a general battle with Sherman, Joseph Johnston withdrew toward the Chattahoochee River, hoping to lure Sherman into striking a well-prepared Confederate position. The Union general refused to be drawn into such an attack, although he experimented with limited assaults on several occasions while maneuvering Johnston out of his fortified lines. Shortly after Sherman crossed the river in July, Davis replaced Johnston with the more aggressive Hood.

JOHN BELL HOOD

JUNE 1, 1831–AUGUST 30, 1879

Born in Kentucky, Hood graduated in the West Point class of 1853 and served in California and Texas. He created an impressive record as a regimental, brigade, and division commander in Virginia early in the Civil War but was injured by artillery fire at Gettysburg, losing the use of an arm. Another serious wound at Chickamauga led to the amputation of his leg. When a third corps was created in the Army of Tennessee, Hood received the command even though the thirty-two-year-old general had to be strapped onto his horse to keep him mounted.

Despite his record, Hood turned in a poor performance as corps commander during the Atlanta campaign. On more than one occasion, he folded under pressure yet privately criticized his superior for constantly falling back without fighting a major battle.

Hood was surprised when appointed Johnston's successor on July 17, 1864. To his credit, he developed good plans for taking the offensive against Sherman, but all of them failed in part because of factors beyond his control. Hood invaded Tennessee in a failed effort to redeem captured Confederate territory and was defeated at Franklin and Nashville.

Hood blamed everyone but himself. He inflamed controversies with Joseph E. Johnston and William J. Hardee that would rage for years to come. Living in New Orleans, he, his wife, and one of their children died of yellow fever in 1879.

Confederates had prepared to block his advance) and subsequent positions until he forced the Army of Tennessee to cross the Chattahoochee River and retire to the outskirts of Atlanta in mid-July.

John Bell Hood replaced Johnston on July 18. His sudden reversal of Confederate strategy failed to halt Union progress. Hood launched an attack on Sherman's line north of Atlanta on July 20, hitting George Thomas's Army of the Cumberland as it crossed Peachtree Creek. Although taken by surprise, the Federals reacted quickly, fought well, and repelled the assault. Hood, whose experience was largely in the Army of Northern Virginia, where he had spearheaded a powerful assault at the battle of Gaines's Mill, was not daunted by the repulse. When James McPherson's Army of the Tennessee approached Atlanta from the east, Hood shifted troops to block the advance and then sent William Hardee's corps on a long march to strike McPherson's left flank on the afternoon of July 22. Hardee caught the Union XVII Corps with its flank in the air, and the Confederates attacked it literally from three sides, but the Federals jumped from one side of their fieldworks to another to fight off the Rebels. Sherman's army group survived its closest brush with disaster in the campaign, while McPherson was killed in the bitter fighting that came to be known as the Battle of Atlanta. When Sherman shifted the Army of the Tennessee to the west side of Atlanta in an effort to approach the railroads supplying the city from the south, the Confederates counterattacked near Ezra Church, where they were repulsed with heavy casualties on July 28.

Having lost 11,000 troops in a little more than a week, Hood now gave up his aggressive tactics and merely extended his outnumbered line to protect the railroad each time Sherman made a move southward. Confederate morale plummeted, supplies became scarce (especially small arms and artillery ammunition), and they had difficulty countering the aggressive skirmishing that the Federals conducted in the semistatic lines outside Atlanta. Nevertheless, while Sherman's troops had deeply penetrated Georgia and won several battles, they seemed stalled outside the gates of the city.[40]

PETERSBURG

In fact, both of the major Federal campaigns seemed to be stalled by August, after suffering about 100,000 casualties. War weariness loomed as Grant tried to find a solution to his dilemma at Petersburg. He had far less room to maneuver than during the Overland campaign, and the Confederates constantly improved their earthworks to the point that they seemed unassailable.

◀ **SECTION OF CONFEDERATE CITY LINE, ATLANTA**
This photograph, taken soon after Sherman captured Atlanta, shows a section of the defenses known as the City Line around the town. Note the inclined and sharpened palisades a few feet in front of a row of upright palisades, with each stake only a few inches apart from the next to allow Confederate infantrymen to fire through the row.

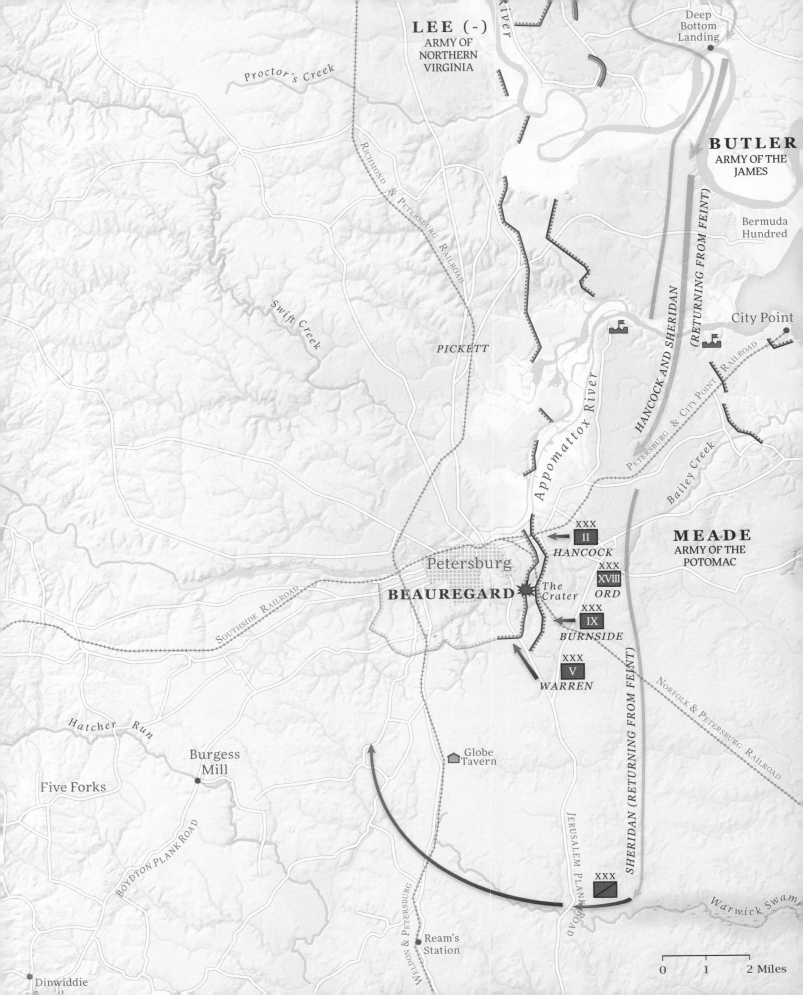

LEE (-)
ARMY OF
NORTHERN
VIRGINIA

Proctor's Creek

Swift Creek

PICKETT

Richmond & Petersburg Railroad

Appomattox River

Deep Bottom Landing

BUTLER
ARMY OF THE JAMES

Bermuda Hundred

City Point

HANCOCK AND SHERIDAN (RETURNING FROM FEINT)

Petersburg & City Point Railroad

Bailey Creek

MEADE
ARMY OF THE POTOMAC

XXX II HANCOCK

Petersburg

BEAUREGARD

The Crater

XXX XVIII ORD

XXX IX BURNSIDE

XXX V WARREN

SOUTHSIDE RAILROAD

Hatcher Run

Burgess Mill

Five Forks

Globe Tavern

Jerusalem Plank Road

SHERIDAN (RETURNING FROM FEINT)

Norfolk & Petersburg Railroad

BOYDTON PLANK ROAD

WELDON & PETERSBURG

Ream's Station

Dinwiddie

XXX

Warwick Swamp

0   1   2 Miles

Initially, Grant merely tried to extend his line as far westward as possible. The Second Union Offensive at Petersburg sent the II and VI Corps west of the Jerusalem Plank Road on June 22 and 23, only to see them surprised and thrown back by adroit Confederate attacks. After this failure, Grant began to plan a more complex operation that centered on digging an underground tunnel (or mine gallery) by the 48th Pennsylvania (commanded by an antebellum mining engineer, and with a number of coal miners in its ranks), designed to blow up a Confederate battery located at a salient in Lee's line. Ambrose Burnside, back in command of the IX Corps after redeeming himself in the West, trained a division of United States Colored Troops specifically for the attack to exploit the breach, a rare example of mission- or operation-specific training in the Civil War.[41]

EARLY'S LUNGE AGAINST WASHINGTON

But before that offensive could begin, Grant had to ward off pressure to abandon his position at Petersburg. Lee had detached his II Corps under Jubal Early to secure the Shenandoah Valley from a Union column under David Hunter, which had advanced up the valley to Lynchburg before Early met and defeated it on June 17–18. Hunter retired to Harpers Ferry, allowing Early to cross the Potomac River and advance toward Washington. Early hoped this move would compel Grant to release his grip on Petersburg.[42]

Although Washington was ringed by a huge system of earthen defenses, Grant had stripped it of troops to add strength to Meade's army for the Overland campaign. The threat to the capital was blunted when Union general Lew Wallace delayed Early's advance by giving battle at a river crossing at Monocacy Junction, Maryland, on July 8, allowing Grant more time to shift troops to Washington. The VI Corps came from Petersburg, and the XIX Corps, which was at sea en route from Louisiana to Petersburg, was diverted as well. When Early reached the defenses of Washington on July 11, the vanguard of the VI Corps was just entering the city. Lincoln came out to Fort Stevens to watch the skirmishing only a few hundred yards away, making him the only president to come under enemy fire while in office. Early continued to skirmish the next day, but then, realizing he had missed his chance, retreated to Virginia.

▲
JUBAL EARLY
Although he probably could have threatened Washington, D.C., if he had arrived a few days sooner, Early would not have been able to hold the city upon the arrival of VI Corps troops. But his raid on the national capital threatened the civilian leadership and led Grant to promote Phil Sheridan to head the Army of the Shenandoah.

◀ **PETERSBURG CAMPAIGN: GRANT'S THIRD OFFENSIVE**
After the initial battles at Petersburg, Grant began extending his lines to the west, hoping to flank the Confederates.

Grant's Third Offensive at Petersburg took place between July 26 and July 30, with the explosion of the 48th Pennsylvania's mine on the last day. Eight tons of black powder tore a gaping hole in the Confederate earthworks, but Meade doubted the ability of the black division to spearhead the attack and feared the political repercussions of that failure. He forced Burnside to alter the plan, and Burnside chose a white division that was woefully understrength, ill led, and had received no special training for the assignment. The follow-up attack was marked by miscommunication and hampered by a drunken division commander (who was dismissed from the army as a result) and the thirty-foot-deep mine crater. Confederate survivors managed to hold Burnside's men, including the division of African American troops (who followed the first wave), until fresh troops arrived to drive them out. It was the first time that the Army of Northern Virginia encountered armed blacks on the battlefield, and the Confederates killed many of the men as they tried to surrender, or even while escorting them away from the battlefield under guard. With casualties of 3,798 out of 16,772 Federals engaged, the Battle of the Crater represented one of the Army of the Potomac's costliest days of fighting.[43]

▼ BATTLE OF THE CRATER

During much of the planning for the Crater, a division of African American soldiers was trained to lead the assault. The day before the attack, Meade worried that the men would not fight well enough and that the army would be criticized for using them. He forced Burnside to put a white division in the lead. This led to a serious breakdown in planning the assault, as Burnside struggled to adjust his arrangements and entrusted his least capable division commander to lead the attack.

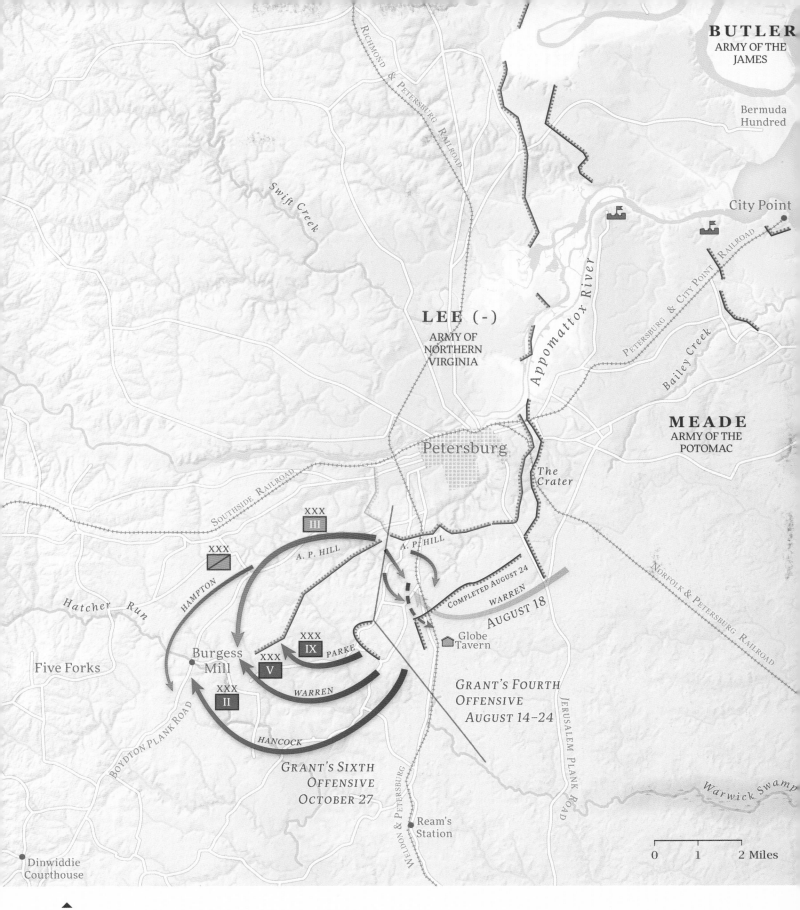

BUTLER
ARMY OF THE JAMES

Bermuda Hundred

City Point

LEE (-)
ARMY OF NORTHERN VIRGINIA

MEADE
ARMY OF THE POTOMAC

Petersburg

The Crater

Globe Tavern

Grant's Fourth Offensive
August 14–24

COMPLETED AUGUST 24   WARREN   AUGUST 18

A. P. HILL

A. P. HILL

XXX III

XXX

HAMPTON

Burgess Mill

XXX IX   PARKE

XXX V

WARREN

XXX II

HANCOCK

Grant's Sixth Offensive
October 27

Five Forks

Hatcher Run

Swift Creek

Appomattox River

Bailey Creek

SOUTHSIDE RAILROAD

RICHMOND & PETERSBURG RAILROAD

PETERSBURG & CITY POINT RAILROAD

NORFOLK & PETERSBURG RAILROAD

BOYDTON PLANK ROAD

JERUSALEM PLANK ROAD

WELDON & PETERSBURG

Ream's Station

Warwick Swamp

Dinwiddie Courthouse

0   1   2 Miles

▲ PETERSBURG CAMPAIGN
After the failure at the Crater, Grant changed his strategy to one of short advances followed by fortifying and holding territory. He continued to extend his line farther west, hoping to either flank the Confederates or force them into overextension.

Grant's next offensive at Petersburg, between August 14 and 25, was a turning point in the campaign. Gouverneur Warren's V Corps crossed the Jerusalem Plank Road and planted itself on the Weldon and Petersburg Railroad, one of Lee's principal supply lines (and the target of Grant's initial plan of operations before the campaign). The Federals repelled several attacks and then connected the newly won ground with Union trenches east of the road. Grant now had a winning tactic: short advances, digging in to stymie Rebel counterattacks, extending the Union works westward, and stretching Lee's army until it broke or the Federals could turn his flank. Bite-and-hold tactics offered Grant a solution to the problem posed by the heavy earthworks outside Petersburg.[44]

Union Offensives and the Election of 1864

National politics seemed to demand more Union victories as the fall approached. Lincoln had been nominated for a second term on June 7 by a temporary coalition of Republicans and War Democrats calling itself the National Union Party. The Democrats nominated George B. McClellan, banking on his military fame. The bloody course of the campaigns in Virginia and Georgia taxed northern morale as war weariness increased. Yet the Democrats were divided. Their platform blasted Lincoln's handling of the war effort as a bloody failure, attacked radical measures such as the Emancipation Proclamation and the suspension of the writ of habeas corpus, and advocated negotiations with the Confederate government. McClellan rejected that last provision, preferring to fight the war to a military conclusion before opening negotiations. Exactly how all this might have played out was anyone's guess, but a Democratic electoral victory could have derailed the intense military effort launched by Grant to win the war.[45]

How real were Lincoln's chances of defeat? We will never really know, but it is certain that by late August, Lincoln himself felt that he probably would lose and that McClellan would be unable to fight the war to a successful conclusion. The Republicans retained a strong, secure political base, rooted in social and economic as well as sectional issues, and they had the support of the War Democrats. But the president and other leaders worried that a continued military stalemate might undermine that support and lead to McClellan's election.[46]

Military success precluded that outcome. Sherman handed the nation a critical victory by capturing Atlanta on September 2. Unable to stretch his entrenchments south to bypass the Confederate earthworks west of the city, Sherman broke contact with Hood's army on August 26 and swung around to cut two railroads south of Atlanta. Hood shifted two of his three corps to fight the last battle of the campaign at Jonesboro. The Confederates attacked on August 31 and were repulsed, suffering twice as many casualties as they inflicted. This ratio held true throughout the campaign around Atlanta, with 14,000 total Confederate losses to 7,700 for the Union forces. The disparity cannot be accounted for solely by foolish tactics, bad command decisions, or the

THE ELECTION OF 1864 ▶

The Democratic Party banked on McClellan's reputation as a general to soothe its pro-war faction and encourage the nation that its ticket would not simply surrender the Union upon inauguration. Here McClellan is depicted as holding the nation together despite the abolitionist Lincoln ("No peace without Abolition!") and the secessionist Davis ("No peace without Separation!").

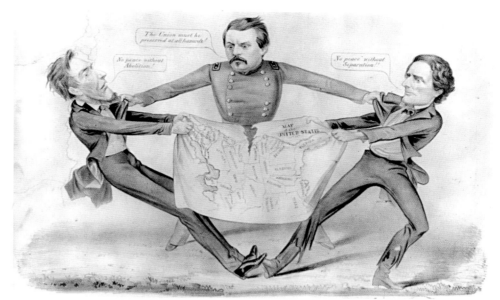

▲
FEDERAL SOLDIERS RELAX AT THEIR GUNS

These Union soldiers occupy one of the Confederate forts on the Atlanta City Line. News of Sherman's capture of Atlanta came during the course of the 1864 Democratic convention, severely undercutting the party's characterization of Lincoln's first term as "four years of failure." Subsequent Union successes in the Shenandoah Valley only deepened the Democrats' internal divisions and paved the way for Lincoln's overwhelming reelection.

defensive power of entrenchments, for the Army of Tennessee proved only minimally capable of coordinating its assaults. That capability deteriorated, along with the army's morale, during August, and Confederate commanders complained openly about the poor spirit and physical deterioration of their troops in the Jonesboro battle. After the repulse, Hood recalled one of those corps to Atlanta, and Sherman drove the other away on September 1. The railroad was securely in Union hands, and Hood had no choice but to evacuate Atlanta.[47]

OPERATIONS IN VIRGINIA: CLEARING THE VALLEY

Continued operations in the Shenandoah Valley also brought Union success. Grant dispatched aggressive cavalry commander Philip Sheridan to deal with Jubal Early, who had retreated from Washington to occupy the lower Valley. Sheridan engaged Early in a series of battles beginning with Third Winchester on September 19, a large and costly engagement that resulted in a significant Union victory. On September 22 he smashed Early's position at Fisher's Hill and inflicted a stunning defeat on the Confederates. As the Rebels retreated, Sheridan was uncertain how far he should pursue because the Valley angled toward the southwest, away from the Union concentration at Petersburg. The Federals went into camp at Cedar Creek as Sheridan consulted his superiors in Washington. Early countered with a surprise attack on October 19 and drove the Federals from their camps, but stiffening resistance and the return of Sheridan, whose dramatic ride onto the battlefield infused new energy into the Union army, concluded in a counterattack that scattered the Rebels, ending major Confederate efforts in the Valley for the remainder of the war.[48]

PHILIP HENRY SHERIDAN

MARCH 6, 1831–AUGUST 5, 1888

Born in Albany, New York, Sheridan grew up in Ohio and graduated in the U.S. Military Academy class of 1853. He served as a quartermaster and commissary until appointed colonel of the 2nd Michigan Cavalry in May 1862. From that point, Sheridan's rise was swift. Commissioned brigadier general in September 1862, he ably commanded a division at Perryville, Stones River, and Missionary Ridge.

Grant chose Sheridan to command the cavalry in the Army of the Potomac. He led that mounted arm with vigor. In his first encounter with J. E. B. Stuart, the Federals defeated the Confederate cavalry and killed Stuart at Yellow Tavern in May 1864.

Named to command the Union troops defending Washington, DC, Sheridan emerged as a major independent commander. He won an important victory near Winchester on September 19 against Jubal Early and smashed Early's subsequent position at Fisher's Hill three days later. Sheridan gained his greatest fame at Cedar Creek, when he rode back to his army in time to rally the troops and defeat Early one last time.

Grant brought Sheridan back to the Army of the Potomac to conduct a sweeping advance around Lee's flank at Petersburg and win an important victory at Five Forks on April 1, 1865. Sheridan also led Grant's pursuit of Lee, preventing the Confederates from moving toward North Carolina and heading them off at Appomattox Court House. Sheridan administered Radical Reconstruction measures in Louisiana and Texas, and fought Native Americans on the Plains.

Sheridan's operations in the Valley also represented a significant escalation in the harshness of Federal policy in the East. Grant wanted Sheridan to destroy food resources in the Shenandoah Valley "so that crows flying over it for the balance of this season will have to carry their provender with them."[49] By early October, Sheridan had burned more than two thousand barns and over seventy mills, and had collected seven thousand head of stock. He predicted that the lower Valley would soon "have but little in it for man or beast."[50]

Grant also kept the election in mind when planning his moves at Petersburg. His Fifth Offensive (September 29 to October 2) resulted in limited success, but the Sixth Offensive (October 27) failed because he used too few troops and expected them to go too far. Grant knew, however, that he could continue making progress in the next bite-and-hold attack, and his October failure did not affect the outcome of the presidential contest. Lincoln won reelection by a huge landslide in the electoral college, an event as important as any military action in determining the outcome of the war. Most northerners were committed to the war effort as Lincoln had pursued it, while critics

▼
PENNSYLVANIA SOLDIERS VOTING
In 1864, Union soldiers serving in the field voted through absentee ballot. Those states that provided for soldier voting saw approximately 80 percent of the military vote go to Abraham Lincoln. While not decisive, it contributed to the overwhelming nature of the incumbent president's victory and signified that the army was solidly behind his goal of winning the war through military means.

The average cavalry trooper did not wear a uniform substantially different from other army branches. The primary difference was the color of cloth piping or tape assigned to that branch. The American army had associated yellow with cavalry since the early 1850s. (Red represented artillery and light blue, infantry.)

Cavalry in the Civil War used a variety of weapons: carbines, shotguns, pistols, and occasionally sabers. Most Union cavalry soldiers were equipped with breech-loading carbines that were shorter than a rifle-musket and easier to reload, both important when firing while riding a horse.

UNION CAVALRY, 1864 ▶

Cavalry was the slowest-developing branch of the Union army during the Civil War. Unlike their European counterparts, American cavalry units were used mostly for screening and scouting operations. The difficult North American terrain made it hard to attempt larger cavalry actions.

Cavalry horses in the Civil War were not the specialized breeds found in many European armies. Few American troopers had the two to three years' training European armies considered necessary for fighting from horseback, and horsemen on both sides often dismounted to fight.

of Lincoln's policies had always remained a minority voice in northern politics. Even Union soldiers, showing they were not demoralized by the year's casualties, voted heavily for Lincoln, contributing greatly to the scale of his victory.[51]

SHERMAN'S MARCH

While Grant maintained nearly continuous contact with Lee from May 5 until the end of the war, Sherman adopted a different strategy when he broke contact with Hood and rested his troops in Atlanta after the fall of the city. Logistics loomed as the most important reason for this decision. Sherman knew that the single-track railroad had barely sufficed to support his army group during the campaign from Chattanooga. He was certain that it could no longer do so if he continued advancing south of Atlanta.[52]

But then Hood embarked on a bold move to seize the strategic initiative in the West. With Davis's approval, he crossed the Chattahoochee River and threatened Sherman's rail line to Chattanooga. As far as Davis knew, Hood's intention was to plant the army on the railroad and fight a climactic battle to decide the fate of Georgia. Instead, Hood led most of Sherman's command on a chase northward. The Confederates tried to capture a large depot of supplies at Allatoona Station on October 5, 1864, but the outnumbered Union garrison fought them off with heavy losses. Hood deliberately avoided a major battle with Sherman, preferring to draw the Federals northward before veering west into northern Alabama.[53]

Sherman refused to let Hood dictate Union strategy. Such a ploy had worked in 1862 when Braxton Bragg invaded Kentucky, because at that time, Don Carlos Buell's Army of the Ohio was the only large force available to contend with Bragg. But the strategic situation was very different in the fall of 1864. Successive calls for new troops by Lincoln, the construction of fortified posts to protect the railroad towns, and Sherman's determination never to give up the strategic initiative confounded Hood's hopes. Although he had chased the Army of Tennessee with six of his seven corps, Sherman stopped as soon as Hood entered Alabama. He then dispatched two of those corps under Brig. Gen. John Schofield to Tennessee, and sent George Thomas to Nashville to coordinate the state's defense. Sherman ordered spare troops from other departments in the Military Division of the Mississippi to reinforce Thomas.

Meanwhile, Sherman intended to take the rest of his command—some 60,000 troops—to reinforce Grant at Petersburg. It would be the largest transfer of troop strength from one region to another by either side in the war. Although Grant initially questioned the wisdom of this move, Sherman convinced him it was sound strategy. Rather than transporting these men by the rail system, which would have taken more than a month and strained the Union logistical system to the breaking point, Sherman preferred to march them from Atlanta to a southern seaport, which would also take about a month to accomplish. From there, the navy could transport them to Virginia. This plan avoided clogging the rail system with 60,000 troops and would allow the Federals to make a powerful statement that the Confederacy was a hollow shell. They

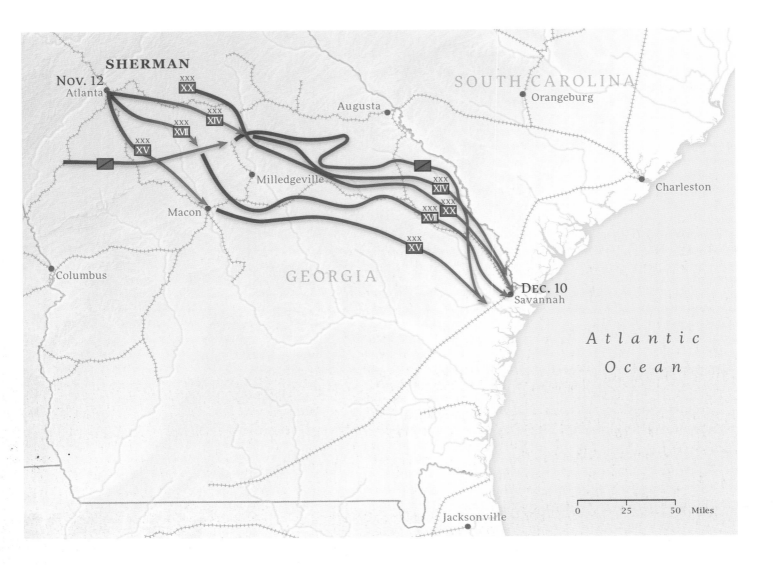

SHERMAN'S MARCH TO THE SEA

Facing minimal resistance from Johnston's army, Sherman pushed across Georgia from Atlanta to Savannah. His army lived off the land, taking the food and supplies it needed, and destroying much of the rest, along with railroads and other Confederate infrastructure.

could forage their way toward the coast, supplying themselves at Rebel expense and destroying railroads and resources in the state that linked the eastern Confederacy with its remaining western territory in Alabama and parts of Mississippi. This moving occupation would be a much more extended version, in both time and space, of Confederate raids like Lee's into Maryland and Pennsylvania—and would prove much more effective, since Hood's army, and those of the Confederacy as a whole, had been so badly damaged by thirty months of attritional battles. The Atlanta campaign had given Sherman a chance to demonstrate his operational agility, maneuvering large armies in difficult terrain against a cagey adversary; the March to the Sea offered him a chance to demonstrate his political-strategic genius on a grand scale.[54]

Sherman now prepared to abandon Atlanta and cut his line of communication with the North, destroying buildings of military value in the city. He intended to live

SHERMAN AT ATLANTA ▶

Sherman rested his army at Atlanta following the city's capture but knew he needed to do something different in order to continue his advance through the South and keep his army properly fed.

"I CAN MAKE THIS MARCH, AND MAKE GEORGIA HOWL"

Following his capture of Atlanta, Sherman prepared to move across the state toward Savannah. By supplying his army from the land, Sherman hoped to demonstrate the irresistible force of northern arms. In this passage, part of his correspondence with Grant proposing the March to the Sea, Sherman lays out his broader strategic goals of destroying a vast swath of Georgia:

I felt compelled to do what is usually a mistake in war, divide my forces, send a part back into Tennessee, retaining the balance here . . . I have in Tennessee a force numerically greater than his, well commanded and well organized, so that I feel no uneasiness on the score of Hood reaching my main communications . . . I propose to act in such a manner against the material resources of the South as utterly to negative Davis' boasted threat and promises of protection. If we can march a well-appointed army right through his territory, it is a demonstration to the world, foreign and domestic, that we have a power which Davis cannot resist. This may not be war, but rather statesmanship, nevertheless it is overwhelming to my mind that there are thousands of people abroad and in the South who will reason thus: If the North can march an army right through the South, it is proof positive that the North can prevail in this contest, leaving only open the question of its willingness to use that power.[55]

off the land and move with dispatch through regions that had never been visited by Federal troops. Setting out on November 14, he arrayed his columns to cover a corridor sixty miles wide and three hundred miles long from Atlanta to Savannah. His men systematically burned railroads, mills, and the recently harvested crops of that region while feeding off the fat of the land. Sherman issued orders to restrain the troops, and they largely avoided personal violence against civilians and concentrated on destroying war materiel, but many private residences were vandalized or destroyed despite officers' efforts. Since Hood had gone north, the Federals were opposed only by militia and a division of Confederate cavalry. In no previous campaign of the Civil War had they enjoyed such a huge disparity of troop strength, nor such ability to do what they wanted, deep behind enemy lines. Hood's move north, the sort of counteroffensive that had always reversed Union initiative before, failed to do so, mirroring the failure of Early's offensive toward Washington during the summer. Grant and Sherman had seized the strategic and operational initiative, and held it until the Confederacy collapsed.[56]

Sherman's columns closed on Savannah by mid-December. A Federal division captured Fort McAllister on December 13, opening communications with the navy, but

► FEDERALS DESTROYING RAILROADS

The most efficient method of wrecking railroads is depicted in this postwar drawing: line up the men on one side, have all of them lift up the end of a tie at the same time, and topple the line over. The Federals then separated the ties from the rails.

◄ BURNING RAILS AND TIES

After dismantling the ties from the rails, the Federals stacked up the ties like crib work, set them afire, and heated the middle of the rails so that they could bend them into unusable shapes by either wrapping them around a tree or telegraph pole or twisting them from both ends. The resulting mutilated rails were often called Sherman's neckties.

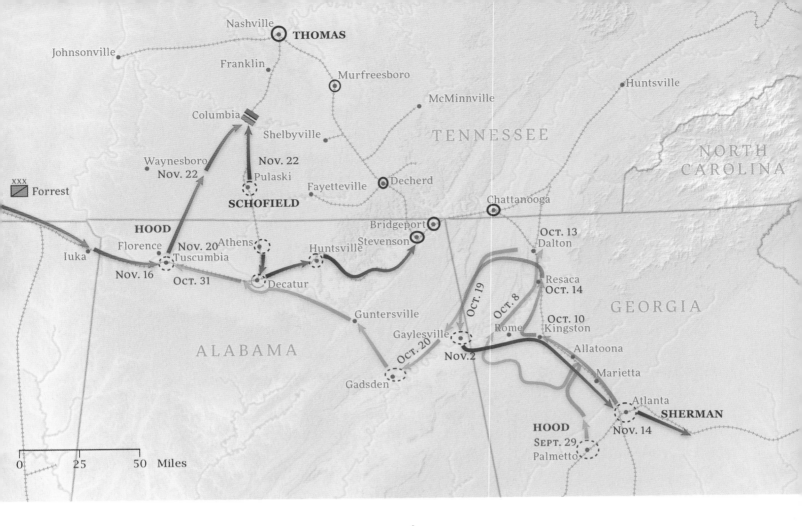

HOOD'S CAMPAIGN IN TENNESSEE
Hoping to draw Sherman away from Atlanta and threaten his supply lines, Hood launched a desperate drive into Tennessee. Sherman, refusing to cede the initiative, left large forces under John Schofield and George Thomas to defend the state.

Savannah's Confederate garrison escaped before Sherman completely invested the city. The Federals entered Savannah a week later.

With minimal fighting, Sherman had moved 60,000 men on the first leg of a long journey to Petersburg and destroyed an estimated $100 million worth of property. That was 18 percent of the $600 million worth of taxable property in the entire state of Georgia, but the destruction was concentrated along a narrow corridor from Atlanta to Savannah, making the example of Federal power even greater. Sherman had also demoralized many Confederates by his march through the heart of their country.[57]

HOOD IN TENNESSEE

The Union troops left behind to deal with Hood experienced some of the most vicious fighting of the war as they defended Tennessee. Hood left northern Alabama on November 21, intending to outflank Schofield's IV and XXIII Corps at Pulaski, Tennessee, and cut them off from George Thomas at Nashville. At Spring Hill, Hood nearly succeeded, but mistakes by his corps commanders and a silent march past sleeping

Rebel soldiers allowed Schofield to escape on the night of November 29. He had to stop at Franklin, thirty miles south of Nashville, to rebuild bridges over the Harpeth River, but his men assumed a good defensive position just south of town behind stout earthworks.

Hood rashly threw his troops into a frontal attack against the Franklin position late in the evening of November 30. Some 20,000 men advanced across open, ascending ground in the Army of Tennessee's last great attack, with more soldiers than in Pickett's Charge at Gettysburg. The Rebels temporarily cracked the Federal line along the Columbia Pike, but, as at Spotsylvania six months before, a reserve brigade contained the penetration. Close-range firing lasted for hours into the night, with frightful losses, but the Federals held their enemy in place and then quietly slipped out of town late that night. Hood held the field but had lost 7,000 men (including 13 out of 28 generals and a total of 65 division, brigade, and regimental commanders) while inflicting only 2,326 losses on his opponent, who safely joined Thomas's concentration at Nashville.[58]

The failure to cut off Schofield left Hood with no choice but to take position on the hills south of Nashville and await developments. He had too few troops and too little logistical support to bypass the stronghold and advance north. There was little to

▼
BATTLE OF FRANKLIN
After losing Atlanta, Hood attempted to draw Sherman's men out of Georgia by threatening Nashville. His defeat while assaulting Union defenses at Franklin allowed Union forces in the region to link up, and led to his overwhelming defeat by George Thomas at Nashville in December.

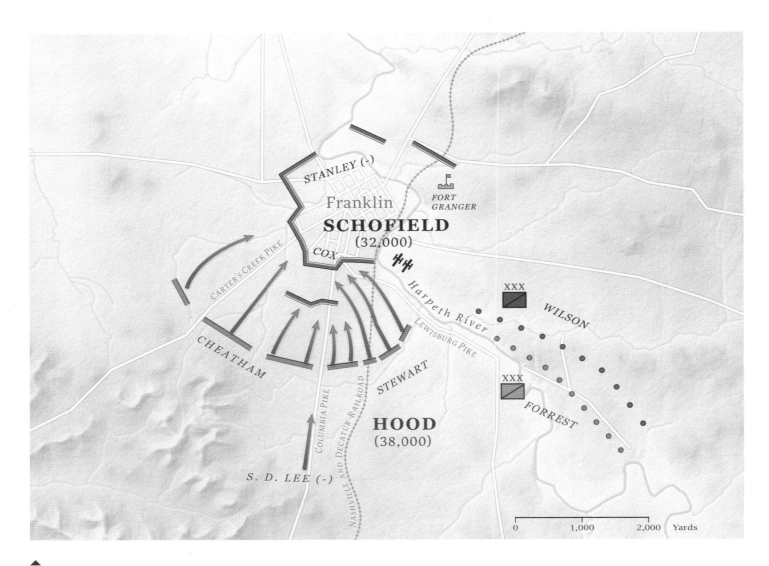

BATTLE OF FRANKLIN

Hoping to regain the strategic initiative, Hood chased down Schofield's army at Franklin. He launched a frontal attack against strong Union lines, and though they briefly broke through, the Confederates could not keep their gains, and lost 7,000 men. Schofield's forces escaped to join Thomas in Nashville.

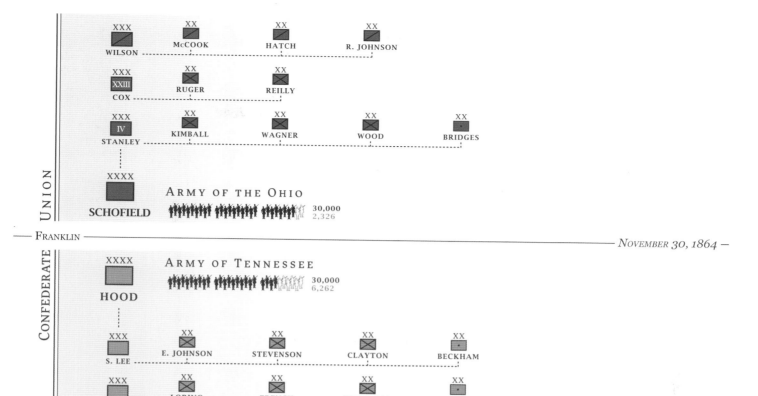

be gained by retreating, for Sherman already was too far away for Hood to catch him. Hood's only choices were to stay near Nashville or take a defensive stance somewhere farther south, and he chose to stay. Outnumbering Hood 55,000 to 21,500, Thomas attacked on December 15 and compelled his opponent to fall back to a new, more compact line. The next day, the Federals renewed the assault, and Hood's army collapsed. The Confederates barely escaped, pursuing Federal cavalry before finding refuge south of the Tennessee River.[59]

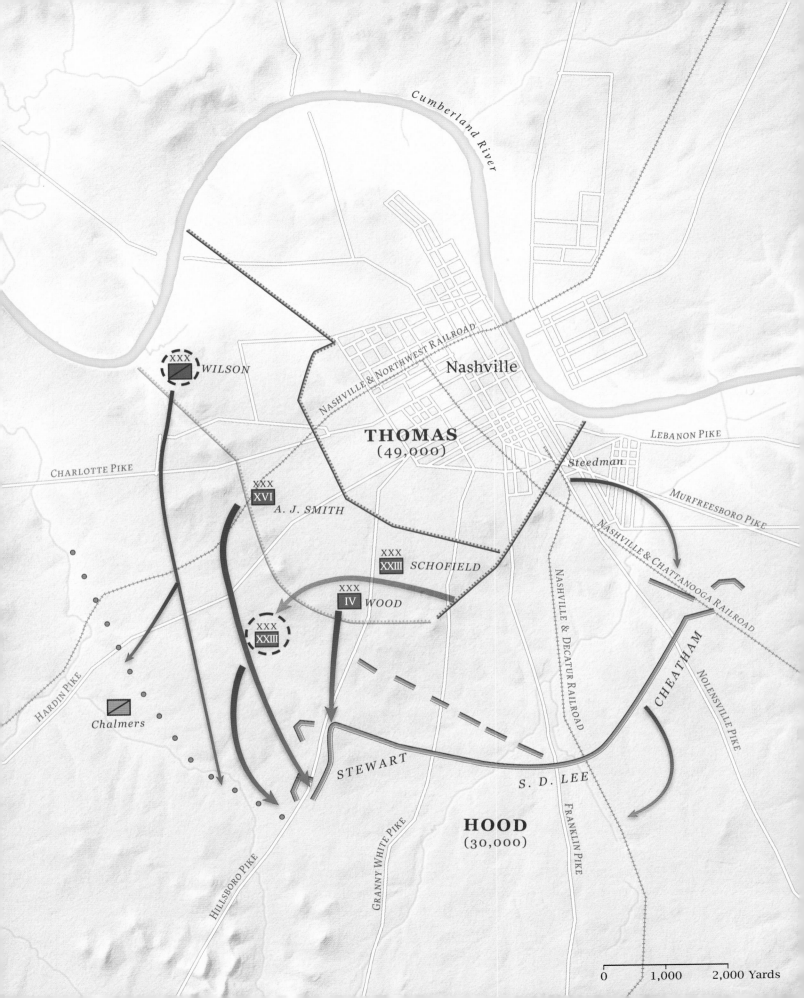

Cumberland River

XXX **WILSON**

Nashville

CHARLOTTE PIKE

THOMAS
(49,000)

Steedman

LEBANON PIKE

XXX
XVI

A. J. SMITH

MURFREESBORO PIKE

XXX
XXIII SCHOFIELD

XXX
IV WOOD

XXX
XXIII

Chalmers

STEWART

CHEATHAM

S. D. LEE

HARDIN PIKE

HILLSBORO PIKE

GRANNY WHITE PIKE

HOOD
(30,000)

FRANKLIN PIKE

NOLENSVILLE PIKE

NASHVILLE & NORTHWEST RAILROAD

NASHVILLE & CHATTANOOGA RAILROAD

NASHVILLE & DECATUR RAILROAD

0   1,000   2,000 Yards

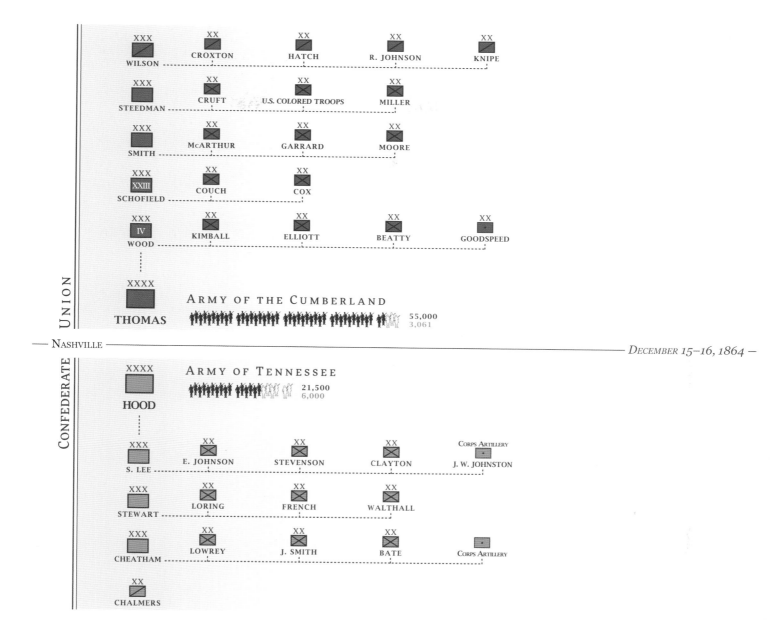

UNION

XXX **WILSON**	XX CROXTON	XX HATCH	XX R. JOHNSON	XX KNIPE
XXX **STEEDMAN**	XX CRUFT	XX U.S. COLORED TROOPS	XX MILLER	
XXX **SMITH**	XX McARTHUR	XX GARRARD	XX MOORE	
XXX XXIII **SCHOFIELD**	XX COUCH	XX COX		
XXX IV **WOOD**	XX KIMBALL	XX ELLIOTT	XX BEATTY	XX GOODSPEED

XXXX **THOMAS** ARMY OF THE CUMBERLAND

55,000
3,061

— NASHVILLE —

— *DECEMBER 15–16, 1864* —

CONFEDERATE

XXXX **HOOD** ARMY OF TENNESSEE

21,500
6,000

XXX **S. LEE**	XX E. JOHNSON	XX STEVENSON	XX CLAYTON	CORPS ARTILLERY J. W. JOHNSTON
XXX **STEWART**	XX LORING	XX FRENCH	XX WALTHALL	
XXX **CHEATHAM**	XX LOWREY	XX J. SMITH	XX BATE	CORPS ARTILLERY
XX **CHALMERS**				

◀ **BATTLE OF NASHVILLE**

Faced with few options, Hood tried to hold the hills south of Nashville and contain the Union army there. With a significant advantage in troop strength, Thomas pushed back the Confederates and nearly destroyed Hood's army.

The battle of Nashville ended major fighting in the western theater. Sherman continued on his way to help Grant at Petersburg. A shortage of coastal shipping forced him to march his troops northward from Savannah through the Carolinas. Beginning the trek in January, the Federals faced a far more difficult time than they had experienced in the March to the Sea. Not only was the distance longer, but their path was bisected by numerous streams, rivers, and swamps. The dirt roads in the region became ribbons of mud with each rainfall. Low-lying ground characterized much of the coastal plain, compelling the Federals to "corduroy" (or lay down a layer of wood along the muddy roads for wagons and artillery) for miles at a time.

The Federals overcame the difficulties of the Carolinas campaign with the perseverance and ingenuity they had developed at Vicksburg and Chattanooga. The "bummers"—soldiers detailed to range freely across the countryside in search of food for their comrades—came into their own. Eager to punish South Carolina, the first state to leave the Union in 1860, the soldiers became more destructive. When Sherman entered Columbia, the city already was in flames because of fires set by the retreating Confederates. Some Federals helped the flames along, while others tried to put them out, until a vicious wind rose to spread the conflagration. More than 260 houses were destroyed that night.[60]

Resistance began to stiffen in North Carolina as the Confederates finally mounted major efforts to find troops to defend their interior. The garrisons of Savannah and Wilmington, supplemented by what was left of the Army of Tennessee, began to gather in Sherman's path. The Confederates had managed to move Hood's battered army from Mississippi to North Carolina, mostly by circuitous rail routes. The ramshackle Confederate force was back under the command of Joseph E. Johnston.

Put in charge of all available troops in North Carolina, about 18,000 men, Johnston tried to stop Sherman. He launched a surprise attack on one of Sherman's columns near Bentonville on March 19, routing a division of Federals until another division stemmed the tide. Sherman brought his other column to the field that night, and both armies remained within striking distance of each other until the Confederates retired on March 21. It was obvious that Johnston could do no more than delay the Federals, who had completed a trek of 425 miles in fifty days.[61]

◀ **FEDERAL LINE NEAR NASHVILLE**

Taken just before the Battle of Nashville, this view shows a portion of the Union infantry line confronting Hood's Army of Tennessee. Note how the tents were arrayed behind the Union line of earthworks.

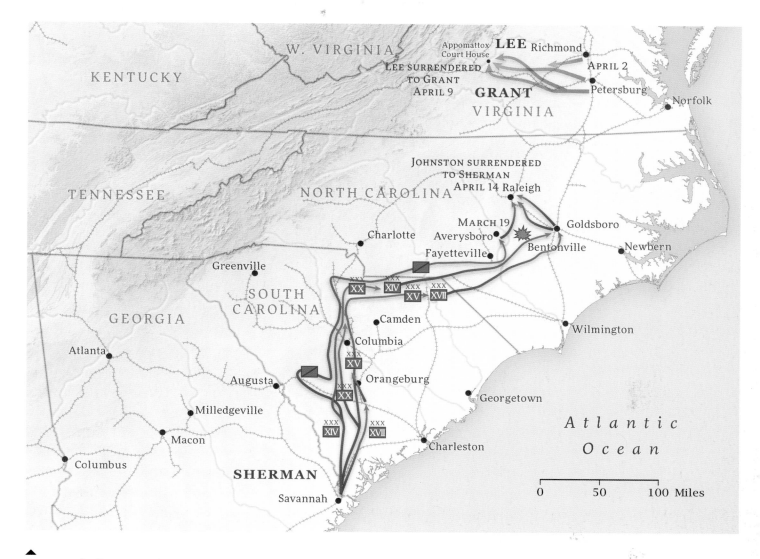

SHERMAN'S CAMPAIGN THROUGH THE CAROLINAS

After the new year, Sherman turned north from Savannah, intending to reinforce Grant at Petersburg. Johnston renewed his feeble attempts at stopping the Union advance, fighting at Bentonville, North Carolina, on March 19 before surrendering in April.

◤ MARCHING THROUGH THE CAROLINAS

Sherman's 60,000 men marched across the level, soggy coastal plain of the Carolinas during the middle of winter, crossing several major rivers and creeks that often flooded wide areas of bottomland. They built corduroy roads for miles on end—that is, cut small pine trees to make a rough wooden pavement over the worst sections of the road.

◀ THE BURNING OF COLUMBIA, SOUTH CAROLINA

Retreating Confederates attempted to burn their supplies in Columbia to prevent Sherman from using them, but the fire raged out of control. In the chaos, various Union units worked either to help or to fight the flames, and much of the state's capital burned.

Lee knew that Sherman was on the way. He had been appointed Confederate general in chief on February 6, 1865, but there was little he could do to coordinate the nation's crumbling defenses. Grant had turned an important corner when his latest bite-and-hold attack, the Seventh Offensive of February 5–7, 1865, secured ground that would enable the Federals to turn Lee's right if they could mount a sweeping movement to the south and west. Doing so would cut Lee's last supply line and make it impossible for his already overextended army to defend Petersburg against Union assault. In short, the Army of the Potomac and the Army of the James were poised to win the contest at Petersburg without Sherman's help.

Grant's Eighth Offensive began on March 29, and resulted in a smashing Union victory at Five Forks on April 1, which finally completed the long effort to turn Lee's flank. Knowing that Lee would be compelled to withdraw, Grant hoped to damage the Army of Northern Virginia as much as possible, so he ordered three major attacks against the front of Lee's position on April 2. This last day of fighting at Petersburg (the Ninth Union Offensive) resulted in a clean breakthrough by the VI Corps. Only heroic fighting by the Confederates staved off disaster long enough for Lee to evacuate his line after dark. Petersburg and Richmond fell into Federal hands as Jefferson Davis and the Rebel government fled.[62]

Lee sought to escape to North Carolina and join Joseph E. Johnston, but Grant mounted the most effective pursuit of a retreating army in the Civil War. Philip Sheridan, who had recently returned from the Shenandoah Valley, took up a fortified position at Jetersville to block Lee's route southward, forcing the Army of Northern Virginia to head west instead. A Federal attack at Sailor's Creek on April 6 smashed Lee's rear guard and garnered 3,400 prisoners. Sheridan's cavalry then cut off Lee's escape at Appomattox Court House, 90 miles west of Petersburg. Blocked on three sides, and realizing the futility of attempting to escape northward, Lee decided to negotiate surrender terms with Grant on April 9.

Grant had earned the nickname Unconditional Surrender because of his actions at Fort Donelson three years before. But now, in accordance with Lincoln's wishes, he offered generous terms that not only eased the pain of Confederate defeat but became a model for terms offered to other Rebel armies over the next two months. Officers were

PETERSBURG CAMPAIGN ▶

Grant began his final offensives at Petersburg in late March, smashing the Confederate defenders at Five Forks. Only desperate fighting allowed Lee enough time to evacuate his lines, ceding Petersburg and Richmond to the Union army.

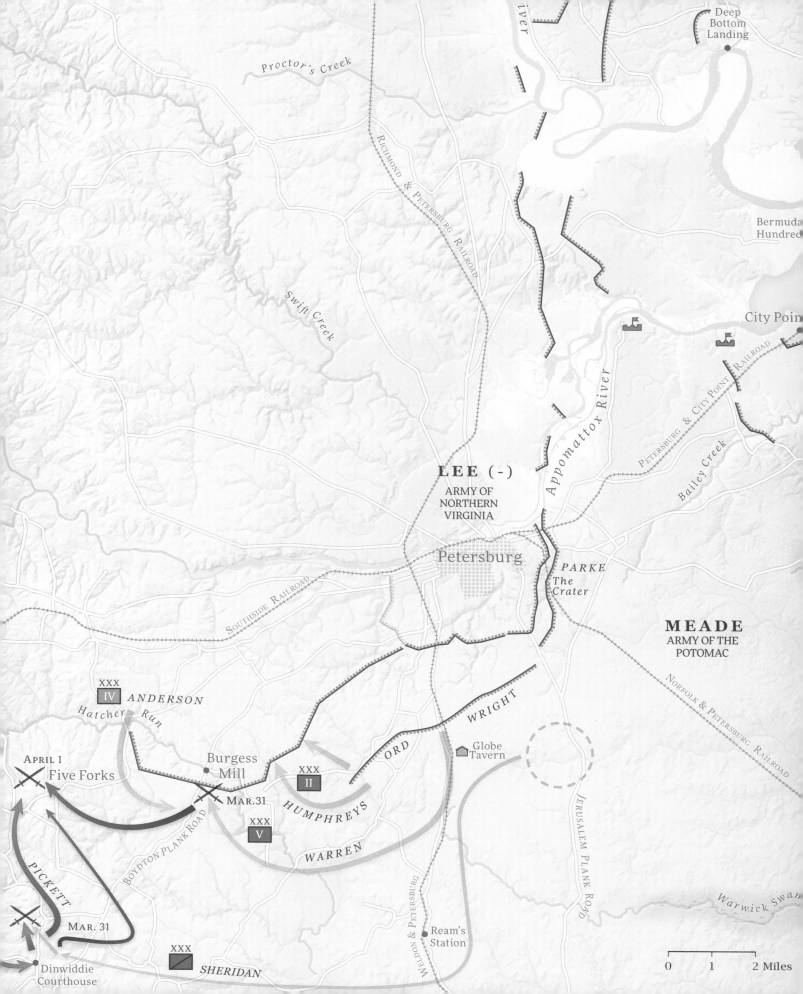

Deep
Bottom
Landing

Proctor's Creek

RICHMOND & PETERSBURG RAILROAD

Swift Creek

Bermuda
Hundred

Appomattox River

City Poin

PETERSBURG & CITY POINT RAILROAD

Bailey Creek

LEE (–)

ARMY OF
NORTHERN
VIRGINIA

Petersburg

SOUTHSIDE RAILROAD

PARKE
The Crater

MEADE

ARMY OF THE
POTOMAC

NORFOLK & PETERSBURG RAILROAD

XXX
IV   *ANDERSON*
Hatcher's Run

ORD

WRIGHT

Globe
Tavern

APRIL 1
Five Forks

Burgess
Mill

XXX
II

MAR. 31

HUMPHREYS

XXX
V

Jerusalem Plank Road

PICKETT

WARREN

Boydton Plank Road

MAR. 31

WELDON & PETERSBURG

Ream's
Station

Warwick Swan

Dinwiddie
Courthouse

XXX

SHERIDAN

0   1   2 Miles

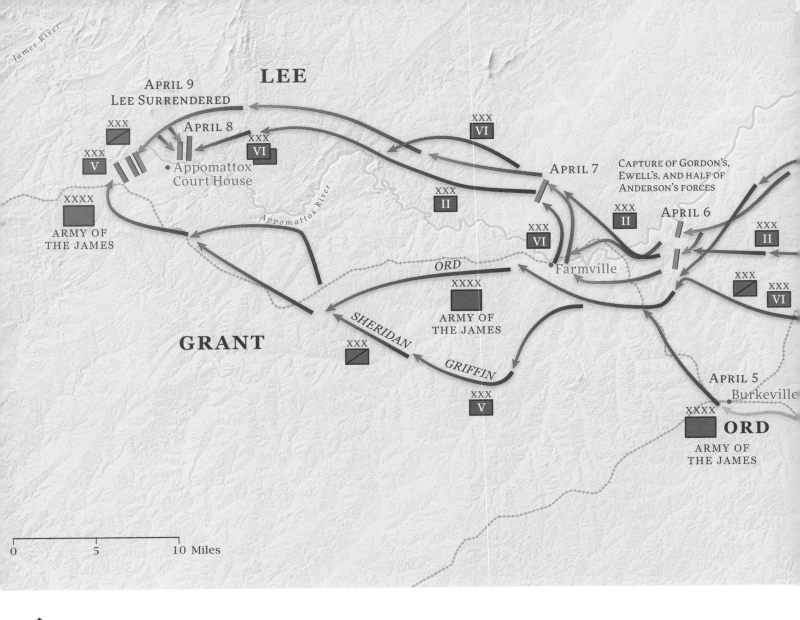

James River

LEE

APRIL 9
LEE SURRENDERED

XXX

APRIL 8

XXX
V

XXX
VI

XXXX

• Appomattox
Court House

Appomattox River

ARMY OF
THE JAMES

XXX
VI

XXX
II

ORD

XXXX

ARMY OF
THE JAMES

GRANT

SHERIDAN

XXX

GRIFFIN

XXX
V

XXX
VI

APRIL 7

CAPTURE OF GORDON'S,
EWELL'S, AND HALF OF
ANDERSON'S FORCES

XXX
II

APRIL 6

XXX
II

Farmville

XXX

XXX
VI

APRIL 5
Burkeville

XXXX ORD

ARMY OF
THE JAMES

0   5   10 Miles

THE DEFEAT OF LEE: PURSUIT TO APPOMATTOX

Lee fled west, hoping to find supplies and escape to North Carolina, where he might be able to meet Johnston and defeat the Union armies separately. For once, Lee could not outrace the Union army and was finally trapped at Appomattox Court House on April 8. Lee surrendered his army the next day.

allowed to retain their sidearms, any Confederate with a horse or mule was allowed to keep it, and Grant offered thousands of rations to feed Lee's starving men. The terms set a precedent for what many hoped would be a lenient effort to rehabilitate secessionists into loyal citizens of the United States.[63]

CONCLUSION

Grant's conduct of the last year of the Civil War was unprecedented in American history. Never before had the United States mobilized such a large military force or engaged troops in such intense action, suffered such heavy casualties, or so damaged its enemy. Grant coordinated overall strategy for widely dispersed forces far more than any previous American commander, enabled by Lincoln's similar concept of strategy, by modern means of communication and transportation, and because he could trust Sherman to support his plans. After three years, the United States had finally mounted

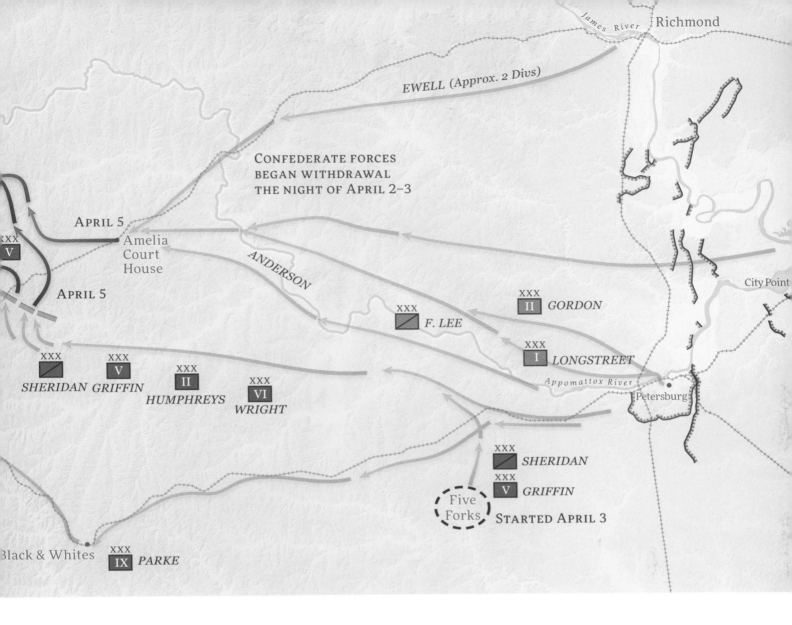

simultaneous offensives in both East and West. Worn down by years of battle and blockade, the Confederacy could not survive Grant's application of military power on both the strategic and operational levels.

It was remarkable that Lee surrendered less than a year after the onset of the Overland campaign and that the fighting mostly came to an end in the West by mid-December 1864. One insight into why that took place lies in the manpower available in the South. The Confederate government managed to maintain its troop strength fairly well through the spring of 1864. The national armies of the Confederacy had 47 percent of the manpower Lincoln's government could muster at the start of the year, and they still had 43.6 percent of Union troop strength in June. But by December, Confederate numbers had slid to only 27.6 percent of Union strength. Many reasons accounted for that decline, including Hood's casualties, attrition at Petersburg, and increasing desertion. Moreover, Davis's government chose to shift a larger proportion of reinforcements to Lee rather than to Johnston or Hood. As a result, the Army of Tennessee suffered a severe decline in its resources, while the Army of Northern Virginia

LEE'S SURRENDER AT ▶ APPOMATTOX COURT HOUSE

Surrounded by Grant's army, Lee surrendered the Army of Northern Virginia on April 9, 1865. Though the largest Confederate army, Lee's force was only the first of several to surrender over the next few months to close out the Civil War.

MAIN BATTERY OF FORT SEDGWICK

The flank protection for the gun emplacements consists entirely of two layers of gabions (wickerwork baskets filled with earth), separated by a row of fascines (bundles of sticks tied together). The men lying on the traverses were Union soldiers helping the photographer by pretending to be dead.

CONFEDERATE DEAD NEAR FORT MAHONE, PETERSBURG ▶

About a hundred photographs were taken of battlefield dead during the Civil War. This Confederate soldier was killed in the fighting of April 2, 1865, the last day of the Petersburg campaign. Rain turned the raw, dug earth into a muddy mess, making the image of battlefield death even more poignant.

was able to prolong the contest. Even so, Lee's troop strength allowed him less than one man for every yard of the thirty-mile-long works at Petersburg by April 2, 1865. For example, only 2,800 Confederates opposed 14,000 Federals along the VI Corps's line that day.[64]

The intense use of field fortifications was a major feature of campaigning in the last year of the Civil War. Fieldworks of all kinds had been common before May 1864, but no one could have predicted the extent of their use in the Overland, Petersburg, and Atlanta campaigns. The primary reason for this was continuous contact between the armies—a result of Grant's determination to wear down the Rebels. Now that they remained within striking distance of each other for months at a time, crude breastworks evolved into massive fieldworks. At Petersburg, a campaign that lasted 292 days, the earthworks were thirty miles long. The Army of Tennessee constructed no fewer than eighteen separate lines of elaborate earthworks during the four-month-long campaign for Atlanta.

The Confederates used fieldworks mostly for defensive purposes and thereby delayed Union operations. Remarkably, the Federals gained an even greater advantage by using earthworks for offensive purposes, in order to turn enemy positions and continue exercising the operational initiative. In all three campaigns, Union commanders held their enemy in place with strong fortifications that the Confederates could not capture, while detaching troops to conduct turning maneuvers that often succeeded in prying the Confederates out of their works. As long as there was room to maneuver, the Federals could overcome the defensive advantage of field fortifications. Lee understood this crucial dynamic when contemplating Grant's relentless advance during the Overland campaign: "If he is allowed to continue that course we shall at last be obliged to take refuge behind the works of Richmond and stand a siege, which would be but a work of time."[65]

This "old" technology proved more important than the new one for which the Civil War is known best. Historians of the Civil War have long thought that the introduction of the rifle musket as a general-issue weapon in the Civil War influenced all aspects of campaigning in that conflict, giving overwhelming strength to the defender. They assumed that the heavy use of fieldworks in the last year of the war was due to the long-range accuracy of this weapon. But this view does not hold up to objective scrutiny. The most important reason for the fieldworks is that Civil War officers and soldiers correctly thought that short-range firing was more effective. In fact, most infantry combat before, during, and even after the Civil War, whatever the small arms used, has been at ranges of one hundred yards or less.[66]

Another marked feature of campaigning in the last year of the war was the deliberate destruction of resources. Individual Federal soldiers, sometimes hungry because of supply deficiencies, or angered by guerrilla attacks, had been eating and burning southern property since the start of the conflict. The difference in 1864 was that high-level directives guided this destruction in the Shenandoah Valley, the March to the Sea, and the Carolinas campaign, followed by an array of raids through the Lower South during the spring of 1865. James H. Wilson's large cavalry force defeated Nathan Bedford Forrest and destroyed the Rebel industrial center at Selma, Alabama, early in April 1865, going on to Columbus and Macon, Georgia, by April 20. George Stoneman

conducted a destructive cavalry raid six hundred miles from Knoxville through western North Carolina and back during that month. Sherman, especially, saw a political purpose behind this effort to deny military resources to the enemy. "This movement is not purely military," he wrote to Halleck, ". . . but will illustrate the vulnerability of the South. They don't know what war means, but when the rich planters of the Oconee and Savannah see their fences and corn and hogs and sheep vanish before their eyes they will have something more than a mean opinion of the 'Yanks.'" Like the Prussian military theorist Carl von Clausewitz, Sherman well understood that the application of military force is simply a form of political pressure.[67]

Stout Confederate resistance and the difficulty of destroying Rebel armies in decisive battles eventually led the United States to turn to more gradual strategies of attrition and exhaustion. The practice of hard war, as historians now call it, had many precedents, stretching at least to the ancient Greeks. The fact that northern soldiers practiced it against other Americans in 1864 created a deep well of bitterness that lasted for generations in the South. But emotion should not obscure the fact that Federal forces acted with considerable restraint even when ordered to systematically destroy war materiel. They did so selectively in a few regions for short periods of time. In any case, the combination of strategies that Grant devised, adopted, or allowed others to employ brought the war to an end faster than if the pace of military operations that characterized the period of 1861 to 1863 had been allowed to continue.[68]

DEFIANCE: INVITING A SHOT BEFORE PETERSBURG
In this 1864 Winslow Homer painting, a Confederate soldier looks to draw sharpshooter fire from the Union line several hundred yards away. The campaign ultimately lasted ten months, as Grant launched nine successive offensives in his efforts to break the Confederate lines.

▲

RETURN OF THE FLAGS

This depiction of the Union Irish Brigade returning to New York reflects the exhausting nature of the recently finished struggle. The end of the fighting, which took place over several months following Appomattox, would mark only the beginning of a conflict over the war's meaning and legacy.

The struggle for union and freedom did not end with Lee's surrender at Appomattox on April 9, 1865, or with Abraham Lincoln's assassination five days later. Congress, the administration, and the press had been debating the shape of national reconstruction since the outbreak of hostilities, and the debate had not been resolved when Lincoln was murdered. Radical Republicans, a substantial force in Congress, sought a thoroughgoing transformation of southern society, breaking the power of the planter elite who had led the charge in secession and war and refashioning the South in the North's image. The president had hoped for both reconciliation between North and South and a degree of equality for the freedpeople (former slaves) of the South, "with malice toward none." His successor, Andrew Johnson, was a Democrat from East Tennessee, put on the 1864 ticket to encourage War Democrats to vote Republican and to promote the resuscitation of loyal government in Unionist regions of the Confederacy. Johnson's views were largely unknown: he hated elitist planters but shared the racism common throughout the nation, especially among Democrats (who had made it a campaign theme for decades). Most northern Democrats continued to hope for the restoration of "the Union as it was," with little social, political, economic, or cultural change. While that might have seemed unlikely after four years of war, Democrats relied on the belief in white supremacy, shared by most whites, North and South, in their hopes for the speedy readmission of the seceded states into the Union with the same rights as other states.[1]

These objectives clashed in several central policy questions. Who would direct Reconstruction policy: Congress, the executive branch, or voters in the southern states? Would the United States Army remain in the South, and for how long? Who would have political authority within the South: the army, civilians sent from the North, or southern whites? Would Confederate leaders be punished for their rebellion, how, and for how long? What would happen to the freedpeople? What rights would they have? How would they feed themselves? What role would they play in the economy and politics? If the South was to be transformed, what would it become?

Lee's decision to surrender the Army of Northern Virginia advanced two crucial outcomes in 1865. First, the Confederate government would not survive intact to have any voice in reconstructing the South. Second, the remaining Confederate field armies and naval forces would eventually capitulate. Yet Confederate military collapse after Appomattox proved haphazard rather than automatic. Toward the end, staunch Confederates desperately pursued a number of alternative strategies in the hope of staving off complete defeat, but none worked. Union military victory gave way to the challenges of demobilizing citizen-soldier armies, securing the border with Mexico, and occupying the defeated South. The federal army kept a small number of troops on occupation duty in the ex-Confederate states for more than a decade, but by 1877, even this mission came to an end. Demobilization meant that the peacetime army would shrink to nearly its antebellum size, remaining about 25,000 strong until the

6

THE END OF THE CIVIL WAR AND RECONSTRUCTION

JAMES K. HOGUE

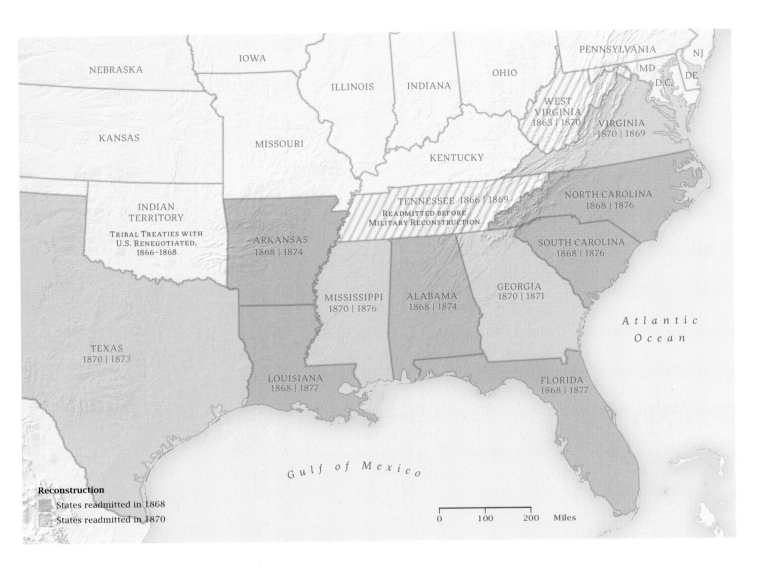

MAP OF RECONSTRUCTION

In the decade after the Civil War, the U.S. government slowly readmitted the states of the former Confederacy. Under each state's name, the map shows two dates: the first year is the state's readmission to the Union, the second the reestablishment of conservative white rule.

Spanish-American War in 1898. This chapter explores these challenges, and assesses why the Confederacy lost and the United States won the Civil War.

THE SERIAL SURRENDER OF CONFEDERATE ARMIES

After learning of Lee's surrender, Gen. Joseph Johnston decided to surrender his army in North Carolina to Sherman, and the two agreed to terms on April 18. Those terms hinted at federal recognition of Confederate state governments, which proved too generous for Andrew Johnson. The new president ordered General Grant to instruct Sherman to renegotiate the surrender with "Appomattox terms" identical to those that Grant had offered to Lee. Johnston signed the revised surrender on April 26, and his soldiers laid down their arms and headed home.[2]

The other major Confederate commands haltingly followed suit. Confederate forces defending Mobile, Alabama, had surrendered three days after Appomattox. Gen. Richard Taylor, son of Mexican War general and U.S. president Zachary Taylor, surrendered all Confederate forces under his command in the Department of Alabama

and Mississippi on May 8.[3] In Texas, Gen. Edmund Kirby Smith signed the surrender of the Army of the Trans-Mississippi on June 2. Frontier Texas was so remote that it took another three weeks before Federal troops arrived to raise the Stars and Stripes over Austin on June 25, 1865, the last state capital reoccupied.[4]

In an era before wireless communication, Confederate ships at sea took even longer to receive news from home. The C.S.S. *Shenandoah*, a commerce raider secretly built and launched from Liverpool, England, in late 1864, sailed halfway around the world by way of the Indian Ocean and Melbourne, Australia, to ravage the northern whaling fleet off Alaska. Its captain did not receive definitive news of Confederate defeat until August 1865, after he had already captured thirty-eight ships. Fearing that he and his crew might be tried and hanged for piracy by U.S. courts, he disguised his ship, struck the Confederate colors, and sailed the rest of the way around the world to Liverpool, where he surrendered to the Royal Navy on November 6, 1865. Organized Confederate military resistance had finally ceased.[5]

JOHNSTON'S SURRENDER

Shortly after hearing of Lee's surrender at Appomattox, Joseph Johnston decided to surrender his Army of Tennessee to William T. Sherman in North Carolina. Sherman provided terms that were considered too generous in Washington, and the government forced him to renegotiate using Grant's terms from Appomattox.

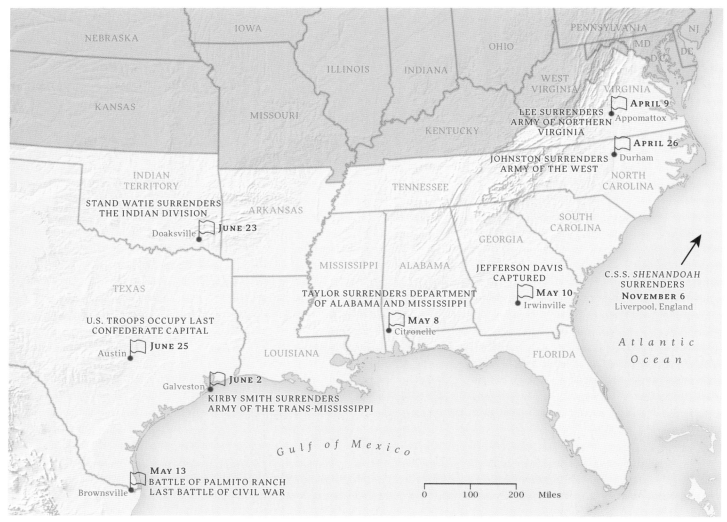

Map of Confederate Surrenders

Lee's surrender at Appomattox marked the beginning of the war's end. In the months that followed, Rebel armies surrendered across the South. The final official surrender of a Confederate force was the crew of the *Shenandoah*, which was in the North Pacific Ocean when it finally received word of the Confederacy's defeat.

Old "Rip" of the *Shenandoah* ▶

The C.S.S. *Shenandoah*, led by Capt. James I. Waddell, did not learn of the war's end until August, which the cartoon here mocks using a reference to Rip van Winkle. Waddell went to Liverpool, England, where he surrendered his ship to the British government in November.

Roads Not Taken:
Confederate Strategic Options in 1865

This protracted collapse serves as a reminder that many Confederates did not believe that defeat was inevitable, even in 1865. Other outcomes still seemed possible to those who refused to give up until they had exhausted every alternative to defeat. Yet none of these options proved realistic after a long war that had devastated much of the Confederacy, demoralized many of its citizens, and made inveterate enemies among northerners.

One alternative was an armistice leading to the voluntary return of Confederate states to the Union. After Lincoln's November 1864 reelection crushed Confederate hopes for a change of administration in Washington, Jefferson Davis authorized a commission led by Vice President Alexander Stephens to conduct talks with U.S. leaders "for the purpose of securing peace to the two countries." Not wanting to refuse any opportunity to shorten the war, Lincoln warily agreed to meet them at Hampton Roads, Virginia, on February 3, 1865. Once there, however, Lincoln refused to negotiate unless the Confederates accepted three conditions: restoration of the national government; abolition of slavery; and disbandment of all Confederate military forces. Stephens had no authority to agree to any preconditions, so the commissioners returned to Richmond empty-handed. Davis used his own commission's failure to argue that Lincoln's stance proved that the war could end only in Confederate independence or total defeat. The war continued.[6]

Some Confederates argued that the government had not tried every source of manpower to refill the army's depleted ranks. The 1862 draft law applied only to white men, not to the Confederacy's four million slaves and free blacks. The Confederate Congress debated proposals to arm slaves during the winter of 1865, but legislators divided bitterly over whether the slaves should—or would—fight for their side, especially after the Union had recruited blacks to fight under a banner promising emancipation.[7]

After Davis finally appointed Lee as general in chief on January 31, 1865, Lee identified manpower as the critical shortage for the spring campaign. He issued a general amnesty for absentees who voluntarily returned to their regiments and then exerted his influence to persuade legislators to pass the so-called Negro Soldier Bill, which Davis signed on March 23. Lee immediately ordered the recruiting of slaves and free blacks in Richmond, but only two companies began mustering before Union forces occupied the city eleven days later. Of the 28,000 Confederates present at the Appomattox surrender, only 39 blacks received paroles. This amounted to just 0.10 percent of Lee's army, an insignificant proportion by any reckoning. The South's last-ditch effort to try arming slaves came far too late to make any difference in the outcome of the war.[8]

Some historians have wondered why Confederates did not disband their conventional armies and adopt guerilla warfare. Many southerners remembered how the British had decisively defeated two conventional Patriot armies after seizing Charleston during the American Revolution. Yet the British never completely snuffed out the

THE RIVER QUEEN

The *River Queen*, seen here in its original job as a ferry in Nantucket, Massachusetts, was commandeered by Grant as a dispatch ship in 1864–65. In February 1865 it was the site of the Hampton Roads Conference, an attempted peace negotiation requested by Confederate vice president Alexander Stephens.

insurgencies in any of the southern colonies. If guerrilla war succeeded for their forefathers, why couldn't it work for them?

Col. Edward Porter Alexander (USMA 1857), put that question directly to Lee on the day before the Appomattox surrender. Doubtlessly thinking of the ruin of Sherman's March to the Sea, Sheridan's ravaging of the Shenandoah Valley, and the draft resisters and bandits already roaming the Confederate interior, Lee replied that he feared Confederate guerrillas "would become mere bands of marauders, and the enemy's cavalry would pursue them and overrun many sections they may never [otherwise] have occasion to visit. We would bring on a state of affairs it would take the country years to recover from."[9] Without Lee's endorsement, Confederates refused to transform what had mostly been a conventional war into a remorseless guerrilla struggle against the massed armies of the United States.

A final option was for the Confederate government to abandon Richmond and continue to direct the fight from somewhere in the far West, though the resources there would be so slim as to virtually require resorting to guerrilla warfare. Jefferson Davis embraced this idea after Grant's forces overran the fortifications outside Petersburg. Accompanied by his cabinet and the treasury, he moved by rail to Danville, Virginia, and then to Greensboro, North Carolina. At Danville, he issued a proclamation to the Confederate people promising that "war would be carried on with renewed vigor."[10] After reaching Greensboro, however, the fugitive government discovered that Yankee cavalry and Confederate deserters blocked the railway ahead. Davis and a smaller party continued on horseback to Charlotte, North Carolina, where his cabinet met until April 26. While there, Davis learned of Lincoln's assassination and Johnston's surrender. A general disintegration followed. Several cabinet members escaped to Florida and then exile in England. Thousands of Confederates crossed the Rio Grande River to seek sanctuary in Mexico. Smaller colonies took refuge in Cuba, Central America, and as far south as Brazil.[11] But Union cavalry captured Davis near Irwinville, Georgia, and the federal government imprisoned him for several years. If moving the capital to the far West had ever been a viable option, Jefferson Davis waited too long to try it.[12]

GUERRILLAS ◥

Though guerrilla raids had been a part of Confederate tactics, especially in the West, Lee refused to sanction the widespread use of such forces, fearing the destruction it would bring to the South. This etching depicts the destruction of Lawrence, Kansas, in August 1863.

THE LAST DAYS OF THE CONFEDERATE GOVERNMENT ▶

After the fall of Richmond, Jefferson Davis and other officials fled south, trying to maintain the government. Here Davis is signing acts into law at a makeshift camp, presumably days before being captured by Union cavalry on May 10, 1865.

UNION VICTORY: THE GRAND REVIEW, MAY 23–24, 1865

After Davis's capture, the Union mood turned celebratory. The federal government organized a grand review and military parade down Washington's Pennsylvania Avenue from the U.S. Capitol to a reviewing stand erected just for the occasion in front of the White House. It was the largest public celebration ever held in the United States up to that time—executed on a scale so vast that it took not one but *two* entire days for well over one hundred thousand soldiers to pass in review. On May 23, 1865, General Meade rode at the head of the Army of the Potomac until he reached the reviewing stand, where he saluted, dismounted, and then shared the dais with President Johnson, General Grant, and Union leaders. For the rest of the day, Meade received salutes from waves of blue regiments fresh from victory over Lee's army. On the following day, General Sherman followed suit with the westerners of the Army of the Tennessee—most of whom were seeing Washington for the first time in their lives. Within days, the men who made up these citizen-soldier armies collected their final pay and discharge papers and headed home.[13] They were tired of war and uncertain about peace, but certain that they had done their duty and saved the Union in an epic struggle that they and the country would never forget.[14]

WHY THE UNION WON, WHY THE CONFEDERACY LOST

Over the past 150 years, Americans have argued endlessly over why the Union won and the Confederacy lost. For the generation of Confederate veterans who felt the sting of defeat, the explanation seemed simple: Johnny Reb fought long and hard and well but could not overcome Billy Yank's many advantages. This explanation took hold immediately after General Lee issued his farewell address on April 10, 1865, the day after he surrendered to Grant. After praising his soldiers for their "unsurpassed courage and fortitude," he wrote, "the Army of Northern Virginia has been compelled to yield to overwhelming numbers and resources."[15] There was the answer in black and white from the greatest Confederate general.

The Confederacy had indeed fought against greater numbers and resources. The North's population outnumbered the South's by two and a half to one. (This figure includes slaves and free blacks, who were frequently compelled to labor on Confederate fortifications or otherwise support the war effort.) Northern railroads had three times the mileage of their southern counterparts. Northern manufacturing outstripped southern by nearly ten to one. The Confederacy had virtually no navy, and the Federal blockade aggravated shortages and stoked inflation across the import-dependent Cotton South, which lacked significant liquid capital. Over time, northerners built more warships, and southern port after southern port fell in a vicious spiral of defeat. Numbers and resources are *external factors* with which states at war with each other must

For two days, May 23 and 24, 1865, soldiers from the main Union armies marched past a reviewing stand for President Andrew Johnson, General Grant, and other Union officials in Washington in a parade to celebrate their victory and the end of the war.

contend. In the Civil War, Union quantitative superiorities shaped strategy, operations, and tactics on both sides.

External factors also shaped the course of land campaigns, although not as quickly and perhaps not as much as might have been expected. Through the first year of the war, Confederate armies generally held their own on the battlefield, especially in the East. After Lee took command in 1862, the Army of Northern Virginia seemed even more capable. By mid-1863, however, Union armies had repulsed Lee's and other Confederate offensives and began to seize the strategic initiative. This was particularly true in the West, where an increasing disparity of numbers allowed Federal forces to maneuver more effectively while guarding long lines of communication. Unlike Confederate armies, they repeatedly replenished their ranks, thanks to the new federal draft law, a continuing stream of immigrant recruits, and Lincoln's decision to enlist black soldiers. Union armies grew better armed and supplied over time as well. The Confederacy did manage to mobilize 80 percent of its free adult white male population for military service—a remarkable feat by any measure—but it was never enough to overcome the Union armies' larger numbers.[16]

External factors remain a favorite explanation among Civil War historians. During the centennial commemoration in 1960, northern-born historian Richard Current reviewed a century of literature on the war and concluded that, "as usual, God was on the

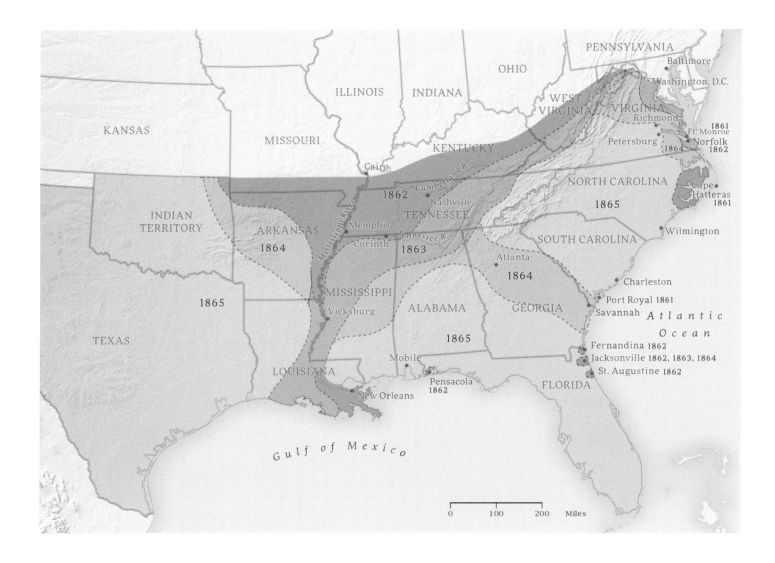

Union Territorial Gains by Year

The Union started the war with a large superiority in nearly every category of material resources. As the Confederacy lost ground in 1862, 1863, and 1864, its disadvantages in population, industry, food production, and wealth became greater and greater.

side of the heaviest battalions."[17] Shelby Foote, southern-born author of a best-selling three-volume history of the war, agreed. After noting the vast disparities between each side's resources, he declared, "I don't think the South ever had a chance to win that war."[18] Acclaimed British military historian John Keegan subscribed to an even more expansive version of this explanation in 2009: "the Union triumphed in the end only because of larger numbers and greater wealth of resources."[19]

There is, however, a fundamental problem with explanations focused narrowly on external factors. Confederates from Jefferson Davis down to rank-and-file privates constantly—perhaps obsessively—looked to their forefathers' example in the American Revolution for inspiration.[20] Americans had prevailed against the world's greatest empire, with its superb navy, well-trained army led by seasoned generals, and a treasury adept at financing multiple campaigns around the world. Like their forefathers, Confederates did not have to conquer and occupy their enemy's country to win their independence. They simply had to convince the Yankees, like the British before them, to stop fighting.

Other wars demonstrate that numerical and material superiority does not guarantee victory, particularly in protracted conflicts fueled by popular will. In the Dutch Revolt (1568–1648), the Netherlands fended off the Spanish in an eighty-year conflict against the most powerful state in Europe. In the twentieth century, the North Vietnamese prevailed in "people's wars" against France and the United States, despite their disadvantages in numbers and technology. Thus, while external factors point to the Union's significant advantages in the conduct of the Civil War, they are *insufficient* by themselves to explain the conflict's outcome.

A second school of thought, particularly strong among historians who study the American South, recognizes the importance of popular will and the problem of divisions within the Confederacy. Southern politicians warned before the war that a powerful central government would trample over states' rights. It was no surprise, then, that Jefferson Davis ran into fierce opposition when he called for greater powers for his national government on the grounds of "military necessity." In February 1862 the Confederate Congress authorized military officers and civilian agents to impress (seize) supplies (most often food and fodder) for the army. In April Davis signed a draft bill that also forced current volunteers to remain on active duty. Failure to keep the volunteers in uniform and draft new recruits, he warned, would be tantamount to defeat.[21] For the rest of the war, Davis argued with state governors, particularly Joseph E. Brown of Georgia and Zebulon Vance of North Carolina, over issues surrounding the legality of the Confederate draft. Both governors withheld state militia that Confederate armies needed badly to fend off the more numerous Yankees. One historian quipped that the Confederacy's epitaph ought to read, "Died of states' rights."[22]

Intertwined with Confederate political divisions over conscription and impressment was the notion that the Civil War was "a rich man's war but a poor man's fight." Enactment of an exemption for one overseer for every twenty slaves (the so-called Twenty Negro Law) antagonized nonslaveholding whites, who made up the majority of Confederate soldiers. (Approximately a quarter of Confederates were slaveholders.) Historian Steven Hahn identifies conflict between slaveholding planters and yeoman farmers as a fundamental source of class tensions within southern society. Large areas of the Confederacy (particularly the Appalachian regions of East Tennessee, western North Carolina, and what became West Virginia) opposed secession, and tens of thousands of white southern men fought for the United States, whether as guerrillas or in organized regiments. These tensions weakened popular will, undermined a sense of shared sacrifice, and paved the way to defeat.[23]

Another internal division argument emphasizes the impact of race and slavery. Some historians argue that *the* critical turning point in the war came with Lincoln's

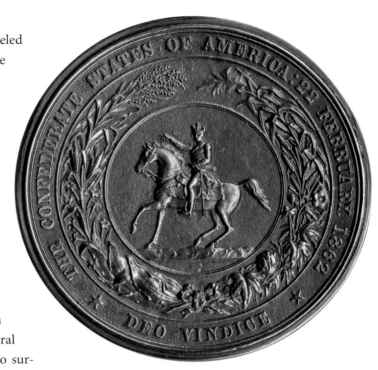

SEAL OF THE CONFEDERATE STATES OF AMERICA

The Confederate government consciously looked to the example of the American Revolution to justify its cause. The Confederate seal focused on an image of George Washington, and dated the foundation of the official government from Jefferson Davis's inauguration on February 22, Washington's birthday.

▲
PRISONERS FROM THE FRONT

Though outmatched in numbers, industry, and logistics, the Confederates fought to the end. This 1866 painting by Winslow Homer (who followed the Union army as a journalist) depicts Confederate prisoners at the end of the war as poorly outfitted; the age of the white-bearded man in the center reflects how heavily the Confederacy had tapped its available manpower.

▲
CHARGE OF THE 22ND U.S. COLORED TROOPS

The use of black troops provided a twofold advantage for the North: providing additional manpower while removing a source of labor for the Confederacy. Though kept in segregated units and mostly relegated to support duty, black troops fought bravely when granted the opportunity.

Emancipation Proclamation on January 1, 1863. Before then, most Confederates believed that their slaves would labor faithfully on the home front. After Lincoln's edict, a surging exodus of slaves escaped from bondage and flooded into Union "contraband camps," crippling the South's agricultural economy. Union forces subsequently enlisted 200,000 black soldiers and sailors, most of whom had been slaves before the war. A pillar of Confederate domestic economic strength morphed into an Achilles' heel.[24]

Feminist scholarship has similarly analyzed gender relations during the war. The Old South, steeped in a culture of traditional patriarchy, was as fearful of northern reforms in gender roles (like suffrage for women) as it was of the abolition of slavery. At first, white women enthusiastically supported the Confederacy when their kinsmen marched off for a brief and glorious war for independence. As the conflict wore on, their enthusiasm declined. Confederate women found themselves burdened by the new demands of taking on "men's work" in farm fields and towns while trying to keep up with traditional "women's work" to sustain home and family. By late 1864, soaring casualties and the grinding privations of war bore down on the home front as never before. Southern women demanded that their men return home, triggering an unprecedented spike in desertion in the winter of 1865. By the next spring, Confederate armies had become too depleted to continue to fight. According to historian Drew Gilpin Faust, the Confederacy did not endure any longer because "so many women did not want it to."[25]

The common problem with many internal division arguments, whether rooted in politics, race, class, gender, or some combination, is that they tend to either ignore or to minimize the importance of external factors, treating them as catalysts for internal divisions rather than causal forces in their own right. Nor, focused narrowly on southern society, do they always acknowledge that there were also divisions within the victorious Union. Indeed, on closer examination, some of the same internal divisions that supposedly explain Confederate defeat seriously divided the Union as well.

The Confederate government began its war for independence more united than the northern states on the questions of slavery and secession. By comparison, Lincoln's new government was a squabbling coalition, paralyzed for weeks over how—or even whether—it should respond to Confederate threats to take Fort Sumter by force. Northern politicians in Congress could not agree on whether to demand the immediate abolition of slavery, restrict its expansion into new territories, or protect it with a constitutional amendment that would somehow lure the Confederate states back into the Union and stave off civil war. To be sure, the Confederate decision to take the fort in Charleston Harbor provoked a tremendous response to Lincoln's subsequent call for volunteers, but that burst of Union sentiment came at the price of losing four more Upper South states (Virginia, North Carolina, Tennessee, and Arkansas), making the Confederacy an even stronger and more formidable opponent.[26]

Divisions within the Union continued through much of the war. Military conscription was less successful and arguably just as divisive in the Union as it was in the Confederacy.[27] In the U.S. Congress, every Republican voted for the draft bill in 1863, but

THE BURIAL OF LATANÉ ▶

Captain William Latané was the only one of Stuart's soldiers killed during his famous 1862 ride around the Army of the Potomac. The funeral was arranged by local women who volunteered to see to his burial. The mourners were limited to women, children, and slaves, because the white men of the plantation were all serving with the army. The ladies' evident sorrow reflects their Confederate patriotism, not family connection. The painting became very famous as an evocation of women's devotion to the Rebel cause.

88 percent of Democrats opposed it as an attack on civil liberties and "class legislation" that let the wealthy buy substitutes to serve in their place.[28] Opposition to the draft erupted in July 1863 in New York City. Marked by violence and arson, it remains the deadliest urban riot in American history. At least one hundred and possibly as many as one thousand people died, including thirty-eight draft officials. Overwhelmed by mobs in the streets, police lost control over parts of the city. In desperation, the authorities summoned six regiments, fresh from Gettysburg, to restore order. Antidraft riots also struck Boston, Albany, Chicago, and other cities. If the Union had lost the war, some historians would probably have argued that the North's greater internal divisions must have caused its defeat.[29]

Gary Gallagher, an expert on the Confederacy, identifies the common underlying problem with overreliance on internal division arguments. He contends that historians are posing the wrong question when they ask why the Confederacy lost, because that was always the most likely outcome of an unequal contest. Gallagher contends that the better historical question lies in asking why the Confederacy lasted as long as it did and why it came as close as it did to winning the war in spite of the constraints of both external factors *and* internal factors. For him, the answer lies in the dynamic relationship between popular will, Confederate nationalism, and the military strategy embodied in Robert E. Lee's generalship. It was for these reasons that, in spite of the South's many handicaps, Lee almost won the war.[30]

Gallagher's emphasis on Lee's generalship has refocused attention on the dynamic nature of the Civil War and the critical factor of leadership that lies at the nexus between internal and external factors. Consider the crucial impact of political leadership on policy and military strategy. Lincoln and Davis are studies in contrast as commanders in chief. Davis was far better prepared for the test of supreme leadership, both by education and experience. He had not only graduated from West Point (USMA 1824) and served in the antebellum army but also had commanded a volunteer regiment in the Mexican War, served as secretary of war, and overseen the making of military policy as a U.S. senator. As Confederate president, however, Davis encountered difficulties largely of his own making: he made bitter enemies among politicians and generals all too easily, and exuded a stiff self-righteousness rather than burying personal differences for the common good. In some of his military appointments, such as Braxton Bragg and Joseph Johnston, he supported personal favorites to the detriment of his armies. He delegated administrative work badly or not at all, repeatedly overworking himself until he was literally too ill to get out of bed and attend to critical affairs of state. While personally devoted to the Confederacy, he often seemed at a loss to summon the rhetorical skills or seize the political opportunities that a great war demands from those in positions of executive power.[31]

Lincoln provides a striking contrast. He had no military education or experience before the Civil War, except for a month as a militia captain in the Black Hawk War thirty years earlier. Yet he readily conceded his lack of preparation and taught himself the rudiments of strategy by studying military treatises from the U.S. Library of Congress and the dispatches his generals sent to the telegraph office in the War Department, which was then literally steps away from the White House. Lincoln undoubtedly made mistakes in directing the Union war effort, but he also unified the factions of the Republican Party behind it. He reached out to his political opponents, most famously in his controversial selection of Andrew Johnson, a southerner and a Democrat from Tennessee, to be his running mate in 1864. Above all, Lincoln developed an impressive range of rhetorical skills suitable for every occasion. Whether employing barnyard humor at cabinet meetings to explain the military strategy for 1864 ("Those not skinning can hold a leg"), or soaring rhetoric in his inaugural addresses and the Gettysburg Address ("that government of the people, by the people, for the people shall not perish from the earth"), Lincoln communicated the Union's war aims in simple yet clear language that helped sustain the people through the years of appalling sacrifice and bloodshed required to win the war, reconstruct the Union, and destroy the centuries-old institution of slavery. The net effect of Lincoln's dynamic leadership was to minimize the internal divisions within the Union while maximizing the external factors that bore down and finally crushed Rebel armies and their government.[32]

Military leadership shaped the conduct of the war just as much as political leadership. Lee's appointment as commander of the Army of Northern Virginia in 1862 began a series of dazzling campaigns, the likes of which had not been seen since Napoleon. While always outnumbered, Lee executed bold and aggressive campaigns that repeatedly thrashed Union armies and inspired tremendous confidence in common soldiers and generals alike. Lee's victories inspired still greater sacrifices from the home front, sustained popular will, and encouraged Confederate nationalism even after those victories began to wane.

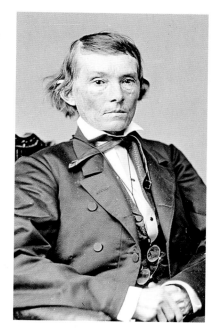

ALEXANDER STEPHENS
Alexander Stephens served as vice president of the Confederacy. In this position, he argued with Davis over Confederate policy. Stephens disagreed with Davis's use of conscription and the suspension of habeas corpus, and lobbied on several occasions for Davis to negotiate an end to the war.

Furling the Flag

Championed by former Confederates such as Jubal Early, "Lost Cause" ideology depicted the Confederacy as the noble defender of old-fashioned chivalry, idealizing Lee, Jackson, and the Army of Northern Virginia. Lost Cause proponents attributed their defeat to overwhelming force, and saw the war and Reconstruction as a deliberate attempt by the North to destroy the more traditional southern way of life.

Reflecting his long study of Napoleon and his personal experience with Winfield Scott's expedition to Mexico, most of Lee's campaigns were stunningly bold offensives. Some historians have criticized the appalling casualties that such aggressiveness produced.[33] Those criticisms—emphasizing that the Confederacy could not sustain such losses over an extended period—are correct as far as they go. Yet balanced against this terrible human toll must be an understanding that the Union's successive military defeats in 1862 and 1863 might have inflicted fatal blows on the morale of northern society, which represented the real center of gravity of the conflict. Lee's crushing victory at Fredericksburg so depressed Lincoln that he privately observed, "If there is a worse place than Hell, I am in it."[34] There was harder to come, in the form of another even worse defeat at Chancellorsville and the humiliation of the invasion of Pennsylvania. Had Lincoln been a prime minister in a parliamentary form of government rather than

General Robert E. Lee ▶

Even during the war, Lee's leadership of the Army of Northern Virginia provided an important symbol for Confederate nationalism.

serving a fixed term as president of a republic, he might well have lost a vote of confidence and been forced to accept an armistice leading to Confederate independence.[35]

The making of the winning team of Union generals was a long, complicated saga. While much of Washington's attention remained riveted on bigger battles in the eastern theater, Ulysses S. Grant compiled a string of victories carried out by a collection of like-minded subordinate generals. From Forts Henry and Donelson, to Vicksburg, to Missionary Ridge, Grant conducted agile offensives that sliced through Confederate territory with unrelenting aggressiveness. His interservice cooperation with navy officers in riverine operations remains underappreciated. As the war progressed, Grant encouraged Sherman and Sheridan toward an emerging practice of "hard war" that fused skillful maneuver and battlefield victories with a determination to destroy the Confederacy's resources.[36] When Lincoln promoted Grant to commanding general in 1864, Grant's strategic plan, which called for simultaneous attacks on all fronts, took time to wear down the Confederacy. That did not stop him from pressing the Army of Northern Virginia relentlessly south, penning it up in Petersburg, and resuming the offensive in the spring of 1865, a testament to his unshakeable determination to finish what he had started.[37]

In addition to battlefield commanders, Lincoln and Secretary of War Edwin Stanton assembled an executive team in Washington with the managerial skills to support multiple campaigns on a continental scale. Henry Halleck, Lincoln's military chief of staff, helped translate the president's policies into military strategy and coordinated the far-flung armies.[38] Montgomery Meigs (USMA 1836), the quartermaster general, oversaw a department employing over a hundred thousand civilians who fed, clothed, armed, and supplied more than a million soldiers, transforming the Union armed forces into "the largest, best equipped, best fed, and most powerful war machine ever assembled in the history of the world to that date."[39] Herman Haupt (USMA 1835) did much the same for the U.S. Military Railroad, in contrast to Jefferson Davis's vacillation over the relationship between railroads and the war effort.

This new Union war machine suited the character of mid-nineteenth-century warfare. In the Crimean War, the American Civil War, and the wars of German and Italian unification, it proved impossible to destroy the armies of industrializing states in a single day's battle, as Napoleon had done to the Prussians at Jena in 1806, or as was done to his own army at Waterloo in 1815.[40] The generals who fought the Civil War had been imbued with a vision of Napoleonic-style decisive battles through a growing literature on the Napoleonic wars and the teachings of Dennis Hart Mahan, professor of military art and engineering at West Point from 1824 to 1871.[41] Those who

ABRAHAM LINCOLN ▶

Far less prepared for wartime leadership than his Confederate counterpart, Lincoln rose to the occasion by utilizing his strengths to close internal divisions while providing the nation a clear rationale for the war.

DAVID GLASGOW FARRAGUT

JULY 5, 1801–AUGUST 14, 1870

The son of a Spanish immigrant, David Farragut was one of the U.S. Navy's first admirals. Born with the name James, Farragut was given up for adoption after the death of his mother and took the name David to honor David Porter (father of fellow future Civil War admiral David Dixon Porter), who took him in. Through the elder Porter, Farragut was commissioned as a midshipman in 1810. He fought in the War of 1812, served in the Mosquito Fleet under Commodore Porter, and in 1859 built the Mare Island Navy Yard near San Francisco.

Though born in the South, married to a Virginian, and living in Norfolk in 1860, Farragut denounced secession as treason and moved to New York. Though early on he served on the Naval Retirement Board, due to concerns over his loyalty, his adopted brother David Dixon Porter assigned him to capture New Orleans. Aboard his flagship the U.S.S. *Hartford*, he successfully ran the guns and captured the city from upriver. His most celebrated victory came in the Battle of Mobile Bay in 1864. Farragut famously told his men to "Damn the torpedoes!" when several ships were sunk by mines (then called torpedoes), racing into the harbor to capture the city. So great was his stature that he served as one of Abraham Lincoln's pallbearers.

After the war, in 1866, he became the first U.S. Navy officer promoted to the rank of admiral. Farragut was given command of the European Squadron from 1867 to 1868. He was one of only six U.S. naval officers in history to have been honored with active duty status "for life."

served with Taylor and Scott in Mexico believed they had seen decisive battles and campaigns themselves. Yet by the 1860s, that decisiveness had disappeared. Civil War generals aimed for Napoleonic battles of annihilation, but what they usually got were campaigns of attrition. Historians still debate the principal causes for this, with many citing the effects of rifle muskets, inexperienced soldiers and commanders with little experience of large-scale warfare, and the growth in the size of armies (unprecedented in the Western Hemisphere to that point in history), all of which hindered battlefield command and control and maneuver. This unexpected tactical stalemate profoundly influenced the course of the war.

Historian James McPherson has argued that the Civil War can best be understood as a series of turning points, each contingent on events on and off the battlefield.[42] The

▲ CONFEDERATE BLOCKADE RUNNERS

As the Union blockade tightened, the Confederates relied on small, fast blockade runners to slip through and bring in supplies from European powers. In spite of Confederate diplomacy, this material support never translated into full military aid.

◀ LINCOLN AND HIS GENERALS

An idealized image of Lincoln consulting with his top officers as they planned the defeat of the Confederates in 1864. It took some time for Lincoln to assemble the right officers to win the war, a task made more difficult by the collective inexperience of the nation in a conflict of the Civil War's scale. (*Left to right*) Porter, Farragut, Lincoln, Sherman, Thomas, Grant, Sheridan.

Montgomery Cunningham Meigs

MAY 3, 1816–JANUARY 2, 1892

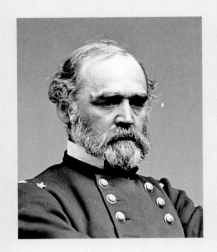

Born in Augusta, Georgia, to a wealthy and well-connected doctor, Meigs was bright and hard working, enrolling at the University of Pennsylvania at age fifteen. He won an appointment to West Point in 1832 and graduated fifth in his class in 1836. Commissioned in the artillery, he mostly served in the Corps of Engineers, building a series of forts across the country. He also supervised the construction of the Washington Aqueduct and the wings and dome of the U.S. Capitol building.

After Lincoln's election, the new president quietly charged him with resupplying Fort Pickens, Florida, which he accomplished in April 1861. A month later, Meigs was promoted to brigadier general, and appointed quartermaster general of the army, replacing Joseph Johnston. Meigs established a reputation for being efficient, hard driving, and scrupulously honest. His department proved vital in supplying the massive Union war effort, and he personally supervised Grant's supply lines at Fredericksburg, and Sherman's resupply in Georgia and the Carolinas.

Though southern born, Meigs hated the Confederacy, and when looking for land for national military cemeteries, chose the suitable lands of the Arlington estate, which had belonged to Robert E. Lee. Burials began at Arlington National Cemetery in June 1864. Meigs was also present at Lincoln's death, standing guard at the door of the Petersen House, where the president died. He continued to supervise the construction of army buildings, most famously the Pension Office Building, before his death from pneumonia in 1892.

first turning point came in 1862, when Confederate armies halted McClellan's Peninsular offensive, preventing the loss of Richmond. Had this offensive succeeded, the rebellion might have collapsed, causing reunion without the abolition of slavery. Instead, Lee went over to the offensive, only to be halted at Antietam in September 1862. In mid-1863 a second turning point occurred with Union victories at Gettysburg, Vicksburg, and Chattanooga. These campaigns shrank the Confederacy's resource base and damaged the offensive capacity of its armies. The final turning point came in 1864, when a weakened Confederacy shifted to a deliberate strategy of exhaustion. Its aim was to convince northern voters that they could not win the war and provoke Lincoln's defeat at the polls. By the late summer of 1864, it seemed as though this strategy just might succeed, but then Sherman seized Atlanta, and Sheridan razed the Shenandoah Valley. The very fact that Lincoln feared as late as August 1864 that he would go down to electoral defeat in November underscores the fact that Union victory remained contingent on events on the battlefield.[43] It was never inevitable.

The elusiveness of decisive battle compelled both sides toward a more total war than either had envisioned in 1861. When limited war failed to deliver victory, the search was on for more comprehensive means to win the war. The effort of total war meant greater manpower mobilization in the form of conscription on both sides

CIVIL WAR PATRIOTIC SCENE ▶

The Union needed strong support from the home front to succeed in the war. Though that support wavered with Union defeats, the North remained committed to maintaining the Union despite the mounting costs of the effort.

and the employment of black troops by the Union. It meant greater mobilization of economic resources: in the North, new forms of taxation and small-denomination bonds marketed to citizens as patriotic contributions; in the South, the impressment of resources deemed critical, including military supplies, machine tools for weapons manufacturing, and railroads. The protracted war transformed the home fronts in turn. After four years of rising federal spending, Union farmers and contractors were still well paid, but Confederate farmers found themselves paid with inflated currency, struggling against impressment of their crops and livestock.

The drive to mobilize resources also meant novel attempts to control friendly and hostile civilian populations. These included an expanding constellation of measures such as military tribunals in place of civilian trials; campaigns to regulate agriculture and ration food; and the creation of intelligence and security agencies. While the absolute level of Union mobilization fell short of that achieved by the great powers in the world wars of the twentieth century, the American Civil War foreshadowed what was to come.[44]

THE ARMY AND THE PROBLEMS OF PEACE

The end of the Civil War left the U.S. Army little opportunity to rest on its laurels. The problems of winning the war abruptly gave way to the problems of winning the peace. As commanding general, Grant had to simultaneously juggle the challenges of occupying the ex-Confederate states; demobilizing more than a million volunteers; and persuading the French to leave Mexico. Each of these missions presented unique problems.

Not wanting to provoke a potentially dangerous alliance between Napoleon III and the Confederacy, Lincoln had declared neutrality toward the French military presence in Mexico during the Civil War, even though it violated the Monroe Doctrine.[45] After the Confederate armies surrendered, President Johnson and Secretary of State William H. Seward decided it was time to persuade the French to leave. Grant ordered Sheridan to move 50,000 troops to Texas to supervise the Confederate surrender there and form an army of observation along the Rio Grande. Sheridan sized up the situation and advised Grant that he could make a quick end of Napoleon III's colonial ambitions: "We should give a permanent government to that republic [Mexico]. Our work in crushing the rebellion will not be done until this takes place. The advent of Maximilian (the emperor of Mexico put in place by the French in 1864) was a portion of the rebellion and his fall should belong to its history."[46] Though these views were widely shared among Republicans and military commanders, the administration proved less interested than "Little Phil" Sheridan in starting a new war, especially after the French emperor signaled that he had tired of the cost of supporting Maximilian and wanted to curtail his Mexican adventure. The last French troops left in February 1867, and Maximilian ended up in front of a Mexican firing squad.

The vast majority of the million soldiers in Union blue wanted nothing more than to resume civilian life as fast as possible. By Christmas, Grant reduced the active duty rolls from over a million to fewer than 200,000; seven months later, the figure was 57,000. Further reductions cut this force to roughly 26,000 officers and soldiers over the following decade, a level the U.S. Army maintained until the Spanish-American War in 1898. This rapid decline in the army's size was understandable. It was politically untenable to keep volunteers in uniform after the Confederate surrender.[47] Concerns over the unprecedented size of the national debt (between $70 billion and $80 billion in 2012 dollars—more than one-third of the nation's gross national product—compared with approximately $1.8 billion in 1860) also played a role in Washington's desire to demobilize the volunteers as quickly as possible. Nevertheless, a rapid return to a traditionally tiny antebellum peacetime army complicated the twin tasks still confronting army commanders: the challenges of Reconstruction and the country's continuing western expansion.[48]

The U.S. Army's immersion in occupation and constabulary duties during the period known as Reconstruction embroiled it in some of the most politically controversial episodes in its history. Confederate defeat left the U.S. Army as the only organization capable of upholding law and order in many parts of the South. Emancipation freed the slaves but did not determine their position in postwar society. Nor did defeat

THE EXECUTION OF MAXIMILIAN I

After the war, the United States was able to put pressure on the French-backed "Mexican Empire." Tired of the cost, Napoleon III withdrew his support from Maximilian's government, and the emperor was executed by firing squad in 1867.

THE VETERAN IN A NEW FIELD

With the war over, many volunteers returned home, expecting to pick up their lives as before. This Winslow Homer painting shows a Union veteran returning to his old life, using a scythe, symbolic of the Grim Reaper and the war's death toll. On the other hand, the veteran is harvesting bountiful wheat, possibly symbolizing northern victory and the reunited nation's new growth.

convince Confederate veterans that their former slaves had become their equals. Consequently, there were frequent and often violent confrontations between black and white southerners. Congress established the Freedmen's Bureau, headed by Maj. Gen. Oliver Otis Howard (USMA 1854), to aid the former slaves' transition to freedom and manage conflicts in the ex-Confederate states. It employed many former Union army officers and authorized them to act as intermediaries in disputes ranging from civil rights to land use and wages.[49]

Lincoln and Congress had never settled on a policy for readmitting the Rebel states to the Union, leaving the country debating, "What would Lincoln do?" It was a question with no simple answer. Lincoln's assassination left a political vacuum filled by a constitutional struggle between the conservative Democrat Andrew Johnson, who soon came to favor the mildest treatment of the former Rebels, and a Republican Congress that wanted to punish secessionists for what they had put the nation through. Army commanders stationed in the ex-Confederacy believed that they were merely the executors of decisions made by Washington, but their visibility as blue-clad conquerors from the north insured that their actions would be interpreted as taking sides in local—and, indeed, national—politics.

As commanding general of the army, Grant found himself walking a tightrope between the president, as constitutional commander in chief, and Congress, which the Constitution empowers to make rules and regulations for the armed forces. Though Republican votes in the North had made him vice president, on becoming president,

Andrew Johnson was born in poverty in Raleigh, North Carolina. He apprenticed as a tailor and settled in Greeneville, Tennessee. After several terms in the Tennessee State House, he was elected to the House of Representatives, and then governor of Tennessee, finally being elected to the Senate in 1857. A dedicated follower of fellow Tennessean Andrew Jackson, Johnson supported territorial acquisition in the West, and defended the rights of slaveholders to bring their property into those territories.

Johnson was also solidly Unionist and refused to leave the government following Tennessee's secession. When Union troops retook the state in 1864, Lincoln named him military governor. Johnson's support for Lincoln's wartime policies, and his status as a southern Democrat, made him an attractive candidate for the fusionist Union Party ticket in 1864, and he replaced Hannibal Hamlin as vice president.

His inaugural address, given shortly before Lincoln's in 1865, was rambling and incoherent, possibly because Johnson was drunk. Lincoln's assassination a month later unexpectedly elevated Johnson to the presidency. Like his predecessor, Johnson advocated a conciliatory approach to reunification, hoping to restore civilian rule in the South as quickly as possible. To that end, he pardoned many Confederate leaders and quarreled with Radical Republicans in Congress. This feud included Johnson's veto of the 1866 Civil Rights bill (overridden by Congress), and culminated with his impeachment.

After violating the politically motivated Tenure of Office Act, Johnson became the first president targeted for impeachment proceedings. He held on to the office by a single vote, but his national political power base had disappeared. Johnson campaigned unsuccessfully for a congressional seat in 1869 and 1872, but won a Senate seat for a special session in 1875. Shortly after the session ended, he suffered a stroke and died.

ANDREW JOHNSON
DECEMBER 29, 1808–JULY 31, 1875

Johnson promptly alienated most congressional Republicans. Nor, after a brief period in which former Confederates appeared cowed or uncertain, did white southerners encourage hopes that they had accepted emancipation, which became law under the Thirteenth Amendment in December 1865. Instead, southern legislatures, still elected by whites alone, were filled with former Confederate officers, who passed a series of "black codes" imposing controls on the freedpeople that resembled slavery.

After Johnson pardoned numerous Confederate leaders and vetoed a civil rights bill, Republicans turned the 1866 midterm elections into a referendum on his policies, urging Union veterans to "vote like you shot." They obliged Republicans with veto-proof landslide victories in both houses. Congressional Republicans then enacted their Military Reconstruction Act over Johnson's veto. This unprecedented law circumvented the president's authority as chief executive and granted army generals broad powers to oversee the readmission of ten of the ex-Confederate states to the Union. Congress exempted Tennessee, Johnson's home state, from the provisions of the law because its state legislature had voted to ratify the Fourteenth Amendment, which made former slaves citizens, mandated equal protection under the law without regard to race, and repudiated Confederate war debt. Johnson opposed the amendment, which was ratified in 1868, and Tennessee was the only one of the eleven ex-Confederate states to ratify it. The law also required each state to enact a new constitution banning racial discrimination in voting as the price of readmission to congressional representation.[50]

At first, Grant tried to support the president. By mid-1866, however, he became convinced that Johnson's actions endangered what Grant called "the fruits of victory."

▲
MARRIAGE BY THE FREEDMEN'S BUREAU

With the help of the army, the Freedmen's Bureau provided a variety of services to former slaves in the South, including education, financial support, and even weddings.

Trust between the two men evaporated. Grant privately warned Sherman and Sheridan that, unwittingly or not, Johnson was encouraging the resumption of the rebellion. Indeed, by the fall of 1866, Grant's relationship with Johnson deteriorated to the point of a potentially explosive crisis in civil-military relations, the depth of which was not revealed until much later. Grant secretly wrote to Sheridan at the time, "I much fear that we are fast approaching the point where he [Johnson] will want to declare the body [Congress] itself illegal, unconstitutional, and revolutionary. Commanders in southern states will have to take great care to see, if a crisis does come, that no armed headway can be made against the Union." Two days later he confided to Sherman that the president wanted Sherman to come to Washington so that he could fire Secretary of War Stanton and appoint Sherman acting secretary. Underlining the political delicacy of the situation in Washington, Grant even warned Sherman that "I will not venture in a letter to say all I think about the matter or that I would say to you in person."[51]

In August 1867 Grant agreed to become acting secretary of war after Johnson removed Secretary Stanton in a deliberate violation of the Tenure of Office Act, which Congress had passed to prevent Johnson from replacing Lincoln's cabinet.[52] The president's action enraged Republicans and triggered his impeachment. When the Senate voted to refuse to accept Stanton's removal in early 1868, Grant returned the keys to Stanton's office in the War Department. Johnson felt betrayed by Grant's symbolic decision to obey Congress and tried to humiliate him in front of a full Cabinet meeting at the White House by openly accusing Grant of disobedience. Though Grant refused

THADDEUS STEVENS AND IMPEACHMENT

Thaddeus Stevens was the leader of the Radical Republican faction that wanted to use Reconstruction to punish the former Confederates and remake southern society. The Radicals feuded with Andrew Johnson over policy, culminating in Johnson's 1868 impeachment.

◀ 'TIS BUT A CHANGE IN BANNERS

Republican politicians tied Democrats to the Confederacy, using concepts such as "vote like you shot" or "waving the bloody shirt," that pinned the war on Democrats. Illustrated by this cartoon, these ideas helped Grant defeat Democrat Horatio Seymour in the 1868 presidential election.

THE ARMY IN RECONSTRUCTION

With the war over, the army now found itself in an uncomfortable position. Troops were needed to maintain order in the states of the former Confederacy until their readmission, while also protecting the rights of newly freed slaves who faced a recalcitrant white population.

to argue with the president, he steadfastly refused to disobey the plain intent of Congress, which made him a heroic figure to Republicans and sealed his nomination for president. Johnson's impeachment trial in 1868 fell one vote short in the Senate, but his career never recovered. That November, Grant defeated former New York governor Horatio Seymour with the campaign slogan "Let Us Have Peace." In 1869 he became the first West Point graduate to become president of the United States.[53]

RECONSTRUCTION AND THE U.S. ARMY

When Grant became president, the United States had a rare moment in its history at which one party simultaneously controlled the presidency, both houses of Congress, and the Supreme Court.[54] Though Radical Republican demands for the redistribution of plantation land (usually held by former Confederates) to the freedpeople (who still worked the land, as wage laborers or, increasingly, sharecroppers) faded in the face of American dedication to claims of private property, the Republicans used their unprecedented power to ratify the Fourteenth and Fifteenth Amendments to the Constitution, which forbade discrimination based on race in civil rights and voting. By 1870, all of the ex-Confederate states had been readmitted to the Union, formally ending the army's occupation role. The vast majority of whites, including most of the former Confederate officers and officials who had been disfranchised during congressional, or "Radical," Reconstruction, were again able to vote and hold office.

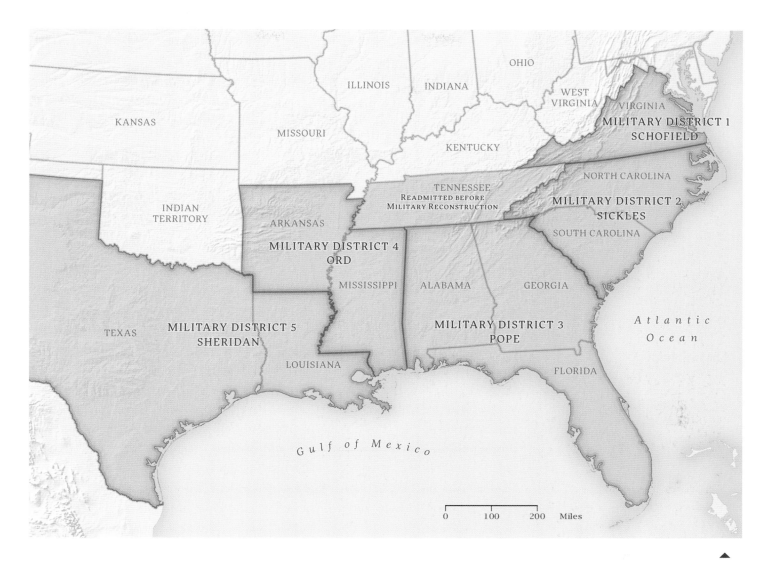

During the occupation of the South, federal troops assumed many civil roles, including conducting voter registration, guarding polling places, organizing state constitutional conventions, and fulfilling police and militia functions.[55] Yet even as the focus of Reconstruction moved away from punishing former secessionists and Rebels and preventing their control over southern states, the plague of racism spurred continuing white resistance to federal authority. Although wartime southern Unionists frequently became Republicans (who continued to dominate politics in areas such as East Tennessee for decades after the war), the majority of southern Republicans were African American. Whether to control politics, to enhance their control over the labor of the freedpeople—still essential to growing the cash crops southern elites still relied on for wealth—or out of racist fears developed over two centuries of slavery, southern whites turned ever more violently against the freedpeople, their leaders, and those who attempted to protect their rights in the South. This ongoing recalcitrance provoked Congress to pass and President Grant to sign the Enforcement Act of 1870, and another in 1871, which became popularly known as the Ku Klux Klan Act. These laws made it a federal crime to conspire against the exercise of civil and political rights. They also gave the president expanded legal authority to suspend the writ of habeas corpus and use the army to combat the Ku Klux Klan and similar terrorist groups.[56]

MILITARY DISTRICTS OF THE SOUTH

The army organized its control over the states of the former Confederacy into five military districts.

▲

LEWIS MERRILL

Lt. Col. Lewis Merrill came to South Carolina with the 7th Cavalry to suppress the Klan in that state. Using counterinsurgency tactics learned from fighting Confederate guerrillas in Missouri, he drove the Klan from its prominent position in South Carolina.

SOUTH CAROLINA, 1871–1873:
THE CAMPAIGN AGAINST THE KU KLUX KLAN

From 1870 until the end of his presidency, Grant repeatedly used the army as a constabulary force in a series of counterinsurgency campaigns to root out white supremacist paramilitary groups trying to terrorize the freedmen and regain control over local governments across the former Confederacy. Two of these campaigns, one in South Carolina and the other in Louisiana, illustrate the potential as well as the problems in using military forces as an instrument of counterinsurgency.

A majority of South Carolina's population had been slaves before the Civil War. Their enfranchisement in 1868 created an instant Republican political majority in a state where Lincoln's name had not even been placed on the ballot in 1860. That prospect traumatized the white population. Racialized violence had been pervasive since the war, but it spiked after black and white Republican legislators amended the state constitution to reelect Governor Robert K. Scott, a former Union general and native of Ohio, in 1870. Scott led the Freedmen's Bureau in the state after the war and campaigned vigorously for black votes. White South Carolinians widely despised him as a "carpetbagger," in the colorful vernacular of the time.

The secretive nature of the Klan makes it impossible to determine precisely the scale of its insurgency, but it probably totaled a thousand or more men in each of a cluster of nine counties in up-country South Carolina. Reports reached Washington that five hundred armed whites had attacked the Union County jail and lynched eight black inmates. In York County, masked men scheduled weekly "night rides" in a terrorist campaign that sent thousands of blacks into hiding in the woods. After York County Klansmen lynched a black militia captain (who was also a Union veteran), Governor Scott appealed to President Grant for federal troops to restore civil order.[57]

Grant responded on November 17, 1871, by proclaiming that a "state of rebellion" existed in the nine counties and suspending the writ of habeas corpus there. As commander in chief, he ordered a detachment of the 7th U.S. Cavalry under its deputy commander, Lt. Col. Lewis Merrill (USMA 1855), to South Carolina. Merrill proved a superb choice for this mission. At the beginning of the Civil War, he had raised a volunteer cavalry regiment and waged a counterinsurgency campaign against Confederate guerrillas in central Missouri. In 1864 the War Department brevetted him to brigadier general and sent him to northern Alabama and Georgia to conduct similar counterinsurgency operations.

In late 1871 and 1872, Merrill moved in tandem with the Justice Department lawyers to suppress the South Carolina Klan. Merrill's experience hunting guerrillas during the Civil War had convinced him of the importance of developing a highly mobile force of cavalry that could cover wide swathes of territory and develop its own intelligence as it moved. Merrill had also seen how effective military commissions could be when used to turn suspects into informants. The 7th Cavalry's descent upon the South Carolina up-country caught the local Ku Klux Klan by surprise, as it had never before seen such mass arrests carried out for crimes that normally would have been tried in the much more friendly confines of local courts. His troopers arrested and detained

◀ **KLANSMEN IN MISSISSIPPI**

Three Mississippi Klansmen arrested while disguised. The masked men were part of a terrorist insurgency group in the South during Reconstruction, which the army battled to protect freedmen and their white sympathizers—many of whom came from the North and were known as "carpetbaggers."

INTIMIDATION AND VIOLENCE

The Klan used physical intimidation to suppress freedmen from participating in civil society. One such victim was Elias Hill of York County, South Carolina, a Baptist preacher who testified to the Congress about the violence he suffered. His introduction describes him as "crippled in both legs and arms, which are shriveled by rheumatism; he cannot walk, cannot help himself." A group of Klansmen had broken into Hill's house, and, after they identified him, dragged him into the yard.

The first thing they asked me was, "Who did the burning? Who burned our houses?"—gin-houses, dwelling-houses and such. Some had been burned in the neighborhood. I told them it was not me; I could not burn houses; it was unreasonable to ask me. Then they hit me with their fists, and said I did it, I ordered it. They went on asking me didn't I tell the black men to ravish all the white women. No, I answered them. They struck me again with their fists on my breast, and then they went on . . .

They pointed pistols at me all around my head once or twice, as if they were going to shoot me, telling me they were going to kill me; wasn't I ready to die, and willing to die? Didn't I preach? That they came to kill me—all the time pointing pistols at me . . . One said "G-d d--n it, hush!" He had a horsewhip, and he told me to pull up my shirt, and he hit me. He told me at every lick, "Hold up your shirt." I made a moan every time he cut with the horsewhip. I reckon he struck me eight cuts right on the hip bone; it was almost the only place he could hit my body, my legs are so short—all my limbs drawn up and withered away with pain . . . They all had disguises on. I then thought they would not kill me. One of them then took a strap, and buckled it around my neck and said, "Let's take him to the river and drown him . . ."[60]

six hundred suspected Klansmen. Five hundred other suspects turned themselves in voluntarily rather than face arrest and detainment. Other Klan suspects fled as far as Canada. Of these eleven hundred suspects, forty-nine pleaded guilty and five were convicted by federal juries composed of blacks and whites.[58] After spending all of 1872 gaining the first five convictions of Klan members, the federal government decided that it lacked the extensive legal machinery of courts, clerks, and prosecuting attorneys to try the twelve hundred suspects that Merrill had caught. Nevertheless, despite the small number of convictions, violence against black and white Republicans in the South Carolina up-country dropped dramatically in 1872 and 1873. Merrill's relentless mass arrests and detentions had "broken the Klan's back" and driven it underground.[59]

LOUISIANA, 1874–1877: THE CAMPAIGN AGAINST THE WHITE LEAGUES

Despite the readmission of the southern states and opposition from the emerging "Liberal Republican" wing (dedicated to limited government and dubious about Radical Reconstruction) in his own party, Grant won reelection by an overwhelming margin in 1872, and Republicans continued to hold both houses of Congress, as they had done since the election of 1860. Yet violence and terrorism against the freedpeople, white Republicans (those born in the South, as well as so-called carpetbaggers), and federal officials did not cease.

Merrill's successful counterinsurgency campaign in South Carolina proved difficult to duplicate in the face of endemic white violence, voter intimidation, and fraud at the ballot box. Like South Carolina, Louisiana was an ex-Confederate state with a black majority population. In 1873 and 1874, the White Leagues, a paramilitary organization similar to the Klan, seized power by ousting Republicans from office in more than a dozen rural parishes (Louisiana's equivalent of counties) with a mixture of targeted assassination, armed intimidation at the polls, and electoral fraud in the counting of ballots. The rise of the White Leagues effectively began with a massacre of black militiamen defending the Grant Parish Courthouse at Colfax, Louisiana, in 1873. An estimated one hundred defenders died in the attack by some four hundred white paramilitaries, led by former Confederate officers.[61] The climax to the White League campaign to overturn democratic government came on September 14, 1874, when two thousand heavily armed insurgents, organized into companies, defeated the Republican-controlled state militia in a deadly street battle in New Orleans. The next day, they overthrew the elected Republican governor and inaugurated their own candidate, a former Confederate colonel.[62]

Grant responded by sending federal troops to New Orleans to restore the Republican governor. He also secretly dispatched General Sheridan to report on the situation. When the opening session of the new state legislature convened on January 5, 1875, dispute over which party's candidates would be seated in five swing elections erupted into a brawl on the floor of the Louisiana House. The governor asked for federal troops to restore order. Sheridan endorsed the request and declared martial law. He justified his actions in a telegram to President Grant:

I think that the terrorism now existing in Louisiana . . . could be entirely removed and confidence and fair dealing established by the arrest and trial of the ringleaders of the armed White Leagues. If Congress would pass a bill declaring them banditti they could be tried by a military commission . . . It is possible that if the President would issue a proclamation declaring them banditti, no further action need be taken, except that which would devolve upon me.[63]

News of the armed intervention by federal troops on the floor of a state legislature and Sheridan's inflammatory "banditti" telegram triggered a national backlash against the Grant administration and its use of the army in the South. Grant's critics, including the Liberal Republican faction in his own party, questioned whether such use of the army was necessary—or even legal. Some of his political opponents even suggested that the former general's actions amounted to an unprecedented exercise of executive power that reflected the president's "Napoleonic ambition." Being depicted as a kind of American dictator-in-waiting no doubt wounded Grant's pride and probably played a role in his reluctance to continue to use the army as a constabulary force in the South as violence escalated in 1875 and 1876. Reconstruction had never been popular with Democrats north or south; now it was unpopular within a substantial wing of the northern Republican Party as well.[64]

◀ GRANT IN LOUISIANA
Grant and Uncle Sam argue over the use of federal troops to control the Louisiana legislature in the aftermath of the Battle of Liberty Place on September 14, 1874. Uncle Sam criticizes Grant's actions, calling them an abuse of power and warning of the possibilities of Grant seeking a third term.

"THE UNION AS IT WAS" ▶

Similar to the Klan, the White League was a paramilitary organization that terrorized freedmen and Republicans in the South during Reconstruction. Attempts to suppress the League in a manner similar to the Klan in South Carolina were less successful, and the survival of these violent groups helped suppress the rights of freedpeople.

THE END OF RECONSTRUCTION

Nor was southern violence the sole problem facing Reconstruction by the middle of the 1870s. Democrats and Republicans had been locked in a furious debate over economic policy, centered around the form and extent of the nation's money supply and how to repay the debts incurred in waging the war. In 1873 the Republican Congress passed a law that would gradually retire the wartime "greenbacks," the first large-scale issue of paper money since the Revolutionary War, from circulation, in favor of gold specie (coins). Their intent was to prevent inflation and maintain credit, but a financial panic soon broke out, plunging the nation into a depression. Democrats immediately blamed the move to gold—"the Crime of '73"—for the panic. Though the panic originated in complex ties with financial centers stretching across the Atlantic, reducing the money supply at that moment aggravated the depression and made economic recovery more difficult. Democrats won control of the House of Representatives in 1874, the first time in a generation, signaling that sectional issues no longer dominated national politics.[65]

After the Louisiana State House fiasco, Grant's Reconstruction policy faced mounting opposition. Traditional Democratic appeals to "home rule," which effectively meant the return of white supremacy and black disfranchisement in the South, gained momentum against the supposed excesses of executive rule, "bayonet rule," and "Black Reconstruction." Union veterans continued to "vote as they shot" for the rest of the century, and politicians north and south both "waved the bloody shirt" to arouse sectional antagonism against their opponents, but amid an economic depression that lasted six years, many northerners, Republican leaders as well as voters, rejected further efforts (expensive by the standards of the nineteenth century) to protect the freedpeople, for whom they ultimately felt little empathy.

Democrats also regained political momentum within the South. But rather than waiting for Democratic victories in the North, they sought to send a message of self-reliance and racial domination. In 1875, under the so-called Mississippi Plan, white supremacists dropped all pretense of the secrecy associated with the Ku Klux Klan's guerrilla-style attacks. They urged whites in Mississippi to openly use violence and electoral fraud to destroy the Republican Party in that state (where the majority of the population was African American) before the fall elections. After doing so enabled them to take over the state legislature, "white liners" impeached the black lieutenant governor and threatened to do the same to Governor Adelbert Ames (USMA 1861). The governor appealed for federal troops to curb the violence, but Grant's political advisers told him that doing so could lead to Republican defeat in the national elections of 1876. In the end, he refused Ames's request and informed the governor that he would have to rely on his own state militia for self-defense. Rather than preside over a race war and massacres like those at Colfax, Ames chose to resign and left the state.[66]

By the national centennial in 1876, the country seemed exhausted with sectional issues. The Republican presidential nominee, Rutherford B. Hayes, pledged to let the South have "home rule," a slogan that promised an end to further military intervention. Democrats chose Samuel J. Tilden of New York, who campaigned against corruption north and south. Political corruption had been a significant failing of Grant's administration, as the president proved a poor judge of civilian character and remained all too loyal to men defrauding the government.

The race was one of the most contentious in U.S. history. Both men went to bed on election eve thinking that Tilden had won, but Republican operatives held on to the electoral votes in Louisiana, South Carolina, and Florida, accurately charging local Democrats with Mississippi-style fraud and intimidation at the polls. When a bipartisan electoral college commission declared Hayes the winner by a single vote, many Americans were disgusted by rumors that the Republicans had traded away local control of these southern states in order to keep the presidency—the so-called Compromise of 1877. Whether this was true or not, Republican leaders had indeed chosen to prioritize their ability to appoint judges and veto Democratic attacks on Republican economic policy. The civil rights of the freedpeople now took a backseat to national economic development and the emergence of a corporate economic order.[67]

The army's involvement in Reconstruction left a controversial record. Suppressing

Hayes was born near Columbus, Ohio, a descendent of New Englanders who settled in the Midwest. He graduated as valedictorian from Kenyon College and then attended Harvard Law School. Hayes nearly enlisted during the Mexican-American War, but was prevented from doing so by a bout of tuberculosis. In 1850 he moved from Sandusky County, Ohio, to Cincinnati, where he became involved in local politics. He rose to prominence as a defense attorney, particularly working for escaped slaves against the 1850 Fugitive Slave Law.

A staunch Republican, Hayes enlisted with the 23rd Ohio Volunteer Infantry as a major following Fort Sumter. The 23rd fought in West Virginia, and joined Pope's Army of Virginia just after Second Bull Run. During the Antietam campaign, Hayes was wounded leading a charge at the Battle of South Mountain, and during his recovery, he was promoted to brigade command and given the rank of brevet brigadier general. Hayes's brigade later fought in the 1864 Shenandoah Valley campaigns against Jubal Early.

While in the Shenandoah, Hayes was nominated for, and won, a seat in the House of Representatives. Like others in a similar position, Hayes refused to leave the army to campaign and won a slim victory over his opponent, the Copperhead Alexander Long. While in Congress, Hayes was considered a moderate, but he voted with the Radicals on many occasions, including the 1866 Civil Rights Act and the Fourteenth Amendment. Though more moderate than other Ohio Republicans, Hayes's war service helped him to the governorship in 1867. At the 1876 convention, Hayes upset James Blaine to win the presidential nomination. He narrowly defeated Samuel Tilden in a controversial election. Tilden supporters reportedly acquiesced to Hayes's victory after he promised to remove troops from the South and agreed to other conciliatory measures.

RUTHERFORD BIRCHARD HAYES
OCTOBER 4, 1822–JANUARY 17, 1893

insurgencies thrust military commanders into the midst of political disputes at the local, state, and national levels, for which they had little professional training. General Sheridan's use of troops on the floor of the Louisiana House and his "banditti" telegram inflamed national opposition to Grant's Reconstruction policy, making the army's use seem heavy-handed, if not downright dangerous to democratic government. Much as army officers and Republican leaders did not fully appreciate the degree of political finesse required to challenge an insurgency with locally broad popular support, so too they did not appreciate how long troops would have to be stationed in the South if they were to create new social norms that would support, or at least permit, the enforcement of the Fourteenth and Fifteenth Amendments—and so uphold the principle of the sovereignty of the Union in all the states, which the military victory in the Civil War was supposed to have guaranteed.

Colonel Merrill appeared to have dismantled the Klan in South Carolina by 1873, so the army withdrew the 7th Cavalry, which was badly needed for Indian fighting in the West. When the political winds shifted, former Klan members resurfaced as part of a new white supremacist paramilitary organization, the Red Shirts, which modeled

◀ PANIC OF 1873
Investors flee the New York Stock Exchange following the collapse of a major bank in September 1873. The Panic of 1873, one of the worst financial crises in American history, weakened support for the Grant administration, and helped to create greater impetus to end Reconstruction.

"A TRUCE, NOT A COMPROMISE" ▶
In this critical cartoon, the North offers to compromise over the end of Reconstruction rather than have the South descend into further violence if Samuel Tilden's challenge to the 1876 election results failed.

its campaign on the Mississippi Plan. In 1876 Red Shirt "rifle clubs" used targeted violence and parades of hundreds of armed riders at local political rallies to intimidate Republicans from voting (a good reason to suspect that the Republicans won, or would otherwise have won, the state's electoral votes). The following January, in the midst of the turmoil that followed the presidential election, thousands of armed Red Shirts converged on the South Carolina state capitol at Columbia to inaugurate Wade Hampton III, the former Confederate general, as governor.[68]

Following the army's deployment against striking workers in 1877, Congress passed and Hayes signed the Posse Comitatus Act of 1878, effectively reversing the Grant administration's interventionism by forbidding the use of the army for local law enforcement, such as protecting polling places in state elections. Constabulary duty had never been popular with army officers bred on leading soldiers in battle, and as time passed, their fears of another great rebellion in the South faded. The country and the army had lost interest in Reconstruction. Former Confederates had regained control of southern politics and soon exercised their power to pass legislation discriminating against a third of the South's population. Though racist violence abated temporarily, segregation and disfranchisement became more formal during the 1890s, creating a kind of American apartheid, reminiscent of slavery, by the turn of the century.[69]

SIGNIFICANCE OF THE CIVIL WAR EXPERIENCE FOR WEST POINT

The Civil War era was a transformative experience for West Point, just as it was for the United States. Only one West Point graduate had attained the rank of brigadier general in the antebellum army when war broke out in 1861. Over the next four years, 294 graduates became generals for the Union, and 151 for the Confederacy.[70] While many generals were commissioned directly from civilian life, West Pointers came to

United Daughters of the Confederacy

The UDC was founded in 1894 to care for former Confederate soldiers and promote Confederate memory, mainly through the Lost Cause lens. The group grew quickly, and by the end of World War I claimed nearly 100,000 members. Because the membership was for women, they were able to organize in public without raising suspicion of insurgent activities.

Reconciliation

After Reconstruction, Americans began supporting a history that emphasized common national ties. Both sides had fought for national ideals they believed in, and had done so honorably and bravely. Here, veterans at the fiftieth Gettysburg reunion shake hands. Though comforting to many Americans, this narrative diminished the role of slavery in starting the war and ignored the contributions of many blacks.

dominate the high commands of both sides. That dominance continued in the post-war era. West Point graduates and Civil War generals Grant, Sherman, Sheridan, and Schofield led the peacetime army in an unbroken chain of commanding generals for the next thirty years. Grant and Sherman wrote their memoirs in the 1880s, both of which became wildly popular bestsellers that burnished their alma mater's fame as well as their own.[71] Grant served two terms as president from 1869 to 1877 and came close to being nominated for an unprecedented third term in 1880. Only Sherman's adamant denial of any interest in the office kept him from being nominated and elected in 1884. Before the Civil War, cadets at the Military Academy studied European military campaigns to understand the art and science of war. Since 1865, they have studied the campaigns of the American Civil War as well. In the end, the service of its graduates in the Civil War made West Point a permanent institution in American public life.[72]

CONCLUSION

The Civil War era remains a unique watershed moment in the history of the United States and its armed forces. For four momentous years, the Union and the Confederacy sought each other's destruction, each pouring every resource it could conceive into its respective war effort. The great disparity in those resources, however, is not sufficient to explain the outcome. The sociopolitical differences between North and South and the contingent decisions of military and political leaders must also be taken into account. If the causes of Union victory can be disputed, the results are relatively clear. The military victory of the United States enabled and confirmed the transformation of what had been a decentralized, largely agricultural society into one of the greatest industrialized states in the world. Political, economic, and social changes also undergirded changes in warfare. Many historians have argued that these changes amounted to a distinctive "American way of war"—a marked preference for offensive campaigns aimed at complete victory that foretold of the drive toward total war in the world wars of the twentieth century. Yet after the war, the U.S. Army shrank back nearly to the tiny numbers of its antebellum days, resuming its reliance on a cadre of long-serving professionals. Civil War generals played important roles in reconstructing the nation, even if it involved them more deeply in the dilemmas of southern politics than most would have preferred. Well into the next century, Civil War veterans carried memories of the war and how every aspect of their lives, and the life of the nation, had been "touched with fire."[73]

MEDAL OF HONOR

The Congressional Medal of Honor was created during the Civil War. The first medals were awarded on March 25, 1863, to several Union soldiers (including Private Jacob Parrott, whose medal is seen here) who captured a Confederate locomotive in northwest Georgia. The incident is known as the Andrews Raid, or the Great Locomotive Chase.

◀ BATTLE MONUMENT: DEDICATED IN 1897 AT WEST POINT

Due to the prominent role played by West Point graduates in fighting the Civil War, the institution's profile rose dramatically in the latter part of the century. Battle Monument memorializes the service of the two thousand Union Regular Army Officers and soldiers killed during the "War of the Rebellion," which was described by Professor Charles Larned as a "mighty struggle for principle, which freed a race and welded a nation."

Civil War

Ultimately, the United States survived the Civil War, remaining a united nation and stepping forward into a more prominent position on the world stage. Though many advances in civil rights remained in the future, the cause of Union had been won at great cost in blood and treasure.

After the Civil War, the nation's long contest between local and federal authority had tipped decidedly toward central federal power. With slavery abolished and a party favorable to industry in command of the White House, America's westward expansion gathered speed, and its economy grew—erratically but exponentially. Domestic divisions remained, especially those emanating from racism and the quest for civil rights, but industrial growth propelled the United States to world influence and power. During the twentieth century, the United States and its army would become enmeshed in resolving global conflicts. Those struggles for freedom encouraged parallel struggles for civil rights at home, and a hundred years after the Civil War, the nation and its army would engage in a second, more successful, Reconstruction.[74]

INTRODUCTION

1. The views expressed here are those of the author and do not reflect the official policy or position of the army, the Defense Department, or the U.S. government.

2. Peter S. Michie, *Emory Upton* (New York: D. Appleton, 1885), 26.

3. Morris Schaff, *The Spirit of Old West Point* (Boston: Houghton Mifflin, 1907), 142–48. For more contemporary accounts of West Point in 1860 and 1861, see Tully McCrea, *Dear Belle: Letters from a Cadet to His Sweetheart, 1858–1865* (Middletown, CT: Wesleyan University Press, 1965); Joseph Person Farley, *West Point in the Early Sixties* (Troy, NY: Pafraets, 1902).

4. Schaff, *Spirit of Old West Point*, 84, 137, 140, 165, 167.

5. Ibid., 142–48.

6. Official Ledger of Casualties, 1861, Records of the United States Military Academy, National Archives Record Group, 404. Hereafter referred to as USMA Archives.

7. Edward Boynton, *History of West Point and Its Military Importance During the American Revolution and the Origin and Progress of the United States Military Academy* (New York: Van Nostrand, 1863), 252.

8. The best account of Beauregard's outlandish attempts to become superintendent despite his vocal support for secession is found in T. Harry Williams, *P. G. T. Beauregard: Napoleon in Gray* (Baton Rouge: Louisiana State University Press, 1955), 44–47; Post Orders 5, 405, 407; Brigadier General John Ross Delafield to Major General Maxwell Taylor, February 20, 1947, USMA Archives.

9. Schaff, *Spirit of Old West Point*, 202–5.

10. Lee and Beauregard were the only superintendents to leave for the South. René DeRussy, although a Virginian, stayed with the Union. The numbers of cadets leaving West Point can be found in James L. Morrison Jr., *"The Best School in the World": West Point in the Pre–Civil War Years, 1833–1866* (Kent, OH: Kent State University Press, 1986), 132.

11. The most effective rebuttal to this claim was given by Senator Garrett Davis of Kentucky, who noted the skill with which West Point–educated generals had served the Confederacy, saying, "For myself, sir, I wish that the armies of the confederates had been commanded in every field by [non–West Point] generals, and that the generals who were educated at West Point had been ever absent from them. The results to our arms would have been very different." *Congressional Globe*, 37th Congress, 1st session, 331.

12. *Congressional Globe*, 37th Congress, 1st session, 328; "House of Representatives," *New York Times*, July 31, 1861.

13. The Naval Academy was not mentioned in the oath legislation. While Congress investigated the Naval Academy's defections, it was not an important institution during the Civil War. At the end of the war, the highest-ranking Naval Academy graduate was only a lieutenant commander. Park Benjamin, *The United States Naval Academy* (New York: G. P. Putnam's Sons, 1900), 195.

14. *Congressional Globe*, 37th Congress, 1st session, 325, 332.

15. G. J. Fieberger, *The Campaign and Battle of Gettysburg* (West Point, NY: U.S. Military Academy Press, 1915), 1.

16. Dwight D. Eisenhower, *At Ease: Stories I Tell My Friends* (New York: Doubleday, 1967), 185.

CHAPTER 1: ORIGINS OF THE CIVIL WAR AND THE CONTEST FOR THE BORDERLANDS

1. *Editors' note:* The extensive bibliographic references in the notes below have been supplied by one of the volume's editors, Professor Sam Watson. Parts of this chapter were generously supplied by West Point faculty.

2. Michael F. Holt, *The Rise and Fall of the American Whig Party: Jacksonian Politics and the Onset of the Civil War* (New York: Oxford University Press, 1999); Daniel Walker Howe, *The Political Culture of the American Whigs* (Chicago: University of Chicago Press, 1984); Thomas Brown,

Politics and Statesmanship: Essays on the American Whig Party (New York: Columbia University Press, 1985). Major works on the second party system include Holt, *Political Parties and American Political Development from the Age of Jackson to the Age of Lincoln* (Baton Rouge: Louisiana State University Press, 1992); Joel H. Silbey, *The American Political Nation, 1838–1893* (Stanford, CA: Stanford University Press, 1991) and *The Partisan Imperative: The Dynamics of American Politics Before the Civil War* (New York: Oxford University Press, 1985); Harry L. Watson, *Liberty and Power: The Politics of Jacksonian America* (New York: Hill and Wang, 1990); Richard L. McCormick, *The Party Period and Public Policy: American Politics from the Age of Jackson to the Progressive Era* (New York: Oxford University Press, 1986); Richard P. McCormick, *The Second American Party System: Party Formation in the Jacksonian Era* (Chapel Hill: University of North Carolina Press, 1966). Richard H. Brown, "The Missouri Crisis, Slavery, and the Politics of Jacksonianism," *South Atlantic Quarterly* 65 (Winter 1966): 55–70, and Leonard L. Richards, "The Jacksonians and Slavery," in *Antislavery Reconsidered: New Perspectives on the Abolitionists,* eds. Lewis Perry and Michael Fellman (Baton Rouge: Louisiana State University Press, 1979), emphasize how the emerging Democratic coalition defended slavery while avoiding overt discussion of the institution.

3. Michael A. Morrison, *Slavery and the American West: The Eclipse of Manifest Destiny* (Chapel Hill: University of North Carolina Press, 1997); Michael F. Holt, *The Fate of the Country: Politicians, Slavery Extension, and the Coming of the Civil War* (New York: Hill and Wang, 2004); Joel H. Silbey, *Storm over Texas: The Annexation Controversy and the Road to Civil War* (New York: Oxford University Press, 2005). The centrality of the defense of slavery to southern politics is explored in William J. Cooper Jr., *The South and the Politics of Slavery, 1828–1856* (Baton Rouge: Louisiana State University Press, 1978), and *Liberty and Slavery: Southern Politics to 1860* (New York: Alfred A. Knopf, 1983). Historians continue to debate the extent to which the North and South were, had become, or were becoming different or distinct from each other; see Edward L. Pessen, "How Different from Each Other Were the Antebellum North and South?," *American Historical Review* 85, no. 5 (December 1980): 1119–49, and Bruce Levine, *Half Slave and Half Free: The Roots of the Civil War* (New York: Hill and Wang, 1992).

4. U.S. Bureau of the Census, *Historical Statistics of the United States, 1789–1945* (Washington, D.C.: Government Printing Office, 1949), 25.

5. See the graph in Ulrich B. Phillips, *American Negro Slavery*, orig. pub. 1918 (Baton Rouge, Louisiana State University Press, 1966), facing p. 370.

6. Don E. Fehrenbacher, *The Slaveholding Republic: An Account of the United States Government's Relations to Slavery*, ed. and completed by Ward M. McAfee (New York: Oxford University Press, 2001).

7. Eric H. Walther, *The Fire-eaters* (Baton Rouge: Louisiana State University Press, 1992).

8. See J. Mills Thornton III, *Politics and Power in a Slaveholding Society: Alabama, 1800–1860* (Baton Rouge: Louisiana State University Press, 1978), for the increasingly intimate relationships southerners saw between the defense of black slavery and that of white freedom; and Stephen E. Maizlish, *The Triumph of Sectionalism: The Transformation of Ohio Politics, 1844–1856* (Kent, OH: Kent State University Press, 1983), for an example of the gradual shift from economic policy to sectional debates.

9. The abolitionists remained a small minority, often scorned for their radicalism by other northerners, throughout the generation before the Civil War. Their numbers notwithstanding, they did press the question of slavery into the spotlight, forcing slaveholders to respond, which they did ever more stridently. See James B. Stewart, *Holy Warriors: The Abolitionists and American Slavery* (New York: Hill and Wang, 1976), and Merton L. Dillon, *Slavery Attacked: Southern Slaves and Their Allies, 1619–1865* (Baton Rouge: Louisiana State University Press, 1990). For antislavery politics more broadly considered, see Richard H. Sewell, *Ballots for Freedom: Antislavery Politics in the United States, 1837–1860* (New York: Oxford University Press, 1976).

10. Harriet Beecher Stowe, *Uncle Tom's Cabin,* 2 vols. (New York: John P. Jewett, 1852); a free audiobook version is available via the Internet Archive, http://archive.org/stream

/uncletomscabino01coopgoog#page/n6/mode/2up, http://archive.org/details/uncle_toms_cabin
_librivox.

. Ira Berlin, *Generations of Captivity: A History of African-American Slaves* (Cambridge, MA: Harvard University Press, 2003), 15.

12. Stanley W. Campbell, *The Slave Catchers: Enforcement of the Fugitive Slave Law, 1850–1860* (Chapel Hill: University of North Carolina Press, 1970). The compromise also provided that the boundaries claimed by Texas were to be shrunk, but the United States would assume responsibility for paying the debts owed to Texas bondholders from their revolution and period of independence.

13. Eric Foner, *Free Soil, Free Labor, Free Men: The Ideology of the Republican Party Before the Civil War* (New York: Oxford University Press, 1970) explores the variety of the Republicans, their views of northern and southern society, and their integration of social, economic, and sectional arguments in the concept of free labor.

14. See David Brion Davis, *The Slave Power Conspiracy and the Paranoid Style* (Baton Rouge: Louisiana State University Press, 1969).

15. The planters of this class constituted around 3 percent of southern families. James L. Huston, *Calculating the Value of the Union: Slavery, Property Rights, and the Economic Origins of the Civil War* (Chapel Hill: University of North Carolina Press, 2003), 28.

16. Clement Eaton, *The Freedom-of-Thought Struggle in the Old South* (New York: Harper & Row, 1964).

17. William W. Freehling, *The Road to Disunion: Secessionists at Bay, 1776–1854* (New York: Oxford University Press, 1990), 308–52.

18. Michael F. Holt, *The Political Crisis of the 1850s* (New York: John Wiley, 1978), 1–38, 151–53.

19. See the still-unsurpassed Ray Allen Billington, *The Protestant Crusade, 1800–1860* (New York: Macmillan, 1938). On the political effects, see Holt, *Political Crisis of the 1850s*, 156–99.

20. Tyler Anbinder, *Nativism and Slavery: The Northern Know Nothings and the Politics of the 1850s* (New York: Oxford University Press, 1992), and Michael F. Holt, *Forging a Majority: The Formation of the Republican Party in Pittsburgh, 1848–1860* (New Haven, CT: Yale University Press, 1969).

21. William E. Gienapp, *The Origins of the Republican Party, 1852–1856* (New York: Oxford University Press, 1987).

22. Nicole Etcheson, *Bleeding Kansas: Contested Liberty in the Civil War Era* (Lawrence: University Press of Kansas, 2004); Stanley Harrold, *Border War: Fighting over Slavery Before the Civil War* (Chapel Hill: University of North Carolina Press: 2010); Tony R. Mullis, *Peacekeeping on the Plains: Army Operations in Bleeding Kansas* (Columbia: University of Missouri Press, 2004); Durwood Ball, *Army Regulars on the Western Frontier* (Norman: University of Oklahoma Press, 2001).

23. Don E. Fehrenbacher, *The Dred Scott Case: Its Significance in American Law and Politics* (1979; reprint ed., New York: Oxford University Press, 2001), condensed as *Slavery, Law, and Politics: The Dred Scott Case in Historical Perspective* (New York: Oxford University Press, 1981). See also Kenneth M. Stampp, *America in 1857: A Nation on the Brink* (New York: Oxford University Press, 1990).

24. See especially David M. Potter, *The Impending Crisis, 1848–1861* (New York: Harper & Row, 1976), 356–84, and Steven A. Channing, *Crisis of Fear: Secession in South Carolina* (New York: W. W. Norton, 1974).

25. Bruce Levine, *The Spirit of 1848: German Immigrants, Labor Conflict, and the Coming of the Civil War* (Urbana: University of Illinois Press, 1992).

26. James L. Huston, *The Panic of 1857 and the Coming of the Civil War* (Baton Rouge: Louisiana State University Press, 1987).

27. Arthur M. Schlesinger Jr., ed., *History of American Presidential Elections, 1789–1968*, 4 vols. (New York: McGraw-Hill, 1971), 2:1152. See also William C. Harris, *Lincoln's Rise to the Presidency* (Lawrence: University Press of Kansas, 2007); Douglas R. Edgerton, *Year of Meteors:*

Stephen Douglas, Abraham Lincoln, and the Election That Brought on the Civil War (New York: Bloomsbury, 2010). The best account of the Democratic schism remains Roy F. Nichols, *The Disruption of American Democracy* (New York: Macmillan, 1948).

28. Roy P. Basler, ed., *The Collected Works of Abraham Lincoln*, 9 vols. (New Brunswick, NJ: Rutgers University Press, 1953–55), 7:499.

29. Major works, not otherwise mentioned herein, that attempt to explain secession include William L. Barney, *The Road to Secession: A New Perspective on the Old South* (Westport, CT: Praeger, 1972), and *The Secessionist Impulse: Alabama and Mississippi in 1860* (Princeton, NJ: Princeton University Press, 1974); Michael P. Johnson, *Toward a Patriarchal Republic: The Secession of Georgia* (Baton Rouge: Louisiana State University Press, 1977); William W. Freehling, *The Reintegration of American History: Slavery and the Civil War* (New York: Oxford University Press, 1994); William A. Link, *Roots of Secession: Slavery and Politics in Antebellum Virginia* (Chapel Hill: University of North Carolina Press, 2003); and Stephanie McCurry, *Confederate Reckoning: Power and Politics in the Civil War South* (Cambridge: Harvard University Press, 2010). See Charles B. Dew, *Apostles of Disunion: Southern Secession Commissioners and the Causes of the Civil War* (Charlottesville: University Press of Virginia, 2001), for the centrality of protecting slavery in the arguments of the emissaries seceded states sent to the conventions in other states.

30. Daniel W. Crofts, *Reluctant Confederates: Upper South Unionists in the Secession Crisis* (Chapel Hill: University of North Carolina Press, 1989).

31. Kenneth M. Stampp, "The Concept of a Perpetual Union," in *The Imperiled Union: Essays on the Background of the Civil War* (New York: Oxford University Press, 1980), 3–38. On the configuring power of the Constitution, see Arthur M. Bestor, "The American Civil War as a Constitutional Crisis," *American Historical Review* 69 (1964), 327–52. For a history of constitutional dilemmas and outcomes from secession to the war's end, see Mark E. Neely Jr., *Lincoln and the Triumph of the Nation: Constitutional Conflict in the American Civil War* (Chapel Hill: University of North Carolina Press, 2011).

32. Lincoln, First Inaugural Address, March 4, 1861, in Roy P. Basler, ed., *The Collected Works of Abraham Lincoln*, 9 vols. (New Brunswick, NJ: Rutgers University Press, 1953–55), 4:268.

33. This followed a line of reasoning in the explication of the Constitution in the Kentucky and Virginia Resolutions of 1798 and 1799 (written by Thomas Jefferson and James Madison, no less).

34. "First Inaugural Address—First Edition and Revisions" in Basler, ed., *Collected Works of Abraham Lincoln*, 4:253.

35. Lincoln to James T. Hale, January 11, 1861, in Basler, ed., *Collected Works of Abraham Lincoln*, 4:172; David M. Potter, *Lincoln and His Party During the Secession Crisis* (New Haven, CT: Yale University Press, 1942).

36. Robert W. Johannsen, ed., *The Letters of Stephen A. Douglas* (Urbana: University of Illinois Press, 1961), 509–513; John G. Nicolay, *The Outbreak of the Rebellion*, intro. by Mark E. Neely Jr. (1881; reprint ed., New York: Da Capo, 1995), 77. Douglas died of illness brought on by rheumatism during his tour. See William J. Cooper, *We Have the War Upon Us: The Onset of the Civil War, November 1860–April 1861* (New York: Alfred A. Knopf, 2012); the wide-ranging essays in Gabor S. Boritt, ed., *Why the War Came* (New York: Oxford University Press, 1996); and the still-classic Kenneth M. Stampp, *And the War Came: The North and the Secession Crisis, 1860–1861* (Baton Rouge: Louisiana State University Press, 1950).

37. Shannon, 1:159–60. For Confederate problems balancing mobilization and states' rights, see David Donald, "Died of Democracy," in Donald, ed., *Why the North Won the Civil War* (Baton Rouge: Louisiana State University Press, 1960), 77–90. For the most comprehensive account of mobilization, continuing through the war, see Paul A. C. Koistinen, *Beating Plowshares into Swords: The Political Economy of American Warfare, 1606–1865* (Lawrence: University Press of Kansas, 1996).

38. This important calculation was made by T. Harry Williams in "The Military Leadership of North and South," in Donald, ed., *Why the North Won*, 23–48.

39. "To the Women of America," *New York Tribune*, April 24, 1863. See Nina Silber, *Daughters of*

the Union: Northern Women Fight the Civil War (Cambridge, MA: Harvard University Press, 2005); Jeanie Attie, *Patriotic Toil: Northern Women and the American Civil War* (Ithaca, NY: Cornell University Press, 1998); Lyde Cullen Sizer, *The Political Work of Northern Women Writers and the Civil War, 1850–1872* (Chapel Hill: University of North Carolina Press, 2000).

40. Ulysses Grant, *The Papers of Ulysses S. Grant,* vol. 2, April–September 1861, ed. John Y. Simon (Carbondale: Southern Illinois University Press, 1969), 3–4, http://digital.library.msstate.edu/cdm/compoundobject/collection/USG_volume/id/15878/rec/2.

41. Melinda Lawson, *Patriot Fires: Forging a New American Nationalism in the Civil War North* (Lawrence: University Press of Kansas, 2002), 14–39.

42. For a contrary view see Drew Gilpin Faust, *Mothers of Invention: Women of the Slaveholding South in the American Civil War* (Chapel Hill: University of North Carolina Press, 1996).

43. Richard N. Current, "God and the Strongest Battalions," in Donald, ed., *Why the North Won,* 3.

44. Richard M. McMurry, *Two Great Rebel Armies: An Essay in Confederate Military History* (Chapel Hill: University of North Carolina Press, 1989), 20.

45. Numbers and sources are cited, with analysis, in Samuel J. Watson, "Continuity in Civil-Military Relations and Expertise: The U.S. Army During the Decade Before the Civil War," *Journal of Military History* 75 (January 2011): 39–41.

46. John Y. Simon, "Abraham Lincoln, Jefferson Davis, and Fort Sumter," in Simon, *The Union Forever: Lincoln, Grant, and the Civil War* (Lexington: University Press of Kentucky, 2012), 53–63.

47. This point is made most effectively by Michael C. C. Adams, *Fighting for Defeat: Union Military Failure in the East, 1861–1865,* originally published as *Our Masters the Rebels: A Speculation on Union Military Failure in the East, 1861–1865* in 1978 (Lincoln: University of Nebraska Press, 1992).

48. *The War of the Rebellion: A Compilation of the Official Records of the Union and Confederate Armies,* 127 vols. (Washington, D.C.: Government Printing Office, 1880–1901), [hereafter abbreviated *OR*] ser. 1, vol. 25, pt. 1, 193.

49. The role of geography is best described by McMurry, *Two Great Rebel Armies,* 10–29. For the blockade, see Robert M. Browning Jr., *Success Is All That Was Expected: The South Atlantic Blockading Squadron During the Civil War* (Washington, D.C.: Potomac Books, 2002), and *From Cape Charles to Cape Fear: The North Atlantic Blockading Squadron During the Civil War* (Tuscaloosa: University of Alabama Press, 2003).

50. See Dennis E. Showalter, *Railroads and Rifles: Soldiers, Technology and the Unification of Germany* (Hamden, CT: Archon Books, 1975); Orlando Figes, *The Crimean War: A History* (New York: Metropolitan, 2011); John Sweetman, *The Crimean War: 1854–1856* (New York: Osprey, 2001); Frederick Schneid, *The Second War of Italian Unification 1859–61* (New York: Osprey, 2012); Jack Green and Alessandro Massignani, *Ironclads at War: The Origin and Development of the Armored Warship, 1854–1891* (Conshohocken, PA: Combined Publishing, 1998); William H. Roberts, *Civil War Ironclads: The U.S. Navy and Industrial Mobilization* (Baltimore: Johns Hopkins University Press, 2002).

51. Earl J. Hess, *The Rifle Musket in Civil War Combat: Reality and Myth* (Lawrence: University Press of Kansas, 2008); Mark Grimsley, "Surviving Military Revolution: The U.S. Civil War," *The Dynamics of Military Revolution,* ed. MacGregor Knox and Williamson Murray (Cambridge: Cambridge University Press, 2001), 76; Geoffrey Wawro, "'An Army of Pigs': The Technical, Social, and Political Bases of Austrian Shock Tactics, 1859–1866," *Journal of Military History* 59 (July 1995): 407–33; Wayne Wei-siang Hsieh, *West Pointers and the Civil War: The Old Army in War and Peace* (Chapel Hill: University of North Carolina Press, 2009). The belief that the rifled musket was revolutionary in the power it gave to the defense, which was standard among historians a generation ago but has come into question by many, is most effectively presented in Perry Jamieson and Grady McWhiney, *Attack and Die! Civil War Military Tactics and the Southern Heritage* (Tuscaloosa: University of Alabama Press, 1984). For Civil War tactics more generally, see Paddy Griffth, *Battle Tactics of the Civil War* (New Haven, CT: Yale University

Press, 1989), which stresses the similarities between Civil War and Napoleonic tactics, and Brent Nosworthy, *The Bloody Crucible of Courage: Fighting Methods and Combat Experience of the Civil War* (New York: Carroll and Graf, 2003).

52. The most comprehensive work is Stephen Z. Starr, *The Union Cavalry in the Civil War,* 3 vols. (Baton Rouge: Louisiana State University Press, 1985).

53. Watson, "Continuity in Civil-Military Relations and Expertise," presents an assessment of the army's capabilities and limitations in 1860.

54. Carol Reardon, *With a Sword in One Hand and Jomini in the Other: The Problem of Military Thought in the Civil War North* (Chapel Hill: University of North Carolina Press, 2012), which observes that Jomini's influence was, in fact, rather limited. See also Morrison, *"Best School in the World."*

55. Mark E. Neely Jr., re strategy, in *The Union Divided: Party Conflict in the Civil War North* (Cambridge, MA: Harvard University Press, 2002), ch. 3.

56. Ernest A. McKay, *The Civil War and New York City* (Syracuse, NY: Syracuse University Press, 1990), 33–38; George C. Rable, *The Confederate Republic: A Revolution Against Politics* (Chapel Hill: University of North Carolina Press, 1994).

57. James M. McPherson, *Battle Cry of Freedom: The Civil War Era* (New York: Oxford University Press, 1988), 284.

58. See William C. Harris, *Lincoln and the Border States: Preserving the Union* (Lawrence: University Press of Kansas, 2011).

59. That is the term used by Michael Fellman in his landmark book *Inside War: The Guerrilla Conflict in Missouri During the American Civil War* (New York: Oxford University Press, 1989), 10.

60. William Garrett Piston and Richard W. Hatcher III, *Wilson's Creek: The Second Battle of the Civil War and the Men Who Fought It* (Chapel Hill: University of North Carolina Press, 2000). In addition to Fellman, see Mark W. Geiger, *Financial Fraud and Guerrilla Violence in Missouri's Civil War, 1861–1865* (New Haven, CT: Yale University Press, 2010).

61. Merryman was "charged with various acts of treason, and with being publicly associated with and holding a commission as lieutenant in a company having in their possession arms belonging to the United States, and avowing his purpose of armed hostility against the government." *OR,* Ser. II, vol. 1, 576.

62. Mark E. Neely Jr., *The Fate of Liberty: Abraham Lincoln and Civil Liberties* (New York: Oxford University Press, 1991). Similar conflicts within the Confederacy are explored in Neely, *Southern Rights: Political Prisoners and the Myth of Confederate Constitutionalism* (Charlottesville: University Press of Virginia, 1999), and Paul D. Escott, *Military Necessity: Civil-Military Relations in the Confederacy* (Westport, CT: Praeger, 2006).

63. Frederick Douglass, "The War and Slavery," in Philip S. Foner and Yuval Taylor, eds., *Frederick Douglass: Selected Speeches and Writings* (Chicago: Lawrence Hill Books, 1999), 464–65, from *Douglass' Monthly* 4, no. 3, August 1861, 1.

64. Abraham Lincoln to Orville H. Browning, September 22, 1861, in Basler, ed., *Collected Works of Abraham Lincoln,* 4:531–32.

65. For a contrary view see Daniel E. Sutherland, "Sideshow No Longer: A Historiographical Review of the Guerrilla War," *Civil War History* 46 (2000): 5–23.

66. James M. McPherson, *War on the Waters: The Union and Confederate Navies, 1861–1865* (Chapel Hill: University of North Carolina Press, 2012), 44–46.

67. Norman Graebner states the issue of interpretation of diplomatic history succinctly and vividly in Norman Graebner, "Northern Diplomacy and European Neutrality," in Donald, ed., *Why the North Won,* 49–75.

68. U.S. Congress, *Report of the Joint Committee on the Conduct of the War* (3 vols., Washington, D.C.: Government Printing Office, 1863), 2:37–38.

69. The best accounts of the campaign and battle are William C. Davis, *The Battle at Bull Run: A History of the First Major Campaign of the Civil War* (Baton Rouge: Louisiana State University

Press, 1981), and Ethan S. Rafuse, *A Single Grand Victory: The First Campaign and Battle of Manassas* (Wilmington, DE: Scholarly Resources, 2002).

70. This interpretation of the meaning of the Bull Run defeat comes from Adams, *Fighting for Defeat*.

71. *Congressional Globe*, 37th Congress, 1st session, 222; also in *OR*, ser. 3, vol. 5, 1008.

72. Valuable discussions may be found in Herman Hattaway and Archer Jones, *How the North Won: A Military History of the Civil War* (Urbana: University of Illinois Press, 1991), and Earl J. Hess, *The Civil War in the West: Victory and Defeat from the Appalachians to the Mississippi* (Chapel Hill: University of North Carolina Press, 2012). Belmont is examined in Nathaniel Cheairs Hughes Jr., *The Battle of Belmont: Grant Strikes South* (Chapel Hill: University of North Carolina Press, 1991). Bruce Catton's *Grant Moves South* (Boston: Little, Brown, 1960) remains a classic.

73. Benjamin F. Cooling, *Forts Henry and Donelson: The Key to the Confederate Heartland* (Knoxville: University of Tennessee Press, 1987); Stephen D. Engle, *Struggle for the Heartland: The Campaigns from Fort Henry to Corinth* (Lincoln: University of Nebraska Press, 2001). Rowena Reed, *Combined Operations in the Civil War* (Annapolis, MD: Naval Institute Press, 1978), is the most comprehensive treatment of riverine operations during the war.

74. Larry J. Daniel and Lynn N. Bock, *Island No. 10: Struggle for the Mississippi Valley* (Tuscaloosa: University of Alabama Press, 1996); William H. Roberts, *Now for the Contest: Coastal and Oceanic Naval Operations in the Civil War* (Lincoln: University of Nebraska Press, 2004), 47–54. See also Chester G. Hearn, *The Capture of New Orleans, 1862* (Baton Rouge: Louisiana State University Press, 1995). Meanwhile, U.S. forces turned back a substantial Confederate thrust in Arkansas at the battle of Pea Ridge (March 6–7); see William L. Shea and Earl J. Hess, *Pea Ridge: Civil War Campaign in the West* (Chapel Hill: University of North Carolina Press, 1992).

75. Edwin M. Stanton to Horace Greeley, February 19, 1862, *New York Tribune*, February 20, 1862.

76. See Neely, *Union Divided*, ch. 3, for the Republican condemnation of "strategy."

77. Larry J. Daniel, *Shiloh: The Battle That Changed the Civil War* (New York: Simon & Schuster, 1997); James McDonough, *Shiloh: In Hell Before Night* (Knoxville: University of Tennessee Press, 1977); Wiley Sword, *Shiloh: Bloody April* (New York: William Morrow, 1974).

78. It must be admitted, though, that the provenance for this anecdote is not very good, as it seems to have been recorded for the first time much later by Charles Frederick Wingate in *What Shall Our Boys Do for a Living?* (New York: Doubleday and McClure, 1898), 213–14. Wingate, however, was an assiduous collector of information about the war during its progress.

79. Hess, *Civil War in the West*, 34–51; Grant, *Personal Memoirs*, 218, http://books.google.com/books?id=Z5B-eOn_Pb4C&pg=PA218.

80. Lincoln speech, July 4, 1861, in Basler, ed., *Collected Works of Abraham Lincoln*, 4:438.

CHAPTER 2: THE WAR IN THE EAST, JULY 1861–SEPTEMBER 1862

1. Joseph T. Glatthaar, *General Lee's Army: From Victory to Collapse* (New York: Free Press, 2008), 55, 62–63. Union commander Brig. Gen. Irvin McDowell had left 10,000 fresh troops some ten miles north of the battlefield as he advanced on the Confederates. Those fresh troops would have prevented any effective pursuit from threatening Washington, D.C. In victory, the Confederates were almost as disorganized as the Federals.

2. Confederates frequently called Federal soldiers Hessians, in reference to mercenaries that the British government hired from various German states in the Revolutionary War.

3. The exemption did not apply if there was a white male adult not liable to conscription available to oversee the slaves. James M. Matthews, *Public Laws of the Confederate States of America, Passed at the Second Session of the First Congress* (Richmond, VA: R. M. Smith, 1862), 77–79. In Virginia, only 2 percent of all exemptions were under the twenty-slave law.

4. Later, Congress extended all enlistments to the duration of the war.

5. Glatthaar, *General Lee's Army*, 66–69.

6. Ibid., 89–94.

7. See William C. Davis, *Jefferson Davis: The Man and His Hour* (New York: HarperCollins, 1991), 357; Johnston to Cooper, July 29, 1861, *The War of the Rebellion: Official Records of the Union and Confederate Armies* (Washington, D.C.: Government Printing Office, 1880–1901) (hereafter *OR*) ser. 1, vol. 2: 1007.

8. Glatthaar, *General Lee's Army*, 94–103; Joseph T. Glatthaar, *Partners in Command: The Relationships Between Leaders in the Civil War* (New York: Free Press, 1994), 95–133. Davis intended that Lee, as his military adviser, issued orders for the commander in chief. The dispute over rank centered around two laws: An Act for the Establishment and Organization of the Army of the Confederate States of America, March 6, 1861, and An Act Amendatory of an Act for the Organization of the Staff Departments of the Army and an Act for the Establishment and Organization of the Army of the Confederate States of America, March 14, 1861, *OR* 4, 1:131 and 164. Cooper was adjutant general (by custom the senior staff officer) in the U.S. and C.S. armies, though his actual rank in the U.S. Army was colonel. Lee and A. S. Johnston were both colonels, but A. S. Johnston outranked Lee because of an honorary ("brevet") promotion for Johnston's command of the expedition against Mormon unrest in Utah in 1857. As a brigadier general, Joe Johnston formally outranked Cooper, Lee, and A. S. Johnston in the U.S. Army, but his general's rank was staff officer (as quartermaster general). Once he vacated that position, he could claim only the rank of a lieutenant colonel in the line. Had Johnston accepted the job of quartermaster general in the C.S. army, he would have outranked Lee, A. S. Johnston, and even Cooper, but he was never offered the position, nor did he want it. Also see Steven H. Newton, *Joseph E. Johnston and the Defense of Richmond* (Lawrence: University Press of Kansas, 1998), 5–7.

9. W. T. Sherman to Ellen, July 28 [1861?]. Brooks D. Simpson and Jean V. Berlin, eds., *Selected Correspondence of William T. Sherman, 1860–1865* (Chapel Hill: University of North Carolina Press, 1999), 125.

10. Confederates under Brig. Gen. Robert S. Garnet, with some 4,600 men, guarded two roads: the Clarksburg-Philippi Road and the Parkersburg-Staunton Turnpike. He posted 1,300 of his men under Lt. Col. John Pegram. McClellan, who had a force of 20,000, moved 3,000 of them along the Clarksburg-Philippi Road to distract the Confederates, while 5,000 came with him along the Parkersburg-Staunton Turnpike to seize Rich Mountain in the Confederate rear. McClellan had Brig. Gen. William S. Rosecrans, with 1,900 men, slipped to the rear of the Confederates. On July 11, 1861, Rosecrans attacked 311 of Pegram's forces from Rich Mountain. McClellan was supposed to attack from the north but did not move, thinking that Rosecrans was repulsed. McClellan did not know of Rosecrans's victory until the next day. Pegram retreated in the direction of Garnett. Upon hearing of Pegram's defeat, Garnett retreated, and he was killed two days later in a rear-guard action. Pegram then was trapped between two Union commands. He and part of his command surrendered. All told, Confederates lost 300 men (killed, wounded, or captured); the Federals lost 46. McClellan received credit for the victory, which resulted in his switch to command the Army of the Potomac. See Ruth Woods Dayton, "The Beginning— Philippi, 1861," *West Virginia History Journal* 13, no. 4 (July 1952): 254–66; Stephen W. Sears, *George B. McClellan: The Young Napoleon* (New York: Ticknor & Fields, 1988), 84–92.

11. For the best biography of McClellan, see Sears, *George B. McClellan*. Also see Ethan Rafuse, *McClellan's War: The Failure of Moderation in the Struggle for the Union* (Indianapolis: Indiana University Press, 2005), for a much more positive spin on the controversial general.

12. Crenshaw Hall to Father, June 26, 1861, Bolling Hall Family Papers, Alabama Department of Archives and History.

13. Napoleons were smoothbore guns named after Napoleon III. They were durable, reliable, and relatively easy to manufacture, firing a twelve-pound solid shot for a mile. They generally fired

solid shot, exploding shells with fuses, case shot, and canister. The Union army also utilized three-inch rifled guns, which had a range of three miles.

14. Americans were accustomed to a relatively high standard of living in peacetime.

15. Report of Brig. Gen. William F. Barry, September 1, 1862. Barry to McClellan, August 23, 1861, *OR* 12 (3):66–69; Report of Quartermaster General Montgomery C. Meigs, November 18, 1862, *OR* 3, 2:797–800. See L. Van Loan Naisawald, *Grape and Canister: The Story of the Field Artillery of the Army of the Potomac* (Washington, D.C.: Zenger Publishing, 1960), 26–41; Edward Hagerman, *The American Civil War and the Origins of Modern Warfare: Ideas, Organization, and Field Command* (Bloomington: Indiana University Press, 1988), 39 and 44–46. For a brilliant article on Civil War logistics, see John G. Moore, "Mobility and Strategy in the Civil War," *Military Affairs* 24 (1960): 68–77.

16. McClellan squabbled with his schoolteacher, claimed that West Point faculty conspired to deny him of the number one rank in his class, offended the chief engineer of the army as a second lieutenant, landed in a dispute with the territorial governor of Oregon, and openly despised the senior officers who observed the Crimean War with him. As chief engineer, he tussled with the directors of the Illinois Central Railroad and was arguing with the administrative superintendent of the Mobile & Ohio Railroad when the war broke out. See Glatthaar, *Partners in Command*, 240–42.

17. McClellan to Wife, July 27, 1861, Sears, ed., *Civil War Papers of McClellan*, 70; McClellan to Lincoln, 4 [2] August 1861, *OR* 5: 6–8; McClellan to Scott, August 8, 1861, *OR* 11 (3):3; McClellan to Wife, August 8 and August 10, 1861; McClellan to Wife, August 16, 1861; McClellan to Wife, August 19, 1861; McClellan to Cameron, September 13, 1861, Sears, *Papers of* McClellan, 81, 85, 87, and 100. McClellan determined the grossly inflated figure before the famed detective Allan Pinkerton conducted spying efforts. As Sears has explained so well, Pinkerton's exaggerated numbers merely verified what McClellan believed to be true: that the Confederates vastly outnumbered his army. On July 10, 1861, the aggregate present was 106,466. By December 1, it was up to 198,213 (*OR* 5:12–13). By contrast, Johnston reported a strength of 45,000 on August 23, 1861, 10,000 of whom were sick; on November 30, 1861, the combined Confederate forces in the Potomac District (I and II Corps), Valley District, and Aquia District totaled 63,929 aggregate present. See Johnston to Davis, August 23, 1861, Lynda Lasswell Crist and Mary Seaton Dix et al., eds., *The Papers of Jefferson Davis* (Baton Rouge: Louisiana State University Press, 1992), 7, 304–6, and *OR* 5:974.

18. McClellan to Wife, August 16, 1861; McClellan to Wife, August 19, 1861; McClellan to Cameron, September 13, 1861; McClellan to Wife, October 11?, 1861; McClellan to Wife, October 31, 1861; McClellan to Wife, November 17, 1861, Sears, *Papers of McClellan*, 85, 87, 100, 107, 114, and 135.

19. See William C. Davis, *Duel Between the First Ironclads* (Garden City, NY: Doubleday, 1975).

20. Glatthaar, *General Lee's Army*, 104–9 and 116–18.

21. See Donald Pfanz, *Richard S. Ewell: A Soldier's Life* (Chapel Hill: University of North Carolina Press, 1998).

22. Lee to Jackson, April 25, 1862, *OR* 12 (3):865–66. See Jackson to Ewell, April 10, 1862; Lee to Jackson and Lee to Ewell, April 21, 1862, *OR* 12 (3):845 and 858–60. Lee had already developed a great command relationship with Jackson when Lee commanded the Virginia Forces and Jackson commanded the troops at Harpers Ferry. See Joseph L. Harsh, *Confederate Tide Rising: Robert E. Lee and the Making of Southern Strategy, 1861–1862* (Kent, OH: Kent State University Press, 1998).

23. Lee to Jackson, May 16, 1862, *OR* 12 (3):892–93. Also see Taylor to Jackson, May 14, 1862, *OR* 12 (3):889. Ewell delayed an attack on the flank, so that when Brig. Gen. Richard Taylor's attack broke the Federal lines, Ewell's men were not in a position to exploit it.

24. See Robert K. Krick, *Conquering the Valley: Stonewall Jackson at Port Republic* (New York: Morrow, 1996); Peter Cozzens, *Shenandoah 1862: Stonewall Jackson's Valley Campaign* (Chapel Hill:

University of North Carolina Press, 2008); Robert G. Tanner, *Stonewall in the Valley: Thomas J. "Stonewall" Jackson's Shenandoah Valley Campaign, Spring 1862* (Mechanicsburg, PA: Stackpole, 1996). For Jackson, see James I. Robertson Jr., *Stonewall Jackson: The Man, the Soldier, the Legend* (New York: Macmillan, 1997).

25. In the early part of the war, staff work was poor. In this case, however, Johnston and Longstreet and not their staffs were at fault. For the Confederate Order of Battle, see *OR* 12 (3):530–33. For Union strength, see *OR* 12 (3):238. For Union Order of Battle, see *OR* 11 (1):757–62, and *OR* 11 (2):24–37.

26. For Daniel Harvey Hill, see Maj. Brit Erslev, U.S. Army, "Daniel Harvey Hill and Southern Memory of the Civil War," PhD diss., University of North Carolina at Chapel Hill, 2011.

27. Steven H. Newton, *The Battle of Seven Pines, May 31–June 1, 1862* (Lynchburg, VA: H. E. Howard, 1993).

28. Winfield Scott to Sec. of War John B. Floyd, May 8, 1857, George Bolling Lee Papers, Virginia Historical Society (hereafter VHS); Lee to Annette Carter, January 16, 1861, Lenning Collection, Washington and Lee University.

29. EKS to Mother, May 10 and May 16, 1861. R2, Edmund Kirby Smith Papers, Southern Historical Collection, University of North Carolina (hereafter SHC, UNC); F. W. Pickens to Bonham, July 7, 1861, Milledge Luke Bonham Papers, University of South Carolina (hereafter UofSC); Sam to wife, May 29, 1861, Samuel Wicliffe Melton Papers, UofSC; Walter Taylor to [Bettie], March 4, 1864, Walter H. Taylor Papers, Norfolk Public Library; Edward A. Pollard, *Southern History of the War: The First Year of the War* (New York: C. B. Richardson, 1864), 168.

30. Ben Allston to Father, December 9, 1861, R. F. W. Allston Papers, South Carolina Historical Society; A. C. Haskell to Mother, January 22, 1862; Alexander C. Haskell Papers, SHC, UNC; Richmond *Enquirer*, September 20, 1861, P1, C3; Armand [Beauregard] to [General Beauregard], October 14, 1863, *OR* 30 (4):746.

31. Lee to wife, October 7, 1861, Robert E. Lee Jr., *Recollections and Letters of General Robert E. Lee* (New York: Doubleday, Page & Co., 1904), 51; R. E. Lee to [Charlotte], December 25, 1862, Lee Family Papers, VHS; Freeman, *R. E. Lee: A Biography* (New York: Charles Scribner's Sons, 1934), 2:598; Davis to Lee, March 2, 1862, *OR* 6:400; Tho S Preston to Wife, March 28, 1862. Preston-Davis Papers, UVA; Catherine Edmonston diary, May 6, 1862. Beth Gilbert Crabtree and James W. Patton, eds., *Journal of a Secesh Lady* (Raleigh: North Carolina Division of Archives and History, 1979), 169; McClellan to Lincoln, April 20, 1862, Stephen Sears, ed., *Papers of McClellan*, 244–45; Glatthaar, *General Lee's Army*, 123–27. McClellan's statement may be a classic case of projection.

32. Jay Luvaas, "Lee and the Operational Art: The Right Place, the Right Time," *Parameters* (Autumn, 1992): 2–18, for a marvelous introduction into Lee and the operational art.

33. GO, No. 15, A & IGO, October 22, 1861, *OR* 5:913–14; SO, No. 22, HQ, June 1, 1862, *OR* 11 (3):569. Lee called it the Army of Northern Virginia in SO, No. 4. HQ, Richmond, VA, April 5, 1862. SO, Virginia Forces, April 29, 1861–May 30, 1862. Record Group 109, National Archives; Glatthaar, *General Lee's Army,* 129–33. For Seven Days Battles, see Brian K. Burton, *Extraordinary Circumstances: The Seven Days Battle* (Bloomington: Indiana University Press, 2001).

34. See James I. Robertson Jr., *A. P. Hill: The Story of a Confederate Warrior* (New York: Random House, 1987).

35. Harold B. Simpson, "Hood's Texas Brigade," www.tshaonline.org/handbook/online/articles/qkh02.

36. The exact number of McClellan's command is subject to some confusion. McClellan admitted to his wife that he had 135,000, and authorities in Washington believed he did. With sicknesses and soldiers detached for various duties, he probably had around 115,000 troops for combat.

37. McClellan to Wife, July 4 and 17 [1862?], Sears, ed., *Papers of McClellan*, 335 and 363.

38. AAR of LTC LA, Grant, July 9, 1862, *OR* 11 (2):478–79.

39. Chilton to Magruder, July 1, 1862, AAR of Lewis Armistead, July 14, 1862, *OR* 11 (2):677 and 819; Robert K. Krick, "Armistead and Garnett: The Parallel Lives of Two Virginia Soldiers," in Gary W. Gallagher, ed., *The Third Day of Gettysburg and Beyond* (Chapel Hill: University of

North Carolina Press, 1994), 99–101; Daniel Harvey Hill, "McClellan's Change of Base and Malvern Hill," in Robert Underwood Johnson and Clarence Clough Buel, eds., *Battles and Leaders of the Civil War* (New York: Thomas Yoseloff, 1956), 2, 394.

40. Charles to Etta, June 19, 1862, Kerrison Family Papers, University of South Carolina.

41. Norton to Sister L., July 7, 1862, Oliver Willcox Norton, *Army Letters, 1861–1865* (Chicago: O. L. Deming, 1903), 95.

42. [Jaspar A. Gillespie] to wife, July 5, 1862, Jaspar A. Gillespie Papers, Georgia Department of Archives and History.

43. McClellan to Stanton, June 25, 1862, and June 27, 1862, *OR* 11 (3):254; McClellan to Stanton, July 28, 1862, *OR* 11 (1):61; McClellan to Lorenzo Thomas, July 1, 1862, *OR* 11, (3):281.

44. McClellan to Wife, [July 7, 1862]; McClellan to Marcy, July 4, 1862, Sears, ed., *Papers of McClellan*, 341 and 334; McClellan to Stanton, July 3, 1862, *OR* 11 (3):291–92; McClellan to Lincoln, July 4, 1862, *OR* 11(1):72. Also see McClellan to Wife, July 8 and [July] 10, 1862, Sears, ed., *Papers of McClellan*, 346 and 348.

45. McClellan to Wife, July 8, [1862], Sears, ed., *Papers of McClellan*, 346; McClellan to Lincoln, July 7, 1862, *OR* 11 (1):73–74.

46. T. Harry Williams in *Lincoln and His Generals* (New York: Knopf, 1952), 133, argues that it might be considered improper today but was not so back then. Stephen Sears in *George B. McClellan*, 227–29, argues that this blending of political and military issues was typical of McClellan. He does not criticize him for it but implies that it was not proper.

47. http://archive.org/details/confiscationact00circgoog.

48. www.history.umd.edu/Freedmen/milact.htm.

49. www.history.umd.edu/Freedmen/conact2.htm.

50. U.S., *Statutes at Large, Treaties, and Proclamations of the United States of America*, 12 (Boston: 1863), 597–600; Sherman to Halleck, December 24, 1864, *OR* 44: 799.

51. Lincoln to Halleck, July 11, 1862, *OR* 11 (3):314; Halleck to McClellan, August 3 and 6, 1862. McClellan to Halleck, August 4, 1862, *OR* 11 (1):80–84.

52. Lincoln Order, June 26, 1862, *OR* 12 (3):435; General Orders, No. 5. General Orders, No. 6. General Orders, No. 7. General Orders, No. 11. July 18, 10 [?], and 23, 1862, *OR* 12 (2):50–52.

53. Lee to Jackson, July 27, 1862, *OR* 12 (3):918–19. See Robert K. Krick, *Stonewall Jackson at Cedar Mountain* (Chapel Hill: University of North Carolina Press, 1990), for the battle and casualty numbers, in appendix III.

54. For Union order of Battle at Second Bull Run, see *OR* 12 (3):581–88. For Confederates, see *OR* 12 (2):546–51.

55. John J. Hennessy, *Return to Bull Run: The Campaign and Battle of Second Manassas* (New York: Simon & Schuster, 1993), 177.

56. McClellan to Lincoln, *OR* 11 (1):98.

57. Pope would later bring up charges against Porter, and a general court-martial dismissed him from the service. After the war, Porter fought the court's decision, had a rehearing, and was exonerated. *OR* 12 (2), supplement.

58. Longstreet to Fitz John Porter, September 23, 1866, and October 31, 1877, box 2, clippings file, Cadmus Wilcox Papers, Library of Congress (hereafter LC); AAR of Lee, June 8, 1863; AAR of Longstreet, October 10, 1862; AAR of Jackson, April 26, 1863, *OR* 12 (2):555, 564–65, and 645–46. For the Battle of Second Bull Run, see Hennessy, *Return to Bull Run*.

59. AAR of Col. Stephen D. Lee, October 2, 1862; AAR of Longstreet, October 10, 1862, *OR* 12 (2):577–78, 565–66.

60. Thomas R. Hay diary, [1] and September 5, 1862, Tyler Dennett, ed., *Lincoln and the Civil War in the Diaries and Letters of John Hay* (New York: Dodd, Mead & Co., 1939), 45 and 47.

61. See Joseph L. Harsh, *Taken at the Flood: Robert E. Lee & Confederate Strategy in the Maryland Campaign of 1862* (Kent, OH: Kent State University Press, 1999); Stephen W. Sears, *Landscape Turned Red: The Battle of Antietam* (New Haven, CT: Ticknor & Fields, 1983); James M. McPherson, *Antietam: Crossroads of Freedom* (New York: Oxford University Press, 2002).

62. Even though McClellan had Lee's plans, he was convinced that Lee had 120,000 troops, and this scared him. In addition, intelligence reports contradicted some of the invasion plans, and McClellan, extremely cautious as an army commander, hesitated to act too aggressively, in case Lee had altered his plans. See Sears, *George B. McClellan*, 284–88, and D. Scott Hartwig, *To Antietam Creek: The Maryland Campaign of September 1862* (Baltimore: Johns Hopkins University Press, 2012), 284–95. McClellan's headquarters most likely knew of the order before noon, and perhaps earlier, and he probably learned of it around 1:30 p.m., after he completed a troop inspection. Between 2:00 and 3:00, he moved two divisions to aid a division and some cavalry at Middleton, which was probably a response to the discovery of the order. At 6:20 p.m. he issued his first plans for attack. Why did his staff not notify him immediately when it received the lost order? While there were some slight discrepancies, ample evidence indicated the veracity of the "lost order." Why did it take him so long to formulate plans? Why did he not move more aggressively? Why did he direct Maj. Gen. William B. Franklin, who was in command of the critical attack, to begin his march at daybreak on September 14? The advance to South Mountain meant that no strong attack could be mounted before nightfall on the thirteenth, but an assault the following dawn might have permitted the Army of the Potomac to move through the gaps on the fourteenth rather than on the fifteenth, perhaps enabling a powerful attack at Antietam on the sixteenth rather than on the seventeenth, before McLaws's and A. P. Hill's divisions arrived.

63. Lee to Davis, September 16, 1862, *OR* 19 (1):141–42; Timothy J. Reese, *High-Water Mark: The 1862 Maryland Campaign in Strategic Perspective* (Baltimore: Butternut and Blue, 2004), 16–21.

64. AAR of Lee, August 19, 1863, AAR of Jackson, April 23, 1863, *OR* 19 (1):147–48 and 954–55; Channing Price to Mother, September 18, 1862, R. Channing Price Papers, SHC, UNC; Jackson to McLaws, September 14, 1862; Chilton to McLaws, September 14, 1862; A. L. Long to McLaws, September 15, 1862, McLaws Papers, SHC, UNC; L. M. McLaws to Miss Lizzie, September 20, 1862, Ewell Papers, LC.

65. Sears, *George B. McClellan*, 298–300.

66. Rufus R. Dawes, *Service in the Sixth Wisconsin Volunteers* (Marietta, OH: E. R. Alderman & Sons, 1890), 90–91.

67. Charles Carleton Coffin, *Stories of Our Soldiers: War Reminiscences*, by "Carleton" and by Soldiers of New England (Boston: Journal Newspaper Company, 1893), 102.

68. Soldier to Messrs. Editors, November 2, 1862, Montgomery (AL) *Advertiser*, November 19, 1862, 1; Robert K. Krick, "It Appeared as Though Mutual Extermination Would Put a Stop to the Awful Carnage: Confederates in Sharpsburg's Bloody Lane," in Gary W. Gallagher, ed., *The Antietam Campaign* (Chapel Hill: University of North Carolina Press, 1999), 231–32.

69. McClellan to Wife, September 18, 1862, Sears, ed., *Papers of McClellan*, 469; McClellan to Halleck, September 19, 1862, *OR* 19 (2):330; McClellan to Wife, September 22, [1862], Sears, ed., *Papers of McClellan*, 477. Also see McClellan to Wife, September 20, [1862], Sears, ed., *Papers of McClellan*, 473 and 476.

CHAPTER 3: LEE'S WAR IN THE EAST

1. For U.S.-British relations, see Howard Jones, *Union in Peril: The Crisis over British Intervention in the Civil War* (Chapel Hill: University of North Carolina Press, 1992).

2. See Richard J. M. Blackett, *Divided Hearts: Britain and the American Civil War* (Baton Rouge: Louisiana State University Press, 2001).

3. See Howard J. Fuller, *Clad in Iron: The American Civil War and the Challenge of British Naval Power* (Annapolis, MD: Naval Institute Press, 2011).

4. General Orders, No. 163, Army of the Potomac, October 7, 1862, *The War of the Rebellion: Official Records of the Union and Confederate Armies* (Washington, D.C.: Government Printing Office, 1880–1901) [heareafter *OR*], series I, vol. 19, part (2):395–96.

5. James M. McPherson, *Antietam: Crossroads of Freedom* (New York: Oxford University Press, 2002), 153–54.

6. Lincoln to McClellan, October 13, 1862, *OR* 19 (1):13–14; Lincoln to McClellan, October 24 [25], 1862, *OR* 19 (2):485.

7. McClellan to Wife, [November 4, 1862]; McClellan to Wife, November 7 [1862], Sears, ed., *Civil War Papers of McClellan*, 518 and 520.

8. See William Marvel, "The Making of a Myth: Ambrose E. Burnside and the Union High Command at Fredericksburg," in *The Fredericksburg Campaign: Decision on the Rappahannock,* ed. Gary W. Gallagher (Chapel Hill: University of North Carolina Press, 1995), and Marvel, *Burnside* (Chapel Hill: University of North Carolina Press, 1991).

9. Burnside to Cullum, November 7, 1862, *OR* 19 (2):552–53. See Marvel, *Burnside*, 164–67; Donald Pfanz on the pontoon problem, http://fredericksburg.com/CivilWar/Battle/0217CW.htm#. See also *The Autobiography of Oliver Otis Howard,* vol. 1 (New York: Baker and Taylor, 1907), 316–17, which should be compared with Burnside's official report in *OR* 21:84–85, 102–104, and Gen. Sumner's testimony in the *Report of the Joint Committee on the Conduct of the War,* vol. 1 (Washington, D.C.: Government Printing Office, 1863), 657. For a superb and insightful study of Fredericksburg, see George C. Rable, *Fredericksburg! Fredericksburg!* (Chapel Hill: University of North Carolina Press, 2002). The best battle study is Francis Augustin O'Reilly, *The Fredericksburg Campaign: Winter War of the Rappahannock,* (Baton Rouge: Louisiana State University Press, 2003). Also see William Marvel, with Donald Pfanz, *The Battle of Fredericksburg* (Spotsylvania, VA: Eastern National, 1993), for a short study.

10. See O'Reilly, *Fredericksburg Campaign*, 152–53 and 164–97, on Meade's penetration.

11. Milton Barrett to Brother and Sister, January 28, 1863, J. Roderick Heller and Carolynn Ayres Heller, eds., *The Confederacy Is On Her Way Up the Spout* (Athens, GA: University of Georgia Press, 1992), 82–83.

12. J. M. C[oker] to Wife, December 18, 1862, Coker Papers, Fredericksburg and Spotsylvania National Battlefield Park (hereafter FSNBP) (originals in Hodgson Heidler Collection, University of Georgia); Summary of Casualties in First Corps. Report of Casualties of Second Corps. Report of Casualties in Union Army, *OR* 21:572, 635, and 142; J. B. Magruder to Papa, December 20, 1862, Magruder Family, Library of Virginia (hereafter LV).

13. Lee to Davis, September 21, 1862, *OR* 19 (1):143; Lee to Davis, September 22, 1862, J. R. Jones to Major Paxton, September 27, 1862, *OR* 19 (2):617–18 and 629–30.

14. W. L. Davis to S. W. Smythe, December 16, 1862, William L. Davis Papers, Mississippi Department of Archives and History (hereafter MDAH).

15. C. C. Blacknall to Jinny, December 18, 1862, Oscar W. Blacknall Papers, North Carolina Division of Archives and History (hereafter NCDAH).

16. Jno. W. Daniels to Grandmama, December 22, 1862, John Warwick Daniel Papers, University of Virginia (hereafter UVA).

17. H. R. Berkeley diary, December 18, 1862, H. R. Berkeley Papers, Museum of the Confederacy (hereafter MC).

18. John S. Foster to Sister Lissie, January 12, 1863, box 18, F194, Joseph F. Waring Papers, Georgia Historical Society.

19. [Thos. Elder] to wife, December 21, 1862, Thomas Elder Papers, Virginia Historical Society (hereafter VHS); James R. Boulware diary, December 28, 1862; Dr. James Richmond Boulware Papers, LV.

20. Lee to Longstreet and Jackson, September 22, 1862, *OR* 19 (2):618–19.

21. On that culture, see Joseph T. Glatthaar, *General Lee's Army*, 174–99.

22. As one private explained, "our men stripped the dead bodies to get clothing to Keep them warm," Edward S. Duffey diary, December 17, 1862, Edward S. Duffey Papers, VHS. Also see AAR of Capt. Greenlee Davidson, Letcher's Artillery, undated, section dated September 19, 1862, Greenlee Davidson Folder, Rockbridge Historical Society Papers, Washington and Lee University; James P. Williams to Aunt Mary, November 18, 1862, James Peter Williams Papers,

UVA; W. B. Bailey to Bro, November 20, 1862, Coco Collection, Harrisburg Civil War Round Table, U.S. Army Military History Institute (hereafter USAMHI); [John W. Daniel] to Sister, December 5, 1863. John Warwick Daniels Papers, UVA. In tabulating the weapons, I merely added up the numbers reported from each of the major campaigns by army commanders. Early in the war, a high percentage of Confederates carried smoothbore weapons. At First Manassas, for example, this was not a disadvantage. Most of the fighting took place within smoothbore range, and Federals had rifled weapons that were sighted for 300 yards, so that their fire frequently went high. In time, Federals added a second sight for shorter ranges.

23. McPherson, *Ordeal by Fire: The Civil War and Reconstruction* (New York: Knopf, 1982), 206; Maj. Francis Rawle to Lieut., December 10, 1862, Frank Rawle Papers, MC; SO, No. ___ HQ, Colquitt's Brigade, December 20, 1862, Colquitt's Brigade, Orders and Circulars of Subcommands, ANV, Record Group (hereafter RG) 109, National Archives (hereafter NA); G. M. Logan to Colonel, March 1, 1863, G. M. Logan Papers, University of South Carolina. It had become 2nd South Carolina Cavalry by then.

24. [Wm. H. Cocke] to [Parents], December 25, 1862, Cocke Family Papers, VHS; B. H. Freeman to Father and Mother and Sisters, November 24, 1862, *Confederate Letters of Benjamin H. Freeman*, ed. Susan T. Wright (Hicksville, NY: Exposition Press, 1974), 19; Circular. Medical Director & Inspector's Office, November 22, 1862, Orders & Circulars Rec'd & Issued, Medical Director's Office, RG 109, NA; J. Scurry to Sarah, February 13, 1863, John G. Scurry Papers, Gilder-Lehrman Collection, Morgan Library; Lewis Leon diary, February 7, 1863; Lewis Leon, *Diary of a Tar Heel Confederate Soldier* (Charlotte, NC: Stone Publishing Co., 1913), 16. By the first winter, locals had become pretty much tapped out. See Christopher to Kate, November 1, 1861, Christopher Winsmith Papers, MC.

25. L. B. Northup to Randolph, November 3, 1862, CSA, Commissary Department, New York Public Library; Lee to Seddon, January 12, 1863, L&TS, ANV. RG 109, NA; Theodore to Father, October 18, 1861, Theodore T. Fogle Papers, Emory University.

26. E. Fontaine to Davis, March 19, 1863, M437, R91, F727. LR, SW; Johnston to War Department, December 3, 1861, LR, SW. WD-8229-1861. RG 109, NA; Report of Forage Received at Milford Station by Railroad for the Army of the 2nd Corps, January 29–April 13, 1863, W. H. Kirker Papers, LV. On spying, see Meriwether Stuart, "Samuel Ruth and General R. E. Lee: Disloyalty and the Line of Supply, 1862–1863," *Virginia Magazine of History and Biography* 70, no. 3 (January 1963): 35–101 (hereafter *VMHB*).

27. W. H. Kirker to Col. _____, February 2, 1863; George G. Thompson to Kirker, March 17, 1863, W. H. Kirker Papers, LV; Lee to Lawton, March 10, 1864, L&TS, ANV. RG 109, NA; Willie to Father, March 28, 1863, Willie Dame Papers, FSNBP; Thos. C. Elder to wife, April 6, 1863, Thomas Elder Papers, VHS; Augustus L. Coble to Turley Coble, February 25, 1863, HCWRT, USAMHI; George H. Sharpe to General, March 21, 1863. Information from Examination of Scouts, Deserters, Etc., Army of the Potomac, RG 108, NA; W. R. Montgomery to Aunt Frank, n.d. April 1863, W. R. Montgomery Papers, V242, FSNBP; R. E. Lee to [Mary], March 6, 1863, Lee Family Papers, VHS; Lee to Longstreet, February 18 and March 27, 1863; Longstreet to Lee, March 18 and 24, 1863, *OR* 18:883–84, 924–25, 933, and 943.

28. GO, No. 119. HQ, ANV, October 16, 1862; GSOCI, ANV. M921, R1, F259. RG 109, NA; Lee to Custis, January 5, 1863, R. E. Lee Papers, DU; Lee to Seddon, December 7, 1862, box 1, Telegraph Book, Ser. a, Lee's Headquarters Papers, VHS; Lee to Davis, February 24, 1863, *Lee's Dispatches*, 72; Lee to Col. Lawrence Baker, March 1, 1863; Lee to Longstreet, March 10, 1863; Lee to Myers, March 21, 1863; Lee to Seddon, March 25, 1863; Lee to Jackson, March 27, 1863; Lee to Anderson, March 28, 1863, L&TS, ANV. RG 109, NA; GO, No. 24. HQ, ANV. 21 March 1863. Wright's Brigade Order Book, Civil War Times Illustrated Collection, USAMHI; SO, No. ___. HQ, Arty. Corps. January 29 and February 4, 1863. Pendleton Order Book, MC; Lee to Longstreet, February 18 and March 27, 1863; Longstreet to Lee, March 18 and 24, 1863, *OR* 18:883–84, http://ebooks.library.cornell.edu/cgi/t/text/pageviewer-idx?c=moawar;cc= moawar;q1=883;rgn=full%20text;idno=waro0026;didno=waro0026;view=image;seq=

0899, 924–25, http://ebooks.library.cornell.edu/cgi/t/text/pageviewer-idx?c=moawar&cc=
moawar&idno=waro0026&q1=883&view=image&seq=940&size=100, 933, http://ebooks
.library.cornell.edu/cgi/t/text/pageviewer-idx?c=moawar&cc=moawar&idno=waro0026&q1=
883&view=image&seq=949&size=100, and 943, http://ebooks.library.cornell.edu/cgi/t/text
/pageviewer-idx?c=moawar&cc=moawar&idno=waro0026&q1=883&view=image&seq=
959&size=100.

29. In early March, he confessed to his wife, "I am in indifferent health myself & feel almost worn out, so that I fear I may be unable in the approaching campaign to go through the work before me." Lee to [Mary], March 6, 1863, Lee Family Papers, VHS; H. E. Y[oung] to Uncle, April 18, 1863, Robert Newman Gourdin Papers, Emory University; C. S. Venable to wife, April 13, 1863, McDowell-Miller-Warner Papers, UVA; D. D. P[endleton] to Mama, October 16, 1863, Dudley D. Pendleton Papers, Duke University. Not everyone agrees that it was a heart attack, but I suspect it was. In fact, when Lee submitted his resignation after Gettysburg, he claimed that his impaired health prevented him from reconnoitering and carrying on the duties of an army commander.

30. Pendleton to Lee, February 11, 1863, GO, No. 26. HQ, ANV; February 15, 1863, *OR* 25 (2): 614–19 and 625–26.

31. Lincoln to Hooker, January 26, 1863, *OR* 25 (2):4. The word *hooker* was already in the vocabulary, but he made it much more famous.

32. Stephen W. Sears, *Chancellorsville* (Boston: Houghton Mifflin, 1996), 1–11, 19–25, 62–68.

33. GO, no. 3, Hdqrs., Army of the Potomac, January 30, 1863; GO, no. 6, Hdqrs., Army of the Potomac, February 5, 1863; GO, no. 9. Hdqrs., Army of the Potomac, February 7, 1863; Circular. Hdqrs., Army of the Potomac, March 21, 1863; SO, No. 129. Hdqrs., Army of the Potomac, May 12, 1863, *OR* 25 (2):11, 51, 57, 152, and 471–72; AAR of Brig. Gen. Henry J. Hunt, August 1, 1863, *OR* 25 (1):252–53; Sears, *Chancellorsville*, 68.

34. It is unclear how large Hooker suspected that Lee's army was. Stephen Sears argues that Hooker had an accurate sense of Lee's strength, but in the congratulatory order to the Army of the Potomac, which was written by Meade's chief of staff and Hooker's former chief of staff, Daniel Butterfield, it praises the army for driving back "an enemy, superior in numbers . . . ," *OR* 27 (3):519; Sears, *Chancellorsville*, 102. Meade believed his force was roughly equal to Lee's, which demonstrates that the Union still overestimated the size of Lee's forces at Gettysburg. In Meade to Reynolds, July 1, 1863, Meade wrote that their numbers ought to equal it and, with the addition of 10,000 reinforcements, which never reached his army, exceed them, *OR* 27 (3):460. Also see H. Haupt to Halleck, July 1, 1863, *OR* 27 (3):476–77.

35. Hotchkiss diary, February 23, 1863, Jedidiah Hotchkiss, *Make Me a Map: The Civil War Journal of Stonewall Jackson's Topographer*, ed. Archie K. McDonald (Dallas: Southern Methodist University Press, 1973), 116; Lee to Seddon, March 25, 1863, L&TS, ANV. RG 109, NA; Lee to Seddon, April 9, 1863; Lee to Davis, April 16, 1863, *OR* 25 (2):713–14 and 724–25; Lee to Dr. A. T. Bledsoe, October 28, 1867; Fitzhugh Lee, *Chancellorsville* (Richmond, VA: G. W. Gary, 1879), 28; T. M. R. Talcott to Long, July 19, 1886, Talcott Family Papers, VHS; AAR of Lee, September 21, 1863, *OR* 25 (1):798; William Allan, Memorandum of Conversations with Lee, in *Lee the Soldier*, ed. Gary W. Gallagher (Lincoln: University of Nebraska Press, 1996), 9.

36. R. E. Willbourn to Sir, December 12, 1863, Dabney-Jackson Papers, LV; [Lane] to Augustus C. Hamlin, n.d., James Lane Papers, Auburn University; [O. C. Hamilton] to Father, May 17, 1863, Colier Green and Oliver Clark Hamilton Papers, NCDAH; Statement of Maj. Sandie Pendleton, July 18, 1863, John Esten Cooke Papers, UVA; H. H. McGuire, "Some Notes in Regard to the Last Days of Jackson," Thomas J. Jackson Papers, New-York Historical Society; Krick, "The Smoothbore Volley That Doomed the Confederacy," in *The Smoothbore Volley That Doomed the Confederacy* (Baton Rouge: Louisiana State University Press, 2002), 1–41, especially 16–18; Robertson, *Stonewall Jackson: The Man, The Soldier, The Legend* (New York: Macmillan, 1997), 725–39; J to [Aunt], April 21, 1863, *Diary of James Keith Boswell*, MC. By sending his cavalry toward Richmond, Hooker was left with only small numbers of scouts, who were overwhelmed

by Stuart's cavalry and could neither detect, nor alert troops of, enemy movements. See Sears, *Chancellorsville*, on Howard's defenses.

37. Shells had fuses that ignited on firing and exploded overhead. They had a range of about 1,300 yards when fired from a twelve-pound Napoleon. Case shot were marble-sized balls packed in a thin iron container. A fuse ignited an explosive charge that scattered the balls up to 800 yards. See Joseph T. Glatthaar, "Battlefield Tactics," in *Writing the Civil War: The Quest to Understand*, eds. James M. McPherson and William J. Cooper Jr. (Columbia: University of South Carolina Press, 2000), 65.

38. AAR of Stuart, May 6, 1863; AAR of Brig. Gen. John W. Geary, May 10, 1863; AAR of Brig. Gen. Alpheus S. Williams, May 15, 1863; AAR of Brig. Gen. E. Porter Alexander, March 7, 1864, *OR* 25 (1):887–88, 730–31, 680–81, and 823–24; S.D.R. to Brother, April 10, [1863], Stephen Dodson Ramseur Papers, Southern Historical Collection, University of North Carolina (hereafter SHC, UNC).

39. Rice C. Bull, *Soldiering: The Civil War Diary of Rice C. Bull*, ed. K. Jack Bauer. (San Rafael, CA: Presidio Press, 1977).

40. Micajah D. Martin to Father and Mother, May 8, 1863, Martin, ed., "Chancellorsville," *VMHB* 37, 3, 226; Charles Marshall, *Lee's Aide-De-Camp* (Lincoln: University of Nebraska Press, 2000), 173.

41. Wilcox authored a book (http://books.google.com/books?id=JNtEAAAAIAAJ) on rifled weapons. At Antietam, his men suffered disastrously when Federals penetrated the Bloody Lane, so at Fredericksburg his men dug zigzag trenches. AAR of Early, May 7, 1863, *OR* 25 (1):1001–2; W. J. Seymour journal, May 4, 1863, Schoff Collection, University of Michigan. McLaws gave muddled explanations in his AAR and his later writings. See AAR of McLaws, May 10, 1863, *OR* 25 (1):827–29; Gary W. Gallagher, "Jubal Early at Second Fredericksburg," in *Chancellorsville: The Battle and Its Aftermath*, ed. Gallagher (Chapel Hill: University of North Carolina Press, 1996), 52–53.

42. J. Thomas Petty diary, May 5, 1863, J. Thomas Petty Papers, MC.

43. See chapter 4 for a full discussion of the Vicksburg campaign.

44. Lee to Seddon, May 10, 1863, *OR* 25 (2):790.

45. Lee to Davis, May 11, 1863, *Wartime Papers of Robert E. Lee*, eds. Clifford Dowdey and Louis Manarin (Boston: Little, Brown, 1961), 482–84; Lee to Davis, June 7, 1863; Lee to Cooper, July 31, 1863, *OR* 27 (2):305.

46. C. R. Phelps to Aunt, June 11, 1863, Charles R. Phelps Papers, UVA; W. O. H[arvie] to Ma, June 14, 1863, Harvie Family Papers, VHS; Quotation in Mac to Bill, June 22, 1863, box 18, F197, Joseph F. Waring Papers, GHS; H. B. McClellan, *I Rode with Jeb Stuart* (Bloomington: Indiana University Press, 1958), 294; Thomas [Rosser] to [Sister], June 11, 1863, Gordon and Rosser Families, UVA.

47. See GO, no. 72, HQ, ANV, June 21, 1863, *OR* 27 (3):912–13; B[uck] to [Parents], May 18, 1863, Cocke Family Papers, VHS.

48. Lee still had two cavalry brigades to guard the wagons and to scout. In a conversation I had with General (Retired) Donn A. Starry, he indicated that he had examined the use of cavalry on the campaign carefully and believed Lee had not utilized them as effectively as he should have. Lee gently chided Stuart in his report, AAR of Lee, n.d. January 1864, *OR* 27 (2):321.

49. Charles E. Belknap diary, June 29, 1863, copy in Brake Collection, USAMHI. Also see Charles C. Perkins diary, June 30, 1863, Civil War Times Illustrated Collection, USAMHI. See also Circular, HQ, Army of the Potomac, June 30, 1863; Meade to [Reynolds], June 30, 1863, *OR* I, 27, (3):417, 420.

50. AAR of Maj. Gen. Henry Heth, September 13, 1863, *OR* 27 (2):637–38; AAR of Col. William W. Robinson, November 18, 1863, *OR* 27 (1):278–80; Joseph T. Glatthaar, "The Common Soldier's Gettysburg Campaign," in *The Gettysburg Nobody Knows*, ed. Gabor S. Boritt (New York: Oxford University Press, 1997), 15.

51. AAR of Brig. Gen. Joseph R. Davis, August 26, 1863; AAR of Rodes, n.d, 1863, *OR* 27

(2):649–50, 552–55, and 562; Alan T. Nolan, *The Iron Brigade: A Military History* (Bloomington: Indiana University Press, 1994), 239; Rufus R. Dawes, *Service with the Sixth Wisconsin Volunteers* (Marietta, OH: E. R. Alderman & Sons, 1890), 169; Louis G. Young to Maj. Barker, February 10, 1864, Francis D. Winston Papers, NCDAH; Jas. H. Wilkes to [Mary], July 16, 1863, Ward Family Papers, LC; Thomas J. Webb to Brother, July 18, 1863, Brake Collection, USAMHI; John W. Daniel on Gettysburg, November 20, 1863, John Warwick Daniel Papers, VHS.

52. See AAR of Ewell, n.d., 1863, *OR* 27 (2):445–46; Edwin B. Coddington, *The Gettysburg Campaign: A Study in Command* (New York: Charles Scribner's Sons, 1968), 271; W. J. H. to Parents, July 7, 1863, Hatchett Family Folder, CWTIC, USAMHI; Jas. H. Wilkes to [Mary], July 16, 1863, Ward Family Papers, LC.

53. AAR of Meade, October 1, 1863, *OR* 27 (1):115–16; AAR of Lee, January 1864, *OR* 27 (2): 317–18.

54. AAR of Lee, January 1864, *OR* 27 (2):318–19.

55. Meade's chief engineer was Gouverner K. Warren. At Chancellorsville, Hooker ordered Sickles to evacuate from the critical piece of terrain called Hazel Grove. Confederates occupied it and were able to hurl converging artillery fire on Sickles's men with heavy losses as a result. He determined not to make that same mistake.

56. As they waited to charge, Col. William C. Oates of the 15th Alabama ordered twenty-two men to collect canteens and return for fresh water. As they searched for their regiment, the party stumbled into Union hands. William C. Oates, *The War Between the Union and the Confederacy and Its Lost Opportunities*, ed. Robert K. Krick (Dayton, OH: Press of Morningside Bookshop, 1985), 212; Maj. Homer R. Stoughton to Capt. John M. Cooney, July 27, 1863, *OR* 27 (1):519; AAR of Col. William C. Oates, August 8, 1863, *OR* 27 (2):392–93; J. H. H[endrick] to Mother, July 8, 1863, Robert James Lowry diary, July 2, 1863, Brake Collection, USAMHI; W. B. Sturtevant to Jimmy, July 27, 1863, W. B. Sturtevant Papers, MC. When Civil War soldiers lacked water, they often urinated in the barrel to clean it. In this instance, due to dehydration, soldiers could not urinate.

57. Circular, HQ, Army of the Potomac, June 30, 1863, *OR* 27 (3):415; Glatthaar, "The Common Soldier's Gettysburg Campaign," 20.

58. Confederates lost 6,500 men that day. McLaws to Wife, July 7, 1863, McLaws Papers, SHC, UNC; S. R. Johnston to Fitz Lee, February 11, 1878, Samuel R. Johnston Papers, VHS; Edward Porter Alexander, *Fighting for the Confederacy*, ed. Gary W. Gallagher (Chapel Hill: University of North Carolina Press, 1989), 236–40; Osmun Latrobe diary, July 2, 1863, Osmun Latrobe Papers, Maryland Historical Society; AAR of Wilcox, July 17, 1863, AAR of Brig. Gen. A. R. Wright, September 28, 1863, *OR* 27 (2):618–19 and 622–23.

59. AAR of Capt. J. J. Young, July 4, 1863, *OR* 27 (2):645. Faulty ammunition prevented Confederates from firing indirectly on Federals while the attack occurred. After the war, individuals began blaming Longstreet for the attack's failure and insisting that he was adamantly opposed to it. There is no contemporary evidence to justify that claim. Hostility toward Longstreet and his performance at Gettysburg emerged largely after Lee's death. McLaws criticized Longstreet in a letter to his wife largely because Longstreet pushed McLaws to attack on the second day and because of what he claimed was interference by Longstreet. See McLaws to Wife, July 7, 1863, Lafayette McLaws, *A Soldier's General: The Civil War Letters of Major General Lafayette McLaws,* ed. John C. Oeffinger (Chapel Hill: University of North Carolina Press, 2002), 197. Although Longstreet affiliated with Republicans during Lee's lifetime, any criticism of him was muffled, because Lee would not have tolerated it. Longstreet's criticism of Lee and his cooperation with Republicans and his old friend President Grant fueled the open criticism after Lee's death on October 12, 1870. During the artillery exchange, Brig. Gen. James L. Kemper of Pickett's Division ordered his men to hug the ground. The Federal shells were accurate, bearing down on his troops and cutting them to shreds even though they lay on the opposite side of the crest. Looking up, Kemper saw Longstreet in front of the Confederate line, astride his great horse, completely impervious to the danger. "His bearing was to me the grandest moral spectacle of the war" (Sears, *Gettysburg,* 404). Longstreet felt the biggest problem the Confederates

had at Gettysburg was that they operated under the assumption that the Union army was not up when it was, and Lee's army was not all on the scene until the last day. See Longstreet to Wigfall, August 2, 1863, Louis Wigfall Papers, LC. Years later, people accused Longstreet of sulking over the infantry assault, but when Kemper saw and spoke to him, Longstreet was a tower of strength, concerned not for his own safety but for Kemper's men. See Kemper to E. P. Alexander, September 20, 1869, Frederick Dearborn Collection, Harvard University. Also see William Garrett Piston, *Lee's Tarnished Lieutenant: James Longstreet and His Place in Southern History* (Athens: University of Georgia, 1990).

60. Special Orders, No. 2. A&IGO, March 14, 1863, Report of Board to Examine the Explosion, March 18, 1863. J. W. Mallet File, Record and Pension Office, RG 94, NA; Josiah Gorgas diary, March 13, 1863, Josiah Gorgas, *The Civil War Diary of Josiah Gorgas*, ed. Frank E. Vandiver (Tuscaloosa: University of Alabama Press, 1947), 25–26; Records of Mary Ryan, U.S. Census, 1860, City of Richmond, VA, 225; Records of Elizabeth Dorson, U.S. Census, 1860, City of Richmond, VA, 28; March–April 1863, Ordnance Department, Time Book, Women Employees, Richmond Arsenal, RG 109, NA; W. P. Heflin, *Blind Man "On the Warpath"* (NP: Published in 1903), 24; Horatio Dana Chapman diary, July 3, 1863; John W. Plummer to brother, undated, in Minneapolis *State Atlas*, August 26, 1863, Brake Collection, USAMHI; John N. Old to Catherine, July 16, 1863, Old Papers, FSNBP; Longstreet to Alexander, July 3, 1863, 11:45 a.m. and 12:15 p.m., Alexander to Longstreet, July 3, 1863, around noon, Edward Porter Alexander Papers, LC. Also see Allan Nevins, ed., *A Diary of Battle: The Personal Journals of Colonel Charles S. Wainwright, 1861–1865* (New York: Harcourt, Brace, 1962), 249.

61. Glatthaar, "Common Soldier's Gettysburg Campaign," 21–22.

62 *Collected Works of Abraham Lincoln*, vol. 6, pp. 327–28.

63. James L. Kemper to Edward Porter Alexander, September 20, 1869, Frederick Dearborn Collection, Houghton Library, Harvard University.

64. Felix Brannigan to Father, n.d. [July 1863], Brake Collection, U.S. Army Military History Institute.

65. Eseck G. Wilbur to [Parents], July 15, 1863, Eseck G. Wilbur Papers, Rice University.

66. Jeffry D. Wert, *The Sword of Lincoln: The Army of the Potomac* (New York: Simon & Schuster, 2006), 308.

67. Lee to Davis, August 8, 1863, Dowdey and Manarin, eds., *Wartime Papers*, 589–90; Lynda Lasswell Crist et al., *Papers of Jefferson Davis*, 9 (*Papers of Jefferson Davis*, vols. 7–11, Baton Rouge: Louisiana State University Press, 1992), 337–38.

68. Longstreet to Wigfall, August 18 and September 12, 1863, Louis T. Wigfall Papers, LC; Longstreet to Lee, September 5, 1863; Lee to Davis, September 6, 1863; Davis to Lee, September 8, [1863]; Lee to Davis, September 9, 1863, *OR* 29 (2):699–702; Maj. Frederick A. Eiserman, "Longstreet's Corps at Chickamauga: Lessons in Inter-Theater Deployment," MMAS thesis, U.S. Army Command and General Staff College, 1985, 35–65; AAR of Longstreet, n.d., October 1863; AAR of Kershaw, October 15, 1863, *OR* 30 (2):287–91; Walter to [Bettie], October 17, 1863, Walter Taylor Papers, Norfolk Public Library; AAR of Hill, October 26, 1863, Return of Casualties of Third Corps, in the Engagement at Bristoe Station, VA, October 14, AAR of Heth, October 24, 1863, List of Casualties of Heth's Division, October 14, 1863, *OR* 29 (1):426–28, http://ebooks.library.cornell.edu/cgi/t/text/pageviewer-idx?c=moawar;cc=moawar; q1=426;rgn=full%20text;idno=waro0048;didno=waro0048;view=image;seq=0444, and 430–33, http://ebooks.library.cornell.edu/cgi/t/text/pageviewer-idx?c=moawar&cc=moawar&idno=waro0048&q1=426&view=image&seq=448&size=100; A.S. Pendleton to ?, [October 16, 1863], William N. Pendleton Papers, SHC, UNC; W. J. Seymour journal, October 15, 1863, Schoff Collection, Clements Library, University of Michigan.

69. Glatthaar, *General Lee's Army*, 302; Adam H. Domby, "'Loyal to the Core from the First to the Last': Remembering the Inner Civil War of Forsyth County, North Carolina, 1862–1876," MA thesis, University of North Carolina at Chapel Hill, 2011; Philip Paludan, *Victims: A True Story of the Civil War* (Knoxville: University of Tennessee Press, 1981).

70. See Glatthaar, *Forged in Battle: The Civil War Alliance of Black Soldiers and Their White Officers* (New York: Free Press, 1990), and Glatthaar, "Black Glory: The African American Role in Confederate Defeat," in *Why the Confederacy Lost the Civil War*, ed. Gabor Boritt (New York: Oxford University Press, 1992), 133–62.

71. Glatthaar, *General Lee's Army*, 402–3. Also see Albert Burton Moore, *Conscription and Conflict in the Confederacy* (New York: Macmillan, 1924).

72. "Bliss copy" refers to a copy of the Gettysburg Address that was kept by Alexander Bliss.

73. Emory Thomas, *Confederate State of Richmond: A Biography of the Capital* (Austin: University of Texas Press, 1971), 119–22; S to Editor, March 19, 1863, Raleigh *Standard*, March 20, 1863; Daniel Brown to Wife, April 5, 1863, Isaac Brown Papers, NCDAH; North Carolina *Standard*, March 20, 1863; Mary J. Wills to my affectionate husband, June 1, 1863, Wills Family Papers, William and Mary College; Paul Escott, *Many Excellent People: Power and Privilege in North Carolina, 1850–1900* (Chapel Hill: University of North Carolina Press, 1985), 64–67; Hillary Hollowood, "A Blessing and a Curse: The North Carolina Railroad and the American Civil War in Rowan County, North Carolina, 1850–1870," honor's thesis at the University of North Carolina at Chapel Hill, 2013. For inflation in the Confederacy, see http://inflationdata.com/Inflation/Inflation_Rate/ConfederateInflation.asp.

74. The term *Copperheads* reflects the poisonous snakes that Ohio Republicans likened to antiwar Democrats. See McPherson, *Battle Cry of Freedom: The Civil War Era* (New York: Oxford University Press, 1988), 493–94. Also see Jennifer L. Weber, *Copperheads: The Rise and Fall of Lincoln's Opponents in the North* (New York: Oxford University Press, 2006).

75. See Iver Bernstein, *New York City Draft Riot: Their Significance for American Society and Politics in the Age of the Civil War* (New York: Oxford University Press, 1990); Eugene Converse Murdock, *One Million Men: The Civil War Draft in the North* (Madison: State Historical Society of Wisconsin, 1971); Grace Palladino, *Another Civil War: Labor, Capital, and the State in the Anthracite Regions of Pennsylvania, 1840–1868* (Urbana: University of Illinois Press, 1990). In 1864 Congress determined that payment exempted the draftee for only a year.

76. McPherson, *Battle Cry of Freedom*, 442–48.

CHAPTER 4: GRANT'S WAR IN THE WEST

1. Brooks D. Simpson, *Ulysses S. Grant: Triumph over Adversity, 1822–1865* (Boston: Houghton Mifflin, 2000), 141.

2. John F. Marszalek, *Commander of All Lincoln's Armies: A Life of General Henry W. Halleck* (Cambridge, MA: Belknap Press of Harvard University Press, 2004); John F. Marszalek, "'A Full Share of All the Credit': Sherman and Grant to the Fall of Vicksburg," in *Grant's Lieutenants: From Cairo to Vicksburg*, ed. Steven E. Woodworth (Lawrence: University Press of Kansas, 2001), 14–15; Steven E. Woodworth, *Nothing but Victory: The Army of the Tennessee, 1861–1865* (New York: Alfred A. Knopf, 2006), 207.

3. Timothy B. Smith, *Corinth 1862: Siege, Battle Occupation* (Lawrence: University Press of Kansas, 2012), 17–102; Stephen D. Engel, *Struggle for the Heartland: The Campaigns from Fort Henry to Corinth* (Lincoln: University of Nebraska Press, 2001), 166–86; Marszalek, *Commander of All Lincoln's Armies*, 123–25; Thomas Lawrence Connelly, *Army of the Heartland: The Army of Tennessee, 1861–1862* (Baton Rouge: Louisiana State University Press, 1967), 176–77; Woodworth, *Nothing but Victory*, 206–8.

4. Jefferson Davis to Varina Davis, June 21, 1862, Jefferson Davis Collection, Eleanor S. Brockenbrough Library, Museum of the Confederacy, Richmond, Virginia.

5. Connelly, *Army of the Heartland*, 177–83; Steven E. Woodworth, *Jefferson Davis and His Generals: The Failure of Confederate Command in the West* (Lawrence: University Press of Kansas, 1990), 104–7.

6. Marszalek, *Commander of All Lincoln's Armies*, 125–26; Woodworth, *Nothing but Victory*, 209.

7. David H. Donald, *Lincoln* (London: Random House, 1995), 410; Marszalek, *Commander of All Lincoln's Armies*, 197–98.

8. Connelly, *Army of the Heartland*, 187–220; Earl J. Hess, *Banners to the Breeze: The Kentucky Campaign, Corinth and Stones River* (Lincoln: University of Nebraska Press, 2000), 22.

9. Connelly, *Army of the Heartland*, 205–8; Hess, *Banners to the Breeze*, 1–29; Woodworth, *Jefferson Davis and His Generals*, 136–37.

10. Kirby Smith was inspired by the exploits of the highly mercurial Col. John H. Morgan, a Kentuckian who, during the summer of 1862, led 900 cavalry on a daring raid far behind Union lines in Kentucky. During the course of the raid, Morgan's men captured and paroled 1,200 Union soldiers and took or destroyed a great deal of property. Yet of even greater interest to Kirby Smith and many other Confederates was the public adulation the flamboyant Morgan enjoyed as his command rode through Kentucky. This seemed to suggest that the population of the Bluegrass State was finally fed up with the Lincoln regime and ready to cast its lot with the Confederacy if given a chance. Bragg brought 20,000 extra rifles to Kentucky to arm the hoped-for flood of recruits, but nearly all of those rifles were still in their crates when Bragg withdrew.

11. Connelly, *Army of the Heartland*, 210–20; Hess, *Banners to the Breeze*, 30–55; Woodworth, *Jefferson Davis and His Generals*, 137–39.

12. Bragg had reached Munfordville, Kentucky, squarely blocking the direct line of supply or retreat for Buell, forty miles to the southwest at Bowling Green. However, part of the reason Bragg had been able to travel faster than Buell was that Bragg's army had few supply wagons, while Buell's had a great many. Bragg's army had lived off the land while on the march, but when it halted to block Buell's retreat to Louisville, supplies began to run short. Buell, on the other hand, had plenty. Bragg lacked enough troops to assault the Army of the Ohio and enough supplies to continue waiting in its path. Kirby Smith was serenely occupying the abundant bluegrass region around Lexington, ninety miles to the northwest, but sent Bragg neither troops nor supplies. Bragg finally gave up the position at Munfordville and marched to join Kirby Smith near Lexington. The actual combination of his and Kirby Smith's previously separate armies finally gave Bragg command of all the Confederate forces in Kentucky, but it was too late to salvage the campaign. For more details, see Woodworth, *Jefferson Davis and His Generals*, 125–61.

13. When a heavily reinforced Buell advanced from Louisville to confront Bragg, the Confederate general's planned counterstroke was halted when subordinate general Leonidas Polk chose not to obey Bragg's order to march his corps so as to make a flank attack against the Union column advancing directly on Frankfort. Forced to abandon Lexington and the state capital at Frankfort, Bragg began withdrawing to the southeast, still looking for an opportunity to defeat Buell and salvage the campaign. He thought he might have found it when elements of the opposing armies blundered into each other while seeking water—a scarce commodity after a summerlong drought—in the valley of Doctor's Creek near Perryville. For more detail, see Kenneth W. Noe, *Perryville: This Grand Havoc of Battle* (Lexington: University Press of Kentucky, 2001), 107–326.

14. For additional reading on the campaign in Kentucky, see Noe's excellent *Perryville*, as well as Connelly, *Army of the Heartland*, 221–80; Hess, *Banners to the Breeze*, 1–120; Woodworth, *Jefferson Davis and His Generals*, 237–61.

15. The ironclad river gunboats of the upstream force had captured Memphis in June, and the seagoing tall ships of the downstream force had taken New Orleans in April. The two naval squadrons had only a single brigade of ground troops with them, however, making Van Dorn's job relatively easy. By late summer, the drought had lowered the river level to the point that the seagoing ships had to head back downstream. For more details, see Michael B. Ballard, *Vicksburg: The Campaign That Opened the Mississippi* (Chapel Hill: University of North Carolina Press, 2004), 31–62.

16. Van Dorn hoped to take Memphis or some other target of opportunity in West Tennessee. For

that purpose, he sent dispatches to get Price's cooperation. Van Dorn outranked Price, but as with Bragg and Kirby Smith simultaneously in Kentucky, Van Dorn could not give orders to Price unless the two had combined their forces. This Price declined to do. Bragg had left him with orders to prevent Grant from reinforcing Buell and/or to proceed into Middle Tennessee, where Bragg had once hoped for a showdown battle with Buell. That, Price insisted, precluded his joining Van Dorn for an incursion into West Tennessee, and he urged Van Dorn to bring his force to join him in a move via northeastern Mississippi in the direction of Middle Tennessee. Van Dorn likewise declined, and thus, for the time being, the two Confederate forces continued to operate independently, with Van Dorn moving north and Price northeast. *OR* vol. 16, pt. 2, pp. 782–83; vol. 17, pt. 2, pp. 662, 667, 675–77, 682, 685, 690–93, 695–98; vol. 53, p. 823; Albert E. Castel, *General Sterling Price and the Civil War in the West* (Baton Rouge: Louisiana State University Press, 1968), 106, http://books.google.com/books?id=rSl0MIy1XuoC&printsec= frontcover&&source=gbs_ge_summary_r&pg=PA106; Woodworth, *Jefferson Davis and His Generals*, 148–53.

17. On Halleck's orders, Grant had detached three divisions to reinforce Buell. Halleck had also directed that Grant keep Price from getting around him into Middle Tennessee or Kentucky. To carry out that mission, Grant concentrated his remaining forces into key garrisons while reserving as much force as he could to reinforce threatened points. When on September 14 Price occupied the northeastern Mississippi town of Iuka, Grant saw an opportunity to trap and crush the Confederate force. Thanks to his judicious arrangement of his forces, Grant was able to cover all the key points in his department while still freeing up 17,000 men to march against Price. At this point, Grant's senior subordinate, Brig. Gen. William S. Rosecrans, spoke up and urged that he, Rosecrans, be permitted to take 9,000 of the available troops and by a roundabout march approach Iuka from the southwest by multiple roads so as to take Price in rear while Grant with the remaining 8,000 men advanced toward the town from the northwest. When Rosecrans was in place, the sound of his guns engaging Price would be the signal for Grant's column, under the direct command of Brig. Gen. E. O. C. Ord, to join the action. Rosecrans was relatively new to Grant's command, having previously won modest recognition for service in western Virginia. In recent weeks, he had commanded the portion of Grant's front that included Iuka and claimed to know the country well and possess superior maps that would make possible the ambitious maneuver against Price's force. Thus Grant agreed and authorized the movement. As might have been predicted of a scheme that complicated, the plan miscarried. Muddy roads slowed Rosecrans's march, throwing the operation far off schedule. Rosecrans then opted to alter the plan so as to keep all his troops on a single road, leaving an escape route open for Price. A subsequent wrong turn by one of his divisions brought further delay. Price discovered Rosecrans's approach and advanced to strike the head of the Union column, precipitating a small but intense battle that raged for several hours on the evening of September 19, a few miles south of Iuka. Atmospheric conditions prevented anyone in Ord's column from hearing the firing, so half Grant's force remained idle. Learning during the night of the intended pincer movement, Price withdrew. Disgusted, Grant returned his troops to their various garrisons. See Ballard, *U.S. Grant*, 67–76; U.S. War Department, *The War of the Rebellion: Official Records of the Union and Confederate Armies*, 128 vols. (Washington, D.C.: Government Printing Office, 1881–1901; hereinafter cited as *OR*; except as otherwise noted all references are to series 1), vol. 17, pt. 1, 65, 117–18, 66–67; Ulysses S. Grant, *Personal Memoirs of Ulysses S. Grant*, 2 vols. (New York: Charles L. Webster & Co., 1885), 1:407–08; John Q. A. Campbell, *The Union Must Stand: The Civil War Diary of John Quincy Adams Campbell, Fifth Iowa Volunteer Infantry*, eds. Mark Grimsley and Todd D. Miller (Knoxville: University of Tennessee Press, 2000), 57; William W. McCarty Reminiscences, William W. McCarty Papers, Civil War Miscellaneous Collection, United States Army Military History Institute, Carlisle, PA; John B. Sanborn, "Battles and Campaigns of September, 1862," in *Papers of the Military Order of the Loyal Legion of the United States*, 56 vols. (various publishers and dates; reprint, Wilmington, NC: Broadfoot Publishing Co., 1994; hereinafter cited as MOLLUS) 30:214; Hess, *Banners to*

the Breeze, 132–33 (Baton Rouge: Louisiana State University Press, 1968), 101–3; Hattaway and Jones, *How the North Won*, 251–52; Woodworth, *Nothing but Victory*, 219–24.

18. From his vantage point in Richmond, Jefferson Davis observed Price's and Van Dorn's actions in Mississippi with dismay. The fact that Bragg had left the two generals in Mississippi with neither in overall command seemed unbelievable to Davis, although it was exactly the situation he had set up in Kentucky when he declined to give Bragg command of Kirby Smith's small army. Of course, Davis had not anticipated that Bragg and Kirby Smith would both end up in Kentucky at the same time any more than Bragg had anticipated that Van Dorn and Price would be in a position to carry out a joint offensive in Mississippi. Frustrated at having to deal with the situation with scanty information from the distance of Richmond, Davis finally issued an order for Van Dorn to take command of all Confederate troops in Mississippi, including Price's, whether the armies had combined or not. In fact, realizing the severe risks they were running by operating separately, Price and Van Dorn had already combined their forces. With the combined army, Van Dorn planned to feign a lunge into West Tennessee before turning sharply back to the southeast to strike at the Union garrison in the most strategic of the northwest Mississippi towns, Corinth itself. Van Dorn hoped thus to surprise the Federals by attacking Corinth from the rear. *OR* vol. 17, pt. 1, 154–55; pt. 2, pp. 698–701, 703–4, 707, 709–10, 715; Van Dorn to Davis, September 9, 1862, Samuel Richey Collection of the Southern Confederacy, Miami University Libraries; John Y. Simon, ed., *Papers of Ulysses S. Grant*, 26 vols. to date (Carbondale: Southern Illinois University Press, 1969–), 6:104–6; Woodworth, *Jefferson Davis and His Generals*, 154.

19. Grant recognized that Van Dorn was aiming at Corinth. Since the Confederate general, who had never numbered logistics among his greatest skills, managed the approach march badly, Grant had time to prepare, reinforcing Rosecrans at Corinth and starting additional troops on the march toward the rail-junction town in hopes of trapping a defeated Van Dorn when he tried to retreat. When Van Dorn at last launched his attack on Corinth, his troops initially made progress amid heavy fighting. Rosecrans had deployed his forces in the extensive breastworks the Confederates had built for a much larger army the preceding spring, and Van Dorn's Rebels were able to drive the overextended bluecoats back into a more substantial and compact inner line of works that the Federals had constructed since taking over the town. As the second day's fighting opened, Confederates in one sector were able to break through the Union line and penetrate into the town itself, threatening the Union baggage wagons. In the midst of the crisis, Rosecrans panicked, galloping this way and that, alternately shouting abuse at his men and announcing that the battle was lost. He ordered the officer in charge of one brigade's baggage train to burn the wagons, but that officer, a chaplain, ignored the order, moved the wagons to safer ground, and rallied teamsters, stragglers, and convalescents for their defense. It did not come to that, however, as the Union troops in that sector, veterans of Fort Donelson and Shiloh, rallied and drove the Confederates out of the position. Elsewhere, Confederate attacks continued throughout the day, climaxing in midafternoon in a bloody repulse. Ballard, *U.S. Grant*, 76; Robert G. Hartje, *Van Dorn: The Life and Times of a Confederate General* (Nashville, TN: Vanderbilt University Press, 1967), 209; Hess, *Banners to the Breeze*, 154–60; Peter Cozzens, *The Darkest Days of the War: The Battles of Iuka and Corinth* (Chapel Hill: University of North Carolina Press, 1997), 194–270; Charles F. Hubert, *History of the Fiftieth Regiment, Illinois Volunteer Infantry in the War of the Union* (Kansas City, MO: Western Veteran, 1885), 147; Woodworth, *Nothing but Victory*, 225–35.

20. As Van Dorn had made his approach toward Corinth and it became apparent that the town was his target, Grant had sent Rosecrans clear and repeated orders that he was to pursue aggressively the moment the Confederates began to retreat. Yet although several hours of daylight remained when Van Dorn marched his battered army away from Corinth, and although about a third of Rosecrans's force had been engaged only very lightly or not at all, the Union commander nevertheless kept his army where it was and spent the afternoon hours riding his lines, congratulating his troops and advising them to rest in preparation for an early start the next

morning. The opportunity to trap Van Dorn was genuine. Because of the Confederates' attempt to surprise the Corinth garrison by approaching it from the rear, the Rebel army would, if it kept to the most reliable roads, have to begin its retreat by marching about twenty miles due west from Corinth to Davis's Bridge over the Hatchie River. Only after crossing the river there could Van Dorn's troops turn south and begin putting more distance between themselves and Grant's various forces in northern Mississippi. Recognizing this, Grant had dispatched Brig. Gen. Stephen Hurlbut's division, about 5,400 men, from Bolivar, Tennessee, to march south along the west bank of the Hatchie the thirty miles to Davis's Bridge, where it could block Van Dorn's escape. Hurlbut marched his troops hard, reached the bridge before the Confederates, and on October 5 repulsed Van Dorn's attempt to force a crossing. For further details, see Woodworth, *Nothing but Victory*, 225–240.

That should have spelled the doom of the Confederate army in Mississippi, but Rosecrans's army marched only eight miles in pursuit that day and was still twelve miles from the Hatchie. With the complete lack of pressure from the east, Van Dorn was able to turn south along the east bank of the Hatchie, proceed by back roads six miles to Crum's Mill, and there make his crossing. After that, there was no chance of catching up with Van Dorn before his army could fall back on the ample supplies and prepare defensive works at Holly Springs, Mississippi. The advantage of the victory at Corinth had been lost. Perversely, Rosecrans then undertook to mount a belated pursuit, but Grant prevented the potentially dangerous consequences of that step by canceling the movement. Rosecrans complained bitterly at thus having, as he imagined, the fruits of his victory snatched from him. A few weeks later, Grant was spared the necessity of further dealings with his increasingly fractious subordinate when Lincoln assigned Rosecrans to replace Buell in command of the Army of the Ohio. Grant, *Personal Memoirs*, 1:417; W. S. Morris, L. D. Hartwell, and J. B. Kuykendall, *History 31st Regiment Illinois Volunteers* (Carbondale: Southern Illinois University Press, 1998; originally published 1902), 49; Augustus L. Chetlain, *Recollections of Seventy Years* (Galena, IL: Gazette, 1899), 95–96; McCord, "Battle of Corinth: the Campaigns Preceding and Leading Up to This Battle and Its Results," in MOLLUS, 29:581–82; Smith, "A Few Days with the Eighth Regiment, Wisconsin Volunteers at Iuka and Corinth," in MOLLUS, 49:66; *OR* vol. 17, pt. 1, 170; Grant, *Personal Memoirs*, 1:420; *OR* vol. 17, pt. 2, 290; Simon, ed., *Papers of U. S. Grant*, 6:180; Smith, *Corinth*, 259–75; Woodworth, *Nothing but Victory*, 235–47.

21. Michael Burlingame, *Abraham Lincoln: A Life*, 2 vols. (Baltimore: John Hopkins University Press, 2008), 1:430.

22. Lincoln and his top advisers in Washington, Stanton and Halleck, had been so disgusted with Buell's sluggish performance in allowing Bragg to get all the way to Kentucky that they had moved to sack him during the middle of the campaign, offering the command instead to Buell's subordinate George H. Thomas. But Thomas had turned it down, and so Lincoln and his advisers had given Buell another chance. John C. Waugh, *Lincoln and McClellan: The Troubled Partnership Between a President and His General* (New York: Palgrave Macmillan, 2010), 179.

23. It was Civil War newspaperman Alexander McClure who, many years later, quoted Lincoln as having said of Grant shortly after the Battle of Shiloh, "I can't spare this man; he fights." Alexander K. McClure, *Abraham Lincoln and Men of War-times: Some Personal Recollections of War and Politics During the Lincoln Administration* (Philadelphia: Times, 1892), 196.

24. After the death of his political mentor Stephen A. Douglas in 1861, McClernand was Illinois's foremost Democratic politician. At the outbreak of war, Lincoln, eager to maintain Democratic support for the war, had appointed him a brigadier general, despite meager military qualifications. Though he had put on a general's uniform, McClernand never put off his nature as an insatiably ambitious politician. He hoped to parlay military victory into electoral success at the highest level and for that purpose was especially eager for an independent command where all the glory would be his. Hitherto in the war, he had served under Grant, usually second only to him in rank, and had compiled a moderately good battlefield record while engaging in nonstop political posturing and glory-hunting. He also sent letters to Lincoln

behind Grant's back, forwarding spurious charges that his commanding officer was a drunk. During the late summer of 1862, McClernand manipulated Illinois governor Richard Yates to get a leave of absence to Illinois and then to Washington, where he relentlessly lobbied Lincoln for the plan he hoped would catapult him to national fame. Woodworth, *Nothing but Victory*, 42–43.

25. Ballard, *Vicksburg*, 24.

26. Simon, ed., *Papers of Ulysses S. Grant*, 6:199–200; Grant, *Personal Memoirs*, 2:422; McClernand to Lincoln, June 20 and September 28, 1862, and Richard Yates et al., to Lincoln, September 26, 1862, Abraham Lincoln Papers, Library of Congress; Richard L. Kiper, *Major General John A. McClernand: Politician in Uniform*, 125–37; *OR* series 3, vol. 1, 582–84; Ballard, *Vicksburg*, 24; Woodworth, *Nothing but Victory*, 248–50.

27. *OR* vol. 17, pt. 2, 282; Kiper, *McClernand*, 140; Edwin C. Bearss, *Vicksburg Is the Key* (Dayton, OH: Morningside Press, 1985), 27; Woodworth, *Nothing but Victory,* 250–53.

28. A Pennsylvania-born West Point graduate who had married a Virginian and sided with the Confederacy, Pemberton was Jefferson Davis's solution to the problem of divided command that had plagued the Confederacy during the Iuka and Corinth campaign that fall.

29. Sherman, *Memoirs*, 303; Simon, ed., *Papers of Ulysses S. Grant*, 6:372; *OR* vol. 17, pt. 1, 473; Woodworth, *Nothing but Victory*, 253–60.

30. Kiper, *Mclernand,* 142.

31. Bearss, *Vicksburg Is the Key*, 27; Kiper, *McClernand*, 140–42; Simon, ed., *Papers of Ulysses S. Grant*, 6:180, 279, 372, 403; *OR* vol. 17, pt. 1, 473–74; Grant, *Personal Memoirs*, 1:428–32; Sherman, *Memoirs*, 304–11; Woodworth, *Nothing but Victory*, 251–52, 260.

32. Simpson and Berlin, eds., *Sherman's Civil War*, 342–3, 348; Crooker, Nourse, and Brown, *The 55th Illinois*, 184–86; Sherman, *Memoirs*, 30; *OR* vol. 17, pt. 2, 426, 434, 441; Wiley, *Civil War Diary*, 26; Sweetman, "Chickasaw Bluffs," *National Tribune*, April 20, 1893, 1; Perry, "The Entering Wedge," in MOLLUS, 24:359; Woodworth, *Nothing but Victory*, 261.

33. Some examples of this shift in attitude can be found in Edward P. Stanfield to "Dear Father," October 12, 1862, Edward P. Stanfield Papers, Indiana Historical Society; John G. Given to "Dear Father and Mother," October 23, 1862, John G. Given Papers, Illinois State Historical Library; *OR* vol. 17, pt. 2, 856. On the development of Union hard-war policies, see Mark Grimsley's excellent book *The Hard Hand of War* (New York: Cambridge University Press, 1995).

34. For an excellent discussion of the impossibility of guerrilla warfare's achieving the results that the Confederacy needed, see Robert G. Tanner, *Retreat to Victory? Confederate Strategy Reconsidered* (Wilmington, DE: Scholarly Resources Books, 2001).

35. A. J. Sweetman, "Chickasaw Bluffs," *National Tribune*, April 20, 1893, 1.

36. *OR* vol. 13, 748–49; vol. 17, pt. 2, 280–81, 285, 287–88; Simpson and Berlin, eds., *Sherman's Civil War*, 346–47; Simon, ed., *Papers of Ulysses S. Grant*, 6:180.

37. Sweetman, "Chickasaw Bluffs," http://chroniclingamerica.loc.gov/lccn/sn82016187/1893-04-20/ed-1/seq-1/; Northup, *Drifting to an Unknown Future*, 54; Alexander Harper to "Dear Father and Mother," December 22, 1862, John and Alexander Harper Papers, Illinois State Historical Library; John M. Roberts Reminiscences, Indiana Historical Society; Munn, Miller, and Newton, *Military History and Reminiscences*, 236; *OR* vol. 17, pt. 2, 434; Sherman, *Memoirs*, 308; Winters, *Musick of the Mocking Birds*, 13; Wiley, *Civil War Diary*, 26–27; Woodworth, *Nothing but Victory*, 262–63, 266.

38. Woodworth, *Nothing but Victory*, 265–67.

39. Lucien B. Crooker, "Chickasaw Bayou," *National Tribune*, September 11, 1884, 3; Sweetman, "Chickasaw Bluffs," 3, http://chroniclingamerica.loc.gov/lccn/sn82016187/1893-04-20/ed-1/seq-3/; Sherman, *Memoirs*, 315–16; Woodworth, *Nothing but Victory*, 267–84; *OR* vol. 17, pt. 2, 570–71; vol. 20, pt. 24, pt. 1, 8; vol. 52, pt. 1, 442; Grant, *Personal Memoirs*, 1:440–41; Woodworth, *Nothing but Victory*, 286–87.

40. See Woodworth, *Jefferson Davis and His Generals*, 180–81.

41. *OR* vol. 17, pt. 2, 757–58; vol. 20, pt. 2, 439; Connelly, *Autumn of Glory: The Army of Tennessee,*

1862–1865 (Baton Rouge: Louisiana State University Press, 1971), 26–27, 93–98; Woodworth, *Jefferson Davis and His Generals*, 180–81.

42. Rowland, *Jefferson Davis, Constitutionalist*, 5:294–95, 384; Johnston, *Narrative of Military Operations*, 151–52; Connelly, *Autumn of Glory*, 40–42; Dodd, *Jefferson Davis*, 294; *OR* vol. 17, pt. 2, 781, 800; vol. 20, pt. 2, 449–50, 492–93; Woodworth, *Jefferson Davis and His Generals*, 182–83.

43. Hartje, *Van Dorn*, 269; *OR* vol. 17, pt. 1, 503, 604, 625; pt. 2, 439–40, 442–43, 482, 811–12; Herman Hattaway, *General Stephen D. Lee* (Jackson: University Press of Mississippi, 1976), 68; Woodworth, *Jefferson Davis and His Generals*, 183–84; Woodworth, *Nothing but Victory*, 264–65.

44. Within days, news of the transfer appeared in the columns of the Chattanooga *Daily Rebel*.

45. *OR* vol. 20, pt. 1, 661, 663–72, 771–79; pt. 2, pp. 463, 468, 479; vol. 52, pt. 2, 401; Stanley Horn, *The Army of Tennessee* (Indianapolis: Bobbs-Merrill, 1941), 196–200; James Lee McDonough, *Stones River: Bloody Winter in Tennessee* (Knoxville: University of Tennessee Press, 1980), 73–227; Connelly, *Autumn of Glory*, 47, 55–60, 84–85; Horn, *Army of Tennessee*, 200; Christopher Losson, "Major General Benjamin Franklin Cheatham and the Battle of Stone's River," *Tennessee Historical Quarterly* (Fall 1982): 279–86; Irving A. Buck, *Cleburne and His Command* (Jackson, TN: McCowat-Mercer, 1958), 119–20; William C. Davis, *Breckinridge*, 336–48; Grady McWhiney, *Braxton Bragg and Confederate Defeat* (New York: Columbia University Press, 1969), 347–64; Woodworth, *Jefferson Davis and His Generals*, 187–93.

46. *OR* vol. 20, pt. 1, 484, 492, 662–72, 699–700; vol. 52, pt. 2, 402; McDonough, *Stones River*, 161–97; Horn, *Army of Tennessee*, 206–08; Woodworth, *Jefferson Davis and His Generals*, 193; Davis, *Breckinridge*, 341–50; Connelly, *Autumn of Glory*, 64–74; Peter Cozzens, *No Better Place to Die: The Battle of Stones River* (Urbana: University of Illinois Press, 1990).

47. Sherman, *Memoirs*, 316–17, 324; Woodworth, *Nothing but Victory*, 285.

48. Rosecrans's defensive victory at Stones River only just avoided plunging the populace into deeper despair. Several months later, Lincoln wrote that had Rosecrans suffered outright defeat there, so soon after Fredericksburg, the country could scarcely have survived it. Roy P. Basler, ed., *Collected Works of Abraham Lincoln* (New Brunswick, NJ: Rutgers University Press, 1953), 6:424.

49. *OR* vol. 24, pt. 1, 8, 10, 14–16, 378, 388, 394; pt. 3, pp. 76, 98, 110; Grant, *Personal Memoirs*, 1:448–53; Simon, ed., *Papers of Ulysses S. Grant*, 7:253–54; Sherman, *Memoirs*, 330–34; Bearss, *Vicksburg Is the Key*, 467–92; Woodworth, *Nothing but Victory*, 287–314.

50. Michael B. Ballard, *U.S. Grant: The Making of a General, 1861–1863* (Lanham, MD: Rowman & Littlefield, 2005), 109–17; Simpson, *Ulysses S. Grant*, 187–90; Woodworth, *Nothing but Victory*, 322–40.

51. Woodworth, *Nothing but Victory*, 340–50.

52. Woodworth, *Nothing but Victory*, 353–62.

53. Ibid., 362–68; Simpson, *Ulysses S. Grant*, 194–98.

54. Johnston's performance in the Vicksburg campaign is ably analyzed in an essay by John R. Lundberg in a chapter of *The Vicksburg Campaign: March 29–May 18, 1863*, ed. Steven E. Woodworth (Carbondale: Southern Illinois University Press, 2013).

55. For the most part, orders issued to general officers during the mid-nineteenth century were always assumed to be at least somewhat discretionary unless worded so as to be peremptory. The latter was almost never done, and a general receiving an order worded in such a way as to be peremptory would likely have requested to be relieved of command, as Stonewall Jackson did (after obeying) when ordered to evacuate the town of Romney, Virginia (now West Virginia), in early 1862. And yet, the matter was even more nuanced than that. Although officers were expected to exercise discretion, they were also expected to try to fulfill their commander's wishes insofar as practical. In some cases, the disobedience of orders did result in at least the threat of court-martial. Officers were more likely to disobey if they lacked respect for their commander or thought him weak, either by nature or because he lacked the support of his own superior. An example would be Jefferson Davis's chronic failure to support Braxton Bragg's authority within

the Army of Tennessee. On the Battle of Champion Hill, see Timothy B. Smith, *Champion Hill: Decisive Battle for Vicksburg* (New York: Savas Beatie, 2004).

56. Grant, *Personal Memoirs*, 1:510–20; Warren Grabau, *Ninety-Eight Days*, 279–80; Woodworth, *Nothing but Victory*, 369–89.

57. Woodworth, *Nothing but Victory*, 390–96.

58. Ibid., 390–99.

59. Ibid., 399–405.

60. Simpson, *Ulysses S. Grant*, 303–5.

61. *OR* vol. 24, pt. 1, 164–65; Woodworth, *Nothing but Victory*, 439–47.

62. *The Century, Illustrated Monthly Magazine*, vol. 30, May 1885 to October 1885.

63. When Vicksburg surrendered, the 29,491 officers and men of Pemberton's army were paroled under the terms of the capitulation. Confederate authorities found that they had to grant the paroled prisoners furloughs or risk having most of them desert. However, contrary to what Grant had expected, a large number of the Confederates reported to their designated reception centers at the conclusion of their furloughs. Confederate Prisoner-of-War Commissioner Robert Ould wrote a letter to his Union counterpart, Brig. Gen. Sullivan A. Meredith, announcing that he had records of enough paroled Union soldiers to justify the immediate exchange (release from parole) of two divisions, a brigade, and the equivalent of another oversized regiment. Ould's assertion was flatly false, and Meredith rejected it. The Confederacy nonetheless placed the units—the cream of Pemberton's army—back on duty. At the Battle of Chattanooga that November, the capture of paroled Vicksburg troops proved what the Confederates had done. The parole system quickly broke down: the Union released an equivalent number of its own paroled soldiers; the Confederacy replied in kind. Soon all paroled prisoners had been released. In response to Union protests, Confederate authorities changed their story and asserted that the Vicksburg and Port Hudson paroles had been invalid due to technical flaws in the parole forms. In April 1864 Grant ordered that all prisoner exchanges cease until the Confederacy recognized the validity of the Vicksburg and Port Hudson paroles. Simultaneously, the prisoner-exchange system was breaking down because of Confederate refusal to exchange captured African Americans, insisting that they should be sold into slavery instead. Grant, with Lincoln's backing, refused to exchange white soldiers if blacks were not to be exchanged on the same terms. Thus there were almost no further prisoner of war exchanges during the remainder of the Civil War. See Edwin C. Bearss, *The Vicksburg Campaign: Volume 3—Unvexed to the Sea* (Dayton, OH: Morningside House, 1986), 1310–11.

64. Hudson Strode, *Jefferson Davis, Confederate President* (New York: Harcourt Brace, 1959), 443–45; Woodworth, *Jefferson Davis and His Generals*, 214–19.

65. During those months, Rosecrans's idleness stood in a mutually enabling relationship with the almost complete dysfunction of the high command in the opposing Confederate Army of Tennessee. In January, in the immediate aftermath of the retreat from Stones River, a staff officer denounced Bragg in an anonymous newspaper article, claiming that he had retreated against the advice of his generals. Knowing that was untrue, Bragg sent a circular to his generals asking if they had counseled retreat and if they still had confidence in him. He ought to have known better. The officer corps of the Army of Tennessee was a virtual snake pit of jealousy and resentment, and corps commanders Leonidas Polk and especially William J. Hardee had done much to turn their subordinates against Bragg. The responses sullenly admitted having advised retreat but, asserting that no one in the army had any confidence in Bragg, insisted he should resign. Getting wind of the affair, Davis had ordered Johnston to Bragg's headquarters to sort things out. Since assuming the western theater command, Johnston had hardly let a day go by without complaining that he would rather be in command of an individual army, so Davis assumed he would fix the mess in the Army of Tennessee by assuming effective command, as his position entitled him to do. Apparently sensing that such was Davis's wish, Johnston did the opposite, insisting that Bragg was fine as an army commander. Davis spent the next several weeks sending orders, advices, and solicitations but could not induce Johnston to relieve Bragg.

When Mississippi began to heat up in May, Davis gave up trying to replace Bragg and ordered Johnston to Mississippi. These controversies gave Rosecrans the leisure to plan his campaign exactly as he wanted it.

66. Bragg was by this time scarcely on speaking terms with his chief subordinates, who had little understanding of his plans and less interest in carrying them out. Before the campaign was over, they were seriously discussing the possibility of mutiny should Bragg fail to heed their advice to retreat without fighting.

67. Connelly, *Autumn of Glory*, 112–34; Steven E. Woodworth, *Six Armies in Tennessee: The Chickamauga and Chattanooga Campaigns* (Lincoln: University of Nebraska Press, 1998), 1–46.

68. Connelly, *Autumn of Glory*, 166–75; Woodworth, *Six Armies in Tennessee*, 47–62.

69. The Army of the Cumberland was on the west side of the eighty-mile-long ridge of Lookout Mountain. The Army of Tennessee was retreating somewhere to the east. Lookout was passable only at widely spaced gaps, and Rosecrans sent each of his three corps through one of the three northernmost gaps, thus spreading his army over nearly forty-five miles, several days' march in this rough country, from the left-flank column to the right-flank one.

70. Connelly, *Autumn of Glory*, 175–89; Woodworth, *Jefferson Davis and His Generals*, 230–33; Woodworth, *Six Armies in Tennessee*, 62–78.

71. Connelly, *Autumn of Glory*, 201–43; Woodworth, *Six Armies in Tennessee*, 79–128.

72. Woodworth, *Six Armies in Tennessee*, 129–36.

73. Ibid., 148.

74. Grant, *Personal Memoirs*, 1:578–81; James Lee McDonough, *Chattanooga: Death Grip on the Confederacy* (Knoxville: University of Tennessee Press, 19), 49; Bruce Catton, *Grant Takes Command* (Boston: Little, Brown, 1968), 25–54; Simpson, *Ulysses S. Grant*, 222–29; Wiley Sword, *Mountains Touched with Fire: Chattanooga Besieged, 1863* (New York: St. Martin's Press, 1995), 53–58, 151–59; Woodworth, *Six Armies in Tennessee*, 150–53.

75. Simpson, *Ulysses S. Grant*, 229-31; Sword, *Mountains Touched with Fire*, 112–52; Woodworth, *Six Armies in Tennessee*, 153–68.

76. Sword, *Mountains Touched with Fire*, 213–21; Woodworth, *Six Armies in Tennessee*, 181–83.

77. Grant, *Personal Memoirs*, 2:76–77; McDonough, *Chattanooga*, 143–60; Catton, *Grant Takes Command*, 77–78; Peter Cozzens, *The Shipwreck of Their Hopes: The Battles for Chattanooga* (Urbana: University of Illinois Press, 1994), 204–43; Connelly, *Autumn of Glory*, 275; John F. Marszalek, *Sherman: A Soldier's Passion for Order* (New York: St. Martin's, 1993), 244; Sword, *Mountains Touched with Fire*, 231–58; Woodworth, *Six Armies in Tennessee*, 191–93.

78. Grant, *Personal Memoirs*, 2:78–79; Cozzens, *Shipwreck of Their Hopes,* 245–48; Catton, *Grant Takes Command*, 79; Sword, *Mountains Touched with Fire*, 259–65; Woodworth, *Six Armies in Tennessee*, 194–96.

79. The geographic crest is the highest point. The military crest is the highest point on the slope from which all points of the slope below it are visible.

80. Woodworth, *Six Armies in Tennessee*, 196–205.

81. Abraham Lincoln to James C. Conkling, August 26, 1863, in *Complete Works of Abraham Lincoln*, eds. John G. Nicolay and John Hay (New York: Francis D. Tandy, 1894), 9:100–101.

82. T. Harry Williams, *Lincoln and His Generals* (New York: Alfred A. Knopf, 1952), 272.

CHAPTER 5: COORDINATED STRATEGY AND HARD WAR

1. Grant was the first United States Army officer promoted to the rank of lieutenant general since George Washington; even Winfield Scott had only held the rank as a brevet.

2. There are several good biographies of Grant; see for example Geoffrey Perret, *Ulysses S. Grant: Soldier and President* (New York: Random House, 1997), and Brooks D. Simpson, *Ulysses S. Grant: Triumph over Adversity, 1822–1865* (Boston: Houghton Mifflin Harcourt, 2000), but the best reading on Grant is the general's own words in Ulysses S. Grant, *Personal Memoirs of U. S.*

Grant (New York: Webster, 1885–86). Simpson correctly points out that Grant's options were not unlimited, but his flexibility was circumscribed by political considerations pushed by Lincoln. See Brooks D. Simpson, "Ulysses S. Grant and the Problems of Command in 1864," in *The Art of Command in the Civil War*, ed. Steven H. Woodworth (Lincoln: University of Nebraska Press, 1998), 137–56. See also Brooks D. Simpson, "Great Expectations: Ulysses S. Grant, the Northern Press, and the Opening of the Wilderness Campaign," in *The Wilderness Campaign,* ed. Gary W. Gallagher (Chapel Hill: University of North Carolina Press, 1997), 1–35.

3. For an overview of the Union war effort during the last year of the conflict, see William Marvel, *Tarnished Victory: Finishing Lincoln's War* (Boston: Houghton Mifflin Harcourt, 2010); on the expenses of the northern war effort, see Mark R. Wilson, *The Business of Civil War, 1861–1865* (Baltimore, MD: Johns Hopkins University Press, 2008), 1.

4. A Western soldier named John F. Brobst of the 25th Wisconsin (XVI Corps, Army of the Tennessee) wrote, "The Army of the Potomac has never done anything and never will. If they had done half as much as the western army, this war would have been rubbed out before this time. This army will have to go down there and take Richmond for them, poor fellows." Margaret Brobst Roth, ed., *Well Mary: Civil War Letters of a Wisconsin Volunteer* (Madison: University of Wisconsin Press, 1960), 37. See also Earl J. Hess*, Civil War in the West: Victory and Defeat from the Appalachians to the Mississippi* (Chapel Hill: University of North Carolina Press, 2012), 311–15.

5. Ulysses S. Grant to Edwin M. Stanton, July 22, 1865, *The War of the Rebellion: A Compilation of the Official Records of the Union and Confederate Armies*, vol. 38, pt. 1 (Washington, D.C.: Government Printing Office, 1891), 1–2. Hereafter cited as *OR.*

6. Tyler Dennett, ed., *Lincoln and the Civil War in the Diaries and Letters of John Hay* (New York, Dodd, Mead, 1939), 179; see also Grant, *Personal Memoirs*, 2:143.

7. An old but good biography of Meade is Freeman Cleaves, *Meade of Gettysburg* (Norman: University of Oklahoma, 1960); see also the short survey by Ethan S. Rafuse, *George Gordon Meade and the War in the East* (Abilene, TX: McWhiney Foundation Press, 2003). For the best biography of Sherman, see John F. Marszalek, *Sherman: A Soldier's Passion for Order* (New York: Free Press, 1993). For a discussion of the Grant-Sherman relationship, consult Joseph T. Glatthaar, *Partners in Command: The Relationships Between Leaders in the Civil War* (New York: Free Press, 1994).

8. About 90 percent of blockade runners made it through the Union blockade in 1861, but only about half were successful by 1865. As pointed out, however, in James M. McPherson, *War on the Waters: The Union and Confederate Navies, 1861–1865* (Chapel Hill: University of North Carolina Press, 2012), 225, one must compare pre–Civil War coastal commerce with the war years to truly understand how the blockade hurt the Confederacy. While 20,000 ships entered or left southern ports from 1856 to 1860, only 8,000 did so during 1861 to 1865.

9. On Confederate troubles in 1864–65, see Richard E. Berringer, Herman Hattaway, Archer Jones, and William N. Still Jr., *Why the South Lost the Civil War* (Athens: University of Georgia Press, 1986); William Blair, *Virginia's Private War: Feeding Body and Soul in the Confederacy, 1861–1865* (New York: Oxford University Press, 1998); and James M. McPherson, *Ordeal by Fire: The Civil War and Reconstruction*, 2nd ed. (New York: McGraw-Hill, 1992), 203. On the two major Confederate field armies, see Richard M. McMurry, *Two Great Rebel Armies: An Essay in Confederate Military History* (Chapel Hill: University of North Carolina Press, 1989); J. Tracy Power, *Lee's Miserables: Life in the Army of Northern Virginia from the Wilderness to Appomattox* (Chapel Hill: University of North Carolina Press, 1998); Steven H. Newton, *Lost for the Cause: The Confederate Army in 1864* (Mason City, IA: Savas Publishing, 2000); Joseph T. Glatthaar, *Soldiering in the Army of Northern Virginia: A Statistical Portrait of the Troops Who Served Under Robert E. Lee* (Chapel Hill: University of North Carolina Press, 2011); Gary W. Gallagher, "Our Hearts Are Full of Hope: The Army of Northern Virginia in the Spring of 1864," in *The Wilderness Campaign,* ed. Gallagher (Chapel Hill: University of North Carolina Press, 1997), 36–65; and John J. Hennessey, "I Dread the Spring: The Army of the Potomac Prepares for the Overland Campaign," in *The Wilderness Campaign.* Douglas Ball has pointed

out the level of financial mismanagement by top Confederate leaders and how that mismanagement crippled the Confederate government's ability to wage a long, demanding war effort. See Douglas B. Ball, *Financial Failure and Confederate Defeat* (Urbana: University of Illinois Press, 1991).

10. For a discussion of Confederate defensive strategy in 1864, see Hattaway and Jones, *How the North Won*, 525–682.

11. John Cimprich, *Fort Pillow: A Civil War Massacre, and Public Memory* (Baton Rouge: Louisiana State University Press, 2005); Earl J. Hess, *Into the Crater: The Mine Attack at Petersburg* (Columbia: University of South Carolina Press, 2010), 200–201; Hess, *Civil War in the West*, 142–44, 164–65, 188–89, 241–44.

12. Charles W. Sanders Jr., *While in the Hands of the Enemy: Military Prisons of the Civil War* (Baton Rouge: Louisiana State University Press, 2005), 1–5.

13. William Glenn Robertson, *Back Door to Richmond: The Bermuda Hundred Campaign, April–June, 1864* (Newark: University of Delaware Press, 1987).

14. William C. Davis, *The Battle of New Market* (Baton Rouge: Louisiana State University Press, 1983).

15. John Sergeant Wise, *The End of an Era* (New York: Thomas Yoseloff, 1965), 298–99.

16. Michael C. C. Adams, *Fighting for Defeat: Union Military Failure in the East, 1861–1865* (Lincoln: University of Nebraska Press, 1992); Grant to Halleck, January 19, 1864, Simon, ed., *Papers of Ulysses S. Grant*, vol. 10 (hereafter *Grant Papers*), 39–40.

17. Grant to Meade, April 9, 1864, *Grant Papers*, vol. 10, 274.

18. Grant to Butler, April 19, 1864, *Grant Papers*, vol. 10, 327.

19. Gordon C. Rhea, *The Battle of the Wilderness, May 5–6, 1864* (Baton Rouge: Louisiana State University Press, 1994).

20. Frank Wilkeson, *Recollections of a Private Soldier in the Army of the Potomac* (New York: G. P. Putnam's Sons, 1887), 78–80.

21. Gilbert Thompson Journal, May 8, 1864, Manuscript Division, Library of Congress.

22. Gordon C. Rhea, *The Battles for Spotsylvania Court House and the Road to Yellow Tavern, May 7–12, 1864* (Baton Rouge: Louisiana State University Press, 1997), 39. For a good short history of the Overland campaign, see Mark Grimsley, *And Keep Moving On: The Virginia Campaign, May–June 1864* (Lincoln: University of Nebraska Press, 2002).

23. Total Union casualties were officially reported at 17,666, which may be an understatement, according to Rhea, *Battle of the Wilderness*, 435. Not enough reports were filed for a good accounting of Confederate casualties, but they can be estimated at 11,000. Rhea, *Battle of the Wilderness*, 440.

24. Rhea, *Battles for Spotsylvania Court House*, 162–88.

25. Ibid., 232–307; Earl J. Hess, *Trench Warfare Under Grant & Lee: Field Fortifications in the Overland Campaign* (Chapel Hill: University of North Carolina Press, 2007), 65–82. For participants' accounts, see Gary W. Gallagher, ed., *Fighting for the Confederacy: The Personal Recollections of General Edward Porter Alexander* (Chapel Hill: University of North Carolina Press, 1989), 371–86, and Francis Channing Barlow, "Capture of the Salient, May 12, 1864," in *The Wilderness Campaign, May–June 1864: Papers of the Military Historical Society of Massachusetts*, vol. 4 (Boston: Cadet Armory, 1905), 245–62, http://archive.org/stream/wildcampaign04bostrich#page/244/mode/1up.

26. Lewis A. Grant, "Review of Major-General Barlow's Paper on the Capture of the Salient at Spottsylvania, May 12, 1864," in *The Wilderness Campaign, May–June 1864: Papers of the Military Historical Society of Massachusetts*, vol. 4, 269–70.

27. Gordon C. Rhea, *To the North Anna River: Grant and Lee, May 13–25, 1864* (Baton Rouge: Louisiana State University Press, 2000). For participants' accounts, see Gallagher, *Fighting for the Confederacy*, 386–94, and Ed Malles, ed., *Bridge Building in Wartime: Colonel Wesley Brainerd's Memoir of the 50th New York Volunteer Engineers* (Knoxville: University of Tennessee Press, 1997), 220–39.

28. Gordon C. Rhea, *Cold Harbor: Grant and Lee, May 26–June 3, 1864* (Baton Rouge: Louisiana State University Press, 2002), 312, 362. "I have always regretted that the last assault at Cold Harbor was ever made," Grant wrote in his memoirs. "I might say the same thing of the assault of the 22d of May, 1863, at Vicksburg. At Cold Harbor no advantage whatever was gained to compensate for the heavy loss we sustained." Ulysses S. Grant, *Personal Memoirs of U. S. Grant*, 2 vols. (New York: Webster, 1885–86), 2:185.

29. Hess, *Trench Warfare Under Grant & Lee*, 155–203.

30. Regarding Federal refusals to attack on June 18, see Earl J. Hess, *In the Trenches at Petersburg: Field Fortifications and Confederate Defeat* (Chapel Hill: University of North Carolina Press, 2009), 33–36.

31. Stephen Minot Weld, *War Diary and Letters of Stephen Minot Weld*, 2nd ed. (Boston: Massachusetts Historical Society, 1979), 318; Allan Nevins, ed., *A Diary of Battle: The Personal Journals of Colonel Charles S. Wainwright, 1861–1865* (New York: Harcourt, Brace, and World, 1962), 426, 431. For the first Union offensive at Petersburg, see Hess, *In the Trenches at Petersburg*, 9–37.

32. Ulysses S. Grant to Henry W. Halleck, May 10, 1864, *Grant Papers*, vol. 10, 418–19 or *OR* 36, part 1, p. 3.

33. For an evaluation of the results of Grant's Overland campaign within the context of the entire war in Virginia, see Hess, *Trench Warfare Under Grant & Lee*, 205–16.

34. Grant's after-dinner comment on the Overland campaign quoted in Henry Yates Thompson diary, April 16, 1866, in Sir Christopher Chancellor, ed., *An Englishman in the American Civil War: The Diaries of Henry Yates Thompson, 1863* (New York: New York University Press, 1971), 4.

35. Capt. Thomas J. Linebarger to family, May 15, 1864, Linebarger-Snuggs Papers, Southern Historical Collection, University of North Carolina at Chapel Hill.

36. William T. Sherman to wife Ellen, May 20, 1864, in Brooks D. Simpson and Jean V. Berlin, eds. *Sherman's Civil War: Selected Correspondence of William T. Sherman, 1860–1865* (Chapel Hill: University of North Carolina Press, 1999), 638; also printed in an older edition available online at http://books.google.com/books?id=nscEAAAAYAAJ&pg=PA291&lpg=PA291.

37. For Union logistics during the Atlanta campaign, see Hess, *Civil War in the West*, 217–20.

38. Buck T. Foster, *Sherman's Mississippi Campaign* (Tuscaloosa: University of Alabama Press, 2006).

39. Hess, *Civil War in the West*, 235–37; Jefferson Davis to Joseph E. Johnston, July 11, 1864, *OR*, vol. 38, pt. 5, 875–76. Many historians have written about the effect of Joseph E. Johnston's replacement by John Bell Hood as commander of the Army of Tennessee; see, for example, Albert Castel, *Decision in the West: The Atlanta Campaign of 1864* (Lawrence: University Press of Kansas, 1992), 363–65. For more details on that topic, see Richard M. McMurry, "Confederate Morale in the Atlanta Campaign of 1864," *Georgia Historical Quarterly* 45 (1970): 226–43, and William J. McNeill, "A Survey of Confederate Soldier Morale During Sherman's Campaign Through Georgia and the Carolinas," *Georgia Historical Quarterly* 45 (1971): 1–25.

40. The standard history of the Atlanta campaign remains Castel, *Decision in the West*. For representative accounts by participants, see Milo M. Quaife, ed., *From the Cannon's Mouth: The Civil War Letters of General Alpheus S. Williams* (Detroit: Wayne State University Press, 1959), 285–354, and R. Lockwood Tower, ed., *A Carolinian Goes to War: The Civil War Narrative of Arthur Middleton Manigault, Brigadier General, C.S.A.* (Columbia: University of South Carolina Press, 1983), 173–272.

41. Hess, *In the Trenches at Petersburg*, 78–89.

42. B. Franklin Cooling, *Jubal Early's Raid on Washington, 1864* (Tuscaloosa: University of Alabama Press, 2007).

43. Hess, *Into the Crater*. For representative personal accounts by participants, see Robert Garth Scott, ed., *Forgotten Valor: The Memoirs, Journals, and Civil War Letters of Orlando B. Willcox* (Kent, OH: Kent State University Press, 1999), 549–64, and John C. Featherston, "Graphic

Account of Battle of Crater," *Southern Historical Society Papers* 33 (1905): 358–74. The mine was not blown until the last day of the offensive because Grant continued to hope that operations against Lee's left flank would succeed, allowing him to avoid conducting a frontal attack against Lee's center, where the mine was located. The mine explosion was the last chance for Union success in the third offensive.

44. Hess, *In the Trenches at Petersburg*, 124–41. For representative accounts by participants, see George K. Dauchy, "The Battle of Ream's Station," *Military Essays and Recollections: Papers Read Before the Commandery of the State of Illinois, Military Order of the Loyal Legion of the United States*, vol. 3 (Chicago: Dial, 1890): 125–40, and W. S. Dunlop, *Lee's Sharpshooters: Or, The Forefront of Battle* (Dayton, OH: Morningside Bookshop, 1982), 193–95.

45. Stephen W. Sears, *George B. McClellan: The Young Napoleon* (New York: Ticknor and Fields, 1988), 370–86. For Confederate ideas about the northern presidential election, see Larry E. Nelson, *Bullets, Ballots, and Rhetoric: Confederate Policy for the United States Presidential Contest of 1864* (Tuscaloosa: University of Alabama Press, 1980).

46. Jack C. Waugh, *Reelecting Lincoln: The Battle for the 1864 Presidency* (New York: Crown, 1997).

47. Castel, *Decision in the West*, 490–529. Following are casualty statistics for the four major battles fought near Atlanta in the latter half of the campaign: 1,900 Union soldiers and 2,500 Confederate soldiers at Peachtree Creek, July 20; 3,722 Union soldiers and 5,500 Confederate soldiers on July 22; 632 Union soldiers and 3,000 Confederate soldiers at Ezra Church, July 28; and 1,444 Union soldiers and about 3,000 Confederate soldiers at Jonesboro on August 31 and September 1.

48. For Philip Sheridan's operations in the Shenandoah Valley in 1864, see P. H. Sheridan, *Personal Memoirs*, vol. 2, 2; Gary W. Gallagher, ed., *The Shenandoah Valley Campaign of 1864* (Chapel Hill: University of North Carolina Press, 2006); Jeffry D. Wert, *From Winchester to Cedar Creek: The Shenandoah Campaign of 1864* (Mechanicsburg, PA: Stackpole Books, 1997).

49. Grant to Halleck, July 14, 1864, *OR*, vol. 40, pt. 3, 223–25.

50. Grant to Sheridan, August 26, 1864, *OR*, vol. 43, pt. 2, 202–4; Sheridan to Grant, October 7, 1864, *OR*, vol. 43, pt. 1, 30–31. For Federal policy in the Shenandoah Valley, see Mark Grimsley, *The Hard Hand of War: Union Military Policy Toward Southern Civilians, 1861–1865* (New York: Cambridge University Press, 1995), and Mark E. Neely Jr., *The Civil War and the Limits of Destruction* (Cambridge, MA: Harvard University Press, 2007), 109–39. Neely points out that Sheridan's destruction of resources in the valley was limited, since his primary objective was defeating Early's force, not laying waste to the countryside. Impressionistic evidence, such as the harsh language used in the dispatches quoted in the text, has to be balanced with statistical evidence. For example, Sheridan destroyed no more than one-third of the hay typically produced every year in Rockingham County. While that county produced 684,239 bushels of wheat in 1860, Sheridan destroyed only 50,000 bushels there in the fall of 1864. As Neely puts it, "Sheridan assigned to his three divisions of cavalry the task of destroying some crops and livestock when they did not have other more important things to do."

51. Lincoln's electoral victory and the soldier vote are discussed in Jack C. Waugh, *Reelecting Lincoln: The Battle for the 1864 Presidency* (New York: Crown, 1997).

52. For a discussion of supply and Sherman's decision to break contact with Hood after the fall of Atlanta, see Hess, *Civil War in the West*, 229–32.

53. For Hood's North Georgia campaign, consult Hess, *Civil War in the West*, 247–52, and J. B. Hood, *Advance and Retreat: Personal Experiences in the United States and Confederate Armies* (Philadelphia: Burk and McFetridge, 1880), 243–69.

54. For Sherman's plans and preparations for the March to the Sea, consult Marszalek, *Sherman*, and William T. Sherman, *Memoirs of General William T. Sherman, by Himself*, vol. 2 (New York: D. Appleton, 1875), 152–69, especially 152–57 and 164–67, along with *OR*, vol. 38, pt. 2, 357–58, for the strategic decision.

55. Sherman to Grant, November 6, 1864, *OR*, vol. 39, pt. 3, 658–60.

56. Joseph T. Glatthaar, *The March to the Sea and Beyond: Sherman's Troops in the Savannah and*

Carolinas Campaigns (New York: New York University Press, 1985), 66–80, 134–37, 141, 145; Sherman, *Memoirs,* 180–245.

57. For the March to the Sea, consult Hess, *Civil War in the West,* 258–67. On the level of taxable property in Georgia, consult C. Mildred Thompson, *Reconstruction in Georgia: Economic, Social, Political, 1865–1872* (Gloucester, MA: Peter Smith, 1964), 28.

58. Wiley Sword, *The Confederacy's Last Hurrah: Spring Hill, Franklin, and Nashville* (Lawrence: University Press of Kansas, 1993), and John M. Schofield, *Forty-Six Years in the Army* (New York: Century Company, 1897), 175–88. Schofield, interestingly, defends Hood's decision to attack as "entirely justifiable" (183–84).

59. James Lee McDonough, *Nashville: The Western Confederacy's Final Gamble* (Knoxville: University of Tennessee Press, 2004). For representative accounts by participants, see Douglas Cater to Fannie, December 15, 1864, and January 12, 1865, Douglas J. Cater and Rufus W. Cater Papers, Library of Congress, and William Dudley Gale to wife, January 14, 1865, Gale and Polk Family Papers, Southern Historical Collection, University of North Carolina, Chapel Hill.

60. Marion Brunson Lucas, *Sherman and the Burning of Columbia* (College Station: Texas A&M University Press, 1976).

61. The standard history of the Carolinas campaign remains John G. Barrett, *Sherman's March Through the Carolinas* (Chapel Hill: University of North Carolina Press, 1956), but see also Mark L. Bradley, *Last Stand in the Carolinas: The Battle of Bentonville* (Campbell, CA: Savas Woodbury, 1996). See also William T. Sherman, *Memoirs,* 276–345.

62. For the seventh, eighth, and ninth offensives at Petersburg, see Hess, *In the Trenches at Petersburg,* 229–79, and for the decisive breaking of Lee's line on April 2, consult A. Wilson Greene, *The Final Battles of the Petersburg Campaign: Breaking the Backbone of the Rebellion* (Knoxville: University of Tennessee Press, 2008). For accounts by participants, see Scott, *Forgotten Valor* (Kent, OH: Kent State University Press, 1999), 614–44, and Nathaniel Harrison Harris, "Defence of Battery Gregg," *Southern Historical Society Papers,* vol. 8 (1880): 475–88.

63. For the Appomattox campaign, see William Marvel, *Lee's Last Retreat: The Flight to Appomattox* (Chapel Hill: University of North Carolina Press, 2002). For participants' accounts, see Gallagher, *Fighting for the Confederacy* (Chapel Hill: University of North Carolina Press, 1989), 510–52, and J. F. J. Caldwell, *The History of a Brigade of South Carolinians Known as "Gregg's," and Subsequently as "McGowan's Brigade"* (Philadelphia: King and Baird, 1866), 226–45.

64. Newton, *Lost for the Cause,* 10, 68, 70–72, 84; Mark A. Weitz, *More Damning Than Slaughter: Desertion in the Confederate Army* (Lincoln: University of Nebraska Press, 2005), 234–94; Hess, *In the Trenches at Petersburg,* 254, 272.

65. Robert E. Lee to A. P. Hill, June [no date], 1864, *OR,* vol. 40, pt. 2, 702–3. For studies of field fortifications in the Virginia campaigns of 1864–1865, consult Hess, *Trench Warfare Under Grant & Lee,* and Hess, *In the Trenches at Petersburg.*

66. For a full discussion of the rifle musket's role in Civil War operations, see Earl J. Hess, *The Rifle Musket in Combat: Reality and Myth* (Lawrence: University Press of Kansas, 2008).

67. William T. Sherman to Henry W. Halleck, October 9, 1864, *OR,* vol. 39, pt. 3, 358. The standard study of Union hard-war policies remains Grimsley, *The Hard Hand of War.*

68. See Grimsley, *The Hard Hand of War,* and Mark Grimsley, "'Rebels and Redskins': U.S. Military Conduct Toward White Southerners and Native Americans in Comparative Perspective," in *Civilians in the Path of War,* eds. Mark Grimsley and Clifford J. Rogers (Lincoln: University of Nebraska Press, 2002), 137–61.

1. See William C. Harris, *With Charity for All: Lincoln and the Restoration of the Union* (Lexington: University Press of Kentucky, 1999). The standard work on Reconstruction, emphasizing its relationship to emancipation during the Civil War but also addressing civil rights in the North, remains Eric Foner, *Reconstruction: America's Unfinished Revolution, 1863–1877* (New York: Harper & Row, 1988). W. E. B. DuBois, *Black Reconstruction in America* (1935; reprint ed., New York: Oxford University Press, 2007) provides both a focus on the centrality of black labor and politics in Reconstruction in the South, and connections with the growth of industrial capitalism in the North.

2. The path to Johnston's decision to surrender is analyzed by Mark Grimsley, "Learning to Say 'Enough': Southern Generals and the Final Weeks of the Confederacy," in *The Collapse of the Confederacy,* eds. Mark Grimsley and Brooks D. Simpson (Lincoln: University of Nebraska Press, 2001), 40–79. The texts of both the April 18 and April 26, 1865, agreements between Sherman and Johnston, along with additional information about their meetings at Bennett Place, North Carolina, can be found at the Bennett Place North Carolina Historic Site website: www.nchistoricsites.org/bennett/bennett.htm.

3. Taylor recalled the uncertainties during the interim between Lee's surrender and the capture of Jefferson Davis in his memoirs: "The surrender of Lee left us little hope of success; but while Johnston remained in arms we must be prepared to fight our way to him. Again, the President and civil authorities of our Government were on their way to the south, and might need our protection. Granting the cause for which we had fought to be lost, we owed it to our own manhood, to the memory of the dead, and the honour of our arms, to remain steadfast to the last. This was received, not with noisy cheers, but solemn murmurs of approval, showing that it was understood and adopted." Richard Taylor, *Destruction and Reconstruction: Personal Experiences of the Late War* (New York: D. Appleton, 1879), 279.

4. Jeffrey S. Prushankin, *A Crisis in Confederate Command: Edmund Kirby Smith, Richard Taylor and the Army of the Trans-Mississippi* (Baton Rouge: Louisiana State University, 2005).

5. Lynn Schooler, *The Last Shot: The Incredible Story of the C.S.S.* Shenandoah *and the True Conclusion of the Civil War* (New York: HarperCollins, 2005); Raimondo Luraghi, *A History of the Confederate Navy* (Annapolis, MD: Naval Institute Press, 1996).

6. Historical controversy continues over what actually transpired at the conference at Hampton Roads, including the respective roles of Presidents Davis and Lincoln, and the instrumental role of General Grant in bringing about the meeting. Lincoln never recorded his personal views on the meeting in the remaining days of his life in any detail, so whether he expected peace could have come from this meeting remains unknowable. Given the long-standing personal antagonism between Davis and Stephens (his vice president), Davis probably intended to use the conference to discredit his domestic political opponents and reverse his growing unpopularity in the winter of 1864–65. Immediately after the return of the commissioners, Davis appeared at a political rally in Richmond, where all the speakers called for a Confederate fight to the finish. For analyses focused on Lincoln and Davis, see William C. Harris, "The Hampton Roads Peace Conference: A Final Test of Lincoln's Presidential Leadership," *Journal of the Abraham Lincoln Association* 21 (January 2000): 30–61; and Charles W. Sanders Jr., "Jefferson Davis and the Hampton Roads Peace Conference: 'To Secure Peace to the Two Countries,'" *Journal of Southern History* 63 (November 1997): 803–26. For an early account of the Hampton Roads Conference, along with the primary source documents compiled by Lincoln's secretaries, see John G. Nicolay and John Hay, "Abraham Lincoln: A History. The Hampton Roads Conference," *The Century* (October 1889): 846–82.

7. Jefferson Davis had secretly ordered the suppression of a petition to arm the slaves that Maj. Gen. Patrick Cleburne circulated in the headquarters of the Army of Tennessee during the winter of 1864, citing its potential danger to Rebel morale. Cleburne was killed at the battle of

Franklin in 1864, so it was not until many years later that his petition was discovered by War Department historians who were assembling the volumes of the official records. See Craig L. Symonds, *Stonewall of the West: Patrick Cleburne and the Civil War* (Lawrence: University Press of Kansas, 1997).

8. The bill as enacted did not explicitly provide for emancipation, but Lee favored recruiting only freed slaves into the army. See Robert E. Lee to Jefferson Davis, March 10, 1865, in Douglas S. Freeman and Grady McWhiney, eds., *Lee's Dispatches: Unpublished Letters of General Robert E. Lee, C.S.A. to Jefferson Davis and the War Department of the Confederate States of America, 1862–1865* (New York: G. P. Putnam's Sons, 1957), 373–74. For additional works on the attempt to arm the slaves, see Robert F. Durden, *The Black and the Gray: The Confederate Debate on Emancipation* (Baton Rouge: Louisiana State University Press, 1972), and Bruce Levine, *Confederate Emancipation: Southern Plans to Free and Arm Slaves During the Civil War* (New York: Oxford University Press, 2007). See also the carefully researched exhibition describing blacks present in Lee's army at the end of the war at Appomattox Court House National Historic Park website: www.nps.gov/apco/black-soldiers.htm.

9. Douglas Southall Freeman, *R. E. Lee: A Biography*, 4 vols. (New York: Scribners, 1934–35), 4:120–23; Edward P. Alexander, *Fighting for the Confederacy: The Personal Recollections of General Edward Porter Alexander*, ed. Gary W. Gallagher (Chapel Hill: University of North Carolina Press, 1998), 531–33. See Paul D. Escott, *Military Necessity: Civil-Military Relations in the Confederacy* (Westport, CT: Praeger Security International, 2006), for a discussion of draft resistance, banditry, and military operations against them in the Confederacy. Lee's distrust of the use of Confederate partisan rangers developed earlier in the war. In early 1864 he wrote to Jefferson Davis complaining that some of Gen. John H. Morgan's rangers had encouraged the absconding of wounded soldiers from a military hospital in Richmond, and arguing that "if this conduct is allowed, that all discipline is destroyed & our armies will be ruined." He also supported the bill that abolished the partisan corps and returned them to the Regular Army. See Lee to Davis, January 20, 1864, in Freeman and McWhiney, eds., *Lee's Dispatches*, 131–33.

10. *Papers Relating to the Foreign Relations of the United States,* Part 1 (Washington: Government Printing Office, 1867), 130.

11. See Matthew Guterl, *American Mediterranean: Southern Slaveholders in the Age of Emancipation* (Cambridge: Harvard University Press, 2008), chaps. 3–5; Cyrus B. Dawsey and James M. Dawsey, eds., *The Confederados: Old South Immigrants in Brazil* (Tuscaloosa: University of Alabama Press, 1995); Andrew F. Rolle, *The Lost Cause: The Confederate Exodus to Mexico* (Norman: University of Oklahoma Press, 1965); Anthony Arthur, *General Jo. Shelby's March* (New York: Random House, 2010).

12. The flight of Jefferson Davis's government from Richmond in 1865 is depicted in vivid detail in William C. Davis, *An Honorable Defeat: The Last Days of the Confederate Government* (New York: Harcourt, 2001). Federal authorities imprisoned Davis because they believed that he must have had some role in Lincoln's assassination and would eventually be indicted, perhaps along with other coconspirators. This charge could not be sustained at the time (Davis was never indicted), or by historians more generally since then. See Edward Steers Jr., *Blood on the Moon: The Assassination of Abraham Lincoln* (Lexington: University Press of Kentucky, 2001).

13. The grand review was like no other victory parade in American history, certainly before the 1860s, and quite possibly since then. Cadets might visualize the grand review by imagining that it would take almost forty consecutive parades of the entire U.S. Corps of Cadets, one after another for two consecutive days, to equal the size of the Union's victory parade in 1865. James M. McPherson and James K. Hogue, *Ordeal by Fire: The Civil War and Reconstruction*, 4th ed. (Boston: McGraw-Hill, 2009), 523–24. For contemporary illustrations of the grand review, see the entire issue of *Harper's Weekly*, vol. 9, no. 441 (June 10, 1865): 353–68.

14. For over a century, the accepted figure of Civil War dead has been 258,000 Confederates and 362,000 Union soldiers, for an estimated total of 620,000—more than the combined total of all other American wars down to the present. These figures were originally compiled by officers

in the War Department, who recognized that they labored under the general problem of the inadequacies of nineteenth century military bureaucracies as well as the special problems created by the destruction, incompleteness, or absence of reliable Confederate records, particularly during the last year of the war. A recent (2011) sophisticated demographic analysis of mortality rates drawn from census data across the mid-nineteenth century has persuasively revised the total number of dead upward to a probable figure of 750,000—an increase of at least 20 percent. See J. David Hacker, "A Census-Based Count of the Civil War Dead," *Civil War History* 57, no. 4 (December 2011): 307–48. Hacker's methodology does not permit him to say with certainty whether these additional deaths were either Union or Confederate, but he reasons that the probability of a significant Confederate undercount is high for a host of plausible reasons. Hacker's assumptions, methodology, and findings will almost certainly be subjected to wide-ranging scholarly scrutiny and the prospect of additional revision, but that is itself an indication of the robust state of study and research of the Civil War in the midst of its sesquicentennial. See Stuart McConnell, *Glorious Contentment: The Grand Army of the Republic, 1865–1900* (Chapel Hill: University of North Carolina Press, 1992), on the primary Union veterans organization.

15. Freeman, *Lee,* 4:154–55.

16. Confederate military necessity was the mother of much invention. Rebel armies had simpler logistical organizations in part because they generally fought on Confederate territory. In comparison, Union armies had to construct much longer and more elaborate lines of supply and depots in order to invade and then occupy the vast expanse of the Confederate States of America. Nevertheless, the breadth and depth of Confederate economic mobilization, however ramshackle it may seem in retrospect, still proved sufficient to keep their armies supplied with food, ammunition, weapons, horses, and military provisions until the last months of the war. See Frank Vandiver, *Ploughshares into Swords: Josiah Gorgas and Confederate Ordnance* (Austin: University of Texas Press, 1952), and Harold S. Wilson, *Confederate Industry: Manufacturers and Quartermasters in the Civil War* (Jackson: University Press of Mississippi, 2002). For additional insight into the creation of a proto–military-industrial complex in one state, see Chad Morgan, *Planters' Progress: Modernizing Confederate Georgia* (Gainesville: University Press of Florida, 2005).

17. Richard N. Current, "God and the Strongest Battalions," in David H. Donald, ed., *Why the North Won the Civil War* (Baton Rouge: Louisiana State University Press, 1960), 3–22.

18. "Men at War: An Interview with Shelby Foote," in Geoffrey C. Ward with Ric Burns and Ken Burns, *The Civil War* (New York: Alfred A. Knopf, 1990), 272.

19. John Keegan, *The American Civil War: A Military History* (New York: Alfred A. Knopf, 2009), 364.

20. Anne Sarah Rubin, "Seventy-six and Sixty-one: Confederates Remember the American Revolution," in *Where These Memories Grow: History, Memory, and Southern Identity,* ed. W. Fitzhugh Brundage (Chapel Hill: University of North Carolina Press, 2000), 85–105; Emory Thomas, "Jefferson Davis and the American Revolutionary Tradition," *Journal of the Illinois State Historical Society* 70 (February 1977): 2–9.

21. Douglas Southall Freeman, Lee's meticulous biographer, established that the draft of the 1862 conscription bill originated in Lee's office while he was Davis's personal military adviser, before Davis appointed him commander of the Army of Northern Virginia in April 1862. See Freeman, *Lee,* 2:25–29. According to Davis's biographer, "Davis acted both boldly and timidly" on the crucial issue of conscription; William J. Cooper Jr., *Jefferson Davis, American* (New York: Alfred A. Knopf, 2000), 384–85. Cooper also noted that the Confederate Congress (which, unlike the Union Congress, had no organized political parties) passed the draft bill by a two-to-one margin in the House and a four-to-one margin in the Senate. However unpopular conscription later became, most Confederate leaders at the time accepted it as a "military necessity." Upon secession, Confederate politicians abandoned antebellum party affiliations, but what ensued was a growing factionalism within the Confederate Congress divided into

pro- and anti-Davis camps. On this curious form of "antipolitics," see especially George C. Rable, *The Confederate Republic: A Revolution Against Politics* (Chapel Hill: University of North Carolina Press, 1994). For additional views that emphasize the impact of southern internal political divisions, see William W. Freehling, *The South vs. The South: How Anti-Confederate Southerners Shaped the Course of the Civil War* (New York: Oxford University Press, 2001); Richard Beringer et al., *Why the South Lost the Civil War* (Athens, GA: University of Georgia Press, 1986); and Escott, *Military Necessity*.

22. Frank L. Owsley, *State Rights in the Confederacy* (Chicago: University of Chicago Press, 1925).

23. Steven Hahn, *The Roots of Southern Populism: Yeoman Farmers and the Transformation of the Georgia Upcountry, 1850–1890* (New York: Oxford University Press, 1983).

24. Ira Berlin et al., *Slaves No More: Three Essays on Emancipation and the Civil War* (New York: Cambridge University Press, 1992). See also Joe Glatthaar, "Black Glory: The African-American Role in Union Victory," in Gabor Boritt, ed., *Why the Confederacy Lost* (New York: Oxford University Press, 1992), 133–62. On the complex dynamic of changing race relations within the Confederacy during the war, see Clarence Mohr, *On the Threshold of Freedom: Masters and Slaves in Civil War Georgia* (Athens, GA: University of Georgia Press, 1986).

25. Drew Gilpin Faust, "Altars of Sacrifice: Confederate Women and the Narratives of War," *Journal of American History* 76 (March 1990): 1228. For a more recent version of this argument that combines a critique of the impacts of race and gender, see Stephanie McCurry, *Confederate Reckoning: Power and Politics in the Civil War South* (Cambridge, MA: Harvard University Press, 2012). For women in the Confederacy more generally, see George Rable, *Civil Wars: Women and the Crisis of Southern Nationalism* (Urbana: University of Illinois Press, 1989).

26. See especially the classic account of the opening crisis of the Union in William A. Swanberg, *First Blood: The Story of Fort Sumter* (New York: Scribner, 1957). Swanberg's day-by-day account illustrates not only the inherited paralysis of the last days of the James Buchanan administration, but also the turmoil that Lincoln encountered within his own cabinet, leaders of Congress, and his principal military adviser, Gen. Winfield Scott, in making vital decisions that would shape the war and public opinion at home and abroad.

27. Conscripts provided only 2 percent, and substitutes 6 percent, or a total of 8 percent (168,000), of all the 2.1 million Union troops enlisted during the war. In stark contrast, conscripts provided 21 percent (210,000) of the Confederacy's estimated one million troops. As the war progressed, the Confederacy expanded the draft age, eliminated exemptions, and banned substitutions. See James W. Tollefson, "Draft Resistance and Evasion," in John Whiteclay Chambers, *The Oxford Companion to American Military History* (New York: Oxford University Press, 1999), 180–82.

28. James M. McPherson, *Battle Cry of Freedom: The Civil War Era* (New York: Oxford University Press, 1988), 608–9.

29. Iver Bernstein, *The New York City Draft Riots: Their Significance for American Society and Politics in the Age of the Civil War* (New York: Oxford University Press, 1990). On the larger issues connecting draft riots to labor unrest in the North, see Phillip Shaw Paludan, *"A People's Contest": The Union and the Civil War, 1861–1865* (New York: Harper & Row), 170–97. Vehement opposition to the draft formed immediately during debate over the bill in Congress and then coalesced at state and national levels with politicians identified as Peace Democrats, also known as Copperheads, for the remainder of the war. Many Peace Democrats were opposed to emancipation as well. For a fuller discussion of internal political opposition in the Union, see Jennifer L. Weber, *Copperheads: The Rise and Fall of Lincoln's Opponents in the North* (New York: Oxford University Press, 2006).

30. Gary W. Gallagher, *The Confederate War: How Popular Will, Nationalism, and Military Strategy Could Not Stave Off Defeat* (Cambridge, MA: Harvard University Press, 1999). Another recent historian of the Army of Northern Virginia agreed that Lee "came close to convincing the Union to give up the fight." See Glatthaar, *General Lee's Army*, xv.

31. For a well-documented and judicious biography of Davis that focuses on his leadership of the Confederacy, see William J. Cooper, *Jefferson Davis, American* (New York: Alfred A. Knopf, 2000). Several historians have suggested that Davis did not manage to strike an effective balance between market and state forces, or public and private enterprise, in the Confederate mobilization and resource management. See Escott, *Military Necessity*, and Paul A. C. Koistinen, *Beating Plowshares into Swords: The Political Economy of American Warfare, 1606–1865* (Lawrence: University Press of Kansas, 1996).

32. The historical literature devoted to Abraham Lincoln is massive and, even more than that of Jefferson Davis, of highly variable quality. A well-researched and written scholarly recent one-volume biography is David H. Donald, *Lincoln* (New York: Simon & Schuster, 1995). This author, however, differs with one of Donald's key conclusions: namely, that Lincoln had an essentially passive personality. Rather, the evidence suggests that Lincoln possessed an extraordinarily keen sense of political timing and the nerve to wait until the moment to act was ripe, regardless of the pressures exerted by friends or rivals in the midst of crisis. These were qualities that he shared with the president who presided over the American war effort in World War II, Franklin D. Roosevelt. For brief essays covering key aspects of Lincoln's leadership in the Civil War era, including his rhetoric, see James M. McPherson, *Abraham Lincoln and the Second American Revolution* (New York: Oxford University Press, 1991). Many historians have commented on Lincoln's fascination with technology in general and the telegraph in particular, but see especially Tom Wheeler, *Mr. Lincoln's T-Mails: How Abraham Lincoln Used the Telegraph to Win the Civil War* (New York: HarperBusiness, 2008). Wheeler points out that Lincoln dispatched nearly a thousand telegrams during four years of war, or roughly one per day. He argues that Lincoln not only mastered this distinctive nineteenth-century method of long-distance communication, but also suggests that the mechanics of telegraphy influenced his economical rhetorical style. On the power of Lincoln's rhetoric in set-piece speeches, see Garry Wills, *Lincoln at Gettysburg: The Words That Remade America* (New York: Simon & Schuster, 1992).

33. "Like Napoleon himself, with his passion for the strategy of annihilation and the climactic, decisive battle as its expression, he [Lee] destroyed in the end not the enemy armies, but his own," in Russell F. Weigley, *The American Way of War: A History of United States Military Strategy and Policy* (Bloomington: Indiana University Press, 1973), 127. The most aggressive critique of Lee's generalship is in Grady P. McWhiney and Perry Jamieson, *Attack and Die! Civil War Military Tactics and the Southern Heritage* (Tuscaloosa: University of Alabama Press, 1984), which also presents the strongest argument for the defensive power of the rifle musket as a reason for the indecisiveness of Civil War battles. For a response to Weigley and other military historians critical of Lee's generalship, see Gary W. Gallagher, *Lee and His Army in Confederate History* (Chapel Hill: University of North Carolina Press, 2001).

34. Lincoln quoted in William Henry Wadsworth to Samuel L. M. Barlow, December 16, 1862, Barlow Papers, Huntington Library, San Marino, CA.

35. It is impossible for a historian to *prove* that something that did not happen, like the defeat of the Union or Lincoln's loss of power in a parliamentary vote of no confidence, *might* have happened. Used with due care, counterfactual and comparative history scenarios can provide points of reference for considering how likely it was for a different outcome to have possibly happened. In this respect, counterfactual history is a sort of literary analogy to wargames and staff rides, which almost always seek to uncover the reversibility of contingent decisions made by commanders in war. See, for example, James M. McPherson, "If the Lost Order Hadn't Been Lost: Robert E. Lee Humbles the Union, 1862," in Robert Cowley, *What Ifs? of American History: Eminent Historians Imagine What Might Have Been* (New York: Berkeley Books, 2003). McPherson argues that, absent the lost order before Antietam, Lee could have decisively defeated McClellan and consequently Lincoln would have been forced to accept an armistice. For a longer counterfactual treatment of the possible mechanics and potential consequences of Confederate victory by a veteran economic historian, see Roger L. Ransom, *The Confederate*

States of America: What Might Have Been (New York: W. W. Norton, 2005). In his opening prologue, Ransom argues, "The 'might-have-beens' of history are not simply idle conjectures; they are an essential part of the historical narrative."

36. Mark Grimsley, *"The Hard Hand of War": Union Military Policy Toward Southern Civilians, 1861–1865* (New York: Cambridge University Press, 1997). Grimsley's careful study of the progression of Union policy during the war has gone far toward demolishing the myth that Yankee barbarians indiscriminately plundered and destroyed the South and everything in their way. See also Glatthaar, *The March to the Sea and Beyond*.

37. See Russell F. Weigley's chapter, "A Strategy of Annihilation: U.S. Grant and the Union," in Weigley, *The American Way of War*, 128–52.

38. Stephen E. Ambrose, *Halleck: Lincoln's Chief of Staff* (Baton Rouge: Louisiana State University Press, 1996), and John F. Marszalek, *Commander of All Lincoln's Armies: A Life of General Henry W. Halleck* (Boston: Harvard University Press, 2004). Halleck's ability as chief of staff was debatable, but Davis had no equivalent subordinate to help coordinate military operations across a half continent.

39. For a biography of Meigs, see Russell F. Weigley, *Quartermaster General of the Union Army: A Biography of Montgomery C. Meigs* (New York: Columbia University Press, 1959). On the enormous expansion of the Quartermaster Department and its unprecedented network of military officials and civilian contractors, see Mark Wilson, *The Business of Civil War: Military Mobilization and the State, 1861–1865* (Baltimore: Johns Hopkins University Press, 2006), 1–2. For the quotation on the size and power of the Union war machine, see Bruce Porter, *War and the Rise of the State: The Military Foundations of Modern Politics* (New York: Free Press, 1994), 258.

40. "The aim of Napoleonic strategy was to bring about the threat or reality of the decisive battle." Peter Paret, "Napoleon and the Revolution in War," in Peter Paret, with Gordon A. Craig and Felix Gilbert, eds., *Makers of Modern Strategy: From Machiavelli to the Nuclear Age* (Princeton, NJ: Princeton University Press, 1986), 131.

41. Antebellum officers with the requisite intellect, education, and opportunity studied Napoleonic campaigns in considerable detail throughout the antebellum era. For example, Robert E. Lee had not been Mahan's student as a cadet, but he attended Mahan's lectures on Napoleon when he returned to West Point as superintendent from 1852 to 1855. While there, he also attended Mahan's meetings of his "Napoleon Club," at which a young George B. McClellan once delivered a paper (now apparently lost). Lee's fluency in the language also permitted him to read a number of military works on the Napoleonic wars in the original French, as is apparent from the list of books he checked out from the West Point Library while he was superintendent. See Freeman, *Lee*, 1:352–58. On the influence of Dennis Hart Mahan on the development of strategic thought in the antebellum army, see Weigley, *The American Way of War*, 77–91.

42. Careful readers of the previous chapter and this one may note that the authors do not fully agree on the impact that rifled muskets and cannon had on Civil War battles. Regardless of the specific reasons, the historical evidence shows that decisive battles were possible during the Napoleonic wars fought with Napoleonic-era weapons. Jena and Waterloo were two such examples, but there were a number of others that came close; see "Appendix I: Selected Battles 1792–1815" in Gunther E. Rothenberg, *The Art of Warfare in the Age of Napoleon* (Bloomington: Indiana University Press, 1980), 247–53. An analogous review of Civil War battles, however, fails to show another Jena or a Waterloo between 1861 and 1865, but not for lack of trying by Civil War generals who had been steeped in Napoleonic warfare and repeatedly struggled to achieve decisive battles. See, for instance, the table of battles at AmericanCivilWar.com (http://americancivilwar.com/cwstats.html).

The reasons for this failure may be subject for debate, but there is little doubt that the impact of repeated failure to achieve decisive victories made itself felt at the strategic level in the Civil War. Tactical failure forced repeated strategic reappraisals by both Union and Confederate policy makers. Hence their halting steps toward "total war."

43. Noah Brooks, *The Life of Lincoln,* vol. 8 of *The Writings of Abraham Lincoln,* ed. Arthur Brooks Lapsley (New York: G. P. Putnam's Sons, 1888), 439.

44. Historians disagree on whether the Civil War was a "total war" or a "modern war," terms whose very definitions are themselves subject to considerable debate. For an introduction to this debate, see the sharply opposing points of view of Mark E. Neely Jr., "Was the Civil War a Total War?" in Stig Förster and Jörg Nagler, eds., *On the Road to Total War: The American Civil War and the German Wars of Unification, 1861–1871* (Cambridge, UK: Cambridge University Press, 1997), 29–52, and James M. McPherson, "From Limited War to Total War in America," ibid., 283–94. For an even wider historical context, see Brian Holden Reid, *The American Civil War and the Wars of the Industrial Revolution* (London: Cassell, 1999). Reid analyzes the Crimean War (1854–56) along with the American Civil War and the German wars of unification (1862–71) as mid-nineteenth-century wars that all presented similar challenges stemming from the general advance of industrialization in Western Europe and North America. A still larger global historical context for an examination of the relationship between war and economic change in the mid-nineteenth century is provided by Paul Kennedy, *The Rise and Fall of the Great Powers: Economic Change and Military Conflict from 1500 to 2000* (New York: Random House, 1987), 178–82.

45. Abraham Lincoln, "Annual Message to Congress," December 6, 1864, in Roy P. Basler, ed. *Collected Works of Abraham Lincoln,* 8 vols. (New Brunswick, NJ: Rutgers University Press, 1953–1990), 8:137.

46. Philip H. Sheridan to John Rawlins [Grant's chief of staff], June 29, 1865, in Simon, ed., *Papers of Ulysses S. Grant*, 31 vols., vol. 15. Grant responded by recommending that Johnson send a general on leave to advise the Mexican government of Benito Juarez. See U. S. Grant to Andrew Johnson, July 15, 1866, in LeRoy P. Graf and Ralph W. Haskins, eds., *The Papers of Andrew Johnson*, 16 vols. (Knoxville, TN: University Press of Tennessee, 1967–2000), 8:410–11. On the French military campaign, see Jean Avenel, *La Campagne du Mexique* (Paris: Economica, 1996). A recent transnational interpretation of the interrelationship of the concurrent wars in Mexico and the United States is found in Patrick J. Kelly, "The American Crisis of the 1860s," *Journal of the Civil War Era* 2, no. 3 (September 2012): 337–68.

47. Remaining on postwar duty in Sheridan's army of occupation and observation was terrifically unpopular with soldiers and officers alike. Maj. Gen. George Armstrong Custer (USMA June 1861), the most famous "boy general" of the war, struggled with indiscipline that bordered on mutiny in volunteer regiments, especially the 2nd Wisconsin Cavalry, where several soldiers concocted a plot to ambush him. See Jeffrey D. Wert, *Custer: The Controversial Life of George Armstrong Custer* (New York: Simon & Schuster, 1996), 241. Maj. Gen. Godfrey Weitzel (USMA 1855), commander of the mostly African American XXV Corps, summed up the dire conditions in South Texas in a personal letter to Benjamin Butler, whom he hoped would intervene politically to have his command demobilized:

> All the officers, myself included, have had the bone break fever and many the chronic diarrhaea. The men are dying fast with scurvy and not a vegetable to be had. I have to-day nearly 2500 cases of scurvy in the corps . . .
>
> I often think it a duty to myself to go home. I have served Uncle Sam long enough in God-forsaken countries and climes.

> Letter, Major General Godfrey Weitzel to [former Maj. Gen.] Benjamin F. Butler, August 14, 1865, Brownsville, TX, Benjamin Butler Papers, Library of Congress.
> See Gerald F. Linderman, *Embattled Courage: The Experience of Combat in the American Civil War* (New York: Free Press, 1987), and the somewhat controversial Eric T. Dean Jr., *Shook over Hell: Post-Traumatic Stress, Vietnam, and the Civil War* (Cambridge, MA: Harvard University Press, 1997), on some of the legacies of the war for veterans.

48. President Johnson's emphasis on the connection between reducing the national debt and reducing the size of the army and navy can be seen in the proximity of his discussion of the

two issues in his 1866 annual message to Congress. See Andrew Johnson, "Annual Message to Congress," December 3, 1866, in *Papers of Andrew Johnson*, 11:508–9, or online via the *American Presidency Project*, www.presidency.ucsb.edu/ws/?pid=29508. For background on debates over the size of the postbellum army, see Russell F. Weigley, *History of the United States Army* (New York: Macmillan, 1967), 262. For a year-by-year breakdown of the overall end strength of the U.S. Army that illustrates the rapidity of demobilization, see ibid., "Appendix, Strength of the Active Army Since 1789," 566–69. For a brief general discussion of the ballooning of the national debt, innovations in national finance by the federal government, and the Civil War's role in bringing about the Panic of 1873, see McPherson and Hogue, *Ordeal by Fire*, 4th ed., 222–26, 642–43. For a sophisticated argument that the Civil War increased the power of the national state, see Richard F. Bensel, *Yankee Leviathan: The Origins of Central State Authority in America, 1859–1877* (Cambridge, UK: Cambridge University Press, 1990).

49. Dan C. Carter, *When the War Was Over: The Failure of Self-Reconstruction in the South, 1865–1867* (Baton Rouge: Louisiana State University Press, 1985); George C. Rable, *But There Was No Peace: The Role of Violence in the Politics of Reconstruction* (Athens: University of Georgia Press, 1984). For an overview of this novel federal agency and the role that army officers played in it, see Paul A. Cimbala and Randall Miller, eds., *The Freedmen's Bureau and Reconstruction* (New York: Fordham University Press, 1999). Joseph G. Dawson, *Army Generals and Reconstruction: Louisiana, 1862–1877* (Baton Rouge: Louisiana State University Press, 1982), profiles each of the major military commanders in one southern state and their attitudes toward Reconstruction. William L. Richter, *The Army in Texas During Reconstruction, 1865–1870* (College Station: Texas A&M University Press, 1987), provides another state-level study. For an excellent selection of primary sources on the subject, see Ira Berlin et al., eds., *Free at Last: A Documentary History of Slavery, Freedom, and the Civil War* (New York: New Press, 1992).

50. For further discussion of the development of Johnson's Reconstruction policy, see Eric L. McKitrick, *Andrew Johnson and Reconstruction* (Chicago: University of Chicago Press, 1960). On the enactment of the first two military reconstruction acts, see McPherson and Hogue, *Ordeal by Fire*, 4th ed., 563–67. For the full text of Johnson's veto of the bill, see Andrew Johnson, "Veto of the First Military Reconstruction Act," March 2, 1867, in *Papers of Andrew Johnson*, 12:82–94.

51. See Ulysses S. Grant to Philip H. Sheridan, October 12, 1866, in *Grant Papers*, 16, 30–31; and Ulysses S. Grant to William T. Sherman, October 18, 1866, ibid., 16:337–38. See also Harold M. Hyman, "Stanton and Grant: A Consideration of the Army's Role in the Events Leading to Impeachment," *American Historical Review* 66, no. 1 (October 1960): 85–100.

52. Congressional Republicans passed the Tenure of Office Act in March 1867 specifically to prevent Johnson from firing Republican officials appointed by Lincoln who they believed were carrying out their vision of a transformed South after the war. The constitutionality of the act was never tested. Secretary of War Stanton, although a Democrat before the war, had become a bitter enemy of Johnson over Reconstruction policy and refused Johnson's request to resign. Grant advised the president not to fire Stanton, but Johnson insisted and then asked the popular war hero to serve as Stanton's successor on an interim basis while retaining his position as commanding general of the U.S. Army beginning in August 1867. See McPherson and Hogue, *Ordeal by Fire*, 4th ed., 566–67. For the text of Johnson's veto of the bill, see Andrew Johnson, "Veto of the Tenure of Office Act," March 2, 1867, in *Papers of Andrew Johnson*, 12:95–96.

53. An extensive and careful reconsideration of the evolution of General Grant's contentious relationship with President Johnson and his decision to run for president is found in Brooks Simpson, *Let Us Have Peace: Ulysses S. Grant and the Politics of War and Reconstruction, 1861–1868* (Chapel Hill: University of North Carolina Press, 1991).

54. The composition of the Supreme Court changed dramatically during Lincoln's presidency. Chief Justice Roger B. Taney, the architect of the infamous 1857 *Dred Scott* decision, which helped ignite the sectional crisis by repudiating the Missouri Compromise, died in 1864. Lincoln appointed former Treasury Secretary Salmon P. Chase to succeed Taney. Chase, who had

been Lincoln's rival for the Republican presidential nomination in 1860, held strong abolitionist views and his appointment was widely understood to be a gesture to the radicals, who sought to repudiate a number of Taney's decisions. Lincoln also appointed four other known Republicans to be associate justices during the war, which gave Republicans a five-to-four majority against the four holdovers, all of whom had been appointed before the war by Democratic presidents. The Chase court played a crucial role in the politics of the Civil War and Reconstruction when it ruled secession unconstitutional in *Texas v. White* (1869), but it also created unresolved Reconstruction enforcement issues when it imposed limitations on the use of military tribunals in *ex parte Milligan* (1866). See Bernard Schwartz, *A History of the Supreme Court* (New York: Oxford University Press, 1993), 147–61.

55. McPherson and Hogue, *Ordeal by Fire*, 4th ed., 563–67, 579–84.

56. Ibid., 612–16. See also Gordon B. McKinney, *Southern Mountain Republicans, 1865–1900: Politics and the Appalachian Community* (Baton Rouge: Louisiana State University Press, 1978), and Richard H. Abbott, *The Republican Party and the South, 1855–1877: The First Southern Strategy* (Chapel Hill: University of North Carolina Press, 1986).

57. On the general historical problem of Klan violence in the post-Confederate South, see Foner, *Reconstruction*, 425–59. For an overview of South Carolina during Reconstruction see Richard Zuczek, *State of Rebellion: Reconstruction in South Carolina* (Columbia: University of South Carolina Press, 1996).

58. Lou Falkner Williams, *The Great South Carolina Ku Klux Klan Trials, 1871–1872* (Athens: University of Georgia Press, 1996), 49.

59. Merrill's counterinsurgency campaign against the South Carolina Klan still awaits a first-rate scholarly monograph. See Foner, *Reconstruction*, 458–59. U.S. Attorney General George A. Williams decided to discontinue or postpone most of the cases in 1873, despite Merrill's perceptive warning that "the blind unreasoning, bigoted hostility to the results of the war is only smothered not appeased or destroyed." Williams, *The Great South Carolina Ku Klux Klan Trials*, 123. Colonel Merrill was on detached duty with the War Department in Washington and therefore survived Custer's campaign with the 7th Cavalry that ended with the Battle of the Little Bighorn in 1876. For the testimony acquired in the pursuit of the Ku Klux Klan, see United States Congress, *Report of the Joint Select Committee to Inquire into the Condition of Affairs in the Late Insurrectionary States*, 13 vols., (Washington, D.C.: U.S. Government Printing Office, 1872).

60. *Report of the Joint Select Committee to Inquire into the Condition of Affairs in the Late Insurrectionary States* (Washington, D.C.: Government Printing Office, 1872), 45–46.

61. See Charles Lane, *The Day Freedom Died: The Colfax Massacre, the Supreme Court, and the Betrayal of Reconstruction* (New York: Henry Holt, 2008), and LeeAnna Keith, *The Colfax Massacre: The Untold Story of Black Power, White Terror, and the Death of Reconstruction* (New York: Oxford University Press, 2009). For a parish-by-parish breakdown of the rise of the White Leagues, see table 2.1 "Growth and Actions of the White Leagues in Louisiana, 1874," in James K. Hogue, *Uncivil War: Five New Orleans Street Battles in the Rise and Fall of Radical Reconstruction* (Baton Rouge: Louisiana State University Press, 2006), 198.

62. Accusations of massive electoral fraud, armed intimidation at the polls, and outright political violence were common in all of the ex-Confederate states during Reconstruction. The outcomes of the Louisiana state elections in 1872, 1874, 1876, and 1878 were contested by both sides before state returning boards as well as congressional investigating committees, whose members could not agree on who won the elections either. White Leaguers justified their coup against the Republican governor in 1874 because they argued that he was a "usurper" who had not been legally elected to the office. See Hogue, *Uncivil War*, 116–43. For Governor Kellogg's own testimony on his election before a congressional investigating committee, see Testimony, W. P. Kellogg, in U.S. House, *Condition of Affairs in the Southern States*, 43rd Congress, 2nd session, 1875, House Report No. 261, 242–68. The governor installed by the White Leagues was Davidson B. Penn, former Confederate colonel and commander of the 7th Louisiana at the Battle of Gettysburg. Penn had run for lieutenant governor in 1874 alongside John O. McEnery,

another former Confederate officer. Both men declined to testify before the investigating committee, probably because they feared they would be prosecuted under the Enforcement Act of 1871.

63. The army restored the Republican governor, William Pitt Kellogg, to office in New Orleans after the street battle of 1874, but White League seizure of power in rural parishes shifted the electoral balance in the Louisiana House against returning Republicans in the November 1874 legislative elections. When the new session of the legislature met in January 1875, Republicans and White League–backed Democrats each held 53 seats, with five seats too uncertain to determine which candidate had won. The incoming House therefore would have to determine who had won those seats—and with them which party would elect the incoming Speaker and control the Louisiana House during the new session. Hence the high stakes and brawl on the floor of the Louisiana House on January 5, 1875. For further details on the White League insurgency of 1873–74, see Hogue, *Uncivil War,* 144–59. For the full text of Sheridan's "banditti" telegram, as it became known, see Telegram, General P. H. Sheridan to Secretary of War W. W. Belknap, January 5, 1875, Records Group 94, Records of the Adjutant General's Office, 1780–1917, National Archives, Washington, D.C.

The term *banditti* came from the Italian term for "bandits." After the unification of Italy in the 1860s, Piedmontese military regiments hunted down outlaws from southern Italy and Sicily for several decades and summarily executed them without recourse to civil trials. The term became popular in the postwar army in the United States where it was used to describe both Indians and desperadoes in the West as those actions cast them outside the law. Hence Sheridan's usage. A detailed after-action report of the events in New Orleans can be found in the papers of the regimental commander of troops assigned the task of securing the Louisiana statehouse. See *Official Report of Colonel Phillipe Regis de Trobriand, January 6, 1875*, Phillipe Regis De Trobriand Papers, United States Military Academy Library Special Collections, West Point, New York.

Colonel de Trobriand had a colorful military career. Born in France, he was the son of one of Napoleon's generals and was educated in French military schools, but emigrated to the United States before the Civil War. He rose to major general of volunteers during the war and is best known for the steady command of his brigade in the fierce fighting at the Wheatfield on the second day of the Battle of Gettysburg. After the war, he was selected for a regular commission as a colonel in the Regular Army and became commander of the 13th U.S. Infantry Regiment.

64. Senator Carl Schurz, "Military Interference in Louisiana," Speech in the United States Senate, January 11, 1875, in Frederic Bancroft, ed., *Speeches, Correspondence and Political Papers of Carl Schurz*, 3 vols. (New York: G. P. Putnam's Sons, 1913), 3:123–26. Senator Schurz's accusations that Grant had endangered democratic government were enhanced by his own military credentials. Schurz had fought against the Prussian Army in the revolution of 1848 and subsequently became a major general of volunteers in the Civil War, commanding many German-speaking soldiers in the Union army. After the war, he was the first German-American to serve as a U.S. senator and cabinet member. On the other hand, Thomas Jefferson had declared counties violating the Embargo Act along the Canadian border in rebellion in 1808, and George Washington had led troops to repress the Whiskey Rebellion in 1794. An 1807 law authorized the use of federal military forces against rebellion (2 *Stat.* 445–46).

65. Gretchen Ritter, *Goldbugs and Greenbacks: The Antimonopoly Tradition and the Politics of Finance in America, 1865–1896* (Cambridge, UK: Cambridge University Press, 1999), and Foner, *Reconstruction,* 512–24.

66. Nicholas Lemann, *Redemption: The Last Battle of the Civil War* (New York: Farrar, Straus & Giroux, 2006), and William C. Harris, *The Day of the Carpetbagger: Republican Reconstruction in Mississippi* (Baton Rouge: Louisiana State University Press, 1979).

67. A recent historical study of the election is Michael F. Holt, *By One Vote: The Disputed Presidential Election of 1876* (Lawrence: University Press of Kansas, 2008). In a much-disputed but

now classic account of the inner dealmaking that attended the resolution of the crisis, C. Vann Woodward, *Reunion and Reaction: The Compromise of 1877 and the End of Reconstruction* (New York: Oxford University Press, 1991), contended that the critical aspect of the Compromise of 1877 was sectional reconciliation based upon shared economic interests between northern and southern business elites.

68. Rod Andrew Jr., *Wade Hampton: Confederate Warrior to Southern Redeemer* (Chapel Hill: University of North Carolina Press, 2008); Jerry Lee West, *The Bloody South Carolina Election of 1876: Wade Hampton III, The Red Shirt Campaign for Governor and the End of Reconstruction* (Jefferson, NC: McFarland & Co., 2011).

69. For additional context on the army's post–Civil War constabulary duties, see Andrew J. Birtle, *U.S. Army Counterinsurgency and Contingency Operations Doctrine, 1860–1941* (Washington, D.C.: U.S. Army Center of Military History, 1998). See also Jerry M. Cooper, "Federal Military Intervention in Domestic Disorders," in Richard H. Kohn, ed., *The United States Military Under the Constitution of the United States, 1789–1989* (New York: New York University Press, 1991).

70. See especially the class-by-class breakdown of Union and Confederate generals from the U.S. Military Academy at http://sunsite.utk.edu/civil-war/wpclasses.html.

71. Ulysses S. Grant, *Memoirs and Selected Letters: Personal Memoirs of U.S. Grant, Selected Letters, 1839–1865* (New York: Library of America, 1990); idem, *Personal Memoirs of U.S. Grant*, 2 vols. (New York: Charles L. Webster, 1885), also available as a free Librivox audiobook; William T. Sherman, *Memoirs of General W. T. Sherman* (New York: D. Appleton, 1886–89), vol. 1.

72. Theodore J. Crackel, *West Point: A Bicentennial History* (Lawrence: University Press of Kansas, 2002), chs. 5–6; Morrison, *"Best School in the World"*; and, more specifically, James Tyrus Seidule, "'Treason Is Treason': Civil War Memory at West Point, 1861–1902," *Journal of Military History* 76 (April 2012): 427–52. For a new and provocative interpretation of the role played by West Pointers in the Civil War, see Wayne Wie-siang Hsieh, *West Pointers and the Civil War: The Old Army in War and Peace* (Chapel Hill: University of North Carolina Press, 2009). For more on the multiple roles that West Point and graduates of West Point played in American history, see the Smithsonian Institute's online exhibit, "West Point in the Making of America," http://americanhistory.si.edu/westpoint/history_1.html.

73. Oliver Wendell Holmes Jr., Memorial Day speech to John Sedgwick Post No. 4, Grand Army of the Republic, May 30, 1884, Keene, NH. Publically expressed memories of the Civil War, their contestation between and within the sections, and their political uses during the late nineteenth century are examined in David W. Blight, *Race and Reunion: The Civil War in American Memory* (Cambridge, MA: Harvard University Press, 2001), and Caroline E. Janney, *Remembering the Civil War: Reunion and the Limits of Reconciliation* (Chapel Hill: University of North Carolina Press, 2013).

74. For the post-Reconstruction "New South," see the still-classic C. Vann Woodward, *The Origins of the New South, 1877–1913* (Baton Rouge: Louisiana State University Press, 1951), and Edward L. Ayers, *The Promise of the New South: Life After Reconstruction* (New York: Oxford University Press, 1992).

INTRODUCTION

1. "Much of the History We Teach Was Made by the People We Taught," United States Military Academy [hereafter USMA] History Department.
2. Brady National Photographic Art Gallery (Washington, DC), *Portrait of Maj. Gen. Emory Upton, Officer of the Federal Army,* Library of Congress.
3. *The Prince of Wales at West Point—Evening Parade—Battalion Passing in Review. Double-Quick Time. October, 1860,* courtesy of the Anne S. K. Brown Military Collection, Brown University Library.
4. *U. S. Grant Oath of Allegiance,* USMA Archives.
5. *D. D. Eisenhower Oath of Allegiance,* USMA Archives.
6. Coupil & Cie (publisher), *Confederate Commanders Trained at the U.S. Military Academy, West Point,* courtesy of the Anne S. K. Brown Military Collection, Brown University Library.
7. *Cadets in Law and History Class,* Stockbridge Collection, Special Collections, USMA Library.
8. *View of Ballroom, Looking Northeast—U.S. Military Academy, Cullum Memorial Hall, West Point, Orange County, NY,* Library of Congress.
9. Insert to "The campaign and battle of Gettysburg," by G. J. Fiebeger, from the book collection of George S. Patton, USMA Archives.
10. *The Panorama of Military History,* Mess Hall Mural, photo by John Pellino/West Point Multimedia.
11. *Our Banner in the Sky* (oil on canvas), Frederic Edwin Church (1826–1900), private collection, photo © Christie's Images, The Bridgeman Art Library.
12. *West Point Cadets,* photo by John Pellino/West Point Multimedia.

CHAPTER 1

13. The United States in 1848, Rowan Technology Solutions, 2014.
    Sources: Territorial Acquisitions, United States Territorial Acquisitions, 1783–1917, in *National Atlas of the United States;* Minnesota Population Center, National Historical Geographic Information System: Version 2.0, Minneapolis, Minn.: University of Minnesota, 2011.
14. The Compromise of 1850, Rowan Technology Solutions, 2014.
    Sources: Territorial Acquisitions, United States Territorial Acquisitions, 1783–1917, in *National Atlas of the United States;* Minnesota Population Center, National Historical Geographic Information System: Version 2.0, Minneapolis, Minn.: University of Minnesota, 2011.
15. *A slave family in a Georgia cotton field, c.1860* (b/w photo, American photographer, 19th century), private collection, Peter Newark American Pictures, The Bridgeman Art Library.
16. A. S. Seer's Union Square Print, *George Peck's grand revival of Stetson's Uncle Tom's cabin, booked by Klaw & Erlanger,* Library of Congress.
17. Kansas-Nebraska Act, Rowan Technology Solutions, 2014.
    Source: Minnesota Population Center, National Historical Geographic Information System: Version 2.0, Minneapolis, Minn.: University of Minnesota, 2011.
18. *Stephen A. Douglas,* Library of Congress.
19. John L. Magee, *Forcing slavery down the throat of a Freesoiler,* Library of Congress.
20. Expansion of Slavery, 1790–1860, Rowan Technology Solutions, 2014.
    Source: Minnesota Population Center, National Historical Geographic Information System: Version 2.0, Minneapolis, Minn.: University of Minnesota, 2011.
21. John Andrews, *Anthony Burns,* Library of Congress.
22. *American 'Know-Nothing' Party Cartoon, 1854* (engraving, American school, 19th century), private collection, Peter Newark American Pictures, the Bridgeman Art Library.
23. *Members of the anti-slavery Free soil Party, 1856* (b/w photo, American photographer, 19th century), private collection, Peter Newark American Pictures, the Bridgeman Art Library.
24. Thomas Hovenden, *The Last Moments of John Brown.*
25. Anthony Berger, *Abraham Lincoln, three-quarter length portrait, seated, facing right; hair parted on Lincoln's right side,* Library of Congress.
26. War Department, Office of the Chief Signal Officer, *Jefferson Davis, ca. 1860-ca. 1865,* National Archives and Records Administration.
27. *The Constitution of the Confederate States of America,* Duke University Libraries.
28. Waves of Secession, Rowan Technology Solutions, 2014.
    Source: Minnesota Population Center, National Historical Geographic Information System: Version 2.0, Minneapolis, Minn.: University of Minnesota, 2011.
29. *Telegram Announcing the Surrender of Fort Sumter* (1861), OurDocuments.gov.
30. *The Union Volunteer, pub. by Currier & Ives, 1861* (color litho, American school, 19th century), American Antiquarian Society, Worcester, Mass., the Bridgeman Art Library.
31. *Attention! Company!, recruiting broadside for New York 156th Infantry, 1862* (litho, American school, 19th century), Gilder Lehrman Collection, New York, N.Y., the Bridgeman Art Library.
32. Morristown, Tennessee: Neal & Roberts, 1861, *Freemen! Of Tennessee!* Rare Book and Special Collections Division, Library of Congress.

IMAGE CREDITS

33. *Federal recruiting poster for 69th Regiment, appealing to Irish immigrants* (color litho, American school, 19th century), private collection, Peter Newark American Pictures, the Bridgeman Art Library.

34. *Drum of the Gray Reserves, First Regiment Infantry* (wood, American School, 19th century), First Regiment Infantry Armory, Philadelphia, Pa., photo © Civil War Archive, the Bridgeman Art Library.

35. P. S. Duval & Son, *Buildings of the Great Central Fair, in aid of the U.S. Sanitary Commission, Logan Square, Philadelphia, June 1864,* Library of Congress.

36. Distribution of White Males, Ages 15–39, Rowan Technology Solutions, 2014.
    Source: Minnesota Population Center, National Historical Geographic Information System: Version 2.0, Minneapolis, Minn.: University of Minnesota, 2011.

37. Value of Crop Production, Rowan Technology Solutions, 2014.
    Source: Minnesota Population Center, National Historical Geographic Information System: Version 2.0, Minneapolis, Minn.: University of Minnesota, 2011.

38. Soldier from the Garibaldi Guards of New Orleans, 1861, Chase Stone, 2014.

39. Unknown Artist, *Zouave Regiment Marching Up Pennsylvania Ave., Washington, D.C., 1861,* oil on canvas, 43 × 53½ inches, courtesy of the West Point Museum Collection, United States Military Academy.

40. Edwin Forbes, *The "reliable contraband,"* Library of Congress.

41. Thomas Nast, *King Cotton,* Library of Congress.

42. Charles Joseph Minard, *Carte figurative et approximative des quantités de coton brut importées en Europe en 1858, en 1864 et en 1865,* Library of Congress.

43. *Battle of Wilson's Creek,* 1893 (color litho), Kurz and Allison (fl.1880–98), Gilder Lehrman Collection, New York, N.Y., the Bridgeman Art Library.

44. *Massachusetts militia passing through Baltimore, Pennsylvania, 1861* (litho), Felix Octavius Carr Darley (1822–88) (after), private collection, Ken Welsh, the Bridgeman Art Library.

45. Frank Leslie, 1861, *Landing of the 7th Regiment at the wharf of the Naval Academy, at Annapolis, Maryland,* courtesy of the Anne S. K. Brown Military Collection, Brown University Library.

46. William Smith Jewett, *John Charles Fremont.*

47. Thomas Butler Gunn, *Capture of secession varmints,* Library of Congress.

48. War Department, Office of the Chief Signal Officer, *General P. G. T. Beauregard, C.S.A, ca. 1860–ca. 1865,* National Archives and Records Administration.

49. J. B. Elliot, *Scott's Great Snake,* Library of Congress, American Memory Project.

50. First Bull Run Campaign, Rowan Technology Solutions, 2014.
    Sources: Railroads, Historical Geographical Information System: The 1861 Railroad System in America, University of Nebraska-Lincoln; military layer based on Frank Martini's map #3 Northern Virginia, 1861, First Bull Run Campaign, Situation 18 July 1861. USMA History Department.

51. Battle of First Bull Run—Order of Battle, Rowan Technology Solutions, 2014.
    Sources: National Park Service website, U.S. Department of the Interior, "Manassas National Battlefield Park—The Battle of First Manassas, Confederate order of battle," accessed April 24, 2014; U.S. War Department, *The War of the Rebellion: A Compilation of the Official Records of the Union and Confederate Armies* [hereafter *OR*], Series I, Volume II (U.S. Government Printing Office, 1891), 314–315.

52. Battle of First Bull Run, Rowan Technology Solutions, 2014.
    Source: Military layer based on Frank Martini's map #3b inset Centreville and Vicinity, 1861, Battle of First Bull Run, Situation 1400 Hours, 21 July 1861. USMA History Department.

53. *Pictorial War Record,* Stearns & Co., 1882, courtesy of the Anne S. K. Brown Military Collection, Brown University Library.

54. Campaign for Forts Henry and Donelson, Rowan Technology Solutions, 2014.
    Sources: Military layer based on Edward Krasnoborski's map #26 Henry and Donelson Campaign, Union Advance on Forts Henry and Donelson and Situation 14 February 1862. *The West Point Atlas of American Wars: Vol.1, 1689–1900* (New York: Praeger, 1959); Frank Martini's map #5 Henry-Donelson Vicinity, 1861, Henry and Donelson Campaign, Union Advance on Forts Henry and Donelson and Situation 14 February 1862. USMA History Department.

55. *Portrait of Admiral Andrew Hull Foote (1806–63)* (litho), Alonzo Chappel (1828–87) (after), private collection, Ken Welsh, The Bridgman Art Library.

56. Battle of Shiloh—Order of Battle, Rowan Technology Solutions, 2014.
    Sources: Civil War Trust website, "The Battle of Shiloh—Summary & Facts," accessed April 24, 2014; Jeffrey J. Gudmens, *Staff Ride Handbook for the Battle of Shiloh, 6–7 April 1862* (Fort Leavenworth, Kans: Combat Studies Institute Press, 2005); *OR*, Series I, Volume X, Part 1, 100–108; *OR*, Series I, Volume LII, Part 1, 26–29.

57. Advance to Shiloh, Rowan Technology Solutions, 2014.
    Source: Military layer based on Edward Krasnoborski's map #31 Shiloh Campaign, Union and Confederate Concentrations and Situation 29 March 1862. *The West Point Atlas of American Wars: Vol.1, 1689–1900.*

58. Battle of Shiloh, Morning, 6 April, Rowan Technology Solutions, 2014.
    Source: Military layer based on Frank Martini's map #8 Shiloh and Vicinity, 1861 Shiloh Campaign, Confederate Attack and Situation at End of the First Day, 6 April 1862. USMA History Department.

59. Battle of Shiloh, Evening, 6 April, Rowan Technology Solutions, 2014.
    Source: Military layer based on Frank Martini's map #8 Shiloh and Vicinity, 1861 Shiloh Campaign, Confederate Attack and Situation at End of the First Day, 6 April 1862. USMA History Department.

60. Battle of Shiloh, Morning, 7 April, Rowan Technology Solutions, 2014.

Source: Military layer based on Frank Martini's map #9 Shiloh and Vicinity, 1861 Shiloh Campaign, Confederate Attack and Situation at Close of the Second Day, 7 April 1862. USMA History Department.

61. Battle of Shiloh, Afternoon, 7 April, Rowan Technology Solutions, 2014.
    Source: Military layer based on Frank Martini's map #9 Shiloh and Vicinity, 1861 Shiloh Campaign, Situation at Close of the Second Day, 7 April 1862. USMA History Department.

62. *The Battle of Shiloh,* Ehrgott, Forbiger & Co., 1862, courtesy of the Anne S. K. Brown Military Collection, Brown University Library.

63. Thure de Thulstrup, *Battle of Shiloh,* Library of Congress.

CHAPTER 2

64. Principal Campaigns in the East, July-September 1863, Rowan Technology Solutions, 2014.
    Source: Military layer based on Frank Martini's map #1 Southeastern United States, 1860, Principal Campaigns of the American Civil War. USMA History Department.

65. William Sartain, *Joseph E. Johnson [i.e., Johnston],* Library of Congress.

66. Currier & Ives, *Southern "volunteers,"* Library of Congress.

67. J. D. Edwards, *Confederate camp, Warrington Navy Yard, Pensacola, Florida,* Library of Congress.

68. W. B. Cox, *The Heroes of Manassas,* c. 1865, oil on canvas, 18 × 24 inches, courtesy of the West Point Museum Collection, United States Military Academy. Photography: Sean T. Smith.

69. *Major Genl. McClellan,* Gibson & Co. (Cincinnati, Ohio), Library of Congress.

70. Edwin Forbes, *Light 12 pdr. Napoleon gun, brass, Rappahannock,* Library of Congress.

71. 39th New York, Chase Stone, 2014.

72. *Gen'l Geo. B. McClellan,* Library of Congress.

73. Thomas Worthington Whittredge, *Civil War Camp Scene at Portsmouth, Rhode Island,* 1861, oil on paper, 10 × 16 inches, courtesy of the West Point Museum Collection, United States Military Academy.

74. Alexander Gardner, *Antietam, Md. President Lincoln and Gen. George B. McClellan in the general's tent; another view,* Library of Congress.

75. Peninsular Campaign, June 1862, Rowan Technology Solutions, 2014.
    Source: Military layer based on map #11 Richmond and Peninsula, 1861, The Peninsular Campaign, March–July 1862. West Point Military Atlas, United States Military Academy.

76. Warden Wood, *U.S.S. Monitor and C.S.S. Virginia (The Monitor and The Merrimack),* undated, watercolor on board, 14½ × 20 inches, courtesy of the West Point Museum Collection, United States Military Academy. Photography: Sean T. Smith.

77. George N. Bernard, *Centreville, Virginia. Quaker gun,* Library of Congress.

78. *Union Mortar Battery Firing,* undated, William T. Trego, oil on canvas, 33 × 29 inches, courtesy of the West Point Museum Collection, United States Military Academy.

79. Thomas Jonathan ("Stonewall") Jackson, three-quarter length portrait, seated, Library of Congress.

80. Edwin Forbes, *The war in the Shenandoah Valley—burning the bridge near Mount Jackson, by order of the Rebel General,* Library of Congress.

81. Jackson's Valley Campaign, Rowan Technology Solutions, 2014.
    Source: Military layer based on Edward Krasnoborski's map #50 Jackson's Valley Campaign, Situations 3–17 April and 29 April 1862. *The West Point Atlas of American Wars: Vol.1, 1689–1900.*

82. Jackson's Valley Campaign, Rowan Technology Solutions, 2014.
    Source: Military layer based on Edward Krasnoborski's map #52 Jackson's Valley Campaign, Situations 29 May and 31 May 1862. *The West Point Atlas of American Wars: Vol.1, 1689–1900.*

83. Jackson's Valley Campaign, Rowan Technology Solutions, 2014.
    Source: Military layer based on Edward Krasnoborski's map #53 Jackson's Valley Campaign, Situations 29 May and 31 May 1862. *The West Point Atlas of American Wars: Vol.1, 1689–1900.*

84. *Little Mac's Union Squeeze,* Library of Congress.

85. Currier & Ives, *Genl. Meagher at the Battle of Fair Oaks, Va., June 1st 1862,* Library of Congress.

86. Julian Vannerson, *Portrait of Gen. Robert E. Lee, officer of the Confederate Army,* Library of Congress.

87. Matthew B. Brady, *Professor Lowe's military balloon near Gaines Mill, Virginia,* Library of Congress.

88. *J. E. B. Stuart leading his men on the famous four day ride through enemy territory in June 1862* (litho), Frank Vizetelly (1830–83), private collection, Peter Newark Military Pictures, the Bridgeman Art Library.

89. James F. Gibson, *White House Landing, Va. "White House on the Pamunkey," residence of Gen. W. H. F. Lee, and headquarters of Gen. George B. McClellan,* Library of Congress.

90. Alfred R. Waud, *After Gaines Mill Sunday June 29th 1862,* Library of Congress.

91. Ludwig Wilhelm Maurer, *The gunboat candidate at the Battle of Malvern Hill,* Library of Congress2.

92. James F. Gibson, *Savage Station, Va. Field hospital after the battle of June 27,* Library of Congress.

93. Currier & Ives, *The battle of Malvern Hill, Va. July 1st 1862,* Library of Congress.

94. Seven Days Battles—Order of Battle, Rowan Technology Solutions, 2014.
    Sources: Stephen W. Sears, *To the Gates of Richmond: The Peninsula Campaign* (New York: Ticknor and Fields, 1992), 195, 243–245; OR, Series I, Volume XI, Part 2, 21–37, 483–489.

95. Seven Days Battles, Rowan Technology Solutions, 2014.
    Sources: Military layer based on Edward Krasnoborski's maps #45a Peninsular Campaign, Battle of Mechanicsville, Situation Just Before Dark, 26 June 1862; #45b Peninsular Campaign, Battle of Gaines's Mill,

27 June 1862; #46a Peninsular Campaign, Situation Late 28 June 1862, During the Retreat to the James River; #46b Peninsular Campaign, Situation Late 29 June 1862, During the Retreat to the James River; #47a Peninsular Campaign, Battle of Frayser's Farm, Situation about Noon, 30 June 1862; #47b Peninsular Campaign, Battle of Malvern Hill, 1 July 1862. *The West Point Atlas of American Wars: Vol.1, 1689–1900.*

96. *Antietam, Md. President Lincoln with Gen. George B. McClellan and group of officers 1862* (photo), Universal History Archive/UIG, the Bridgeman Art Library.

97. James F. Gibson, *Cumberland Landing, Va. Group of "contrabands" at Foller's house,* Library of Congress.

98. *African American man, sitting outside a military camp tent,* Library of Congress.

99. J. A. Scholten, *Portrait of Maj. Gen. Henry W. Halleck, officer of the Federal Army,* Library of Congress.

100. Brady National Photographic Art Gallery (Washington, D.C.), *Portrait of Brig. Gen. John Pope, officer of the Federal Army (Maj. Gen. after Mar. 21, 1862),* Library of Congress.

101. Second Battle of Bull Run—Order of Battle, Rowan Technology Solutions, 2014.
Sources: Darrell L. Collins, *The Army of the Potomac: Order of Battle, 1861–1865, with Commanders, Strengths, Losses and More* (Jefferson, N.C.: McFarland & Company, 2013), 45–56; David J. Eicher, *The Longest Night: A Military History of the Civil War* (New York: Simon & Schuster, 2001), 327; National Parks Service website, U.S. Department of the Interior, "Confederate Order of Battle—Second Manassas—Manassas National Battlefield Park," accessed April 29, 2014; *OR,* Series I, Volume XII, Part 3, 581–588; Jennings Cropper Wise, *The Long Arm of Lee* (Lynchburg, Va.: J. P. Bell and Company, 1915), 259.

102. Second Bull Run Campaign, Rowan Technology Solutions, 2014.
Source: Military layer based on Frank Martini's map #12 Northern Virginia, 1861, Second Bull Run Campaign, Maneuvers Prior to Battle, 29–30 August 1862. USMA History Department.

103. Second Bull Run Campaign, Rowan Technology Solutions, 2014.
Source: Military layer based on Edward Krasnoborski's map #60 Second Bull Run Campaign, Situation at 5:30 PM, 28 August and Movements since Midnight, 27–28 August 1862. *The West Point Atlas of American Wars: Vol.1, 1689–1900.*

104. Battle of Second Bull Run, Rowan Technology Solutions, 2014.
Source: Based on Hal Jespersen, Second Battle of Bull Run, Actions Noon, August 29, 1862, www.cwmaps .com.

105. Battle of Second Bull Run, Rowan Technology Solutions, 2014.
Source: Based on Hal Jespersen, Second Battle of Bull Run, Actions 1500, August 30, 1862, www.cwmaps .com.

106. Battle of Second Bull Run, Rowan Technology Solutions, 2014.
Source: Based on Hal Jespersen, Second Battle of Bull Run, Actions 1700, August 30, 1862, www.cwmaps .com.

107. Edwin Forbes, *Officers and soldiers on the battlefield of the second Bull Run, recognizing the remains of their comrades,* Library of Congress.

108. *The rebel chivalry as the fancy of "My Maryland" painted them; as "My Maryland" found them,* Library of Congress

109. Antietam Campaign, Rowan Technology Solutions, 2014.
Source: Military layer based on Edward Krasnoborski's map #65a Antietam Campaign, Situation 7 September 1862. *The West Point Atlas of American Wars: Vol.1, 1689–1900.*

110. *The battle of South Mountain, MD. Sunday, Sept. 14, 1862,* Library of Congress.

111. David Hunter Strother, *The burning of the United States arsenal at Harper's Ferry, 10 P.M. April 18, 1861,* Library of Congress.

112. *Battle of Antietam,* undated, Julian Scott, oil on canvas, 39 × 51 inches, courtesy of the West Point Museum Collection, United States Military Academy.

113. Antietam Campaign, Rowan Technology Solutions, 2014.
Source: Military layer based on Edward Krasnoborski's map #65b Antietam Campaign, Situation on the Evening of 13 September 1862. *The West Point Atlas of American Wars: Vol.1, 1689–1900.*

114. Edwin Forbes, *Battle of Antietam, Maryland—Burnside's division carrying the bridge over the Antietam Creek, and storming the Rebel position, after a desperate conflict of four hours, Wednesday, September 17,* Library of Congress.

CHAPTER 3

115. Principal Campaigns in the East, December 1862–July 1863, Rowan Technology Solutions, 2014.
Source: Military layer based on Frank Martini's map #1 Southeastern United States, 1860, Principal Campaigns of the American Civil War. USMA History Department.

116. Currier & Ives, *John Bull makes a discovery,* Library of Congress.

117. John Tenniel, "Abe Lincoln's Last Card; Or, Rouge-et-Noir (Red and Black)," *Punch,* Volume 34, October 18, 1862, 161.

118. Edward Stauch, *Uncle Sam protecting his property against the encroachments of his cousin John,* Library of Congress.

119. G. W. Bromley & Co./Kimmel & Forster, *Political caricature. No. 4, The miscegenation ball,* Library of Congress.

120. *General M'Clellan Taking Leave of His Army,* Harper's, 1862, courtesy of the Anne S. K. Brown Military Collection, Brown University Library.

121. Brady National Photographic Art Gallery (Washington, D.C.), *Portrait of Maj. Gen. Ambrose E. Burnside, officer of the Federal Army,* Library of Congress.

122. Battle of Fredericksburg—Order of Battle, Rowan Technology Solutions, 2014.
Sources: Civil War Trust website, "The Battle of Fredericksburg—Summary and Facts." accessed April 29, 2014; G. F. R. Henderson, *The Campaign of Fredericksburg, Nov.-Dec. 1862* (London: Chatham, Gale & Polden, 1891), 14–15; *OR,* Series I, Volume XXI, Part 1, 48–61, 538–545.

123. Fredericksburg, Rowan Technology Solutions, 2014.
Source: Military layer based on Edward Krasnoborski's map #72a Fredericksburg Campaign, Situation Early 13 December 1862. *The West Point Atlas of American Wars: Vol.1, 1689–1900.*

124. Fredericksburg, Rowan Technology Solutions, 2014.
Source: Military layer based on Edward Krasnoborski's map #72b Fredericksburg Campaign, Situation about 1:00 PM, 13 December 1862. *The West Point Atlas of American Wars: Vol.1, 1689–1900.*

125. Fredericksburg, Rowan Technology Solutions, 2014.
Source: Military layer based on Edward Krasnoborski's map #73a Fredericksburg Campaign, Situation about 3:30 PM, 13 December 1862. *The West Point Atlas of American Wars: Vol.1, 1689–1900.*

126. Fredericksburg, Rowan Technology Solutions, 2014.
Source: Military layer based on Edward Krasnoborski's map #73b Fredericksburg Campaign, Situation about Dark, 13 December 1862. *The West Point Atlas of American Wars: Vol.1, 1689–1900.*

127. *American Civil War 1861–1865: Battle of Fredericksburg, Virginia, 11–15 December 1862. Army of the Potomac (Union) under Burnside crossing the Rappahannock, 13 December. Confederate victory under Lee.* Kurz & Allison, ca. 1888, Universal History Archive/UIG, the Bridgeman Art Library.

128. *Burial Scene after the Battle of Fredericksburg, 1862* (b/w photo), Mathew Brady (1823–96) & studio, private collection, Stapleton Collection, the Bridgeman Art Library.

129. *The Mud March,* undated, Giovanni Ponticelli, oil on canvas, 24¼ × 43½ inches, courtesy of the West Point Museum Collection, United States Military Academy.

130. 1st Texas, Chase Stone, 2014.

131. Julian Vannerson, *General Robert E. Lee, full-length portrait, standing, facing front, with left hand at waist, on sword, wearing military uniform,* Library of Congress.

132. *Hardtack, possibly from the Scottish fishing vessel 'Resolute,' 1864,* Vancouver Maritime Museum, Canada, the Bridgeman Art Library.

133. Edwin Forbes, *Culpepper [i.e., Culpeper], Va.—Stacking wheat,* Library of Congress.

134. *Richmond, Va. Damaged locomotives,* Library of Congress.

135. *A Confederate Scout of General Turner Ashby at the Valley near Luray and New Hacket* (oil on canvas), J. A. Collins (19th century), © Chicago History Museum, the Bridgeman Art Library.

136. L. E. Faber, *Major General Joseph Hooker (1815–1879, USMA 1837),* undated, oil on canvas, 72 × 47¾ inches, courtesy of the West Point Museum Collection, United States Military Academy. Photography: Sean T. Smith.

137. James Magee, *Civil War envelope showing Army of the Potomac, 6th Corps, 3rd Division, badge with blue cross,* Library of Congress.

138. *The stampede of the Eleventh Corps—Berry's corps checking the pursuit,* Library of Congress.

139. Currier & Ives, *Death of "Stonewall" Jackson,* Library of Congress.

140. Battle of Chancellorsville—Order of Battle, Rowan Technology Solutions, 2014.
Sources: Eicher, *The Longest Night,* 475, 488; *OR,* Series I, Volume XXV, Part 1, 156–170, 789–794.

141. Chancellorsville, Rowan Technology Solutions, 2014.
Source: Military layer based on Edward Krasnoborski's map #84 Chancellorsville Campaign, Situation Late 30 April 1863 and Movements since 27 April 1863. *The West Point Atlas of American Wars: Vol.1, 1689–1900.*

142. Chancellorsville, Rowan Technology Solutions, 2014.
Source: Military layer based on Edward Krasnoborski's map #87 Chancellorsville Campaign, Situation at 6:00 PM, 2 May 1863. *The West Point Atlas of American Wars: Vol.1, 1689–1900.*

143. Chancellorsville, Rowan Technology Solutions, 2014.
Source: Military layer based on Edward Krasnoborski's map #88 Chancellorsville Campaign, Situation Early 3 May 1863. *The West Point Atlas of American Wars: Vol.1, 1689–1900.*

144. Chancellorsville, Rowan Technology Solutions, 2014.
Source: Military layer based on Edward Krasnoborski's map #89 Chancellorsville Campaign, Battle of Salem Church, Situation at 4:00 PM, 3 May 1863. *The West Point Atlas of American Wars: Vol.1, 1689–1900.*

145. *Gen. Longstreet, C.S.A.,* Library of Congress.

146. Gettysburg Campaign, Rowan Technology Solutions, 2014.
Sources: Military layer based on Edward Krasnoborski's map #93a Gettysburg Campaign, Situation 9 June and 17 June 1863; map #93b Gettysburg Campaign, Situation 24 June 1863. *The West Point Atlas of American Wars: Vol.1, 1689–1900.*

147. *General "Jeb" Stuart, Confederate States of America, 1863,* National Archives and Records Administration.

148. T. Henry Smith, *George G. Meade (1815–1872, USMA 1835),* 1890, oil on canvas, 56½ × 40¼ inches, courtesy of the West Point Museum Collection, United States Military Academy. Photography: Sean T. Smith.

149. *Gettysburg, The First Day,* undated, James Walker, oil on canvas, 24 × 42 inches, courtesy of the West Point Museum Collection, United States Military Academy.

150. *Devil's Den, Gettysburg,* Library of Congress.

151. Alexander Gardner, *Gettysburg, Pa. Dead Confederate soldiers in the "slaughter pen" at the foot of Little Round Top,* Library of Congress.

152. Timothy H. O'Sullivan, *Gettysburg, Pennsylvania. View in the wheatfield opposite our extreme left,* Library of Congress.

153. Edwin Forbes, *Scene behind the breastworks on Culps Hill, morning of July 3rd 1862,* Library of Congress.

154. *General Pickett taking the order to charge from General Longstreet, Battle of Gettysburg, 3rd July 1863* (color litho), Henry Alexander Ogden (1856–1936) (after), private collection, Ken Welsh, the Bridgeman Art Library.

155. *Pickett's Charge, Battle of Gettysburg in 1863* (colored etching), Charles Prosper Sainton (1861–1914), private collection, the Bridgeman Art Library.

CHAPTER 4

156. Principal Campaigns in the West, 1862–1863, Rowan Technology Solutions, 2014.
Source: Military layer based on Frank Martini's map #1 Southeastern United States, 1860, Principal Campaigns of the American Civil War. USMA History Department.

157. *U.S. gunboat Lexington [i.e. Tyler]—Mississippi River Fleet,* Library of Congress.

158. Mathew B. Brady, *President Ulysses S. Grant, half-length portrait, seated, facing right,* Library of Congress.

159. Corinth, Rowan Technology Solutions, 2014.
Source: Based on Frank Martini's map #15a inset Kentucky—Tennessee, 1861, Developments Between the Battle of Shiloh, 6–7 April 1862, and the Confederate Invasion of Kentucky, Which Began in August 1862. USMA History Department.

160. *Lt. Gen. Edmund Kirby Smith,* Library of Congress.

161. *Third Kentucky Confederate Infantry at Corinth, Mississippi, May 11, 1862,* ca.1867 (engraving), Conrad Wise Chapman (1842–1910), © Boston Athenaeum, the Bridgeman Art Library.

162. *General Braxton Bragg,* Library of Congress.

163. Kentucky Campaign, Rowan Technology Solutions, 2014.
Sources: Military layer based on Edward Krasnoborski's map #75 Stones River Campaign, Bragg's Invasion of Kentucky and the Situation 17 September 1862; map #76 Stones River Campaign, Situation 26 December 1862 and Movements since 17 September. *The West Point Atlas of American Wars: Vol.1, 1689–1900.*

164. Brady National Photographic Art Gallery (Washington, D.C.), *Portrait of Maj. Gen. William S. Rosecrans, officer of the Federal Army,* Library of Congress.

165. Battle of Corinth, Rowan Technology Solutions, 2014.
Sources: Based on Hal Jespersen, Battle of Corinth, Actions October 3, 1862; Battle of Corinth, Actions October 4, 1862, www.cwmaps.com.

166. Battle of Corinth—Order of Battle, Rowan Technology Solutions, 2014.
Sources: Eicher, *The Longest Night,* 374–378; OR, Series I, Volume XVII, Part 1, 173–176, 374–375.

167. Detroit Publishing Co., *General view of battle ground, Vicksburg, Mississippi,* Library of Congress.

168. *David Dixon Porter, Rear Admiral,* Library of Congress.

169. Brady National Photographic Art Gallery (Washington, D.C.), *Portrait of Maj. Gen. John A. McClernand, officer of the Federal Army,* Library of Congress.

170. Grant's First Vicksburg Campaign, Rowan Technology Solutions, 2014.
Source: Based on Frank Martini's map #19a Southeastern Lower Mississippi River Valley and Vicinity, 1861, Vicksburg Campaign, Unsuccessful Federal Attempts to Reach Vicksburg, 2 November 1862 to 15 January 1863. USMA History Department.

171. Thomas Nast, *A Rebel guerrilla raid in a western town,* Library of Congress.

172. *Formation of guerrilla bands,* c.1880–90 (etching), Adalbert John Volck, (1828–1912), Gilder Lehrman Collection, New York, the Bridgeman Art Library.

173. Wm. R. Pywell, *Chickasaw Bayou, Mississippi. The poison spring. Battlefield of Chickasaw Bayou,* Library of Congress.

174. *General Nathan B. Forrest,* Library of Congress.

175. Battle of Stones River, Rowan Technology Solutions, 2014.
Source: Military layer based on Edward Krasnoborski's map #79 Stones River Campaign, Situation about 8:00 AM, 31 December 1862. *The West Point Atlas of American Wars: Vol.1, 1689–1900.*

176. Henri Lovie, *The head of the canal, opposite Vicksburg, Miss., now being cut by command of Gen. Grant,* Library of Congress.

177. Grant's Second Vicksburg Campaign, Rowan Technology Solutions, 2014.
Source: Based on Frank Martini's map #19b Lower Mississippi River Valley and Vicinity, 1861, The Bayous and the Canal, January through April 1863, and Grant's Preliminary Diversions before his Final Campaign. USMA History Department.

178. *Grant's transports running the batteries,* Library of Congress.

179. Grant's Final Vicksburg Campaign, Rowan Technology Solutions, 2014.
Source: Based on Frank Martini's map #20 Vicksburg and Vicinity, 1863, Vicksburg Campaign, The Crossing of the River and the Advance to Jackson, 29 April–14 May 1863. USMA History Department.

180. Gilford Photography, *North (front) elevation—Coker House, Champion Hill, Edwards, Hinds County, MS,* Library of Congress.

181. *Battle of Champion-Hills, 16th May, 1863,* engraved by Kurz & Allison (colou litho, American school, 19th century), private collection, Peter Newark American Pictures, the Bridgeman Art Library.
182. Battle of Champion Hill, Rowan Technology Solutions, 2014.
     Source: Based on Frank Martini's map #21c Vicksburg and Vicinity, 1863, Battle of Champion's Hill, Withdrawal Late 16 May 1863. USMA History Department.
183. *Siege of Vicksburg,* Library of Congress.
184. *First at Vicksburg,* U.S. Army Center of Military History.
185. Grant's Final Vicksburg Campaign, Rowan Technology Solutions, 2014
     Source: Military layer based on Edward Krasnoborski's map #105 Vicksburg Campaign, Union Advance from Jackson to Vicksburg, 15–19 May 1863. *The West Point Atlas of American Wars: Vol.1, 1689–1900.*
186. Vicksburg Siege, Rowan Technology Solutions, 2014
     Source: Based on Frank Martini's map #22b Vicksburg, 1861, The Siege of Vicksburg, Situation 3 July 1863, Near End of Siege, Showing Field Works. USMA History Department.
187. Siege of Vicksburg—Order of Battle, Rowan Technology Solutions, 2014.
     Sources: Frances H. Kennedy, ed., *The Civil War Battlefield Guide.* 2nd ed. (Boston: Houghton Mifflin Co., 1998), 172–173; *OR,* Series I, Volume XXIV, Part 2, 148–158, 326–328.
188. Middleton, Strobridge & Co., *The siege of Vicksburg, the fight in the crater of Fort Hill, after the explosion, June 25 63,* Library of Congress.
189. *Assault of the Second Louisiana (Colored) regiment on the Rebel works at Port Hudson, May 27,* Library of Congress.
190. Adalbert John Volck, *Cave life in Vicksburg,* Library of Congress.
191. Donaldson & Elmes, *The Army of the Cumberland in front of Chattanooga,* Library of Congress.
192. Rosecrans Advance to Chattanooga, Rowan Technology Solutions, 2014.
     Sources: Based on Frank Martini's map #39 Chattanooga and Vicinity, 1863, Middle Tennessee Campaign, Situation 30 June and Movements since 24 June 1863; map #40 Chattanooga and Vicinity, 1863, The Advance of Chattanooga, Situation 15 August and Federal Advance, 16–30 August 1863. USMA History Department.
193. Battle of Chickamauga, Rowan Technology Solutions, 2014.
     Source: Based on Frank Martini's map #41b McLemore's Cove and Vicinity, 1863, The Fall of Chattanooga, Bragg's Counterattack, Situation at Dusk, 12 September 1863. USMA History Department.
194. Battle of Chickamauga—Order of Battle, Rowan Technology Solutions, 2014.
     Sources: Civil War Trust website, "The Battle of Chickamauga—Summary & Facts," accessed May 7, 2014; *OR,* Series I, Volume XXX, Part 1, 40–47, and Part 2, 11–20.
195. Battle of Chickamauga, Rowan Technology Solutions, 2014.
     Source: Based on Frank Martini's map #42a Chickamauga Creek and Vicinity, 1863, Battle of Chattanooga, Situation at Dawn, 19 September 1863. USMA History Department.
196. Battle of Chickamauga, Rowan Technology Solutions, 2014.
     Source: Based on Frank Martini's map #42b Chickamauga Creek and Vicinity, 1863, Battle of Chattanooga, Situation at 1130 Hours, 20 September 1863. USMA History Department.
197. Alfred R. Waud, *Chickamauga,* Library of Congress.
198. Brady National Photographic Art Gallery (Washington, D.C.), *Portrait of Maj. Gen. George H. Thomas, officer of the Federal Army,* Library of Congress.
199. *Chattanooga, Tenn. U.S. military train at depot; Lookout Mountain in background,* Library of Congress.
200. L. Prang & Co., *Battle of Chattanooga,* Library of Congress.
201. Opening the Cracker Line, Rowan Technology Solutions, 2014.
     Sources: Based on Frank Martini's map #44a Raccoon Mountain and Vicinity, 1863, Opening the Gateway, Situation at Dark, 28 October 1863, Union Movements since 25 October, and the "Cracker Line". USMA History Department.
202. *Missionary Ridge,* undated, Horace Rawdon, satercolor on paper, 11 × 31 inches, courtesy of the West Point Museum Collection, United States Military Academy.

CHAPTER 5

203. Principal Campaigns of 1864, Rowan Technology Solutions, 2014.
     Source: Military layer based on Frank Martini's map #1 Southeastern United States, 1860, Principal Campaigns of the American Civil War. USMA History Department.
204. George P. A. Healy, *The Peacemakers,* The White House Historical Association (White House Collection).
205. *Headquarters, Army of Potomac—Brandy Station, April 1864. Camp of Provost Guard—114th Pennsylvania Infantry,* Library of Congress.
206. Grant's Plan, Rowan Technology Solutions, 2014.
     Source: Military layer based on Frank Martini's map #45 Southeastern United States, 1864, Grant's Plan for the 1864 Campaign. USMA History Department.
207. *Photographs of six pieces of Confederate paper currency,* Library of Congress.
208. Julian Scott, *Confederate Prison Scene,* 1873, oil on canvas, 24 × 18 inches, courtesy of the West Point Museum Collection, United States Military Academy. Photography: Sean T. Smith.
209. David Bustill Bowser, *We will prove ourselves men—127th Regt. U.S. Colored Troops,* Library of Congress.

210. The Overland Campaign, 3–26 May 1864, Rowan Technology Solutions, 2014.
    Source: Military layer based on Frank Martini's map #46a Eastern Virginia, 1864, The Road to Richmond, The Federal Advance from Rapidan to the North Anna, 3–26 May 1864. USMA History Department.

211. The Battle of the Wilderness, Rowan Technology Solutions, 2014.
    Source: Military layer based on Frank Martini's map #46b Eastern Virginia, 1864, Wilderness Campaign, Situation about 0700 Hours, 7 May 1864, 3–26 May 1864. USMA History Department.

212. The Battle of Spotsylvania Court House, Rowan Technology Solutions, 2014.
    Source: Military layer based on Edward Krasnoborski's map #130 Battle of Spotsylvania, Federal Attacks 12 May 1864. *The West Point Atlas of American Wars: Vol.1, 1689–1900.*

213. *Wilderness, CS Earthworks,* Military History Institute.

214. *Spotsylvania, CS Muleshoe Salient,* Military History Institute.

215. *General Ulysses S. Grant at his headquarters in Cold Harbor, Virginia,* Library of Congress.

216. *Digging in at Cold Harbor,* Battles & Leaders of the Civil War.

217. *Cavalry Charge at Yellow Tavern, VA, May 11, 1864,* 1871, H. W. Chaloner, oil on canvas, 31 × 47⅞ inches, courtesy of the West Point Museum Collection, United States Military Academy.

218. The Overland Campaign, 27 May–18 June 1864, Rowan Technology Solutions, 2014.
    Source: Military layer based on Frank Martini's map #47a Eastern Virginia, 1864, The Road to Richmond, The Federal Advance from the North Anna River to Petersburg, 27 May–18 June 1864. USMA History Department.

219. Overland Campaign—Order of Battle, Rowan Technology Solutions, 2014.
    Sources: Eicher, *The Longest Night,* 660; Gordon C. Rhea, *In the Footsteps of Grant and Lee: The Wilderness Through Cold Harbor* (Baton Rouge: Louisiana State University Press, 2007); *OR,* Series I, Volume XXXVI, Part 1, 106–116, 1021–1027.

220. Battle at the North Anna River, Rowan Technology Solutions, 2014.
    Source: Military layer based on Frank Martini's map #46d Eastern Virginia, 1864, Battle of the North Anna, 23–26 May 1864. USMA History Department.

221. Battle of Cold Harbor, Rowan Technology Solutions, 2014
    Source: Military layer based on John Weyss's map "Richmond. From Surveys under the direction of Bvt. Brig. Gen N. Michler, Maj. of Engineers and Bvt. Lieut. Col. P. S. Michie, Capt. of Engineers By Command of Bvt. Maj. Genl. A. A. Humphreys, Brig. Genl. & Chief of Engineers. 1867." Surveyed & drawn by Maj. J. E. Weyss, assisted by F. Theilkuhl, J. Strasser & G. Thompson. Photolith by the N.Y. Lithographing, Engraving & Printing Co., Julius Bien, Supt. Accessed from David Rumsey Collection, www.davidrumsey.com, Image # 3881009.

222. Petersburg Campaign, 18 June 1864, Rowan Technology Solutions, 2014.
    Source: Based on Frank Martini's map # 47d Eastern Virginia, 1864, Siege of Petersburg, Federal Attacks 18 June 1864. USMA History Department.

223. *Maj. Gen. William T. Sherman,* Library of Congress.

224. Atlanta Campaign, Rowan Technology Solutions, 2014.
    Source: Based on map from Robert Doughty and Ira Gruber, eds., *Warfare in the Western World,* Vol.1. (Stamford, Conn.: Cengage Learning, 1995), 439.

225. Atlanta Campaign—Order of Battle, Rowan Technology Solutions, 2014.
    Source: *OR,* Series I, Volume XXXVIII, Part 1, 89–114, and Part 3, 638–675.

226. *J. B. Hood,* Library of Congress.

227. George N. Barnard, *Atlanta, Ga. Confederate palisades, on north side of city,* Library of Congress.

228. Petersburg Campaign, Rowan Technology Solutions, 2014.
    Source: Based on Frank Martini's map # 54a Petersburg and Vicinity, 1864, The Siege of Petersburg, Hancock's Movements, 26–29 July and the Federal Plan of Attack Following the Explosion of the Mine, 30 July 1864. USMA History Department.

229. *Confederate General Jubal Early, head-and-shoulders portrait, facing front,* Library of Congress.

230. Alfred R. Waud, *Scene of the explosion Saturday July 30th,* Library of Congress.

231. Petersburg Campaign, Rowan Technology Solutions, 2014.
    Sources: Based on Frank Martini's map # 54a Petersburg and Vicinity, 1864, The Siege of Petersburg, Hancock's Movements, 26–29 July and the Federal Plan of Attack Following the Explosion of the Mine, 30 July 1864. USMA History Department; Edward Krasnoborski's map #141 Siege of Petersburg, Operations 27 October and Situation October-November 1864, *The West Point Atlas of American Wars: Vol.1, 1689–1900.*

232. Currier & Ives, *The true issue or "That's what's the matter,"* Library of Congress.

233. George N. Barnard, *Atlanta, Ga. Federal soldiers relaxing by guns of captured fort,* Library of Congress.

234. *Gen. Phil Sheridan,* Library of Congress.

235. William Waud, *Head-quarters, Army of the James—Pennsylvania soldiers voting,* Library of Congress.

236. Union Cavalry, 1864, Chase Stone, 2014.

237. Sherman's March to the Sea, Rowan Technology Solutions, 2014.
    Source: Military layer based on Edward Krasnoborski's map #154b Sherman's March to the Sea, 12 November 1864 to 13 April 1865. *The West Point Atlas of American Wars: Vol.1, 1689–1900.*

238. George N. Barnard, *Atlanta, Ga. Gen. William T. Sherman on horseback at Federal Fort No. 7,* Library of Congress.

239. *Federals Destroying Railroads,* Battles & Leaders of the Civil War.

240. *Method of destroying railroads,* Library of Congress.

241. Hood's Campaign in Tennessee, Rowan Technology Solutions, 2014.
    Sources: Based on Frank Martini's map #50 Petersburg and Vicinity, Tennessee-Alabama, 1864, Franklin and Nashville Campaign, Situation 26 November and Movements since 29 September 1864. USMA History Department.
242. Kurz & Allison, *Battle of Franklin. November 30, 1864–Union (Gen. Schofield) . . . Conf. (Gen. Hood),* Library of Congress.
243. Battle of Franklin, Rowan Technology Solutions, 2014.
    Sources: Based on Frank Martini's map #51b Franklin, Tennessee and Vicinity, 1864, Franklin and Nashville Campaign, Battle of Franklin, Situation at 1530 Hours and Confederate Attack at 1600 Hours, 30 November 1864. USMA History Department.
244. Battle of Franklin—Order of Battle, Rowan Technology Solutions, 2014.
    Sources: Civil War Trust website, "The Battle of Franklin—Summary & Facts," accessed May 7, 2014; Civil War Trust website, "Confederate Order of Battle," accessed May 7, 2014; *OR,* Series I, Volume XLV, Part 1, 1197–1205.
245. Battle of Nashville, Rowan Technology Solutions, 2014.
    Sources: Based on Frank Martini's map #52a Nashville and Vicinity, 1864, Franklin and Nashville Campaign, Battle of Nashville, Situation about 1300 Hours, 15 December 1864. USMA History Department.
246. Battle of Nashville—Order of Battle, Rowan Technology Solutions, 2014.
    Sources: Eicher, *The Longest Night,* 780; *OR,* Series I, Volume XLV, Part 1, 90–96, 664–669.
247. Jacob F. Coonley, *Nashville, Tenn. Federal outer line,* Library of Congress.
248. *Marching through the Carolinas,* Battles & Leaders of the Civil War.
249. William Waud, *The burning of Columbia, South Carolina, February 17, 1865,* Library of Congress.
250. Sherman's Campaign through the Carolinas, Rowan Technology Solutions, 2014.
    Sources: Military layer based on Edward Krasnoborski's map #154b Sherman's March to the Sea, 12 November 1864 to 13 April 1865. *The West Point Atlas of American Wars: Vol.1, 1689–1900.*
251. Petersburg Campaign, Rowan Technology Solutions, 2014.
    Sources: Based on Frank Martini's map #54a Petersburg and Vicinity, 1864, The Siege of Petersburg, Hancock's Movements, 26–29 July and the Federal Plan of Attack Following the Explosion of the Mine, 30 July 1864. USMA History Department;Edward Krasnoborski's map #142 Siege of Petersburg, Federal Movements 29–31 March and Battle of Five Forks 1 April 1865, *The West Point Atlas of American Wars: Vol.1, 1689–1900.*
252. The Defeat of Lee: Pursuit to Appomattox, Rowan Technology Solutions, 2014.
    Source: Military layer based on Edward Krasnoborski's map #144 Grant's Pursuit of Lee to Appomattox Court House, 3–9 April 1865. *The West Point Atlas of American Wars: Vol.1, 1689–1900.*
253. *Lee's Surrender at Appomattox Court House* (color litho), Tom Lovell (1909–97), National Geographic Creative, the Bridgeman Art Library.
254. *Petersburg, Virginia. Fort Sedgwick,* Library of Congress.
255. Thomas C. Roche, *Petersburg, Virginia. Dead Confederate soldier in the trenches of Fort Mahone,* Library of Congress.
256. *Defiance: Inviting a Shot Before Petersburg,* 1864 (oil on panel), Winslow Homer (1836–1910), Detroit Institute of Arts, Founders Society purchase and Dexter M. Ferry Jr. fund, the Bridgeman Art Library.

CHAPTER 6

257. *The Return of the Flags, 1865,* 1869, Thomas Waterman Wood, oil on canvas, 37 × 30 inches, courtesy of the West Point Museum Collection, United States Military Academy.
258. Map of Reconstruction, Rowan Technology Solutions, 2014.
    Source: Data based on LEARN NC map "North Carolina in the Civil War and Reconstruction," www.learnnc.org.
259. *American Civil War 1861–1865: William Tecumseh Sherman (1820–1891) left, Unionist (northern) general, meeting General Joseph E. Johnston to discuss terms of surrender of Confederate (southern) forces in North Carolina.* After Currier & Ives lithograph, Universal History Archive/UIG, the Bridgeman Art Library.
260. Map of Confederate Surrenders, Rowan Technology Solutions, 2014.
261. *The old rip of the "SHENANDOAH",* Library of Congress.
262. Charles H. Shute & Son, *Sidewheel steamer River Queen at the wharf in Nantucket, probably taken during the late 1860s,* www.oldtimeislands.org.
263. *The destruction of the city of Lawrence, Kansas, and the massacre of its inhabitants by the Rebel guerrillas, August 21, 1863,* Library of Congress.
264. *The Last Days of the Confederate Government—Mr. Jefferson Davis Signing Acts of Government by the Roadside,* 22nd July 1865 (engraving, American school, 19th century), photo © Liszt Collection, the Bridgeman Art Library.
265. E. Sachse & Co., *The grand review at Washington May 23th 1865 The glorious Army of the Potomac passing the head stand,* Library of Congress.
266. Advance of Union Armies, Rowan Technology Solutions, 2014.
    Source: Data based on The Civil War 1861–1865, Office of the Chief of Military History, United States Army—American Military History, Army Historical Series Perry-Castañeda Library Map of the Civil War 1861–1865 Map Collection.

267. Joseph Shepherd Wyon, *The Seal of the Confederacy,* U.S. Diplomacy Center (State Department).
268. Winslow Homer, *Prisoners from the Front,* Metropolitan Museum of Art.
269. *Charge of the 22nd Negro Regiment—Civil War,* 1892, André Castaigne, oil on canvas, 23½ × 30½ inches, courtesy of the West Point Museum Collection, United States Military Academy.
270. *The Burial of Latane,* William D. Washington, www.the-athenaeum.org.
271. *Alexander Hamilton Stephens, Vice President of the CSA,* National Archives and Records Administration.
272. *Furling the Flag,* 1872, Richard Norris Brooke, oil on canvas, 22 × 30 inches, courtesy of the West Point Museum Collection, United States Military Academy.
273. *Generals Curtis Lee, Robert E. Lee and Lieutenant Colonel Walter Taylor,* hand-colored photograph, 1865, private collection, J. T. Vintage, the Bridgeman Art Library.
274. George Peter Alexander Healy, *Abraham Lincoln,* The White House Historical Association (White House Collection).
275. War Department, Office of the Chief Signal Officer, Admiral David G. Farragut, ca. 1860-ca. 1865, National Archives and Records Administration.
276. Jones & Clark, *Lincoln and his Generals,* Library of Congress.
277. William Torgerson, *Confederate Blockade Runners in Harbor,* 1881, oil on canvas, 34 × 52 inches, courtesy of the West Point Museum Collection, United States Military Academy. Photography: Sean T. Smith.
278. *Gen. Montgomery Meigs, U.S.A.,* Library of Congress.
279. *Civil War Patriotic Scene,* ca. 1861, William Winner, oil on canvas on wood panel, 16 × 11¾ inches, courtesy of the West Point Museum Collection, United States Military Academy.
280. *The Execution of Maximilian I* (1832–67) (oil on canvas, Mexican school, 19th century), Museo Nacional de Historia, Castillo de Chapultepec, Mexico, Giraudon, the Bridgeman Art Library.
281. *The Veteran in a New Field,* Winslow Homer (1836–1910), Metropolitan Museum of Art, New York, the Bridgeman Art Library.
282. Eliphalet Frazer Andrews, *Official Presidential portrait of Andrew Johnson,* The White House Historical Association.
283. Alfred R. Waud, *Marriage of a colored solider at Vicksburg by Chaplain Warren of the Freedmen's Bureau,* Library of Congress.
284. Theodore R. Davis, *The Last speech on impeachment—Thaddeus Stevens closing the debate in the House, March 2,* Library of Congress.
285. *Harper's Weekly, 'Tis But a Change in Banners—CSA KKK.*
286. Alfred R. Waud, *The Freedmen's Bureau,* Library of Congress.
287. Military Districts of the South, Rowan Technology Solutions, 2014.
Sources: Data based on LEARN NC map "North Carolina in the Civil War and Reconstruction," www.learnnc.org.
288. *General Lewis Merrill,* Library of Congress.
289. *Mississippi Ku-Klux in the disguises in which they were captured,* Library of Congress.
290. Joseph Ferdinand Keppler, *Grant's last outrage in Louisiana,* Library of Congress.
291. Thomas Nast, *The Union as it Was The lost cause, worse than slavery,* Library of Congress.
292. *The Rush from the New York Stock Exchange on September 18, 1873,* from E. Benjamin Andrews, "A History of the Last Quarter Century," *Scribner's,* July 1895 (oil on canvas), Howard Pyle, (1853–1911), Delaware Art Museum, Wilmington, the Bridgeman Art Library.
293. Daniel Huntington, *Official Presidential portrait of Rutherford Birchard Hayes,* White House Historical Association.
294. Thomas Nast, *A truce—not a compromise, but a chance for high-toned gentlemen to retire gracefully from their very civil declarations of war,* Library of Congress.
295. *Monument to Gen. John H. Morgan and his men, and some of the members of the U.D.C. Committee that built it,* Library of Congress.
296. *The Blue and the Gray at Gettysburg, Assembly Tent, Gettysburg Celebration, Pennsylvania,* Library of Congress.
297. Battle Monument, photo by John Pellino/West Point Multimedia.
298. Jacob Parrott Medal of Honor, courtesy of the West Point Museum Collection, United States Military Academy. Photography: Sean T. Smith.
299. *Union Troops Capturing Confederate Fort,* 1864, G. deNigri, oil on canvas, 21¾ × 32¾ inches, courtesy of the West Point Museum Collection, United States Military Academy.

Antietam Gatefold

Image 1. Carol M. Highsmith, *Antietam Battle Field, "Bloody Lane," Sharpsburg, Maryland,* Library of Congress.
Image 2. Carol M. Highsmith, *Burnside Bridge at Antietam National Park, Maryland,* Library of Congress.
300. Antietam, Rowan Technology Solutions, 2014.
Sources: Military layer based on Frank Martini's map #67a Sharpsburg and Vicinity, Antietam Campaign, Situation at 1800 Hours, 16 September 1862. USMA History Department; Bradley M. Gottfried, *The Maps of Antietam: An Atlas of the Antietam (Sharpsburg) Campaign, Including the Battle of South Mountain, September 2–20, 1862* (El Dorado Hills, Calif.: Savas Beatie, 2012). Imagery from National Agriculture Imagery Program (NAIP), data available from the U.S. Geological Survey.

301. Battle of Antietam—Order of Battle, Rowan Technology Solutions, 2014.
    Sources: Civil War Trust website, "The Battle of Antietam—Summary & Facts," accessed April 29, 2014; Eicher, *The Longest Night,* 363; *OR,* Series I, Volume XIX, Part 1, pages 169–180, 803–810.
302. Alexander Gardner, *Completely silenced! Dead Confederate artillery men, as they lay around their battery after the Battle of Antietam,* Library of Congress.
303. *The First Reading of the Emancipation Proclamation* (oil on canvas), Francis Bicknell Carpenter (1830–1900), Library of Congress, Washington D.C., USA, the Bridgeman Art Library.

GETTYSBURG GATEFOLD

Image 1. *Valley of Death and the Wheatfield [i.e. Wheat Field], Gettysburg,* Library of Congress.
304. Gettysburg, Rowan Technology Solutions, 2014.
    Sources: Military layer based on Frank Martini's map #35b Gettysburg and Vicinity, 1863, Gettysburg Campaign, Situation at 1430 Hours, 1 July 1863; map #36a Situation 1800 Hours, 1 July 1863; map #37b Situation 1430 Hours, 3 July 1863 and Pickett's Charge; Philip Laino, *Gettysburg Campaign Atlas* 2nd Edition, Revised (Dayton, Ohio: Gatehouse Press, 2009); National Agriculture Imagery Program (NAIP), data available from the U.S. Geological Survey.
305. Battle of Gettysburg—Order of Battle, Rowan Technology Solutions, 2014.
    Source: Laino, *Gettysburg Campaign Atlas,* 429–457.
306. Alexander Gardner, *Gettysburg, Pa. Confederate dead at the edge of the Rose woods, July 5, 1863,* Library of Congress.
307. *Lincoln's Gettysburg Address, Gettysburg,* Library of Congress.
308. Currier & Ives, *The Dis-United States. Or the Southern Confederacy,* Library of Congress.
309. Currier & Ives, *Jeff Davis's last appeal to arms,* Library of Congress.
310. *The copperhead party—in favor of a vigorous prosecution of peace!* Library of Congress.
311. *Draft riots in New York, 'The mob burning the Provost Marshal's office,'* 1863 (litho, American school, 19th century), private collection, Peter Newark American Pictures, the Bridgeman Art Library.

CHATTANOOGA GATEFOLD

Image 1. [*Three unidentified soldiers at Point Lookout, Tennessee*], Library of Congress.
Image 2. *Missionary Ridge,* Library of Congress.
312. Battle of Chattanooga, Rowan Technology Solutions, 2014.
    Sources: Based on Frank Martini's map #44b Chattanooga and Vicinity, 1863, Opening the Gateway, Battle of Lookout Mountain, Situation at Noon, 24 November 1863; map #44c Battle of Missionary Ridge, Situation at Dawn, 25 November 1863; map #44d Battle of Missionary Ridge, Situation at 1530 Hours, 25 November 1863. USMA History Department; National Agriculture Imagery Program (NAIP), data available from the U.S. Geological Survey.
313. Battle of Chattanooga—Order of Battle, Rowan Technology Solutions, 2014.
    Sources: Civil War Trust website, "The Battle of Chattanooga—Summary & Facts," accessed May 7, 2014; *OR,* Series I, Volume XXXI, Part 2, 14–24, 657–664.
314. *Chattanooga, Tenn. Confederate prisoners at railroad depot,* Library of Congress.
315. Currier & Ives, *The old bulldog on the right track,* Library of Congress.

A

B

Burnside, Ambrose P.—battles/campaigns and
    Antietam campaign, *125*, 126, 128, *129*,
       130, 131, *142*
    Battle of the Crater, 278, *278*
    Cold Harbor, *267*
    First Battle of Bull Run, *56*, *142*
    Fredericksburg, *142*, 143, 144, *145*, 146,
       147, 148, *149*, 150, 215
    Knoxville Battle, *142*, 183, 231
    North Anna River Battle, *266*
    Overland Campaign, *265*
    Petersburg Campaign, *268*, *276*, 278, *278*
    Petersburg Mine Assault, *142*
    Roanoke Island capture, *142*
    Second Battle of Bull Run, *116–17*
    Spotsylvania, *258*
    Wilderness campaign, *142*, 256
Burnside's Bridge, *130*
Butler, Benjamin
    Bermuda Hundred and, 253
    confiscation of slaves by, 110
    and demobilization of Union Army,
      395*n*47
    Grant's strategy and, *250*, 253, 254, 259
    and operations in Virginia, 253, 254, 259
    and Petersburg Campaign, 253, *276*, 279
    and Richmond, *250*, 253
Butterfield, Daniel, *115*, 121, *143*, 144, *145*,
    146, *273*, 371*n*34

C

Cabell, Sergeant, *254*
Cadet Mess Hall (West Point): Panorama of
    Military History mural in, *10–11*
Cadet Oath, *4*, *5*, 6
cadet review parade, West Point, *3*
Calhoun, John C., 20, 23
California: Compromise of 1850 and, *14*, *15*,
    19
Cameron, Simon, 3
camp tent: escaped slaves at, *112*, *113*
Carolinas, Sherman's March through the, *271*,
    297, 298–99, 308, *309*, *332*
Carpenter, Francis Bicknell, *132–33*
carpetbaggers, 342, *343*, 344
Carr, Joseph Brandford, *227*
Cass, Lewis, 19
casualties
    African Americans as, 278
    at Antietam, 127, 128, *130*, 131, *131*
    in Atlanta Campaign, 275, 280, 282, 387*n*47
    at Bristoe Station Battle, 183
    at Chancellorsville, 161, 162, 183
    and Chattanooga Campaign, 240
    at Chickasaw Bayou, 211–12
    at Cold Harbor, 261, 266
    and comparison of North and South, 37
    and conclusions about early years of war in
      Eastern Theater, 190
    at Corinth, 203
    at Culp's Hill, 178, 373*n*58
    effects on home front of, 183, 186

and end of War, 303
at Ezra Church, 387*n*47
at First Battle of Bull Run, 57
at Franklin, *292*
at Fredericksburg, *149*, 150, 151
at Gaines Mill, 100
at Gettysburg, 104, 173, *176–77*, 178, 179,
    182–83, 183
and Grant's strategy, *262*, 302
Grant's views about, 266
Hood and, 303
at Island No. 10, 62
at Jonesboro, 280, 387*n*47
at Kennesaw Mountain, 271
Lee's leadership and, 326
at Malvern Hill, 104
among North Carolina troops, 183, 185
and Overland Campaign, 269
at Peachtree Creek, 387*n*47
at Perryville, 202
and Petersburg Campaign, 278, *306–7*
plundering of, 151, 369*n*22
prisoners of war as, 251
and recruiting from local communities, *35*
at Rich Mountain, 364*n*10
and role of Southern women, 323
at Second Battle of Bull Run, 117, 118, *123*
and Seven Days Battles, 104, *109*
at Seven Pines, 97
at Shiloh, *70–71*, 71, 195
and soldiers' voting in elections of 1864,
    285
at Spotsylvania, 259, 260
at Stones River, 214
total Civil War, 390–91*n*14
Union, 98, 269–70
and Vicksburg Campaign, 212, 214, 223, 224
at Wilderness Battle, 257, 385*n*23
Catholicism, 23, 26
cavalry, 43, *284*, 289, 342, 372*n*48. *See also*
    specific commander
Cedar Creek, Battle of, 282, *282*
Cedar Mountain, Battle of, *91*, 113, *116–17*
Cemetery Hill/Cemetery Ridge, Battle of, 171,
    172, 173, *181*
Chalmers, James Ronald, *293*, *294*, 295
Chamberlain, Joshua, 172
Champion Hill, Battle of, 219, *219*, 220–21,
    221, *222*, 224
Chancellorsville, Battle of
    casualties at, 161, 162, 183
    and conclusions about early years of war in
      Eastern Theater, 187
    Confederate mobility at, 191
    forces at, *163*
    Hooker at, *158*, 159–60, 161, 162, *163*,
      164, 165, 187, 257, 371*n*34, 371–72*n*36,
      373*n*55
    Jackson at, *91*, 160, *160*, 162, *162*, 163, *164*,
      166, *170*
    Lee at, 159, 160–61, 162, *162*, 163, *164*, 165,
      257, 326, 371*n*34
    maps of, *164–65*
    Meade at, *163*, 164, 165, 171, 371*n*34
    prisoners of war at, *161*

and supplies for Army of Northern
    Virginia, 156
timeline for, *136–37*, 193
wounded at, *161*
Chandler, Zachariah, 3
Charleston
    Beauregard as commander of coastal
      defense in, 52
    Lee in, 98
Chase, Salmon P., 23, *132–33*, 396–97*n*54
Chattanooga Campaign
    Bragg and, 197–98, 199, 231, *231–34*, 235,
      241, *241*, 242, 243
    Buell and, 197–98, 199
    casualties in, 240
    "Cracker Line" in, 241, *241*
    and factors influencing the outcome of the
      Civil War, 332
    Grant and, *195*, 199, 240–44, *240*, *241*
    Hooker and, 242
    prisoners of war and, 242, 251, 382*n*63
    role in Civil War of, 244
    Rosecrans and, 202, 230–31, *230*, *231–34*,
      240, *241*
    Sherman and, 241, 242, *242*, 243, 244
    timeline for, *136–37*, 193
    and Union capture of Chattanooga, 191
    See also specific battle
Chattanooga, Tennessee
    as Confederate headquarters in Western
      Theater, 212
    importance of, 238–39
Cheat Mountain, Battle of, *98*
Cheatham, Benjamin F.
    and Atlanta Campaign, *273*
    and Chattanooga Campaign, *234*
    at Chickamauga, 235, *236*, 237
    at Franklin, *292*, 293
    at Nashville, *294*, 295
    at Shiloh, 63
    at Stones River Battle, *213*
Chickamauga, Battle of
    Bragg at, 183, *199*, *202*, 231, 235, *236*, 237,
      238
    forces at, *235*, 236
    Grant and, 244
    importance to Confederacy of, 240
    Lee and, 183
    Longstreet at, *167*, 183, 235, *236*, 237
    map of, *236*, 237
    Rosecrans at, *202*, 231, 235, *236*, 238, 240,
      244
    Thomas at, 231, *235*, 237, 238, *239*
    timeline for, *193*
    Waud sketch of, *238*
Chickasaw Bayou, Battle of, *207*, 211–12, *211*,
    214, 215, 221
Church, Frederic Edwin, *12*, *13*
City Line (Atlanta), *275*, *281*
civil liberties, 51, 186
civil rights
    and Civil War as watershed in American
      history, 354, *354*
    and constitutional amendments, 340
    elections of 1876 and, 347
    Enforcement Act and, 341

Johnson (Andrew) and, 337
  See also specific constitutional amendment
Civil Rights Act (1866), *337, 349*
Civil War
  border states role in, 46–48, 50
  and comparison of Union and Confederate
    states, 36–37, 41–42
  expansion of, 109, 111, 248
  expenditures for, 245, 346
  factors influencing the outcome of, 318–21,
    320, 321, 323–26, *326–27,* 328, *328–29,*
    331, 353, 393*n*31, 393*n*32, 393*n*33,
    394*n*38, 395*n*44
  as "hard war," *210*
  meaning and legacy of, *310*
  mobilization and national assets and, 33,
    34, 35, 36–42, 72
  origins of, 15–31, 194, *351,* 358*n*9
  popular support for, *80–81*
  purpose of, 349
  reconciliation and, *351*
  significance for West Point of, 350, 353
  as total war, 332, 334, 395*n*43
  as watershed in American history, 353–54,
    354
  why the Confederacy lost the, 318–21, *320,*
    323–26, 328, 331–32, 334
  why the Union won the, 318–21, *320,*
    323–26, 328, 331–32, 334
Clark, Charles, *63*
class divisions, 185–86, 321, 324
Clausewitz, Carl von, 148, 309
Clayton, Henry D., *293, 295*
Cleburne, Patrick R.
  and arming of slaves, 389*n*7
  and Atlanta Campaign, *273*
  and Chattanooga Campaign, *233, 234,* 242,
    243, 244
  at Chickamauga, *235*
  death of, 389–90*n*7
  at Franklin, *293,* 389–90*n*7
  and Stones River Battle, *213*
Cobb, Thomas R., *107*
Cocke, Philip St. George, *55, 56, 107*
Coker House, *220–21*
Cold Harbor, Battle of, 261–62, *262, 263, 264,*
  266–67, 386*n*28
Colfax, Louisiana, massacre at, 344, 347
Colored Troops, U.S. (USCT), 250, 277, *322.*
    See also African Americans: in Union
    Army
Colston, Raleigh E., *163, 164, 165*
Columbia, South Carolina: burning of, 297,
  298–99
command and control, 44, 159
"common property" doctrine, 20, 23
"compact theory." *See* state's rights theory
Compromise of 1850, *14, 15,* 19, *19,* 359*n*12
Compromise of 1877, 347, 399*n*67
Confederacy
  Constitution of, 30, *30*
  Davis named president of, *29,* 30
  divisions within, 321, 323, 324
  economy of the, 249, *251,* 334
  foreign relations and, 52, 135, 138, *138,*
    139, 140

and government in exile, 316, *316–17,*
  390*n*12
home front of, 183, 185–86
impact of war on, 135
last days of, 316, *316–17*
morale in, 249, 290
naval blockade of, 42, 44, 45, 135, 249, *251,*
  318, *331,* 384*n*8
pardoning of leadership of, *337, 337*
punishment of leaders of, 311, 336, *339,* 341
readmission of states in, 311, *312,* 336, 337,
  340
Reconstruction role of, 311
seal of the, *321*
and states' rights, *187*
strategic options in 1865 of, 315–16
strategies for victory of the, 45–46, 332
Union states compared with, 36–37, 41–42,
  135
and why the Confederacy lost the Civil War,
  318–21, *320,* 323–26, 328, 331–32, 334
  See also South; *specific person, state, or topic*
Confederate Army
  civil-military relations and, 76–77
  conscription/recruiting for, 33, *35,* 73, 76,
    77, 123, 185, 315, 319, 321, *322,* 391*n*16,
    391*n*21, 392*n*27
  culture of, 151
  Davis as general in chief of, 249
  demobilization of, 311
  depletion of, 315
  differences among high command in, *79*
  discipline and supply for, 150–51, *152, 153,*
    154–56, *154, 155, 156–57,* 158
  disobeying of orders in, 381–82*n*55
  divided command problem in, 380*n*28
  food and supplies for, 123, *124,* 151,
    154–56, 158, 166, 321
  and Hampton Roads peace negotiations,
    315
  health issues in, 76, *78–79*
  Lee as general in chief of, 300, 315
  McClellan's estimation of, *84,* 87, *89, 99,*
    100, 128
  manpower shortage in, 315
  mobilization of, 33, *35,* 123, 319, 391*n*16,
    393*n*31
  morale in, 275, 290
  motivation of, 73
  partisan rangers and, 390*n*9
  picket duty in, *80*
  rank, structure and organization of, 73,
    76–77, *152,* 364*n*8, 391*n*16
  slaves in, 389*n*7, 390*n*8
  strategic options in 1865 of, 315
  strategy of, 249–50
  strength of, *84,* 87, *89, 99,* 100, 128, 245,
    249, 303, 365*n*17
  surrender of, 311, 312–13, *314*
  veterans of, *351*
  volunteers in, 76, 321
  wagons and animals for, 151, 154
  in West, 41–42
  West Point graduates in, 6, *6,* 350, 353
  and West Point memorials, *8*
    See also specific person, army, or battle

Confederate Congress, 73, 76, 77, 185, 315,
  321, 391–92*n*21
Confiscation Acts, 110–11
Congress, U.S.
  and conscription/draft, 323–24, 364*n*4,
    392*n*29
  divisions in, 392*n*29
  and escalation of war, 109, 111
  and factors influencing the outcome of the
    Civil War, 323
  and First Battle of Bull Run, 57–58
  Freedman's Bureau and, 336
  and funding for West Point, 3
  "gag rule" in, 23
  and Grant-Johnson (Andrew) relationship,
    336–37
  Grant presidency and, 340
  Lincoln's relations with, 392*n*26
  and mobilization for war, 33
  powers of, 48
  and punishment of former Rebels, 336
  violence in, 24
  and warfare in 1860, 44
    *See also specific person, election, or
    legislation*
Congressional Medal of Honor, *353*
conscription/enlistments
  in Confederate Army, 33, *35,* 73, 76, *77,*
    123, 185, 315, 319, 321, *322,* 391*n*16,
    391*n*21, 392*n*27
  effects on home front of, 186–87
  evasion of, 185, 245, 316
  exemptions from, 185, 321, 363*n*3, 375*n*75,
    392*n*27
  and factors influencing the outcome of the
    Civil War, 323–24, 332, 334
  substitutions for, 392*n*27
  for Union Army, 186–87, 249–50, 319,
    323–24, 392*n*27
Constitution, Confederate, 30, *30*
Constitution, U.S.
  Crittenden Resolutions and, 58
  emancipation and, 51
  and origins of Civil War, 17, 20, 23, 28,
    29–30, 31
  and presidential powers, 72
  and suspension of habeas corpus, 48
    See also specific amendment
Constitutional Union Party, 28
contraband, slaves as, 110, *111, 112, 113,*
  323
Cooper, Samuel, 77, 364*n*8
Copperheads, 186, *189,* 349, 375*n*74, 392*n*29
Corinth Campaign
  and advance to Shiloh, *64–65*
  Bragg and, 202, 203
  casualties in, 203
  Confederate divided command problem in,
    380*n*28
  first, 194–97, *196*
  forces in, *204*
  Grant and, 65, 203, 378*n*19, 378–79*n*20
  Halleck at, 111, *113,* 196, *196*
  public opinion about, 197
  Rosecrans and, *202,* 203, 204, *204,* 231,
    378*n*19, 378–79*n*20

E

Early, Jubal
    at Bull Run, *55, 56*
    at Cedar Creek, *282, 282*
    at Chancellorsville, *163, 164, 165*
    at Cold Harbor, *267*
    at Fisher's Hill, *282*
    at Fredericksburg, *144, 145, 146, 147*, 159,
        162
    and Gettysburg Campaign, 171
    "Lost Cause" ideology of, *326*
    and Overland Campaign, *265*
    in Shenandoah Valley, 277, *282, 349,*
        387n50
    and Spotsylvania, *258*
    as threat to Washington, D.C., 277, *277,*
        289
    at Winchester, *282*
Eastern Theater
    conclusions about early years of war in,
        187, 190
    importance of, 191
    Lee's war in, 135–90
    maps of, *74–75, 136–37*
    strategy and operations during first year of
        war in, 52–53, *54, 55, 56, 57–58*, 134
    timeline for battles in, *136–37*
    See also specific commander or battle
economy
    and Army size, *395–96n48*
    and Civil War as watershed in American
        history, 354
    and demobilization of armies, 335
    elections of 1876 and, 347
    and factors influencing the outcome of the
        Civil War, 318, 323, 334
    and mobilization of Confederate Army,
        391n16
    Panic of 1873 and, 346, 347, *348–49*
    Reconstruction and, 335, 347
    and warfare, *395n44*
    and western expansion, 335
education: and warfare in 1860, 44
Eisenhower, Dwight D., *5, 7, 8*
elections of 1848, 18–19
elections of 1852, 19
elections of 1856, 24, 26
elections of 1858, *19*, 25, 26
elections of 1860
    Douglas and, *19*, 47
    and influence of Civil War on West Point,
        1, 2
    Lincoln and, 1, 2, 26, 47, 342, *397n54*
    and origins of the Civil War, 26, 28
    Republican Party and, 26
    results of, 28
    and role of border states in Civil War, 47
elections of 1862, 123, 141
elections of 1864
    Atlanta Campaign and, *281*
    cartoon about, *281*
    and conclusions about early years of war in
        Eastern Theater, 190
    Confederate strategy and, 249

Davis and, *281*
Democrats and, 269, 280, *281*, 311
Grant and, 280, 283
influence of battles/campaigns on, 183
Johnson (Andrew) and, *337*
Lincoln and, *243, 245, 249*, 269, 280, *281,*
    283, *283*, 311, 315, 325, 332
McClellan and, *102–3, 243*, 280, *281*
Overland Campaign and, 264
peace negotiations and, 280, *281*
Union offensives and, 280, 282
and Union strategy and victories, 245
voting by soldiers in, *283, 285*
elections of 1866, 337
elections of 1868, *339, 340*
elections of 1872, 344
elections of 1874, 346
elections of 1876, 347, *349, 350*
elections of 1884, 353
Elliott, Stephen, *273, 295*
emancipation, 50–51, *50, 50*, 110, *140*, 185, 186,
    337, *392n29*. *See also* Emancipation
    Proclamation
Emancipation Proclamation, 111, *132–33, 134,*
    135, 138, *139*, 141, *212*, 269, 280, 321,
    323, 335
Enfield rifles, 135, *152*
Enforcement Act (1870, 1871), 341, *398n62*
Esposito, Vincent, 8
European Squadron, 330
Evans, Nathan George, at Bull Run, *55, 56*
Everett, Edward, 186
Ewell, Richard S.
    and end of war, *302–3*
    at First Battle of Bull Run, *55, 56–57*
    at Fredericksburg, *143*
    and Gettysburg Campaign, 166–67, 171,
        174, 175, *178*
    and Grant's pursuit of Lee, *302–3*
    at North Anna River Battle, *266*
    and Overland Campaign, *265*
    and reorganization of Army of Northern
        Virginia, 166
    at Second Battle of Bull Run, *115*
    at Seven Days Battle, *107*
    at Spotsylvania, *258*
    and Valley Campaign, 91, 92, *93, 94, 365n23*
    and Wilderness Campaign, *256, 260*
Ewing, Thomas, 271
Ezra Church, Battle at, *387n47*

F

faculty, West Point: in Confederate Army, 3
Fair Oaks, Battle of. *See* Seven Pines, Battle of
Farley, Henry C., 2
Farragut, David G., 63, *330, 331*
Faust, Drew Gilpin, 323
Ferrero, Edward, *265*
Field, Charles W., *265*
field fortifications, 308
Fifteenth Amendment, 340, 349

15th Alabama, *373n56*
Fillmore, Millard, 24
1st Battalion, 13th Infantry (US), *223, 224*
1st Cavalry (US), *170*
1st Division (US), *159*
1st Minnesota Infantry (US), 173, 175, *176*
1st Regiment Pennsylvania Infantry, drum
    of, *36*
1st Rhode Island Infantry (US), *142*
1st Texas Infantry (CSA), 127, *152. See also*
    Texas Brigade
1st Virginia Cavalry (CSA), *170*
Fisher's Hill, Battle of, *282*
Five Forks, Battle of, *282*, 300, *300*
flags, return of the, *310*
Florida, 17, 29, 347
Floyd, John, 59, *61, 62*
foot cavalry, 92, 95
Foote, Andrew H., 59, *60–61, 62, 62*, 195
Foote, Samuel A., *62*
Foote, Shelby, 320
foreign relations
    Confederacy and, 52, 135, 138, *138, 139,*
        140
    effects on Civil War of, 187
    Lincoln and, 140
    and naval blockade of Confederacy, *331*
    See also specific nation
Forney, John H., *226, 227*
Forrest, Nathan Bedford
    and Atlanta Campaign, 270–71
    and Chattanooga Campaign, *232–33, 234*
    at Chickamauga, *235, 236, 237*
    at Fort Donelson, 62
    at Franklin, *292, 293*
    Hood as replacement for, 271
    at Selma, 308
    at Shiloh, *69*
    and Vicksburg Campaign, 207, 212, *212*
Fort Donelson
    and advance to Shiloh, *64–65*
    Grant and, *58, 59, 59, 62, 62*, 113, 194, *195,*
        204, 300, 328
    and Grant-Halleck relations, 195
    impact on Confederacy of loss of, 199, 244
    map about, *59, 60–61*
    timeline for, *75*
Fort Fisher, *206*
Fort Henry
    and advance to Shiloh, *64–65*
    Grant and, 59, *59, 60–61, 62*, 113, 194, *195,*
        204, 328
    and Grant-Halleck relations, 195
    impact on Confederacy of loss of, 199, 244
    and joint military-naval operations, 59,
        59, 62
    timeline for, *75*
Fort Hill, Battle of, *228*
Fort Mahone, *306*
Fort McAllister, 289–90
Fort Monroe, 109
Fort Pickens, 30, *332*
Fort Pillow, *64–65*, 250
Fort Randolph, *64–65*
Fort Sedgwick, *306*
Fort Stevens, Lincoln's visit to, 277

Fort Sumter
　Anderson's surrender of, *32–33*
　and Church's *Our Banner in the Sky*
　　painting, *12, 13*
　firing on, 2, 30–31, *31*, 37, *52*
　Lincoln administration response to, 323
　surrender of, *32, 33*
　volunteer sentiment following, 35
48th Pennsylvania (US), 277, 278
Fourteenth Amendment, 337, 340, 349, *349*
France, 45, *45*, 123, 135, 334, *335*. *See also*
　Crimean War
Franklin, Battle of, *246–47, 274*, 291, *291, 292,
　293*, 389–90*n*7
Franklin, William B.
　and Antietam Campaign, *125, 129*, 368*n*62
　and dissension within Army of the
　　Potomac, 159
　at First Battle of Bull Run, *56*
　at Fredericksburg, *143*, 144, 145, 146, *147*,
　　148, 149, 150
　and Peninsular campaign, *86–87*
　removal as division commander of, 159
　at Second Battle of Bull Run, *116–17*
　at Seven Days Battle, *107, 108–9*
Frayser's Farm, Battle of, 104, *108–9*
Fredericksburg, Battle of
　Burnside at, *142, 143*, 144, 145, 146, *147,
　　148, 149*, 150, 215
　casualties at, *149*, 150, 151
　and conclusions about early years of war in
　　Eastern Theater, 187
　Confederate mobility at, 191
　crossing the Rappahannock during, *148,
　　148*, 159
　Early at, 144, 145, 146, *147*, 159, 162
　forces at, *143*, 144–47
　Grant and, *332*
　Hooker at, *143*, 144, 145, 146, 148, 150,
　　158
　Jackson at, *91*, 143, 144, 145, 146, *147*,
　　148–49, 150
　Lee at, *143*, 144, 145, 146, *147*, 148, 326
　maps of, *144–47*
　Meade at, *143, 145*, 149, *171*
　plundering after, 151
　and Shenandoah Valley Campaign, *91*
　timeline for, *136–37, 193*
Free Soil Party, 19, 20, *20*, 24, 26
Freedmen's Bureau, 336, *338*, 342
Frémont, John C., 24, 26, 50–51, *50*, 92, *93,
　94, 95*
French North African soldiers, *40, 41*
French, William H., *143, 163, 273, 293, 295*
Friar's Point, Mississippi: guerrillas at, *209*
Front Royal, Battle of, *94*
Fugitive Slave Law (1850), 15, 18–19, *23*

G

Gaines's Mill, Battle of, 100, *102–3, 105, 108–9*,
　126, 275
Gallagher, Gary, 324

Gardner, Alexander, *131*
Gardner, Franklin, *216–17*, 230
Garibaldi, Giuseppe, *39*
Garibaldi Guards
　New Orleans, *39*
　39th New York Regiment as, *39*
Garnet, Robert S., 364*n*10
Garrard, Kenner, *273, 295*
Geary, John W., *163, 273*
Georgia
　Bragg in, 183
　Longstreet in, 183
　secession of, 29
　Union drive into, 191
　See also Atlanta Campaign
German Americans, 23, 26, 47, 187, 398*n*64
Getty, George W., *143*, 265
Gettysburg Address, Lincoln's, *186*, 325
Gettysburg Campaign
　casualties at, 104, 173, *176–77*, 178, 179,
　　182–83, 183
　and conclusions about early years of war in
　　Eastern Theater, 187, 190
　and Confederate mobility, 191
　and Davis' call to arms, *188*
　and factors influencing the outcome of the
　　Civil War, 332
　first day of, *172*
　Grant and, 166
　and influence of Civil War on West
　　Point, 6
　Lee and, *98*, 166, 167, *167*, 170, 171, *171*,
　　175, *178*, 179, 181, 183, *183*, 371*n*34,
　　372*n*48, 374*n*59
　Lincoln and, 166, 179, 181, *184–85*
　Longstreet and, *167, 167*, 171–72, *173*, 175,
　　180, 373–74*n*59
　maps of, *167–69*
　Meade and, *167*, 170, 171, *171*, 172, 173,
　　174, 175, *176*, 179, 181, *183*
　and *Panorama of Military History* mural,
　　11
　Pickett's Charge during, 291
　plundering during, 171
　and prisoners of war, *171*, 181
　Stuart at, 166, 167, *170*, 175, 372*n*48
　and teaching the Civil War at West Point,
　　7–8, *7, 9*
　timeline for, *136–37, 193*
　veterans of, *351*
　See also Cemetery Hill/Cemetery Ridge,
　　Battle of; Culp's Hill, Battle of; Little
　　Round Top, Battle of; Wheatfield, Battle
　　of
Gibbes, Wade Hampton, 2, *2*
Gibbon, John, *143, 163*, 173, *265*
Gist, States Rights, *235*
Gladstone, William, 135, 138
"God and the Strongest Battalions" (Current),
　36
Gordon, John B., 127–28, *302–3*
Gordonsville, Virginia, Pope at, 113
Grand Review (Washington, 1865), 318, *319*,
　390*n*13
Granger, Gordon, *232–33, 234*, 235, *236*
Grant, Lewis A., *259*

Grant, Ulysses S.
　as acting secretary of war, 338, 340, 396*n*52
　and Army–Ku Klux Klan clashes, 342
　with the Army of the Potomac, 195, *249*
　"bull dog" cartoon about, *243*
　Cadet Oath taken by, *4*
　casualties among troops of, 270
　casualty views of, *266*
　as commander of Military Division of the
　　Mississippi, *271*
　corruption in administration of, 347
　cotton views of, 35
　criticisms of, *71*, 195, 269, 345, *345*,
　　398*n*64
　and defense of Washington, *277, 277*
　and demobilization of troops, 334–35
　election as president of, *271*
　elections of 1864 and, 280, 283
　elections of 1868 and, *271*, 339, 340
　elections of 1872 and, 344
　and end of war, 300, 302–3
　and Enforcement Act, 341
　enlistment of, *35*
　as general in chief of Union Army, *195, 243*,
　　245, *271*, 328
　and Grand Review, 318, *319*
　as greatest of nineteenth-century generals,
　　191
　Halleck and, *113*, 195, 197, 205, 206, 208
　and Hampton Roads peace negotiations,
　　248, 389*n*6
　headquarters of, 248
　health of, 195
　importance of command of, 269
　and influence of Civil War on West Point, 6
　Johnson (Andrew) and, 336–38, 340
　and Johnson-Stanton relationship, 396*n*52
　and joint military-naval operations, 254,
　　328
　leadership abilities of, 328
　Lee's surrender to, 300, 302, *302*, 303–5,
　　312, *313*
　lieutenant general appointment of, *171*
　Lincoln and, 204–5, 244, 248, 254, *331*,
　　379*n*23, 384*n*2
　and Lincoln's views about warfare, 28
　Longstreet and, 373*n*59
　and McClernand-Lincoln relationship,
　　379–80*n*24
　and Meade, *171*, 195
　memoir of, 353
　and Mexico-France relationship, 334
　in Mississippi, 166, 197, 205
　nickname of, *58*, 300
　personality and character of, *71*, 204–5, *214*,
　　269, 270
　politics and, 214, 254, 353, 384*n*2
　Posse Comitatus Act and, 350
　and post-war role of the Army, 334–38
　and prisoners of war, 382*n*63
　professional background of, *195*
　rank of, 383*n*1
　Reconstruction and, 346–47, *348, 349*
　on recruiting poster, *1*
　Republicans and, 340, 345
　resignation from army of, 62

and *River Queen, 316*
Rosecrans and, *202,* 203, 241, 379*n*20
Schurz and, 398*n*64
and Sheridan-White League clash in
Louisiana, 344–45, *345*
and Sheridan's promotion as commander of
the Army of the Shenandoah, *277*
Sherman's relationship with, 195, 210, 245,
248, 249, 270, *271,* 285, 302
and significance of Civil War for West
Point, 353
slavery views of, *35*
Stanton and, 241
strategy of, 245, 248–51, *248, 250,* 262, 269,
270, *279,* 285, 289, 302–3, 308, 309, *309,*
328, 384*n*2
suspension of habeas corpus by, 342
talents of, *113*
and Union Army mobility, 82
warfare views of, 71
as West Point graduate in Union Army, *6, 7*
West Point memorials to, *1, 8*
Grant, Ulysses S.—battles/campaigns and
and advance to Shiloh, *64–65, 65*
Champion Hill, *222*
Chattanooga Campaign, *195, 199,* 240–44,
240, 241, 242, 243
Chickamauga, 244
Cold Harbor, 261, *262,* 266–67, 386*n*28
Corinth Campaign, 65, 203, 378*n*19,
378–79*n*20
Fort Donelson, *58, 59, 59,* 62, *62, 113,* 194,
195, 204, 300, 328
Fort Henry, 59, *59, 60–61,* 62, *113,* 194, *195,*
204, 328
Fredericksburg, *332*
Gettysburg Campaign, 166
Iuka, *202,* 203, 377*n*17
Kentucky Campaign, *200,* 377*n*16
Missionary Ridge, 328
and move into Virginia, 253–54, 257, 270
Overland Campaign, *249, 254, 254–55, 256,*
257, 259, 265, 269, 270, 275, 308
Petersburg Campaign, 262, *265,* 269, 270,
275, *276–77,* 277, 278, *279,* 280, 283,
285, 297, *299,* 300, *300–301,* 316, 328,
387*n*43
pursuit of Lee, *246–47,* 282, 300, *302–3*
and Sheridan in Shenandoah Valley, 282,
282
and Sherman's March to the Sea, 289
Shiloh, *52, 63, 66, 67, 68, 69,* 71, *71,* 195,
195, 204, 379*n*23
Spotsylvania, *258, 259,* 260
Vicksburg Campaign, 82, 166, *195,* 206,
206, 207, 208, 210, 212, *212,* 214–15,
215, 216–17, 217, *218–19,* 219, 221–22,
222, 223, 224, *224–25, 226, 227, 228,*
244, 254, 328, 386*n*28
and Western victory, 63, 65
Wilderness Campaign, *256,* 257
Great Britain
Confederate strategic options in 1865 and,
315–16
and Confederate strategies for victory, 45,
45, 46, 135, 138, *138, 139,* 140

and diplomatic recognition for
Confederacy, 123
Mexico invasion by, 135
Shenandoah/Waddell surrender to, 313, *314*
and *Trent* affair, *51, 52,* 140
wait-and-see diplomacy of, 52
See also Crimean War
Great Locomotive Chase, 353
Gregg, John, 219, *265*
Gresham, Walter Q., 273
Grierson, Benjamin, *216–17,* 217
Griffin, Charles, *143, 163, 265,* 302–3
guerrillas, 48, 50, 198, *208,* 209–10, *209, 210,* 214,
230, 308, 315–16, *316–17,* 321, 342, *342*
gunboats, 191, *194,* 217, *217*

H

habeas corpus
Davis's suspension of, *29, 325*
Enforcement Act and, 341
Grant's suspension of, 342
Lincoln's suspension of, 48, *49,* 280
Hacker, J. David, 390–91*n*14
Hahn, Steven, 321
Hall, Bolling, *80*
Hall, Crenshaw, *80*
Halleck, Henry Wager
appointment as commanding general of,
111, *113,* 197
and Army of the Mississippi, 195
and Army of the Ohio, 195
and Army of the Tennessee, 195
Buell and, 379*n*22
as chief of staff, *113*
and Corinth Campaign, 111, *113,* 196, *196*
and Forts Henry and Donelson, *113*
and Fredericksburg, 148
Grant and, *113,* 195, *195,* 197, 205, 206, 208,
377*n*17
and Grant's strategy, 269
and Harpers Ferry, 123
Hooker's relationship with, *158*
leadership abilities of, 328, 394*n*38
Lincoln and, 111, *113,* 197
McClellan and, 111, 113, 134
and McClernand's expedition to Vicksburg,
206, 208
nickname for, 197
and Peninsula Campaign, *113*
professional background of, *113*
Rosecrans and, 230
and Second Battle of Bull Run, 117
Sherman and, *113*
and Sherman's deliberate destruction of
resources, 309
and Western Theater, 195, *195,* 198
Hamilton, Schuyler, *204*
Hamlin, Hannibal, *337*
Hampton Legion (CSA), 154
Hampton Roads, Virginia
Monitor-Virginia battle at, 88, *88*
peace negotiations at, *248,* 315, *316,* 389*n*6

Hampton, Wade III, *265, 279,* 350
Hancock, Winfield Scott
at Chancellorsville, *163*
at Cold Harbor, *267*
at Fredericksburg, *143*
at North Anna River Battle, *266*
and Overland Campaign, *265*
and Peninsular campaign, *86–87*
and Petersburg Campaign, 269, *276, 279*
at Spotsylvania, *258, 259*
and Wilderness Campaign, *256*
"hard war," 109–11, *210,* 245, 309, 328
Hardee, William J., *63, 66–68, 213, 241, 273,*
274, 275, 382*n*65
Harpers Ferry, Virginia
and Antietam campaign, 123–24, 126, *127,*
131, 134
Hunter at, 277
Jackson at, 92, 124, 126, 365*n*22
John Brown's raid on, 1, 25–26, *26, 27, 170*
Johnston at, 77
Harrow, William, 273
Hartford, U.S.S., *330*
Hatch, John Porter, *121, 122,* 293, *295*
Haupt, Herman, 328
Hayes, Rutherford B., 347, *349,* 350
Hébert, Louis, *203, 204*
Heintzelman, Samuel
and Antietam Campaign, *125, 129*
at First Battle of Bull Run, *55*
and Peninsular campaign, *86–87*
at Second Battle of Bull Run, *115, 116–17,*
120, 121
at Seven Days Battle, *107, 108–9*
Henry House Hill, 55, *57,* 118, *122*
Herron, Francis J., *227*
Heth, Henry, *165, 265*
Hill, A.P.
and Antietam campaign, 126, 131, 368*n*62
at Bristoe Station Battle, 183
at Chancellorsville, *163, 164*
at Cold Harbor, *267*
at Fredericksburg, *143, 144, 145, 146, 147*
and Gettysburg Campaign, 167, 170, 171,
175
media and, 105
at North Anna River Battle, *266*
and Overland Campaign, *265*
and Peninsular Campaign, *86–87*
and Petersburg Campaign, *279*
and reorganization of Army of Northern
Virginia, 166
at Second Battle of Bull Run, *115, 120, 121*
at Seven Days Battle, 100, 102, 105, *107,*
108–9
and Wilderness Campaign, *256*
Hill, Daniel Harvey "D.H."
and Antietam campaign, 124, *129*
and Chattanooga Campaign, *233*
at Chickamauga, *235*
at Fredericksburg, *143, 144, 145, 146, 147*
and Lee's push into Maryland, 124
and Peninsular campaign, *86–87*
at Seven Days Battle, 100, 104, *107, 108–9*
at Seven Pines, 96
at Turner's Gap, 124

Grant's relationship with, 336–38, 340
impeachment of, *337*, 338, *339*, 340
inaugural address of, *337*
as Lincoln supporter, *337*
and Mexico-French relations, 334, 395*n*46
Military Reconstruction Act and, 337
pardoning of Confederate leaders by, 336, 337, *337*
personal and professional background of, *337*
post-war policies of, 311
and Reconstruction, 396*n*52
Republicans and, 336–37, *337*, *339*
and reunification, *337*
and Sherman-Johnston surrender, 312
and size of the Army, 395–96*n*48
Stanton and, 338, 396*n*52
and Tenure of Office Act, *337*, 338, 396*n*52
and western expansion, *337*
Johnson, B.R., *234*, *235*, 236
Johnson, E., *265*, *293*, *295*
Johnson, R., 236, *293*, *295*
Johnston, Albert Sidney
at Bull Run, *54–55*
at Corinth, 65, *199*
Davis and, 197
death of, *52*, *67*, 195, 197
rank of, 77, 364*n*8
Shiloh and, *63*, *64–65*, 65, *66*, *67*, 71, 195, 197
in Tennessee, *52*
in Utah, 364*n*8
and Western Theater, 195
Johnston, Joseph E.
Bragg and, 382–83*n*65
Chattanooga as headquarters for, 212
as commander of the Army of Northern Virginia, *76*
as commander of the Army of Tennessee, *76*, 248, 297, 382*n*65
as commander in Western Theater, 212
Davis and, *76*, *76*, 77, 98, 212, 219, 325, 382–83*n*65
and end of the war, 300, *302*, 303, 389*n*3
estimation of Confederate strength by, 365*n*17
Hood as replacement for, 271, 273, *274*, 275
Lee as replacement for, *98*, 134
Lee's relationship with, 77
Longstreet and, *167*
McClellan's views about, 98
media and, 105
Meigs as replacement for, *332*
in Mississippi, 383*n*65
personal and professional background of, *76*
personality and character of, 76, *76*
rank of, *76*, 77, 364*n*8
and reorganization of Confederate troops, 73
reputation of, 77

strategy of, 303
surrender of, *76*, 299, 312, *313*, *314*, 316
as West Point graduate in Confederacy, 6, *76*
wounding of, *76*, 96, 134
Johnston, Joseph E.—battles/campaigns and
Atlanta campaign, *76*, 271, *272*, *273*, 275
Bentonville, North Carolina, *76*
First Battle of Bull Run, *52*, *55*, *56*
Harpers Ferry, 77
Kennesaw Mountain, 271, 275
Manassas, *79*
Peninsular campaign, *76*, 87, *87*, 89
Port Hudson, *76*
Seven Days Battle, 105
Seven Pines-Fair Oaks Battle, *76*, 96, 97
Shenandoah Valley Campaign, *93*
Sherman's March to the Sea, *286*
Sherman's March through the Carolinas, 297
Sherman's pursuit of Johnston, *246–47*
Vicksburg Campaign, *76*, 212, *218–19*, 219, 221, 224, *225*, 230
Johnston, J.W., *295*
joint military-naval operations
at Forts Henry and Donelson, 59, *59*, 62
and Grant's leadership abilities, 328
and Kentucky Campaign, 376*n*15
in New Orleans, 376*n*15
and Vicksburg Campaign, 202, *206*, 210, *215*, 215, 217, *217*
in Western Theater, 191, 254
Jomini, Antoine-Henri, 44, 362*n*54
Jones, D.R., *55*, *56–57*, *107*, *115*, *121*, *122*
Jonesboro, Battle of, 280, 282, 387*n*47
Judah, Henry M., *273*
Justice Department, U.S., 342

K

Kansas, 24, *25*
Kansas-Nebraska Act (1854), *18*, 19, *19*, 23
Kearny, Philip, *107*, *115*, *120*, *121*, *122*
Keegan, John, 320
Kellogg, William Pitt, 397*n*62, 398*n*63
Kelly, John H., *273*
Kemper, James, *115*, *121*, *180*, 373*n*59, 374*n*59
Kennesaw Mountain, Battle at, 271, *272*, 275
Kentucky
and Confederate strategies for victory, 45
guerrilla warfare in, 50
neutrality of, *198*
role in Civil War of, 46, 48, 50, 51
and secession, 29
Kentucky Campaign
Bragg and, 138, *193*, 202, 285, 376*n*10, 376*n*12, 376*n*13, 379*n*22
Buell and, 199, *199–201*, 202, 285, 376*n*12, 376*n*13, 379*n*22
impact of battles at Fort Donelson and Fort Henry on, 62

Kirby Smith and, *197*, 198–99, *198*, *199–201*, 202, 376*n*10, 376*n*12, 377*n*16, 378*n*18
Lincoln and, 376*n*10
Polk in, *198*
and prisoners of war, 376*n*10
and Western Theater, 197–99, *199–200*, 202
Kentucky Resolution (1798), 360*n*33
Kernstown, Battle of, *93*
Kershaw, Joseph B., *235*, *265*
Keyes, Erasmus D., *56*, *86–87*, *107*, *108–9*
Kilpatrick, Hugh Judson, *273*
Kimball, Nathan, *227*, *293*, *295*
King, Rufus, *115*
Kirby Smith, Edmund
Bragg and, 198–99, *199–201*, 202, 203, 377*n*16, 378*n*18
at Bull Run, *55*, *56*
and Kentucky Campaign, *197*, *199–201*, 202, 376*n*10, 376*n*12, 377*n*16, 378*n*18
and surrender of Confederate forces in Texas, 313, *314*
Knipe, Joseph F., *295*
Know-Nothing Party, 23, 24, *24*, 26
Knoxville, Battle of, *142*, 183, 231
Krasnoborski, Edward, 8
Ku Klux Klan, 341, 342, *342*, 343, 344, *346*, 347, *347*, 349, 397*n*59
Ku Klux Klan Act (1871), 341

L

Lamon, Ward Hill, *185*
Larned, Charles, *353*
Latané, William, *324*
Lauman, Jacob G., *227*
Law, Evander C., 126, *172*, *235*
Lawrence, Amos Adams, *23*
Lawrence, Kansas, guerrilla destruction in, *316–17*
Lawton, Henry W., *120*, *121*
leadership
and factors influencing outcome of Civil War, 324–26, *326–27*, 328, *328–29*, 331, 353, 393*n*32, 393*n*33, 394*n*38
Johnson's pardoning of Confederate, 337, *337*
military, 325–26, *326–27*, 328, 331, 353
political, 324–25, 353, 394*n*38
punishment of Confederate, 311, *339*, 341
See also specific person
LeCompton Constitution, 25
Lee, Fitzhugh, 8, 159–60, *165*, *265*, *302–3*
Lee, Robert E.
and Arlington National Cemetery, *332*
and casualties, 326
in Charleston, 98
as commander of Army of Northern Virginia, *76*, 98–99, *170*, 195, 319, 325, 365*n*22, 366*n*33
and conclusions about early years of war in Eastern Theater, 187, 190

McMurry, Richard, 36, 41
McPherson, James B.
    and Atlanta Campaign, *272*, *273*, 275
    and Corinth Campaign, *204*
    death of, 275
    and Vicksburg Campaign, 218–19, *219*, 221,
        222, *225*, *226*, *227*
McPherson, James M., 46, 331–32
Madison, James, 360*n*33
Magruder, John B.
    and Peninsular campaign, *86–87*, 88–89
    at Seven Days Battle, 100, 102, 104, *107*,
        108–9
Mahan, Dennis Hart, 3, 7, 44, 328, 394*n*41
Malvern Hill, Battle of, *102–3*, 104, *106*, *108–9*
Manassas, 53, 77, *78–79*, 87, 104, *116–17*, 117,
    118. *See also* Bull Run, First Battle of;
    Bull Run, Second Battle of
Mansfield, Joseph, *125*, 127, *129*
manufacturing, 46, 318
March to the Sea, Sherman's, 246–47, *271*,
    285–90, *286*, *289*, 297, 308, 316, *332*
March through the Carolinas, Sherman's, *271*,
    297, *298–99*, 308, 309, *332*
Marcy, William L., 106
Mare Island Navy Yard, *330*
Martha (slave), *229*
Martin, James Green, *235*, *273*
Marye's Heights, Battle of, *145*, *146*, 149, *149*,
    162
Maryland
    Confederate recruiting in, 123
    and Confederate strategies for victory, 45
    Jackson in, *91*
    Lee's push into, 123–24, *125*, 134, 138,
        150–51, 159, 166, 286
    role in Civil War of, 46, 48, 50
    and secession, 29
"Maryland, My Maryland" (song), *124*
Mason, James M., 52
Maury, Dabney H., *203*, *204*
Maximilian I (emperor of Mexico), 334, *335*
Meade, George Gordon
    casualties among troops of, 269–70
    as commander of the Army of the Potomac,
        167, *171*, *249*
    criticisms of, 181
    and Early's threat to Washington D.C., 277
    and Grand Review, 318
    Grant compared with, 270
    Grant's headquarters with, 248
    Grant's relationship with, *171*, 195
    and Grant's strategy, 250, 254
    and influence of Civil War on West Point, 6
    Lincoln's relationship with, *171*, 179, 181
    and operations in Virginia, 254
    personality and character of, *171*
    professional background of, *171*
    as West Point graduate in Union Army, 6
Meade, George Gordon—battles/campaigns
    and
    Antietam, *171*
    Battle of the Crater, 278, *278*
    Bristoe Station, 183
    Chancellorsville, *163*, *164*, *165*, *171*, 371*n*34
    Cold Harbor, 267

Fredericksburg, *143*, *145*, 149, *171*
Gettysburg Campaign, 6, *11*, 167, 170, 171,
    171, 172, 173, 174, 175, 176, 179, 181, *183*
Mine Run Battle, 183
North Anna River Battle, *266*
Overland Campaign, *254–55*, *264*, *265*, 277
Peninsula Campaign, *171*
Petersburg Campaign, 262, *265*, 268, 269,
    276, 278, *278*, *279*, *300*
Second Battle of Bull Run, *171*
Seven Days Battle, *171*
Spotsylvania, *258*
Wilderness Campaign, *256*
Meagher, Thomas, *97*
Medal of Honor, Congressional, *353*
media
    and First Battle of Bull Run, 57
    Lee and, 105
    and Seven Days Battle, 104–5
medical services, 33, 36
Meigs, Montgomery Cunningham, 328, *332*
Memphis & Charleston Railroad, 196, 197, 198
Meredith, Sullivan A., 382*n*63
Meridian, Mississippi: Sherman at, 271
Merrill, Lewis, 342, *342*, 344, 349, 397*n*59
Merrimack, C.S.S., 88
Merryman, John, 48, 362*n*61
Mexican-American War
    Compromise of 1850 and, 15
    and Eastern strategy and operations during
        first year of war, 53
    Grant's views about, *195*
    Lincoln's views about, *28*
    and origins of the Civil War, 15
    and warfare in 1860, 42, 43, 44
    See also specific person or battle
Mexico
    as Confederate sanctuary, 316
    European nations invasion of, 135
    French in, 135, 334
    and Johnson administration, 395*n*46
    Maximilian's government in, 334, *335*
    and Monroe Doctrine, 135, 334
    in post-war years, 311
Michie, Peter, 1
Miles, D.S., 55, *129*
Military Division of the Mississippi, 248, *271*,
    273, 285
Military Division of the Pacific, 239
Military Railroad, U.S., 328
Military Reconstruction Act, 337
Militia Act, 110–11
Mill Springs, Battle of, *239*
Miller, William, 295
Mine Run (Petersburg), Battle of, *142*, 183, 277
Minié ball, 43, *83*, 127
Miscegenation Ball (cartoon), *140*
Missionary Ridge, Battle of, 240, *240*, 241,
    242–44, *242*, *271*, 282, 328
Mississippi
    Grant in, 166, 205
    Ku Klux Klan in, *343*
    secession of, 29
    white supremacy in, 347
Mississippi Central Campaign, 166, 204–6,
    208–12, 214

Mississippi Central Railroad, 206, 212
Mississippi Plan (1875), 347, 350
Mississippi River
    and Eastern strategy and operations during
        first year of war, 52–53
    Farragut flotilla on, 63
    importance of, 191, 194
    and role of border states in Civil War, 50
    Union control of, 191, 244
    and Vicksburg Campaign, 230
    and Western strategy and operations during
        first year of war, 62
Mississippi River Squadron, *62*, 206
Missouri
    and Battle of Wilson's Creek, *47*, 48
    and Confederate strategies for victory, 45
    and elections of 1860, 47
    Frémont in, 50, *50*
    guerrillas in, 48, 50, *208*, *209*, 342, *342*
    role in Civil War of, 46, 47–48, 50–51
    and secession, 29, 47
    slavery in, 50–51, *50*
Missouri Compromise of 1820, 18, 19,
    20, 30
Mitchell, Robert B., 235
Mizner, Henry R., *204*
Mobile & Ohio Railroad, 196, 365*n*16
Mobile, Alabama
    and Grant's strategy, *250*
    surrender of Confederate forces at, 312
Mobile Bay, Battle of, 246–47, *330*
mobilization
    for Civil War, 33, *34*, *35*, 36–42, 72, 123,
        319, 391*n*16, 393*n*31
    and factors influencing outcome of Civil
        War, 334, 393*n*31
    See also conscription/enlistments
Monitor, U.S.S., 88, *88*
Monocacy Junction, Battle of, 277
Monroe Doctrine (1823), 135, 334
Monroe, James, 135
Moore, John C., *295*
Morell, George W., *107*
Morgan, John Hunt, *207*, 376*n*10, 390*n*9
Mott, Gershom, *265*
"Mud March," *142*, 150, *150*
"Mule Shoe," *258*, *259*, *259*, 260, *261*
music: role in Civil War of, *36*

N

Napoleon Bonaparte, 43, 44, 53, 80, 98, *206*,
    325, 326, 328, 393*n*33, 394*n*40, 394*n*41,
    394*n*42
"Napoleon Club" (West Point), 44, 394*n*41
Napoleon guns, *82*, *138*, 334, *335*, 364–65*n*13,
    372*n*37
Napoleon III, *82*, *138*, 334, *335*
Nashville, Tennessee
    Battle of, *239*, 246–47, 274, 294–95, 296–97,
        297
    and Hood's campaign in Tennessee, 291,
        291, *292*

S